Game Programming Gems 7

Edited by
Scott Jacobs

Charles River Media

A part of Course Technology, Cengage Learning

COURSE TECHNOLOGY
CENGAGE Learning™

Australia • Brazil • Japan • Korea • Mexico • Singapore • Spain • United Kingdom • United States

COURSE TECHNOLOGY
CENGAGE Learning™

Publisher and General Manager, Course Technology PTR: Stacy L. Hiquet

Associate Director of Marketing: Sarah Panella

Manager of Editorial Services: Heather Talbot

Marketing Manager: Jordan Casey

Senior Acquisitions Editor: Emi Smith

Project/Copy Editor: Kezia Endsley

CRM Editorial Services Coordinator: Jen Blaney

Interior Layout Tech: Judith Littlefield

Cover Designer: Tyler Creative Services

CD-ROM Producer: Brandon Penticuff

Indexer: Valerie Haynes Perry

Proofreader: Sue Boshers

Library of Congress Control Number: 2007939358
ISBN-13: 978-1-58450-527-3
ISBN-10: 1-58450-527-3

Course Technology
25 Thomson Place
Boston, MA 02210
USA

Cengage Learning is a leading provider of customized learning solutions with office locations around the globe, including Singapore, the United Kingdom, Australia, Mexico, Brazil, and Japan. Locate your local office at: **international.cengage.com/region**

Cengage Learning products are represented in Canada by Nelson Education, Ltd.

For your lifelong learning solutions, visit **courseptr.com**
Visit our corporate website at **cengage.com**

Printed in Canada
2 3 4 5 6 7 11 10 09 08

Contents

Preface ix

About the Cover Image xiii

Acknowledgments xv

Contributor Bios xvii

SECTION 1 GENERAL PROGRAMMING 1

Introduction 3
Adam Lake, Graphics Software Architect

1.1 **Efficient Cache Replacement Using the Age and Cost Metrics** 5
Colt "MainRoach" McAnlis, Microsoft Ensemble Studios

1.2 **High Performance Heap Allocator** 15
Dimitar Lazarov, Luxoflux

1.3 **Optical Flow for Video Games Played with Webcams** 25
Arnau Ramisa, Institut d'Investigació, en Intelligència Artificial
Enric Vergara, GeoVirtual
Enric Martí, Universitat Autónoma de Barcelona

1.4 **Design and Implementation of a Multi-Platform Threading Engine** . . . 35
Michael Ramsey

1.5 **For Bees and Gamers: How to Handle Hexagonal Tiles** 47
Thomas Jahn, King Art
Jörn Loviscach, Hochschule Bremen

1.6 **A Sketch-Based Interface to Real-Time Strategy Games Based on a Cellular Automaton** 59
Carlos A. Dietrich, Luciana P. Nedel, João L. D. Comba

1.7 **Foot Navigation Technique for First-Person Shooting Games** 69
Marcus Aurelius C. Farias, Daniela G. Trevisan, Luciana P. Nedel

1.8 **Deferred Function Call Invocation System** 81
Mark Jawad, Nintendo of America Inc.

1.9 **Multithread Job and Dependency System** 87
Julien Hamaide

1.10 **Advanced Debugging Techniques** 97
Martin Fleisz

SECTION 2 MATH AND PHYSICS 107

Introduction 109
Graham Rhodes, Applied Research Associates, Inc.

2.1 **Random Number Generation** 113
Chris Lomont

2.2 **Fast Generic Ray Queries for Games** 127
Jacco Bikker, IGAD/NHTV University of Applied Sciences—Breda, The Netherlands

2.3 **Fast Rigid-Body Collision Detection Using Farthest Feature Maps** . . 143
Rahul Sathe, Advanced Visual Computing, SSG, Intel Corp.
Dillon Sharlet, University of Colorado at Boulder

2.4 **Using Projective Space to Improve Precision of Geometric Computations** 153
Krzysztof Kluczek, Gda'nsk University of Technology

2.5 **XenoCollide: Complex Collision Made Simple** 165
Gary Snethen, Crystal Dynamics

2.6 **Efficient Collision Detection Using Transformation Semantics** 179
José Gilvan Rodrigues Maia, UFC
Creto Augusto Vidal, UFC
Joaquim Bento Cavalcante-Neto, UFC

2.7 **Trigonometric Splines** 191
Tony Barrera, Barrera Kristiansen AB
Anders Hast, Creative Media Lab, University of Gävle
Ewert Bengtsson, Centre For Image Analysis, Uppsala University

2.8 **Using Gaussian Randomness to Realistically Vary Projectile Paths** . 199
Steve Rabin, Nintendo of America Inc.

SECTION 3 AI 205

Introduction 207
Brian Schwab

3.1 **Creating Interesting Agents with Behavior Cloning** 209
John Harger
Nathan Fabian

3.2 **Designing a Realistic and Unified Agent-Sensing Model** 217
Steve Rabin, Nintendo of America Inc.
Michael Delp, WXP Inc.

3.3 **Managing AI Algorithmic Complexity: Generic Programming Approach** 229
Iskander Umarov
Anatoli Beliaev

3.4 **All About Attitude: Building Blocks for Opinion, Reputation, and NPC Personalities** 249
Michael F. Lynch, Ph.D., Rensselaer Polytechnic Institute, Troy, NY

3.5 **Understanding Intelligence in Games Using Player Traces and Interactive Player Graphs** 265
G. Michael Youngblood, UNC Charlotte
Priyesh N. Dixit, UNC Charlotte

3.6 **Goal-Oriented Plan Merging** 281
Michael Dawe

3.7 **Beyond A*: IDA* and Fringe Search** 289
Robert Kirk DeLisle

SECTION 4 AUDIO 295

Introduction 297
Alexander Brandon

4.1 **Audio Signal Processing Using Programmable Graphics Hardware** . 299
Mark France

4.2 **MultiStream—The Art of Writing a Next-Gen Audio Engine** 305
Jason Page, Sony Computer Entertainment, Europe

4.3 **Listen Carefully, You Probably Won't Hear This Again** 321
Stephan Schütze

4.4 **Real-Time Audio Effects Applied** 331
Ken Noland

4.5 **Context-Driven, Layered Mixing** 341
Robert Sparks

SECTION 5 GRAPHICS. 349

Introduction 351
Timothy E. Roden, Angelo State University

5.1 **Advanced Particle Deposition 353**
Jeremy Hayes, Intel Corporation

5.2 **Reducing Cumulative Errors in Skeletal Animations 365**
Bill Budge, Sony Entertainment of America

5.3 **An Alternative Model for Shading of Diffuse Light for Rough Materials. 373**
Tony Barrera, Barrera Kristiansen AB
Anders Hast, Creative Media Lab, University of Gävle
Ewert Bengtsson, Centre For Image Analysis, Uppsala University

5.4 **High-Performance Subdivision Surfaces 381**
Chris Lomont

5.5 **Animating Relief Impostors Using Radial Basis Functions Textures . 401**
Vitor Fernando Pamplona, Instituto de Informática: UFRGS
Manuel M. Oliveira, Instituto de Informática: UFRGS
Luciana Porcher Nedel, Instituto de Informática: UFRGS

5.6 **Clipmapping on SM1.1 and Higher 413**
Ben Garney

5.7 **An Advanced Decal System 423**
Joris Mans
Dmitry Andreev

5.8 **Mapping Large Textures for Outdoor Terrain Rendering. 435**
Antonio Seoane, Javier Taibo, Luis Hernández, and
Alberto Jaspe, VideaLAB, University of La Coruña

5.9 **Art-Based Rendering with Graftal Imposters. 447**
Joshua A. Doss, Advanced Visual Computing, Intel Corporation

5.10 **Cheap Talk: Dynamic Real-Time Lipsync. 455**
Timothy E. Roden, Angelo State University

SECTION 6 NETWORKING AND MULTIPLAYER 463

Introduction 465
Diana Stelmack

6.1 **High-Level Abstraction of Game World Synchronization** 467
Hyun-jik Baeb

6.2 **Authentication for Online Games** 481
Jon Watte

6.3 **Game Network Debugging with Smart Packet Sniffers** 491
David L. Koenig, The Whole Experience, Inc.

SECTION 7 SCRIPTING AND DATA-DRIVEN SYSTEMS 499

Introduction 501
Scott Jacobs

7.1 **Automatic Lua Binding System** 503
Julien Hamaide

7.2 **Serializing C++ Objects Into a Database Using Introspection** 517
Joris Mans

7.3 **Dataports** 535
Martin Linklater

7.4 **Support Your Local Artist: Adding Shaders to Your Engine** 541
Curtiss Murphy, Alion Science and Technology

7.5 **Dance with Python's AST** 555
Zou Guangxian

About the CD-ROM 561

Index 563

Preface

Six volumes of *Game Programming Gems* have preceded the edition now in your hands. Useful, practical ideas and techniques have spilled out of each and every one of them. Referred to in online discussions, contemplated by inquisitive readers, and consulted by both amateur and professional game developers, I believe the previous editions have contributed toward making the games we all play more innovative, entertaining, and satisfying. Significant efforts have been made so that this 7th volume continues this tradition.

Passion for Game Development

Game development is a fantastic endeavor of which to be a part. It can be a true meritocracy allowing passion and talent to shine. Degrees and experience can help get you in the door, but it often comes down to results. Is your code maintainable? Does its performance meet or exceed targets? Are the visuals and audio compelling? Is the gameplay fun? The challenge of excelling in these areas certainly contributes to the excitement of game development and I imagine is one of the motivations that inspired the authors of the following gems to share their ideas and experiences. I hope the same desires to excel have brought you to this book, as the intention of this volume and indeed the entire series is to provide tools and inspiration to do so.

There are not many industries where passion for the work runs so high that working professionals gather together with interested amateurs for weekend "jams" to do almost exactly what they just spent the previous five days doing. Maybe some of the lumberjack competitions I've seen on TV come close. But how many lumberjacks have a logging project going on at home just to try out some new ideas for fun and experience?

The necessity of domain expertise requirements means that often game developers become relegated to a particular role: graphics programmer, AI programmer, and so on. The sections of this book certainly reflect some of the common dividing lines between disciplines, although I must respect those who wish to quarrel with a few of the classifications within those categories as they sometimes don't always easily fall into just a single area. While I hope those with a more narrow focus find gems to suit their interests, I'm very excited about the diverse range and ability to appeal to those with a passion for all areas of game development. I want graphics programmers to read audio gems and vice versa!

Wanting to Make Games

Enthusiasm for game development from industry insiders may help explain why so many seem so eager to join up as game developers. Although self-taught independent renegades can still get their foot in the door (sometimes even making their own fantastic doors!), it is becoming increasingly easy to find quality educational help for those trying to enter game development as a first career choice. Besides the traditional math and computer science educational routes and a wealth of quality introductory to advanced publications, specialized game development degrees and courses are available at secondary schools and universities around the world, sometimes working in close collaboration with professional development studios. A wide variety of game genres are represented by published titles able to be modded, offering unprecedented access to cutting-edge multi-million-dollar game engines and a great way to enhance your experience or demo portfolio. Additionally, for most genres of games you can easily locate quality Open Source titles or engines available for inspection, experimentation, and contribution.

The opportunity to contribute to gaming also looks good for those passionate amateurs with significant non-game-related software development experience. We can use them. As game designs, target hardware, and development teams themselves become increasingly large and complex, the industry finds itself continuing its voracious appetite for good ideas from the rest of the software development industry. Does your development team include a DBA (pipe down, MMO developers!)? Inside you'll find a gem that suggests ways to integrate your object system with a relational database. We have a networking gem that applies tools to multiplayer development that are common to many network administrators, but may not yet have widespread use in our industry. Recognizing trends and successes in the wider software development community, development teams are increasingly adopting formalized project management and production methodologies like Agile and Scrum, where we can benefit from the general experience of our colleagues outside of game development. Making games isn't like making word processors, but good solutions for managing ever increasing team sizes, facilitating efficient intra-team communication, and managing customer (publisher!) relationships can't help but be similar to good solutions to the same problems experienced by those outside our industry. The shift to multi-core machines, whether on a PC or current-day consoles, has developers looking beyond the traditional C/C++ programming languages to solve problems of concurrency and synchronization and we are actively seeking out the experiences of those versed in languages like Haskell and Erlang to see of what we may make use.

Passion for Fun

Games are appealing because of their ability to challenge, amuse, and entertain. Many of our gems deal with the messy behind-the-curtain bits that don't directly contribute to making a game fun. A genre re-definer played over and over again and a clunker abandoned prior to the first boss fight can be using the same collision detection system or C++ to scripting language interface. It is the experience created by playing the game that produces the fun. So, in addition to gems addressing core bits, there are gems that contribute directly to a player's experience of the game, including audio production gems and human-game interactions. People are hungry for and eager to try new ways to interact with their games. The recent successes of *Rock Band,* the Guitar Hero franchise, *Dance Dance Revolution,* and of course, Nintendo's Wii, have demonstrated this without a doubt. New interfaces have given long-time gamers new experiences as well as tempted those not normally enticed by electronic games to give them a try, often opening a whole new avenue of fun for them, and new markets for us. I'm proud that this volume introduces three gems related to under-explored ideas in human-game interaction and greatly look forward to what will come in the future as these ideas and others are tried and refined.

Into this world of passionate developers, eager newcomers, voracious production requirements, and demands for innovating and entertaining gameplay and design comes this volume. Asking one book to meet the needs of all these interests is a tall order, but I feel confident that what follows will deliver, and I hope you agree. Let me know when your game is released. I want to check it out!

About the Cover Image

Christopher Scot Roby created the *Game Programming Gems 7* cover. The cover represents a few of the early steps in producing content for a game. Starting with the very left edge of the image, there are remnants of the original sketch, which was later painted on in Photoshop, resulting in the concept art seen on the left. The right portion reflects one of the very latest procedures for turning concepts into playable assets. Google Sketchup's Photo Match feature is used to block in geometry conforming to the concept image. Depending upon the pipeline, this geometry can then be directly exported into a form usable by a game, greatly speeding up the process of going from concept to something playable!

Acknowledgments

I must start by thanking Jenifer Niles and the *Game Programming Gems 6* editor Michael Dickheiser for giving me the opportunity and enjoyable burden of editing this volume. I also need to thank my section editors, both returning veterans and eager newcomers. Without these people and the years of experience they bring, I would have been overwhelmed by the fantastic articles supplied by our gems authors, many well outside my areas of expertise. I cannot overstate how much of their hard work is directly reflected in these pages.

Additionally, I would like to thank for their patience and efforts working with me to bring this book and accompanying CD-ROM together Emi Smith from Cengage, Kezia Endsley, Brandon Penticuff, and the unmet people undoubtedly supporting them.

My wife Veronica Noechel needs to be acknowledged for her understanding each time another night went by with cage cleanings postponed, TVs asked to be turned down, and cooking duties unshared. My parents should be thanked for so much as well, but I'll specially call out all the times my father brought home for my use his work PC. Honestly, they really used to be quite expensive, heavy, and require multiple trips across the parking lot to the car!

Contributor Bios

Contains bios for those contributors who submitted one.

Dmitry Andreev

Dmitry is a software engineer specializing in 3D graphics and tools at 10Tacle Studios, Belgium. Previously, he was a lead programmer at Burut CT/World Forge, the founder of the X-Tend gaming technology used in numerous releases, including the recent *UberSoldier* and *Sparta: Ancient Wars*. Dmitry started programming on ZX-Spectrum about 17 years ago. He is a well known demomaker and a two-time winner in 64K intro competition at the Assembly demo party. He has a B.S. in Applied Mathematics and Mechanics.

Hyun-jik Bae

After Hyun-jik Bae developed the *Speed Game* (see his Bio in *Game Programming Gems 5*), he developed *Boom Boom Car* (similar to *Rally-X*) by using Turbo Pascal when he was 11. *Boom Boom Car* was also mentioned by the hero actor in the movie *Who Are You?"* (from a love story of a gamer and a game developer). He is now a director with Dyson Interactive Inc. and developing another online game title. His major interests include designing and implementing high-performance game servers, scalable database applications, realistic renderers, and physics simulators, as well as piano, golf, and touring with his wife and son.

Tony Barrera

Tony Barrera is an autodidact mathematician and computer graphics researcher. He specializes in algorithms for performing efficient mathematical calculations, especially in connection with computer graphics. He published his first paper "An Integer Based Square-Root Algorithm" in *BIT* 1993 and has since published more than 20 papers. He has worked as a consultant for several companies in computer graphics and related fields. Currently, he is developing computationally efficient basic graphics algorithms together with Ewert Bengtsson and Anders Hast.

Anatoli Beliaev

Anatoli Beliaev (beliaev@trusoft.com) is a software engineer with more than 15 years of diverse development experience. Since 2001, he has been working for TruSoft as Lead Engineer responsible for the architecture of behavior-capture AI technologies. He is especially focused on adaptive and generic programming approaches, and their application to constructing highly efficient and flexible software in performance-demanding areas. Mr. Beliaev graduated from Bauman Moscow State Technical University with an M.S. in Computer Science.

Ewert Bengtsson

Ewert Bengtsson has been professor of Computerized Image Analysis at Uppsala University since 1988 and is currently head of the Centre for Image Analysis in Uppsala. His main research interests are to develop methods and tools for biomedical applications of image analysis and computer assisted visualization of 3D biomedical images. He is also interested it computationally efficient algorithms in graphics and visualization. He has published about 130 international research papers and supervised about 30 Ph.D. students. He is a senior member of IEEE and member of the Royal Swedish Academy of Engineering Sciences.

Jacco Bikker

Bikker is a lecturer for the International Architecture and Design course of the University of Applied Sciences, Breda, the Netherlands. Before that, he worked in the Dutch game industry for 10 years, for companies such as Lost Boys Interactive, Davilex, Overloaded PocketMedia, and W!Games. Besides his job, he has written articles on topics such as ray tracing, rasterization, visibility determination, artificial intelligence, and game development for developer Websites such as Flipcode.com and Gamasutra.

Bill Budge

Ever since he got his first set of blocks at age 2, Bill Budge has loved building things. At age 15, he discovered computer programming, the greatest set of blocks ever invented. Since then, his life's work has been to use these "blocks" to build even better sets of blocks. Among these have been *Bill Budge's 3D Game Toolkit* and *Pinball Construction Set.* He is currently building game editors in the Tools and Technology Group at Sony Computer Entertainment, America.

Joaquim Bento Cavalcante-Neto

Joaquim Bento Cavalcante-Neto is a professor of Computer Graphics in the Department of Computing at the Federal University of Ceará (UFC) in Brazil. He received his Ph.D. in Civil Engineering from the Pontifical Catholic University of Rio de Janeiro (PUC-Rio), Brazil, in 1998. While pursuing his Ph.D., he spent a year working with Computer Graphics/Civil Engineering at Cornell University. He was also a post-doctoral research associate at Cornell University from 2002 to 2003. During both his Ph.D. and post-doc, he worked with applied computer graphics. His current research interests are computer graphics, virtual reality, and computer animation. He also works with numerical methods, computational geometry, and computational mechanics. He has been the coordinator of several government-sponsored projects and the coordinator of the graduate program (master's and Ph.D. programs) in computer science at the Federal University of Ceará (UFC).

Michael Dawe

Michael's route to joining the games industry after college included three years in the consulting industry, two cross-country moves, and one summer devoted entirely to finishing his thesis. After earning a B.S. in Computer Science and a B.S. in Philosophy from Rensselaer Polytechnic Institute, Michael went on to earn an M.S. in Computer Science from DigiPen Institute of Technology while cutting his teeth in the industry at Amaze Entertainment. Michael is currently employed as an artificial intelligence and gameplay programmer at Big Huge Games.

Robert (Kirk) DeLisle

Robert (Kirk) DeLisle started programming in the early 1980s and has always had an interest in artificial intelligence, numerical analysis, and algorithms. During graduate school, he developed applications for his laboratory that were used for analysis of molecular biological data and were distributed internationally. Currently, he works as a Computational Chemist developing and applying artificial intelligence methods to computer-aided drug design and cheminformatics. He is author of a number publications and is named as co-inventor of various patents in the fields of computational chemistry and drug development.

Michael Delp

Michael is the Lead Artificial Intelligence Engineer at WXP Inc. in Seattle where he built an FPS AI from scratch in four months, which won critical acclaim. He's been an AI, physics, and gameplay software engineer throughout his career, including work on FPS, sports, and vehicle AI at small companies, like his current one, as well as large ones like EA and Sega. He has also lectured at the Game Developers Conference and taught an AI course for the University of Washington Extension. He earned his Computer Science degree at UC Berkeley.

Carlos Dietrich

Carlos Augusto Dietrich received a B.S. in Computer Science from the Federal University of Santa Maria, Brazil, and an M.S. in Computer Science from the Federal University of Rio Grande do Sul, Brazil. His research interests include graphics, visualization, and the use of GPUs as general purpose processors. He is currently a third-year Ph.D. student working in the Computer Graphics Group at the Federal University of Rio Grande do Sul, Brazil.

João Dihl

João Luiz Dihl Comba received a B.S. in Computer Science from the Federal University of Rio Grande do Sul, Brazil, and an M.S. in Computer Science from the Federal University of Rio de Janeiro, Brazil. After that, he received a Ph.D. in Computer Science from Stanford University. He is an associate professor of computer science at the Federal University of Rio Grande do Sul, Brazil. His main research interests are in graphics, visualization, spatial data structures, and applied computational geometry. His current projects include the development of algorithms for large-scale scientific visualization, data structures for point-based modeling and rendering, and general-purpose computing using graphics hardware. He is a member of the ACM SIGGRAPH.

Priyesh N. Dixit

Priyesh N. Dixit is a games researcher in the Department of Computer Science at The University of North Carolina at Charlotte and part of the Game Intelligence Group (playground.uncc.edu). His primary focus these days is in contributing to the development of the Common Games Understanding and Learning (CGUL) toolkit. He is the designer and developer of the CGUL PlayerViz and HIIVVE tools. He received his Bachelor of Science in Computer Science from UNC Charlotte and will complete his master's degree in Spring 2008 with the Game Design and Development certificate. His areas of interest are in learning and understanding from playtesting, building tools to support interactive artificial intelligence, and working on all types of computer games.

Joshua A. Doss

Joshua Doss started his career at 3Dlabs in the Developer Relations division creating several tools and samples for the professional graphics developer community. His software contributions include ShaderGen, an Open Source application that dynamically creates programmable shaders to emulate most fixed-function OpenGL as well as several of the first high-level GLSL shaders. Joshua is currently at Intel Corporation working with the Advanced Visual Computing team to create world-class graphics tools and samples for game developers.

Nathan Fabian

Nathan is a veteran hobbyist game developer, with 12 years' experience working satellite projects for Sandia National Labs. He's often thought about joining the game industry proper, but never taken the plunge. He has tinkered with various game technologies for over 20 years and cannot decide whether he prefers graphics special effects, physics simulation, or artificial intelligence. In the end, he'd really like to make a game involving 3D sound localization as a key element. Until then, he's finishing his master's degree in Computer Science at the University of New Mexico.

Marcus Aurelius Cordenunsi Farias

Marcus Aurelius Cordenunsi Farias graduated with a degree in Computer Science from Universidade Federal de Santa Maria (UFSM), Brazil in 2004. He obtained his master's degree in Computer Science (Computer Graphics) from Universidade Federal do Rio Grande do Sul, Brazil (UFRGS), in 2006. Last year, he worked in developing new interaction techniques for casual games for Zupple Games, a startup enterprise in Brazil. He has experience in the development of new interaction modalities for games, including computer vision and noise-detection techniques. Currently, he is working at CWI Software company in Porto Alegre, Rio Grande do Sul, Brazil.

Mark France

Mark recently graduated with a B.S. in Computer Games Technology. He is also a cofounder of the independent game development studio "Raccoon Games."

Ben Garney

Ben Garney has been working at GarageGames since it was eight guys in a tiny tworoom office. He sat in the hallway and documented the Torque Game Engine. Since then, he's done a lot with the Torque family of engines, working on graphics, networking, scripting, and physics. He's also helped out on nearly every game from GG—most notably *Marble Blast Ultra* and *Zap*. More recently, he's re-learning Flash and PHP for an avatar-creation Website. In his spare time, Ben plays piano, climbs buttes, and finds ways to survive living with his fuzzy kitty, Tiffany.

Julien Hamaide

Julien started programming a text game on his Commodore 64 at the age of eight. His first assembly programs followed soon after. He has always been self-taught, reading all of the books his parents were able to buy. He graduated four years ago at the age of 21 as a Multimedia Electrical Engineer at the Faculté Polytechnique de Mons in Belgium. After two years working on speech and image processing at TCTS/Multitel, he is now working as lead programmer on next-generation consoles at 10Tacle Studios Belgium/Elsewhere Entertainment. Julien has contributed several articles to the *Game Programming Gems* and *AI Game Programming Wisdom* series.

Anders Hast

Anders Hast has been a lecturer in computer science at the University of Gävle since 1996. In 2004, he received his Ph.D. from Uppsala University based on a thesis about computationally efficient fundamental algorithms for computer graphics. He has published more than 20 papers in that field. He is currently working part time as Visualization Expert at Uppsala Multidisciplinary Center for Advanced Computational Science.

Jeremy Hayes

Jeremy Hayes is a software engineer in the Advanced Visual Computing group at Intel. Before he joined Intel, Jeremy was part of the Developer Relations group at 3Dlabs. His research interests include procedural content generation (especially terrain), independent game design, and Dodge Vipers.

Scott Jacobs

Scott Jacobs has been working in the games industry since 1995. Currently, he is a Senior Software Engineer at Destineer. Prior to this he worked as a software engineer at the serious games company Virtual Heroes, two Ubisoft studios including Redstorm Entertainment, and began in the game development industry at Interactive Magic. He also served as the Network & Multiplayer section editor for *Game Programming Gems 6*. He lives in North Carolina with his wife and a house full of creatures.

Thomas Jahn

Thomas Jahn has been studying multimedia engineering at the Hochschule Bremen since 2002. In addition to his studies, he began working for KING Art Entertainment in 2005, where he contributed to the development of a turn-based strategy game. Intrigued by the tiling characteristics of hexagons, he dedicated his final thesis to hexagonal grids. After receiving his degree in Computer Science in the summer of 2007, Thomas was offered a full-time position at KING Art, Bremen, where he is currently working on the adventure game *Black Mirror 2*.

Alberto Jaspe

Alberto Jaspe was born in 1981 in La Coruña, Spain. His interest in computer graphics started with the demoscene movement when he was 15. During his studies of computer science at the University of La Coruña, he was developing 3D medical image visualization systems at the RNASA-Lab. Since 2003, he has been working as software engineer and researcher at the computer graphics group VideaLAB, taking part in different projects and publications, from terrain visualization to virtual reality and rendering.

Mark Jawad

Mark began programming when he was in the second grade, and never bothered to stop. He began his career in the videogame industry when he was 21, and soon specialized in Nintendo's hardware and software platforms. He spent eight years in Los Angeles writing many games, tools, and engines for systems like the N64, Game Boy Advance, GAMECUBE, and Nintendo DS. Mark moved to Redmond in 2005 to join Nintendo of America's developer support group, where he currently serves as the team's Technical Leader. In his spare time, he enjoys studying compilers and runtime systems, and spending time with his family.

Krzysztof Kluczek

Krzysztof was interested in game programming since he was 10. As 3D technology in games began evolving, he became more and more interested in the graphical aspect of 3D games. He received his master's degree in Computer Science at Gdansk University of Technology. Currently, he is pursuing his Ph.D. degree there, enjoying learning new technologies, making games, and being a part of the gamedev.pl community in his free time.

David L. Koenig

David L. Koenig is a Senior Software Engineer with The Whole Experience, Inc. in Seattle. His main focus is on network and resource loading code. He serves as an instructor for the networking and multiplayer programming course at the University of Washington. David is a returning author to the *Game Programming Gems* series. His work has contributed to many titles, including *SceneIt? Lights, Camera, Action* (Xbox 360), *Greg Hastings' Tournament Paintball Max'd* (PS2), *Tron 2.0* (PC), *Chicago Enforcer* (Xbox), and many more titles. He holds a bachelor's degree in Computer Engineering Technology from the University of Houston. His personal Website is http://www.rancidmeat.com.

Adam Lake

Adam Lake is a Graphics Software Architect in the Software Solutions Group leading development of a Graphics SDK at Intel. Adam has held a number of positions during his nine years at Intel, including research in non-photorealistic rendering and delivering the shockwave3D engine. He has designed a stream-programming architecture that included the design and implementation of simulators, assemblers, compilers, and programming models. Previous to working at Intel, he obtained an M.S. in computer graphics at UNC-Chapel Hill and worked in the Computational Science methods group at Los Alamos National Laboratory. More information is available at www.cs.unc.edu/~lake/vitae.html. He has several publications in computer graphics, and has reviewed papers for SIGGRAPH, IEEE, and several book chapters on computer graphics, and has over 35 patents or pending patents in computer graphics and computer architecture. In his spare time he is a mountain biker, road cyclist, hiker, camper, avid reader, snowboarder, and Sunday driver.

Dimitar Lazarov

Dimitar Lazarov is a senior software engineer at Luxoflux (an Activision owned studio). He has more than 10 years of experience in the game industry and has worked on a variety of games, ranging from children-oriented titles such as *Tyco RC, Casper,* and *Kung Fu Panda,* to more mature titles such as *Medal of Honor* and *True Crime*. He considers himself a generalist programmer with passion for graphics, special effects, animations, system libraries, low-level programming, and optimizations. He also has a recurring dream of writing his own programming language one day. In his spare time, Dimitar likes to read books, travel, play sports, and relax on the beach with his wife.

Martin Linklater

Martin Linklater is currently a lead programmer at SCEE Liverpool (UK). He has 14 years of experience in the games industry and has worked on many titles, including *Wipeout HD, Wipeout Pure,* and *Quantum Redshift.*

Chris Lomont

Chris Lomont, http://www.lomont.org, is a research scientist working on government sponsored projects at Cybernet Systems Corporation in Ann Arbor. He is currently researching image processing for NASA and designing hardware/software to prevent malware from infecting PCs for Homeland Security. At Cybernet, he has worked in quantum computing, has taught advanced C++ programming, and has unleashed chaos. Chris specializes in algorithms and mathematics, rendering, computer security, and high-performance scientific computing. After obtaining a triple B.S. in math, physics, and computer science, he spent several years programming in Chicago. He eventually left the video game company in Chicago for graduate school at Purdue, West Lafayette, resulting in a Ph.D. in mathematics, with additional graduate coursework in computer science. His hobbies include building gadgets (http://www.hypnocube.com), playing sports, hiking, biking, kayaking, reading, learning math and physics, traveling, watching movies with his wife Melissa, and dropping superballs on unsuspecting coworkers. He has two previous gems.

Jörn Loviscach

Jörn Loviscach has been a professor of computer graphics, animation, and simulation at Hochschule Bremen (University of Applied Sciences) since 2000. Before that, he was deputy editor-in-chief at *c't* computer magazine in Hanover, Germany. Jörn also possesses a Ph.D. in Physics. Since his return to academia he has contributed to *GPU Gems*, *Shader X3*, *Shader X5*, and *Game Programming Gems 6*. Additionally, he has authored and co-authored a number of works on computer graphics and interactive techniques presented at conferences such as Eurographics and SIGGRAPH.

Michael F. Lynch, Ph.D.

Dr. Lynch's background is in Electrical Engineering where he worked in various tech jobs before returning to grad school at an advanced age, where he crossed the great chasm over to the social sciences. Today he is a member of the faculty for the new Games and Simulations Arts and Sciences (GSAS) major at Rensselaer Polytechnic

Institute in Troy, New York, where he teaches "A History and Culture of Games" and a forthcoming course in AI for games. In his spare time, he does a little gourmet cooking, plays strange electronic music, and occasionally samples the Interactive Storytelling kool-aid (and plays games, too).

José Gilvan Rodrigues Maia

José Gilvan Rodrigues Maia is a doctoral student in the Department of Computing at the Federal University of Ceará (UFC) in Brazil. He received a B.S. and an M.S. in Computer Science from the Department of Computing at the Federal University of Ceará (UFC) in Brazil. During his M.S., he spent two years working with computer game technologies, specially rendering and collision detection. His current research interests are computer graphics, computer games, and computer vision. He has been working on research projects at the Federal University of Ceará (UFC).

Joris Mans

Joris Mans has a master's in Computer Science from the Free University, Brussels. Combining the knowledge gathered during his education and the hands-on experience as a developer in the demo-scene allowed him to start working in the games industry directly after graduating. He currently works as a lead programmer at 10Tacle Studios Belgium, poking around with stuff ranging from console data cache optimization to database backends.

Enric Martí

Enric Martí joined the Computer Science department at the Universitat Autònoma de Barcelona (UAB) in 1986. In 1991, he received a Ph.D. at the UAB with a thesis about the analysis of handmade line drawings as 3D objects. That same year he also became an associate professor. Currently, he is a researcher at the Computer Vision Center (CVC) and is interested in document analysis, and more specifically, Web document analysis, graphics recognition, computer graphics, mixed reality and human computer interaction. He is working on text segmentation in low-resolution Web images (for example, CIF and JPEG) using wavelets to extract text information from Web pages. Additionally, he is working on the development of a mixed-reality environment with 3D interfaces (data glove and optical lenses). He is also the reviewer of the *Computer & Graphics* and *Electronic Letters on Computer Vision and Image Analysis* (ELCVIA) journals.

Colt McAnlis

Colt "MainRoach" McAnlis is a graphics programmer at Microsoft Ensemble Studios specializing in rendering techniques and systems programming. He is also an adjunct professor at SMU's Guildhall school of game development where he teaches advanced rendering and mathematics courses. After receiving an advanced degree from the Advanced Technologies Academy in Las Vegas Nevada, Colt earned his B.S. in Computer Science from Texas Christian University.

Curtiss Murphy

Curtiss Murphy has been developing and managing software projects for 15 years. As a project engineer, he leads the design and development of several Serious Game efforts for a variety of Marine, Navy, and Joint government and military organizations. Curtiss routinely speaks at conferences with the intent to help the government leverage low-cost, game-based technologies to enhance training. Recent game efforts include a dozen projects based on the Open Source gaming engine, Delta3D (www.delta3d.org) and a public affairs game for the Office of Naval Research based on *America's Army*. Curtiss holds a B.S. in Computer Science from Virginia Polytechnic University and currently works for Alion Science and Technology in Norfolk, Virginia.

Luciana Nedel

Luciana Porcher Nedel received a Ph.D. in Computer Science from the Swiss Federal Institute of Technology in Lausanne, Switzerland, under the supervision of Prof. Daniel Thalmann in 1998. She received an M.S. in Computer Science from the Federal University of Rio Grande do Sul, Brazil, and a B.S. in Computer Science from the Pontifical Catholic University, Brazil. During her sabbatical in 2005, she spent two months at the Université Paul Sabatier in Toulouse, France, and two months at the Université Catholique de Louvain in Louvain-la-Neuve, Belgium, doing research on interaction. She is an assistant professor at the Federal University of Rio Grande do Sul, Brazil. Since 1991 she has been involved in computer animation research and since 1996 she has been doing research in virtual reality. Her current projects include deformation methods, virtual humans simulation, interactive animation, and 3D interaction using virtual reality devices.

Ken Noland

Ken Noland is a programmer at Whatif Productions and has worked on several internal projects that extend the technology and the infrastructure of the proprietary game engine. His focus tends to be on audio, networking, and gameplay, and he also works on the code behind the elusive content-driven technology that drives the Whatif engine, also known as the WorLd Processor. He's been involved in the games industry in one form or another for over six years. When not actively working, you can generally find him walking around town in a daze wondering what to do with this thing called "free time."

Jason Page

Jason Page has worked in the computer games industry since 1988 and has held job positions of games programmer, audio programmer, "musician" (audio engineer/ content creator), and currently is the Audio Manager at Sony Computer Entertainment Europe's R&D division. This role includes managing, designing, and programming various parts of the PlayStation 3 audio SDK libraries (the PS3 audio library "MultiStream" is used by many developers worldwide), as well as supporting developers on all PlayStation platforms with any audio issues. Of course, none of this would be possible without the hard work of his staff—so thanks also to them. Jason's past work as a audio content creator includes music and sound effects for titles such as *Rainbow Islands, The Chaos Engine, Sensible World of Soccer, Cool Boarders 2,* and *Gran Turismo.* Although he no longer creates music for games, he still writes various pieces for events such as the SCEE DevStation conference. Finally, he would like to say thank you to his wife, Emma, for putting up with his constant "I've just got to answer a developer's email" when at home. Jason personally still blames the invention of laptops and WiFi.

Vitor Fernando Pamplona

Vitor Fernando Pamplona received his B.S. in Computer Science from Fundação Universidade Regional de Blumenau. Since 2006 he has been a Ph.D. student at Universidade Federal do Rio Grande do Sul, Brazil. His research interests are in computer graphics, agile development, and free software. He also manages the java virtual community called JavaFree.org and leads seven free software projects.

Steve Rabin

Steve is a Principal Software Engineer at Nintendo of America, where he researches new techniques for Nintendo's next generation systems, develops tools, and supports Nintendo developers. Before Nintendo, Steve worked primarily as an AI engineer at several Seattle start-ups including Gas Powered Games, WizBang Software Productions, and Surreal Software. He managed and edited the *AI Game Programming Wisdom* series of books, the book *Introduction to Game Development*, and has over a dozen articles published in the *Game Programming Gems* series. He's spoken at the Game Developers Conference and currently moderates the AI roundtables. Steve is an instructor for the Game Development Certificate Program through the University of Washington Extension and is also an instructor at the DigiPen Institute of Technology. Steve earned a B.S. in Computer Engineering and an M.S. in Computer Science, both from the University of Washington.

Arnau Ramisa

Arnau Ramisa graduated with a degree in Computer Science from the Universitat Autònoma de Barcelona and is now working on a Ph.D. in Computer Vision and Artificial Intelligence at the Institut d'Investigació in Intelligència Artificial. He is interested in computer vision, augmented reality, human-machine interfaces and, of course, video games.

Mike Ramsey

Mike Ramsey is the principle programmer and scientist on the GLR-Cognition Engine. After earning a B.S. in Computer Science from MSCD, Mike has gone on to develop core technologies for the Xbox 360 and PC. He has shipped a variety of games, including *Men of Valor* (Xbox and PC), *Master of the Empire,* and several *Zoo Tycoon 2* products, among others. He has also contributed multiple gems to both the *Game Programming Gems* and *AI Wisdom* series. Mike's publications can be found at http://www.masterempire.com. He also has an upcoming book entitled, *A Practical Cognitive Engine for AI.* In his spare time, Mike enjoys strawberry and blueberry picking and playing badminton with his awesome daughter Gwynn!

Graham Rhodes

Graham Rhodes is a principal scientist at the Southeast Division of Applied Research Associates, Inc., in Raleigh, North Carolina. Graham was the lead software developer for a variety of Serious Games projects, including a series of sponsored educational mini-games for the *World Book Multimedia Encyclopedia*; and more recently, first/third-person action/role-playing games for industrial safety and humanitarian demining training. He is currently involved in developing software that provides procedural modeling and physics-based solutions for simulation and training. Graham contributed articles to several books in the *Game Programming Gems* series, and authored the section on real-time physics for *Introduction to Game Development.* He is the moderator and frequent contributor to the math and physics section at gamedev.net, has presented at the annual Game Developer's Conference (GDC) and other industry events, and regularly attends GDC and the annual ACM/SIGGRAPH conference. He is a member of ACM/SIGGRAPH, the International Game Developer's Association (IGDA), and the North Carolina Advanced Learning Technologies Association (NC ALTA).

Timothy E. Roden

Timothy Roden is an associate professor and head of the Department of Computer Science at Angelo State University in San Angelo, Texas. He teaches courses in game development, computer graphics, and programming. His research interests include entertainment computing with a focus on procedural content creation. His published papers in entertainment computing appear in *ACM Computers in Entertainment, International Conference on Advances in Entertainment Technology,* the International Conference on Entertainment Computing and Microsoft Academic Days on Game Development Conference. He also contributed to *Game Programming Gems 5*. Before joining academia, Roden spent 10 years as a graphics software developer in the simulation industry.

Rahul Sathe

Rahul P. Sathe is working as a software engineer in the Advanced Visual Computing Group at Intel Corp where he is developing an SDK for next generation high-end graphics hardware. He's currently involved in designing advanced graphics algorithms for game developers. Earlier in his career, he worked on various aspects of CPU architecture and design. He holds a bachelor's degree from Mumbai University (1997) in Electronics Engineering and his master's in Computer Engineering from Clemson University (1999). He has prior publications in the computer architecture area. His current interests include graphics, mathematics, and computer architecture.

Stephan Schütze

Stephan Schütze currently resides in Tokyo where he is working in both the anime and game industries while trying to learn both the Japanese language and its culture. See Stephan@stephanschutze.com and www.stephanschutze.com.

Antonio Seoane

Antonio Seoane is a researcher who works in "VideaLAB" (http://videalab.udc.es), the Visualization For Engineering, Architecture, and Urban Design Group of the University of A Coruña, in Spain. He has been working for 10 years in the research and development of real-time graphics applications focused on topics like simulation, civil engineering, urban design, cultural heritage, terrain visualization, and virtual reality. Main research interests and experiences are terrain visualization (http://videalab.udc.es/santi/), and in recent years working on GPGPU and Artificial Intelligence.

Dillon Sharlet

Dillon Sharlet is an undergraduate student in Mathematics and Electrical Engineering at the University of Colorado at Boulder. He has been interested in computer graphics for years. He likes exploring new algorithms in graphics. In his free time, he likes to go climbing and skiing.

Gary Snethen

Gary's passion for computing began before he had access to a computer. He taught himself to program from examples in computer magazines, and wrote and "ran" his first programs using pencil and paper. When his parents balked at buying a computer, Gary set out to create his own. When his parents discovered hand-drawn schematics for functional digital adders and multipliers, they decided it was more than a passing interest and purchased his first computer. Gary's early interests were focused heavily on games and 3D graphics. Gary wrote his first wireframe renderer at age 12, and spent many late nights throughout his teens writing one-on-one modem games to share with his friends.

Gary is currently a principal programmer at Crystal Dynamics, where he shipped *Legacy of Kain: Defiance* and *Tomb Raider Legend.* Gary's current professional interests include constrained dynamics, advanced collision detection, physics-based animation, and techniques for improving character fidelity in games.

Robert Sparks

This is Robert's seventh year programming audio in the games industry. Most recently he was a technical lead on *Scarface: The World Is Yours* (Radical Entertainment, Vancouver, Canada). His past game credits include *The Simpsons: Hit & Run*, *The Simpsons: Road Rage*, *The Hulk*, *Tetris Worlds*, *Dark Angel*, and *Monsters, Inc.*

Diana Stelmack

Diana Stelmack works at Red Storm Entertainment, where she has worked on the *Ghost Recon* series since Spring 2001. Since the PC version of this title, Xbox Live Online services and multiplayer game system support have become her development focus. Prior to games, her network background included telecommunications, IP Security, and DoD Network communications. Just remember "If you stumble, make it look like part of the dance"!

Javier Taibo

Javier Taibo graduated in computer science at the University of Coruña in 1998. He has worked on computer graphics R&D projects in the "Visualization for Engineering, Architecture and Urban Design Group" (a.k.a. VideaLAB). The fields he has been working on include real-time 3D terrain rendering and GIS visualization, virtual reality, and panoramic image and video. At present he is also teaching computer animation and 3D interaction at the University of A Coruña.

Daniela Gorski Trevisan

Daniela Gorski Trevisan graduated with a degree in Informatics from Universidade Federal de Santa Maria (UFSM), Brazil, in 1997. She obtained her master's degree in Computer Science (Computer Graphics) from Universidade Federal do Rio Grande do Sul (UFRGS), Porto Alegre, Brazil, in 2000. She earned her Ph.D. degree in applied sciences from Université catholique de Louvain (UcL), Belgium, in 2006. Nowadays she is a CNPq researcher and member of the Computer Graphics group of Informatics Institute at UFRGS. Her research interest topics are focused on the development and evaluation of alternative interaction systems, including multimodal, augmented, and mixed reality technologies.

Iskander Umarov

Iskander Umarov (umarov@trusoft.com) is the technical director of TruSoft (www.trusoft.com). TruSoft develops behavior-capture AI technologies and provides AI middleware and consulting services to other companies to implement innovative AI solutions for computer and video games and simulation applications on PC, PlayStation 2, PlayStation 3, and Xbox 360 platforms. Mr. Umarov authored the original ideas behind TruSoft's Artificial Contender AI technology. Artificial Contender provides behavior-capture AI agents for games and simulation applications. These AI agents capture human behavior, learn, and adapt. Mr. Umarov is currently responsible for managing development of TruSoft's AI solutions and leads TruSoft's R&D efforts, including joint projects with Sony, Electronic Arts, and Lockheed Martin. Mr. Umarov holds a B.S. in Applied Mathematics and an M.S. in Computer Science, both from Moscow Technological University, where he specialized in instance-based learning methods and graph theory.

Enric Vergara

Enric Vergara is a computer engineer at the Universitat Autònoma de Barcelona and recently received a master's degree in Video Games Creation at Pompeu Fabra University. He now works as a C++ programmer for GeoVirtual.

Creto Augusto Vidal

Creto Augusto Vidal is an associate professor of computer graphics in the Department of Computing at the Federal University of Ceará in Brazil. He received his Ph.D. in civil engineering from the University of Illinois at Urbana-Champaign in 1992 and was a post-doctoral research associate at the Department of Mechanical and Industrial Engineering at the University of Illinois at Urbana-Champaign from 1992 to 1994. He is currently a visiting researcher at VRLab at EPFL (École Polytechnique Fédérale de Lausanne) in Switzerland. His current research interests are computer graphics, virtual reality applications, and computer animation. He has been the coordinator of several government-sponsored projects investigating the use of networked virtual environments for training and education.

Jon Watte

In addition to his job as CTO of serious virtual world platform company Forterra Systems, Jon is a regular contributor to the independent game development community. As a Microsoft DirectX/XNA MVP and moderator of the Multiplayer and Networking forum on the independent games site GameDev.Net, he enjoys sharing experience from his time in the business, with his earliest shipping title a cassette-based game for the Commodore VIC 20. Prior to heading up Forterra Systems, Jon worked on products such as There.com, BeOS, and Metrowerks CodeWarrior.

G. Michael Youngblood

G. Michael Youngblood, Ph.D., is an Assistant Professor in the Department of Computer Science at The University of North Carolina at Charlotte, co-director of the Games + Learning Lab, and head of the Games Intelligence Group (playground.uncc.edu). His work studies how artificial agents and real people interact in virtual environments, including computer games and high-fidelity simulations in order to understand the elements and patterns of learning for the development of better artificial agents. He has worked with real-time computer games, intelligent environments, and robotics since 1997. His research interests are in interactive artificial intelligence, entertainment computing, and intelligent systems.

SECTION

1

GENERAL PROGRAMMING

Introduction

Adam Lake, Graphics Software Architect, Advanced Visual Computing Group (AVC), Intel

adam.t.lake@intel.com

Game development continues to undergo significant changes in every aspect. Extracting performance in previous generations of hardware meant a focus on scheduling assembly instructions, exploiting small vector instructions (SSE, for example), and ensuring data remains in registers or cache while processing. Although these issues are still relevant, they are now secondary relative to exploiting the multithreaded hardware in current generation consoles and PCs. To this end, we have included articles on tools and techniques for game programmers to take advantage of this new hardware: *Design and Implementation of a Multi-Platform Threading Engine* by Michael Ramsey, an implementation of a *Multithread Job and Dependency System* by Julien Hamaide, and a *Deferred Function Call Invocation System* by Mark Jawad. These issues have become more prevalent in the time since the last *Game Programming Gems* publication.

In the category of systems we have three articles. Two systems software articles include *High Performance Heap Allocator* by Dimitar Lazarov and *Efficient Cache Replacement Using the Age and Cost Metrics* by Colt McAnlis. Martin Fleisz also brings us an article on *Advanced Debugging Techniques*. Martin covers issues related to exception handling, stack overflows, and memory leaks—common issues we all encounter during application development.

We also have an exciting set of articles in this edition related to user interfaces for games. Carlos Dietrich et al. have an article on sketch-based interfaces for real-time strategy games. Arnau Ramisa et al. have written an article on optical flow for video games played with a Webcam, and Marcus C. Farias et al, have described a new first-person shooter interface in *Foot Navigation Technique for First-Person Shooting Games*. Finally, a wonderful paper on using hexagonal tiling instead of a traditional square grid is presented by Thomas Jahn and Jörn Loviscach entitled *For Bees and Gamers: How to Handle Hexagonal Tiles*.

Each of these authors brings to the table his or her own unique perspective, personality, and vast technical experience. My hope is that you benefit from these articles and that these authors inspire you to give back when you too have a gem to share. Enjoy.

1.1

Efficient Cache Replacement Using the Age and Cost Metrics

Colt "MainRoach" McAnlis
Microsoft Ensemble Studios
cmcanlis@ensemblestudios.com

In memory-constrained game environments, custom media caches are used to amplify the amount of data in a scene, while leaving a smaller memory footprint than containing the entire media in memory at once. The most difficult aspect of using a cache system is identifying the proper victim page to vacate when the cache fills to its upper bounds. As cache misses occur, the choice of page-replacement algorithm is essential—this choice is directly linked to the performance and efficiency of hardware memory usage for your game. A bad algorithm will often destroy the performance of your title, whereas a well implemented algorithm will enhance the quality of your game by a significant factor, without affecting performance. Popular cache-replacement algorithms, such as LRU, work well for their intended environment, but often struggle in situations that require more data to make accurate victim page identifications. This gem presents the Age and Cost metrics to be used as values in constructing the cache-replacement algorithm that best fits your game's needs.

Overview

When data is requested from main memory, operating systems will pull the data into a temporary area of memory (called a *cache*), which can be accessed at a faster speed than main memory. The cache itself is a predefined size, segmented into smaller sets of memory called *pages*. As memory accesses occur, the cache itself can get filled, at which time the operating system must choose a page from the cache in which to replace with the incoming page data. This occurrence is called a *cache miss*. When the amount of needed pages exceeds the size of the cache by a significant amount (usually 2x or more) a *thrash* occurs, that is, the entire cache will be dumped in order to make room for the entirety of the incoming data set. Thrashing is considered the worst-case scenario for any caching algorithm, and is the focal point of any performance testing of cache replacements.

Each time the memory handler has to fetch information from main memory, there is an associated cost involved with it. Reading from the cached memory has a smaller cost, usually due to introduction of an extra memory chip closer to the processor itself. So, in determining which page to dump from memory when a cache miss occurs, one of the key goals is to pick a page that does not need an active spot in the cache. For instance, if you randomly chose a page to evict during the fault, and that page happens to be needed immediately after its eviction, you would incur another performance overhead to re-fetch that data from the main memory. The goal is to create an algorithm that best describes which page is ideal to remove from the cache to reduce the amount of cache misses and performance burden.

These types of algorithms, called *victim page determination* or *page-replacement* algorithms were a hot topic in the 1960s and 1970s, and reached a plateau with the introduction of the Least Recently Used (LRU) algorithm (as well as other working-set systems). Since that time, derivations of these algorithms have been generated in order to address some of the issues that LRU presents when working in specific subject areas. For example, [O'Neil93] described an offshoot of LRU, called LRU-K, which was described to work more efficiently in software database systems. Adaptive Replacement Cache (ARC) is an algorithm developed by IBM used both in hardware controllers as well as other popular database systems [Megiddo03]. (See the "References" section at the end of this gem for more information.)

In game development, programmers have to deal with caches both on the hardware and on the software level, especially in the game console arena where programmers constantly struggle to increase the amount of content in the game while still fitting within memory constraints. Like many other replacement algorithms tailor-made to solve a specific problem, there are common game and graphics systems that require a replacement system that better resembles the memory patterns and usage models. This gem describes two cache page metrics that can be interweaved together in a way that better fits into the video game development environment.

Cache-Replacement Algorithms

Since their creation, cache-replacement systems have been an active area of research, resulting in a large number of various algorithms custom tuned to solve various instances of the problem space. In order to have a frame of reference, I'll cover a few of the most common algorithms here.

Belady's Min (OPT)

The most efficient replacement algorithm would always replace the page that would not be needed for the longest period of time since its eviction from the cache. Implementing this type of algorithm in a working system would require the foreknowledge of system usage, which would be impossible to define. The results of implementing OPT in test situations where the inputs over time are known can be used as a benchmark to test other algorithms.

In a multithreaded environment, where there is a producer-consumer architecture between threads, it is possible to get close to OPT using information from the producer thread if the producer thread is multiple frames ahead of the consumer.

Least Recently Used (LRU)

The LRU algorithm replaces the page that hasn't been used for the longest amount of time. When a new page is loaded into the cache, data is kept per page that represents how long since the given page has been used. Upon a cache miss, the victim page is then the one that hasn't been used in the longest time span. LRU does some cool things, but is prone to excessive thrashing. That is, you'll always have an oldest page in the cache, which means that unless you're careful, you can actually clear the entire cache when workloads are large.

Most Recently Used (MRU)

MRU replaces the page that was just replaced. That is, the youngest page in the cache. MRU will not replace the entire cache; rather, during heavy thrashing it will always choose to replace the same page. Although not as popular and robust as LRU, MRU has its uses.

In [Carmack00], John Carmack lists a nice hybrid system between LRU and MRU for texture cache page replacement. In short, it works in the form that you use LRU most of the time, until you reach the point that you need to evict an entry every frame, at which time you switch to an MRU replacement policy. As mentioned previously, LRU has the problem that it will potentially thrash your entire cache if not enough space is available. Swapping to MRU at the point you would begin to thrash the cache creates a *scratch pad* in memory for one page, leaving most of the cache unharmed. This can be useful if the amount of textures being used between frames is relatively low. When you're dealing with a situation in which the extra pages needed are double the available cache size this method degenerates; this might stall the rendering process.

Not Frequently Used (NFU)

The not frequently used (NFU) page-replacement algorithm changes the access heuristic to keep a running counter of accesses for every page in the cache. Starting at zero, any page accessed during the current time interval will increase their counter by one. The result is a numeric qualifier referencing how often a page has been used. To replace a page, you then must look for the page with the lowest counter during the current interval.

The most serious problem with this system is that the counter metric does not keep track of access patterns. That is, a page that was used heavily upon load and hasn't been used since then can have the same count as a page used every other frame for the same time interval. The information needed to differentiate these two usage patterns is not available from a single variable. The Age metric, presented in the next section, is a modification of NFU that changes how the counter is represented, so that you can derive extra information from it during thrashing.

For a more expansive list of algorithms, hit up your favorite search engine with "Page Replacement Algorithms," or dust off your operating systems textbook from college.

Age and Cost Metrics

For the purpose of illustration, the rest of the gem references a problem facing most games in the current generation of hardware: the design of a custom texture cache. To do this, you will reserve a static one-dimensional array of cache pages into which data can be loaded and unloaded. Assume that you are working with a multi-dimensional texture cache; that is, the data that you're placing in the cache is of texture origin. The cache is multi-dimensional in the sense that multiple textures of various sizes could fit into a single cache page. For example, if the cache page size fits a 256 × 256 texture, you can also support four 64 × 64 textures, 16 32 × 32 textures, and so on, including multiples of each size existing in the same page in harmony.

Even in this simple example, you have already laid the groundwork for standard replacement functions to under-perform. Consider the case of the multi-dimensional cache where you need to insert a new 256 × 256 page into the cache when it is entirely filled with only 32 × 32 textures. Simple LRU/MRU schemes do not have the required data available to properly calculate which full cache page is the optimal one to replace and which group of 32 × 32 textures needs to be dumped as the access patterns depend greatly on more than the time at which the page was last replaced. To this purpose, a new set of replacement metrics are presented in order to better analyze the best pages to replace when in such a situation.

The Age Algorithm

The OPT algorithm knows the amount of usage for a page in the cache and replaces the one that will be used the farthest away in time. Most replacement algorithms attempt their best to emulate this algorithm with various data access patterns. The Age algorithm emulates this process by keeping a concept of usage over the previous frames in order to best predict future usage; that is, you need to keep track of how many times a page has been accessed in a window of time. To accomplish this task, every page in the cache keeps a 32-bit integer variable that is initialized to 1 (0x00000001) when the page first enters the cache.

Every frame, all active pages in the cache are bit-shifted left by one bit, signifying their deprecation over time. If an active page is used in this frame, the least significant bit of the Age variable is set to one (1); otherwise, it is set to zero (0). This shifting and setting pattern allows you to keep a usage evaluation for the past 32 frames.

For example, a page that is accessed every other frame would have an Age variable 0xAAAAAAAA (010101010....01), whereas a page that was accessed heavily when it was first loaded, and has not been used since, would have an Age variable 0xFFFF0000 (1111...1100000...00).

To show how the Age variable evolves over time, consider a page that is used in the first, third, fourth, and eighth frames over an eight-frame window. The Age variable would change like such:

```
frame1 - 00000001 (used)
frame2 - 00000010 (not used)
frame3 - 00000101 (used)
frame4 - 00001011 (used)
frame5 - 00010110 (not used)
frame6 - 00101100 (not used)
frame7 - 01011000 (not used)
frame8 - 10110001 (used)
```

With this information layout, you can calculate the Age Percentage Cost (APC) of the given window. You average the number of frames a page has been used versus the number of pages not used by dividing the number of frames used (ones) by the total number of frames in the Age variable. This data can be extracted using assembly and processor heuristics rather than higher-level code. Although you can represent this data your own way, the APC presented exists as a normalized single value between [0, 1], and as described in the "Age and Cost" section, can be used as a scalar against other metrics.

When using age to determine the target victim page, you seek to choose the pages that have not been used in a certain time, as well as pages that are not frequently used in general. For example, a page that has been accessed every frame in the window will have a 100% APC and will be almost impossible to replace, whereas a page with an APC of 25% will have a higher chance of being replaced.

What I like about Age is that it gives a number of implicit benefits:

- It biases old textures, forcing textures to prove that they are needed for the scene. Once they prove this fact, they are kept around. Once an APC gets above 50%, it gets difficult to release it from the cache.
- It creates a scratch pad. New textures that haven't proved they are valuable yet are turned into scratch pads. This is a good thing, as new textures can often be temporary and have a high probability to vanish the next frame
- It is a modified NRU (not recently used) scheme. Textures that might have been visible a high percentage for a short time could easily shoot up to 50% APC, but then drop out, and slowly work their APC back down over a number of frames. Age offers a modified representation of the access variable, and allows extra analysis, so if the APC > 60%, but the texture hasn't been used in the most recent X frames, you can check for this and eliminate it early.

The APC variable as presented so far is powerful, but not without fault—multiple pages in the cache can have radically different access patterns but have the same APC value. That is, 0xAAAAAAAA and 0xFFFF0000 have the same usage percentage but it's easy to see that the usage patterns for these two Age variables are dramatically different. Subsequent analysis patterns on the binary data in the basic Age variable could help separate those pages with similar APC values (such as analyzing sub-windows for secondary APC values) but fall into similar problems.

Expanded Age Algorithm

The previously presented Age algorithm makes the assumption that you'd like to keep the memory required to deduce page information fairly low; hence storing a used/unused flag per frame over a window of 32 frames. It should be noted, however, that in situations where the required page amount is larger by a significant factor, the Age algorithm degenerates just as any others would. If, for example, you had 50 textures that were used every frame, and only 12 cache pages in which to put them, there would not be enough space in the cache for your entire memory footprint at once. Every frame would thrash the entire cache, replacing each page.

In this situation, the constant loading/reloading of pages and textures would cause every page to have an Age counter set to 1, and thus would lack any additional information that would be helpful in the identification of specific victim pages. To help solve this problem, the Age variable can store more information per frame than just a used/unused bit, and, in fact, store the usage count of a texture instead. So rather than storing a 0/1 in a single 32-bit integer variable, you could store a list of numbers, each storing how often that page was used in the frame. This would resemble a list of [1, 18, 25, 6, 0, 0,...1] rather than 01001010011..1. This extra information is particularly helpful in the degenerate case, as you now have additional data to assist in the identification of a victim page.

For example, consider two pages (TextureA and TextureB) loaded into the cache at the same time with TextureA being used on 50% of the objects in the scene and TextureB being used on 10%. At this point, both pages would have the same APC value, although clearly, you can identify that these two textures have dramatically different usage amounts. When a victim page must be found, you must take into account that TextureA, being used a larger amount in the current frame, increases the probability that it will be used in the subsequent frame as well. Thus a lower usage texture, TextureB, should be replaced instead.

By storing this extra data per frame, you make available other statistical analysis operations to help identify the best page to evict from the cache:

- The APC variable can still be derived from the expanded Age algorithm by dividing the number of non-zero frames in the window by the total frames.
- Finding the page with the MIN usages in a given frame window will identify the least used page in general, which is helpful to identify victims.
- Using the MAX analysis, you could identify the pages with the most accesses in your window, in order to help avoid dumping them from the cache.
- Finding the AVG usage in the window is just as easy and derives a second simplistic variable similar to APC.

Depending on your implementation needs and data formats, either the simple Age algorithm or the Expanded Age algorithm are viable. The best idea is to sit down and analyze your data to decide which is the most efficient and useful algorithm for your title.

The Cost of Doing Replacements

Most victim page identification algorithms use only a single heuristic. That is, their algorithms are tailor-made to specialize to the access patterns that result in the least amount of cache page misses. For example, LRU only keeps a pointer to the oldest page. However, for a custom software cache there often is a second heuristic that is involved with a cache miss—the cost of filling the page of the cache with the new data. For most hardware caches this is a constant cost associated with the time it takes the memory handler to access main memory and retrieve the desired data.

For your software needs, however, this cost can often fluctuate between pages themselves. Therefore, it would make sense that the victim page determination takes into account the amount of performance hit involved with actually filling a page with a given chunk of memory. This performance cost (or just *cost*) can come from a number of sources. It can be hand-defined by an external data set (for example, an XML file that defines which textures are really used) or it can be defined by the actual cost of filling the page.

Consider that in the previous example, an incoming texture page is generated by streaming it off an optical drive. So, larger textures have a larger performance time involved with getting them into the cache, because they have more information to be streamed from media, whereas smaller or simpler textures have fractions of that cost. In this situation, it would make a great deal of sense to consider the cost involved with potentially replacing a page in memory during victim page determination. If you victimize a page that has a high cost associated with it, you can incur unneeded overhead in the next few frames if that page is required. If, instead, you eliminate a page that has a lower cost, the performance hit from incorrectly removing it from the cache is much lower. In a nutshell, factoring in cost as a page-replacement variable allows you to answer the question "Is it cheaper to dump five smaller textures to make space for 1 larger texture?"

To review, cost allows you to be concerned with how much a given page will hurt performance to reload it into the cache. If required, an expansion of this system allows a victim page identification function to be more concerned about performance cost of a miss, as opposed to coherence between frames.

By itself, cost contains the same problems that other cache replacement algorithms have. When a thrash occurs, you find the cheapest texture in the cache and get rid of it. Because there's always a cheaper page available, the entire cache could potentially thrash if the load is big enough. This algorithm also has the problem that it can leave highly expensive pages in the cache indefinitely. If something like a skybox texture is loaded into the cache, this is a good trait as the skybox will be active every frame and most likely not want to be removed from the cache due to its large size. Most of the time, this is a bad trait and one that needs constant attention.

Cost is a powerful ally when combined with other heuristics. By biasing the replacement identification of access pattern algorithms with replacement metrics, you allow your cache to find a nice medium between page-replacement requirements and thrashing. Additionally, the access pattern identification helps remove the problems involved with pure cost metrics, allowing high-cost items to eventually be freed from the cache when they reach the state that they are no longer needed.

Age and Cost (A&C)

The previous example assumed that each page in the texture cache had an associative APC as well as a relative cost (RC), and was updated every frame. This example assumes that the RC is a more important metric and allows that value to be an integer variable that has no upper limit. For example, if you are moving textures into your cache by streaming them from disk, the RC may be a result of the texture size divided by the time it takes to stream a fraction of that texture from the media. Consider the APC a normalized floating-point variable between (0,1).

In a simple implementation, you can combine these two values into a single result where the APC acts as a scalar of the RC, thus giving ThrashCost = RC*APC. In general, this turns out to be a very nice heuristic for identifying the proper victim page. To prove this, I've provided a few examples of APC/RC ratio, and a description of the replacement pattern. For the following data, assume that the highest RC value can be 10.

APC	RC	TC	Pattern
1.0	10	10	This page is highly expensive to replace, thus will be a hard candidate to move. With the APC of 1.0, this identifies that the page has been used every frame over the Age window. At this point, the only way this page can be replaced is if it's forced by a full cache dump, which might not be allowed depending on your implementation.
0.2	8	4	This page has a relatively high RC, but its APC shows that it's rarely used, and thus could be considered as a valid replacement. However, because the RC is so high, it's worth doing a second APC test on sub-windows of the data in order to determine if this texture should really be replaced.
1.0	5	5	This page is at the halfway point. That is, it's relatively cheap to replace, however its APC says that it will be needed next frame. Replacing this page would be no problem, but due to the high APC, it might be worth the extra search to find another page with a higher RC but lower APC.
0.01	10	0.1	This page has an extremely low APC, which points to the fact that it has either just been introduced to the cache, or it is infrequently used. In either case, the TC is so low that other pages with lower RCs could bump it if their APC is higher. Because the RC is so high, however, it's worth doing a second APC test on sub-windows of the data in order to determine if this texture should really be replaced.

As seen in this table, using the simplistic RC*APC value can result in pages with differing APC/RC values having the same ThrashCost. This will mean that texture A with an APC/RC relation of 0.5/100 can have the same cost as texture B with an APC/RC of 1.0/50. The question here is how do you determine which page to replace? In theory, either page is a valid target, both containing the same numerical weight for potential replacement. Texture A has a higher cost, and thus would be more expensive to replace if it were needed in the next frame. Texture B has a lower cost, but has an APC value of 100%, so there's a high probability that this page will be needed immediately.

In practice, I've found that biasing this decision to replace a lower APC when multiple pages return the same value works much better. In fact, that's why the Age metric is used. By analyzing the usage pattern, along with cost, you can see that although a page is more expensive, it is used less often, and thus has a lower probability of being incorrectly thrashed. In these situations, it's a good idea to re-scan the cache to find a page with a higher ThrashCost, but with a lower APC value. If one isn't found, it's safe to assume that this page may need to be replaced for the sake of the cache. However, depending on your system, the better page to replace may vary.

This table mentions one other instance that needs discussing. As mentioned, the A&C system has the ability to introduce a page that can become static. This can be a good thing if your cache includes textures that are visible from most every camera angle, such as a skybox texture, or an avatar skin. This can also be bad, however, if this is not desired. If too many of these pages are introduced into the cache, the available working size shrinks considerably, causing more cache misses and overall less cache efficiency. If this is the case, it might be wise to generate a separate cache for these static textures.

Conclusion

Custom media cache systems are critical for any high-performance environment. As the usage of out-of-core media increases, the need for an accurate control model also increases for game environments. Because older replacement algorithms were designed with operating system memory management and hardware memory access patterns in mind, they lack some key properties that allow them to evaluate the more complex replacement situations that can exist. Using a combination of the Age and Cost metrics introduces a great deal of additional information, for a very low overhead, that fits and works well in gaming environments. The Cost metric introduces a concept of overall performance in page loading, which for an on-demand out-of-core system can become a major bottleneck. The Age metric allows a more per-frame based view of usage patterns that ties easier into the concept of the game simulation than traditional metrics, and also contains enough usable information to create valid replacement cases in any environment-specific edge case. Because cache replacement needs change over the course of simulation, this allows a great deal of customization and second order analysis to evaluate the best victim page for best results.

The advantage of using this powerful duo of metrics is an overall increase in cache-page replacement performance, resulting in a lower overhead of thrashes and general cost required to fill the cache. At the end of the day, that's really what you're looking for.

Acknowledgments

Big thanks to John Brooks at Blue Shift for the metric in the "Expanded Age Algorithm" section, as well as help getting all this off the ground!

References

[Carmack00] Carmack, J. "Virtualized Video Card Local Memory Is the Right Thing," Carmack .Plan file, March 07, 2000.

[Megiddo03] Megiddo, Nimrod and Modha, Dharmendra S. "ARC: A Self-Tuning, Low Overhead Replacement Cache," USENIX File and Storage Technologies (FAST), March 31, 2003, San Francisco, CA.

[O'Neil93] O'Neil, Elizabeth J. and others. "The LRU-K Page-Replacement Algorithm for Database Disk Buffering," ACM SIGMOD Conf., pp. 297–306, 1993.

1.2

High Performance Heap Allocator

Dimitar Lazarov, Luxoflux

dimitar.lazarov@usa.net

This gem shows you a novel technique for building a high performance heap allocator, with specific focus on portability, full alignment support, low fragmentation, and low bookkeeping overhead. Additionally, it shows you how to extend the allocator with debugging features and additional interface functions to achieve better performance and usability.

Introduction

There is a common perception that heap allocation is slow and inefficient, causing all kinds of problems from fragmentation to unpredictable calls to the OS and other undesirable effects for embedded systems such as game consoles. To a large extent this has been true, mostly because historically console manufacturers didn't spend a lot of time or effort implementing high-performance standard C libraries, which include all the heap allocation support. As a result many game developers recommend not using heap allocation, or go as far as outright banning its use in runtime components of the game engine. In its place, many teams use hand-tuned memory pools, which unfortunately is a continuous and laborious process that is debatably inflexible and error-prone. All this goes against a lot of the modern C++ usage patterns, and more specifically the use of STL containers, strings, smart pointers, and so on. Arguably, all these provide a lot of powerful features that could dramatically improve code development, so it's not so difficult to see why you would want to have the best of both worlds. With this in mind, we set out to create a heap allocator that can give the programmer the performance characteristics of a memory pool but without the need to manually tinker with thousands of lines of allocation-related code.

Related Works

A popular open source allocator by [Lea87], regarded as the benchmark in heap allocation, uses a hybrid approach, where allocations are handled by two separate methods, based on the requested allocation size. Small allocations are handled by bins of linked lists of similarly sized chunks, whereas large allocations are handled by bins of "trie" binary tree structures. In both cases, a "header" structure is allocated together with every requested block. This structure is crucial in determining the size of the block during a free operation, and also for coalescing with other neighboring blocks. Allocations with non-default alignment are handled by over-allocating and shifting the start address to the correct alignment.

Both of these factors, header structure and over-allocating, contribute unfavorably to alignment heavy usage patterns as is common in game programming. A slightly different approach by [Alexandrescu01] suggests using a per-size template pool-style allocator. A pool-style allocator uses a large chunk of memory, divided into smaller chunks of equally sized blocks that are managed by a single linked list of free blocks, commonly known as the *free-list*. This has the nice property of not needing a header structure and hence has zero memory overhead and naturally gets perfect alignment for its elements. Unfortunately, during deallocation, you have to either perform a search to determine where the block came from or the original size of the block needs to be supplied as an additional parameter. Combining ideas from the previously described work and adding our little gem, we arrive at our solution.

Our Solution

Our solution uses a hybrid approach, whereby we split our allocator in two parts—one handling small allocations and the other handling the rest.

Small Allocator

The minimum and maximum small allocations are configurable and are set by default to 8 and 256 bytes, respectively. All sizes in this range are then rounded up to the nearest multiple of the smallest allocation, which by default would create 32 bins that handle sizes 8, 16, 24, 32, and so on, all the way to 256, as shown in Figure 1.2.1.

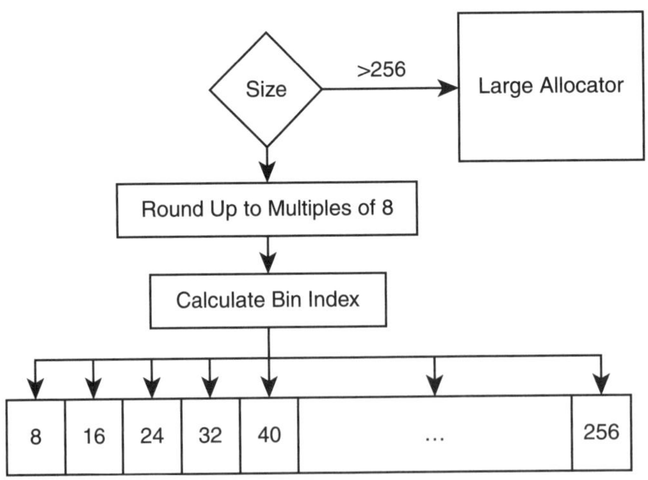

FIGURE 1.2.1 Selection of the appropriate bin based upon allocation size.

Notice that since the small allocations are arranged into bins of specific sizes, you can keep any size-related information just once for the whole bin, instead of with every allocation. Although this saves memory overhead, you might rightly wonder how you find this information when, during a free operation, you are supplied only with the address of the payload block.

To explain this, we need to establish how the small allocator would deal with managing memory. You might want to allocate large blocks of memory from the OS, as is traditionally done with pool-style allocators, but let's do it on demand so as to minimize fragmentation and wasted memory. Additionally, you want to return those same large blocks (let's call them *pages*) back to the OS once you know when they are not used anymore and you need the memory somewhere else.

What is important to note here, for the correctness of this method, is that it asks for naturally aligned pages from the OS. In other words, if the selected page size is 64KB, this method expects it to be 64KB aligned.

Once a naturally aligned page is acquired, the method places the bookkeeping information at the back of the page. There, it stores a free-list that manages all elements inside the page. A use count determines when the page is completely empty, and a bin index determines which bin this page belongs to. Most importantly, all pages that belong to the same bin are linked in a doubly-linked list, so that you can easily add, remove, or arrange pages.

The last piece of the puzzle is almost straightforward—during a free operation, the provided payload address is aligned with the page boundary. Then you can access the free list and the rest of the bookkeeping information, as shown in Figure 1.2.2.

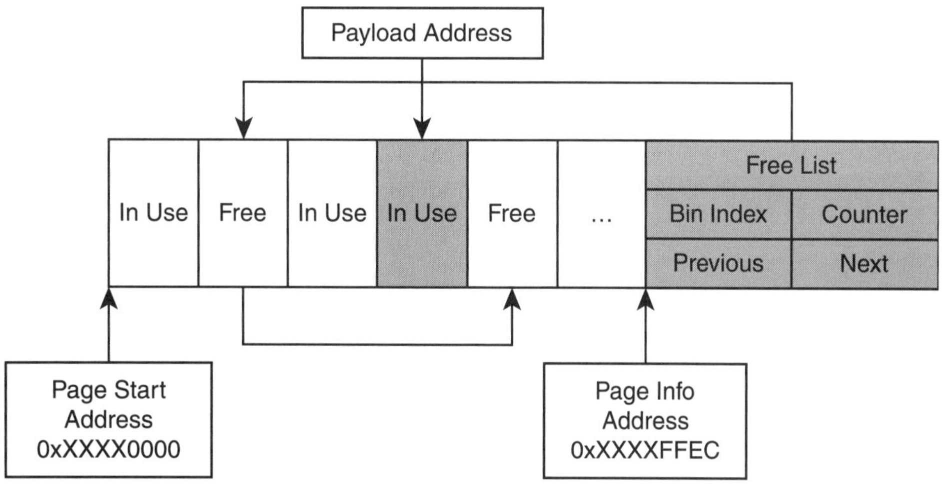

FIGURE 1.2.2 The layout of a single page in a bin.

This method places the bookkeeping information at the back of the page, as opposed to the front, because there is often a small piece of remaining memory at the back, due to the page size not being exactly divisible by the element size. Therefore, you get the bookkeeping cost for free in those situations.

This method also ensures that whenever a page becomes completely full it is placed at the back of the list of pages for the corresponding bin. This way, you just need to check the very first page's free-list to see whether you have a free element available. If no elements are available, the method requests an additional page from the OS, initializes its free-list and other bookkeeping information, and inserts it at the front of the bin's page list.

With this setup, small allocations and deallocations become trivially simple. For example, when the allocation size is known in advance, as is the case with "new"-ing objects, the compiler can completely inline and remove any bin index calculations and the final code becomes very comparable in speed and size to an object specific pool-style allocator.

Large Allocator

The small allocator is simple and fast; however, as allocation sizes grow, the benefits of binning and pool allocations quickly disappear. To combat this, this solution switches to a different allocator that uses a header structure and an embedded red-black tree to manage the free nodes. A red-black tree has several nice properties that are helpful in this scenario. First, it self-balances and thus provides a guaranteed O(log(N)) search, where N is the number of free nodes. Second, it also provides a sorted traversal which is very important when dealing with alignment constraints. Finally, it is very handy to have an embedded red-black tree implementation around.

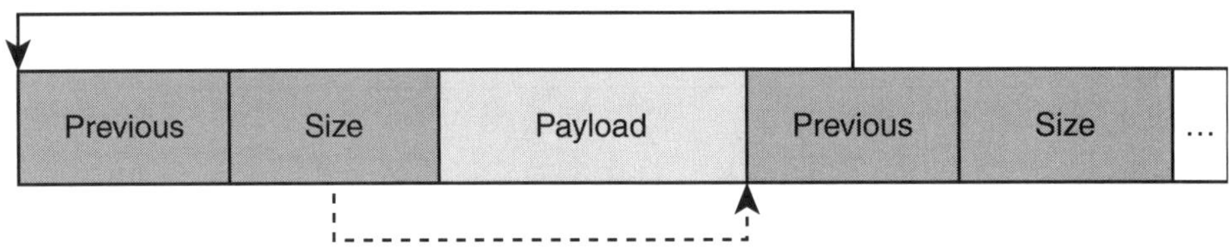

FIGURE 1.2.3 Layout of memory use in the large allocator.

As shown in Figure 1.2.3, the header structures are organized in a linked list of memory blocks arranged in order of their respective addresses. There is no explicit "next" pointer, because the location of the next header structure can be computed implicitly from the current header structure plus the size of the payload memory block. In addition to this, you need to store information about whether a block is currently free. This information can be stored in the least significant bit of the "size" field, because the requested sizes for large allocations are rounded up to the size of the header structure (8 bytes). This rounding is necessary to allow header structures to naturally align between payload blocks.

When a block is freed, you use the empty space to store the previously mentioned red-black tree node. The red-black tree is a straightforward implementation, as in [Cormen90], with a few notable modifications.

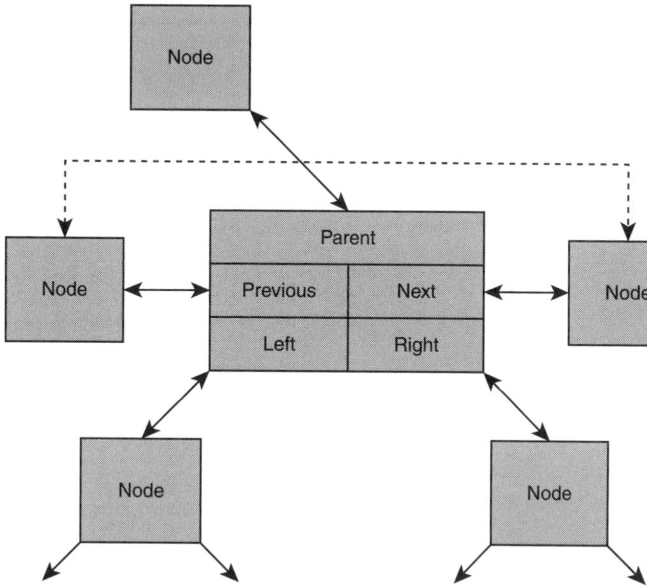

FIGURE 1.2.4 The layout of the red-black tree nodes.

As shown in Figure 1.2.4, you have the classic left, right and parent pointers. There are also two additional pointers, previous and next, that form a linked list of nodes that have the same key value as the current node. This helps tremendously with performance, because it's quite common to have lots of free blocks with identical sizes. In contrast, a traditional red-black tree would store same key value nodes as either left or right children, depending on convention. This would predictably reduce performance, because when searching through these nodes, the search space is not halved as usual to achieve O(log(N)) speed, but is merely walked in a linear fashion of O(N).

Both left/right and previous/next pointers are organized as arrays of two entries. This is done mostly to simplify operations such as "rotate left" and "predecessor," which normally have mirrored counterparts such as "rotate right" and "successor." Using an index to signify left or right, you can then have a generic version that can become either.

Furthermore, in each node, you keep information on which side of its parent that node is attached—left or right—as well as its "color"—red or black. This allocator uses a similar packing trick as with the header structure, and places the parent side index and the node color in the two least significant bits of the parent pointer. The parent side index is quite important for performance, especially when combined with a red-black tree that uses the so-called "nil" node, because the essential "rotate" operation can then become completely branch-free.

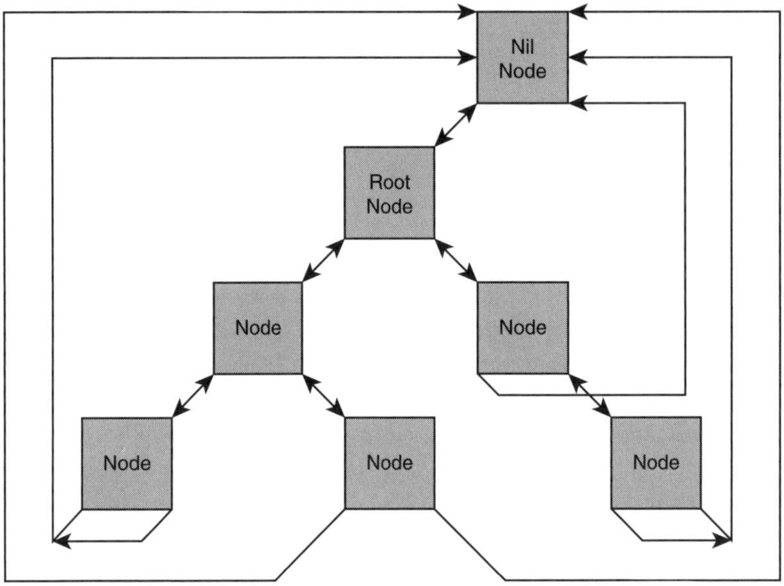

FIGURE 1.2.5 The nil node's place in the tree.

As shown in Figure 1.2.5, the "nil" node is a special node that all terminal nodes point to, and is also the node to which the root of the tree is attached. The fact that the root is to the left side of the "nil" node might appear random, but in fact this is very important for traversal operations. It is easy to notice that running a predecessor operation on the "nil" node would give the maximum element in the tree, which is exactly what you want to happen when you iterate the tree backward starting from the "nil" node—in STL terminology that is the "end" of the container. This way, the predecessor operation doesn't need to handle any special cases.

With all this setup done, during an allocation you search the red-black tree for the appropriate size. If the acquired block is too big, it is chopped up and the remainder is returned to the tree. If there are no available blocks, more are requested from the OS, usually in multiples of large pages.

During a free operation, you look up the header structure and determine whether any of the neighbors are free so they can be coalesced. Because the coalescing is done for every freed block, there could be no more than one adjacent free block on each side, and thus this operation needs to check only two neighbors. The resulting free block is then added to the red-black tree.

The more interesting use of the red-black tree happens when you need to allocate with non-default alignment. This allocator uses the fact that you can iterate a binary tree in sorted order, and notice that you need to check nodes with sizes equal or larger than the requested size, but smaller than the requested size plus the requested alignment. You then can use the binary tree operations "lower bound" with the requested size and "upper bound" with the requested size plus alignment. You can then iterate through this range until you find a block that satisfies the alignment constraint. Iterating through a red-black tree is an O(log(N)) operation, so obviously larger alignments would take longer to find. The important thing to notice is that this will guarantee the smallest-fit block criteria, which is considered to be one of the major factors in reducing fragmentation, something that the traditional approach of over-allocating and shifting doesn't satisfy very well.

Combining the Allocators

Now that you have two allocators, there is another problem. The small allocator relies on the page alignment to find its bookkeeping information. With two allocators though, you need a way to distinguish which allocator a given address comes from. There are several solutions, none of them is perfect, but one is the simplest. You go ahead and access the page info structure, and try to recognize it. You need to make sure the large allocator always uses pages that are at least as large as the small allocator's pages, which makes accessing the page info safe. You place a per bin marker that gets hashed with the page info address and store it inside the page info. Then, during a free operation, you access the page info and compute the hash again. If it matches, you accept the address as originating from the small allocator; otherwise, you forward it to the large allocator. This solution is very simple and fast, but it has the nagging problem that it might, with a very small probability, match the incorrect page. There is a way to detect this mistake and in the reference implementation this verification is performed for debug builds. If a misdetection ever happens, one can increase the security by using bigger hashes or extra checks.

There are at least a few other ways to solve this problem. One is to use a bit array, one bit for every page in the address space. On 32-bit machines with 64KB pages, this bit array is merely 8KB, but unfortunately this doesn't scale very well to 64-bit machines.

A second solution is to keep an array of pointers in every bin, each entry pointing back at their respective page, while the page itself has a bin and array offset indices. This guarantees that the page truly belongs to that bin, but unfortunately makes the memory management of that array quite complicated.

A third solution is to use a reserved virtual address range for all small allocations, and with a simple check you can immediately determine whether a pointer belongs to it or not. Of course, this requires the use of virtual memory, which is either not present or severely limited on many game consoles, and most importantly requires specifying some upper bound on small allocations that might not be possible in certain situations.

Multithreading

It is quite important these days to have robust multithreading, and the allocator is often the very first thing that needs to be properly implemented. Our solution is not ground-breaking but provides good efficiency in mild levels of contention. Notice that the small allocator can have a mutex per bin because once the bin is selected there is no sharing of data between bins. This means that allocations that go to different bins can proceed in full parallel. On the other hand, the large allocator is more complicated and you need to lock it as soon as an operation needs access to the red-black tree.

The only faster alternative to having a mutex per bin is to use thread local storage. That might be feasible especially on systems that can afford some additional memory slack per thread. Unfortunately, thread local store is still non-portable and has all kinds of quirks.

Debugging Features

So far, we have a high-performance allocator that can easily be used as a `malloc/free` replacement. Now, you can easily add features that can help you with debugging or extracting additional performance or functionality.

There are many ways to add debugging support and the reference implementation takes a classic approach of keeping debug records for every allocation made. These records are kept in separately managed memory so that they interfere with the payload as little as possible. We reuse several of the methods developed for the main allocator, specifically we use an embedded red-black tree to quickly search debug records and also we use a novel container that we call a *book*. The idea is that we have a hybrid data structure similar to a list which we manage in "pages" and we can only add elements to the end, as one would write words in a book, hence the name. The need for such a specific structure arises from the fact that you need to use large memory chunks directly from the OS and you want the data structure to take care of that memory, similar to how dynamic arrays over-allocate and then fill in elements one at a time.

When you combine the embedded red-black tree with the "book" container, you can manage the debug records quite efficiently. Besides the size and the address of the payload block, the debug record stores a partial copy of the call stack at the time of the allocation request, which can be quite useful for tracking memory leaks. Additionally, you can store the so-called "debug guard," which is a series of bytes of memory that is over-allocated with the payload and is filled with a sequence of numbers.

Then, during a free operation, the "debug guard" is examined to verify the integrity of the block. If the expected sequence of numbers is not found, it's highly likely there is some memory stomping going on. It is a bit more difficult to determine who exactly did the stomping, but often it is code related to whoever allocated that block, so that's a good starting point. If the stomp is reproducible, a well placed hardware breakpoint can quickly reveal the offender.

Extensions

So far, this allocator follows quite closely the `malloc/free/realloc` interface. We have found that exposing a bit more functionality can be very beneficial for performance.

The first addition is what we call "resize"—the ability to change the size of an already allocated block, but without changing the address of that block. Obviously, this means the block can only grow from the back, and even though that seems limited, it turns out it can be very useful for implementing dynamic arrays or other structures that need to periodically expand.

Another extension is the provision of free operations that take as additional parameters the original requested size and alignment. This is beneficial to this allocator because it can use that size to determine whether the small or the large allocator should free that block. These additional functions cannot be used on blocks that have been reallocated or resized, and the only significant use for these additional functions would be to implement high-performance "new" and "delete" replacements.

On the CD

ON THE CD

There is a reference implementation of the allocator on the included CD. It has been used in practice in a next generation game engine together with a custom STL implementation that takes advantage of our allocator's features and extensions. We also provide a simple synthetic benchmark to verify that the allocator has any performance advantages.

Furthermore, we show several ways to integrate this allocator with existing or future C++ code. The easiest way, of course, is to just override the global new and delete operators. This has several disadvantages, but most notably it is not an appropriate solution for a middleware library. Per class new and delete operators, as tempting as they sound, in practice prove to be quite difficult to work with and tend to have frustrating limitations. We show one possible way to have correct custom per object new and delete functionality with template functions.

References

[Alexandrescu01] Alexandrescu, Andrei. *Modern C++ Design,* Addison-Wesley Longman, 2001.

[Berger01] Berger, Emery D. "Composing High-Performance Memory Allocators," available online at ftp://ftp.cs.utexas.edu/pub/emery/papers/pldi2001.pdf.

[Cormen90] Cormen, Thomas. *Introduction to Algorithms,* The MIT Press, 1990.

[Hoard00] Berger, Emery. "The Hoard Memory Allocator," available online at http://www.hoard.org/.

[Lea87] Lea, Doug. "A Memory Allocator," available online at http://g.oswego.edu/dl/html/malloc.html.

1.3

Optical Flow for Video Games Played with Webcams

Arnau Ramisa, Institut d'Investigació en Intelligència Artificial

aramisa@iiia.csic.es

Enric Vergara, GeoVirtual

evergara@geovirtual.com

Enric Martí, Universitat Autónoma de Barcelona

Enric.Marti@uab.cat

One of the most widely used techniques in computer vision commercial games is the concept of *optical flow.* Optical flow is the movement between the pixels of successive frames of a video stream provided, for example, by a modern Webcam.

Multiple techniques, with different properties, exist in the computer vision literature to determine the optical flow field between a pair of images [Beauchemin95]. This gem explains three of these techniques—the direct subtraction of successive frames, motion history, and a more advanced technique called the Lucas and Kanade algorithm. These three techniques have a different degree of robustness and also a different computational cost, therefore the choice depends on the requirements of each application.

Introduction

The proposed algorithms are prepared and ready to use, with many other computer vision techniques, in the OpenCV library. This library is an open source project that implements in C the most important algorithms and data structures used in computer vision applications. In 2006, the first stable version of OpenCV (1.0) was released after five years of development. *Game Programming Gems 6* contains an article where this library is used to detect in which position the face of the player is located [Ramisa06]. This information was used to map the action of leaning around a corner in a third- or first-person shooter.

The optical flow is an array of vectors that describes the movement that has occurred by pixels between successive frames of a video sequence. Usually it is taken as an approximation to the real movement of the objects in the world. The optical flow information is used not only by many computer vision applications, but also by biological systems such as flying insects or even humans. An example of this application is the MPEG4 video compression standard, which uses the optical flow of blocks of pixels to eliminate redundant information in video files.

In computer vision games, the optical flow is used to determine if a particular pixel of the screen is "activated" or not. If enough pixels of a certain area are activated, one can consider that a "button" has been pressed or, in general, that an action has been performed.

For this, it is usually not necessary to estimate the full optical flow field and computationally cheaper methods that compute only if a given pixel has changed with respect to the previous frame can be used.

OpenCV Code

This section explains the most important functions of the `webcamInput` class. The usage of the class is structured around a main loop where new frames are acquired from the Webcam.

```
#define ESC_KEY 27
webcamInput webcam(true,1);
   // method = (1: Lucas-Kanade,  2: Differences, 3: Motion History)

while(1)
{
     webcam.queryFlow();

     if(cvWaitKey(10)==ESC_KEY)
          break;
}
```

In this code, a new `webcamInput` object called `webcam` is created. This object encapsulated all the logic to acquire images through the camera and process them. The constructor requires two parameters: a Boolean that indicates if the camera connection should be initialized during the object construction or not, and an integer from 1 to 3 that indicates which method of the optical flow will be used. Later, inside the loop, the `queryFlow()` function is used to acquire a new frame and process it. Finally, `cvWaitKey()` is used to pause for 10ms waiting for the Escape key to possibly stop the process.

During initialization all required variables, depending on the method, are allocated in memory:

```
void webcamInput::queryFlow()
{
    getImage();

    switch(method)
    {
    case 1:
        lucaskanade();
    break;
    case 2:
        differences();
    break;
    case 3:
        flowHistory();
    break;
    }

    flowRegions();

    cvCopy( image, imageOld );
      //to save the previous image to do optical flow
}
```

The function `getImage()` acquires a new image from the Webcam and converts it to gray-level, then, depending on the method chosen, the appropriate function is called. Finally, `flowRegions()` is used to count the activated pixels in the defined regions of interest, and the current image is copied to `imageOld` for using it in the next optical flow computation.

First Method: Image Differences

In this section, the three methods used are explained. The first method is the simplest one: image differences. This method is really simple, and consists of subtracting the current camera image from the previous one:

```
void webcamInput::differences()
{
   cvSmooth( image, image, CV_GAUSSIAN, 5, 5);
   cvAbsDiff( imageOld, image, mask );
   cvThreshold( mask, mask, 5, 255, CV_THRESH_BINARY ); // and
   threshold it
   /* OPTIONAL */ cvMorphologyEx(mask, mask, NULL,kernel,
   CV_MOP_CLOSE ,1);
   cvShowImage("differences", mask);
}
```

The `cvAbsDiff` function subtracts `image` from `imageOld`, which are the current and previous images of the Webcam. The result of the operation is stored in `mask`, and in the next line its content is binarized: all pixels with a value lower than 5 (which indicates similar pixels in `image` and `imageOld`) are discarded, whereas the ones with a higher value are marked as active. This threshold depends on the sensitivity of the used Webcam. If a lower value is used, more valid active pixels would be correctly detected, but at the same time more false active pixels would appear, generated by noise in the images. To reduce the effect of noise in the estimation, the first step consists in smoothing the image using a Gaussian kernel of 5×5 pixels. This is done using the function `cvSmooth()`.

Individual or small groups of activated pixels are not likely to correspond to real moving objects, therefore the function `cvMorphologyEx()` applies a closure to eliminate these spurious activated pixels while not changing the correct ones [Morphology]. The size and shape of the morphologic operator is defined in the structure `kernel`. Finally, the last parameter specifies the number of times in a row that the erosion and dilation are performed. The closure is a powerful yet computationally expensive operation, and can be avoided if the noise level of the images is low, or by raising the value of the threshold.

This method is faster than the Lucas and Kanade method, but it is not as robust at handling bad camera quality.

Second Method: Motion History

The second method is called motion history. It uses the same principle of the image differences but uses more than just the previous image, and "remembers" recently active pixels.

```
void webcamInput::flowHistory()
{
   //FLOW HISTORY

   cvSmooth( image, image, CV_GAUSSIAN, 5, 5);
   cvCopy( image, buf[last]);
     IplImage* silh;

     int idx2;
     int idx1=last;
     idx2 = (last + 1) % N; // index of (last - (N-1))th frame
     last=idx2;
     int diff_threshold=30;

     silh = buf[idx2];
     double timestamp = (double)clock()/CLOCKS_PER_SEC;

     cvAbsDiff( buf[idx1], buf[idx2], silh );

     cvThreshold( silh, silh, diff_threshold, 1, CV_THRESH_BINARY );
     cvUpdateMotionHistory( silh, mhi, timestamp, MHI_DURATION );
     cvCvtScale( mhi, mask, 255./MHI_DURATION,
           (MHI_DURATION - timestamp)*255./MHI_DURATION );

     cvShowImage("M_history",mask);
}
```

In this function, `buff` is a cycling buffer where the last N images from the Webcam are stored. When a new image enters the buffer, the oldest and the new image are subtracted, and the result is thresholded to find pixels where reliable change has occurred. Then the motion history image `mhi` is updated with this new information and the timestamp for the latest frame. Finally, the new motion history image is scaled to an 8 bits per pixel mask image. Moreover, this motion history image can be used to determine the motion gradient and to segment different moving objects. A complete example of this method can be found in the `motempl.c` file of the OpenCV samples.

Third Method: Lucas and Kanade Algorithm

The first two methods don't give as output the real optical flow, they just detect pixels where motion has occurred. However, in this case, you can trade the destination position of the moved pixels for less computational load. The last method presented is the optical flow estimation method by Lucas and Kanade [Lucas81]. This method estimates the position where a given pixel has moved using a procedure similar to how the Newton-Raphson method finds the zeroes of a function.

```
void webcamInput::lucaskanade()
{
    cvCalcOpticalFlowLK(imageOld,image,cvSize
          (SIZE_OF,SIZE_OF), flowX, flowY);

    cvPow( flowX, flowXX, 2 );
    cvPow( flowY, flowYY, 2 );
    cvAdd( flowXX, flowYY, flowMOD );
    cvPow( flowMOD, flowMOD, 0.5 );

    cvThreshold( flowMOD, flowAUX, 10, 255, CV_THRESH_BINARY );
    /* OPTIONAL */ cvMorphologyEx
       (flowAUX, flowAUX, NULL,kernel, CV_MOP_CLOSE ,1);

    cvShowImage("LUKAS_KANADE",flowAUX);
}
```

The function `cvCalcOpticalFlowLK()` computes the optical flow between the gray-level images `imageOld` and `image` using the Lucas and Kanade method. The remaining parameters of the function are `cvSize(SIZE_OF,SIZE_OF)`, which specifies the size of the window that will be used to locate the corresponding pixel in the other image, and `flowX` and `flowY`, where the components of the optical flow vectors will be stored. You are interested in the module of the vectors, which indicates the strength of the movement. Once you have the module, you threshold it to eliminate all active pixels caused by noise. If the camera is really noisy, it is also possible to use a morphological closure to remove isolated pixels.

The time values shown in Table 1.3.1 were obtained on a Pentium IV 3GHz computer running the openSUSE 10.2 operating system where the execution time was measured over 100 iterations. The image size was 640 × 480.

Table 1.3.1 Time Required for Each Iteration of the Motion Detection Algorithms

	Mean	Median	Std
Image differences	0.020867s	0.025000s	0.0063869s
Motion history	0.027794s	0.025000s	0.0056899s
Lucas and Kanade	0.21114s	0.19500s	0.043091s

Optical Flow Game

In order to see the results of the optical flow in a real application, we developed a simple game resembling *Eye Toy: Play* (a game developed by SCEE London, using a digital camera similar to a Web camera, for PlayStation 2). The idea behind the game is very simple: clean the stains that appear on the screen through bodily movements (see Figure 1.3.1).

Because players could move their arms about frantically, thereby cleaning all stains as they appear without any difficulty, we added some toxic stains that players have to avoid in order to keep on playing. This forces players to be careful with their movements, introducing an element of skill which makes the game more fun.

FIGURE 1.3.1 A screenshot of the game.

The point is to use the optical flow in the game, so we have encapsulated the functionality described previously in a C++ class called `webcamInput`, which makes it easier to apply to the game. The public interface of this class is as follows:

```
class webcamInput
{
public:

    webcamInput( int method=1 );
      // method = (1: Lukas-Kanade,  2: Differences, 3: M History)
   ~webcamInput( );

    void      GetSizeImage         ( int &w, int &h );
    uchar*    GetImageForRender    ( void );

    void      QueryFlow            ( void );
    void      AddRegion            ( int x, int y, int w, int h );
    std::vector<float> FlowRegions ( void );

private:
      ...
}
```

In the class's constructor, you can decide which method, from the three introduced in the previous section, you want to use in order to calculate the optical flow. As the default, we use the Lucas and Kanade method, which seems to yield the best results.

In order to show on the screen the color image coming from the Webcam (the player's body), this class provides two important functions. The first one is `GetSizeImage()`, which informs you of the size of the image coming from the Webcam. The second function is `GetImageForRender()`, which returns an array of `unsigned char` values that represent the RGB (red, green, blue) components of the pixels, ordered in rows. By means of the `QueryFlow()` function, you can calculate the optical flow of the current frame.

Yet, what you need for the game is to be able to query the amount of movement that has taken place in a particular area of the image (the one occupied by a stain to be cleaned). To achieve this, at the beginning of the game you can define as many regions as you want by making use of the function `AddRegion(int x, int y, int w, int h)`. This function creates a region with its origin at the coordinates (x, y) of the image generated by the Webcam and a width and height given by `(w, h)`.

Once the regions have been defined, every time `QueryFlow()` is called, you can get the extent of the movement in each region by using the function `FlowRegions()`. This function returns a list of floating-point values (as a `std::vector<float>`) comprising values within the [0,1] range that represent the percentage of pixels where movement has been detected.

In the game, you have to instantiate an object (`mWebCam`) of this class, subsequently calling its functions from several parts of the code, as described here:

1. Upon game initialization, as we have already pointed out, you need to partition the query for optical flow in several distinct regions. In particular you have to divide the initial image into 16 regions as a 4 × 4 grid (see Figure 1.3.2). In order to achieve this, you need to use the function `mWebCam.AddRegion()` as follows:

```
int width, height;
mWebCam.GetSizeImage( width, height );
for(int col = 0; col < 4; col++)
{
    for(int row = 0; row < 4; row++)
    {
        mWebCam.AddRegion(col* (width/4), row*(height/4),
            width/4, height/4);
    }
}
```

2. During rendering, you can call the function `mWebCam.GetImageForRender()` in order to paint the colour image coming from the Webcam. On top of the image, you paint the stains with a certain alpha component, depending on how clean they are. The image of the stains will occupy all the space determined by every one of the 16 regions.
3. During the game updates, the function `mWebCam.QueryFlow()` will be called first, followed by a call to `mWebCam.FlowRegions()`. This way, you know the extent of the movement that has taken place in each one of the 16 regions, making more and more transparent (based on the movement detected) the images of the stains that are active at that particular moment. Stains vanish as they become completely transparent.

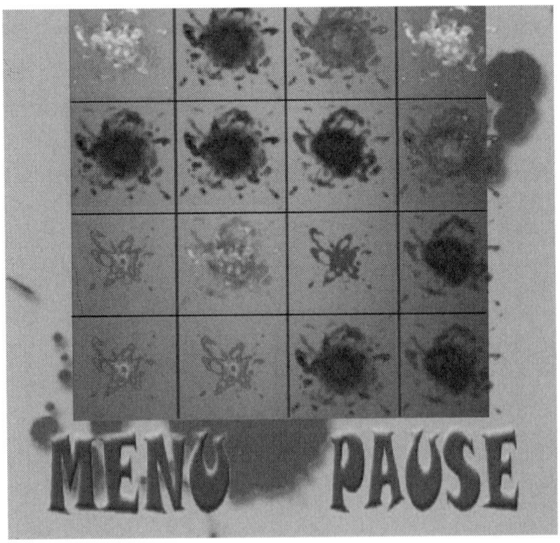

FIGURE 1.3.2 Screenshot of the game, partitioning the screen in several regions.

In order to keep an acceptable frame rate, you need to consider two points. The first one is that the `Update()` function of the game should not call `QueryFlow()` every time, as the latter method is computationally very costly. To circumvent this problem, you can restrict the call to `QueryFlow()` to a certain frequency, x times per second, lower than that of the update calls. This will make the game run smoothly on most modern computers without the game's responsiveness being affected.

A further consideration that needs to be taken into account affects the resolution of the image coming from the Webcam. That is, the higher the resolution, the more calculations the CPU will have to carry out before obtaining the optical flow. This means that you have to set that parameter to, for example, 320 × 240 pixels.

ON THE CD

As a final remark, the CD that accompanies this book contains not only an executable version of the project for Microsoft Windows, but also the source code for it, as well as a .pdf file with the UML class diagram. The game has been programmed in C++, with Microsoft Visual Studio 2005, and using the DirectX and OpenCV libraries.

References

[Beauchemin95] Beauchemin, S.S and Barron, J.L. "The Computation of Optical Flow," ACM Computing Surveys (CSUR), Vol. 27, No. 3, pp. 433–466, ACM Press New York, NY, USA, 1995.

[Lucas81] Lucas, B.D. and Kanade, T. "An Iterative Image Registration Technique with an Application to Stereo Vision."

[Morphology] "Morphological Image Processing," available online at http://en.wikipedia.org/wiki/Morphological_image_processing.

[Ramisa06] Ramisa, A., Vergara, E., and Marti, E. "Computer Vision in Games Using the OpenCV Library," *Game Programming Gems 6,* edited by M. Dickheiser, Charles River Media, 2006, pp. 25–37.

1.4

Design and Implementation of a Multi-Platform Threading Engine

Michael Ramsey

miker@masterempire.com

Engine development is changing. As the paint of an ancient masterpiece fades over time, so are some of the tried and true techniques of the past era of single-core engine development. Developers must now embrace architectures that execute their games on multi-core systems. In some cases, performance differs on a per-core basis! The development of an architecture in a multi-core environment must be acknowledged, designed, planned, and finally implemented. The implementation aspect is where this gem assists, by providing a theoretical foundation and a practical framework for a multi-platform threading system.

A fundamental precept for a game engine architecture is the requirement that it be able to exploit a multi-core environment. The exploitation of the environment is a system that by definition allows for multiple tasks to be executed in parallel. Additionally, you want the performance of the system in question to be real-time; this real-time performance requirement demands that the threading system also be lightweight. Data structures, object construction, cache concerns, and data access patterns are just a few of the issues that you must be continuously aware of during development of objects that will use the threading system.

This gem focuses on the development of a threading engine that has been engineered for both an Xbox 360 and a standard multi-core PC game engine. With that being said, I've provided details on the core systems that are applicable to all architectures, not just a multi-core desktop (Windows/Linux) or Xbox 360. So while you will read about cache lines, they will focus on the principles that make them important across multi-platforms and operating systems.

System Design for a Practical Threading Architecture

One of the most important aspects of designing a multithreaded program is spending the time upfront to design and plan your game architecture. Some of the high-level issues that need to be addressed include the following:

- Task dependencies
- Data sharing
- Data synchronization
- Acknowledgment and flow of data access patterns
- Decoupling of communication points to allow for reading, but not necessarily writing, data
- Minimizing event synchronization

One of the most basic, yet the most efficient, principles of threading a game system is to identify large systems that have relatively few dependencies (or even focused points of intersystem communication) and thread them. If the points of communication between the systems are focused enough, a few simple synchronization primitives (such as a spinlock or mutex) are usually sufficient. If a stall is ever detected, it is straightforward to identify and reduce the granularity of that particular event through routing to a different interobject manager. It is important when designing a multithreaded game engine to not only be stable but to also strive for extensibility.

A Pragmatic Threading Architecture

ON THE CD

On the book's CD, you'll find the source to a complete multi-platform threading system. The GLRThreading library has been engineered in a platform-agnostic manner with a provided implementation for the Windows operating system. The interfaces are conducive to expansion onto the Xbox 360. The GLRThreading library supports all general threading features from the Win32 API. Some functionality has been encapsulated for ease of use (for example, `GLRThreadExecutionProperties`). The standard Win32 model of threading is preemptive in nature. What *preemptive* means in this context is that any thread can be suspended by the operating system to allow for another thread to execute. This allows the OS to simulate multiple processes while only having a single processor. Preempting can be directly influenced by an attributed `GLRThreadTask` property, but generally you should be aware that once a task has been executed or resumed inside the GLRThreading library (that is, made available to the Windows OS), it could and most likely will be preempted or have its execution time reduced/increased by the operating system.

Basic Components of the GLRThreading Library

As you learn about the structure of the GLRThreading library, use Figure 1.4.1 to better understand the system's components and dependencies. The foundational interface to the GLRThreading system is aptly named `GLRThreadFoundation`. `GLRThreadFoundation` is a singleton that should be available to all game systems that need access to threading capabilities. Usually, `GLRThreadFoundation` is placed inside a precompiled header, which is then subsequently included in all files inside an engine. Through `GLRThreadFoundation` you control the submission of tasks. But before you can look at that, you have to determine and define some basic properties for the execution environment; this is where the system descriptions come in.

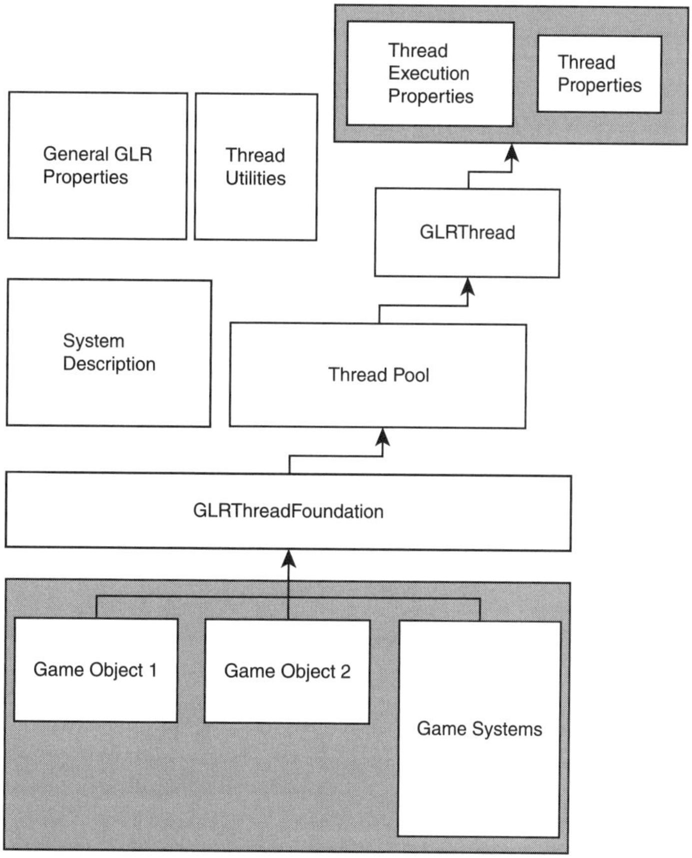

FIGURE 1.4.1 The GLR thread library.

In order to execute properly, the threading system needs the ability to query information about its environment. This includes determining the number of processors, the memory load, and whether or not hyper-threading is supported. To accommodate this in a platform-agnostic manner, there is the `GLRISystemDescription`. The platform-specific implementations are derived from this basic interface. The system description for MS Windows is the `GLRWindowSysDesc`, and the Xbox 360 is implemented by `GLRXBox360SysDesc`.

GLRThreadFoundation Usage

The `GLRThreadFoundation` is the focal point for all threading interactions. The types of threading interactions that you can execute include the ability to execute tasks from a game's objects, as well as accessing threads from the pool. Inside the codebase there will be a single instance of the thread foundation. For example:

```
GLRThreadFoundation glrThreadingSystem;
```

To access functionality inside the threading system, you use the following method syntax:

```
glrThreadingSystem.FunctionName();
```

where `FunctionName` is any of the platform-agnostic functions that can be executed by the game level components.

Threads

Threads are segments of code that can be scheduled for execution by the operating system or by an internal scheduling system. See Figure 1.4.2 for a comparison between a typical single-threaded environment and its multithreaded counterpart. These code snippets can be single functions, objects, or they can be entire systems. The GLRThreading libraries interface is designed to be platform-agnostic, so all manipulation is done on the `GLRThread` level.

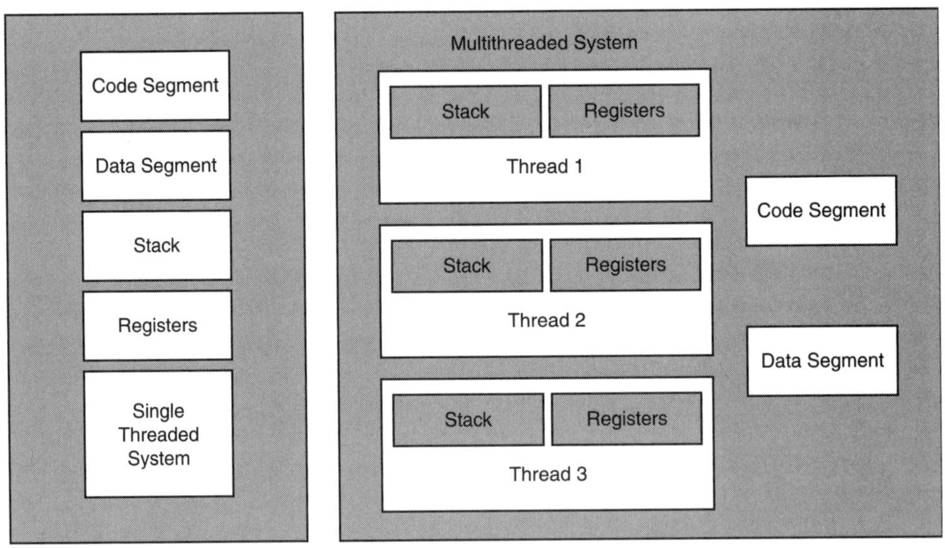

FIGURE 1.4.2 Comparison between a single threaded and multithreaded programming model.

`GLRThread` is the platform-agnostic implementation for a thread within the GLRThreading library. The `GLRThread` interface allows the following operations on a platform-implemented thread:

- Creating a thread
- Executing a thread
- Altering a thread's properties
- Resuming a thread
- Terminating a thread
- Temporarily suspending a thread
- Querying the status of a thread

There are several variations of property management and thread execution. Also associated with a GLRThread are the following control mechanisms: `GLRThreadProperties` and `GLRThreadTask`. These mechanisms control (among other aspects) where and generally how a thread will execute a task.

Preemptible and Simultaneously Executed Threads

It is vital that every engine developer be aware of the performance characteristics of the cores that their engine not only targets but also is developed on. This is because a significant amount of development is initially implemented on a desktop PC, which usually has very different execution characteristics from a typical multi-core console. One of the most important aspects of engineering a threading system is the consideration of threads that can be preempted and those that are agnostically called non-preemptible. One of the standard paradigms that a thread follows is that an OS can suspend execution of a thread to allow another thread to execute. When the OS decides to suspend execution of a current thread, it will save the context of the currently executing thread and restore the context state of the next thread. Context switching is not free; there is some overhead but generally the cost of idling a thread to not incur the overhead of a context switch is not worth the added code complexity. The switching of threads creates the illusion of a multitasking system.

There is also support on consoles for the ability to create threads that are essentially non-preemptible. A non-preemptible thread is a thread that *cannot* be interrupted by the OS. This power is not the pinnacle of blissfulness. The independent execution of threads (on the same core) usually share the same L1 cache, which generally means you still want like tasks to execute on the same core in order to utilize any cache coherency inherent in the data structures. This is to minimize the cache thrashing that could occur when two disparate systems execute tasks on the same core.

Thread Properties

`GLRThreadProperties` is the general mechanism that stores a particular thread handle and its associated ID. There is also the ability to alter the thread's default stack size. The thread's stack is the location for its variables as well as its call stack. The OS can automatically grow the stack for you, but this is a performance hit on consoles. To avoid changing thread stacks on the fly, you should anticipate and set the stack size beforehand.

Thread context switching is in general pretty fast—but as with anything there are associated costs. One of these costs is memory associated with the thread to store its context information. The size of the default `GLRThread` context is 64KB. This 64KB can and should be manually adjusted depending on the platform that you are targeting. If you need to increase the size of thread stacks on a Windows-based OS (such as a PC or Xbox 360), there is a property that can be set from the Visual Studio development environment.

One of the gotchas to be on the lookout for is when your stack needs to be 128KB or 256KB. This type of situation usually requires a scaling down of either the size of the task that is being executed (that is, reducing the granularity) or identifying objects that can be further decomposed into smaller implementations, as in [Ramsey05].

Thread Execution Properties

A thread execution property is a platform-agnostic interface that allows for more granular control over a task's execution. `GLRThreadExecutionProps` provides for a number of properties such as defining a task's preferred processing element, a task's priority, and a task's affinity mask. A thread's execution property also has the ability to define its ideal processor element. This allows for a management system to group like tasks on a particular processor for execution. This is defined inside GLRThreadExecutionProps.h.

On a single physical processor with hyper-thread capabilities, the `GetProcessAffinityMask()` will return bits 1 and 2 with bit 3 set as well, to indicate that you have at least one physical CPU with two logical CPUs. On a dual CPU (physical) machine with hyper-threading capabilities, `GetProcessAffinityMask()` would show 1 + 2 + 4 + 8 = 15. This indicates two physical CPUs with two logical CPUs apiece. CPUs begin their identification at 1. It should be noted that the implementation of `GLRThreadExecutionProps` is inside the GLRThreadExecutionProps.h header.

Processor Affinity

Affinity requests threads to execute on a specific processor. This allows the system developer to target specific processors for repeated operations. By way of repeated operations, you can also group associated operations together, to further increase the cache coherency of similar objects. Some systems may regard thread affinity as a hint and not a requirement, so check the documentation before assuming any problems in your threading libraries.

Specifying a task's affinity is done through a simple label of either PA_HARD or PA_SOFT. These flags tell the OS to either use a particular processor or just the specified processing element as a hint, respectively. This is defined in GLRThreadExecutionProps.h.

Task Priority

Changing the priority on a thread is suggested only for certain systems. The GLRThreading library allows you to designate a thread's priority according to the following scale:

- TP_Low
- TP_Normal
- TP_High
- TP_Critical
- TP_TimeCritical

The default setting for newly created thread execution properties priority is normal. This can be changed depending upon a particular tasks requirements. This is defined inside GLRThreadExecutionProps.h.

Thread Allocation Strategies

There are numerous ways to build a threading system, from the naive allocation of threads on the fly to the more sophisticated implementation of preallocated work systems. One of the underlying paradigms for the GLRThreading system is that you want to do as much allocation up front as possible. This is important in developing a console title, because you not only want to be aware of the memory consumption at start-up, but also memory usage of system-level components at runtime.

Naive Allocation

The simplest and most straightforward way to create a threading system is to have a thread manager object, implemented as a singleton, that processes requests in a create-for-use paradigm. Whereas this is probably the easiest way to get started, it is not an advantageous decision when factoring in the complete length of a product cycle as well as the runtime performance of constantly allocating and deallocating a thread.

Thread Pools

With the underlying principle of front-loading system level allocations in mind, the innards of the GLRThreadingPool rely upon as much preallocation as possible. The thread pool is a system that front-loads the creation of threads. This obviates the need for runtime creation of resources that can be dealt with once and for all upon start-up. Whereas the creation of a single thread is not that expensive, the constant allocation and deallocation during runtime is an unnecessary burden. For instance, the system experiences memory fragmentation if threads are constantly allocated and deallocated. The actual number of threads created for the pool is dependent on the system and can be modified based upon the game's needs and performance criteria.

The thread pool is a subsystem that works off of the time-tested paradigm of task submission. At regular intervals, worker threads look for a task to execute. If there is work available, the execution attributes are set up and the thread is resumed. Once the task has been executed, the thread is suspended and made available for subsequent tasks.

Thread Pool Properties

The thread pool has properties that allow for the defining of several characteristics that will prove useful when the system is used in various games. The thread pool needs the ability to change the number of created threads, the number of tasks that the threads can work on, and the ability to lock the task pool at any particular time.

Multiple Pools

So you might be asking yourself if one pool is good, then possibly creating multiple thread pools for different subsystems in a game engine might be an even better idea. The issues with introducing multiple pools are manifold—the primary issue is that if you have multiple pools, with differing performance characteristics (through the use of thread properties, task scheduling, and so on), you have to introduce another layer of complexity into the system—the need for interpool communication. This complexity is simply not wanted in such a performance-critical system; the more straightforward the underlying thread system is, the more likely it is you'll avoid difficulties introduced through the complexity of the system.

Object Threading

The GLRThreading library provides its threading capabilities through a process of creating an object and then submitting that newly created object to the threading library. To submit an object to the GLRThreading system, you just need to make the call:

```
GLRThreadFoundation.submitTask(&newGameSystemFunction);
```

To actually have the worker threads grab tasks from the task list inside the threading pool, you need to make a call to `distribute()` using this call:

```
GLRThreadFoundation.distribute();
```

Your object is now off and running on the same processor as the invoking process. To make the execution of the objects easier, the process of allowing threads to execute should be inserted in your main game update. In this manner, game systems can just create tasks, submit them, and let the threading system deal with allocation, execution, and all the details.

Thread Safety, Reentrancy, Object Synchronicity, and Data Access

Dealing with issues of designing game systems that are thread-safe and reentrant is a thorny business and is beyond the scope of this gem. A lot of the issues are highly dependent on the architecture and data-access patterns of the game. There are a few principles and practices to keep in mind when creating threadable objects and systems.

A rule of thumb about reentrancy is that you should make a system reentrant only if it needs to be. It costs a lot of time and involves a lot of effort to make your underlying game libraries 100% reentrant and the truth of the matter is that the majority of them don't have to be reentrant. Sure, libraries such as your memory manager and task submission system need to be reentrant and thread-safe, but a lot of the managerial systems can serve as a gatekeeper through the use of a cheap synchronization construct. By using something as simple as a hardware-based spinlock, you can push the burden of thread safety up to the system managers. This makes even more sense, because they should control their own data flow. So, once you've identified the general data flow inside your engine, the process of determining what actually has to be reentrant is usually clear.

Dancing the Line (or Cache Coherency)

Object alignment along cache boundaries is important for a standard single-core engine but it becomes paramount when you develop for a multi-core environment. Normally, a cache is broken into cache lines of 32 or 64 bytes. When main memory is *direct-mapped* to the cache, the general strategy is to not be concerned with the amount of memory being mapped, but with the number of cache lines that are being accessed. There are three basic types of cache misses:

- *Compulsory miss.* This occurs the first time a block of memory is read into the cache.
- *Capacity miss.* This occurs when a memory block is too large for the cache to hold.
- *Conflict miss.* This occurs when you have memory blocks that map to the same cache line. In a multi-core environment, conflict misses should be attacked with a vengeance. Conflict misses are usually systemic of an engine's architecture that contains poorly designed data structures. It's the coupling of these data structures with the general non-deterministic pattern of the threads' executions that causes conflict misses to negatively affect performance.

The GLRThreading library includes a basic utility that will aid you in creating cache-aligned data structures. The principle utility is the `GLRCachePad` macro.

```
#define GLRCachePad(Name,BytesSoFar) \
  GLRByte Name[CACHE_ALIGNMENT - (BytesSoFar) %
      CACHE_ALIGNMENT)]
```

The GLRCachePad macro groups the data together in cache line(size) chunks and on cache line boundaries. You want the access pattern of different CPUs to be separated by at least one cache line boundary. The cache alignment value is different from platform to platform, so you might need to implement a different cache-padding scheme depending on your target system. The final caveat is that you want the GLRCachePad call to occur at the end of a data structure; this will force the following data structure to a new cache line [Culler99].

How to Use the GLRThreading Library

This section illustrates a simple example of how to use the threading system. A typical game object will be defined and is called TestSystem (see Listing 1.4.1).

Listing 1.4.1 The Test Game Object

```
class TestSystem
{
   public:
          TestSystem();
         ~TestSystem();
         void theIncredibleGameObject( void );
         void objectThreadPump( void );

   private:
         GLRThreadedTask<TestSystem> mThreadedTask;
         GLRThreadExecutionProps    *mThreadedProps;
};
```

The TestSystem game object has two private data structures: a GLRThreadedTask and a GLRThreadExecutionProps. The GLRThreadedTask member is used to reference this particular object and a function within the object that will be executed by the threading system. Listing 1.4.2 contains an example of how to register an instantiated object, as well as the function that will be distributed for execution.

Listing 1.4.2 The Implementation of the Game Object's Threadable Function

```
void TestSystem::objectThreadPump( void )
 {
     mThreadedTask.createThreadedTask(this,
     &TestSystem::theIncredibleGameObject,mThreadedProps );
     glrThreadingSystem.submitTask( &mThreadedTask );
 }
```

The sample code in Listing 1.4.3 shows how you use the TestSystem object from Listing 1.4.1. Listing 1.4.3 shows how to instantiate the two threadable objects, myTestObject and myTestObject2. As noted previously, when you call objectThreadPump, you create a task, which in turn obtains a thread from the thread pool and then submits a new task (`myTestObject` and `myTestObject2`) for execution to the GLRThreadingSystem. The tasks are not instantly executed; they've only been added to the task queue for execution. This allows a scheduler to rearrange submitted tasks based upon the game's load and the tasks' similarities. An eventual call to `distribute()` is required to start the execution of these objects.

Listing 1.4.3 Code That Creates and Executes the Test Objects

```
//Create a couple test objects to thread
TestSystem myTestObject;
myTestObject.objectThreadPump();

TestSystem myTestObject2;
myTestObject2.objectThreadPump();

//This call should be placed in your main game loop.
glrThreadingSystem.distribute();
```

ON THE CD

On the CD enclosed with this book, you will find a solution that allows you to compile and execute this example code.

Conclusion

This gem has covered a lot of ground, including the architecture of a practical threading engine that is functional and efficient on multiple platforms. You've also looked at a couple different methods to allocate threads, read about task execution, and finally looked briefly at a method for more efficient data structure usage in a multi-core environment. So as you begin developing or retrofitting your engine for the multi-core market, keep in mind some of the paint strokes that this article has covered and use them to start painting your own masterpiece.

References

[Bevridge96] Bevridge, Jim. *Multithreading Applications in Win32: The Complete Guide to Threads,* Addison-Wesley, 1996.

[Culler99] Culler, David E. *Parallel Computer Architecture*, Morgan Kaufmann, 1999.

[Geist94] Geist, A. PVM. MIT Press, 1996.

[Gerber04] Gerber, Richard. *Programming with Hyper-Threading Technology*, Intel Press, 2004.

[Hughes04] Hughes, Cameron. *Parallel and Distributed Programming Using C++*, Addison-Wesley, 2004.

[Nichols96] Nichols, Bradford. *Pthreads Programming: A POSIX Standard for Better Multiprocessing*, O'Reilly, 1996.

[Ramsey05] Ramsey, Michael. "Parallel AI Development with PVM," In *Game Programming Gems 5*, Charles River Media, 2005.

[Ramsey08] Ramsey, Michael. *A Practical Cognitive Engine for AI*, To Be Published, 2008.

[Richter99] Richter, Jeffrey. *Programming Applications for Microsoft Windows*, Microsoft Press, 1999.

1.5

For Bees and Gamers: How to Handle Hexagonal Tiles

Thomas Jahn, King Art

tjahn@kingart.de

Jörn Loviscach, Hochschule Bremen

jlovisca@informatik.hs-bremen.de

Grids are the one of the most prominent tools to simplify complex structures and relationships in order to simulate or visualize them. Their use in games ranges from the graphical tiles of 8 × 8 pixels used in handheld games to the space representation for AI agents. The typical choice, a square grid, is biased by the square's simple computational rules; they do not show a surpassing behavior in simulation. Hexagonal tiles, in contrast, offer highly attractive features in both logic and look. However, hexagonal grids are awkward in software development. This gem introduces concepts and techniques to deal with this issue.

Introduction

A *tiling* is created when a shape or a fixed set of shapes is repeated endlessly to cover the infinite plane without any gaps or overlaps. Tilings come in a two variations—whereas non-periodic tilings are used to create textures, most applications rely on periodic tilings, which are much easier to handle computationally. To increase symmetry, regular tilings are used, where the tiling is formed from a regular polygon such as a square, an equilateral hexagon, or an equilateral triangle.

For their space-filling efficiency, biology prefers hexagonal grids to square grids: They appear in the layout of honeycombs and the placement of the light receptors in the retina. Even though hexagonal grids have a number of other benefits, they require complex and thus error-prone code. Object-oriented abstraction comes to the rescue. This gem describes a software design to hide the intricacies in a framework.

The Pros and Cons of Hexagonal Tilings

To be able to judge whether a square or a hexagonal tiling fits the task best, you have to consider a number of aspects ranging from adjacency to the choice of a coordinate system.

Neighborhoods and Stride Distances

In a square tiling, there are two common definitions of neighborhoods. Neighbors either have to share an edge (4-neighborhood) or it suffices that they share a vertex (8-neighborhood). This ambiguity has its consequences. Take a strategy game that is based on square tiles as an example. Any movement is broken into a series of steps, where a step means the transition from one tile to one of its neighbor tiles. Now you as the developer have to make a choice. You can allow transitions in only four directions, which means it will take 41% more steps to move the same distance along a diagonal axis than along a vertical or horizontal axis, as shown in Figure 1.5.1. However, allowing transitions in eight directions isn't much better—now the distance covered by moving a number of steps along a diagonal axis will be larger by 41% than along a vertical/horizontal axis. To avoid this distortion, diagonal transitions have to be handled differently, adding to the complexity of both the code and the game's rules.

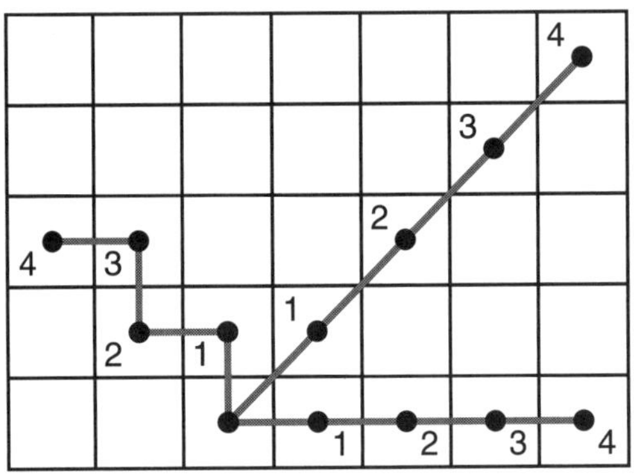

FIGURE 1.5.1 Marching on a square grid shows fast and slow directions, no matter which definition of neighborhood is employed.

Hexagonal tilings offer an advantage here. Each tile has six equidistant neighbors, each of which connects to a different edge. No two tiles share only one vertex or more than one edge. Thus, the notion of a neighbor isn't ambiguous for hexagonal grids. In addition, the distance covered by moving a number of steps in an arbitrary direction will vary by only 15%. See Figure 1.5.2.

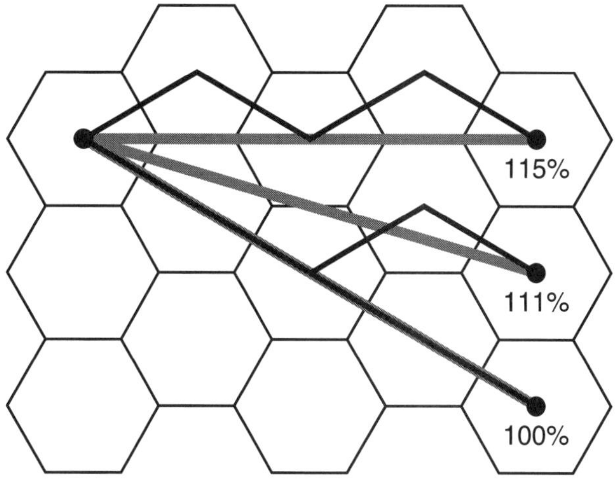

FIGURE 1.5.2 The length of the shortest connection on a hexagonal grid is close to that of a straight line.

Isotropy and Packing Density

Of all shapes that can tile the plane, regular hexagons have the smallest perimeter for a given area, meaning there's no "rounder" type of tile. Thus, whenever a grid has to represent a continuous structure with no inherently preferred directions, a hexagonal tiling will work best. This is a major reason to pursue image processing with hexagonal pixels [Middleton05].

Thanks to their compact shape, regular hexagons form the tiling with the highest packing density. A circular disk inscribed in a square occupies 79% of its area, as opposed to 91% percent for a circular disk inscribed in a hexagon. Thus, with a hexagonal grid you can reach the accuracy of a square grid with about 10% fewer cells. This is a chance to reduce the memory consumption and improve the speed of grid-based algorithms by roughly the same number.

Visual Appearance

In games, grids are often used to represent playing fields. This has a major impact on visual appearance. A square grid is suited well to create cities and indoor scenes. The edges of hexagons, however, connect more smoothly, forming angles of 120 degrees. Assemblies of hexagonal tiles possess slightly jagged-looking outlines because no parallel line segments are connected directly. This and the absence of sharp edges make this type of grid more suited for the representation of natural scenes, as you can see in Figure 1.5.3.

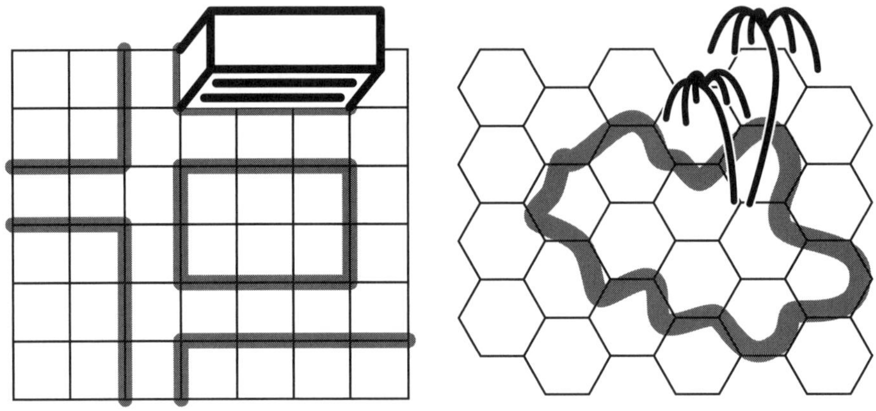

FIGURE 1.5.3 Whereas square tiles are ideal for cities (left), hexagonal tiles lend themselves to organic shapes.

Axes of Symmetry

A square grid can be mapped easily to an ordinary Cartesian system of integer coordinates. These can also be employed as indices of a two-dimensional array. Apart from the two directions of symmetry parallel to the square's sides, there are two diagonal directions of symmetry. Although rarely seen in practice, these could serve as coordinate axes, too.

Hexagonal grids, however, possess 12 directions of symmetry that one could use as coordinate axes. There are two basic layouts, as shown in Figure 1.5.4—a hexagonal grid with horizontally aligned tiles, where every second row is indented by half the width of a tile, and a vertically aligned grid.

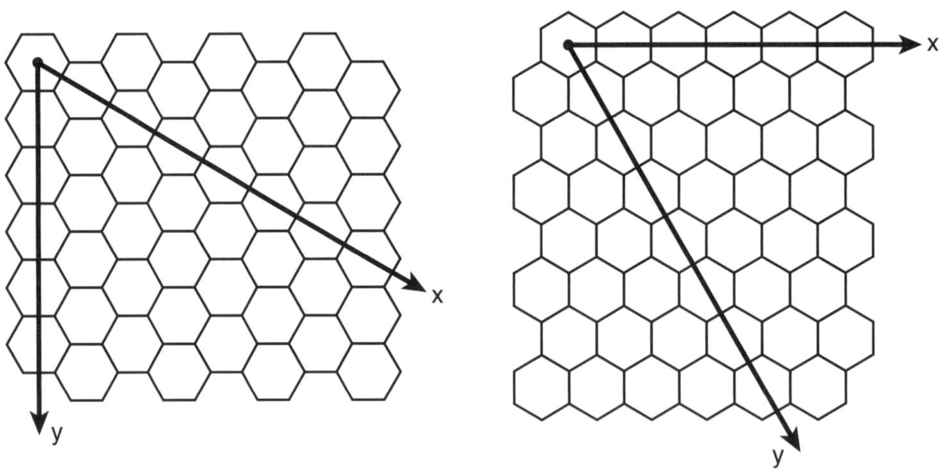

FIGURE 1.5.4 Depending on which direction of symmetry is employed as the *x* axis, the tiles of a hexagonal appear horizontally or vertically aligned.

Any pair of axes that you can choose suffers from one of two defects—if the axes are perpendicular to each other, they will not be geometrically equivalent. In particular, one of the axes runs parallel to some edges of the lattice whereas the other does not. On top of that, you have to deal with fractional coordinates; see Figure 1.5.5. If the axes indeed are chosen to be geometrically equivalent, they will enclose an angle of 60 degrees, meaning for instance that distances can't be computed naively through the Pythagorean Theorem. To better display the symmetry, you might even work with three barycentric coordinates, one of which is redundant.

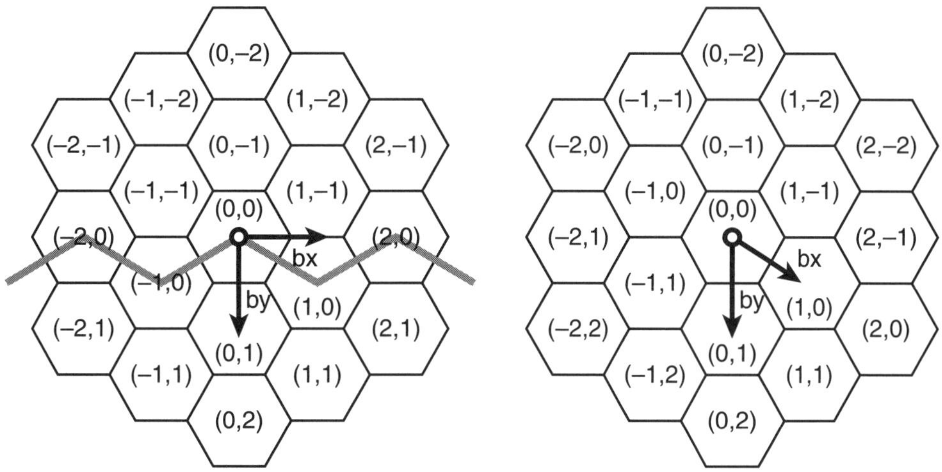

FIGURE 1.5.5 A hexagonal grid allows perpendicular coordinate axes with half-integer values or skewed coordinate axes.

Mastering the Hexagonal Grid

Thanks to object-oriented programming, the issues of a hexagonal grid can be hidden behind an elegant façade. Actually, this gem proposes two software layers at an increasing level of abstraction: addressing and accessing.

Address Layer

Every scheme to translate an address into a spatial location on a hexagonal grid and vice versa has its benefits and limitations. Thus, the first step is to hide the addressing behind a layer of abstraction. Data container classes supporting random access and classes representing addressing schemes that map grid addresses to container elements.

The first option for the container is an indexed random-access container such as the `vector` of the C++ Standard Template Library (STL). Its index can be computed from the tile's address given in perpendicular or skewed coordinates. Because the index range of the container is limited, so has to be the range of addresses. If perpendicular coordinate axes are used, a rectangular section of cells can be defined through an upper and lower boundary for each coefficient. In this case, the index can be computed like `index = y * width + x`.

If the coordinate system has skewed axes, this approach would result in a trapezoidal set of cells. This can be avoided by altering the computation of the index so that the indices again point to a rectangular patch of cells. In this case, the index calculation could look similar to this: `index = Math.Floor(y * (width + 0.5) + x)`. See Figure 1.5.6.

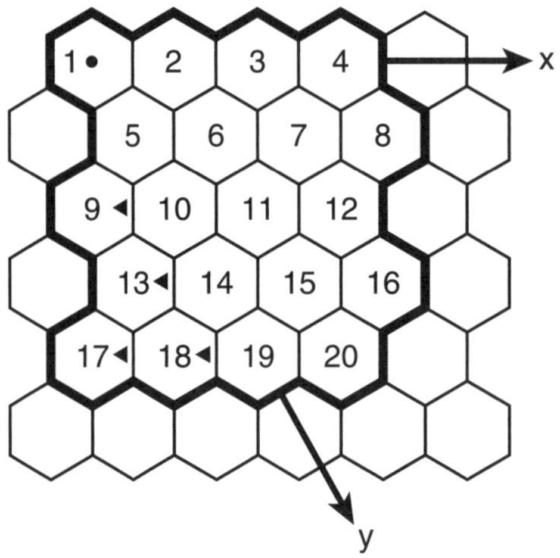

FIGURE 1.5.6 Through a shift in the index computation, skewed axes, too, can be used to define a rectangular domain.

The second option for the container is a key-based random-access container such as C++ STL `map`. Whereas these containers access data slower than indexed containers, you can use the cell addresses directly as keys. The biggest benefits are that there is no built-in limit to the address range and that empty cells don't consume memory. Thus, a map is a good choice for sparse data points.

To support a highly specific setting, you can use a standard container wrapped by a class that implements the addressing scheme of your choice. The next step toward flexibility would be to make this class generic through type parameters so that it isn't limited in which kind of data it can store.

To achieve ultimate flexibility, you can split the functionality into two classes, keeping the actual storage and the addressing scheme apart. That way it's possible to pick the optimal combination of an addressing scheme and a container for the task at hand. Here, the class that deals with the mapping between addresses and data is called `AddressingScheme`.

Access Layer

The second layer is built on top of the addressing scheme. This layer employs the iterator design pattern, which is also used in the STL. An iterator serves as a pointer to an element stored in a container. All of the STL containers provide the same basic interface regarding iterators, hiding the details of the container's implementation. Thus, code that is based on iterators can be used with any container. In addition to being flexible, iterators are also simple to use. You can ask any container for an iterator to its first element; you can just call the iterator's `next()` method until you reach the last element in the list.

A similar strategy can be employed to avoid much hassle with the addressing schemes of hexagonal grids. We suggest two different approaches:

- The first one can be called a `Walker` class. Its instance can be set to represent any cell in the grid and provides an interface to read and write the target cell's data. After the initialization, the referenced cell can be changed by calling a method similar to an iterator's `next()`. Instead of iterating through the cells in a pre-determined sequence, the `Walker` class offers a `move(dir)` method taking an argument that specifies one of the six natural directions on the grid. Calling this method will cause the `Walker` object to point to the neighbor of the old target that is specified by the passed direction; see Figure 1.5.7. This class provides free movement on the grid, hence its name.
- The second approach, the `Enumerator` class, works exactly like an iterator, but only steps through a sequence of cells that represent a specific subset of the grid—for example, only the next neighbors of a given cell. The framework provides `Enumerator` classes to iterate over different neighborhoods, even customized ones like all cells within a certain radius of a given center cell or all cells currently visible on the screen. In a strategy game, an `Enumerator` could provide access to all cells within the attack or viewing range of a certain unit or all cells that are occupied by enemies. Decoupling the logic of the grid from your actual game logic makes the code a lot cleaner and better to maintain.

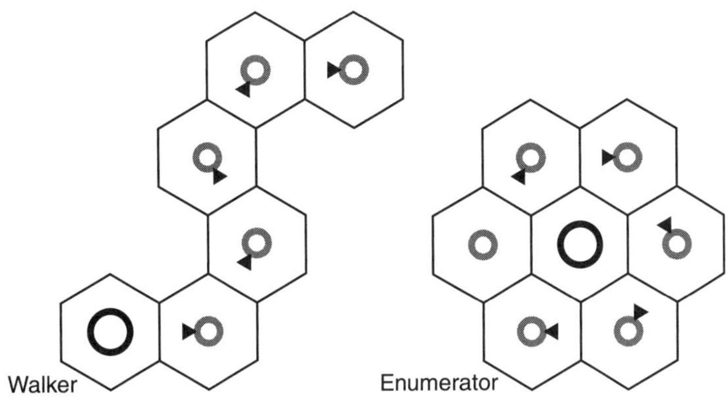

FIGURE 1.5.7 Whereas a `Walker` can access any neighbor of a tile, the `Enumerator` iterates over a predefined pattern of tiles in the vicinity.

Implementation Tips

Many algorithms never need to know actual addresses. They can use `Walker` objects to write and read the data. Thus, we suggest basing as much code as possible on an abstract `Walker` base class that defines a common interface but doesn't rely on a specific addressing scheme. After you have decided on which kind of addressing you want and have implemented a matching `AddressingScheme` class, you can write a compatible `Walker` inheriting the abstract base.

Another suggestion is to implement these classes as generics, such as C++'s class templates. This will allow specifying the data access independent from the data's type.

C# and Java (but not C++) provide specific interfaces to implement, resulting in neater code on the client side. For instance, by implementing C#'s `IEnumeration` interface, it's possible to step through all the cells in the specific selection using a `foreach` loop with the same syntax as the regular `for` loop (unlike the `for_each` of the C++ STL). Assume that a cell in the grid is of type `CellData` and you have a generic `Enumerator` called `Neighborhood` and a `Walker` class `CellPointer`. The instance of `Neighborhood` is created and initialized by passing a `Walker` instance center defining which cells neighborhood you want neighbors to list. As `Neighborhood` implements the `IEnumeration` interface, iterating through all the neighbors of the center cell becomes as easy as this:

```
foreach(CellPointer<DataType> cell
      in new Neighborhood<DataType>(center))
{
      // do something with cell
}
```

The core functionality of the `AddressingScheme` is to provide data access on a grid address layer. However, there is additional functionality this class could provide. Many use cases require you to find a cell based on screen or world coordinates. This is trivial with a rectangular grid, so we suggest the following approach. Partition a hexagonal grid into rectangular sections as shown in Figure 1.5.8. To resolve a coordinate pair *xy*,

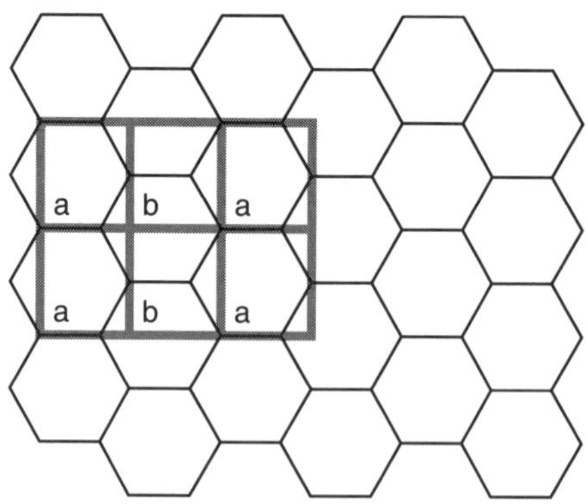

FIGURE 1.5.8 Partitioning the grid into rectangular cells allows simple hit-test computations.

the first step is to decide in which section the point lies. A section has one of two possible layouts; in both cases it is divided into three subsections, each associated with a different tile. Once you have resolved your coordinate to a location within a sector, there are only three choices left and it becomes trivial to compute the correct cell address.

Applications

To show some practical benefits, consider three scenarios where hexagonal grids may be used.

Spatial Search

A game world is populated by numerous entities with the ability to interact if they are within a certain range of each other. When a specific entity has to decide whether an interaction is possible, it would be computationally expensive to consider all other active entities. Instead, a grid can be used to preselect objects within a certain radius. The grid divides the game world into tiles that behave as cells; based on its location, each entity is registered at one of these cells. To find all entities within a certain radius of a game object it suffices to consider objects registered with cells that contain points within the search radius.

If the region to be searched is circular, hexagonal grids would be the optimal choice. Furthermore, with an adequate abstraction the code to perform the search can be very simple.

```
foreach(CellPointer<List<GameObject>> cell
        in new SearchZone<List<GameObject>>(center))
{
    foreach(GameObject obj in cell.GetData())
    {
        // do something with obj
    }
}
```

Each cell consists of a list of instances of `GameObject`. A child `SearchZone` of the `Enumerator` class is defined that allows iteration through all cells in the search zone. It yields a `Walker` object pointing to a specific `cell`. As the `cell`'s data is a list of `GameObjects`, another `foreach` loop can be used to iterate through the game objects associated with this cell.

Pathfinding

A number of games use tiles as building blocks for their game worlds. If agents are required to move within the world, path finding has to take place on the grid level. A transition is possible only between adjacent tiles, where some neighbors may even be blocked, for instance, because they contain walls. This calls for a standard algorithm such as Dijkstra's or A* [Mesdaghi04] to be implemented in the object-oriented framework.

The basic idea is to expand the start node until the goal is reached. On the address level, this is cumbersome. Six different offsets have to be applied to the current cells address to access adjacent cells. For an orthogonal addressing scheme, these offsets will vary depending on whether the current cell is in an even or odd row (or column, if the grid is aligned vertically).

The listing below performs a simple breadth-first search on a grid of cells to find the shortest sequence of moveable cells connecting `startCell` with `goalCell`. The neighbors of a cell are accessed using a matching neighborhood enumerator. Thanks to object-oriented abstraction, the algorithm becomes independent of a specific grid layout or addressing scheme.

```
Queue<CellPointer<PathCell>> openCells
    = new Queue<CellPointer<PathCell>>();
openCells.Enqueue(startCell);

// expand
while(openCells.Count > 0)
{
    CellPointer<PathCell> current
        = openCells.Dequeue();
    foreach(CellPointer<PathCell> cell
            in new Neighborhood(current))
    {
        if(cell.GetData().Moveable &&
           cell.GetData().ExpandedFrom == null)
        {
            cell.GetData().ExpandedFrom
                = current.GetData();
            openCells.Enqueue(cell);
        }
    }
}

// resolve
Stack<PathCell> path= new Stack<PathCell>();
PathCell pc = goalCell.GetData().ExpandedFrom;
while(pc != null && pc != m_Start.GetData())
{
    path.Push(pc);
    pc = pc.ExpandedFrom;
}
```

Cellular Automata

Cellular automata [Wolfram02] can be used to model and simulate complex dynamic systems by letting a virtually infinite number of simple components interact locally. In the two-dimensional setting, the interacting components are usually cells on a grid where the next state of a cell is computed based on the current state of itself and the adjacent cells.

The direction insensitivity of hexagonal grids makes them attractive for cellular automata as well, for instance for the simulation of liquids. The obvious choice for the set of cells that determine a cell's next state is itself and its six direct neighbors (see Figure 1.5.9), even though sometimes other neighborhoods are used. A smaller set of only three neighbors may be sufficient and allow for faster simulation. In other cases, six neighbors might not provide enough data, so the selection is expanded to the closest 12 or even 18 cells.

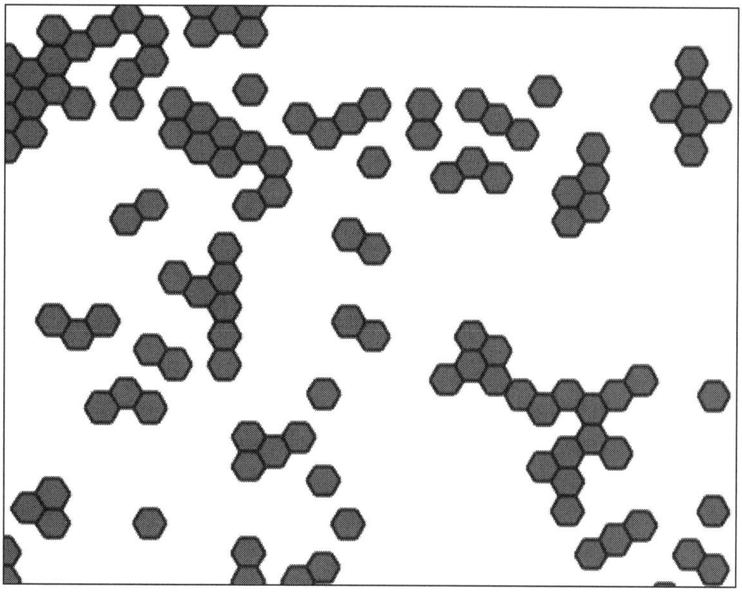

FIGURE 1.5.9 To start with a simple set of rules, *Conway's Game of Life,* the classic 2D cellular automaton, can be carried over to hexagonal tiles.

If the simulation code is directly operating on cell addresses, it is hard to experiment with different selections of influencing cells. If, however, an `Enumerator` provides the collection of influencing cells, the choice of cells can be changed with ease, even at runtime.

Conclusion

By introducing another layer of abstraction on top of the address layer, it is possible to write code that's highly decoupled from the addressing scheme and the storage of the cell data. This not only increases maintainability and flexibility, but also greatly simplifies working on a hexagonal grid. You can keep your game logic clean of all the nasty details that make hexagonal grids so cumbersome to work with.

References

[Mesdaghi04] Mesdaghi, Syrus. "Path Planning Tutorial," *AI Game Programming Wisdom 2,* CD-ROM, Charles River Media Inc., 2004.

[Middleton05] Middleton, Lee, and Sivaswamy, Jayanthi. *Hexagonal Image Processing—A Practical Approach,* Springer New York Inc., 2005.

[Wolfram02] Wolfram, Stephen. *A New Kind of Science,* Wolfram Media Inc., 2002.

1.6

A Sketch-Based Interface to Real-Time Strategy Games Based on a Cellular Automaton

Carlos A. Dietrich

Luciana P. Nedel

João L. D. Comba

Real-time strategy games (RTS) are one of the most popular game genres in the world. The combination of action and strategy is simply addictive, with lots of devoted players spending days on game campaigns or instant battles over the Internet.

We have not been seeing, however, significant improvements in the RTS game-play in recent years. By comparing a recent title to the very early ones, you can say that now there are more units on the screen (maybe hundreds of them), new beautiful graphical engines, and wider battlefields than ever before, but the essence of the gameplay is still the same—selecting units and defining their tasks by clicking with the mouse. This process entails a very simple and efficient interface, on which players are usually well trained. But what should you do when the game demands more? How can you control hundreds of units in a realistic and efficient way? And because the interface is designed for hand-to-hand combat, what should you do when the army becomes huge and there is no clear way to direct it? We are facing such situations in current game titles, and, despite recent improvements, common unit-based interfaces sometimes leave players frustrated.

This gem describes an alternative that may improve gameplay in such situations. We propose a one-click higher-level interface that controls the movement of entire armies or groups of soldiers. The idea behind this approach is very simple, and can be illustrated with any battlefield map from the old history books, such as the one shown in Figure 1.6.1.

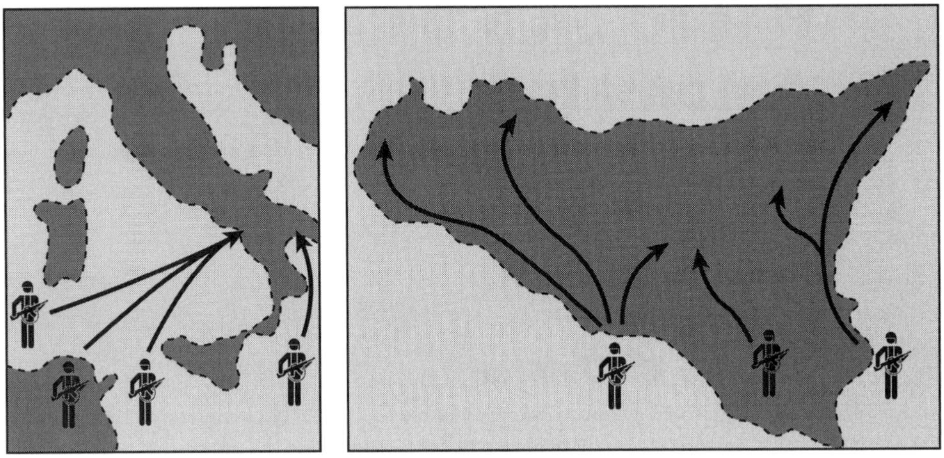

FIGURE 1.6.1 Movements of soldier troops in Italy (left) and Sicily (right) invasions during WWII, 1943.

In Figure 1.6.1, the troop movements are illustrated by arrows that indicate the direction of movement of some soldiers or entire battalions. Note that there is no specific information on the individual tasks each soldier performs or which formation they kept during the movement. And why should there be? In a battlefield, it is nearly impossible to call soldiers by name or give them specific tasks, such as to attack this or that enemy. The commander shouts an instruction to the battalion commanders, which propagates the instruction to company commanders, and so on along the line of command, until some soldiers hear and follow their instructions.

We designed a tool that tries to simulate this behavior by allowing the users to sketch a path or a target on the screen that units must follow or stay. The user interface is very simple: using the mouse, the user draws a sketch line (or point) on the screen, which is then converted into a path (or target) on the battlefield (see Figure 1.6.2). This sketch creates an "influence zone" in the battlefield, and every unit inside this zone must follow the sketched path or target.

Similar attempts to create such a tool have surfaced in recent RTS titles [Bosch06], but we believe there is still lots of room for improvements, mainly in the implementation of the interface infrastructure. The goal with this work is to augment such approaches with a more dynamic control, designed to be used inside the battle, which allows improved gameplay and strategy planning while playing RTS games. The next sections summarize our approach and illustrate it with some examples.

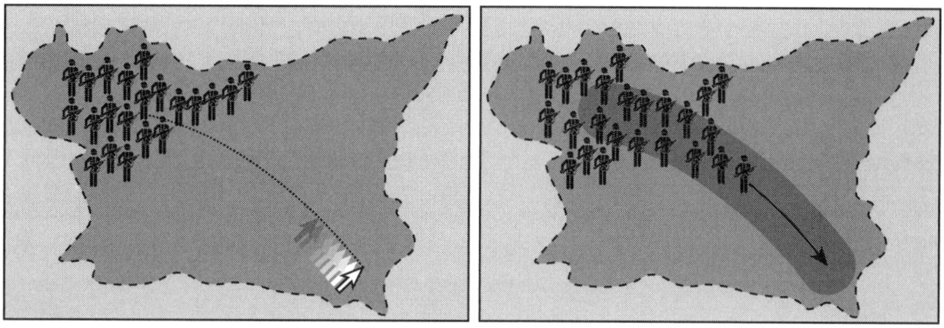

FIGURE 1.6.2 By using the mouse, the user draws a sketch on the screen, which pushes the units inside the sketch influence zone to the desired target.

Focus-Context Control Level

In the hierarchical structure of an army, generals do not deal directly with soldiers, but instead their orders follow the chain of command until reaching lower ranked units. In modern RTS interfaces, however, the general (represented by the player) deals directly with soldiers (the units). This interface keeps the player focus on the hand-to-hand combat instead of the context (army placement). In such interfaces, no matter how good the players are, the one who clicks faster wins [Philip07]. In some circumstances, however, the player must deal with soldiers. For instance, when the combat starts, a detailed control to instruct the units on how to pursue desired targets is necessary.

The proposed interface presents a focus context combination of both approaches—the sketch-based interface that allows macro-management of the context, and a unit-based interface to control the micro-management of the unit's movement (see Figure 1.6.3).

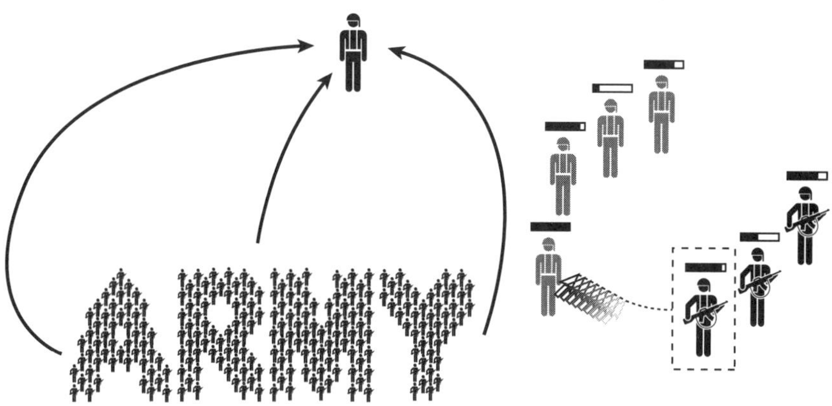

FIGURE 1.6.3 Focus-context interface: combination of a sketch-based interface that controls the context (army disposal, at left) and unit-based interface that controls the micro-management (hand-to-hand fight, at right).

It is easy to see a situation where you could arrange the army disposal with the help of sketches, from a far view, and turn to the unit-based interface when soldiers engage in hand-to-hand combat.

Implementation Details

There are many ways to implement a sketch-based interface and the most important aspect is to choose an efficient way to communicate user intentions to units on the battlefield. We propose here an implementation based on a totalistic cellular automaton [Weisstein07b], which is simple and fast enough to be added to any game engine.

The implementation has two major stages:

- User input capture
- Command propagation in the battlefield

Capturing the user input is very simple, and is discussed in the "Patch Sketching" section. Processing of user commands uses a totalistic cellular automaton, which is responsible for iteratively spreading the command on the battlefield. This cellular automaton is discussed in the section entitled "Moving the Soldiers." Finally, in the section entitled "Putting It All Together," we explain how this is used in a game interface.

Path Sketching

As explained previously, we propose an interface where the user controls an army by sketching curves or points directly on the battlefield. This implementation is straightforward, and must accomplish two tasks:

- Capture of screen coordinates from user input
- Projection of these coordinates onto the battlefield

In the first task, let's assume that the player creates the sketch by simply clicking and dragging the mouse on the screen (creating a path), or simply clicking on the screen (creating a target). The outcome from this operation is an array of one or more points given in 2D screen coordinates (see Figure 1.6.4). These points are stored internally, without worrying if they form a continuous line, which will be taken into account in the second stage.

In the second task, we unproject each 2D point onto a 3D position in the battlefield. Using standard graphics API features such as the `gluUnProject` function from OpenGL, we map window coordinates to object coordinates using the transform and viewport matrices. Care must be taken with battlefield obstacles and screen positions, which have no correspondent positions on the battlefield. This can be avoided by rendering the battlefield at a coarser resolution first, and using the generated depth buffer as input to `gluUnProject`. This simplifies the test for invalid projections, and eliminates the interference of battlefield obstacles. As a result we obtain an array of 3D points on the battlefield, which will be the entry for the second stage of the implementation.

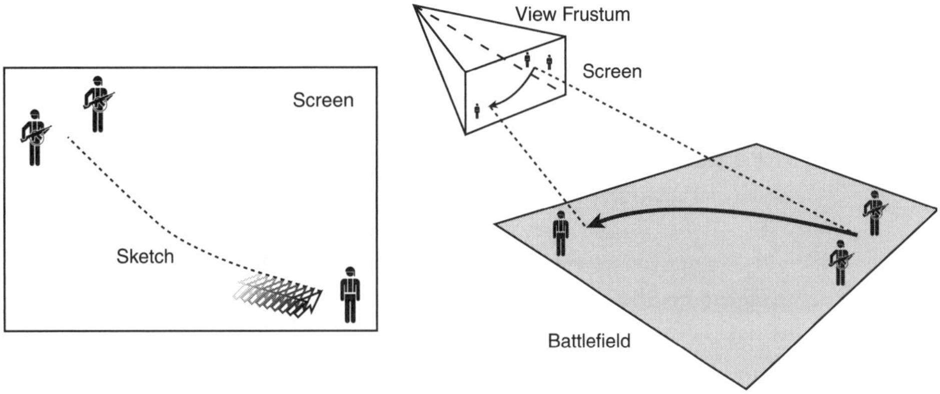

FIGURE 1.6.4 In the first stage of the implementation, 2D coordinates of the sketch (left) are captured and projected on the battlefield (right). The result is an array of 3D points that serves as input to the cellular automaton.

Moving the Soldiers

The second stage of the implementation is responsible for handling the reaction of units to the sketches. In this approach, each sketch is converted into forces that act directly over units by pushing them to desired positions on the battlefield. A grid discretization of the battlefield is used here, storing at each cell a vector representing a force that indicates the direction in which you want to move the units. Forces are updated throughout time and vary according with the user sketch. As Figure 1.6.5 illustrates, forces are stronger in cells closer to the sketch, and are linearly attenuated as they move away from the sketch. This brings the notion of *range* of the sketch into play, which resembles the behavior of a command in a real battlefield.

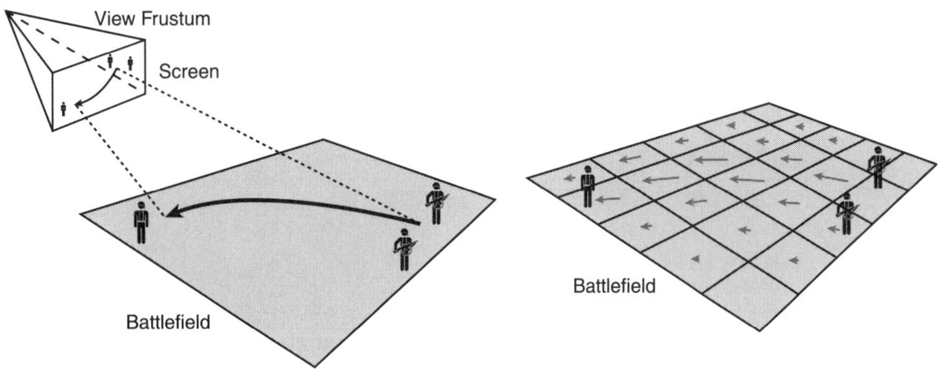

FIGURE 1.6.5 A sketch (left) and its underlying discretization as a grid of forces on the battlefield (right). Forces affect the unit's movement, pushing them to desired positions on the battlefield.

The proposed representation and sketch update can be efficiently done with a cellular automaton, which is simply a grid of cells encoding information that evolves through time according to a set of rules [Weisstein07]. Each rule is locally evaluated for each cell based on information stored in neighboring cells.

Figure 1.6.5 shows a rectangular grid of square cells, which is the configuration of the cellular automaton. The update of the grid information is made by a very simple totalistic rule. As previously stated, each cell stores a force (a vector quantity), which is given by the sketch position and direction on the grid (see Figure 1.6.6). Forces are spread out on the battlefield, attenuated by the distance to the sketch. We implement this with a rule that propagates the state of each cell to its neighbors iteratively until the system reaches the equilibrium. The update of each cell corresponds to *averaging* the quantities of the neighboring cells through time.

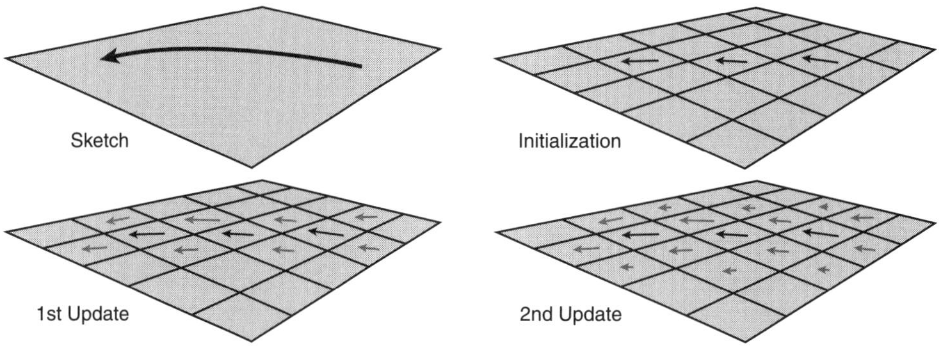

FIGURE 1.6.6 The 3D coordinates of the sketch (see Figure 1.6.4) are converted to 2D coordinates in the cellular automaton grid. Each point on the grid corresponding to a sketch point is marked with a force vector, which is iteratively smoothed through time.

As previously mentioned, such an automaton is formally called a *totalistic cellular automaton*. You have a continuous range of states (because forces can be given in any magnitude at each cell), a simple neighborhood (you are only looking to adjacent cells' states to update each cell), and the rule depends only on the average of the values of the neighboring cells. This last defines a totalistic cellular automaton [Weisstein07b], a complex name for a simple technique.

Putting It All Together

In order to use the proposed approach in real RTS environments, you need a way to define commands by sketches and to integrate the sketch-based interface with the current unit-based interfaces. We propose some useful commands that can be translated to the force grid approach, and also suggest a simple way to integrate sketch-based unit management in an existing implementation.

In RTS gameplay, you frequently need to move troops through the battlefield, guiding them around and in between natural obstacles, until you find some interesting target. These two commands (guide and point targets) have a natural translation with this approach. Guiding units can be made by line sketches, which are directly converted to force vectors on the grid (see Figure 1.6.7). It can be necessary, however, to ensure that the sketch is represented by a sufficient number of points on the grid. This can be accomplished by rasterizing the lines defined between the sketch points directly over the automaton grid.

Pointing out a target on the battlefield can be made by means of a small circular sketch (or even a point), which is then converted to a set of vectors around the sketch, pointing to the sketch center, as shown in Figure 1.6.7. The update of vectors around the sketch creates a vector field pointing to the sketch center, which pushes units closer to the desired target.

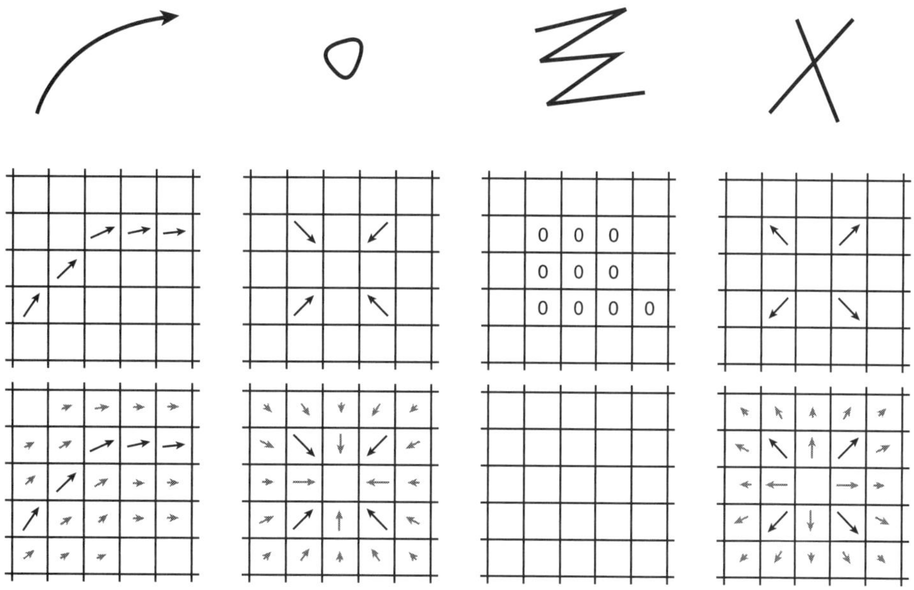

FIGURE 1.6.7 Different types of sketches (first row), their representation in the automaton grid (middle row), and the resulting vector field (last row). The sketch footprint is stored in the grid, which automatically updates the vector field through time. The "erase" command (illustrated in the third column) is a special case, where the sketch cancels the forces of the grid.

It is easy to see, however, that the insertion of some vectors in the automaton grid is not enough to create a stable vector field. The update mechanism smooths the cell contents every timestep, and this information quickly fades away. In order to prevent this from happening, we suggest the use of a command *lifetime*. The command lifetime is the number of iterations in which cells containing vectors originated by the command are not updated, thus allowing more time for the command to spread on the grid. The lifetime can be adjusted for each command type, being naturally high in long sketches (giving more time to units traveling along the battlefield) and small in sketches indicating target or smaller movements.

The integration of a sketch-based interface with an existing unit-based interface is simple because both implementations are independent (one does not affect the other). The sketch-based approach just adds a new item in the unit movement equation, which is a vector quantity indicating a direction to follow. All vectors are stored in a grid, which has a homeomorphic (one-to-one) mapping to the battlefield, which means that any unit on the battlefield can query the grid for the direction in which it should go. The grid update can be made in parallel, because it is independent of any other process. This suggests that you can encapsulate the sketch control in a black box that receives arrays of 2D points from the application interface. The sketch control can then be queried for forces in any battlefield position (see Figure 1.6.8).

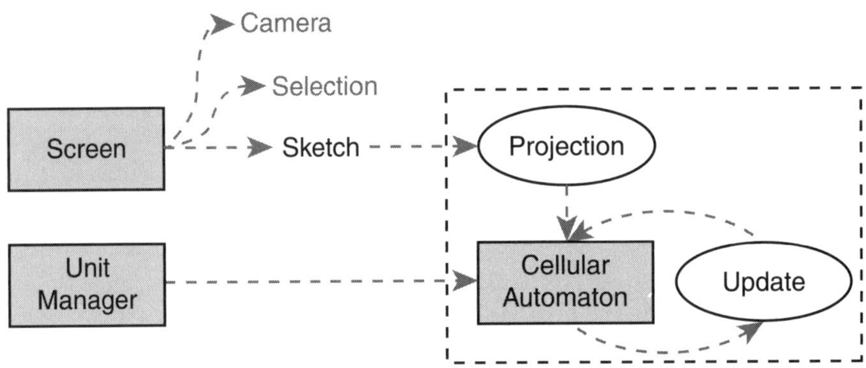

FIGURE 1.6.8 A possible integration of sketch- and unit-based interfaces. The sketch control can be seen as a black box, which receives arrays of 2D points from the application interface and can be queried for forces in any battlefield position.

Conclusion

This gem discussed a simple and efficient approach for implementing sketch-based interfaces. The efficiency comes primarily from the simplicity of the algorithms involved (such as projection of points and grid update through a cellular automaton), thus allowing an easy port for any RTS game engine. It is important to observe, however, that the chosen grid resolution plays a fundamental role on the performance and memory requirements of the application. In our experiments, we observed that a good compromise between reasonable sketch drawings and performance (or memory consumption) can be obtained with very small grids (30 × 30 or 50 × 50 cells). On the other hand, large grids are in general too expensive and tend to create smaller influence zones, which results in lines of units crossing the battlefield.

Our proposal can be easily extended to other types of grid patterns, which might be necessary on other applications. For instance, you can use a hexagonal grid to avoid the repetitive patterns of movement directions that we experience with rectangular grids, or even more general irregular grids can be employed to represent battlefields with many obstacles, such as mountains or rivers. The only modification to accommodate other grid types relies on smaller modifications of the automaton-updating rule, which can be easily adjusted to each grid type by accessing their neighborhood information.

References

[Bosch06] Bosch, Marc ten. "InkBattle," available online at http://inkbattle.marctenbosch.com, May 6, 2006.

[Philip07] Philip G. "Too Many Clicks! Unit-Based Interfaces Considered Harmful," available online at http://gamasutra.com/features/20060823/goetz_01.shtml, June 23, 2007.

[Weisstein07] Weisstein, Eric W. "Cellular Automaton," available online at http://mathworld.wolfram.com/CellularAutomaton.html, June 23, 2007.

[Weisstein07b] Weisstein, Eric W. "Totalistic Cellular Automaton," available online at http://mathworld.wolfram.com/TotalisticCellularAutomaton.html, June 23, 2007.

1.7

Foot Navigation Technique for First-Person Shooting Games

Marcus Aurelius C. Farias

Daniela G. Trevisan

Luciana P. Nedel

Interaction control in first-person shooting (FPS) games is a complex task that normally involves the use of the mouse and the keyboard simultaneously, and the memorization of many shortcuts. Because FPS games are based on the character movement in the virtual world, a combination of left and right hands (keyboard and mouse) is used to control navigation and action. This gem proposes a technique where the player controls navigation with the foot, keeping both hands free for other types of interaction, such as shooting, weapon selection, or object manipulation.

This foot-based navigation technique allows walking forward and backward, turning left and right, and controlling acceleration. The tracking of the foot can be done by using any motion capture device with at least two degrees of freedom, one translation and one rotation, although one or two additional degrees of freedom can be useful too.

Introduction

We implemented the navigation technique in two ways. In the first implementation, a very precise magnetic tracker (Flock of Birds from Ascension Technology Corporation) was used to capture foot translation and rotation (see Figure 1.7.1 for an example of this setup). Despite the very good results produced, this device is too expensive for domestic users.

Then, we tested a low cost and wireless solution for the same problem. In the second implementation, we used ARToolKit—an open source library—and a regular Webcam to capture and identify the translation and orientation of a printed marker attached to the player's foot (see Figure 1.7.1 for an overview of the setup). Because this second implementation also presented good results and can be easily reproduced by everyone with average programming skills, we present it in detail in this gem, avoiding explanation of the first implementation. However, the code for the first implementation is available in the CD.

The following sections present the fundamentals of the foot-based navigation technique, as well as how we implemented this using computer vision—in other words, by exploring ARToolKit features. This gem also provides a sample game developed with the specific purpose of evaluating the technique's usability and precision. User tests reveal that because most players are used to playing with keyboard and mouse, they were not as fast and precise with the use of the foot as a video game controller as expected. However, all of them completed the experience in reasonable time and were able to avoid all obstacles easily. These results encourage us to believe that with some training, users can rapidly increase their performance and become familiar with this new interaction technique, in the same way they are becoming experts with the new Nintendo Wii controller, for example.

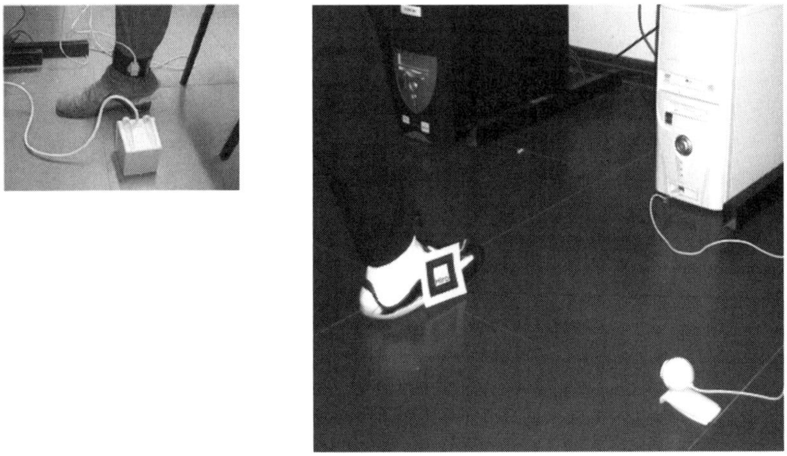

FIGURE 1.7.1 Environment setup using Flock of Birds motion capture device (left), and a square marker pattern attached to the player's foot and a Webcam (right).

Navigating with the Foot

The navigation technique proposed allows the players to control their movement speed and direction in an FPS game by using only one of their feet. First, users can choose if they want to sit down or stand up to play. Then, to start walking at a constant speed, they must move their foot forward (see Figure 1.7.2(c)). The farther forward the users place their feet, the faster they will move in the virtual environment. To stop, they simply move back to the starting position (see Figure 1.7.2(b)). To walk backward, the players slightly move their foot a few centimeters back (see Figure 1.7.2(a)). If the players want to turn left or right, they just turn their foot left or right, as can be seen in Figure 1.7.2(d–f).

The following sections explain how to implement this navigation technique using computer vision.

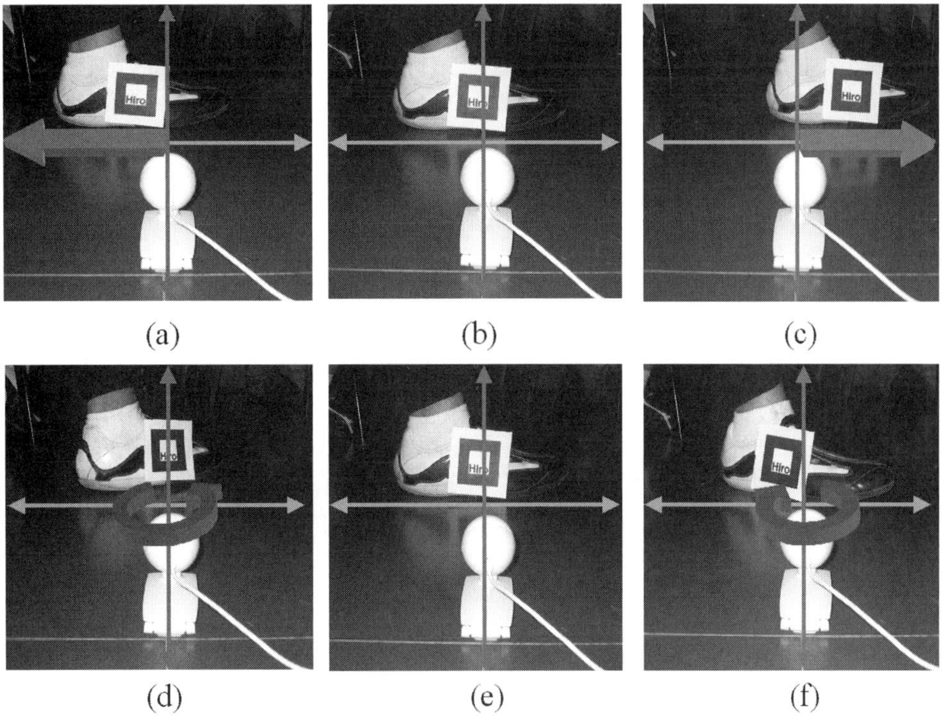

FIGURE 1.7.2 Game navigation control using the right foot: backward (a); rest position (b); forward (c); turn left (d); rest position (e); and turn right (f).

Requirements for an Implementation Based on Computer Vision

Because the computer can interpret the users' movements, gestures, and glances, computer vision is a potentially powerful tool to facilitate human-computer interaction. Some basic vision-based algorithms include tracking, shape recognition, and motion analysis. In this gem, we propose the use of a marker-based approach provided by ARToolKit (http://sourceforge.net/projects/artoolkit), an open source library for building augmented reality applications we used to capture the movement of the player's foot. More details about the ARToolKit marker-recognition principle can be found at http://www.hitl.washington.edu/artoolkit/documentation/index.html.

We used a 3GHz Pentium 4 CPU, with 1GB of RAM, and an NVIDIA GeForce 5200 graphics card. Taking into account the scenario shown in Figure 1.7.1 and considering that the captured image has 320 × 240 pixels, we achieve approximately 1 millisecond for the marker recognition process. Such processing does not introduce any kind of delay in the interactive game response. More details involving performance studies and the minimum CPU requirements can be found at the ARToolKit Website.

ARToolKit can track the position and orientation of special markers—black squares with a pattern in the middle—that can be easily printed and used to provide interactive response to a player's hand or body positions. In this case, the marker should be printed and attached on the player's foot in such a way that it remains always visible to the Webcam, as shown in Figure 1.7.1.

ON THE CD

The technique detailed in the next section requires that you print out the fiducial marker defined in the file hiroPatt.pdf, available on the CD-ROM. Best performance is achieved if this is glued to a piece of cardboard, keeping it flat.

Interaction implementation is almost trivial once you know how to extract the right information from ARToolKit. The first step consists of checking the foot rotation and detecting whether it is rotated to the left, to the right, or if it is pointing forward or backward. You might need to use a different multiplier for each direction, because most people will find it easier to turn to one direction than the other depending on whether the right or the left foot is used to control the program.

First, define a minimum value that will make the character start moving. When you detect that the player's foot has moved farther than this threshold, the character will start moving accordingly, forward or backward. The farther the players move their foot, the faster they will go. The "Implementation" section discusses more details about this.

Implementation

The initialization of ARToolKit requires a few steps, but it is not hard to follow. We set up the camera and load the file that describes the pattern to be detected. There is also an XML file (not shown here) with a few configurations, such as pixel format. It can also be set up to show the settings at start-up so the users will be able to select the preferred camera settings. The following code is based on sample programs that come with ARToolKit.

```
#include <AR/config.h>
#include <AR/video.h>
#include <AR/param.h>
#include <AR/ar.h>
#include <AR/gsub_lite.h>

ARGL_CONTEXT_SETTINGS_REF argl_settings = NULL;
int patt_id;
```

```
void setup()
{
    const char *cparam_name = "Data/camera_para.dat";
    const char *patt_name = "Data/patt.hiro";
    char vconf[] = "Data/WDM_camera.xml";

    setup_camera(cparam_name, vconf, &artcparam);

    // Set up argl library for current context.
    // Don't forget to catch these exceptions :-)
    if((argl_settings = arglSetupForCurrentContext()) == NULL){
        throw runtime_error(
            "Error in arglSetupForCurrentContext().\n");
}
```

Read the pattern definition with the default pattern file Data/patt.hiro:

```
    if((patt_id = arLoadPatt(patt_name)) < 0){
        throw runtime_error("Pattern load error!!");
    }
    atexit(quit);
}
```

`patt_id` is a pattern identification previously identified.

```
void setup_camera(
    const char *cparam_name, char *vconf, ARParam *cparam)
{
    ARParam wparam;
    int xsize, ysize;

    // Open the video path
    if(arVideoOpen(vconf) < 0){
        throw runtime_error("Unable to open connection to camera.\n");
}

    // Find the size of the window
    if(arVideoInqSize(&xsize, &ysize) < 0)
        throw runtime_error("Unable to set up AR camera.");
    fprintf(
        stdout, "Camera image size (x,y) = (%d,%d)\n", xsize, ysize);

    // Load the camera parameters, resize for the window and init
    if (arParamLoad(cparam_name, 1, &wparam) < 0) {
        throw runtime_error((boost::format(
            "Error loading parameter file %s for camera.\n") %
            cparam_name).str());
}
```

Next, parameters are transformed for the current image size, because camera parameters change depending on the image size, even if the same camera is used.

```
    arParamChangeSize(&wparam, xsize, ysize, cparam);
```

The camera parameters are set to those read in and printed on the screen:

```
        fprintf(stdout, "*** Camera Parameter ***\n");
        arParamDisp(cparam);
        arInitCparam(cparam);
        if(arVideoCapStart() != 0){
            throw runtime_error(
                "Unable to begin camera data capture.\n");
        }
    }
```

The `quit` function, referenced by `setup`, releases the resources previously allocated by ARToolKit.

```
    void quit()
    {
        arglCleanup(argl_settings);
        arVideoCapStop();
        arVideoClose();
    }
```

Let's now show some sample code illustrating how to get the position of the marker using ARToolKit. You first detect the marker in the frame using `arDetectMarker` in this way:

```
    ARMarkerInfo *marker_info;
    int marker_num; // Count the amount of markers detected
    arDetectMarker(image, thresh, &marker_info, &marker_num);
```

The markers found in the image by the library are returned in an array. This is useful if you need to detect several markers at the same time. You can tell which marker was found using `marker_info[i].id` and comparing it with the identifier returned by `arLoadPatt`. In the following code, you will see how to get the transformation matrix for the marker found at `marker_info[i]`.

```
    double patt_centre[2] = {0.0, 0.0};
    double patt_width = 80.0;
    double patt_trans[3][4];
    double m[16];
    arGetTransMat(&marker_info[i], patt_centre, patt_width, patt_trans);
    arglCameraViewRH(patt_trans, m, 1.0);
```

As you can see, you need to call two functions: `arGetTransMat` and `arglCameraViewRH`. The former retrieves the transformation matrix used by ARToolKit, whereas the latter converts it to the same format used by OpenGL so that you can use it to transform scene objects (not needed here) or simply to see the transformation in a format with which you are more familiar.

You then extract the translations and the rotation around the y-axis from matrix m.

```
// m[12], m[13], m[14] == x, y, z
if(m[12] > start_position_x + mov_eps){
    walk_fwd(m[12] * mov_mult);
}else if(m[12] < start_position_x - mov_eps){
    walk_bck(m[12] * mov_mult);
}

double angle_y = asin(mat[8]);
if(angle_y > rot_eps){
    turn_left(angle_y);
}else if(angle_y < -rot_eps){
    turn_right(angle_y);
}
```

As explained, the previous code can be used when the camera is on the player's right side, so that it can see the right leg of the user. You just need to reverse the signs if you prefer to put the camera on the left.

You will also need some multipliers and *epsilon* values to adjust control sensitivity. We suggest 10 for `move_eps` and 0.3 for `rot_eps` as start values (you can tweak the values according to your needs). We used 0.0625 for `mov_mult`, but this value depends on the scale used in your virtual world. The variable `start_position_x` must be initialized with the position that you want to use as neutral; that is, a position that guarantees the character will not move. The simplest implementation is to assign to the first `m[12]` captured by ARToolKit when the program starts.

There are other values that can be useful in matrix `m`, including `m[13]` and `m[14]`, because they inform the translation in the other two axes. For example, `m[13]` can be used for jumping and `m[14]` for strafing (sidestepping). However, you'll likely find that it's too hard to control rotation and walk/strafe at the same time, so choose the controls for your game wisely. The other rotation axes do not make much sense in this context, so we will not discuss them.

A Sample Game

In order to evaluate usability and playability of an FPS using foot navigation, we implemented a sample FPS game containing a simple map that the user can explore using the navigation technique proposed here.

In the first contact with the game, the player can interact in the training zone, the first area of the map (see Figure 1.7.3), gaining confidence and permitting input calibration. The game starts only when the user passes over the cyan tile (see Figure 1.7.4). In the remaining regions of the environment, there are a few obstacles and some red checkpoints on the floor that become green when crossed by the user (see Figure 1.7.5). Collisions with obstacles, including walls, are detected and visual feedback (screen changes color, as shown in Figure 1.7.6) is sent to the player each time it happens. The game is over when, after passing over all checkpoints, the player attains the exit shown in Figure 1.7.3 as the "end point." The player's goal is to complete this task in the shortest time with as few collisions with obstacles and walls as possible.

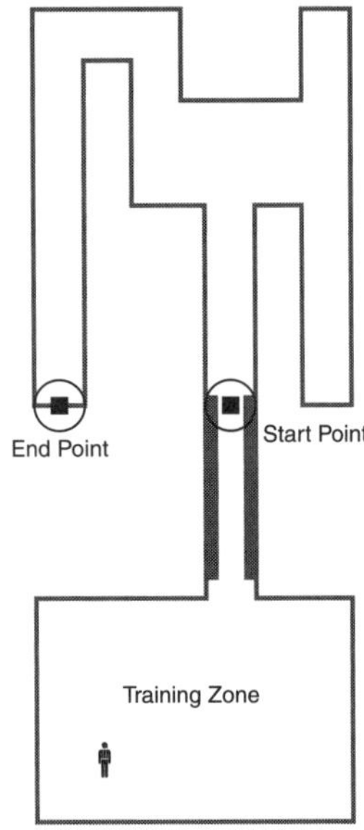

FIGURE 1.7.3 Sketch of the game circuit.

FIGURE 1.7.4 Game start indicator, indicated by the lighter tile in the foreground.

FIGURE 1.7.5 View of the scenario with a checkpoint to be reached (left) and the same checkpoint reached (right).

FIGURE 1.7.6 Two frames of a game—before (left) and after (right) a collision with an obstacle.

All game events are logged in a text file, so you can detect when users have trouble avoiding a wall or finding a checkpoint.

Tests with Real Users

We have tested the proposed navigation technique with 15 people who played the sample game so we could measure their performance and hear their suggestions. We asked how comfortable they felt playing the game, how easy it was to use and learn, and how efficient they think it is. Six people found the navigation with the foot comfortable, whereas four others found it more or less comfortable. Only one person considered the technique hard to use. Three people found the technique hard to learn (as opposed to "hard to use"). Regarding the efficiency, three people thought the technique is inefficient, seven rated it as more or less efficient, and five people found it is efficient.

This data shows us that the interaction is intuitive and reasonably easy to use after some practice. In the sample game, we measured the number of collisions and the time the users took to cross all checkpoints and reach the end goal. Because most users had experience in the use of a keyboard and mouse combination, it is expected that they were not as fast when using their foot as a video game controller. However, everyone completed the task in a reasonable time and easily avoided all obstacles. We noticed that it is especially easy to move fast and suddenly stop, because the acceleration control is intuitive (you just move your foot forward as far as you can, as long as the camera still sees it) and when you want to stop, you need only to go back to the rest position).

Conclusion

This gem presented a new technique to allow navigation for FPS games using one of the player's feet. It also described a low-cost solution to implement it using computer vision, more specifically ARToolKit open source library that easily tracks foot movements and then transforms them into interaction controls for the game environment.

There are some limitations inherent in purely computer-vision-based systems. Naturally, the marker position is computed only when the tracking marks are in the camera's field of view. This may limit the movement of the interaction, also meaning that if the users cover up part of the pattern with other objects, navigation is stopped. Other factors such as *range issues, pattern complexity, marker orientation relative to the camera, and lighting conditions influence detection of the pattern.*

On the other hand, there are basically three advantages in this technique against traditional approaches. First, by using a tracker, users have more degrees of freedom to work with. The users can move their foot in the 1D, 2D, or 3D space and rotate around one axis (left-right rotation). Moreover, the mouse and keyboard could be used in other ways, because navigation is no longer a concern. For example, they can be used for aiming, shooting, selecting, and manipulating on-screen objects. Lastly, using the whole body to interact with the game gives a deeper immersion for the player, as games for the Nintendo Wii console have shown.

Future Work

There are many ways to explore the possibilities of this interaction technique. The first one is to add new simple commands, such as jump or sidestepping. Another alternative is to reuse the mouse and keyboard commands that are no longer needed and to assign more ergonomic commands to them.

Multiplayer games are also an untapped possibility, because the marker-based interaction technique, as well as the Flock of Birds, allow a multiplayer functionality. It is possible to attach and track a different marker for each player as long as the Webcam can capture them. If this is not the case, it is always possible to use two or more cameras concurrently.

To address portability, as well as to avoid the occlusion problem that can occur between the Webcam and the markers, some kind of interaction based on remote controlled devices could be implemented. The main idea remains the same, namely: the controller should be attached to the user's foot while movements should be performed in exactly the same way. Finally, we estimate a different game design, such as a *Super Monkey Ball* style–game, could be more attractive to this type of control.

Acknowledgments

The authors would like to thank Fábio Dapper and Alexandre Azevedo for their work in the conception and first implementation of this technique, as well as all people who played the game, giving us valuable feedback. Finally, we thank the Brazilian Council for Research and Development (CNPq) for financial support.

1.8

Deferred Function Call Invocation System

Mark Jawad, Nintendo of America Inc.

mark.jawad@gmail.com

It seems that lately it has become common for most computing systems to be designed around multiple processors; in fact that appears to be a core design axiom within the engineering community right now. Modern video game machines are no exception to the trend, with multi-core CPU designs being prevalent in many of the game machines on sale today. Additionally, most of them rely on auxiliary processing acceleration chips such as programmable IO controllers, DMA engines, math co-processors, and so on. These run in parallel with the CPU(s), and are there as part of the system so that we as artists can push our craft ever farther. Each of these components may complete their tasks independently of the others, but all send along a notification to the game when the task is done (usually in the form of an interrupt), so that the game can schedule other work.

The way in which a game handles these notifications can either lead to a fairly painless and bug-free experience, or to a frustrating world of head-scratching, bug-chasing hurt. This article discusses the implications of asynchronous events and other timing-related issues, and provides a system to handle them gracefully.

A Matter of Time

From the game's point of view, these notifications may happen at any time, and thus should be treated as true asynchronous events. These event notifications are great because the game can run on the main processor at the pace it desires, while other processors do auxiliary work at whatever rate they can. However, there are some problems. If handled improperly, these notifications can lead to timing-related bugs or system instability. Timing-related bugs are notoriously difficult to track down, and can happen if you try to use memory before another system client is done with it, or if you change the game state without proper synchronization primitives. System instability bugs are even worse, and can occur if a callback/interrupt handler runs for too long during an interrupt period, thus causing other interrupt signals (or subsequent interrupt signals of the same type) to be missed. Such a situation can lead to all sorts of odd program behavior.

Developers working on handheld gaming systems are faced not only with these issues but additional ones as well. A major focus that these systems have is the concept of a *vertical blanking period,* which is the point in time where the graphics engine(s) go idle while the display device prepares for the next frame of output. It is during this small window of time that developers are allowed to access the memory and registers of the graphics system. During this time, you need to quickly determine what new data is to be uploaded, as well as what settings need to change on the graphics chip. A developer must make the changes and data uploads as quickly as possible. If they fail to do the work within the window, the graphics may show corruption or other noticeable artifacts.

These various issues all deal with time in some form or another—time is always an enemy of game developers and we never seem to get enough of it. Because we probably can't get more time in which to do work, we'll have to settle for making smarter use of the time that we've got. One approach is that instead of doing all the work at once, you do some of it now and the rest of it later. In essence, you're making a decision now but deferring the actual work to some point in the future. Because most work is handled by making function calls, this gem uses a system that queues up function calls and their parameters, and has the ability to invoke them sometime later—hence, a deferred function call system.

Case Studies

Let's examine the vertical blank period where you have very limited time. The ideal situation is to not do any time-consuming logic at all during this window; rather you should be purely focused on uploading lots of new data as quickly as possible. So why not do all of the logic relating to what data to upload (and where to put it) earlier on in the frame when you are not under such extreme time pressure? You queue up source and destination addresses, transfer size, and perhaps take note of the "type" of data (textures, palettes, and so on). Then when the blanking window opens, you run through the queue and do all of the transfers.

But what happens if the type of data determines the choice of function used to upload the data? Well, then you have a `switch` statement, jump table, or cascading series of `if` statements in order to determine which function to call. Such an approach isn't worth a second thought on a PC or home console. On a portable machine with a low clock speed it is definitely worth a second thought, especially given the small blanking window coupled with how precious each cycle is. Therefore, the ideal approach is to also pre-determine the function to call when you're setting up the addresses and transfer sizes. Then, during the vertical blanking window, all you have to do is load the function's address along with the necessary parameters and jump off to it. In essence, you're setting up the function call earlier in the game loop, but deferring the actual invocation until the vertical blank period arrives.

The same tactic can be used on home consoles to deal with asynchronous notifications. Maybe you get a callback that informs you that a certain file read has completed, or a memory card was inserted, or that the user has inserted or removed a controller peripheral. Some of these situations require more work than others, but most of them are such that you don't need to do the bulk of the work *right there and then*. Yes, the game logic needs to know about the file read completion, or the new controller, but why not schedule the real processing of the event sometime later near the end of the current processing frame?

Queue up the incoming notification parameters (taking care to save any important temporal data that might get lost) and deal with them later. This way you exit the callback/interrupt as fast as possible, which is always a good thing. By hoisting the notification processing out of the interrupt handler and into a dedicated place in your game loop, you help keep the game behavior deterministic. This in turn nearly eliminates timing-related bugs. An additional benefit of the approach is that you can guarantee that no one on the team will mistakenly run a process that takes "too long" while interrupts are disabled, because the handling process is now at a known point in the simulation loop and not in an interrupt handler. So it can take all the time it needs.

Categorizing a Function Call

Most functions are set up to take their arguments directly in the function parameters, such as this one from the C standard library

```
void *memccpy(void *dest, const void *src, int c, size_t count);
```

which takes four parameters in its argument list. This is the most common function call type in C-derived languages today, and is categorized as taking "direct" parameters. Other functions, such as this one from the Windows SDK

```
ATOM RegisterClassEx(CONST WNDCLASSEX *lpwcx);
```

take a single argument, but really that argument just points to a control structure where the 12 "actual" parameters reside. This type of call can be categorized as a function that takes an "indirect" parameter. Often, the parameter for the indirect argument sits on the stack of the callee (as opposed to being stored in the heap), and is therefore lost once the callee exits.

On the surface, it would appear that the second type is just a subset of the first. However, there is an important distinction that you need to make note of. As mentioned earlier, sometimes you need to store data temporally. In the case of a deferred function, where do you store indirect argument data blocks? The callee function that would normally have created the argument structure will be long gone by the time the deferred function is called (and with it, the data that was in its stack frame). The solution is to hand out a pool of memory large enough to store the argument. This pool will come from the deferred system itself, and the argument will be constructed in-place there instead of on the stack.

A Look at the System

The header file for the system, deferred_proc.h, is quite small, and should be trivial to integrate into your game. The header contains one function for initializing an instance of the system, a couple of functions and macros for adding deferred calls to lists of direct-argument (DA) or indirect-argument (IA) functions, and one for executing the deferred functions (and then resetting the lists when that is done).

The majority of the code is presented in C, although there is one function that must be written in assembly code. That function is the *deferred function caller*. This one function is platform-dependent, and must take into account the ABI (application binary interface) of the platform that it's being run on. So to port the system, you need only to rewrite the deferred function caller.

Please note that the system presented herein is limited to making function calls that only use arguments kept in general purpose registers (GPRs). Floating point values, native floating point vectors, or other data types that aren't intended for a general purpose register are not allowed as parameters to the deferred functions. This is done to keep the system simple, although support for such things could be added if needed. Also in keeping things simple the system allows a maximum of four parameters.

I've found four parameters to be sufficient for most cases. One consideration was that if more than four are used, you might have to transfer some of the parameters in registers and others on the stack, depending on the platform being targeted, which again could increase complexity—and complexity is something that this system actively tries to avoid.

Because this system is limited to four direct parameters, you must use the indirect call for anything where five or more parameters are needed. (Don't forget that the hidden `this` parameter of C++ instance functions counts as one of the four parameters that you can accept for direct-argument function calls!)

The deferred function caller, `dfpProcessAndClear`, may be a little difficult to understand because it's in assembly, but the idea behind it is very simple. All it has to do is loop through the contents of the list and dispatch (call) each entry. At each loop iteration, it needs to load at minimum a control word that describes the following:

- The function type (DA or IA)
- The number of GPR parameters it should load
- Any additional bytes of data that the call took from the list

Of course, it will also need to load the target function's address. Then it needs to load any parameters stored for use with the function. Once this information is loaded it can branch off to the target function. When that function returns, you go on to the next iteration of the loop. Once done, you reset the list and exit. Please note that the sample code is not thread-safe. Please see the CD for the complete source code.

ON THE CD

Conclusion

Deferred functions are an extremely useful tool for game developers on all platforms, especially those working on home consoles or handheld systems. Their existence can help make the most of time critical sections of code, such as the vertical blank period and interrupt processing sequences, and the system that tracks them can handle many different types of function signatures. The idea is flexible, easily extendable, efficient, and very portable—traits that all of us can surely appreciate.

References

[Earnshaw07] Earnshaw, Richard. "Procedure Call Standard for the ARM Architecture," available online at http://www.arm.com/pdfs/aapcs.pdf, January 19, 2007.

1.9

Multithread Job and Dependency System

Julien Hamaide

Julien.hamaide@gmail.com

This gem puts next generation multi-core capabilities into the hands of all programmers without the need to comprehend more complex multithreading concepts to create tasks. By providing a simple system that automatically manages dependencies between tasks, there is almost no need of other more specific synchronization mechanisms. The system is adapted for small- to medium-sized tasks such as animation blending or particle system updates.

Introduction

When thinking about multithreading, synchronization problems come quickly to mind. Deadlock is a fear for every programmer. Even for small projects, a multithreading solution is typically rewritten every time due to the interdependencies unique to the project. Therefore, programmers require knowledge of synchronization primitives and their intricacies. For example, if the system is time-critical, a lock-free algorithm must be used. Additionally, the more complex the system, the higher the chance of creating bugs.

The primary goal of the system is to provide a cross-platform framework that hides the complexity of multithreading issues. Any programmer, even those not familiar with common multithreading concepts, should be able to use the system. There is no concept of threads in the system; it is replaced by the concept of *jobs,* which are defined as units of work.

The process of creating a job is shown in the following code. Cross-platform compatibility is achieved by encapsulating primitives such as critical sections and threads in classes. The framework code is then created with those classes. The demo on the CD contains the job manager and the wrapper classes.

ON THE CD

```
void MultithreadEntryFunction( void * context )
{
    //Do your stuff here
}

PARALLEL_JOB_HANDLE handle;
```

```
handle = PARALLEL_JOB_MANAGER_CreateJob(
    &MultithreadEntryFunction, context);

PARALLEL_JOB_MANAGER_ScheduleJob( handle );
```

The performance of the system is also optimized by preventing thread creation and deletion for small-sized tasks. The framework creates a thread pool that executes the tasks given to the system. The threads are created only once at the launch of the application. The number of threads depends on the platform and is dynamically evaluated if necessary. (On a PC, the number of cores on the target platform may not be known at compile time.) This approach is similar to *OpenMP*'s approach to distributing work over multiple threads [OpenMP].

The system also supports prioritization of tasks. If some tasks take more time or have many dependent tasks, their priority can be increased to ensure early execution. Support for idle tasks is reviewed in the future work section, but has not yet been implemented.

The synchronization of jobs is handled by a dependency system. It allows the creation of synchronization points and job dependencies. The dependency system is covered in detail in following sections.

The Job System

The job system is mainly composed of four types of objects:

- The *job,* which is unit of work delimited in a callback function. It must be designed to be thread-safe.
- The *manager,* which maintains the job list by priority and type.
- The *scheduler,* which chooses the task that suits best depending on priority and type.
- The *workers,* which execute the jobs assigned to them.

Job

Jobs are represented by the class shown in the following code. It simply encapsulates a closure (a function with a predefined argument). The structure also contains the priority and the handle of the job. `PARALLEL_JOB_PRIORITY` is an enum containing classic priority values (that is, High, Low, and so on). The handle identifies the job in the system. It is the object that is used outside the system to reference a job. The `Type` field is explained later.

```
class PARALLEL_JOB
{
public :
    void Execute()
    {
        Function( Context );
    }
```

```
private :

    PARALLEL_JOB_HANDLE
        JobHandle;
    PARALLEL_JOB_PRIORITY
        Priority;
    PARALLEL_JOB_TYPE
        Type;
    PARALLEL_JOB_FUNCTION
        Function;
    void
        * Context;
};
```

Manager

The manager class is a singleton providing the public interface of the system. As the system's central point, it maintains the list of jobs in a multithread-safe manner. The manager is responsible for worker and scheduler thread creation and initialization. The interface of the manager is shown in the following code. The creation and scheduling of jobs is separated to allow the user to add dependencies to and on the created job. In the demo code, every call is protected with critical sections [MSDN1]. Lock-free algorithms are better choices but increase the complexity of the system. To ease the understanding of concepts, only the critical section version is given. Implementation of lock-free algorithms is left as an exercise for the developers.

```
typedef void (*PARALLEL_JOB_FUNCTION )( void* );

PARALLEL_JOB_HANDLE CreateJob(
    PARALLEL_JOB_FUNCTION function,
        void * context,
        PARALLEL_JOB_PRIORITY priority = PARALLEL_JOB_PRIORITY_Default
        );

PARALLEL_JOB_HANDLE CreateAndScheduleJob(
        PARALLEL_JOB_FUNCTION function,
        void * context,
        PARALLEL_JOB_PRIORITY priority = PARALLEL_JOB_PRIORITY_Default
        );

void ScheduleJob(
     PARALLEL_JOB_HANDLE job_handle
    );
```

The `PARALLEL_JOB_HANDLE` is a structure that contains a unique identifier and a dependency index. The dependency index is covered in the following sections.

Scheduler

The scheduler is a thread object that waits for the worker threads to finish. As soon as one is free, it selects the next job, assigns it to the worker thread, and puts itself back to sleep. The following code shows the main loop of the scheduler in pseudocode.

PARALLEL_JOB_MANAGER_GetNextJob returns the best job to be executed next. The decision rules are presented later. The WaitForJobEvent allows the scheduler to sleep if there is no new job available and some worker threads are free. When new jobs are available, the WaitForJobEvent is signaled; otherwise, it is reset [MSDN2].

```
while ( !ThreadMustStop )
{
    thread_index
        = PARALLEL_WaitMultipleObjects( worker_thread_table );

    if( PARALLEL_JOB_MANAGER_GetNextJob( next_job, thread_index ) )
    {
        worker_thread_table[ thread_index ]->SetAssignedJob(next_job);
        worker_thread_table[ thread_index ]->WakeUp();
    }
    else
    {
        WaitForJobEvent.Wait();
    }
}
```

Worker Threads

The worker does the dirty work. When the operating system permits, it is assigned to a processor. The pseudocode is shown in the following code. The worker waits for DataIsReadyEvent to be signaled, meaning it has been assigned to a new job. It then executes it. When finished, it informs the dependency manager that its job is finished. Finally, it signals the scheduler that it is waiting for a new job.

In the implementation, the number of worker threads is set to the number of available processors. If the main thread is always busy, it can be useful to set the number of worker threads to the number of available processors, minus one.

```
while ( !ThreadMustStop )
{
    PARALLEL_WaitObject( DataIsReadyEvent, INFINITE );
    AssignedJob.Execute();
    PARALLEL_DEPENDENCY_MANAGER_SetJobIsFinished( AssignedJob );
    WaitingForDataEvent.Signal();
}
```

Cache Coherency

To ensure code and data cache coherency, both jobs and worker threads have been assigned types. The type of the job can be anything you want, depending on your system. In this implementation, we choose types such as particle systems, animation, pathfinding, and so on. The type will be used in job selection, so choose them carefully. The cache coherency is really specific to each platform. Some tuning can be necessary to achieve the maximum speed.

Job Selection

When the scheduler asks for the next job to execute, the manager uses simple rules to choose it. The pseudocode is shown here after. The selection tries to balance between thread type changes and high priority tasks. This algorithm is not adaptive, but the highest priority thread can be boosted every time a lower priority thread is chosen due to a type difference. In this way, you can allow scheduling of only two or three lower priority threads before the highest priority thread is scheduled.

```
current_type = type of worker thread
if( job of type current_type exists )
{
    new_job = job of type current_type with highest priority
    if( priority of new_job – highest priority available > 2 )
    {
        new_job = job with highest priority
        worker thread type = new job type
    }
}
else
{
    new_job = job with highest priority
    worker thread type = new job type
}
```

The Dependency Manager

The dependency manager is an object-based system that ensures synchronization of tasks. The current implementation has two types of entry: jobs and groups. The system constructs a graph of dependencies between entries. Groups allow the users to create synchronization points such as the start of rendering. Figure 1.9.1 shows a typical dependency graph created by the system.

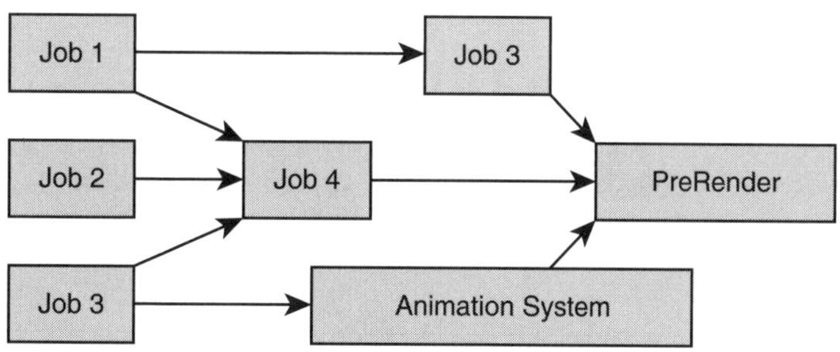

FIGURE 1.9.1 Example dependency graph.

The Dependency Graph

The dependency graph is stored inside dependency entries. Each stores a list of dependent objects. A dependency can be in two states: met or blocked. If a dependency entry is met, it means that every other entry that depends on it can be executed. If only one of its dependencies is blocked, an entry is also blocked.

To prevent polling of dependencies, an entry contains a dependency count. For each blocked dependency an entry depends upon, the counter is increased. When the counter is zero, the dependency is met; otherwise, it is blocked. When a dependency enters the met state, it iterates over all its dependent objects to decrease their counts. Similarly, when a dependency becomes blocking, it iterates all its dependent objects to increase their counts. The met and blocked information is propagated along the graph. Figures 1.9.2 and 1.9.3 show a step of propagation. When job 1 becomes met, the Animation group also becomes met. The dependency count of job 3 decreases by 1, whereas the dependency count of PreRender group decreases by 2.

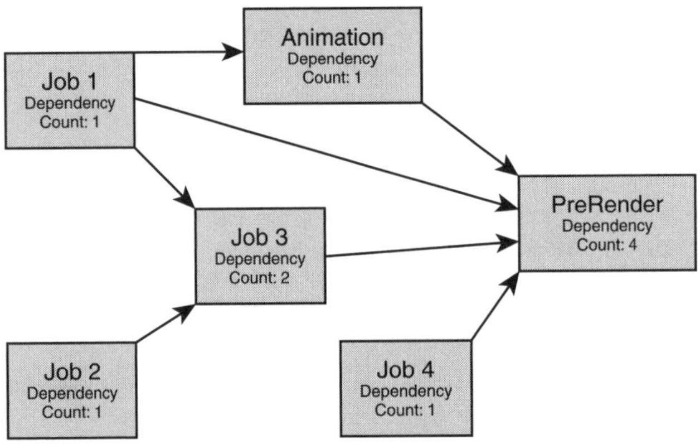

FIGURE 1.9.2 Initial graph with dependency count.

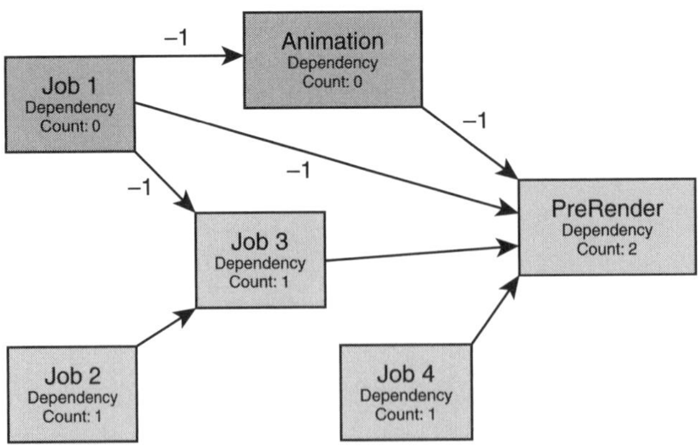

FIGURE 1.9.3 Graph after propagation.

Dependency Storage

The dependency table is a sparse vector of pointers to entries. An index dispenser is used to allocate a free slot to the current dependencies. The table grows if necessary, but never shrinks. When an entry is created, an index is requested from the index dispenser. On deletion its index is recycled and will be used by the next entry created. This recycling means that the dependency cannot be identified by its index alone. The `PARALLEL_DEPENDENCY_IDENTIFIER` has been introduced to solve this problem. This structure contains an index to the table of dependency entries and a unique index. This identifier serves as a handle for the users.

The following code shows the creation of a dependency group and links. In this example, the PreRender group will wait until the Animation group is met. This can be used to ensure that all animations are computed before the rendering occurs. All animation jobs will set up a dependency over the Animation group. Figure 1.9.4 shows the graph created by such a construction. If a dependency no longer exists (that is, the job is finished), it is considered as met.

```
PARALLEL_DEPENDENCY_IDENTIFIER
   animation_identifier, prerender_identifier;

prerender_identifier
   = PARALLEL_DEPENDENCY_MANAGER_CreateEntry( "PreRender
        Synchronization");

animation_identifier
   = PARALLEL_DEPENDENCY_MANAGER_CreateEntry( "Animation
       Synchronization");

PARALLEL_DEPENDENCY_MANAGER_AddDependency(
   animation_identifier, prerender_identifier );

// during the game
blend_job_handle
   = PARALLEL_JOB_MANAGER_CreateJob( &MultithreadBlendAnim, context);

PARALLEL_DEPENDENCY_MANAGER_AddDependency(
    blend_job_handle, animation_identifier );

PARALLEL_JOB_MANAGER_ScheduleJob( handle );
```

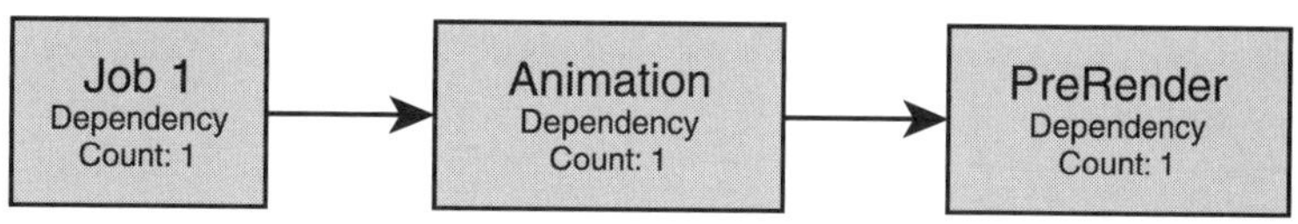

FIGURE 1.9.4 Dependency graph created by previous example.

This example raises a problem—the job is a volatile object and when finished, it is destructed. Groups are stable entries. To address these needs, two types of link have been created:

- *Dynamic link:* As soon as the dependency is met, the link is removed.
- *Static link:* The link is established at launch and always remains valid.

The entry contains two tables, one for static links and one for dynamic links. When the entry is met, the dynamic link table is emptied. In the previous example, the link between the Animation Synchronization entry and the PreRender Synchronization entry is transformed into a static link. This example is used in the demo.

Group Entry

A group entry creates a synchronization point. The manager provides a way to wait until the dependency is met. A call to `PARALLEL_DEPENDENCY_MANAGER_WaitForDependency` will stall until the dependency is met. It is useful, for example, to wait for all computations to finish before starting the rendering. This behavior is implemented with events. An event is created for each instance of a group. This means that an event is created for each group, even if you don't want to be able to wait for it in your code. If you want to avoid this waste of events, you can create two types of groups—waitable and non-waitable groups.

Job Entry

A job entry is used for two purposes:

- To synchronize other entries with the job
- To synchronize the launch of the job

The entry is created with a dependency count set to one. This represents the dependency that the execution of the job sets on the entry. To prevent the need for two entries, one for the launch and one for the end of the job, the entry count is polled by the job manager. If the entry's dependency count is one, there is no dependency left other than the job execution itself, so the job can be executed. As shown in the worker thread pseudocode, it reports that the job is finished to the dependency manager. The dependency count is then set to zero, and the entry becomes met and propagates the information to all entries that depend on it.

Future Work

The following sections discuss the future work—areas of this system that might be good candidates for enhancements and extensions.

Idle Tasks and Preemption

In the presented system, every started task occupies its worker thread until it is finished. This constraint prevents users from scheduling low priority tasks that can be computed over several frames. Three solutions are possible to fix this problem:

- *Preemption*: Low-priority tasks could be preempted if a new job is pushed into the system. Not all operating systems allow the users to code their own version of thread context switching. This solution is also platform-specific.
- *Cooperative multithreading:* Low-priority tasks can be implemented using cooperative multithreading, but each task should use a special function to allow the system the opportunity to execute higher-priority jobs. Such a system can be implemented using, for example, Windows fibers [MSDN3].
- *Low-priority thread:* The system can create new lower-priority threads, letting the operating system scheduler preempt them when other worker threads are working. This solution is cross-platform and easy to implement as long as the OS scheduler is good enough.

The first solution is the best from a control point of view. No special work is needed in the job code, you control exactly when the job is preempted but it is platform-specific and can be tricky to implement. The second solution is easier to implement, but it is still platform-specific. Another drawback is that the job code must be adapted to allow preemption. The third solution is by far the easiest to implement, but you don't have much control about when and how your thread will be preempted. Ideally, the third solution should be implemented first, with a view to switching to other solutions if necessary.

Integration of Synchronization Primitives into the Dependency System

The dependency system supports only two types of entry: job and group. It means that you can't interface the system with an already existing synchronization mechanism. For example, a loading thread can use semaphores to communicate with other threads. If you want your job to wait for some resource to be loaded, the system does not allow it. A solution is to extend the entry to other types: semaphores, events, and so on. The dependency system has been designed to be extensible. The `PARALLEL_DEPENDENCY_ENTRY` can be derived to support primitives easily. Virtual functions that inform the dependency state of the new synchronization mechanism must be written. The job is complete when the implementation of those virtual functions has been written. The new system is then ready to interact with the dependency system.

Conclusion

The presented system provides the power of multithreading to all programmers. It abstracts the complexity and the danger of using synchronization primitives. The critical code is consolidated in a single place and synchronization issues are solved only once. By providing a dependency graph system, the jobs can be chained without any other action than creating a dependency link between them. Already rather complete, the system has been designed to be extensible. The implementation is cross-platform; the only things you need to port are the wrapper classes provided in the demo package (mainly thread, critical section, and event). Performance is also targeted by limiting the overhead of thread creation. The system can also interface with existing synchronization techniques with the help of the `PARALLEL_DEPENDENCY_ENTRY` interface. All your programmers should now be able to create and schedule a job enjoying considerably less threading-related complexity than without this gem. Enjoy!

References

[MSDN1] "Critical Section Objects (Windows)," available online at http://msdn2.microsoft.com/en-us/library/ms682530.aspx, June 1, 2007.

[MSDN2] "Event Objects (Windows)," available online at http://msdn2.microsoft.com/en-us/library/ms682655.aspx, June 1, 2007.

[MSDN3] "Fibers (Windows)," available online at http://msdn2.microsoft.com/en-us/library/ms682661.aspx, June 1, 2007.

[OpenMP] OpenMP Architecture Review Board. "OpenMP: Simple, Portable, Scalable SMP Programming," available online at http://www.openmp.org.

1.10

Advanced Debugging Techniques

Martin Fleisz

Martin.fleisz@kabsi.at

Due to the high expectations that players have in games nowadays, development gets more and more complex. Adding new features or supporting new technologies often requires more code to be written, which automatically leads to more bugs. Game projects are usually tightly scheduled and hard-to-find bugs are often the cause for delays. Although you cannot avoid that erroneous code is written, you can try to improve the process of finding and fixing these errors. If an application crashes or does something wrong, information about the crash becomes the most important data in order to find the cause of a malfunction. Therefore, this gem presents a small framework that detects and reports a vast number of programming errors and can be easily integrated into any existing project.

Application Crashes

The reasons that an application crashes are manifold. Stack overflows, dividing by zero, or accessing an invalid memory address are just a few of them. All of these errors are signaled to the application through exceptions, which, if you fail to handle them properly, will terminate the game. You can distinguish between two different types of exceptions. *Asynchronous exceptions* are unexpected and often caused by the hardware (for example, when your application is accessing an invalid memory address). *Synchronous exceptions* are expected and usually handled in an organized manner. These exceptions are explicitly thrown by the application—that is, using the `throw` keyword in C++.

Exception Handling

The C++ language offers built-in support for handling synchronous exceptions (through the `try`/`throw`/`catch` keywords). However, this is not the case for handling asynchronous exceptions. Their handling depends on how the underlying platform implements them.

Microsoft unified the handling of both exception types on their Windows platforms and refers to it under the term Structured Exception Handling (SEH). If you want to know how SEH and the new Vectored Exception Handling technologies work in detail, refer to [Pietrek97] and [Pietrek01].

What you have to know is what happens if the operating system does not find a handler for an exception. In this case, the `UnhandledExceptionFilter` function is called by the kernel. [Pietrek97] shows a pseudocode sample of what this function does in detail. The most interesting part is that the function will execute a user-defined callback that you can register using the `SetUnhandledExceptionFilter` API. Using this callback, you will be notified when your application crashes so that you can do the error reporting.

UNIX-based operating systems use a different approach. In the case of an asynchronous exception, the system sends a signal to the application, at which time its normal execution flow is stopped and the application's signal handler is called. Using the `sigaction` function, you can install custom signal handlers where you are going to do your error reporting later on.

Besides doing some error reporting, you might want to consider saving the current game in your exception handler. Nothing bothers a gamer more than a crashing game after having played for hours and not having saved. Of course such tasks should all be done after you have finished your reporting.

Reporting Unhandled Exceptions

If an unhandled exception occurs and the process is being debugged, the debugger will break at the code location that caused the error. Of course it would be nice to have similar information about crashes even if there is no debugger attached to the application. For this purpose, you can utilize crash dump files that contain a snapshot of the process at the time of the crash.

On Windows platforms, you can use the Microsoft Debugging Tools API that is provided by the dbghelp.dll library. With help of the `MiniDumpWriteDump` function, you can create a mini-dump file of the running process. Unlike a usual crash dump, like the ones the old Dr. Watson utility created, a mini-dump does not have to contain the whole process space. Some sections are simply not required for most debugging, like the ones that contain loaded modules. You just need to know the version information of these files so that you can provide them to the debugger later on. This means that the dump files created with this API are usually much smaller in size than a full dump.

The information stored in a dump file can be controlled with the `DumpType` parameter. Whereas `MiniDumpNormal` includes only basic information like stack traces and the thread listing, `MiniDumpWithFullMemory` writes all accessible process memory to the file. To find out what dump type is the right one for you, I recommend reading [Starodumov05]. For further information about the `MiniDumpWriteDump` API and its parameters, refer to [MSDNDump07]. You should also consider distributing the latest version of dbghelp.dll when releasing your game because older versions of this library (like the one that comes with Windows 2000) do not have the right exports. Also keep in mind that the API exposed by dbghelp.dll is not thread safe! This means it is the caller's responsibility to synchronize calls to any of these functions.

In order to explicitly create a core dump on UNIX platforms, you have to use a third-party tool. The Google coredumper project [Google05] is an open source library that provides a simple API for creating core dumps of a running process. The `WriteCoreDump` function writes a dump of the current process into a specified file for you. Alternatively, you can also use `WriteCompressedCoreDump` which writes the dump in either bzip2 or gzip compressed format. Finally, there is `GetCoreDump`, which creates a copy-on-write snapshot of the process and returns a file handle from which the dump can be read. Currently the library supports x86, x64, and ARM systems and is pretty easy to include in a project.

Handling Stack Overflows

So far, this implementation can handle almost all cases that can cause an application to crash. The only condition where the error handling fails is in case of a stack overflow. Before being able to handle this special error situation, you need to know the status of the thread after a stack overflow. When the application starts, the stack is initially set to a small size (see Figure 1.10.1a). After the last page of the stack, a so-called guard page is placed. If the game consumes all of the reserved stack memory, the following things happen (see Figure 1.10.1b):

1. When accessing the stack while the stack pointer is pointing to the guard page, a `STATUS_GUARD_PAGE_VIOLATION` exception is raised.
2. The guard protection is removed from the page, which now becomes part of the stack.
3. A new guard page is allocated, one page below the last one.
4. Execution is continued from the instruction that caused the exception.

If the stack reaches its maximum size, the allocation of a new guard page in step 3 fails. In this case, a stack overflow exception is raised, which can be handled by the thread's exception block. As you can see in Figure 1.10.1c, the stack now has just one free page left to work with. If you take up all of this space in the exception handler, you will cause an access violation and the application will be terminated by the operating system.

This means you do not have a large scope left to work with. For instance, if you are calling `MiniDumpWriteDump` or even `MessageBox`, the game will cause an access violation because the functions have too large stack overhead. However, you can overcome this problem with a rather simple trick. Because you have enough space left to call the `CreateThread` function, you can move all the exception handling into a new thread. Then you can work with a clean stack and do whatever kind of reporting you want. In the exception handler, you wait until the worker thread has finished its work and returns.

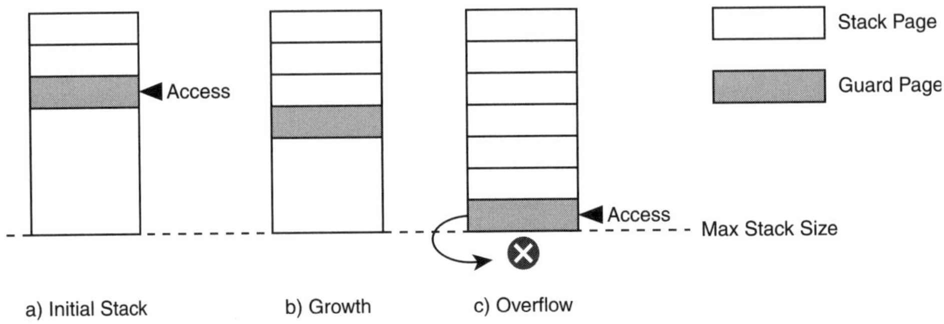

FIGURE 1.10.1 Initial stack, stack growth, and stack overflow.

Unfortunately, this approach does not work on UNIX platforms. When the signal handler is called, the stack is so exhausted that you can't properly report the error. The only way to overcome this problem is by using the `sigaltstack` function to install an alternative stack for the signal handler. All signal handlers that are installed with the `SA_ONSTACK` flag will be delivered on that stack, whereas all other handlers will still be executed on the current stack.

In order to successfully create a core dump, you have to allocate at least 40KB of memory for the alternative stack. In case you want to do even more reporting in the handler, the size should be adjusted appropriately. When using `sigaltstack`, you should check its documentation for your target platform because some implementations can cause problems when used in multithreaded applications.

Memory Leaks

If you are not using a global memory manager to satisfy the memory needs of your game, you should certainly think about using a memory leak detector. There are a vast amount of tools available that can help you find memory leaks. However, using them is not always straightforward and can often be a real pain. One of the techniques used most often is to overload the `new`/`delete` operators. However, this approach has quite a few flaws:

- System headers must be included before the operator overloading while project headers must be included afterward. Violating this rule can result in erroneous leak reports or even application crashes.
- Leaks caused by allocations using `malloc` won't be detected.
- Conflicts with other libraries that overload these operators (MFC, for instance) are possible.

Of course there are also various external leak detection tools available; however, they are usually quite expensive. The leak detector presented in this article uses so-called *allocation hooks* for tracking the application's memory requests. Allocation hooks are provided by the C runtime library and allow you to override memory management functions like malloc or free. The advantage of using hooks is that no matter where or how memory is allocated or freed, you will be notified by the runtime library through the hook functions. The only thing you have to do is install the hooks before doing any allocations.

Installing Allocation Hooks

The Microsoft CRT allows you to install an allocation hook through its _CrtSetAllocHook function. When or where do you install an allocation hook? The answer is as soon as possible so that you are not missing any allocation requests. However, this is not as easy as it sounds. Inside the main method can be too late if there are global objects that dynamically allocate memory on construction. Even if you define the leak detector as a global instance, there is no guarantee it will be initialized before any other global object. One way to overcome this problem is to use the Microsoft specific #pragma init_seg(lib) directive. By using this preprocessor command, you can tell the compiler to initialize the objects defined in the current source file before any other objects (this does not include CRT library initializations).

The GNU C library even allows you to completely replace the memory functions using global hook variables defined in malloc.h. By assigning your own handlers to __malloc_hook, __realloc_hook, and __free_hook, you gain full control over all memory-management requests. Initialization of the hooks can be easily achieved using the __malloc_initialize_hook handler. This is a simple function without parameters or return value that is called after the library finishes installing its default allocation hooks. It is important to back up the default hooks for later use in your own hook functions. Otherwise, you would have to provide a complete implementation for the overloaded memory functions.

Implementing Allocation Hooks

The leak detector manages an allocation registry that contains information about the allocated memory blocks. Each of these blocks contains a unique identifier, the requested block size, and the call stack during the allocation request. The call stack data will be used during the reporting for symbol resolving to get meaningful information. After a memory block is freed its block information is removed from the registry. When the application ends, you have to enumerate the entries left in the registry and report them as memory leaks. The task for the allocation hooks is to update that registry on each memory request with the required information.

The hook function passed to _CrtSetAllocHook must have the following signature:

```
int AllocHook(int allocType, void* data, size_t size, int blockType,
    long request, const unsigned char* filename, int line);
```

The most interesting parameters are allocType, blockType, and request. The allocType parameter specifies what operation was triggered (_HOOK_ALLOC, _HOOK_

REALLOC, or _HOOK_FREE). blockType specifies the memory block type that can be used to filter memory allocations (in this implementation, I exclude all CRT allocations from leak detection). Finally, request specifies the order of the allocation, which you can use as a unique ID for bookkeeping. When the function has finished its work, it returns an integer that specifies whether the allocation succeeds (returns TRUE) or fails (returns FALSE). For more information on the allocation hook function, refer to [MSDNHook07].

The signature of the GNU C library hooking functions is similar to the runtime functions they overload. Each function receives one additional parameter that contains the return address found on the stack when malloc, realloc, or free was called. The hook functions all work in the following way:

1. The original hook functions are restored.
2. Call malloc, realloc or free.
3. Update information for the memory leak detection.
4. Back up the current hook functions.
5. Install the custom hook functions.

This is the recommended workflow for allocation hooks, as described in the GNU C library documentation [GNUC06]. Instead of the request ID, use the address returned by malloc or realloc as the unique memory block ID.

Windows Error Reporting (WER)

With Windows Vista Microsoft introduced the Windows Feedback Platform that allows vendors and developers to access crash dumps sent through WER to Microsoft. This is done through the Windows Quality Online Services (WinQual), an online portal offered by Microsoft. The service is free but requires a VeriSign Code Signing ID to verify the identity of a company that is submitting software or accessing the WER database. WinQual organizes crash dumps into so-called buckets where each bucket contains crash reports caused by the same bug. The following parameters are used for bucket organization:

- Application name—For example, game.exe
- Application version—For example, 1.0.1234.0
- Module name—For example, input.dll
- Module version—For example, 1.0.123.1
- Offset into module—For example, 00003cbb

By default, WER calls dwwin.exe, which collects the bucket data and creates a mini-dump of the crashed process. WinQual additionally offers the possibility to specify feedback or request further information on a bucket. If users experience an already known bug, they will be notified by WER. The users may be pointed to the vendor's support site to download a hotfix, or can be informed of the current state of any bug fixes. Vendors can also request further information by executing WMI queries, listing registry keys, or asking users to fill out a questionnaire.

The Client API

On Windows XP, the WER implementation is rather simple. Just two APIs (`ReportFault` and `AddERExcludedApplication`) are available to the developer. The `ReportFault` API invokes WER and must be called inside the application's exception handler. It will execute the operating system utility dwwin.exe, which creates the crash report and prompts the users to send it to Microsoft. `AddERExcludedApplication` can be used to exclude an application from error reporting (this function requires write access to `HKEY_LOCAL_MACHINE` in the Windows Registry).

Windows Vista offers a completely new API to work with WER. The library includes several functions to create and submit error reports. Another difference from the old WER API is that reports can be generated at any time during execution. The following table gives a short overview of the most important functions offered by WER on Windows Vista. For a complete listing of available WER functions, refer to [MSDNWER07].

Function	Description
`WerAddExcludedApplication`	Excludes the specified application from error reporting.
`WerRegisterFile`	Registers a file to be added to reports generated for the current process.
`WerRemoveExcludedApplication`	Reverts a previous call to `WerAddExcludedApplication`.
`WerReportAddDump`	Adds a dump to the report.
`WerReportAddFile`	Adds a file to the report.
`WerReportCloseHandle`	Closes the report.
`WerReportCreate`	Creates a new report.
`WerReportSetUIOption`	Sets the user interface options.
`WerReportSubmit`	Submits the report.
`WerUnregisterFile`	Removes a file from the reports generated for the current process.

Another feature introduced with Windows Vista is the new Application Recovery and Restart API. It enables an application to register itself to get restarted or recovered after a crash. Especially interesting is the `RegisterApplicationRecoveryCallback` function, which enables you to register a recovery callback. This function will be called by WER when an application becomes unresponsive or encounters an unhandled exception. This would be the ideal place to try saving game and player data, enabling the player to continue the game later. For detailed information about this new Vista API, refer to [MSDNARR07].

The Framework

ON THE CD

This section provides a short overview of the debugging framework provided on the CD. The `CDebugHelp` class contains helper functions for creating dumps and call stacks. Inside of DebugHelp.cpp, you will also find `CdbgHelpDll`, which is a wrapper class for Microsoft's Debugging Tools API. It will automatically try to load the newest dbghelp.dll instead of taking the default one in the system directory. Maybe you also noticed the `MiniDumpCallback` function? `MiniDumpWriteDump` allows you to specify a callback to control what information is added to the dump. In my implementation, I exclude the exception handler thread that you start when handling a stack overflow exception. The UNIX implementation of these functions is simple and doesn't require any further explanation (documentation for `backtrace` and `backtrace_symbols` can be found at [GNUC06]).

Exception Handling

The exception handlers are part of the `CDebugFx` class declared in DebugFx.h. On Windows, you install an `UnhandledExceptionFilter` that creates a mini-dump and calls a user-defined callback to do any more work when an exception occurs. In the UNIX implementation, the framework registers signal handlers for SIGSEGV and SIGABRT. I included the source of the Google coredumper into the library to eliminate the dependency on an external library.

Memory Leak Detector

The memory leak detector is globally instanced and automatically active as soon as you link the debugging framework to your application. Reporting is done via a reporting API so that the users can implement their own reporting. The default reporter will write the leak information into the debug output window when run on a Windows platform and to the error output on UNIX. Another feature of the default reporter is the filtering of useless information from the call stack. Listing function calls for operator new or the CRT allocation functions only bloats the output and doesn't help in finding bugs.

Sometimes there are problems with the symbol resolving, in particular when a module that is referenced in the call stack was already unloaded. In this case, the symbol resolving APIs cannot resolve the address to a symbolic name. On Windows, you can reload the symbol table of a module using the `SymLoadModule64` function. To use this function, you just have to store the module base address (which is equal to the module handle) and the module name, along with the allocation information. Unfortunately, the GNU C library provides only a single function (`backtrace_symbols`) for symbol resolving. The only solution on this platform is to store the resolved symbols instead of the call stack for all allocations. Because this method would result in a huge memory overhead and decreased performance, the leak detector currently doesn't support this feature on UNIX platforms.

Conclusion

With the proper handling of application crashes, you can gain invaluable information that can help you during debugging. Depending on the platform, you have different methods to handle unexpected exceptions, like Windows Unhandled Exception Filters or UNIX signal handlers. Crash dumps are a great tool for post-mortem debugging of your application because they provide a snapshot of the process when it crashed. By using a threaded exception handler on Windows or an alternative signal handler stack on UNIX, you can even handle stack overflows. You can also get rid of nasty memory leaks with a memory leak detector. Using allocation hooks, provided by the CRTs, you can report all leaks with a complete stack trace when your game exits. Finally, you get a complete debugging framework providing unhandled exception handling with crash dump creation using the `CDebugFx` class. Memory leak detection is implemented in the `CMemLeakDetector` class and is automatically enabled when you link the library to your game. With this set of tools, bugs won't have any chance in your future projects.

References

[GNUC06] GNU C library documentation. "The GNU C library," available online at http://www.gnu.org/software/libc/manual/, December 6, 2006.

[Google05] Google coredumper library available online at http://code.google.com/p/google-coredumper/, 2005.

[Pietrek97] Pietrek, Matt. "A Crash Course on the Depths of Win32 Structured Exception Handling," available online at http://www.microsoft.com/msj/0197/exception/exception.aspx, *Microsoft Systems Journal,* January, 1997.

[Pietrek01] Pietrek, Matt. "New Vectored Exception Handling in Windows XP," available online at http://msdn.microsoft.com/msdnmag/issues/01/09/hood/default.aspx, *MSDN Magazine,* September, 2001.

[MSDNDump07] MSDN Library. "MiniDumpWriteDump," available online at http://msdn2.microsoft.com/en-us/library/ms680360.aspx, June 1, 2007.

[MSDNHook07] MSDN Library. "Run-Time Library Reference—_CrtSetAllocHook," available online at http://msdn2.microsoft.com/en-us/library/820k4tb8(VS.80).aspx, June 1, 2007.

[MSDNWER07] MSDN Library. "WER Functions," available online at http://msdn2.microsoft.com/en-us/library/bb513635.aspx, June 1, 2007.

[MSDNARR07] MSDN Library. "Application Recover and Restart Reference," available online at http://msdn2.microsoft.com/en-us/library/aa373342.aspx, June 1, 2007.

[Starodumov05] Starodumov O. "Effective Mini-Dumps," available online at http://www.debuginfo.com/articles/effminidumps.html, July 2, 2005.

[Wikipedia] Wikipedia. "Signal (Computing)," available online at http://en.wikipedia.org/wiki/Signal_(computing)#List_of_signals.

SECTION

2

MATH AND PHYSICS

Introduction

Graham Rhodes, Applied Research Associates, Inc.

grhodes@nc.rr.com

Mathematics makes the world go around! At least within the realm of electronic game development, there is real truth in that statement. We use math, in one way or another, for just about everything. The heaviest uses of math by game developers these days lie in the rendering of game worlds, both two- and three-dimensional, artificial intelligence algorithms of all sorts, and physics-based simulation, which is evolving at a frantic pace. I'm awed by the current level of sophistication being applied in all of these areas! Model surfaces rendered in real-time 3D no longer resemble shiny plastic, thanks to the advent of programmable graphics hardware and the ability to apply advanced physically-based lighting and material models on a per-pixel basis.

Character AI sits on the cusp of Mori's uncanny valley, and we are starting to see flash glimpses that one day it might be crossed. Crossing that valley visually, within the realm of real-time game simulation, will rely not only on AI, but also on physically-based animation techniques that enable game characters to interact with a dynamic game world where collectible items are not necessarily located at scripted locations, and where the game world itself is subject to play-driven geometric change. Some of these physically-based character animation technologies are already appearing in middleware products that are emerging into the industry. The dynamically-changing game worlds themselves, with which sophisticated characters must interact, are also becoming more physically based each year. Several current games, released or imminent, feature fully dynamic environments that exploit the many robust physics engines that are available today. Mankind's and nature's mathematical models enable all of these great entertainment technologies, of course.

I would like to make a few brief comments about one important emerging area of game development that is heavily math-driven. And that is the area of procedural modeling, otherwise known as procedural generation, generative modeling, and probably a dozen other terms. One fact of commercial game development has been that the cost of content development using traditional digital content-creation tools has increased significantly as computer hardware and game engines have become able to support all of the features mentioned previously. The tools also have evolved, and artists can work more efficiently than ever before. But it is often the sheer volume of content that becomes a problem.

So large studios are now beginning to pay homage, in a way, to the game development ways of old, and are mimicking developers from the demo scene who have been inventing content-generating algorithms for years. Procedural modeling, in all its many forms, can greatly reduce the cost of content development, by effectively removing the need for an art team to model and place every tree/bush/clump of grass that is to appear in a scene. Procedural modeling of flora for game levels is currently quite heavily used for commercial game development. Tools exist, but are not yet ubiquitous, for the procedural modeling of other game level elements, such as buildings and structures with interiors and exteriors modeled at multiple levels of detail, auto-populated with furniture and clutter, with everything looking good from a first-person camera. There is even a highly anticipated game in development that claims to apply procedural modeling to create cellular organisms, planets, stars, nebulae, and many things in between.

It is clear to me that there is going to be a strong future for procedural modeling in games, although artists should not worry that they may be out of a job as a result! (That won't be the case.) For this to work, of course, tools and game developers must apply the proper mathematical or physically-based techniques.

In this section, you will find a variety of useful gems that provide insight into classical techniques, as well as new techniques that you can apply to core problems. A duo of gems provides you with a deeper understanding of random number generation, for application toward artificial intelligence, physics techniques, and procedural generation. Chris Lomont provides a comprehensive overview of random number generation techniques, their strengths, weakness, and occasionally dramatic failures, whereas Steve Rabin's gem on Gaussian randomness provides a highly efficient implementation.

Tony Barrera, Anders Hast, and Ewert Bengtsson summarize an efficient technique for evaluating trigonometric splines, which can be used to generate curves made from straight line segments and perfect elliptical arcs. Combining several of these trigonometric splines can generate curves that are visually more elegant and contain fewer curvature artifacts than other piecewise spline techniques such as traditional cubic polynomial splines—just perfect for digital content-creation tools as well as in-engine procedural generation of model geometry. Krzysztof Kluczek continues the presentation of techniques that are quite useful for procedural model generation in his chapter, describing the use of a projective space to enable highly robust geometric operations while reducing storage requirements and computational expense compared with other techniques for achieving similar results.

The last four gems focus on a variety of techniques for collision detection and other geometric queries, which continue to be areas of active research within the industry and academia alike. Jacco Bikker provides a fantastic summary of the kD-tree spatial partitioning technique, with a strong practical focus on minimizing storage requirements and on building trees that are optimized according to query type. He also describes approaches for dealing with dynamic scenes. José Gilvan Rodrigues Maia, Creto Augusto Vidal, and Joaquim Bento Cavalcante-Neto describe transformation semantics, giving a sort of geometric intuition to the interpretation of transformation matrices. Their discussion shows how this intuition can be applied in practice to the various phases that are common to modern collision detection algorithms.

Rahul Sathe and Dillon Sharlet describe a new technique for collision detection that can be applied from broad phase through narrow phase. Finally, Gary Snethen describes a collision detection technique inspired by the GJK algorithm that is elegant in its simplicity and intuitiveness, while being also quite flexible. Take these ideas, young men and women and go forth and develop!

2.1

Random Number Generation

Chris Lomont

www.lomont.org

This article is an introduction to random number generators (RNGs). The main goal is to present a starting point for programmers needing to make decisions about RNG choice and implementation. A second goal is to present better alternatives for the ubiquitous Mersenne Twister (MT). A final goal is to cover various classes of random number generators, providing strengths and weaknesses of each.

Background: Random Number Generation

Random number generators (RNGs) are essential to many computing applications. For some problems, algorithms employing random choices perform better than any known algorithm not using random choices. It is often easier to find an algorithm to solve a given problem if randomness is allowed. (The class of problems efficiently solvable on a [Turing] machine equipped with a random number generator is BPP, and it is an open problem if BPP=P, P being the class of problems efficiently solvable on a computer without random choice.)

Most random numbers used in computing are not considered truly random, but are created using pseudo-random number generators (PRNGs). PRNGs are deterministic algorithms, and are the only type of random number that can be algorithmically generated without an external source of entropy, such as thermal noise or user movements.

Designing good RNGs is hard and best left to professionals. (Robert R. Coveyou of Oak Ridge National Laboratory humorously once titled an article, "The Generation of Random Numbers Is Too Important to Be Left to Chance." Like cryptography, the history of RNGs is littered with bad algorithms and the consequences of using them. A few historical mistakes are covered near the end of this article.

Uses

Random numbers are used in many applications, including the following:

- AI algorithms, such as genetic algorithms and automated opponents.
- Random game content and level generation.
- Simulation of complex phenomena such as weather and fire.

- Numerical methods such as Monte-Carlo integration.
- Until recently, primality proving used randomized algorithms.
- Cryptography algorithms such as RSA use random numbers for key generation.
- Weather simulation and other statistical physics testing.
- Optimization algorithms use random numbers significantly—simulated annealing, large space searching, and combinatorial searching.

Hardware RNGs

Because an algorithm cannot create "true" random numbers, many hardware-based RNGs have been devised. Quantum mechanical events cannot be predicted, and are considered a very good source of randomness. Such quantum phenomena include:

- Nuclear decay detection, similar to a smoke detector.
- Quantum mechanical noise source in electronic circuits called "shot noise."
- Photon streams through a partially silvered mirror.
- Particle spins created from high energy x-rays.

Other sources of physical randomness are as follows:

- Atmospheric noise (see www.freewebs.com/pmutaf/iwrandom.html for a way to get random numbers from WiFi noise).
- Thermal noise in electronics.

Other physical phenomena are often used on computers, like clock drift, mouse and keyboard input, network traffic, add-on hardware devices, or images gathered from moving scenery. Each source must be analyzed to determine how much entropy the source has, and then how many high-quality random bits can be extracted.

Here are a few Websites offering random bits of noise and the method used to obtain them:

- http://random.org/—Atmospheric noise.
- http://www.fourmilab.ch/hotbits/—Radioactive decay of Cesium-137.
- http://www.lavarnd.org/—Noise in CCD images.

Pseudo-Random Number Generators (PRNGs)

PRNGs generate a sequence of "random" numbers using an algorithm, operating on an internal state. The initial state is called the *seed*, and selecting a good seed for a given algorithm is often difficult. Often the internal state is also the returned value. Due to the state being finite, the PRNG will repeat at some point, and the *period* of an RNG is how many numbers it can return before repeating. A PRNG using n bits for its state has a period of at most 2^n. Starting a PRNG with the same seed allows repeatable random sequences, which is very useful for debugging among other things. When a PRNG needs a "random" seed, often sources of entropy from the system or external hardware are used to seed the PRNG.

Due to computational needs, memory requirements, security needs, and desired random number "quality," there are many different RNG algorithms. No one algorithm is suitable for all cases, in the same way that no sorting algorithm is best in all situations. Many people default to C/C++ `rand()` or the Mersenne Twister, both of which have their uses. Both are covered in this gem.

Common Distributions

Most RNGs return an integer selected uniformly from the range $[0,m]$ for some maximum value m. C/C++ implementations provide the `rand()` function, with m being `#defined` as `RAND_MAX`, quite often the 15-bit value, 32767. `srand(seed)` sets the initial seed, often using the current time as an entropy source like `srand(time(NULL))`. Most C/C++ `rand()` functions are Linear Congruential Generators, which are poor choices for cryptography. Most C/C++ implementations (as well as other languages) generate poor quality random numbers that exhibit various kinds of bias.

The most common distribution used in games is a *uniform distribution*, where equally likely random integers are needed in a range $[a,b]$. A common mistake is to use C code like `(rand()%(b-a+1)) + a`. The mistake is that not all values are equally likely to occur due to modulus wrapping around. This only works if $b - a + 1$ divides `RAND_MAX+1`. For example, if `RAND_MAX` is 32767, then trying to generate numbers in the range [0,32766] using this method causes 0 to be twice as likely as any other single value. A valid (although slower) solution is to scale the rand output to [0,1] and back to $[a,b]$, using:

```
double v = (static_cast<double>( rand()) ) / RAND_MAX;
return static_cast<long>(v*(b-a+1)+a);
```

The second most commonly used distribution is a *Gaussian Distribution*, which can be generated from a uniform distribution. Let `randf()` return uniformly distributed real numbers in [0,1]. Then the polar form of the Box-Muller transformation gives two Gaussian values, `y1` and `y2`, per call.

```
float x1, x2, w, y1, y2;
do {
   x1 = 2.0 * randf() - 1.0;
   x2 = 2.0 * randf() - 1.0;
   w  = x1 * x1 + x2 * x2;
   } while ( w >= 1.0 );
w = sqrt( (-2.0 * log( w ) ) / w );
y1 = x1 * w;
y2 = x2 * w;
```

Boost [Boost07] documents techniques for generating other distributions starting with a uniform distribution.

Randomness Testing

To test if a sequence is "random," a definition of "random" is needed. However "randomness" is very difficult to make precise. In practice (because many PRNGs are useful) tests have been designed to test the quality of RNGs by detecting sequence behavior that does not behave like a random sequence should.

The most famous randomness-testing suite is DIEHARD [Marsaglia95], made of 12 tests (for more information, see http://en.wikipedia.org/wiki/Diehard_tests). DIEHARD has been expanded into the open source (GPL) set of tests DieHarder [Brown06], which includes the DIEHARD tests as well as many new ones. Also included are many RNGs and a harness to add new ones easily. A third testing framework is TestU01 [L'Ecuyer06]. Each framework provides some assurance a tested RNG is not clearly bad.

Software Whitening

Many sources of random bits have some bias or bit correlation, and methods to remove the bias and correlation are known as *whitening* algorithms. Some choices:

- John von Neumann. Take bits two at a time, discard 00 and 11 cases, and output 1 for 01 and 0 for 10, removing uniform bias, at the cost of needing more bits.
- Flip every other bit, removing uniform bias.
- XOR with another known good source of bits, as in Blum Blum Shub.
- Apply cryptographic hashes like Whirlpool or RIPEMD-160. Note MD5 is no longer considered secure.

These whitened streams should still not be considered a secure source of random bits without further processing.

Non-Cryptographic RNG Methods

Non-cryptographically secure methods are usually faster than cryptographic methods, but should *not* be used when security is needed, hence the classification. Each of the following methods is a PRNG with output sequence X_n. Some have a hidden internal state S_n from which X_n is derived. Either X_0 or S_0 is the seed, as appropriate.

Middle Square Method

This was suggested by John von Neumann in 1946—take a 10-digit number as a seed, square it, and return the middle 10 digits as the next number and seed. It was used in ENIAC, is a poor method with statistical weaknesses, and is no longer used.

Linear Congruential Generator (LCG)

These are the most common methods in widespread use, but are slowly being replaced by newer methods. They are computed with $X_{n+1} = (aX_n + b) \text{mod} m$, for constants a

and b. The modulus m is often chosen as a power of 2, making it efficiently implemented as a bitmask. Careful choice of a and b is required to guarantee maximal period and avoid other problem cases. LCGs have various pathologies, one of which is that choosing points in three-tuples and plotting them in space shows the points fall onto planes, as exhibited later in the section on RANDU, and is a result of linear relations between successive points. LCGs with power-of-two modulus $m = 2^e$ are known to be badly behaved, especially in their least significant bits [L'Ecuyer90]. For example *Numerical Recipes in C* [Press06] recommends $a = 1664525$, $b = 1013904223$, $m = 2\char94 32$, and the lowest order bit then merely alternates.

LCGs' strengths are they are relatively fast and use a small state, making them useful in many places including embedded applications. If the modulus is not a power of two then the modulus operation is often expensive.

Representing an LCG as LCG(m, a, b), Table 2.1.1 shows some LCGs in use.

Table 2.1.1 Some LCGs in Use

LCG	Use
LCG(2^{31}, 65539, 0)	The infamous RANDU covered later in this gem.
LCG(2^{24}, 16598013, 12820163)	Microsoft VisualBasic 6.0.
LCG(2^{48}, 25214903917, 11)	drand48 from the UNIX standard library; was used in java.util.Random.
LCG($10^{12} - 11$, 427419669081, 0)	Used in Maple 9.5 and in MuPAD 3. Replaced by MT19937 (below) in Maple 10.

Truncated Linear Congruential Generator (TLCG)

These store an internal state S_i updated using an LCG, which in turn is used to generate the output X_i. Symbolically, $S_{n+1} = (aS_n + b)\bmod m$, $X_{n+1} = Floor\left[\frac{S_{n+1}}{K}\right]$. This allows using the fast m as a power of two but avoids the poor low order bits in the LCGs. If K is a power of 2, the division is also fast. This algorithm is used extensively throughout Microsoft products (likely as a result of being compiled with VC++), including VC++ `rand()`, with the implementation

```
/* MS algorithm for rand() */
static unsigned long seed;
seed = 214013L * seed + 2531011L;
return (seed>>16)&0x7FFF; // return bits 16-30
```

This is not secure. In fact, for a cryptographic analysis project, this author has determined only three successive outputs from this algorithm are enough to determine the internal state (up to an unneeded most significant bit), and thereby know all future output. A simple way to compute the state is to notice the top bit of the state has no bearing on future output; so only 31 bits are unknown. The first output gives 15 bits of the state, leaving 17 bits unknown. Now, given two more outputs, take the first known 15 bits and test each of the possible 2^{17} unknown bit states to see which gives the other two known outputs. This probably determines the internal state. Two outputs are not enough because they do not uniquely determine the state.

Borland C++ and TurboC also used TLCGs with a = 22695477 and b = 1. Although the C specification does not force a `rand` implementation, the example one in the *C Programming Language* [Kernighan91] is a TLCG with a = 113515245 and b = 12345, with a `RAND_MAX` of the minimum allowable 32767.

Linear Feedback Shift Register (LFSR)

A Linear Feedback Shift Register (LFSR, see Figure 2.1.1) generates bits from an internal state by shifting them out, one at a time. New bits are shifted into the state, and are a linear function of bits already in the state. LFSRs are popular because they are fast, easy to do in hardware, and can generate a wide range of sequences. Tap sequences can be chosen to make an n bit LFSR have period $2^n - 1$. Given $2n$ bits of output the structure and feedback connections can be deduced, so they are definitely not secure.

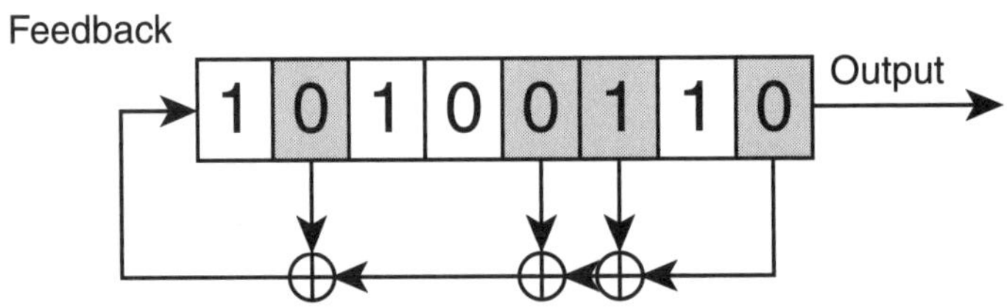

FIGURE 2.1.1 Linear Feedback Shift Register (LFSR).

Inversive Congruential Generator

These are similar to LCGs but are nonlinear, using $X_{n+1} = (aX_n^{-1} + b)\text{mod}m$, where X_n^{-1} is the multiplicative inverse mod$m$, that is, $X_n X_n^{-1} \equiv 1\text{mod}m$. These are expensive to compute due to the inverse operation, and are not often used.

Lagged Fibonacci Generator (LFG)

Use k words of state $X_n = (X_{n-j} \otimes X_{n-k})\text{mod}m$, $O < j < k$ where $\otimes$ is some binary operation (plus, times, xor, others). These are very hard to get to work well and hard to initialize. The period depends on a starting seed and the space of reached values breaks into hard to predict cycles. They are now disfavored due to the Mersenne Twister and later generators. Boost [Boost07] includes variants of LFGs.

Cellular Automata

Mathematica prior to Version 6.0 uses the cellular automata Wolfram rule 30 to generate large integers (see http://mathworld.wolfram.com/Rule30.html). Version 6.0 uses a variety of methods.

Linear Recurrence Generators

These are a generalization of the LFSRs, and most fast modern PRNGs are derived from these over binary finite fields. Note that none of these pass linear recurrence testing due to being linear functions. The next few are special examples of this type of PRNG, and are considered the best general-purpose RNGs.

Mersenne Twister

In 1997, Makoto Matsumoto and Takuji Nishimura published the Mersenne Twister algorithm [Matsumoto98], which avoided many of the problems with earlier generators. They presented two versions, MT11213 and MT19937, with periods of $2^{11213-1}$ and $2^{19937-1}$ (approximately 10^{6001}), which represents far more computation than is likely possible in the lifetime of the entire universe. MT19937 uses an internal state of 624 longs, or 19968 bits, which is about expected for the huge period. It is (perhaps surprisingly) faster than the LCGs, is equidistributed in up to 623 dimensions, and has become the main RNG used in statistical simulations.

The speed comes from only updating a small part of the state for each random number generated, and moving through the state over multiple calls. Mersenne Twister is a Twisted Generalized Feedback Shift register (TGFSR). It is not cryptographically secure: observing 624 sequential outputs allows you to determine the internal state, and then predict the remaining sequence. Mersenne Twister has some flaws, covered in the "WELL Algorithm" section that follows.

LFSR113, LFSR258

[L'Ecuyer99] introduces combined LFSR Tausworthe generators LFSR113 and LFSR258 designed specially for 32-bit and 64-bit computers, respectively, with periods of approximately 2^{113} and 2^{258}, respectively. They are fast, simple, and have a small memory footprint. For example, here is C/C++ code for LFSR113 that returns a 32-bit value:

```
unsigned long z1, z2, z3, z4; /* the state  */
/* NOTE: the seed MUST satisfy
      z1 > 1, z2 > 7, z3 > 15, and z4 > 127 */
unsigned long lfsr113(void)
   { /* Generates random 32 bit numbers.    */
   unsigned long b;
   b  = (((z1 << 6) ^ z1)   >> 13);
   z1 = (((z1 & 4294967294) << 18) ^ b);
   b  = (((z2 << 2) ^ z2)   >> 27);
   z2 = (((z2 & 4294967288) <<  2) ^ b);
   b  = (((z3 << 13) ^ z3)  >> 21);
   z3 = (((z3 & 4294967280) <<  7) ^ b);
```

```
b  = (((z4 << 3) ^ z4)   >> 12);
z4 = (((z4 & 4294967168) << 13) ^ b);
return (z1 ^ z2 ^ z3 ^ z4);
}
```

Because 2^{113} is approximately 10^{34}, this already represents a huge number of values, and has a much smaller footprint than MT19937. The LFSR generators also are well equidistributed, and avoid LCGs problems.

WELL Algorithm

Matsumoto (co-creator of the Mersenne Twister), L'Ecuyer (a major RNG researcher), and Panneton introduced another class of TGFSR PRNGs in 2006 [Panneton06]. These algorithms produce numbers with better equidistribution than MT19937 and improve upon "bit-mixing" properties. WELL stands for Well Equidistributed Long-Period Linear, and they seem to be better choices for anywhere MT19937 is currently used. They are fast, come in many sizes, and most importantly produce higher quality random numbers.

WELL period sizes are presented for period 2^n for n = 512, 521, 607, 800, 1024, 19937, 21701, 23209, and 44497, with corresponding state sizes. This allows users to trade period length for state size. All run at similar speed. 2^{512} is about 10^{154}, and it is unlikely any video game will ever need that many random numbers, because it is far larger than the number of particles in the universe. The larger period ones aren't really needed except for computations like weather modeling or earth simulations. A standard PC needs over a *googol* of years to count to 2^{512}. (A googol is 10^{100}. Google it.)

A significant place the WELL PRNGs perform better than MT19937 is in escaping states with a large number of zeros. If MT19937 is seeded with many zeros, or somehow falls into such a state, the generated numbers have heavy bias toward zeros for many iterations. The WELL algorithms behave much better, escaping zero bias states quickly.

The only downside is that they are slightly slower than MT19937, but not much. The upside is the numbers are considered to be higher quality, and the code is significantly simpler. Here is WELL512 C/C++ code written by the author and placed in the public domain (if you use it, I'd appreciate a reference or at least an email with thanks). It is about 40% faster than the code presented on L'Ecuyer's site, and is about 40% faster than MT19937 presented on Matsumoto's site.

```
/* initialize state to random bits  */
static unsigned long state[16];
/* init should also reset this to 0 */
static unsigned int index = 0;
/* return 32 bit random number      */
unsigned long WELLRNG512(void)
    {
    unsigned long a, b, c, d;
    a  = state[index];
    c  = state[(index+13)&15];
    b  = a^c^(a<<16)^(c<<15);
```

```
c  = state[(index+9)&15];
c ^= (c>>11);
a  = state[index] = b^c;
d  = a^((a<<5)&0xDA442D20UL);
index = (index + 15)&15;
a  = state[index];
state[index] = a^b^d^(a<<2)^(b<<18)^(c<<28);
return state[index];
}
```

Cryptographic RNG Methods

Cryptographically Secure PRNGs (CSPRNGs) make it hard for an attacker to deduce the internal state of the generator or to predict future output given large amounts of output. Several CSPRNGs have been standardized and can be found online (check out http://en.wikipedia.org/wiki/CSPRNG). Two RFCs dealing with randomness requirements for security are RFC1750 and RFC4086 (see www.ietf.org/rfc). Any implementation of these methods has to be done very carefully to avoid many pitfalls. Whenever possible, use an implementation from a trusted and competent source.

Blum Blum Shub

Published in 1986 by Lenore Blum, Manuel Blum, and Michael Shub, Blum Blum Shub [Blum86] is considered a secure PRNG. It is computed via $S_{n+1} = (S_n^2)\bmod m$ where $m = pq$ for two properly chosen large primes p,q. Then the output X_{n+1} is some function on S_{n+1}, which often is taken as bit parity or some particular bits of S_{n+1}. Its strength relies on the hardness of integer factoring, which is the same problem RSA public key encryption relies on for security. Blum Blum Shub is only useful for cryptography, because it is much slower than the non-cryptographic PRNGs. (Note Shor's quantum factoring algorithm factors integers efficiently, so once quantum computers are in use Blum Blum Shub will become insecure.)

ISAAC, ISAAC+

[Jenkins96] introduced ISAAC, a CSPRNG based on a variant of the RC4 cipher. It is relatively fast for a CSPRNG, requiring an amortized 18.75 instructions to produce a 32-bit value. There are no cycles in ISAAC shorter than 2^{40} values, and the expected cycle length is 2^{8295} values. ISAAC-64, a version for 64-bit machines, requires 19 instructions to produce a 64-bit result.

/dev/random

Although not a specific algorithm, Linux and many UNIX flavors implement a source of randomness in /dev/random, which returns random numbers based on system entropy, so it is considered a true random number generator. /dev/random blocks, that is, does not return until enough entropy has been gathered to satisfy the request.

As a result, many programs use the non-blocking /dev/urandom. However, these numbers are not as secure, and use of /dev/urandom depletes system entropy, allowing some attacks on bad implementations. The underlying algorithm is not specified; some systems use Yarrow as mentioned in a following section.

[Gutterman06] revealed exploitable weaknesses in the Linux implementation at the time, which should have been fixed by now. Overall /dev/random is the preferred place on Linux to get CSPRNGs.

Microsoft's CryptGenRandom

Microsoft's CryptoAPI function CryptGenRandom function fills a buffer with cryptographically secure random bytes. Like /dev/random, it is considered a true random number generator. Although closed source, it is FIPS validated, and is considered secure. This author is unaware of any weaknesses with recent implementations. On Windows, it is the preferred source of CSPRNGs.

Yarrow

[Kelsey99] introduces Yarrow, which uses system entropy to generate random numbers. It is explicitly unpatented and royalty-free, and no license is required to use it. Yarrow is used in Mac OS X and FreeBSD to implement /dev/random. Yarrow is no longer supported by the designers, who have released an improved design titled Fortuna.

Fortuna

Fortuna is another CSPRNG from the book *Practical Cryptography* [Ferguson03]. The generator is based on any good block cipher, and encrypts in counter mode, encrypting successive values of a counter. The key is changed periodically to prevent some statistical weaknesses. It uses entropy pools that gather information from random sources available to the system, and is considered a true RNG because it uses external entropy.

Common Mistakes in Creating Random Number Generators

Creation of good RNGs is not trivial and the history of RNGs is scattered with examples of bad design. You can always learn something from the failures of others, so let's take a look at some common mistakes in this area.

Knuth Example

Even algorithm master Donald Knuth tells a story in [Knuth98] about trying his hand at making a random number generator by creating a "super-random" generator. His first run settled onto a 10-digit number that then repeated forever. His second run began to repeat itself after 7401 values with a cycle of 3178.

Here are a few more examples that hopefully will prevent people from using homemade RNGs in critical applications.

RANDU

RANDU is an infamous LCG used since the 1960s; it is LGC($2^{31,65539,0}$), and requires an odd initial seed. The constants were chosen for easy and fast implementation. As all LCGs, it suffers from linear relations between successive numbers. Figure 2.1.2 shows the output of 10,000 triplets (x,y,z) plotted in 3D, which happen to fall into planes.

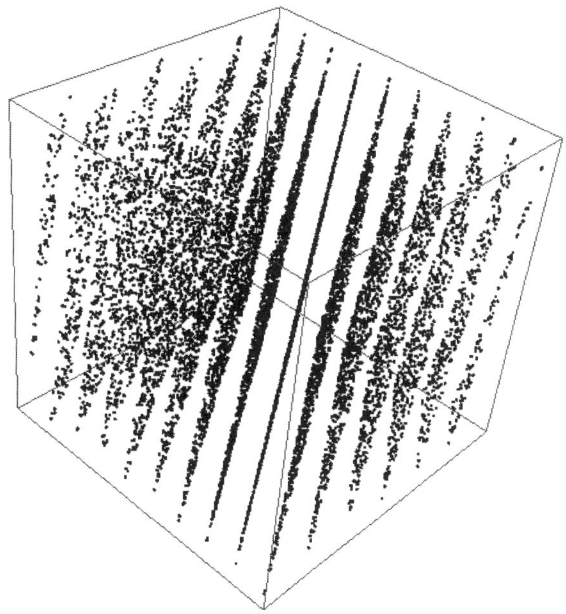

FIGURE 2.1.2 LCG bias.

Netscape

An early version of Netscape needed a CSPRNG, but seeded it with three values that weren't very well spread out (time of day, process ID, and parent process ID) and used the result for cryptography. [Goldberg96] published a successful attack on Netscape's SSL protocol, with the exploitable flaw being a poor choice of seed.

Folklore Algorithms

The author encountered a folklore algorithm from a game programmer around 1992, who explained that he had a fast and simple PRNG for his NES code. The basic idea was to shift bits out of a seed, and whenever the seed had 1 bit about to shift off, exclusive-or in a constant. This was fast and looked nice in assembly, but being a skeptic this author thought about the claim of randomness, and said this should produce numbers that tend to decrease, and every so often jump back up, making saw tooth outputs. This led the original programmer to discover a bug in his AI that was using the PRNG which he hadn't suspected (he had used the PRNG for years). Although anecdotal, it is wise to test a new RNG and see that it behaves as expected before committing it to your toolbox.

One last particularly funny example is the xkcd Webcomic version of a random number generator at http://xkcd.com/c221.html, reproduced for your viewing pleasure:

```
int getRandomNumber()
  {
  return 4; // chosen by fair dice roll.
            // guaranteed to be random.
  }
```

Code

There are many online places to obtain source code for the algorithms covered in this article. Boost [Boost07] contains high-quality implementations for many of them, and Wikipedia contains more information and links to most of the presented topics. L'Ecuyer's Web page (www.iro.umontreal.ca/~lecuyer/papers.html) is a good source of papers and many implementations. In addition, *Technical Review 1* (TR1) for the C++ language includes many distributions and generators (including MT19337), so it is likely C++ will someday have some of these features built-in.

Conclusion

This gem has provided basics of RNGs, including many common algorithms. LFSR113, LFSR258, and the WELL generators offer better choices than the Mersenne Twister for many applications, and this presentation brings knowledge of them to a wider audience. Strengths and weaknesses were presented for algorithms where possible. Knowledge about RNG types and when to apply them should be in the toolkit of any serious developer, just as any serious developer should know multiple sorting algorithms, or numerous tree structures. Hopefully, this gem provides you with a base and reference for such knowledge.

References

[Blum86] Blum, Lenore, Blum, Manuel, and Shub, Michael. "A Simple Unpredictable Pseudo-Random Number Generator," *SIAM Journal on Computing,* Vol. 15, pp. 364–383, May 1986.

[Boost07] "The Boost C++ Library," 2007, www.boost.org.

[Brown06] Brown, Robert G., and Eddelbuettel, Dirk. "DieHarder: A Random Number Test Suite Version 2.24.4," available online at www.phy.duke.edu/~rgb/General/rand_rate.php.

[Ferguson03] Ferguson, Niels, and Schneier, Bruce. *Practical Cryptography*, Wiley, 2003. ISBN 0-471-22357-3.

[Goldberg96] Goldberg, Ian, and Wagner, David. "Randomness and the Netscape Browser," *Dr. Dobb's Journal,* January 1996, pp. 66–70. Available online at www.cs.berkeley.edu/~daw/papers/ddj-netscape.html.

[Gutterman06] Gutterman, Pinkas, and Reinman. "Open to Attack: Vulnerabilities of the Linux Random Number Generator," March 2006, Black Hat 2006, www.pinkas.net/PAPERS/gpr06.pdf.

[Jenkins96] Jenkins, Bob. "ISAAC and RC4," www.burtleburtle.net/bob/rand/isaac.html as of 2007.

[Kelsey99] Kelsey, J., Schneier, B., and Ferguson, N. "Yarrow-160: Notes on the Design and Analysis of the Yarrow Cryptographic Pseudorandom Number Generator," Sixth Annual Workshop on Selected Areas in Cryptography, Springer Verlag, August 1999, www.schneier.com/paper-yarrow.html.

[Kernighan91] Kernighan, B., and Ritchie, Dennis. *The C Programming Language, Second Edition*, Prentice-Hall, 1991.

[Knuth98] Knuth, Donald. *The Art of Computer Programming, Volume 2: Seminumerical Algorithms, Third Edition,* Addison-Wesley, 1998.

[L'Ecuyer90] L'Ecuyer, P. "Random Numbers for Simulation," Communications of the ACM, 33 (1990), pp. 85–98, www.iro.umontreal.ca/~lecuyer/papers.html.

[L'Ecuyer99] L'Ecuyer, P. "Tables of Maximally-Equidistributed Combined LFSR Generators," *Mathematics of Computation,* 68, 225 (1999), pp. 261–269, www.iro.umontreal.ca/~lecuyer/papers.html.

[L'Ecuyer06] L'Ecuyer, P. and Simard, R. "TestU01: A C Library for Empirical Testing of Random Number Generators," May 2006, Revised November 2006, *ACM Transactions on Mathematical Software,* 33, 4, Article 1, December 2007, to appear. www.iro.umontreal.ca/~lecuyer/papers.html.

[Marsaglia95] Marsaglia, George. "DIEHARD," http://www.csis.hku.hk/~diehard/.

[Matsumoto98] Matsumoto, M., and Nishimura, T. "Mersenne Twister: A 623-Dimensionally Equidistributed Uniform Pseudorandom Number Generator," *ACM Trans. Model. Comput. Simul.* 8, 3 (1998), www.math.sci.hiroshima-u.ac.jp/~m-mat/MT/emt.html.

[Panneton06] Panneton, F., L'Ecuyer, P., and Matsumoto, M. "Improved Long-Period Generators Based on Linear Recurrences Modulo 2," *ACM Transactions on Mathematical Software,* 32, 1 (2006), pp. 1–16, www.iro.umontreal.ca/~lecuyer/papers.html.

[Press06] Press, William H. (Editor), Teukolsky, Saul A., Vetterling, William T., and Flannery, Brian P. *Numerical Recipes in C++: The Art of Scientific Computing*, Cambridge University Press, 2nd edition, 2002.

2.2

Fast Generic Ray Queries for Games

Jacco Bikker, IGAD/NHTV University of Applied Sciences—Breda, The Netherlands

bikker.j@nhtv.nl

Recently, real-time ray tracing on consumer PCs has become possible. A real-time ray tracer traces millions of rays per second, per core, using instruction-level parallelism (in particular, SIMD code [Wald04]). Thread-level parallelism allows you to scale this number almost linearly with the number of cores.

Ray tracing is useful for more than just rendering. This gem describes implementation details for a generic ray tracer that can be used for various parts of a game, such as line-of-sight queries, physics, and sound propagation. The focus is on efficient traversal of individual rays.

The kD-tree, built using the surface area heuristic (SAH) [McDonald90], is an efficient spatial subdivision for ray queries in a static scene. This gem describes some approaches to extend this algorithm to support dynamic scenery.

Introduction to Ray Tracing

Ray tracing is a simple algorithm. When applied to rendering, the core algorithm looks like this:

```
for each screen pixel
    construct a ray from the camera to the pixel
    intersect the ray with each primitive in the scene
    shade the pixel based on the intersection results
```

Here, a *ray* is an infinite line with an origin, O, and a direction, D, as shown in Figure 2.2.1.

Tracing a single ray is referred to as *ray casting*. The basic algorithm was invented by Appel in 1963 [Appel63]. In 1979, Whitted extended this process by adding recursion [Whitted79]. At the intersection point, a new ray to each light source is created, to see whether the light affects the intersection point. If the material at the intersection point is reflective or refractive, this will also recursively spawn new rays.

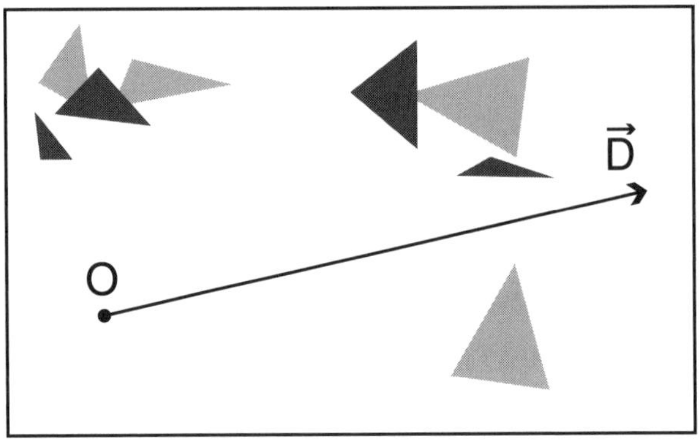

FIGURE 2.2.1 A ray consists of an origin and a direction.

If you look at the process of tracing a single ray alone, you see a visibility query. The camera needs to know which primitive is visible through a screen pixel; the intersection point wants to know which lights are visible from that point. Queries like this are very useful in a game:

- An enemy AI wants to know if the player is visible or audible.
- The user highlights an object in the scene to select it.
- A sniper fires a bullet at the player. The bullet ricochets around the scenery if it misses the player, or if it cannot hit the player directly. Or perhaps it simply continues its path after it pierced through the player.
- A hovering vehicle tries to avoid obstacles and probes the surroundings to do so.
- A destroyed opponent emits a collectable item that should drop until it hits the floor.

Some of these obviously require a ray query (player visibility, bullets, and ray picking), and some are often left to the physics engine's internal collision detection system (when dropping items), even though they could be easily implemented using one or more rays. Most 3D engines support ray queries in one form or another, but often for performance reasons game developers choose not to use them; they are assumed to be too slow. If rays are traced using a naive search of the scene geometry, this is a good assumption. However, we can do (much) better. Using an optimized spatial subdivision, a ray query can be reduced to a few tree traversal steps and a limited number of ray/triangle intersections.

The remainder of this gem describes the kD-tree, considered to be the most efficient acceleration structure for ray tracing [Havran01], and approaches to a highly efficient implementation. Because this structure takes some preprocessing time, it is best used for static scenery. Because of the importance in games and other real-time interactive applications, this gem presents alternatives for dynamic scenery as well. You can combine these for mixed environments. This is demonstrated in the accompanying demo application on the CD-ROM.

ON THE CD

kD-Tree Concepts and Storage Considerations

The kD-tree (*k*-dimensional tree) is a structure that recursively splits space in two halves. In this sense, it is a BSP tree. There is, however, a restriction—the splitting planes are axis-aligned, instead of the arbitrary planes that a generic BSP tree uses. An example is shown in Figure 2.2.2.

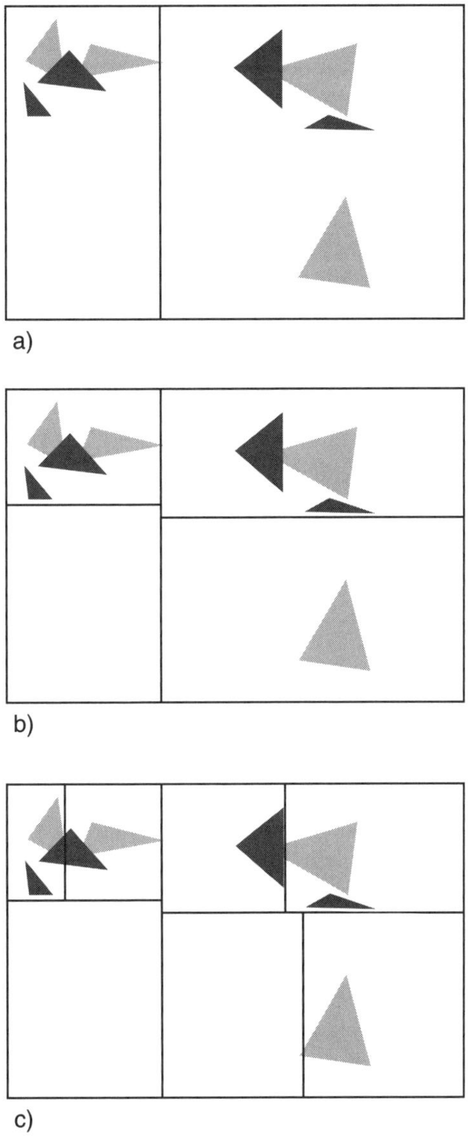

FIGURE 2.2.2 Three iterations of the kD-tree splitting process.

Note that in the third iteration (c), the bottom-left cell is not split, because it does not contain any geometry. Also note how geometry is quickly isolated from empty space, because of the arbitrary split plane position.

Making the split planes axis-aligned may seem limiting. In practice, however, it allows you to traverse a ray more efficiently. Finding the intersection of a ray with an axis-aligned plane is computationally very efficient, as shown in the following equation:

```
t = (splitpos[axis] – ray.origin[axis]) / ray.direction[axis]    (1)
```

Here, `t` is the distance along the ray, starting at the origin. By pre-calculating the reciprocal of the ray direction, this is reduced to a subtraction and a multiplication.

A kD-tree node thus contains a split plane position and an orientation. Because this can be the x, y, or z axis, two bits suffice to store the orientation. Besides the split plane, a node stores a list of primitives or as a pointer to a left and right child node. Finally, a flag is stored to identify a node as either an internal node (which has no geometry but is split into two child nodes) or a leaf node (which has geometry but no child nodes).

```
struct KdTreeNode
{
   float splitpos;
   int axis;
   KdTreeNode* left, *right;
   bool leaf;
   Primitive** primitive;
   int primcount;
};
```

Using a careful layout of the data, this can be stored in just eight bytes:

- By allocating child nodes at each split in pairs, the `KdTreeNode` that the `right` pointer points to is simply `left + 1`. This way, only a single child node pointer needs to be stored.
- By storing pointers to primitives in a separate array, you can index this array from the kD-tree node using an index and a count (see Figure 2.2.3). In order to be able to store both the index and the count in a single unsigned integer, you must use five bits for the count and the remaining 27 bits to index the array.
- If a node is a leaf, it doesn't require the child node pointer. If it is an internal node, it doesn't reference primitives. These can thus safely occupy the same variable in the `KdTreeNode` data structure.
- An optimized `KdTreeNode` requires eight bytes of storage. By aligning `KdTreeNodes` to 8-byte boundaries, the address of a `KdTreeNode` (and thus the value of the `left` pointer) is guaranteed to be a multiple of 8. The lowest bits are thus zero; these can be used for the `leaf` flag (1 bit) and the split plane axis (2 bits). Because this data is shared by the object list index and count, this data must also be shifted by three bits.

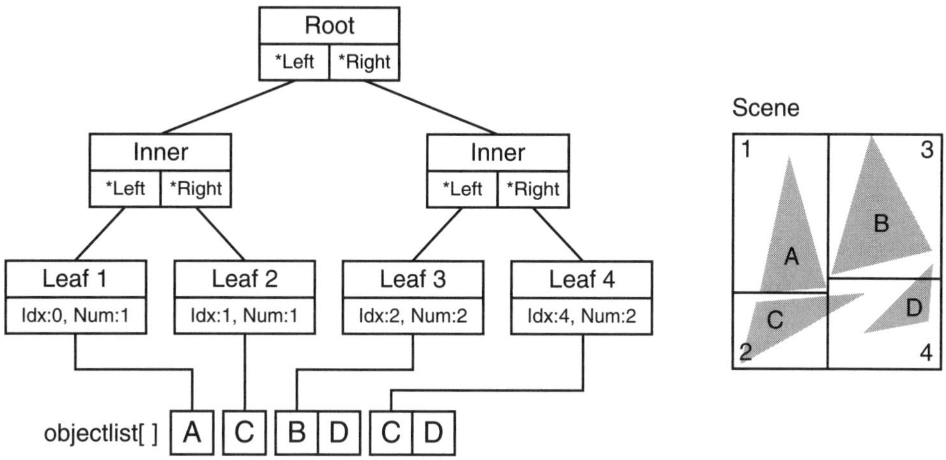

FIGURE 2.2.3 A kD-tree showing the use of an intermediate data structure to reduce the size of the nodes.

The `KdTreeNode` structure now becomes:

```
struct KdTreeNode
{
    // member data access methods
    void SetAxis( int a_Axis ) { m_Data = (m_Data & -4) + a_Axis; }

    int GetAxis(){ return m_Data & 3; }

    void SetLeft( KdTreeNode* a_Left )
    { m_Data = (unsigned long)a_Left + (m_Data & 7); }

    KdTreeNode* GetLeft(){ return (KdTreeNode*)(m_Data & -8); }

    KdTreeNode* GetRight(){ return GetLeft() + 1; }

    int IsLeaf() { return (m_Data & 4); }

    void SetLeaf( bool a_Leaf )
    {m_Data = (a_Leaf)?(m_Data|4):(m_Data & -5);}

    int GetObjOffset() { return (m_Data >> 8); }

    int GetObjCount() { return (m_Data & 248) >> 3; }

    // member data
    float m_Split;
    unsigned long m_Data;
};
```

In this structure, the `m_Data` member contains the `leaf` bit, the split plane axis, and either a pointer to the left child node or a pointer to an entry in the primitive pointer array, plus a primitive count. The various `Get` and `Set` methods filter out the relevant bits for the requested information.

kD-Tree Construction

The previous section described the basic concept of a kD-tree, along with its efficient storage. The biggest unanswered question is how to determine the split plane position.

Exactly what makes a good kD-tree depends on what you want to use it for. If the goal is to walk a list of primitives front-to-back in as few steps as possible, you will probably want a balanced tree with few primitives spanning split planes. For ray tracing, you have a different objective—reduce the number of triangles that you need to intersect. And that means that you would rather traverse empty space. Consider a scene with a single tiny triangle in the top-left corner, as shown in Figure 2.2.4.

FIGURE 2.2.4 Finding the optimal split plane position.

What is the optimal tree for this situation? There are a few options:

- No split at all.
- A single vertical split through the right vertex of the triangle.
- A single horizontal split through the bottom vertex of the triangle.
- Multiple splits.

Note that splits will always occur at bounding box extrema; all other positions will either split the triangle or will add empty space to a node. No split at all means that every ray will be tested against the triangle. A single vertical split will prevent this for some percentage of the rays, and so does a horizontal split. Several splits will reduce this percentage even further. It turns out that, for the illustrated case, the vertical split is the best option. In 3D, the chance that you hit any node with the triangle is proportional to the area of the bounding surface of the node. The vertical split produces a non-empty leaf node with a smaller area than the horizontal split, so it reduces the chance that a ray needs to be intersected with the triangle more than the horizontal split.

Whether or not a split is needed at all depends on the *cost* of intersecting a triangle, versus the cost of traversing one level of the kD-tree. Usually, intersecting a triangle is more expensive and so it pays to do a split, and perhaps more than a single split. This is the idea of the *surface area heuristic* (SAH)—determining the best split plane position, calculating an expected cost for each candidate position, and choosing the split with the lowest expected cost. You should perform a split only if that cost is lower than the cost of not splitting at all.

The cost of a given split can be computed using the following equation:

```
cost_nosplit = primitive_count * total_area * intersection_cost;  (2)
```

The cost of a split can be expressed as the following:

```
left_cost = left_count * intersection_cost;
right_cost = right_count * intersection_cost;  (3)
split_cost = traversal_cost + left_area * left_cost
             + right_area * right_cost;
```

You now have a heuristic to find the best plane, and a termination criterion: If you cannot find a cost lower than the cost of not splitting at all, you do not split. Additionally, it is a good idea to stop splitting at a certain depth, to limit memory usage and construction time.

Even though the SAH is elegant and produces high-quality trees, it needs some intervention to produce trees that are more suitable for fast ray tracing. By itself, the SAH will not try to isolate empty space. To encourage empty space cutoff, scores for splits that produce empty leafs are lowered.

Fast kD-Tree Construction

Constructing the kD-tree using the surface area heuristic is a potentially time-consuming process. Because you need the number of triangles to the left and right of each possible split plane, you must walk the list of triangles 2N times per split, per axis, which amounts to $6N^2$ iterations of the inner loop. Because you are building a tree, the expected runtime of the build process is thus $O(N^2 \log N)$. For any realistic scene, this will take too long. This can be improved however, as shown by Wald and Havran [Wald06a]. As pointed out, the main bottleneck in the SAH algorithm is the triangle counting. Luckily, you can get rid of this expensive process altogether.

In Figure 2.2.5, a simple scene of two triangles is shown. There are four possible split plane positions along the horizontal axis. At the first position, the number of triangles to the left is zero, and the number of triangles to the right is two. Now, whenever a new triangle begins (left side of bounding box), the left count increases.

Whenever a triangle ends, the right count decreases. So, if you create a sorted list of these events (start events and end events), the left and right triangle counts can be updated incrementally, while walking the list of events from left to right.

Although this already improves performance considerably, there are some remaining problems. First of all, the events need to be sorted per axis. Secondly, at each level of the tree, the events need to be resorted, because many triangles will no longer be in the list, whereas others were clipped, introducing new events.

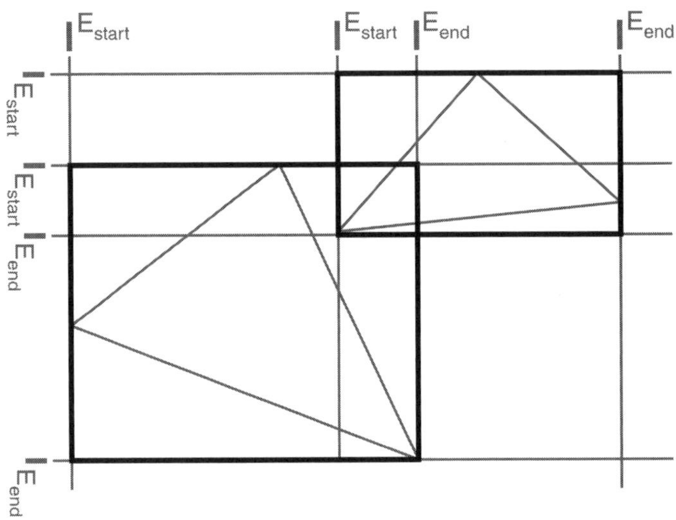

FIGURE 2.2.5 Bounding box start and end events.

It turns out that it is possible to do the sorting just once, at the top level of the tree. For this, you use a rather complex data structure. The `EventBox` (see the code that follows), is a linked list with no less than six next pointers, one for each side of a primitive bounding box, for each axis in 3D space.

For the scene shown in Figure 2.2.5, two `EventBoxes` are needed, storing four events per axis. Consider the `EventBox` for the left triangle: It has two next pointers per axis—one of them points to the start event of the second `EventBox`, the other one points to the end event of the second `EventBox`.

```
struct EventBox
{
    EventBoxSide side[2];
    Primitive* prim;
};
```

The first EventBoxSide contains the start events for the x, y, and z axes. The second element contains the end events. Using two instances of the EventBoxSide object allows you to point from one side to another. Each EventBoxSide instance stores a position along each axis, three next pointers, and the side. The pointers and the side value are stored in a single 32-bit value for efficiency.

```
struct EventBoxSide
{
    EventBoxSide* next( int axis ) { return (EventBoxSide*)
    (n[axis] & -3); }
    void next( int axis, EventBoxSide* p )
    {
        n[axis] = (n[axis] & 3) + (unsigned long)p;
    }
    int side( int axis ) { return n[axis] & 3; }
    void side( int axis, int side ) { n[axis] = (n[axis] & -3)
    + side; }
    unsigned long n[3];
    float pos[3];
};
```

Once the list is constructed, it can be updated on-the-fly. This way, sorting is limited to a single sort at the top level of the tree; tree construction time is now reduced to O(NlogN).

kD-Tree Traversal

Ordered traversal (front-to-back, for ray tracing) of a kD-tree is identical to BSP tree traversal. Traversal starts by finding the leaf node that contains the ray origin. For each node, the side of the split plane that the origin is on is determined, and the branch for that side is followed, while the other side is pushed on a stack. Once a leaf is found, a node is popped from the stack, and the process is continued until the stack is empty. For ray queries, there is an extra termination criterion—once an intersection is found, there is no need to look beyond the current node.

This process visits nodes in the correct order. However, for ray queries it needs some adjustments. Specifically, you need the exact entry and exit points for the ray in the current node, t_{min} and t_{max}. These values are needed because some intersection points might be outside the current node, illustrated in Figure 2.2.6.

The large triangle resides partially in the node that contains the ray origin. If you allow intersections outside the current node, intersecting the ray with this triangle will result in a hit, and so traversal is terminated. The smaller triangle is thus never considered.

You must therefore keep track of t_{min} and t_{max}. To do this, you first calculate t_{min} and t_{max} by clipping the ray against the scene bounding box. After that, t_{min} and t_{max} are incrementally updated.

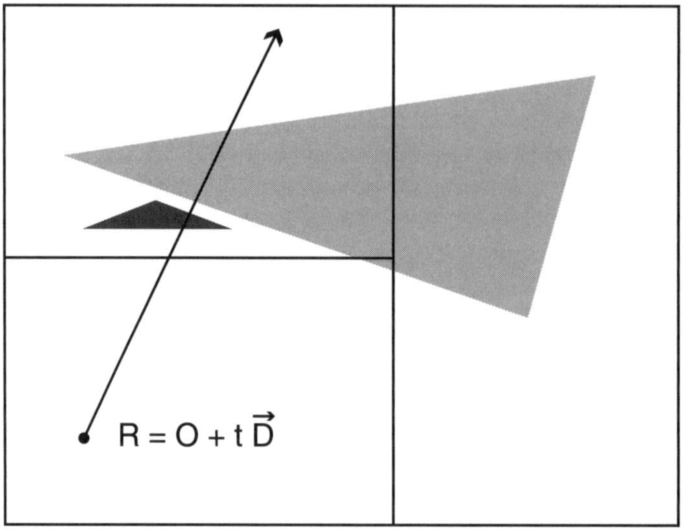

FIGURE 2.2.6 False hit for the larger triangle in the first node.

The three situations that can occur during traversal are shown in Figure 2.2.7:

- (Figure 2.2.7a): The intersection of the line with the split plane (t_{split}) lies between t_{min} and t_{max}. The left node is traversed first, with $t_{max} = t_{split}$. The right node is pushed on the stack, with $t_{min} = t_{split}$.
- (Figure 2.2.7b): t_{split} lies beyond t_{max}. You need only to traverse the left node, and no changes to the interval are needed.
- (Figure 2.2.7c): t_{split} lies before t_{min}. You need only to traverse the right node, and no changes to the interval are needed.

Rays that hit the split plane from the right side are handled in the same manner; the only difference is that the left and right child nodes are now swapped.

This translates to the following code:

```
// precomputed data
int raydir[8][3][2];
for ( int i = 0; i < 8; i++ )
{
    int rdx = i & 1;
    int rdy = (i >> 1) & 1;
    int rdz = (i >> 2) & 1;
    raydir[i][0][0] = rdx, raydir[i][0][1] = rdx ^ 1;
    raydir[i][1][0] = rdy, raydir[i][1][1] = rdy ^ 1;
    raydir[i][2][0] = rdz, raydir[i][2][1] = rdz ^ 1;
}
```

```
// prepare data for traversal
KdTreeNode* node = Scene::GetKdTree()->GetRoot();
vector3 O = ray.origin;
vector3 D = ray.direction;
vector3 R( 1 / ray.direction.x,
           1 / ray.direction.y,
           1 / ray.direction.z );
int oct = ((D.x < 0)?1:0) + ((D.y < 0)?2:0) + ((D.z < 0)?4:0);
int* rdir = &raydir[oct][0][0];
int stackptr = 0;

// actual traversal
while (1)
{
    while (!node->IsLeaf())
    {
      int axis = node->GetAxis();
      KdTreeNode* front = node->GetLeft() + rdir[axis * 2];
      KdTreeNode* back  = node->GetLeft() + rdir[axis * 2 + 1];
      float tsplit = (node->m_Split - O.cell[axis]) * R.cell[axis];
      node = back;
      if (tsplit < tnear) continue;
      node = front;
      if (tsplit > tfar) continue;
      stack[stackptr].tfar = tfar;
      stack[stackptr++].node = back;
      tfar = MIN( tfar, tsplit );
    }

    // leaf node found, process triangles
    int start = node->GetObjOffset();
    int count = node->GetObjCount();
    for (int i = 0; i < count; i++ ) // intersect triangles

    // terminate, or pop node from stack
    if ((dist < tfar) || (!stackptr)) break;
    node = stack[--stackptr].node;
    tnear = tfar;
    tfar = stack[stackptr].tfar;
}
```

The array `raydir` is used to swap the left and right child nodes efficiently. The layout of this array is `[octant][axis][child]`. Each entry in the array contains the offset of the near and far nodes (with respect to the ray direction) for an axis, for an octant.

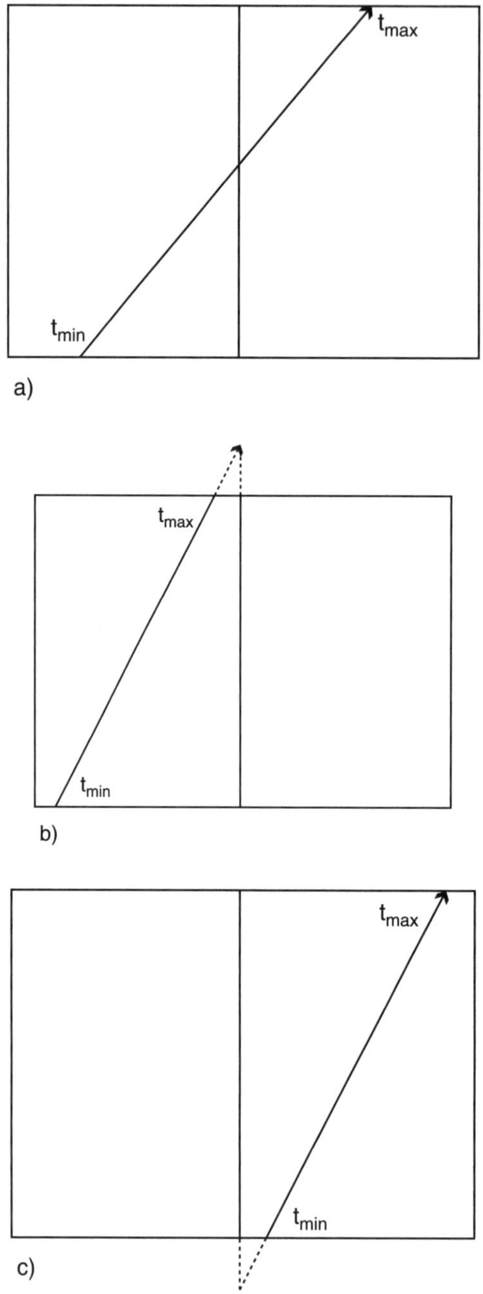

FIGURE 2.2.7 kD-tree traversal cases.

Dynamic Objects

The method for performing ray queries described so far relies on the availability of a high-quality kD-tree, a structure that generally requires offline precomputations. The scenery therefore must be static: In a game, this is generally not the case. There is no easy solution to this problem. Ray tracing dynamic scenes is an area of active research. Depending on your specific needs, there are several possible solutions.

The main reason for not updating the kD-tree every frame is the expensive SAH heuristic. You can however use two trees. The first tree contains the static geometry, whereas the second one contains only the dynamic objects. Tracing rays in a mixed environment (dynamic and static triangles) is then implemented using a two-stage traversal process. First, the ray traverses the tree for the static scenery; then, the ray traverses the tree that contains the dynamic triangles. This may seem inefficient at first, but in practice, most rays will miss the dynamic geometry, because this geometry typically covers only a small area of the screen. Most of these rays will therefore travel a small number of empty nodes, without intersecting any triangles.

In the proposed scheme, the tree containing the dynamic triangles is rebuilt each frame. Using the SAH, determining the split plane position is by far the most expensive part. By fixing plane positions, a tree for the dynamic triangles can be built in very little time. One way to do this is to choose the spatial median for alternating axes. This essentially creates an *octree*. Using a separate tree for dynamic triangles assumes the scenery contains more static geometry than dynamic geometry, which is generally the case.

Alternatively, the kD-tree can be abandoned altogether. Different acceleration structures yield reasonable results, but can be built in less time than a kD-tree. Examples are bounding volume hierarchies (BVHs) [Wald07], the bounding interval hierarchy [Wächter06], and nested grids [Wald06b].

Demo Application

ON THE CD

The demo application on the CD-ROM demonstrates the described concepts. It reads a scene file (in OBJ format) and displays a wireframe representation of the mesh. A small dynamic object is also loaded. Per frame, the dynamic object is rotated, and a small kD-tree is built. The beam consists of 5,000 rays, of which every 64th ray is drawn. These rays are traced through the static kD-tree and the dynamic kD-tree to determine visibility from the center of the scene. Figure 2.2.8 is a screenshot from the demo. Note that even though the visualization is 2D, the actual data is 3D, and so are the ray queries.

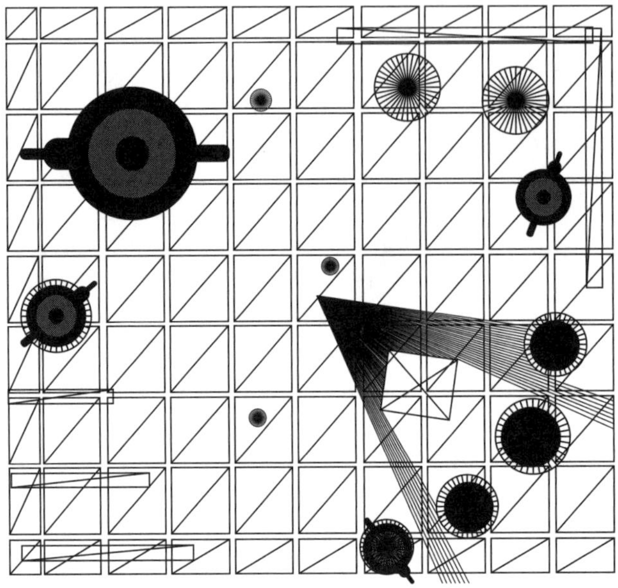

FIGURE 2.2.8 The demo application displays a wireframe representation of the mesh.

Conclusion

Generic ray queries in a polygonal environment offer a powerful tool for many operations in a game. This gem described how these queries are efficiently implemented using a high-quality kD-tree based on the surface area heuristic. Dynamic geometry is stored in a less efficient kD-tree, which can however be built much quicker.

Implemented well, the presented approach lets you trace 1 million rays per second easily. Should you need more, it is worthwhile to explore SIMD-enhanced *packet traversal* (traversing multiples of four rays simultaneously).

You might even want to explore the fascinating world of real-time ray traced graphics, one of those rare algorithms that you can never throw enough processing power at. You will love the intuitive nature of ray tracing—whether you use it for graphics or other purposes.

References

[Appel63] Appel, A. "Some Techniques for Shading Machine Renderings of Solids," *Proceedings of the Spring Joint Computer Conference* 32 (1968), pp. 37–45.

[Havran01] Havran, V. "Heuristic Ray Shooting Algorithms," PhD thesis, Czech Technical University, Praha, Czech Republic, 2001.

[McDonald90] MacDonald, J., and Booth, K. "Heuristics for Ray Tracing using Space Subdivision," *The Visual Computer,* Vol. 6, No. 3 (June 1990), pp. 153–166.

[Wächter06] Wächter, C., and Keller, A. "Instant Ray Tracing: The Bounding Interval Hierarchy," In *Rendering Techniques 2006, Proceedings of the 17th Eurographics Symposium on Rendering* (2006), pp. 139–149.

[Wald04] Wald, I. "Realtime Ray Tracing and Interactive Global Illumination," PhD thesis, Saarland University, 2004.

[Wald06a] Wald, I., and Havran, V. "On Building Fast kD-trees for Ray Tracing, and On Doing That in O(NlogN)," *Proceedings of the 2006 IEEE Symposium on Interactive Ray Tracing* (2006), pp. 61–69.

[Wald06b] I. Wald, I., Ize, T., Kensler, A., Knoll, A., and Parker, S. "Ray Tracing Animated Scenes Using Coherent Grid Traversal," *ACM Transactions on Graphics,* Proceedings of ACM SIGGRAPH 2006, pp. 485–493.

[Wald07] Wald, I., Boulos, S., and Shirley, P. "Ray Tracing Deformable Scenes Using Dynamic Bounding Volume Hierarchies," *ACM Transactions on Graphics* (2007), Vol. 26, No. 1.

[Whitted79] Whitted, T. "An Improved Illumination Model for Shaded Display," *Communications of the ACM* (August 1979), Vol. 23, No. 6, pp. 343–349.

2.3

Fast Rigid-Body Collision Detection Using Farthest Feature Maps

Rahul Sathe, Advanced Visual Computing, SSG, Intel Corp.

rahul.p.sathe@intel.com

Dillon Sharlet, University of Colorado at Boulder

dillon.sharlet@colorado.edu

With the rapidly increasing horsepower of processors and graphics cards, physics has become an important aspect of real-time interactive graphics and games. Without physics, although every frame might look quite realistic, the overall realism will be missing during the gameplay. Modeling of real-world physical phenomena can be quite mathematical in nature and computationally intensive. Game developers usually try to simplify the models without compromising visual fidelity. At the same time, they try to improve the computational efficiency of the models. One of the most computationally intensive tasks is collision detection of objects in gameplay. This involves determining whether two objects are colliding (or have collided in the last timestep). If they are colliding, the physical simulation requires some more quantities like penetration depth and a separating axis.

This gem tries to solve some of the complexities involved in the process using some acceleration data structures. It introduces a new data structure called the *farthest feature map* that is used to accelerate the discovery of a *potentially colliding set* (PCS) of triangles at runtime. This algorithm, like our previous algorithm based on distance cube-maps, works only with convex rigid bodies and has a preprocessing step and a runtime step.

The intuition behind this new proposed approach is as follows—convex rigid bodies when far from each other behave roughly like point masses. However, when they approach each other, this point mass approximation is not good enough. At that point, you must perform more detailed analysis using the local properties of the bodies near the contact manifold.

Background

Collision detection can be modeled in two ways—discrete collision detection or continuous collision detection. The former updates the positions of the game objects at discrete timesteps and tries to find out if two objects are intersecting at a moment in time. One technical approach to discrete collision detection tries to find intersecting triangles by using a recursively subdivided hierarchy of bounding boxes that are either axes aligned (AABB) [Bergen97] or oriented (OBB) [Gottschalk96]. Continuous collision detection systems use a variable timestep and modify that timestep for each potentially colliding pair such that two objects never intersect each other. Continuous collision detection is often modeled by algorithms like the one by Gilbert Johnson and Keerthy [GJK88]. Refer to these and other references for further details on the fundamentals of each approach.

Our recent work tries to move a lot of work to the preprocessing step for rigid bodies [Sathe07]. At runtime, all you do is access the distance cube-maps to find the collision. Distance cube-maps access can be hardware accelerated but there is some room for improvement and optimization, which the new *farthest feature map* concept can provide.

Following are some terms that are used throughout this gem:

- *Principle curvatures:* In differential geometry, principle curvatures at any point on a surface are the curvatures corresponding to the curves with maximum and minimum curvature at that point. These curves are always at right angles to each other.
- *Mean curvature:* The average of principle curvatures is called the mean curvature.
- *Best-fitting sphere:* For the typical game mesh, represented by planar triangles with creases at neighboring edges rather than continuous geometry with smooth derivatives at every seam, the curvature definitions cannot be applied in a meaningful way to many algorithms that require geometric interrogation. So you have to come up with some approximation of the curvatures. The *ring-1 neighborhood* of a vertex is the triangle fan around that vertex. We consider the ring-1 neighborhood around a given vertex and try to find the sphere that has center along the normal axis passing through that vertex. This circle is a crude approximation of the sphere with the radius equal to that corresponding to mean curvature for a triangle mesh.

Preprocessing

This approach uses a data structure that is similar to a cube-map; that is, it is a directional lookup, although the stored data exceeds the capacity of cube-map texture formats for current generation graphics hardware. Place the object's centroid at the origin. Then imagine an axis-aligned cube centered at the origin and then shoot rays from the origin through all the pixel centers on the faces of the cube-map. For each of these rays, you project the line segment from the centroid to the vertices on this ray. You select the maxima of these projections and store the corresponding vertex (vertices) for that sampled direction. We call this data structure a *farthest feature* in that sampled direction.

An intuitive way to visualize a *farthest feature map* is to think of a perpendicular plane for a given sampled direction. Then, think of moving that plane outward from the centroid keeping it perpendicular to that sampled direction. This plane will intersect with the convex object to yield some polygon in that plane. If you keep on moving this plane outward, eventually the plane will intersect with one or more of the vertices of the convex model. As you continue moving the plane farther away from the centroid, it will eventually move far enough to not intersect with the convex geometry. At this point, the distance to the perpendicular plane is the farthest distance in that direction and any vertices from geometry that lay on the plane just prior to the farthest distance are the farthest features.

Figures 2.3.1 through 2.3.3 show this in the 2D case. Here, the thick solid line is the convex geometry of the game object being processed. The geometry is defined here by vertices V_0 through V_4. The plane is shown in thick dotted lines. Arrows represent the directions that they are being moved in order to find the farthest features for the two sampled directions dir_1 and dir_2.

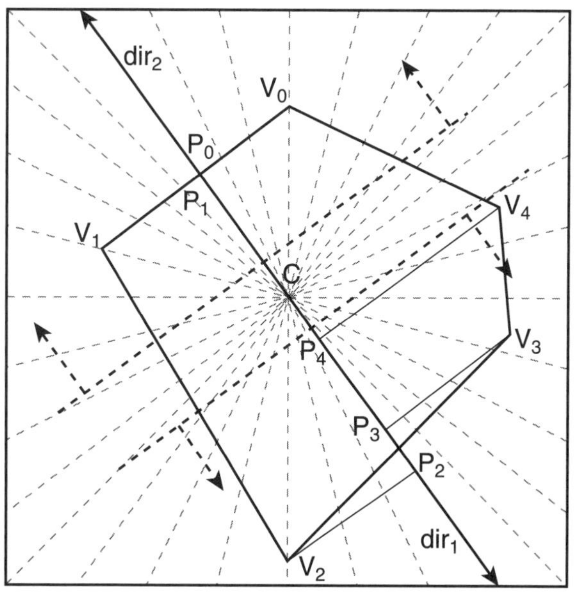

CP_n = Projection of CV_n on dir_1 or dir_2

FIGURE 2.3.1 Planes perpendicular to the sampled directions dir_1 and dir_2 are shown in dotted lines. They are moving away from the centroid.

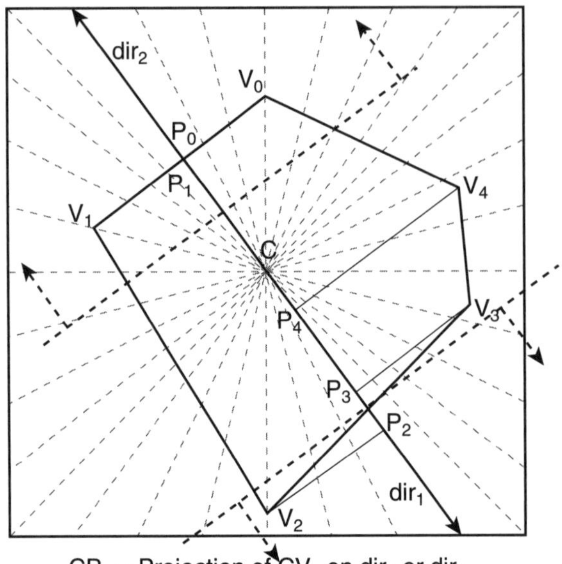

FIGURE 2.3.2 Planes moving farther away from the centroid.

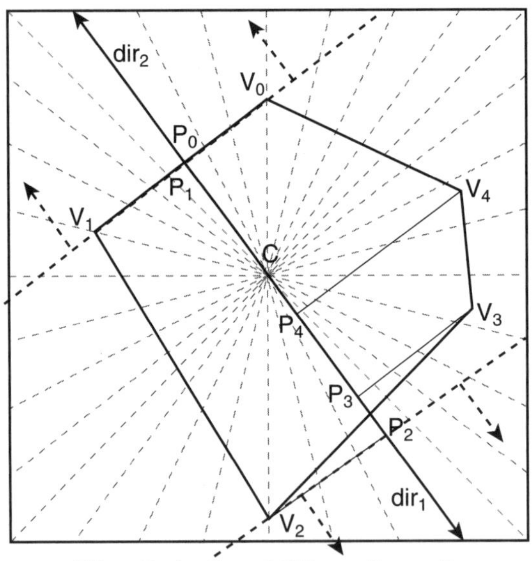

FIGURE 2.3.3 Planes perpendicular to the sampled directions dir_1 and dir_2 in their farthest positions. V_0 and V_1 form the farthest features in dir_2 direction and V_2 is the farthest feature in dir_1 direction.

Figures 2.3.4 and 2.3.5 illustrate the construction of the farthest feature map in 3D, showing the farthest features in two different sampled directions.

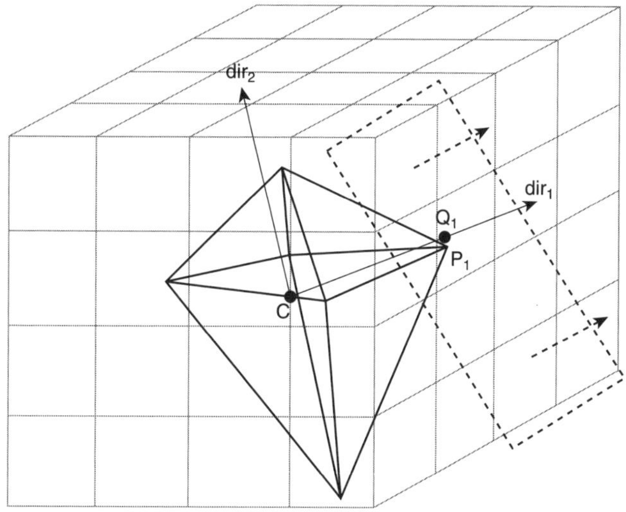

FIGURE 2.3.4 The plane that is perpendicular to dir_1 moving away from the centroid C is in its final position. CQ_1 is the projection of CP_1 on dir_1. P_1 and Q_1 lie on the plane.

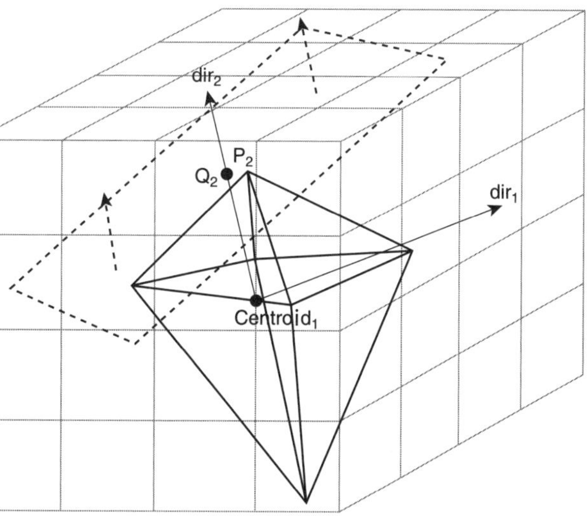

FIGURE 2.3.5 The plane that is perpendicular to dir_2 moving away from the centroid C is in its final position. CQ_2 is the projection of CP_2 on dir_2. P_2 and Q_2 lie on the plane.

The data that you store in a given sampled direction (equivalent to a single pixel center in the cube-map analogy) is represented by class `Node`. Here, you store the index of the vertex representing the farthest feature along the direction. If there is more than one vertex, you store the index of all of them for this direction. At runtime, you can start off with any one of these features.

The detailed farthest feature information for the vertices is stored separately. For every vertex, you store its neighborhood information as shown in the class `VertexNeighborhood`. You store the following data per vertex—the center of the best fitting sphere, as well as equations of planes, face IDs, and edges. You also store the normal and center for the best-fitting sphere for each of the vertices that form the farthest feature for a given direction. Edges are used to find edge-edge intersections.

The reason for splitting this into per vertex and per direction (farthest feature map) is storage optimization. For low poly objects, if you oversample the farthest feature map, you want to store as little information as possible per sample; for example, the indices into the `VertexNeighborhood` buffer.

```
Class Node
{
    int *Index;
}

Class VertexNeighborhood
{
    Vector < Plane > Faces;
    Vector < DWORD > Triangles;
    Vector < Pair < DWORD, DWORD > > Edges;
    Vector3 CenterOfBestFittingSphere;
}
```

The best fitting sphere at the farthest feature is the sphere that best fits the triangle fan around the farthest feature. In the 2D case, this will correspond to a circle that best fits the ring-1 neighborhood of the vertex, which for a 2D piecewise linear curve is always two vertices. It's always possible to find the exact circle that passes through three points (unless they are collinear). This is shown in Figure 2.3.6. In the 3D case, it usually is not possible to find a sphere that exactly passes through all of the ring-1 vertices, because ring-1 will usually contain more vertices than needed to minimally define a sphere, and the surface will rarely happen to be exactly spherical at any given point.

Runtime Queries

At runtime, you start off with the assumption that two convex meshes under consideration behave like a point mass. This assumption is true when they are far away from each other. The question that you have to answer then is how far is far enough? It turns out that you can approximate these objects with point masses so long as their bounding volumes do not intersect each other. The bounding volumes that are used to approximate the object determine how far the objects can be. Bounding spheres, axis-aligned bounding boxes, and oriented bounded boxes are popular bounding volume approximations.

At runtime, you proceed as follows. First, connect the two centroids. Along this direction connecting two centroids, find the farthest features of the two objects using farthest feature-maps that were created during preprocessing. In some sense, you have used the farthest feature map to quickly generate the bounding volumes. However, they differ from conventional bounding volumes because they can be different along any direction. In this case, you are looking at the bounds along the line joining two centroids.

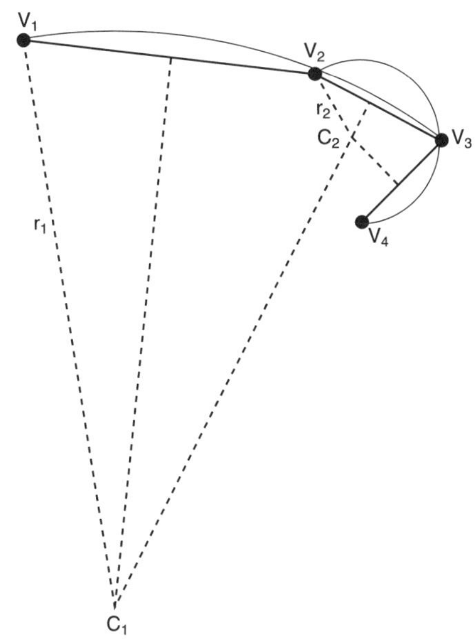

FIGURE 2.3.6 Best fitting circle in 2D.

If the sum of the distances to the farthest feature maps from the respective centroids along the line joining centroids is more than the distance between the centroids, you know that the bounding volume test along this axis has failed, and the objects belong to the potentially colliding set. At this point, you lose the liberty to treat convex objects as point masses located at their centroids and you have to perform a more detailed analysis.

In this case, you query the farthest feature map to find the center of the best fitting sphere at the farthest features for both the objects. Then, connect these centers of best fitting spheres at farthest features of the two objects. This step in some sense approximates the two interacting objects locally with spheres of radii corresponding to the best fitting spheres. The important thing to note here is that the approximation is only a "local" approximation. Find the farthest features along the line joining these centers and do the distance test that you did earlier when you joined the centroids. If the distance test fails, continue finding the best fitting spheres at the farthest features until, at two successive steps, you find the same farthest feature. At this point, you conclude the algorithm.

The pseudocode for the algorithm follows:

```
lastC1 = lastC2 = null;
Connect the two centroids C1C2
Find the distance C1C2 between two centroids
Find the distance d1 and d2 to farthest features along C1C2

while (C1C2 < d1+d2 || lastC1 != C1 || lastC2 != C2)
{
    lastC1 = C1
    lastC2 = C2
    C1 = center of best fitting sphere at farthest feature
        Of object 1
    C2 = center of best fitting sphere at farthest feature
        Of object 2
    d1 = Distance to farthest feature along C1C2 from C1
    d2 = Distance to farthest feature along C2C1 from C2
}
```

When you conclude the algorithm, you are left with two farthest features from two objects and their ring-1 neighborhoods. For a typical game mesh, these two triangle fans will have around six triangles each. At this point, you have to determine if a triangle from the triangle-fan for one object intersects with any triangle from the triangle-fan corresponding to the other object. You thus are left with having to do triangle-triangle intersection tests for typically 36 (triangle-triangle) pairs. All these triangle-triangle intersection tests can be performed in parallel, using the appropriate processor technology and programming language.

Performance Analysis and Concluding Remarks

In most cases, the algorithm converges in O(1) time. This will be the case when the distribution of the vertex density of the two convex meshes doesn't vary too much with the directions. If the contact point is in the region where concentration of vertices is higher, the algorithm takes longer to converge.

It will be interesting to see how this algorithm can be extended to work with concave objects. With the ever-increasing general programmability of the graphics hardware, we want to look at how one can exploit a flexible cube-map that can store more than just a fixed format texture data. Adaptively sampled cube-maps will save a lot of storage but will increase the lookup costs. Some clever encoding scheme that solves this problem will be nice.

Acknowledgments

We would like to thank the management group in Advanced Visual Computing Group, SSG at Intel for allowing us to pursue this work. We would also like to thank our co-workers Adam Lake and Oliver Heim for their help at various stages of this work.

References

[Bergen97] Van den Bergen, G. "Efficient Collision Detection of Complex Deformable Models Using AABB Trees," *Journal of Graphics Tools,* Vol. 2, No. 4, pp. 1–14, 1997.

[GJK88] Gilbert, E.G., Johnson, D.W., and Keerthi, S.S. "A Fast Procedure for Computing the Distance Between Objects in 3 Dimensional Space," *IEEE Journal of Robotics and Automation,* Vol. RA-4, pp. 193–203, 1988.

[Gottschalk96] Gottschalk, S., Lin, M.C., and Manocha, D. "OBBTree: A Hierarchical Structure for Rapid Interference Detection," *Proc. SIGGRAPH 1996,* pp. 171–180.

[Sathe07] Sathe, Rahul. "Collision Detection Shader Using Cube-Maps," *ShaderX^5 Advanced Rendering Techniques,* Charles River Media, 2007.

2.4

Using Projective Space to Improve Precision of Geometric Computations

Krzysztof Kluczek, Gdańsk University of Technology

krzych82@poczta.onet.pl

Many geometric algorithms used in modeling, rendering, physics, and AI modules depend on point-line and, in case of three-dimensional space, point-plane tests. The finite precision of computing introduces problems when collinear or coplanar cases are to be detected. A common solution to this problem is detecting such cases based on a set minimum distance (epsilon), below which elements being processed are assumed to be collinear or coplanar. This set minimum distance solves the problem only partially because checking results against such a distance is prone to signaling false-positives, which reduces the overall robustness of any algorithm using such a solution.

In order to create robust geometric algorithms that will operate correctly in every case, you can't use any operations that will truncate intermediate results (for example, operations on floating-point numbers). Truncation leads to loss of information, which under certain circumstances can be needed to obtain results. This leaves math based on integers the only way to ensure that truncation doesn't happen. The straightforward representation of points using integer Cartesian coordinates isn't the solution because the intersection of a pair of lines with endpoints with integer coordinates doesn't necessarily occur at integer coordinates. Using rational numbers can solve the problem (see [Young02]), but this requires storing six integer values per vector (numerator and denominator for each component) and implementations of efficient operations on such vectors aren't straightforward in three-dimensional space. Using projective space can reduce this number to four integers per vector by using vectors with one extra dimension and storing only a single integer per vector component, which is demonstrated in this chapter.

Projective Space

The concept of *projective space* is fundamental to understanding algorithms presented here. $\mathbf{RP}^2$ projective space can be described as a space of all lines in $\mathbf{R}^3$ space passing through point [0,0,0], as shown on Figure 2.4.1. Each line can be uniquely identified by a point in $\mathbf{R}^3/[0,0,0]$, which lies on the line, and so you can use an $[x,y,z]$ coordinate vector to identify each element in this space, where $[x,y,z] \neq [0,0,0]$. Still, you have to keep in mind that any pair of vectors **P** and **Q** identifies the same line if $\mathbf{P} = \mathbf{Q}c$ for certain scalars $c \neq 0$. Representation of the elements of $\mathbf{RP}^2$ as $[x,y,z]$ vectors is known as *homogeneous coordinate* representation. Keeping in mind that elements of $\mathbf{RP}^2$ can be understood as lines crossing the origin of $\mathbf{R}^3$, let's define a $z = 1$ plane in this $\mathbf{R}^3$ space. Every line crosses the $z = 1$ plane exactly once, unless it's parallel to this plane. The intersection point can be calculated from the line equation and in the case of lines crossing the origin it is located at $[x/z,y/z,1]$ where $[x,y,z]$ is any point on the line other than [0,0,0]. Therefore, you can easily relate points in $\mathbf{R}^2$ and elements of $\mathbf{RP}^2$. Any point $[s,t]$ in $\mathbf{R}^2$ can be represented by element $[s,t,1]$ in $\mathbf{RP}^2$ or in general, any $[s,z,tz,z]$ where $z \neq 0$. Therefore, any vector $[x,y,z]$ with $z \neq 0$ representing an element of $\mathbf{RP}^2$ space will represent point $[x/z,y/z]$ in $\mathbf{R}^2$ space. This representation can be easily extended to higher-dimensional spaces, where $[p_1,\ldots,p_n,w]$ in $\mathbf{RP}^n$ is related to $[p_1/w,\ldots,p_n/w]$ in $\mathbf{R}^n$.

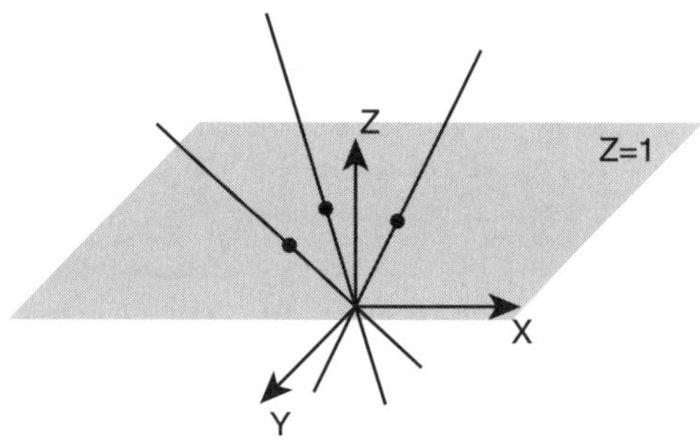

FIGURE 2.4.1 $\mathbf{RP}^2$ projective space as a space of lines in $\mathbf{R}^3$ crossing at the origin. Each line can be uniquely identified by a point in $\mathbf{R}^3/[0,0,0]$ and each line crosses the Z = 1 plane exactly once unless it's parallel to it.

This gem focuses on the representation of $\mathbf{R}^2$ space by $\mathbf{RP}^2$ projective space and representation of $\mathbf{R}^3$ space by $\mathbf{RP}^3$ space. The printed portion of this gem focuses on operations in $\mathbf{R}^2$ space using $\mathbf{RP}^2$ projective space. Because a point in $\mathbf{RP}^2$ space can be represented by a three-component vector, computations on such data are far easier to imagine and understand than computations on four-component vectors used to represent elements in $\mathbf{RP}^3$ space. The CD-ROM contains a separate document that expands the concepts described for $\mathbf{RP}^2$ space for application to $\mathbf{RP}^3$ space to allow computations on three-dimensional data.

ON THE CD

Basic Objects in $\mathbf{R}^2$

In two-dimensional space $\mathbf{R}^2$, you will focus on two types of objects, points and directed lines, which let you define more complex structures. You define a directed line in $\mathbf{R}^2$ space as a line with specified running direction, which allows us to define left and right sides of the line with respect to its running direction. This directional feature of the line definition is essential for efficient polygon representation, where we can assume that the interior of the polygon lies on a certain side of the line. In the case of convex polygons, which can be represented by an ordered list of directed lines defining its boundary, the above assumption can lead to very efficient algorithms for operating on such polygons. Just like convex polygons, many other objects in $\mathbf{R}^2$ such as segments and rays (half-lines) can be represented using points and directed lines, so it's safe to focus only on these two types of objects.

Points and Directed Lines in $\mathbf{RP}^2$

As it was defined at the beginning of this chapter, a point $[s,t]$ in $\mathbf{R}^2$ can be represented by element $[s,t,1]$ in $\mathbf{RP}^2$ space, so conversion from $\mathbf{R}^2$ to $\mathbf{RP}^2$ space is straightforward. Because scaling vectors in $\mathbf{RP}^2$ space doesn't affect their meaning, point $[s,t]$ can be represented by any vector $[sz,tz,z]$ where $z \neq 0$. For simplicity of future computations, let's assume $z > 0$. If this is not the case, the entire vector can be scaled by –1 to fix this. Recall that vectors with $z = 0$ don't represent valid points in $\mathbf{R}^2$. To obtain the formula for conversion of vectors from $\mathbf{RP}^2$ projective space to points in $\mathbf{R}^2$ space, you can use the same rule. Every vector $[x,y,z]$ in $\mathbf{RP}^2$ space represents the point $[x/z,y/z]$ in $\mathbf{R}^2$ space. This is similar to perspective projection onto $z = 1$ plane with the center of projection placed at the origin. Therefore, you can think of $\mathbf{RP}^2$ space almost like $\mathbf{R}^3$ space keeping in mind that it is not the vector $[x,y,z]$ that is important, but its perspective projection onto the $z = 1$ plane, which results in the vector $[x/z,y/z,1]$ representing point $[x/z,y/z]$ in $\mathbf{R}^2$ space. As you can see, this is very similar to the representation of points in $\mathbf{RP}^2$ using rational coordinates with a common denominator (in this case z), but defining it as a vector in $\mathbf{RP}^2$ space will give you efficient tools for performing computations on such points. Functions used to perform transformations of points between $\mathbf{R}^2$ and $\mathbf{RP}^2$ spaces are shown in Equations 2.4.1 and 2.4.2. Note that these functions operate on elements of $\mathbf{R}^3$ space as they take an argument or result in a vector in $\mathbf{R}^3$ referring to one of the elements (lines passing through the origin) of $\mathbf{RP}^2$ projective space and not the element of $\mathbf{RP}^2$ projective space itself.

$$f:\mathbf{R}^2 \to \mathbf{R}^3, \quad f([s,t]) = [s,t,1] \tag{2.4.1}$$

$$g:\mathbf{R}^3_{z\neq 0} \to \mathbf{R}^2 \quad g([x,y,z]) = [x/z,y/z] \tag{2.4.2}$$

The other object in $\mathbf{R}^2$ space of particular interest is a directed line. Just as points are perspective projections of vectors onto the $z = 1$ plane, lines in $\mathbf{RP}^2$ are perspective projections of planes onto the $z = 1$ plane. The only case when perspective projection of a plane results in a line is when the plane passes through the center of the projection, so every plane you use to define a line has to pass through point [0,0,0]. In fact, according to the definition of $\mathbf{RP}^2$ space you use, you can't define a plane in this space that does not pass through the origin, because $\mathbf{RP}^2$ space elements are lines passing through the origin and every plane you define in $\mathbf{RP}^2$ must contain entire lines. The $z = 1$ plane is the only exception to this rule because it is used only for projection of $\mathbf{RP}^2$ space to $\mathbf{R}^2$ space. Considering that every plane is passing through the origin, the definition of a line as projection of a plane in $\mathbf{RP}^2$ onto $z = 1$ plane can be simplified. The defined line is simply the intersection of the given plane and the $z = 1$ plane. Again, because all such planes pass through the origin, it's sufficient to store only their normal vectors. You don't require a normal to be normalized and in general it won't be normalized, because you will be using only integer coordinates for the normal vectors.

The previous definition of a line can be extended to a definition of a directed line by simply taking into account the direction of the normal vector of the plane used for this representation. You define the positive side of a plane as a half-space containing all vectors for which the dot product with the normal of this plane results in a positive value. To put it more straightforward, the positive side of the plane is the half-space the normal vector is pointing at. Similarly, you can define the negative side of this plane. Because a line represented with a plane is an intersection of this plane with the $z = 1$ plane, the plane divides the $z = 1$ plane into two half-planes, one lying in the positive half-space and the other in the negative one. You can call the half-plane on the positive side the *right side* of the directed line and the other half-plane the *left side*. From this, you can derive the direction of the directed line, which makes complete definition of representation of a directed line with a plane in $\mathbf{RP}^2$ space. Figure 2.4.2a contains an example representation of a directed line with a plane in $\mathbf{RP}^3$ projective space.

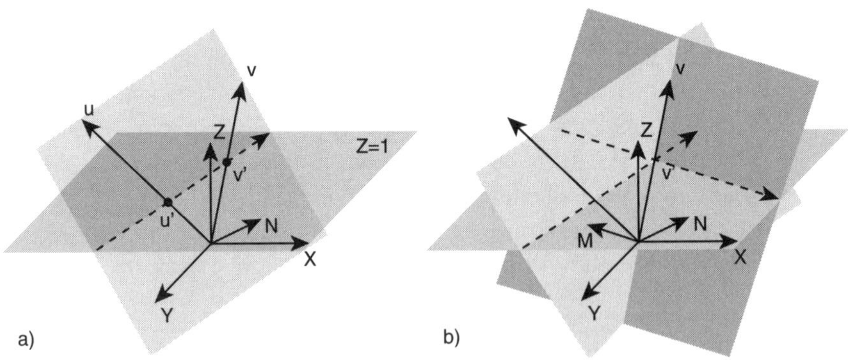

FIGURE 2.4.2 Points and lines in $\mathbf{RP}^2$ projective space: (a) a line passing through a pair of points; vectors **u** and **v** represent points **u**' and **v**' and the line is represented by a plane with normal **N**, (b) intersection of a pair of lines; **N** and **M** are normals of planes representing the lines and their cross product results in a vector representing the intersection point.

Basic Operations in $\mathbf{RP}^2$

There are three basic operations on points and directed lines. Given an ordered pair of points, you can find a directed line passing through them in the given order. Given a point and a directed line, you can determine which side of the line the point lies on or if it lies on the line. Finally, given a pair of directed lines you can find their intersection point. All these operations are fairly easy and straightforward in $\mathbf{RP}^2$ space.

Given a pair of vectors representing two points in $\mathbf{RP}^2$ space, you can look for a directed line passing through the points. Because of the nature of $\mathbf{RP}^2$ space, both vectors representing the points have to lie on the plane representing the line you are looking for; otherwise, the points resulting from their perspective projection wouldn't lay on this plane as every vector lying on the plane is parallel to the plane normal. Given a pair of such vectors, you can find the normal you are looking for using the cross product of these vectors. An example of a line led through a pair of points is shown in Figure 2.4.2a. The normal computed this way will correctly define the plane in $\mathbf{RP}^2$ space representing the directed line you are looking for. The direction of the line depends on the ordering of points used to compute the line, because swapping components of cross product inverts the result. It's desired that the line computed in this operation will be directed in such a way that its running direction will be the direction from first point to the second one, so you have to make sure that computed normal correctly defines the right side of the directed line by correctly defining the positive side of the plane in $\mathbf{RP}^2$ space. Because this depends on the handedness of the coordinate system being used, be sure to check this during the implementation of this operation and reverse the order of the vectors in the cross product if needed.

Another operation of particular interest is a *point-line test*, where you can find where a given point lies with respect to a given directed line. As stated previously, when a point lies on the line, the vector in $\mathbf{RP}^2$ space representing the point will lie on the plane representing this line and therefore it will be perpendicular to the plane's normal. This makes the dot product the perfect tool for this check. If a result of a dot product of vector representing the point and the normal of the plane is zero we can be sure that the point lies on the line. Because the normal of the plane defines its positive side and the right side of the directed line, if the point doesn't lie on the line, you can use the sign of the dot product to determine the side of the line the point lies on. Thanks to the assumption of $z > 0$ for coordinates of the vector representing the point, the result of the dot product will always be positive when the point lies on the right side of the directed line and it will always be negative when it lies on the left side of this line.

The last important basic operation on points and directed lines is finding the intersection point of a pair of lines. Again, the vector representing the point you are looking for has to be perpendicular to the normals of both planes representing the given directed lines, as shown on Figure 2.4.2b. By performing the cross product on these normals, you can find the vector in $\mathbf{RP}^2$ space representing the point you are looking for. To make sure that the $z > 0$ condition is met, even when $z < 0$ in the resulting vector, the entire vector has to be scaled by –1 to obtain the proper vector representing the point. If the given directed lines are parallel, the resulting vector will have the coordinate $z = 0$, which indicates that intersection point of these lines doesn't exist.

Precise Geometrical Computations in RP² Using Integer Coordinates

All of the operations described previously are based mainly on basic comparisons and dot and cross products of vectors. Both dot and cross products require addition, subtraction, and multiplication to implement. Note that if only vectors with integer coordinates are used, none of these operations will result in a fractional number, or a vector with fractional components. Therefore, by using only points with integer coordinates, these operations are guaranteed to return exact results, free of numerical errors that are inherent to floating point computations. Unfortunately, to make such a system usable, you have to make sure it works correctly with floating point input data as most existing systems, like modeling packages, can provide only floating point data. In most cases, you can choose a certain finite precision (for example, 10^{-3}), scale the data up, round it to nearest integers and, after performing all necessary operations, scale the result back. Note that rounding used here only affects positions of input points, but doesn't affect further operations, especially tests where it should be determined whether or not a point lies on a line.

Number Range Limits in Geometrical Computations in RP²

Because integer multiplication is a frequent operation in computations described in this chapter, you have to be aware of range limits of an integer representation. Consecutive multiplications quickly make the values you operate on large. To estimate ranges used in each stage of computations, you can use symmetrical range estimates $[-a,a]$ that define the minimum and maximum values that can be achieved at a given stage in a worst-case scenario. Knowing the range of input values, you can easily estimate the range of results of operations such as addition, subtraction, and multiplication and using this, the range of results of more complex operations like dot and cross products can be estimated. Having two values within ranges $[-a,a]$ and $[-b,b]$, you can be sure that their sum will be within range $[-a-b,a+b]$. Because the estimated ranges are symmetrical, the difference of a pair of given values results in values within exactly the same range $[-a-b,a+b]$. Similarly, the result of multiplication of two values within ranges $[-a,a]$ and $[-b,b]$ can be proven to lie within the range $[-ab,ab]$. Knowing this, you can analyze the numerical ranges required for performing computations at every step.

Because consecutive operations on points result in consecutive multiplications introducing large numbers, you can limit operations to three classes of objects that are enough for most geometric computations. The first class is a point being a part of input data. Such a point has its coordinates in $\mathbf{R}^2$ space given explicitly (for example, imported from a digital content creation program) and therefore you can easily predict the range of its coordinates based on game level extents and the required precision of its representation. The extents and precision are used for scaling model coordinates during the import of the data. Although it is desired to increase allowed range of coordinates of input points because it allows for larger game levels and/or more precision, this range is the main factor influencing all numerical ranges used in computations. The numerical range analysis aims to find a compromise between algorithm efficiency (depending on ranges of intermediate values) and range and precision of input data, because large integers require both more storage space as well as more processing power.

The second class of objects is directed lines computed as lines passing through a pair of points from input data. Input point coordinates are given explicitly, so the normal vectors of planes representing directed lines of this class are obtained using a single cross product. You can easily estimate the ranges required to represent components of normal vectors of planes representing such lines.

The last class of objects being used is a class of points obtained as a result of intersection of a pair of lines of previous class. Vectors representing such points in $\mathbf{RP}^2$ space are the results of cross products on normal vectors of planes representing the lines, which make these vectors the results of two consecutive cross products. In effect, the range of their coordinates is larger than the range of coordinates of vectors representing other classes of objects.

Because of a growing numerical range of coordinates used with the various classes of objects, you should aim to use only these three classes of objects (points from input data, lines led through such points, and intersection points of these lines). Operations resulting in objects outside these three classes, like defining a directed line passing through an intersection point, should be avoided because they can make resulting numbers grow without a control. Fortunately, many geometrical algorithms, including *constructive solid geometry* (CSG) algorithms, can be implemented in a way that doesn't require operations on objects outside the three classes specified. If for some reason an algorithm cannot be implemented with just the three listed classes, you can introduce new classes of objects, such as lines passing through a pair of intersection points. But be aware that the numerical range required for operations on these new classes can grow exponentially with the number of classes of objects and this range should be estimated for each introduced class.

The analysis of numerical range being used in described operations is shown in Table 2.4.1. It can be seen that subsequent operations make numerical range of resulting values grow quickly. Table 2.4.2 shows the maximum ranges of input point coordinates and ranges of further computation results depending on number of bits used to perform the computations. Even with 64-bit integers, the allowed input point coordinate range is only [–20936,20936]. In some applications, the [–20936,20936] range can be sufficient and in this case algorithms described can be implemented without much effort, allowing geometric computations even on devices lacking floating point support (for example, cell phones). However, in many applications this range won't allow for required precision and game level extents. For these applications, long integer math can provide a solution.

Table 2.4.1 Numerical Ranges of Results in Used Projective Space Operations for Two-Dimensional Geometry

Object	Equation	Coordinates	Range
Input point (**P**)	$\mathbf{P} = [x,y,1]$	x,y	$[-n,n]$
		z	1
Normal of a plane (**N**)	$\mathbf{N} = \mathbf{P}_1 \times \mathbf{P}_2$	x,y	$[-2n,2n]$
		z	$[-2n^2,2n^2]$
Intersection point (**Q**)	$\mathbf{Q} = \mathbf{N}_1 \times \mathbf{N}_2$	x,y	$[-8n^3,8n^3]$
		z	$[-8n^2,8n^2]$
Input point check versus line	$\mathbf{N} \cdot \mathbf{P}$		$[-6n^2,6n^2]$
Intersection point check versus line	$\mathbf{N} \cdot \mathbf{Q}$		$[-48n^4,48n^4]$

Table 2.4.2 Maximum Values Allowed at Every Step with Respect to Length of Used Integer Representation

Range	16 Bits	32 Bits	64 Bits
$[-n,n]$	5	81	20 936
$[-2n,2n]$	10	162	41 872
$[-2n^2,2n^2]$	50	13 122	876 632 192
$[-8n^2,8n^2]$	200	52 488	3 506 528 768
$[-8n^3,8n^3]$	1 000	4 251 528	73 412 686 286 848
$[-48n^4,48n^4]$	30 000	2 066 242 608	9 221 808 000 608 698 368
Maximum value	32 767	2 147 483 647	9 223 372 036 854 775 807

To find out the length of the integer representation required for a given application, you have to decide how large the game level extents are and how much precision you need. With that information, you can derive the required range of integer coordinates being used. For example, if desired workspace size is [–1000,1000] range of point coordinates and required precision is 0.01, after scaling the point data during the import, the required range of input coordinates of points used in further operations is equal to [–100000,100000]. Then you can find out the ranges required to carry out operations being used without risking overflows. This in turn gives you the number of bits required for geometry representation with integers (be sure to include the sign bit in this number of bits).

Although the maximum range used can require a large number of bits for integer representation (often over 64 bits), this number is required only for the most complex cases; most basic operations can be performed using much shorter integers. To find the number of bits required, in every case an analysis similar to the one given previously should be done. The range estimates given in Table 2.4.1 can be useful during implementation of used long integer math, because these estimates can be used to find required range of integers according to input data point coordinate range.

Example Application of Operations in $\mathbf{RP}^2$

To prove the usefulness of geometric operations in $\mathbf{RP}^2$ space, a simple algorithm performing Boolean operations on polygons is presented. For simplicity, polygons are assumed to be convex, as every set of input polygons can be partitioned into a set of convex polygons. A convex polygon can be described with a loop of edges. Each edge is defined by its points and a directed line running along the edge in such a direction that the interior of the polygon lies on the right side of this line. The example assumes that in a polygon no three vertices are collinear.

The basic operation useful during Boolean operations on convex polygons is cutting a polygon with a directed line. This operation can be accomplished using the following algorithm, which is illustrated in Figure 2.4.3:

1. For each polygon vertex, determine which side of the cutting line the vertex lies on or whether it lies on the line.
2. If there are no vertices on the right side of the cutting line or there are no vertices on its left side, stop. The line doesn't intersect the interior of the polygon.
3. Split each edge for which starting and ending points lie on opposite sides of the cutting line. Two edges are created in place of the edge being split. The middle point of the split is the intersection of the line running along the edge and the cutting line.
4. Create the first of resulting polygons from edges lying on the right side of the cutting line. Close this polygon by adding an edge running along the cutting line between vertices lying on this line (if the initial polygon was correct, there are exactly two such vertices).
5. Similarly, create the second resulting polygon from edges lying on the left side of the cutting line. Close this polygon by adding an edge running along the cutting line, but in the opposite direction (reverse the normal of the plane defining the cutting line in $\mathbf{RP}^2$ space).

It's worthwhile to note that this algorithm uses only the three classes of objects in $\mathbf{RP}^2$ space listed earlier. In step 3, new intersection points are introduced to the polygon and in steps 3, 4, and 5, existing directed lines are used to define polygon edges. The algorithm doesn't create new lines using existing points, so it isn't important whether the vertices in the initial polygon are points from input data or intersection points.

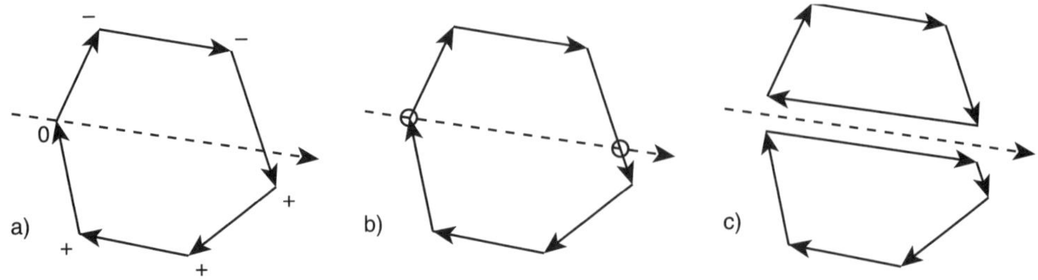

FIGURE 2.4.3 Cutting a polygon with a line: (a) determining which side of the line each vertex lies on (steps 1 and 2), (b) finding intersection vertices and splitting edges (step 3), (c) separating edges and closing resulting polygons (steps 4 and 5).

The algorithm will work flawlessly on both types of vertices. It's also worthwhile to note that in step 3, the splitting point of the edge has to be computed as an intersection of a pair of lines. In the case of floating point–based computations this point could have been computed using linear interpolation of edge endpoints based on distances of these points to the cutting line. In the case of integer-based operations using **RP**^{2} space, you don't have an operation computing point-line distance defined. However, as this algorithm shows, this operation isn't required in this case.

Although cutting polygons with lines can be a useful operation by itself, you can use this operation to implement Boolean set operations on polygons. The following algorithm describes the initial steps required to perform such operations, which is illustrated in Figure 2.4.4.

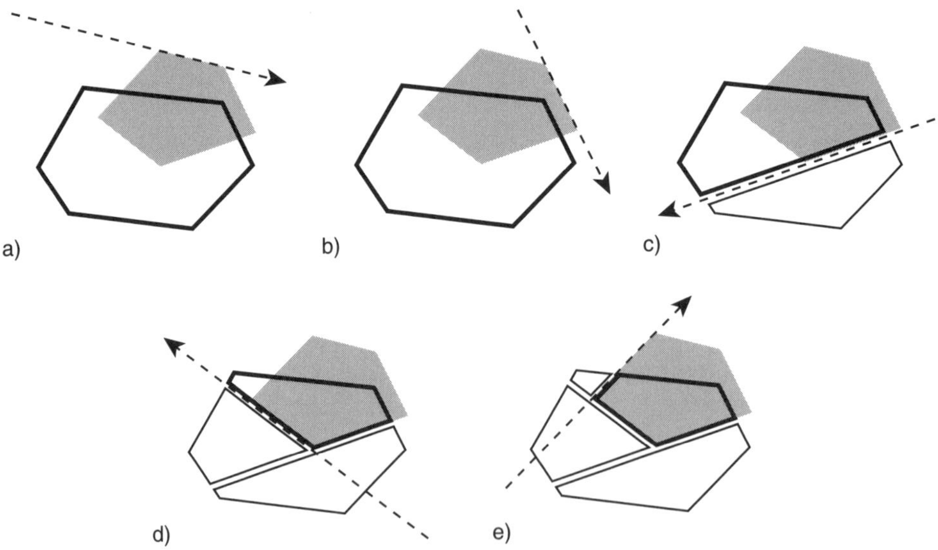

FIGURE 2.4.4 Finding the intersection of a pair of polygons. Steps (a) to (c) show resulting polygons after each cut done during step 3 of the algorithm. Initial polygon **B** is filled gray, current polygon **C** is outlined with thick line, and polygons in set **outA** have normal outline.

1. Let **A** and **B** be a pair of given polygons.
2. Let **C** be a copy of **A** that will be used for finding the intersection.
3. For each edge of polygon **B**, cut polygon **C** using directed line associated with this edge. Add the part of former **C** lying on the left side of the cutting line to set **outA** and replace polygon **C** with the part of this polygon lying on the right side of the cutting line. If no part of **C** lies on the right side of the line, stop, as polygons **A** and **B** don't intersect.
4. Repeat step 3 for each edge of **B** until all edges have been considered (unless the algorithm was stopped).

When this algorithm finishes, providing that initial polygons **A** and **B** intersected (indicating that the algorithm didn't stop early), the polygon **C** after all operations will be the intersection of initial polygons **A** and **B** and set **outA** will contain parts of initial polygon **A** lying outside polygon **B**. Basic Boolean operations on initial **A** and **B** can be expressed as follows, which can be seen in Figure 2.4.5.

$$\mathbf{A} \cup \mathbf{B} = \mathbf{outA} \cup \mathbf{B}$$
$$\mathbf{A} \cap \mathbf{B} = \mathbf{C}$$
$$\mathbf{A} \backslash \mathbf{B} = \mathbf{outA}$$

In these formulas, ∪ is the union of a pair polygons, ∩ is their intersection, and \ is their difference. When operating on sets of polygons, ∪ is a union of a pair of sets. When polygons in set **outA** and polygon **B** don't overlap, the union **outA** ∪ **B** can be computed by simply adding polygon **B** to set **outA**.

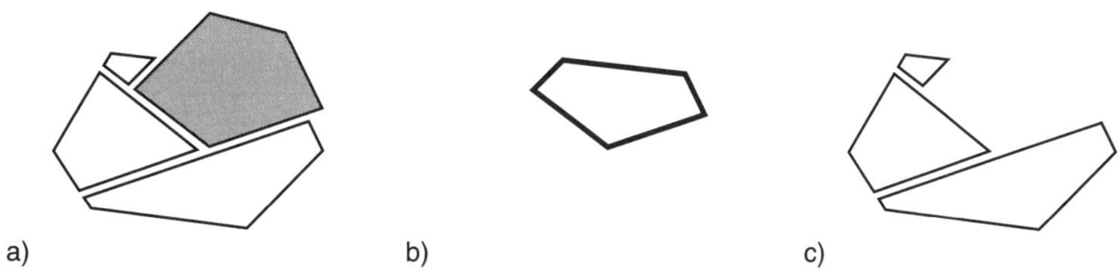

FIGURE 2.4.5 Boolean operations on polygons: (a) sum of polygons **A** and **B** as a sum of **outA** and **B**, (b) intersection of polygons **A** and **B** as resulting polygon **C**, (c) difference of polygons **A** and **B** as resulting set **outA**.

Because this algorithm is based entirely on integer operations in $\mathbf{RP}^2$ space, it can be proven to work with all possible sets of valid input data, which is rarely the case when it comes to algorithms performing Boolean operations. However, this algorithm might not be useable in all applications because it can generate T-intersections in a resulting polygon mesh. To address this problem, the algorithm could be extended to work on mesh data with connectivity information—for example, using a half-edge data structure. But this extension is outside of the scope of this chapter and is not presented here—this algorithm is demonstrated only as a proof-of-concept for integer operations using **RP**^{2} space.

Extension into the Third Dimension

The previous discussion introduced the use of projective space for efficient and error-free computational geometry operations in two-dimensional space. The extension to the third dimension, critical for most of today's games, is straightforward, but it requires using four-dimensional vectors and operations on them. The CD-ROM contains a document providing a discussion similar to the one you've read here, for three-dimensional space and **RP**^{3} projective space.

ON THE CD

Conclusion

Many geometric algorithms suffer from rounding and loss of precision due to used numerical representation, which may lead to wrong behavior of such algorithms in the case of nearly collinear or coplanar points in input data. This is especially true for constructive solid geometry (CSG) algorithms, because collinear and coplanar cases present a serious problem in many implementations. The presented operations in projective space allow implementation of most of these algorithms in such a way that they can be proven to operate correctly for all cases of valid input data. This is done at the cost of additional computational power required for operations on large integers, but resulting robustness of the algorithms based on operations in projective space may be worth its cost. On the other hand, as 64-bit processors and their new instruction sets extensions will become more and more common, the extra computational cost of such algorithms doesn't have to be very large if long integer math is implemented in an efficient way.

Robust CSG algorithms used in a digital content creation tool or in-engine level editor will give artists and "mod" developers more freedom and will save development time when they would otherwise have to find workarounds where other CSG algorithms failed. Also, the robustness of a CSG algorithm can be critical when such an algorithm is used in the game itself, allowing the player to interact with the environment in every imaginable way without concern that a CSG failure will result in a catastrophic gameplay bug.

References

[Hollash91] Hollasch, Steven R. "2.1 Vector Operations and Points in Four-Dimensional Space," in "Four-Space Visualization of 4D Objects," Chapter 2, available online at http://steve.hollasch.net/thesis/chapter2.html.

[Young02] Young, Thomas. "Using Vector Fractions for Exact Geometry," *Game Programming Gems 3,* pp. 160–169.

2.5

XenoCollide: Complex Collision Made Simple

Gary Snethen, Crystal Dynamics

gary@snethen.com

This gem introduces a new collision algorithm that works on a limitless variety of convex shapes, including boxes, spheres, ellipsoids, capsules, cylinders, cones, pyramids, frustums, prisms, pie slices, convex polytopes, and many other common shapes. The algorithm detects overlap and can also provide contact normals, points of contact, and penetration depths for rigid body dynamics. A working implementation, along with a simple rigid body simulator, is provided on the CD-ROM for immediate use and experimentation.

ON THE CD

The algorithm is simple and geometric in nature, so it's easy to visualize and debug. The algorithm reduces to a series of point-plane clipping checks, so the math can be understood by anyone familiar with dot products and cross products.

Introduction

Creating a robust collision system can require a great deal of time and effort. The most common approach is to choose a handful of basic primitives and create $O(N^2)$ separate collision routines, one for each possible pair of primitives. Using this approach, the amount of coding, testing, and debugging can quickly balloon out of control. Even a small set of four simple primitives, such as spheres, boxes, capsules, and triangles will require 10 separate collision routines. Each of these routines will have special cases and failure modes that need to be tested and debugged. Each time an additional collision primitive is added, multiple new collision routines need to be created, one for each pre-existing primitive plus an additional routine to collide the new primitive with itself.

This gem introduces an efficient and compact collision algorithm that works on every convex shape commonly found in real-time collision systems. New shapes can be quickly and easily introduced without changing the algorithm's implementation. All that's required to add a new shape is a simple mathematical description of the shape. If desired, collision shapes can be inexpensively modified in real-time for use on animated objects.

The algorithm is named *XenoCollide.* It is an example of a broader class of algorithms based on a technique called *Minkowski Portal Refinement* (MPR).

XenoCollide and the MPR technique presented in this gem are novel, but they share important similarities to the GJK collision detection algorithm introduced by [GJK88]. The differences are outlined in the section entitled "Comparison of MPR and GJK."

This gem proceeds by introducing support mappings and Minkowski differences. If you are already comfortable with these concepts, you can skip ahead to the section entitled "Detecting Collision Using Minkowski Portal Refinement."

Representing Shapes with Support Mappings

Algorithms that work on a large number of shapes need a uniform way to represent those shapes. XenoCollide relies on support mappings to fill this role. Support mappings provide a simple and elegant way to represent a limitless variety of convex shapes.

A *support mapping* is a mathematical function (often a very simple one) that takes a direction vector as input and returns the point on a convex shape that lies farthest in that direction. (Support mappings are frequently defined as returning the point farthest in the direction opposite the normal. I've chosen the opposite convention to avoid an excessive number of confusing negations in the equations.) If multiple points satisfy the requirement, any one of the points can be chosen, so long as the same point is always returned for any given input.

Support mappings are intuitive and easy to visualize. Imagine that you are given the normal of a plane. If you slide this plane toward a convex shape along the plane's normal, the plane and the shape will eventually touch, as illustrated in Figure 2.5.1.

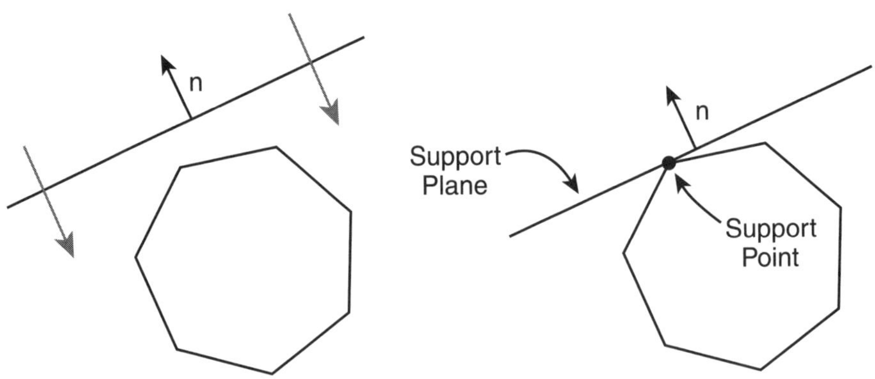

FIGURE 2.5.1 Visualization of a support mapping as a moving plane.

At the moment they touch, the shape is being supported by the plane and the point on the shape that is touching the plane is the *support point* for that plane.

If an entire edge or face touches the plane, any one of the points on the edge or face can be chosen as the support point for that normal, as shown in Figure 2.5.2.

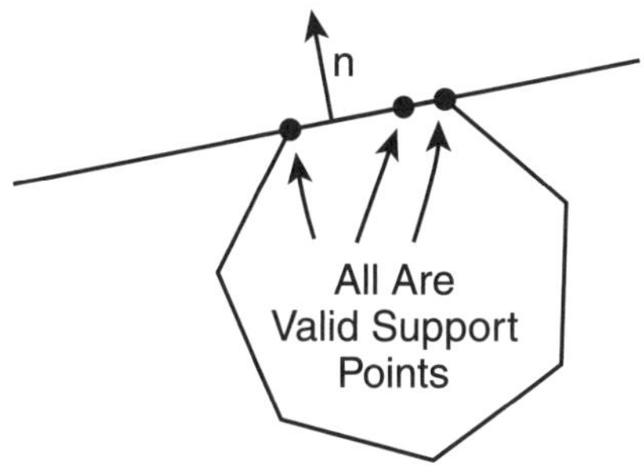

FIGURE 2.5.2 Choosing a support point when an entire edge supports the plane.

Basic Shapes

Many common shapes have simple support mappings. Consider a sphere of radius r, centered at the origin. If you slide a plane from any direction, **n**, the first point you will encounter on the sphere will be in the direction **n** from the origin at a distance r, as illustrated in Figure 2.5.3.

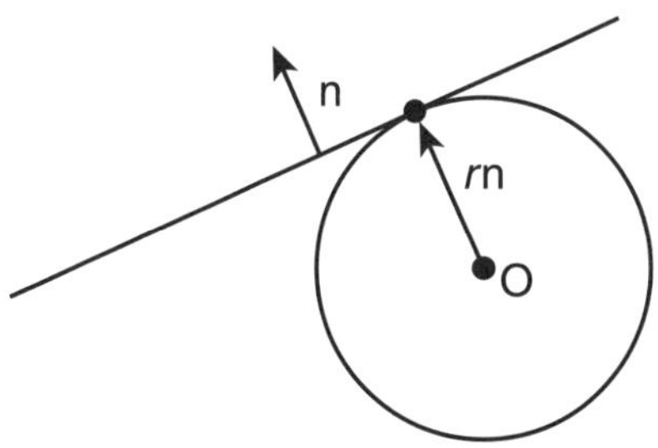

FIGURE 2.5.3 Support mapping of a sphere.

Written as a function, the support mapping for the sphere is as follows:

$$\mathbf{S}_{\text{sphere}}(\mathbf{n}) = r\mathbf{n} \tag{2.5.1}$$

Table 2.5.1 lists the support mappings for several other common shapes.

Table 2.5.1 Support Mappings for Simple Basic Shapes

Shape	Description	Support Mapping
•	Point	$\mathbf{p}$
	Segment	$\begin{bmatrix} r_x \operatorname{sgn} n_x & 0 & 0 \end{bmatrix}$
	Rectangle	$\begin{bmatrix} r_x \operatorname{sgn} n_x & 0 & 0 \end{bmatrix}$
	Box	$\begin{bmatrix} r_x \operatorname{sgn} n_x & r_y \operatorname{sgn} n_y & r_z \operatorname{sgn} n_z \end{bmatrix}$
	Disc	$r \frac{\begin{bmatrix} n_x & n_y & 0 \end{bmatrix}}{\left\| \begin{bmatrix} n_x & n_y & 0 \end{bmatrix} \right\|}$
	Sphere	$r\mathbf{n}$
	Ellipse	$\frac{\begin{bmatrix} r_x^2 n_x & r_y^2 n_y & 0 \end{bmatrix}}{\left\| \begin{bmatrix} r_x n_x & r_y n_y & 0 \end{bmatrix} \right\|}$
	Ellipsoid	$\frac{\begin{bmatrix} r_x^2 n_x & r_y^2 n_y & r_z^2 n_z \end{bmatrix}}{\left\| \begin{bmatrix} r_x n_x & r_y n_y & r_z n_z \end{bmatrix} \right\|}$

Translating and Rotating Support Mappings

The support mappings in Table 2.5.1 represent shapes that are axis-aligned and centered at the origin. To support shapes in world space, you need to rotate and translate support mappings.

The support mapping for a rotated and translated object can be found by first transforming $\mathbf{n}$ into the object's local space, and then finding the support point in local space, and finally transforming the resulting support point back into world space:

$$\mathbf{S}_{\text{world}}(\mathbf{n}) = \mathbf{R}\,\mathbf{S}_{\text{local}}(\mathbf{R}^{-1}\,\mathbf{n}) + \mathbf{T} \tag{2.5.2}$$

For the remainder of this gem, all support mappings are in world coordinates and account for the rotation and translation of their respective shapes.

Compound Support Mappings

Support mappings provide an efficient and compact way to represent basic shapes. They can also be used to represent more complex shapes. This is done by mathematically combining the support mappings of two or more simple primitives.

You can "shrink-wrap" a set of shapes by finding the support points for each shape and returning the point that is farthest along the direction vector. For example, a disc centered at the origin can be shrink-wrapped with a translated point to create a cone, as given by Equation 2.5.3.

$$\mathbf{S}_{\text{cone}}(\mathbf{n}) = \mathbf{maxsupport}\left(\mathbf{S}_{point}(\mathbf{n}), \mathbf{S}_{disc}(\mathbf{n})\right) \quad (2.5.3)$$

To simplify the appearance of compound support mappings, drop the (**n**) from the function names. Every support mapping requires a normal, so you can assume it's always present:

$$\mathbf{S}_{\text{cone}} = \mathbf{maxsupport}\left(\mathbf{S}_{point}, \mathbf{S}_{disc}\right) \quad (2.5.4)$$

A second way to combine support mappings is to add them together. This results in one shape being "inflated by" or "swept about" the other. For example, if you add the support mapping of a small sphere to the support mapping of a large box, you'll get a larger box with rounded corners, as given by Equation 2.5.5:

$$\mathbf{S}_{\text{smoothbox}} = \mathbf{S}_{box} + \mathbf{S}_{sphere} \quad (2.5.5)$$

Some useful combinations of support mappings are listed in Table 2.5.2.

Table 2.5.2 Support Mappings for Compound Shapes

Shape	Description	Support Mapping
	Capsule	maxsupport($\mathbf{S}_{sphere}$,$\mathbf{S}_{sphere}$ + [*length* 0 0]) or $\mathbf{S}_{edge}$ + $\mathbf{S}_{sphere}$
	Lozenge	$\mathbf{S}_{rectangle}$ + $\mathbf{S}_{sphere}$
	Rounded box	$\mathbf{S}_{box}$ + $\mathbf{S}_{sphere}$
	Cylinder	maxsupport($\mathbf{S}_{disc}$,$\mathbf{S}_{disc}$ + [0 0 *height*]) or $\mathbf{S}_{edge}$ + $\mathbf{S}_{disc}$

→

Table 2.5.2 (Continued)

Shape	Description	Support Mapping
	Cone	maxsupport($\mathbf{S}_{disc}$,$\mathbf{S}_{point}$ + [0 0 *height*])
	Wheel	$\mathbf{S}_{disc} + \mathbf{S}_{sphere}$
	Frustum	maxsupport($\mathbf{S}_{rectangle1}$,$\mathbf{S}_{rectangle2}$ + [0 0 *height*])
	Polygon Polyhedron	maxsupport(S_{vert1},S_{vert2},...)

Extremely complex shapes can be easily created by algebraically combining many basic and compound shapes. These algebraic operations can be turned into intuitive controls for content creators as well. Artists and designers can use the basic shapes to sketch out the major external features of an object and then use interactive shrink-wrapping and sweeping/extruding to handle the rest.

Simplifying Collision Detection Using Minkowski Differences

Every convex shape can be treated as a convex set of points in world space. Something interesting happens if you subtract every point in one solid shape from every point in a second solid shape. If the two shapes overlap, there will be at least one point within shape A that shares the same position in world space as a point within shape B.

When one of these points is subtracted from the other, the result will be the zero vector (that is, the origin). Similarly, if the two shapes do not overlap, no point from the first shape will be equal to any point in the second shape and the new shape will not contain the origin.

Therefore, if you can detect whether the origin is in the new shape, you have detected whether or not the two original shapes are colliding.

The shape that's formed by the subtraction of one convex shape from another is called the *Minkowski difference* of the two shapes. The Minkowski difference, B–A, is also a convex shape. If B–A contains the origin, A and B must overlap. If B–A does not contain the origin, A and B are disjoint.

It would be prohibitively expensive to actually subtract every point in one shape from every point in the other. However, you can easily determine the support mapping of the Minkowski difference B–A if you're given the support mappings of A and B. Using Equation 2.5.6, you can reduce the problem of detecting collision between two convex shapes, A and B to that of determining whether the origin lies within a single convex shape, B–A.

$$\mathbf{S}_{\text{B-A}}(\mathbf{n}) = \mathbf{S}_B(\mathbf{n}) - \mathbf{S}_A(-\mathbf{n}) \tag{2.5.6}$$

Detecting Collision Using Minkowski Portal Refinement

Up to this point, everything described applies equally well to GJK and XenoCollide. For the remainder of this gem, the discussion will focus on XenoCollide and the MPR technique. If you're interested in reading more about GJK, [van den Bergen03], [GJK88], and [Cameron97] are excellent references. If you want additional background and details on XenoCollide, please see [Snethen07].

Here's the pseudocode for XenoCollide:

```
// Phase 1: Portal Discovery
find_origin_ray();
find_candidate_portal();
while ( origin ray does not intersect candidate )
{
    choose_new_candidate();
}

// Phase 2: Portal Refinement
while (true)
{
    if (origin inside portal) return hit;
    find_support_in_direction_of_portal();
    if (origin outside support plane) return miss;
    if (support plane close to portal) return miss;
    choose_new_portal();
}
```

Each step is described in detail next.

The *find_origin_ray();* Step

Start by finding a point known to be in the interior of the Minkowski difference B–A. Such a point can be easily obtained by taking a point known to be inside B and subtracting a point known to be inside A. The geometric center (or center of mass) is a convenient point to use. However, any deep interior point will work. The point that results from the subtraction is the *interior point* of B–A. The interior point is labeled V0 in Figure 2.5.4.

The interior point is important because it lies on the inside of B–A. If the ray drawn from the interior point through the origin, called the *origin ray*, passes through the surface of B–A before it encounters the origin, the origin lies outside of B–A. Conversely, if the ray passes through the origin before the surface, the origin is inside of B–A.

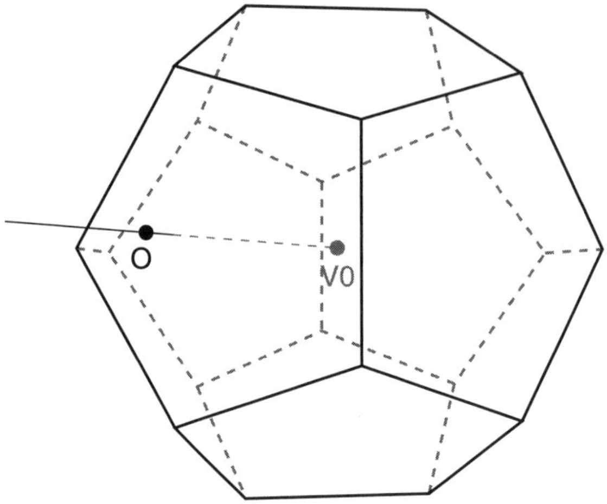

FIGURE 2.5.4 Step 1 involves finding the origin ray.

The *find_candidate_portal();* Step

This step of the algorithm uses the support mapping of B–A to find three non-collinear points on the surface of B–A that form a triangular portal through which the origin ray may (or may not) pass. See Figure 2.5.5.

There are many ways to obtain three non-collinear surface points. XenoCollide uses the following support points:

```
// Find support in the direction of the origin ray
V1 = S( normalize(-V0) );

// Find support perpendicular to plane containing
// origin, interior point, and first support
V2 = S( normalize(V1 x V0) );

// Find support perpendicular to plane containing
// interior point and first two supports
V3 = S( normalize((V2-V0) x (V1-V0)) );
```

The *while (origin ray does not intersect candidate)* Step

You now test the candidate triangle to determine whether the origin ray intersects it. You do this by testing whether the origin lies on the inside of each of the three planes formed by the triangle edges and the interior point—(v0,v1,v2); (v0, v2, v3); and (v0,v3,v1). If the origin lies within all three planes, you've found a valid portal and can move on to the next step. If not, you need to choose a new portal candidate and try again.

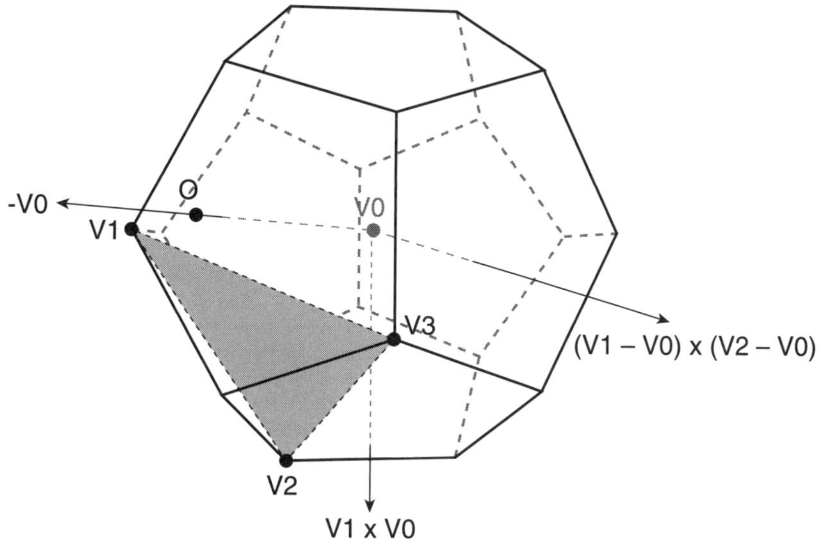

FIGURE 2.5.5 Step 2 involves finding a candidate portal.

The *choose_new_candidate();* Step

If the origin lies outside one of the planes, use that plane's outer-facing normal to find a new support point, as illustrated in Figure 2.5.6.

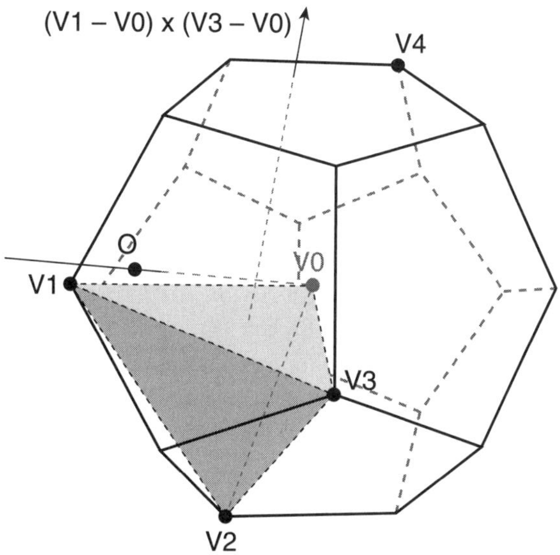

FIGURE 2.5.6 Step 3 involves finding a new candidate portal.

This new support point is used to replace the triangle vertex that lies on the inside of the plane. The resulting support points provide you with a new portal candidate (see Figure 2.5.7); repeat the loop until you obtain a hit.

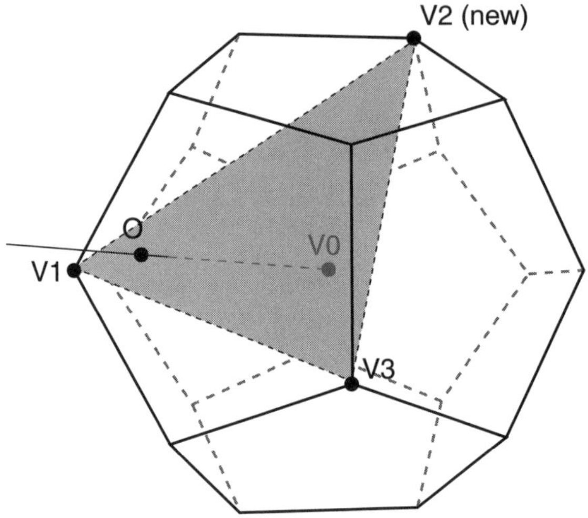

FIGURE 2.5.7 Step 4 involves finding a valid portal.

The *if (origin inside portal) return hit;* Step

The points V0, V1, V2, and V3 form a tetrahedron. Due to the convexity of B–A, this entire tetrahedron lies inside B–A. If the origin lies within the tetrahedron, it must also lie within B–A. You know that the origin lies within three of these faces, because the origin ray starts at V0 and passes through the portal, which forms the opposite side of the tetrahedron. If the origin lies within the portal, it lies within the tetrahedron and therefore lies within B–A. In this case, you return with a hit.

The *find_support_in_direction_of_portal();* Step

If you make it here, the origin lies on the far side of the portal. However, you don't know whether it lies within B–A nearby on the outside of the portal or whether it lies completely outside of B–A. You need more information about what lies on the far side of the portal, so you should use the exterior facing normal of the portal to obtain a new support point that lies outside of the portal's plane. See Figure 2.5.8.

The *if (origin outside support plane) return miss;* Step

If the origin lies outside of the new support plane formed by the support normal and the new support point, the origin lies outside B–A and the algorithm reports a miss.

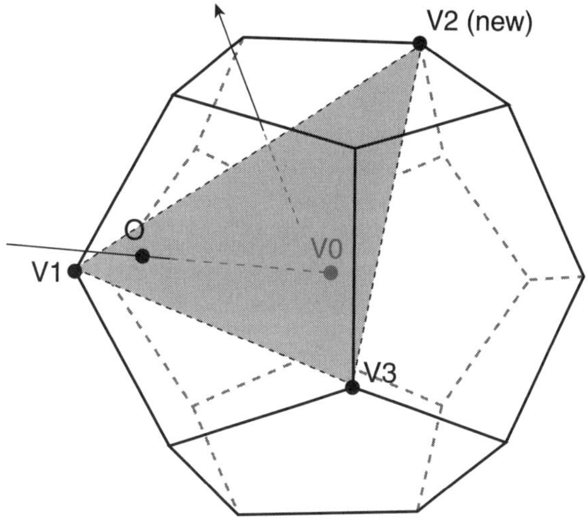

FIGURE 2.5.8 Step 5 involves finding a new support point in direction of portal.

The *choose_new_portal();* Step

The origin lies between the portal and the support plane, so you need to refine your search by finding a new portal that is closer to the surface of B–A. Consider the tetrahedron formed by the support point and the portal.

The origin passes into the tetrahedron through the portal and is therefore guaranteed to exit the tetrahedron through one of the three outer faces formed by the support point and the three edges of the portal. This step determines which of the three outer faces the ray passes through and replaces the old portal with this new portal. To determine which of the three outer faces the origin ray passes through, you test the origin against the three planes—(V4, V0, V1); (V4, V0, V2); and (V4, V0, V3).

The origin will lie on the same side of two of these planes. The face that borders these two planes becomes the new portal, as illustrated in Figure 2.5.9.

The *if (support plane close to portal) return miss;* Step

As the algorithm iterates, the refined portals will rapidly approach the surface of B–A; however, if B–A has a curved surface, the origin may lie infinitesimally close to this curved surface. In this case, the refined portals may require an arbitrary number of iterations to pass the origin. To terminate under these conditions, you have to rely on a tolerance. When the portal gets sufficiently close to the surface (as measured by the distance between the portal and its parallel support plane), you terminate the algorithm. You can terminate with a hit or a miss, depending on whether you prefer to err on the side of imprecise positive or negative results.

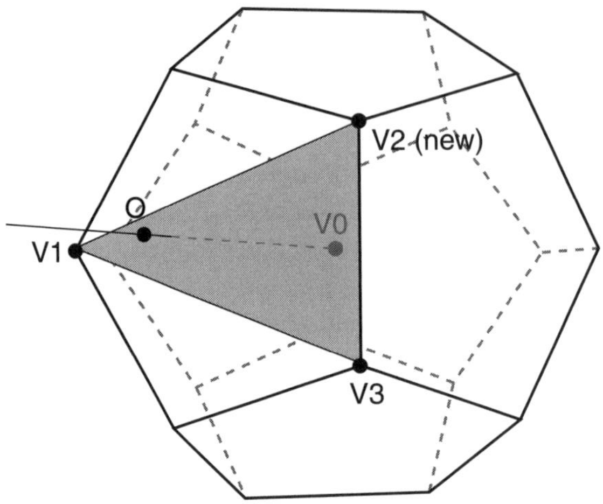

FIGURE 2.5.9 Step 6 involves establishing the new portal.

For physical simulation, it's generally better to err on the side of a false negative (that is, returning a miss even though the point may be slightly below the surface). Very slight penetration won't be noticed, but any visible gap at the contact point would appear unnatural.

Termination

The algorithm will continue running until one of the following conditions is met:

- The origin lies on the inside of a portal (hit)
- The origin lies on the outside of a support plane (miss)
- The distance between the portal and its parallel support plane drops below a small tolerance (close call—can be treated as a hit or miss depending on the application)

A formal proof of termination is beyond the scope of this gem. However, an informal proof can be found in [Snethen07].

Using MPR for Contact Information

If you need only to detect overlap, MPR can be terminated as soon as the portal passes the origin. However, if your application requires contact information, MPR can continue executing to discover a contact point, contact normal, and penetration depth.

MPR offers several possible ways of acquiring contact information. The technique employed by XenoCollide is to simply continue projecting the origin ray out to the surface of the Minkowski difference. This represents pushing the objects away from each other along the line connecting their interior points until they are just touching and then using the normal of this first contact as the collision normal. This is efficient and simple, and it results in stable contact information.

A second choice is to find the relative velocity of a pair of overlapping points, one from each object, and then project a new ray from the origin to the surface of B–A along the negative direction of the velocity vector. This results in a calculation of penetration along the direction of motion, which may result in more realistic dynamic collisions.

Additional Optimizations

XenoCollide exhibits good performance. However, highly optimized routines that target specific pairs of shapes will inevitably be faster than any general-purpose routine. Readers interested in pursuing ideal performance can begin with XenoCollide as a foundation to handle all shapes and then add special-case routines for handling the pairs of shapes that will benefit the most from optimization later in development. One obvious candidate for optimization is a sphere-sphere check, which has minimal cost when implemented as a special case.

Another important optimization is caching the results of each collision test to bootstrap the same check in the next timestep. If a separating support plane is found that proves that two objects do not collide, this same separating plane can be used as an early-out separation test in subsequent frames. Likewise, if a portal is found that lies outside the origin, this same portal can often be used to quickly verify that the objects are still in contact.

The support mapping functions are called multiple times during each collision check. To maximize performance, transform, normalization, and function call overhead should be kept to a minimum. In some cases, it may be better to perform the support mapping evaluation in world space. For example, it's generally less expensive to check a segment using dot(**n**, **d**) in world space than it is to transform **n** to local space, test only the *x* component, and then transform the result back again.

Comparison of MPR and GJK

GJK was one of the inspirations for MPR. GJK also supports a limitless variety of convex shapes, but it suffers from several limitations that MPR attempts to correct:

- The simplex refinement algorithm in GJK is based on an algebraic formulation that isn't intuitive to most game programmers. This formulation relies on determinants and cofactors, which are notoriously sensitive to floating point precision problems. The combination of precision issues and hard-to-visualize mathematics makes it difficult for many game developers to implement GJK robustly.
- As a result of the previous issue, many variations on GJK have been created that attempt to frame GJK as a geometric problem rather than an algebraic one. However, every approach to GJK requires considering the Voronoi regions of 8 to 15 features (points, edges, faces, and interior) of a tetrahedron, to see which is closest to the origin. This can be a complex and potentially expensive task due to the many different conditions and branching operations.

- In the general case, GJK doesn't provide an accurate contact normal, penetration depth, or point of surface contact. A separate algorithm, such as EPA [van den Bergen03], is required to obtain this information.

MPR addresses each of these issues:

- MPR is simple and geometric. Each step of the technique can be easily visualized and verified on-screen, which makes it easier to understand, test, and debug.
- MPR requires fewer branching tests. Instead of choosing among 8 to 15 separate features, only 2 or 3 need to be evaluated.
- MPR can be used both to detect collision and to identify collision details that are well-behaved and consistent from frame to frame.

Conclusion

This gem introduced a simple algorithm for detecting collision among shapes chosen from a limitless pool of useful convex designs. Introducing new shapes is extremely easy and can be wrapped in a graphical user interface for artists and designers. The algorithm provides a robust foundation for a general purpose collision system for gameplay and rigid body dynamics. The algorithm is efficient; however, if additional performance is ever required, optimized pair-specific routines can be layered on the generic framework as needed.

Acknowledgements

The author wishes to thank the managers, programmers, and developers of Crystal Dynamics for their support and review of this gem. The author would also like to thank Erin Catto, for his friendship and encouragement to share this work.

References

[Cameron97] Cameron, S. "Enhancing GJK: Computing Minimum and Penetration Distances Between Convex Polyhedra," *Proceedings of IEEE International Conference on Robotics and Automation (1997)*, pp. 3112–3117.

[GJK88] Gilbert, E.G., Johnson, D.W., and Keerthi, S.S. "A Fast Procedure for Computing the Distance Between Complex Objects in Three-Dimensional Space," *IEEE Journal of Robotics and Automation*, Vol. 4, No. 2 (1988), pp. 193–203.

[Snethen07] Snethen, Gary. "XenoCollide Website," available online at http://www.xenocollide.com, September, 2007.

[van den Bergen03] van den Bergen, Gino. *Collision Detection in Interactive 3D Environments*, Morgan Kauffman, 2003.

2.6

Efficient Collision Detection Using Transformation Semantics

José Gilvan Rodrigues Maia, UFC

gilvanmaia@gmail.com

Creto Augusto Vidal, UFC

cvidal@lia.ufc.br

Joaquim Bento Cavalcante-Neto, UFC

joaquimb@lia.ufc.br

How does a first-person shooter game determine whether a shot hit the head of an enemy? How can you avoid game objects passing through walls or falling to infinity? How do you check whether the player touched an item or reached a checkpoint? How does an engine determine intersections for a dynamics simulation? Although there are many possible ways for solving these problems, collision detection (CD) is a very important tool for dealing with such situations. CD allows for checking whether a given set of geometric entities are overlapping. Because of this, it plays an essential role in almost any computer game.

Current rendering technology provides support for placing geometry in a scene by means of transformation matrices. Therefore, it is important for a game programmer to know how to construct and manipulate these matrices. Moreover, collision detection methods must consider not only the shape of objects but also their corresponding matrices in order to carry out intersection tests.

This gem shows you a method for inverting transformation matrices used for placing models in games and for extracting useful *semantic* information from them. It also explains how this information can be used for implementing efficient collision detection tasks.

Affine Transforms and Games

This section briefly discusses a few concepts of linear algebra. Affine transforms are used to map between two vector spaces by means of a linear transformation (that is, a matrix multiplication) followed by an *origin shift* vector that is added to the result. An *affine transform* (also called *affine mapping*) is defined as follows:

$$\mathbf{q} = \mathbf{A}\mathbf{p} + \mathbf{t} \tag{2.6.1}$$

Affine mappings are used in many computer graphics applications. Vertex transformation from world space to camera space in a transformation pipeline, for example, is implemented using a change of basis—a particular type of affine mapping. Because computer graphics systems implement linear transformations using 4 × 4 matrices, we define the mapping in Equation 2.6.1 using block matrix form:

$$\mathbf{M} = \begin{bmatrix} \mathbf{A} & \mathbf{t} \\ \mathbf{0} & 1 \end{bmatrix} \tag{2.6.2}$$

Observe that in Equation 2.6.2 the affine mapping, **A**, is a 3 × 3 matrix and the origin shift, **t**, is a 3 × 1 (column) matrix. Except for the last item, all components in the fourth row are defined as zero. For computer games, it can be assumed that input vertices to be transformed have their homogeneous w component set to 1 before the matrix multiplication is carried out. Three-dimensional geometry is specified using ordinary Cartesian coordinates, and vertices are then processed in homogeneous coordinates.

From the game programming perspective, the problem is to detect collisions between the models in a scene. Recall that each model has a corresponding matrix that places it in world coordinates; hence, this matrix must be considered for collision detection against a given model.

Observe that typical matrices placing models in world space are affine mappings matching Equation 2.6.2, because these matrices usually arise from a combination of basic transformations, each in itself an affine mapping—scaling, rotation, and translation. These basic transformations can be used to "explain" matrices and answer some common questions about the placement of a model. What is its size? Which direction is the model facing? Where is the model's origin? Because of this, scaling, rotation, and translation are called *transformation semantics*.

Semantics can be used to simplify and speed up computations involved in the collision detection process. The next section presents an efficient decomposition method for both inverting and obtaining semantics from a transformation matrix. This answers the following questions—given a 4 × 4 array representing an affine mapping, what is its inverse, and what are its corresponding scaling, rotation, and translation parts?

Extracting Semantics from Matrices

Some semantics information can be obtained in the general case, as shown briefly next. However, in game development, you are not usually interested in a method that decomposes an arbitrary affine mapping. Instead, most of this gem focuses on matrices such as those described previously, used to place models in a typical game. This enables you to apply a more efficient method.

The General Affine Mapping Case

Can you extract some semantics from any affine mapping? Yes, you can. As shown in Equation 2.6.2, **t** represents an origin shift. Hence, the translation part is available for free—you just get it from the last column of the given matrix. Some orientation information can also be extracted easily. Take a closer look at matrix multiplication over a given vertex:

$$\mathbf{Ap} = \begin{bmatrix} A_{11} & A_{12} & A_{13} \\ A_{21} & A_{22} & A_{23} \\ A_{31} & A_{32} & A_{33} \end{bmatrix} \begin{bmatrix} p_x \\ p_y \\ p_z \end{bmatrix} = \begin{bmatrix} p_x A_{11} + p_y A_{12} + p_z A_{13} \\ p_x A_{21} + p_y A_{22} + p_z A_{23} \\ p_x A_{31} + p_y A_{32} + p_z A_{33} \end{bmatrix} \quad (2.6.3)$$

Grouping Equation 2.6.3 by each axis-aligned component from **p**, you obtain:

$$\mathbf{Ap} = p_x \begin{bmatrix} A_{11} \\ A_{21} \\ A_{31} \end{bmatrix} + p_y \begin{bmatrix} A_{12} \\ A_{22} \\ A_{32} \end{bmatrix} + p_z \begin{bmatrix} A_{13} \\ A_{23} \\ A_{33} \end{bmatrix} \quad (2.6.4)$$

Using Equation 2.6.4, it is clear that the first, second, and third columns from **A** represent the new *x*, *y*, and *z* axes, respectively, after a point gets transformed. This means you can use columns from your affine transform for solving problems considering orientation and scale—a convenient example is detailed later. Although Equation 2.6.4 provides a clear view about how the orientation of vertices is modified by matrices, only translation and orientation semantics are obtained through this analysis.

The inverse of an affine matrix is well-known, and can be written as:

$$\mathbf{M}^{-1} = \begin{bmatrix} \mathbf{A} & \mathbf{t} \\ \mathbf{0} & 1 \end{bmatrix}^{-1} = \begin{bmatrix} \mathbf{A}^{-1} & -\mathbf{A}^{-1}\mathbf{t} \\ \mathbf{0} & 1 \end{bmatrix} \quad (2.6.5)$$

Readers interested in inverting a general affine mapping Equation 2.6.2 are invited to take a look at Kevin Wu's article about this matter [Wu91].

Our Specific Case: Model Matrices

Consider a transformation matrix **M** that transforms a model from its local space into world coordinates. You can assume **M** results from a composition of a non-uniform scaling matrix, followed by as many rotations and translations as needed, in this order. This assumption is reasonable because such form is compatible with most scene representations, such as scene graphs. For convenience, **M** can be written as the product of just three matrices—**S** (scaling), **R** (rotation), and **T** (translation):

$$\mathbf{M} = \mathbf{M}_1 \ldots \mathbf{M}_k \mathbf{S} = \mathbf{TRS} \tag{2.6.6}$$

Here, each $\mathbf{M}_i$ represents rotations or translations.

Kevin Wu [Wu94] used an equivalent matrix form in his gem, and described a simple and efficient method for inverting either matrices that preserve angles between vectors or matrices that preserve vector lengths. However, his method only considers uniform scaling. Our matrix representation is more general (considers non-uniform scales) and can be rewritten using a block matrix format:

$$\mathbf{M} = \mathbf{TRS} = \begin{bmatrix} \mathbf{I} & \mathbf{t} \\ \mathbf{0} & 1 \end{bmatrix} \begin{bmatrix} \mathbf{i} & \mathbf{j} & \mathbf{k} & \mathbf{0} \\ 0 & 0 & 0 & 1 \end{bmatrix} \begin{bmatrix} s_x & 0 & 0 & 0 \\ 0 & s_y & 0 & 0 \\ 0 & 0 & s_z & 0 \\ 0 & 0 & 0 & 1 \end{bmatrix} = \begin{bmatrix} s_x\mathbf{i} & s_y\mathbf{j} & s_z\mathbf{k} & \mathbf{t} \\ 0 & 0 & 0 & 1 \end{bmatrix} \tag{2.6.7}$$

Some details about this representation must be observed: **t** represents the translation part; **i**, **j**, and **k** are column matrices that form an orthonormal basis; and s_x, s_y, and s_z are non-zero (otherwise **M** is singular) scaling factors. As **M** results from a product of basic transforms, its inverse is known and can be written as:

$$\mathbf{M}^{-1} = \left(\mathbf{TRS}\right)^{-1} = \mathbf{S}^{-1}\mathbf{R}^{-1}\mathbf{T}^{-1} = \begin{bmatrix} \mathbf{i}^{\mathrm{T}}/s_x & -\mathbf{i}\cdot\mathbf{t}/s_x \\ \mathbf{j}^{\mathrm{T}}/s_y & -\mathbf{j}\cdot\mathbf{t}/s_y \\ \mathbf{k}^{\mathrm{T}}/s_z & -\mathbf{k}\cdot\mathbf{t}/s_z \\ \mathbf{0} & \mathbf{1} \end{bmatrix} \tag{2.6.8}$$

Now, let's see how a matrix in this form can be inverted without computing any square roots. Because **i** is a unit vector, the squared scale factor in the x axis can be computed by taking the dot product of the first column with itself:

$$\left(s_x\mathbf{i}\right)\cdot\left(s_x\mathbf{i}\right) = s_x^2\left(\mathbf{i}\cdot\mathbf{i}\right) = s_x^2\left(1\right) = s_x^2 \tag{2.6.9}$$

This also holds for the second and third columns

$$\left(s_y\mathbf{j}\right)\cdot\left(s_y\mathbf{j}\right)=s_y^2\left(\mathbf{j}\cdot\mathbf{j}\right)=s_y^2\left(1\right)=s_y^2 \tag{2.6.10}$$

$$\left(s_z\mathbf{k}\right)\cdot\left(s_z\mathbf{k}\right)=s_z^2\left(\mathbf{k}\cdot\mathbf{k}\right)=s_z^2\left(1\right)=s_z^2 \tag{2.6.11}$$

This property becomes quite useful, because the squared scale factor can be used to compute the first row of the 3 × 3 part of $\mathbf{M}^{-1}$ (Equation 2.6.8) by simple division:

$$\left(\frac{s_x\mathbf{i}}{s_x^2}\right)^T=\frac{\mathbf{i}^T}{s_x} \tag{2.6.12}$$

Knowing that, you can compute the inverse as follows: compute the squared scale factors using Equations 2.6.9, 2.6.10, and 2.6.11; transpose the 3 × 3 submatrix **A** of Equation 2.6.2; and divide its resulting rows by the corresponding squared scale factors. Observe that, at this point, you have computed $\mathbf{A}^{-1}$. Finally, the product $-\mathbf{A}^{-1}\mathbf{t}$ corresponding to the last column is easily computed.

This inversion method offers the flexibility of supporting non-uniform scale, and it is quite efficient. Only 27 multiplications, three divisions, and 12 additions are required. Table 2.6.1 provides a comparison of this method with the brute-force methods (Cofactors and Gaussian Elimination with pivoting), with Wu's method for affine mappings [Wu91], and with Wu's method for angle-preserving matrices [Wu94], which only supports uniform scaling. In Table 2.6.1, only a "raw" C implementation is considered. Readers are encouraged to implement these methods using SIMD/MIMD instructions—SSE, SSE2, and so on.

Table 2.6.1 Comparison of Matrix Inversion Methods in Terms of Required Operations

Inversion Method	Divisions	Multiplications	Additions
[Wu94] (angle-preserving)	1	21	8
Our method	3	27	12
[Wu91] (general case)	1	48	22
Cofactors	1	280	101
Gaussian elimination with partial pivoting	10	51	47

Transformation semantics extraction requires a slight modification of the method presented here. As shown in Equation 2.6.2, the translation part comes for free. Square root computation over Equations 2.6.9, 2.6.10, and 2.6.11 gives you the scale factors. The rotation part can be obtained dividing the first three columns by the corresponding scale factors. Therefore, semantics extraction demands three square roots, three divisions, 18 multiplications, and six additions.

When only uniform scaling is considered, it is evident that the inversion method is reduced to Wu's method for angle-preserving matrices [Wu94]. Moreover, semantics extraction in this case demands one square root, one division, 12 multiplications, and two additions.

Now you can invert and extract semantics efficiently from a typical matrix that places models in a scene. The next section explains how semantics information can be used when performing collision detection tasks.

Using Semantics for Collision Detection Tasks

Collision detection methods for real-world applications must consider a given set of models, and this work is usually split into two successive tasks. The first task, known as *broad phase* or *collision culling*, is responsible for finding all object pairs that are in proximity—the potentially colliding set. More importantly, this phase aims at discarding distant pairs that cannot collide, thus avoiding expensive intersection tests. The next task, known as *narrow phase* or *pair processing*, consists of effective intersection tests over object pairs collected during the broad phase. Transformation semantics can be used in these collision detection tasks.

Speeding Up Broad Phase

Given N objects, potentially $O(N^2)$ pairs have to be checked for collision. Nevertheless, it happens that objects in most pairs are not even close to each other, so, many pairs can be discarded quickly—this explains why this phase is also known as *collision culling*. Spatial hashing and sweep-and-prune methods, among others, were specially designed for this purpose. Common implementations of these techniques require knowledge of the axis-aligned bounding box (AABB) tightly fitting each model in world coordinates.

Scene representations usually maintain a *local* AABB per geometric model; for example, an AABB in the model's own local space. This box also gets transformed by the model's matrix, so that it becomes an oriented bounding box (OBB) in world space. The problem at this point is the following: how can you efficiently compute the model's global AABB from its local AABB and a transformation matrix **M**? A brute-force approach transforms all eight corner vertices from the AABB first and then computes the AABB of the transformed vertices—this requires 21 branches. Avoiding not only computations but also branches is very important for improved performance. Although modern CPUs can predict the behavior of code before it is executed, branchless code may still run a bit faster.

Charles Bloom proposed an elegant, efficient solution for this problem in his game engine [Bloom06]. His approach is purely geometric and is based on the orientation semantics shown in Equation 2.6.4. Consider a min-max representation for AABBs. First, the minimum extreme vertex is transformed using the model's matrix, as usual, obtaining a point **p**. Orientation semantics are used in order to obtain the new axes in world coordinates after the model gets transformed by **M**. These axes are then multiplied by the respective box dimensions, obtaining the transformed box's edge vectors. Each sign of each component of these edges is then checked.

Observe that negative components "move" **p** towards the global AABB's minimum extreme vertex, so this extreme point is obtained by adding all negative edge components to **p**. Conversely, all positive edge components are added to **p** in order to obtain the maximum extreme vertex—this requires only nine branches. See Figure 2.6.1.

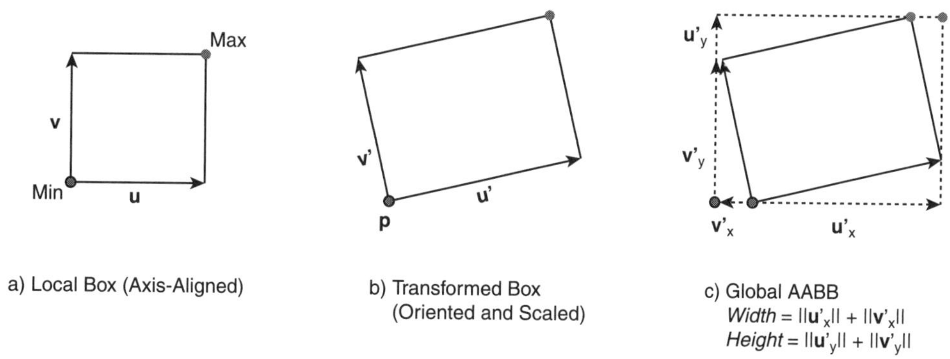

FIGURE 2.6.1 A local AABB fitting a given model (a) is transformed into world coordinates through a matrix (b). Observe that **p** lies on the boundary of the global AABB that tightly fits the transformed AABB. The global box is obtained by adding the components of the edge vectors (c) to the minima point, moving it toward the global extreme vertices.

In a gem from the previous edition, Chris Lomont explained how to perform many tricks efficiently, using floating points [Lomont07]. His approaches can be used for sign bit extraction in order to come up with a branchless implementation of this method, which is provided on the CD-ROM.

ON THE CD

Narrow Phase

The final step for collision detection is to process all pairs reported from broad phase. This task must consider two models A and B, as well as their respective transformation matrices $\mathbf{M}_A$ and $\mathbf{M}_B$. The following question must be answered: do the models intersect after they are transformed? A list of intersecting primitive pairs (that is, triangles) describing the contact surface is reported in case the models intersect.

Bounding volume hierarchies are well-suited for this problem because they provide a multi-resolution representation of the models that is useful for discarding non-intersecting parts. AABB-trees are particularly useful for dealing with deformable models (characters, for example) because they are much cheaper to refit as geometry gets deformed [Bergen97].

Let's define two useful matrices:

$$\mathbf{M}_{AB} = \mathbf{M}_B^{-1}\mathbf{M}_A \quad (2.6.13)$$

$$\mathbf{M}_{BA} = \mathbf{M}_A^{-1}\mathbf{M}_B \quad (2.6.14)$$

$\mathbf{M}_{AB}$ maps geometry from A's local space into B's local space. Conversely, $\mathbf{M}_{BA}$ maps geometry from B's local space into A's local space. These matrices can be obtained using the presented inversion method followed by a matrix multiplication. Triangles can be mapped from the local space of one object into that of another object, providing support for direct intersection tests.

Actually, transformation semantics provides flexibility for processing geometry coming from a given space (A, B, or world spaces) in a common space where computations can be carried out more comfortably. Using this approach, you can choose from seven coordinate systems for performing computations, as illustrated in Figure 2.6.2.

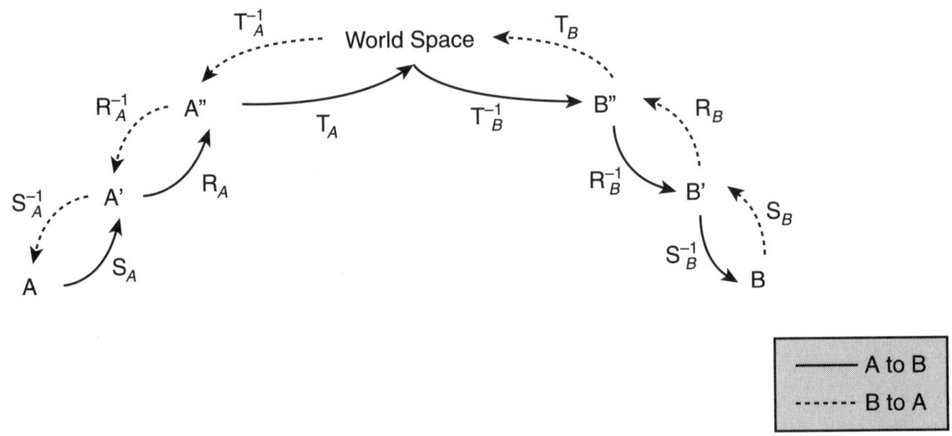

FIGURE 2.6.2 Schematic view illustrating how transformation semantics can be used for processing geometry coming from different local spaces.

In Figure 2.6.2, arrows show how geometry coming from a given space (A, B, or world) is transformed into a common space, which is more adequate for processing. Following this scheme, it can be seen that a mapping from B to A' space corresponds to $\mathbf{R}_A^{-1}\mathbf{T}_A^{-1}\mathbf{T}_B\mathbf{R}_B\mathbf{S}_B$ (transformations are ordered from right to left).

The box-box overlap test is also necessary in order to perform collision detection between a pair of AABB-trees. It is important to notice that occurrence of a non-intersecting box pair avoids many triangle-triangle tests because entire subtrees cannot collide given that their bounding boxes are not overlapping. Moreover, the box-box overlap test also allows for computing collision detection between a model and an oriented box placed in world coordinates. In a game, this can be used to determine whether the player has touched an important item in order to trigger some AI, for example.

The box-box test is usually implemented using the Separating Axis Theorem [Gottschalk96], also known as SAT. This method allows for very early exits based on iterative search for a separating axis, so that box projection intervals over that axis are not overlapping. The given boxes are intersecting only when there is no separation along any of the 15 potentially separating axes.

Bergen pointed out that about 60% of the separating axes found in SAT correspond to the normal of a box's face [Bergen97]. Based on this, he adopted an approximate intersection test between boxes (SAT-lite) that checks only this kind of separating axes. Although all separation cases cannot be handled, this test provides faster collision culling because only 6 of 15 axes are tested.

Using transformation semantics, the box-box test using SAT can be performed as follows. First, scale each box using the scale semantics extracted from its respective model's transformation matrix; after this, the intersection method can be carried out normally considering only the rotation and translation semantics during the search for a separating axis using either SAT or SAT-lite. Observe that this scale adjust causes the test to be performed as boxes are coming from A' and B' spaces (see Figure 2.6.2). Of course, any box-box intersection method can benefit from this slight modification in order to provide support for scaling models. Moreover, only 12 additional multiplications are necessary, which is not excessive given that scaling is supported efficiently.

In this example, only AABB-trees are considered in collision tests. Actually, other useful intersection tests can be performed against a model using volumes, rays, or lines placed in world space. Examples of volumes are sphere, cone, AABB, OBB, and capsule (also called a line-swept sphere).

Basically, support for testing a given primitive against an AABB-tree requires two intersection methods. The first method checks whether the primitive intersects a box coming from the transformed AABB-tree, providing means for fast collision culling of subtrees. Finally, the second method checks overlap between the primitive and a triangle from the model. This second method can be implemented by transforming triangles using the model's matrix before carrying out the intersection test.

As shown in Figure 2.6.2, transformation semantics extraction allows for choosing one of seven coordinate systems in order to carry out tests. This choice affects both the complexity and efficiency of intersection tests. For example, choosing to transform a sphere from world coordinates into the local space of a model (A, for example) may cause the deformation of a sphere into an ellipsoid due to non-uniform scaling, giving rise to a more complicated intersection tests. On the other hand, the sphere can be transformed into the A' space, allowing for simpler intersection tests: just scale triangles and boxes before carrying out the computations.

You might deduce from this that avoiding the local model space during intersection tests provides simpler and faster intersection tests. Actually, this does not hold when considering a model against a ray. Transforming a ray into the model's local space can distort its direction and length. As result, unit vectors representing the ray direction in world space may not be unit after they are transformed into the model's local space.

However, observe that this process is based on a linear transformation. Because of this, any parametric point reported in this local space is still mapped at the same position in world space by using the same parameter. Hence, a faster computation is obtained by using an intersection test that does not rely on unit direction vectors and pre-computing the ray in A space. Our tests on a Pentium D processor using different models in a ray-casting algorithm pointed out that performing intersection computations in the model's local space (A) is about 57% faster when compared to an implementation based on the A' space.

Conclusion

This gem covered how to use semantics information in order to speed up and simplify computations arising from collision detection tasks. You have seen how to efficiently invert and extract semantics information from matrices placing models in a typical game. Moreover, now you can efficiently perform collision detection tasks using transformation semantics. Although only the 3D case was shown, the concepts presented in this gem are straightforward and could be used in other dimensions and in other sorts of problems.

Ideas presented here were used to modify OPCODE [Terdiman03], an existing optimized collision detection library written by Pierre Terdiman, in order to add support for scaling models. The modified version also provides support for non-indexed geometry, as well for triangle fans, strips, and point grids representing terrain. This version is being used in a number of open source projects, and can be obtained at the following link: http://www.vdl.ufc.br/gilvan/coll/opcode/.

References

[Bergen97] Bergen, G. Van Den. "Efficient Collision Detection of Complex Deformable Models Using AABB Trees," *Journal of Graphics Tools,* Vol. 2, No. 4, pp. 1–13, 1997.

[Bloom06] Bloom, Charles. "Galaxy3," available online at http://www.cbloom.com/3d/galaxy3/index.html, January 22, 2006.

[Cohen95] Cohen, J.D., Lin, M.C., Manocha, D., and Ponamgi, M.K. "I-COLLIDE: An Interactive and Exact Collision Detection System for Large-Scale Environments," *Symposium on Interactive 3D Graphics,* pp. 189–196, 1995.

[Gottschalk96] Gottschalk, S. "Separating Axis Theorem," Technical Report TR96–024, Dept. of Computer Science, UNC Chapel Hill, 1996.

[Lomont07] Lomont, Chris. "Floating-Point Tricks," *Game Programming Gems 6,* Charles River Media, 2007.

[Terdiman03] Terdiman, Pierre. "OPCODE," available online at http://www.coder-corner.com/Opcode.htm, December 13, 2003.

[Wu91] Wu, Kevin. "Fast Matrix Inversion," *Graphics Gems II,* Academic Press, Inc., 1991.

[Wu94] Wu, Kevin. "Fast Inversion of Length- and Angle-Preserving Matrices," *Graphics Gems IV,* Academic Press, Inc., 1994.

2.7

Trigonometric Splines

Tony Barrera, Barrera Kristiansen AB

tony.barrera@spray.se

Anders Hast, Creative Media Lab, University of Gävle

aht@hig.se

Ewert Bengtsson, Centre For Image Analysis, Uppsala University

ewert@cb.uu.se

The user interfaces, level, and actor designs for modern games, both 2D and 3D, often contain geometry that an artist intended to be a perfect circle or elliptical arc. The mathematics of gameplay in some cases requires that a game's runtime engine be capable of generating the same types of shapes as efficiently as possible and with minimal error. There are numerous mathematical techniques that can be used to generate arcs, and each has its benefits and weaknesses. The robustness of digital content-creation tools, level editors, and game runtime code can be maximized if developers use a unified approach for generating geometric shapes, rather than having special case math for different basic types of shapes.

This gem shows you how splines can be constructed that can create both straight lines and perfect circle arcs. The latter is not possible with ordinary cubic splines and the trigonometric spline will make it possible to create new forms for 3D models. Furthermore, this gem will show you that the trigonometric functions involved can be computed without the use of the sine and cosine functions in the inner loop, which enables higher performance.

Background

Cubic splines cannot be used to create perfect circle arcs but trigonometric splines can be used for this purpose. Trigonometric splines were introduced by Schoenberg [Schoenberg64] and are sometimes called *trigonometric polynomials.* They have been investigated extensively in the literature of math and computer-aided geometry and some examples are found in [Lyche79] and [Han03]. However, they have not gained much interest in the computer graphics community, perhaps because they involve the computation of trigonometric functions which are relatively computationally expensive. As hardware becomes faster they may gain more interest in the field of computer graphics as a modelling tool, because it is possible to construct everything from straight lines to perfect circle arcs. A later section shows how you can evaluate a trigonometric polynomial without using sine and cosine in the loop and this enables fast evaluation, even if no specialized graphics hardware is available.

Trigonometric Splines

A trigonometric spline [Alba04] can be constructed from a truncated Fourier series [Schoenberg64]. The Hermite spline is defined by two points and the tangents at these points, which are depicted in Figure 2.7.1.

$$\begin{aligned} \mathbf{P}(0) &= \mathbf{P}_0 \\ \mathbf{P}(1) &= \mathbf{P}_1 \\ \mathbf{P}'(0) &= \mathbf{T}_0 \\ \mathbf{P}'(1) &= \mathbf{T}_1 \end{aligned} \tag{2.7.1}$$

Therefore, you need four terms in the Fourier series. The trigonometric curve is defined over the interval $[0,\pi/2]$ as:

$$\mathbf{P}(\theta) = \mathbf{a} + \mathbf{b}\cos\theta + \mathbf{c}\sin\theta + \mathbf{d}\cos 2\theta \tag{2.7.2}$$

The coefficients for the curve can be found by using the constraints in Equation 2.7.1, producing the following system which must be solved:

$$\begin{bmatrix} 1 & 1 & 0 & 1 \\ 1 & 0 & 1 & -1 \\ 0 & 0 & 1 & 0 \\ 0 & -1 & 0 & 0 \end{bmatrix} \begin{bmatrix} \mathbf{a} \\ \mathbf{b} \\ \mathbf{c} \\ \mathbf{d} \end{bmatrix} = \begin{bmatrix} \mathbf{P}_0 \\ \mathbf{P}_1 \\ \mathbf{T}_0 \\ \mathbf{T}_1 \end{bmatrix} \tag{2.7.3}$$

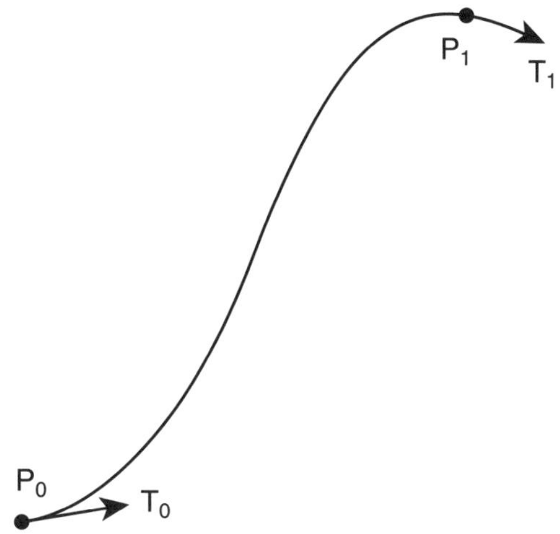

FIGURE 2.7.1 A trigonometric curve and its constraints.

The solution for this equation is:

$$\begin{aligned}\mathbf{a} &= \frac{1}{2}\left(\mathbf{P}_0 + \mathbf{P}_1 - \mathbf{T}_0 + \mathbf{T}_1\right)\\ \mathbf{b} &= -\mathbf{T}_1\\ \mathbf{c} &= \mathbf{T}_0\\ \mathbf{d} &= \frac{1}{2}\left(\mathbf{P}_0 - \mathbf{P}_1 + \mathbf{T}_0 + \mathbf{T}_1\right)\end{aligned} \tag{2.7.4}$$

It should also be noted that the trigonometric Hermite spline can also be written in the following form:

$$\mathbf{P}(\theta) = \mathbf{A}\cos\theta + \mathbf{B}\cos^2\theta + \mathbf{C}\sin\theta + \mathbf{D}\sin^2\theta \tag{2.7.5}$$

Here, the coefficients **A**, **B**, **C**, and **D** are different from **a**, **b**, **c**, and **d**. You can prove this by starting with Equation 2.7.2 and first expanding $\cos 2\theta$ to obtain the following:

$$\mathbf{P}(\theta) = \mathbf{a} + \mathbf{b}\cos\theta + \mathbf{c}\sin\theta + \mathbf{d}(2\cos^2\theta - 1) = \mathbf{a} - \mathbf{d} + \mathbf{b}\cos\theta + \mathbf{c}\sin\theta + 2\mathbf{d}\cos^2\theta \tag{2.7.6}$$

Then you put Equation 2.7.4 into Equation 2.7.6 to obtain:

$$\begin{aligned}\mathbf{P}(\theta) &= \frac{1}{2}\left(\mathbf{P}_0 + \mathbf{P}_1 - \mathbf{T}_0 + \mathbf{T}_1\right) - \frac{1}{2}\left(\mathbf{P}_0 - \mathbf{P}_1 + \mathbf{T}_0 + \mathbf{T}_1\right)\\ &-\mathbf{T}_1\cos\theta + \mathbf{T}_0\sin\theta + 2\frac{1}{2}\left(\mathbf{P}_0 - \mathbf{P}_1 + \mathbf{T}_0 + \mathbf{T}_1\right)\cos^2\theta\end{aligned} \tag{2.7.7}$$

Simplify and you get:

$$\mathbf{P}(\theta) = \mathbf{P}_1 - \mathbf{T}_0 - \mathbf{T}_1 \cos\theta + \mathbf{T}_0 \sin\theta + \left(\mathbf{P}_0 - \mathbf{P}_1 + \mathbf{T}_0 + \mathbf{T}_1\right)\cos^2\theta \qquad (2.7.8)$$

You can split the last term in two parts and rewrite one of them using the trigonometric identity:

$$\mathbf{P}(\theta) = \mathbf{P}_1 - \mathbf{T}_0 - \mathbf{T}_1 \cos\theta + \mathbf{T}_0 \sin\theta + (\mathbf{P}_0 + \mathbf{T}_1)\cos^2\theta + \left(\mathbf{T}_0 - \mathbf{P}_1\right)\left(1 - \sin^2\theta\right) \qquad (2.7.9)$$

Finally, simplifying you get:

$$\mathbf{P}(\theta) = -\mathbf{T}_1 \cos\theta + \mathbf{T}_0 \sin\theta + (\mathbf{P}_0 + \mathbf{T}_1)\cos^2\theta + \left(\mathbf{P}_1 - \mathbf{T}_0\right)\sin^2\theta \qquad (2.7.10)$$

This shows that you can rewrite the curve in different forms. You can use Equation 2.7.2 or Equation 2.7.10. But you can also use Equation 2.7.8. This flexibility will be useful when you evaluate the function, as shown in the next section.

Fast Evaluation of the Trigonometric Functions

[Barrera04] illustrated a technique for efficiently interpolating between vectors or quaternions. The main idea is to use spherical linear interpolation (SLERP), which was introduced to the computer graphics society by Shoemake [Shoemake85]. SLERP is different from linear interpolation in the way that the angle between each vector or quaternion will be constant; that is, the movement will have a constant speed. SLERP can be set up between two orthogonal unit vectors **A** and **B** as:

$$\mathbf{P}(\theta) = \mathbf{A}\cos\theta + \mathbf{B}\sin\theta \qquad (2.7.11)$$

In this case, both the cosine and sine functions need to be evaluated per step in the interpolation. In [Barrera04] it is shown how this can be done for *k* steps using C++ code in the following way:

```
#include <math.h>
#include <stdio.h>
#define M_PI        3.14159265358979323846
void main() {
    int k=10; // nr of steps
    double A[2]={1,0};
    double B[2]={0,1};

    double tm1[2];
    double t0[2];
    double tp1[2];
    double t=M_PI/2.0;
    double kt=t/k; // step angle
```

```
        tm1[0]=A[0]*cos(kt)-B[0]*sin(kt);
        tm1[1]=A[1]*cos(kt)-B[1]*sin(kt);

        t0[0]=A[0];
        t0[1]=A[1];

        double u=2*cos(kt);

        tp1[0]=t0[0];
        tp1[1]=t0[1];
        printf("%f %f\n", tp1[0], tp1[1]);

        for(int n=2; n<=k+1; n++) {
            tp1[0]=u*t0[0]-tm1[0];
            tp1[1]=u*t0[1]-tm1[1];
            printf("%f %f\n",tp1[0], tp1[1]);

            // switch
            tm1[0]=t0[0];
            tm1[1]=t0[1];
            t0[0]=tp1[0];
            t0[1]=tp1[1];
        }
    }
```

This code prints the cosine and sine between **A** and **B** and the result is in the variable `tp1`. If you want to compute cosine and sine between two arbitrary vectors, you can compute an orthogonal vector using the Gram Schmidt orthogonalization algorithm, as shown in the referenced paper.

Discussion

By forcing **d** to be equal to zero in Equation 2.7.2, you get

$$\mathbf{P}(\theta) = \mathbf{a} + \mathbf{b}\cos\theta + \mathbf{c}\sin\theta \tag{2.7.12}$$

This is obviously the equation for an ellipse and this proves that it is possible to construct a perfect circle/elliptical arc with the trigonometric splines. Moreover, because the curve is parametric, it is possible to construct straight lines using the trigonometric splines. The coefficients are vectors and the function produces a point in space. Each coordinate has its own expression and the only thing that differs is the coefficients. Therefore, it is no problem to construct a straight line even though trigonometric functions are involved. Figure 2.7.2. shows a perfect arc drawn using the trigonometric spline.

Note also that when you set $\mathbf{d} = 0$, $\mathbf{T}_0 + \mathbf{T}_1 = \mathbf{P}_1 - \mathbf{P}_0$ from Equation 2.7.4.

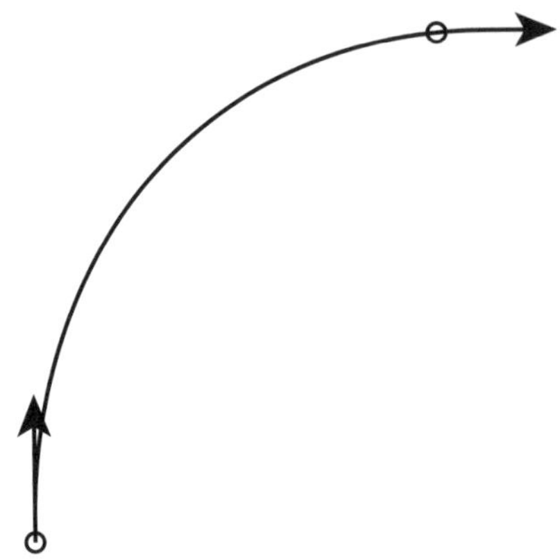

FIGURE 2.7.2 A circle arc is drawn using the trigonometric curve.

Conclusion

The trigonometric spline is interesting because it is possible to construct perfect circle arcs. The trigonometric nature of the spline makes it possible to construct splines and surfaces that are not really possible with ordinary cubic splines, unless the surface is approximated with several cubic splines, in which case ripples in curvature can create geometric artifacts that are visually obvious and undesirable.

Although this discussion has been purely theoretical, we believe trigonometric splines have great potential for solving certain problems that occur in modern game development.

One natural place for the application of trigonometric splines is within digital content-creation (DCC) tools. These splines are a perfect, simple solution to the problem of modelling game geometry that needs to be a pristine conic section.

Beyond DCC, these splines can make an impact within a game's runtime environment as well. We envision a technique, for example, using trigonometric splines to implement specialized game physics solutions, such as simulating various "machinery" and Rube Goldberg machines with perfect arcs that osculate at perfect tangents, in a beautiful way that is visually free of aliasing that piecewise polylines or traditional cubic splines might introduce.

We also believe that there is great potential to apply this technique to various procedural geometry, procedural texturing, and procedural animation techniques. The technique is fairly efficient, and may be suitable for implementation in the geometry shader stage introduced with the most recent graphics hardware. Imagine the possibilities that might include a whole new generation of awesome roller coaster games!

References

[Alba04] Alba-Fernandez, V., Ibanez-Perez, M.J., and Jimenez-Gamero, M. D. "A Bootstrap Algorithm for the Two-Sample Problem Using Trigonometric Hermite Spline Interpolation," *Communications in Nonlinear Science and Numerical Simulation* (April 2004), Vol. 9, No. 2, pp. 275–286.

[Barrera04] Barrera, T., Hast, A., and Bengtsson, E. "Incremental Spherical Linear Interpolation," *Proceedings of SIGRAD (2004),* Vol. 13, pp. 7–10.

[Han03] Han, X. "Piecewise Quadratic Trigonometric Polynomial Curves," Mathematics of Computation (July 2003), Vol. 72, No. 243, pp. 1369–1377.

[Lyche79] Lyche, T. "A Newton Form for Trigonometric Hermite Interpolation," *BIT Numerical Mathematics (June 1979),* Vol. 19, No. 2, pp. 229–235.

[Schoenberg64] Schoenberg, I. J. "On Trigonometric Spline Interpolation," *Journal of Mathematics and Mechanics* (1964), Vol. 13, No. 5, pp. 795–825.

[Shoemake85] Shoemake, K. "Animating Rotation with Quaternion Curves," *Proceedings of the 12th Annual Conference on Computer Graphics and Interactive Techniques, ACM SIGGRAPH (1985),* Vol. 19, No. 3, pp. 245–254.

2.8

Using Gaussian Randomness to Realistically Vary Projectile Paths

Steve Rabin, Nintendo of America Inc.

steve.rabin@gmail.com

Whether shooting a gun or firing off some arrows, we all have an intuitive sense of what the shot distribution on a bull's eye target should look like. Shots will generally be peppered near the center with a few straying shots. This isn't the kind of distribution generated from `rand()`, but rather a special kind of randomness commonly represented by a bell curve. Fortunately, there are random number generators that are capable of generating this type of Gaussian randomness. This gem discusses a very efficient Gaussian random number generator, detailing how it should be applied to simulate natural variations in the paths of projectiles.

Gaussian Distribution

Pseudo-random number generators (PRNGs) like `rand()` produce uniform distributions, in which there is an equal (or uniform) chance of any given number being selected from a given range. For example, in the range [0, 1], the odds of selecting 0.3 or 0.5 are the same. A Gaussian distribution, which is sometimes known as a normal distribution, favors positive and negative numbers centered near zero. When the standard deviation of this distribution is 1.0, it is called a standard normal distribution, as shown in Figure 2.8.1. This distribution is often referred to as a bell curve because of its shape.

To interpret Figure 2.8.1, consider the 68–95–99.7 rule. According to this rule, 68% of the values lie within one standard deviation of the mean [–1, 1], 95% of the values lie within two standard deviations [–2, 2], and 99.7 % of the values lie within three standard deviations [–3, 3]. The remaining 0.3% of the values lie beyond this range, with the chance of seeing numbers beyond [±]5.0 being less than one in a million.

Now that you have a better feel for what a Gaussian distribution looks like, let's look at a few random number generators that can create such distributions.

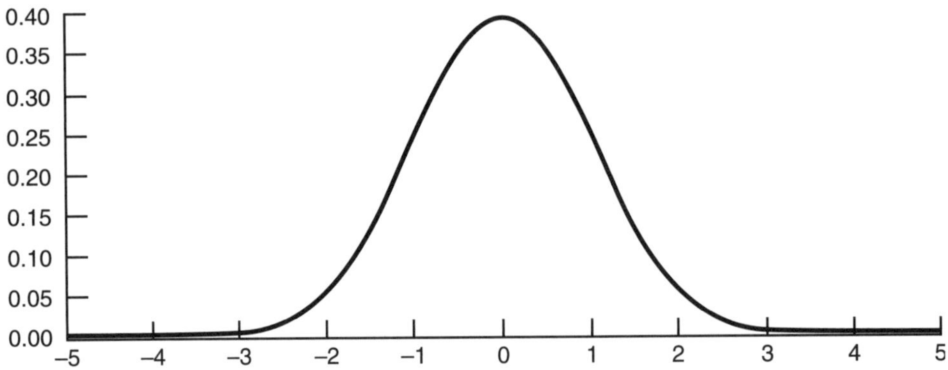

FIGURE 2.8.1 Gaussian distribution (normal distribution) with a mean of zero and a standard deviation of 1.0. The horizontal axis represents the value of the random numbers generated and the vertical axis is the likelihood of seeing any particular value. The tails of this distribution are the seldom-seen values beyond three standard deviations (less than –3.0 and more than 3.0).

Generating Gaussian Randomness

Gaussian random number generators (GRNGs) are useful for statistical analysis and have been studied in-depth for both speed and quality [Thomas07]. Speed is a concern because large simulations require billions of normally distributed random numbers. These simulations, which might perform communications or financial modeling, are concerned with the quality and accuracy of the distribution in the far tails (beyond six standard deviations). The reason is that extremely rare events can affect the outcome of important features that these simulations wish to explore.

Fortunately, video games don't require this level of rigor. In fact, games have the opposite problem in that a GRNG shouldn't generate extreme, but rare, numbers because they would appear as an error to the player. For example, if tree heights were determined with a GRNG, it would be odd to see most trees between 10 and 15 meters with just one really tall 30 meter tree. Consequently, for most purposes, any GRNG you use should reject (but not clamp) values beyond three standard deviations.

Gaussian Random Number Generators

One popular high-quality GRNG is *polar-rejection* [Knop69] (also known as the polar form of the Box-Mueller transform). This algorithm was made popular by its inclusion in the book *Numerical Recipes in C* [Press97] and is notable because its most expensive operations consist of only one logarithm and one square root (avoiding sine and cosine, which are required in the original Box-Mueller transform [Box58]). Although this is a reasonable GRNG, there are faster algorithms.

The *ziggurat* method [Marsaglia00] is a second popular GRNG and is often cited as the best algorithm given speed versus quality tradeoffs [Thomas07]. It's faster than polar-rejection, due to 1KB of lookup tables and very rare calls to transcendental functions. However, for game development, accessing these lookup tables will result in data cache pollution, causing the game to run slower than with polar-rejection, due to the high cost of memory access relative to the CPU speed on most platforms. For example, while the ziggurat method is actually very fast, the lookups will evict other parts of the game program from the cache, negatively affecting the overall game speed more than polar-rejection.

Given that the two previous algorithms are overkill for game applications, the best method is a simple and efficient technique called the *central limit theorem*, sometimes referred to as the *sum-of-uniforms* [Thomas07]. This algorithm takes several uniform random numbers, such as those generated by a PRNG like `rand()`, and adds them. According to the central limit theorem, the sum of these uniform random numbers will result in a single Gaussian distributed random number. This algorithm performs poorly in the tails, but this is acceptable because you generally aren't interested in values beyond three standard deviations.

More precisely, the central limit theorem states that the sum of K uniform random numbers in the range [–1, 1] will approach a Gaussian distribution with mean zero and standard deviation $\sqrt{K/3}$. For example, if you add three uniform random numbers, they will have a mean of zero and a standard deviation of $\sqrt{3/3} = 1.0$ (which is very convenient because the mean and standard deviation are identical to a standard normal distribution). The following code generates a Gaussian distribution by adding three 32-bit signed uniform random numbers (generated by a very fast xorshift PRNG [Marsaglia03]).

```
double gaussrand(void)
{
    static unsigned long seed = 61829450;
    double sum = 0;
    for(int i=0; i<3; i++)
    {
       unsigned long hold = seed;
       seed^=seed<<13; seed^=seed>>17; seed^=seed<<5;
       long r = hold+seed;
       sum += (double)r * (1.0/0x7FFFFFFF);
    }
    return sum; //Returns [-3.0,3.0]
}
```

The function `gaussrand()` returns a `double` in the range [–3.0, 3.0]. If you want a number in the [–1.0, 1.0] range, simply divide the result by 3.0 (which will consequently shrink the standard deviation to 0.33). The distribution roughly follows the 68–95–99.7 rule, but because the tails are missing, the distribution for this particular algorithm (with this seed) is 66.7–95.8–100.

The central limit theorem method can be made more accurate, especially in the tails beyond three standard deviations, by summing more numbers (increased K). However, this makes the algorithm slower for not much benefit, because you generally don't care about the tails.

Varying Projectile Paths

An ideal application for a GRNG in games is adding random variation to projectile paths. As discussed earlier, projectiles, like bullets and arrows, are expected to have some variation that follows a Gaussian distribution (probably due to many random variables like wind, hand shakiness, and projectile irregularities that additively contribute to the final path). However, this Gaussian distribution needs to be expanded into 2D, as shown in Figure 2.8.2.

FIGURE 2.8.2 The left target shows a Gaussian probability distribution in 2D. This can best be visualized as the middle figure, which is a Gaussian distribution revolved around the center. The right target is an example of 30 bullets perturbed by the revolved Gaussian distribution. Because the rings are placed at one and two standard deviations, roughly 68 % of the bullets strike within the smallest ring and 95% of the bullets strike within the two smallest rings.

The distribution in Figure 2.8.2 was created with the help of polar coordinates. This requires two random numbers for each 2D point: an angle and a distance. The bullets in Figure 2.8.2 were computed by generating a uniform random angle in the range $[0, 2\pi]$, along with the absolute value of a Gaussian random distance in the range $[-1, 1]$. By using a uniform random number for the angle, you guarantee that the bullets are evenly distributed at all angles around the center. By using a Gaussian random number for the distance, you guarantee that the bullets are concentrated near the center, following a normal distribution and the 68–95–99.7 rule.

The 2D distribution in Figure 2.8.2 is not technically a 2D Gaussian distribution (also known as a multivariate normal distribution). A true 2D Gaussian distribution is constructed with two Gaussian random numbers plotted against each other in Cartesian coordinates (not polar coordinates). This distribution is useful in statistics, but is not desirable for what you're trying to model.

The flaw in this kind of a distribution, for these purposes, can be seen in the following example. If *x* is a Gaussian random number and *y* is a Gaussian random number, a coordinate of (1.41, 1.41) is statistically less likely than a coordinate of (2.0, 0.0), even though these coordinates are equidistant from the origin. Therefore, a true 2D Gaussian distribution will favor the coordinate axes over the diagonals, which is undesirable for a 2D projectile distribution.

Additional Applications

Gaussian randomness is useful for many game applications other than projectiles. For example, if there are multiple characters or vehicles that move together, there is a tendency to see lockstep movement. This can be avoided by perturbing each agent's acceleration, top velocity, or animation speed by a GRNG. This will cause small variations around an average that will break up any synchronized movement or animations. The result is subtle variations with a few outliers.

Another application is to use a GRNG to perturb the heights of characters, trees, or buildings. If you have algorithmic control over the geometry of objects in your game, realistic variability can be created with a GRNG. This helps when the number of visible objects at any one time is large and you need natural variation. In general, many physical characteristics or attributes that should be randomized around an average will likely benefit from a Gaussian distribution.

Gaussian Distributions in Nature

Why do many distributions in nature follow a Gaussian distribution (or bell curve), such as human intelligence or the heights of trees? The central limit theorem alludes to the answer. When there are many uniform (or even non-uniform) random variations that contribute to a given property, the distribution of that property becomes more normal (rather than remaining uniform). Although this is a gross simplification of most systems in nature, it does shed light on why so many properties and systems roughly display a Gaussian distribution.

For example, if scores on an IQ test are influenced by genetics, diet, schooling, life experiences, and environment, each of these variables combine into the single IQ score. If all of these variables were uniform and weighted equally, the central limit theorem says that the result would be a normal distribution. Of course, each of these variables is not likely to be uniform, but rather the sum of other random variables, which are in turn affected by even more random variables. Therefore, many of these random variations like diet or schooling that influence IQ probably already follow a normal distribution. Ultimately, you can approximate many properties in nature by assuming that many small, independent effects are additively contributing to a given property.

Conclusion

Generating Gaussian randomness for games is embarrassingly simple and efficient using the central limit theorem. However, many game programmers aren't even aware of this type of random number generator. Therefore, the biggest challenge is simply getting the word out and letting developers know that this extra tool exists.

Many physical systems and characteristics tend to have a normal distribution that can be modeled using Gaussian randomness. By combining uniform randomness with Gaussian randomness in polar coordinates, applications like adding realistic variation to projectiles can easily be accomplished.

References

[Box58] Box, G.E.P. and Muller, Mervin E. "A Note on the Generation of Random Normal Deviates," *The Annals of Mathematical Statistics* (1958), Vol. 29, No. 2, pp. 610–611.

[Knop69] Knop, R. "Remark on Algorithm 334 [g5]: Normal Random Deviates," *Commun. ACM*, 12(5), 1969.

[Marsaglia00] Marsaglia, George, and Tsang, Wai Wan. "The Ziggurat Method for Generating Random Variables," *Journal of Statistical Software*, Vol. 5, 2000, paper and code available online at http://www.jstatsoft.org/index.php?vol=5.

[Marsaglia03] Marsaglia, George. "Xorshift RNGs," *Journal of Statistical Software*, Vol. 8, 2003, available online at http://www.jstatsoft.org/v08/i14/xorshift.pdf.

[Press97] Press, W.H., Teukolsky, S. A., Vetterling, W. T., and Flannery, B. P. *Numerical Recipes in C*, 2nd edition, Cambridge University Press, 1997.

[Thomas07] Thomas, David B., Leong, Philip G.W., Luk, Wayne, and Villasenor, John D. "Gaussian Random Number Generators," *ACM Computing Surveys 39*, 2007.

http://www.jstatsoft.org/v08/i14/paper

SECTION 3

AI

Introduction

Brian Schwab

Every year, new games come out. Game programmers rush to see what they'll do to further our ideas of what a game can accomplish. Will they be photo-realistic? Will all physical interactions be modeled with true-to-life physics? Will the audio make you feel like you're six feet from the action, and your heart pumping hard with the music? Finally, and most importantly to this section of *Game Programming Gems 7,* will the in-game characters have half a damn brain?

AI is one of the hardest categories to get right. Sure, art and music are pretty subjective, but what seems *intelligent* to people is an individual distinction on a whole other level. Take for instance a gut level reaction. You're walking down the street, and a full grown, adult male lion steps out from behind the next tree in front of you. What's the *intelligent* thing to do? The vast majority of people would say one of the following things:

- Run.
- Wait and see what's going to happen.
- Walk backward slowly and don't make any sudden moves.

However, any kind of question like this would also guarantee you plenty of not-so-common responses:

- Look for something to defend yourself with.
- Flag down a cab and get out of there.
- Throw your huge leather purse at the lion, hoping he'd stop to eat it.
- Scream at the top of your lungs, scaring him off.
- Pepper spray him.

Which one is correct? The answer might easily be *all of them*. In real life, roughly 70% of all people in this situation would freeze exactly like a deer in the headlights. We're hardwired to sit perfectly still, mostly because during evolution, we learned that most of our predators had motion-based eyesight (meaning, they see motion much better than other types of visual stimulus, like color or shape). Had lions and hyenas on the plains of Africa during our evolution instead been equipped with color-based eyesight, humans might today be able to change color like the chameleon, which would be a tragedy if you're a tattoo artist.

Obviously, we can't model that kind of standstill in games. If you came around the corner in a shooter and pretty much everybody froze, players would likely think the game was broken. However, if everybody ran, the game would get monotonous quick (although this still might work for some games). If everybody readied a weapon of some sort, you've got a pretty overwhelming scene. But a combination of these can work. You can even tune what mix of them they use in order to get the degree of challenge you want the player to overcome.

The point is, you can't always base your game's AI behaviors on realism. You also can't base your AI on what any one of us might think is the correct behavior, because people's notion of what constitutes an intelligent response can vary so greatly. Only by continuing the search for new techniques can you ever hope to convey a little perceived "intelligence" from your creations.

The gems in this section show just how far AI is coming. No longer is the development community as concerned about the trivial matters of AI implementation. Now we're delving into issues like more realistic perception models, using new programming techniques to simplify the creation of our AI systems, giving our AI characters true personality traits, and analysis of our AI at a statistical trend level.

John Harger and Nathan Fabian have written a gem in which you'll learn how to use a supervised learning technique called behavior cloning, which can be used to capture human performances. Steve Rabin and Michael Delp detail a unified sensing model, showing that you can model large portions of reality quite effectively with a nice, orderly, systemic approach. Iskander Umarov and Anatoli Beliaev explain how to use generic programming to create and manage hugely complex AI systems using code that is small, fast, and robust. Michael F. Lynch brings you a detailed gem concerning modeling attitudes within your AI agents. G. Michael Youngblood and Priyesh N. Dixit describe advanced player logging analysis, which can uncover useful patterns of gameplay and player interaction that can be difficult to see with just cursory observation. Michael Dawe shows you how to improve your planning systems by using plan merging to increase the reactivity of your systems without incurring full re-planning costs. Finally, because you might never tire of hearing about ways to improve usage and understanding of path-finding algorithms, Robert Kirk DeLisle provides insight into an A* technique called fringe search.

3.1

Creating Interesting Agents with Behavior Cloning

John Harger

Nathan Fabian

Human opponents are interesting. The popularity of gaming online may have something to do with the kinds of opponents you find there (or maybe mostly the idea that you can "pwn some noobs") but regardless of why it's popular, it wouldn't hurt to breathe some life into the offline, single player opponents (or even allies). This gem explains how to use a machine-learning technique called *behavior cloning* [Sammut92] to borrow from styles and strategies of humans playing the game and place them into game agents.

Behavior cloning is essentially a version of supervised learning. In supervised learning, the idea is that the human trainer provides a set of labels for particular objects and the algorithm learns to recognize, or predict, labels based on the attributes of those objects. When it sees similar characteristics in a new object, it should correctly label it. In behavior cloning, the trainer acts in response to a stimulus. The response becomes the label associated with the stimulus, which is the object. The algorithm then learns to repeat the same kinds of actions in the presence of the same kinds of stimuli.

This extends very nicely into games where it's easy to find the response a person will make to a stimulus, that is, the game state. (In the game nearly all interaction takes place within the game context and each game session is fairly similar to the last. It is important to note, however, that in some cases the game can include out-of-band information like clan membership and rivalries that the agent wouldn't be able to simulate.)

Because there is so much similarity between supervised learning and behavior cloning, this technique can be done with any off-the-shelf supervised learning algorithm. This gem uses a decision tree because the output is easier to edit than, say, the weights on a neural net.

In other words, it is not necessary to become a machine learning expert to exploit advances using this technique. Even better, the game playing trainers don't even need to know that the learning is going on in order for it to be effective. This gem shows you how well the tried-and-true decision tree learning algorithm works when borrowing human characteristics to create interesting, playable game agents.

Example: The Demo Game

Throughout this gem, the examples refer to a game design that resembles the classic computer game *Space War.* That is, two ships face off on an infinite 2D playing field; the goal of the game is to destroy the other ship. This simple design provides an easy-to-understand game environment in which you can train an agent.

How to Set Up the Feature Space Output

The feature space is the most important thing in instance-based machine learning, which is what you use to do behavior cloning. It is a set of attributes or "features" used to record instances of the game state for learning (see Figure 3.1.1). You must carefully consider the design of the features to be able to train interesting agents, and perhaps to be able to train an agent at all.

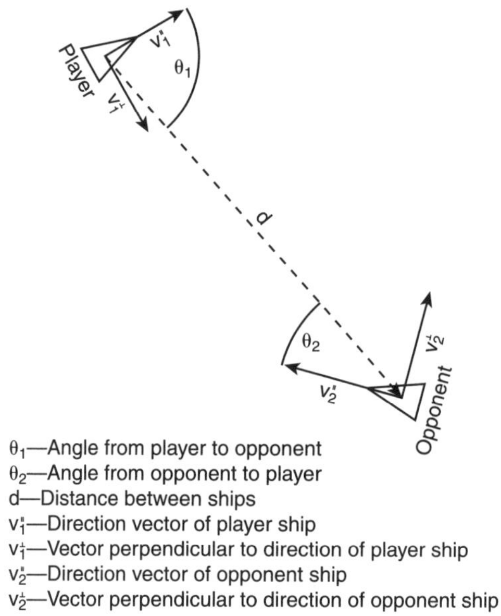

Figure 3.1.1 Example of a feature space.

The features must provide enough information to make decisions. Remember, the goal is to train an agent to behave like a particular human. Try thinking of how you would approach the situation; you might consider the distance to your opponent's ship, the direction of his or her ship from your current heading and even the direction he or she is facing from you. Don't be afraid to keep adding features; some players might act differently if their opponent is "off radar," and that distinction is going to provide more information than distance alone. It might take the learning algorithm 30 minutes to train an agent with detailed features, but it will likely produce a richer one.

However, you should be careful not to use absolute values for information such as position and orientation. If the agent is trained to accelerate based on an absolute direction, the resulting actions might be the opposite of what was expected! For example, if your ship is at point (2,1) and the enemy is at (0,0), you may have turned right. If this is what the agent learns, it will always turn right when its opponent is located at (0,0), even if the trainer would have turned left. If the feature was relative, such as 15° to the left (±2.5°), the agent will turn right when the opponent is just to the left, regardless of its absolute position. Think of it this way—would you consider your absolute heading, latitude and longitude when entering a brawl? Neither should the agent—at least if you want it to act realistic.

In addition to erratic behavior, absolute values can give a search space that might be much too large to process. If the range of location is infinite, the learning algorithm might never be able to classify behavior correctly. Instead of a tight, well structured tree, you end up with a noisy mess.

Table 3.1.1 Equations for Calculating the Features Shown in Figure 3.1.1

Name	Equation	Description
Distance	$\lvert\vec{d}\rvert$	Distance between the two ships
DirectionTo	$\theta_1 = \tan^{-1}\frac{\vec{d}\cdot\vec{v}_1^{\perp}}{\vec{d}\cdot\vec{v}_1^{\parallel}}$	Angle to Ship2 from Ship1's facing direction (–180° to 180°)
DirectionFrom	$\theta_2 = \tan^{-1}\frac{\vec{d}\cdot\vec{v}_2^{\perp}}{\vec{d}\cdot\vec{v}_2^{\parallel}}$	Angle from Ship2's facing direction to Ship1 (–180° to 180°)
VNorm	$\lvert\vec{d}\rvert_{\tau} - \lvert d\rvert_{\tau-1}$	Change in distance between ships
DDirectionTo	$\theta_{1\tau} - \theta_{1(\tau-1)}$	Change in DirectionTo
DDirectionFrom	$\theta_{2\tau} - \theta_{2(\tau-1)}$	Change in DirectionFrom

Training an Agent

Now comes the fun part: training the agent. This can be done with nearly any machine-learning technique available. When developing your own game, feel free to experiment with existing implementations or write your own. If you are interested in machine learning, take a look at [Witten99].

We chose to create our own simple decision tree implementation. It is certainly not the best—because it performs no linear regression, it is limited to working with discreet values. Because predefined linear ranges must be mapped to integers, the trees produced are probably not going to fit the data as tightly as they could otherwise. As a result, if distance 0.5 through 1.0 is a predefined interval, and one trainer tended to react at 0.54 and the other at 0.98, they both would branch at distance 1.0, giving both agents a similar feel.

ON THE CD

When you run our demo AIShooter, found on the CD-ROM, the game records the state 100 times a second. These states fill in the feature space defined earlier: the distance between the two ships, their relative directions to each other, and so on. In addition, the states of the player's controls are also recorded, such as turning left or right and accelerating forward or backward, and you offset these controls by 150ms to account for human reaction time. This is the stimulus/response information you need to build the decision tree.

Building the Trees from the Samples

Once you have a game session recorded, shown in Table 3.1.2, you can use that information to build the decision trees. Different control groups are split between different trees. Forward, Reverse, and None are the possible decisions for one tree. Left, Right, and None are possible decisions for another tree. The nodes of the tree test for all the values that one feature takes on. There is one child and one path down the tree for each value the feature can take on. Each child is passed from its parent all the data that corresponds to the value of that feature for that path. Recursively then, the child node determines whether the data is pure (meaning all the same).

Table 3.1.2 Sample Recorded Game State Data

Distance	DirectionFrom	Hitpoints	Turning
"2 to ∞"	1	100	RIGHT
"0 to 1"	1	100	LEFT
"0 to 1"	1	100	LEFT
"1 to 2"	1	100	NONE
"0 to 1"	3	100	NONE
"2 to ∞"	2	100	LEFT
"1 to 2"	2	100	NONE
"2 to ∞"	3	100	RIGHT
"0 to 1"	3	100	RIGHT
"2 to ∞"	2	100	LEFT
"0 to 1"	3	100	RIGHT

There is enough data left to make the determination and undergo searches for a feature, if so. If not, the node is a leaf and determines which label (that is, Forward) is the majority in its data and sets that as the return value. Listing 3.1.1 shows the recursive algorithm for Node learning.

Listing 3.1.1 Recursive Node Learning Algorithm

```
TreeNode* DataSet::learnNode (const string& targetName,
    const string& columnName, const col_t& column,
    const col_set_t& workingSet, unsigned int threshold)
{
    col_t newTarget = getColumn (targetName, workingSet);
    int majority = for_each (newTarget.begin (), newTarget.end (),
       Majority ());
    float purity = (float) count (column.begin (), column.end (),
       majority) / (float) column.size ();

    if (column.size () <= threshold || purity >= 0.99f) {
       return new TreeNode (majority);
    }
    int max = *max_element (column.begin (), column.end ());

    TreeNode *node = new TreeNode (columnName, 0, max);

    for (int i = 0; i <= max; i ++) {
       col_set_t newWorkingSet = getAllWhere (columnName, i,
       workingSet);
       newWorkingSet.erase (columnName);
       if (newWorkingSet.empty ()) {
          continue;
       }
       pair<string, col_t> best = getBest (targetName,
          newWorkingSet);
       node->addChild (i, learnNode (targetName, best.first,
          best.second, newWorkingSet, threshold));
       }
    node->fillIn();
    return node;
}
```

To determine which feature to use for the node, you must find the feature that leads to the most uniform data. Because the tree is trying to find the one label that makes sense for a given state, you want to find the set of states that describe that one label. This is the crux of what the decision tree does by encoding the features of those states that correspond to the label. Ideally, when the tree is at a leaf node, as described previously, there is one label in every state.

For example, assume you are training a tree from the data in Table 3.1.2 for deciding whether to turn, and your feature space defines distance on three intervals: 0 to 1, 1 to 2, and 2 to infinity. Let's take a look at the distance feature in terms of information gain. First, look at Equation 3.1.1 for computing the information in a set of data.

$$Info(V) = \frac{\left(-\sum_{v \in V} v \log_2 v\right) + n \log_2 n}{n}, n = \sum_{v \in V} v \qquad (3.1.1)$$

Without going into detail on the meaning of information theory, the purpose here is to track how different the data is. The less information the better because it means the labels are more uniform. In the example, there are three None, four Left, and four Right labels, giving an information of Info([3,4,4]) = $(-3 \log_2 3 - 4 \log_2 4 - 4 \log_2 4 + 11 \log_2 11)/11 = 1.5726$.

If you look at only those labels where Distance is "1 to 2," you have only two instances and both are None, giving you Info([2]) = $(-2 \log_2 2 + 2 \log_2 2)/2 = 0$. In other words, there is no information in that set because they are all the same.

The information in "0 to 1" is Info([1,2,2]) = 1.5219, and "2 to ∞" is Info([2,2]) = 1. Notice these are both close to the original information because the distributions of values are very similar.

Now you find the gain as $1.5726 - 3/11 * 0 - 4/11 * 1.5219 - 4/11 * 1 = 0.6555$. It is very easy to see that the gain on the hitpoints would be 0, as there is no change. The gain using direction is 0.4816. Getting a uniform set in one of those examples really helps the gain when you use distance.

$$Gain(O;F) = Info(O) - Info(O \mid F) \tag{3.1.2}$$

In each of the three new nodes, you pass the subset of data that corresponds with that value of distance and recurse using only that. There is no reason to use distance again in the second pass (it would no longer improve the information), so direction becomes an obvious choice as hitpoints still provides no information about the labels. The tree is shown in Figure 3.1.2. Notice again for distance "1 to 2" that since the set is already pure you just return that label; there is no reason to continue the recursion.

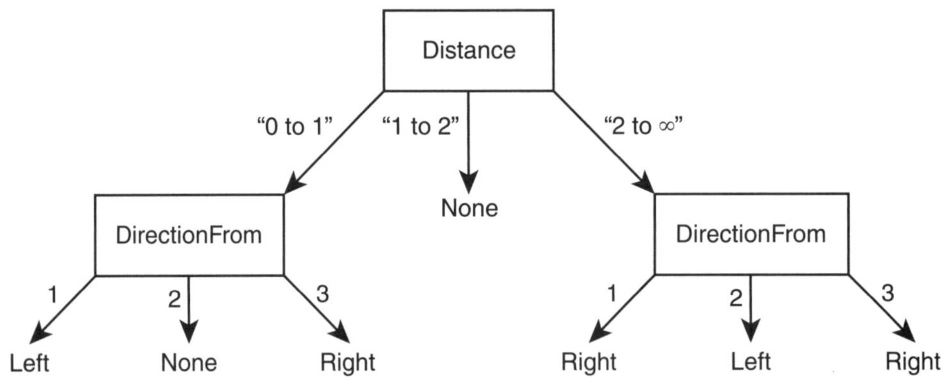

Figure 3.1.2 Example decision tree.

You pick the label, or control, by finding the majority value of that set. It is important to note that for a majority to make sense in statistics, you want to make sure there are enough samples to make the data meaningful. In Listing 3.1.1 for `learnNode`, you'll notice a check against the column to ensure that there are at least a certain number of rows. This is the "no free lunch" rule of machine learning. There is always one free parameter and it often depends on the data. We use 250 as we guess that seeing about 2.5 seconds worth of a game is enough to counteract any accidental key presses, which are considered noise. Additionally, we offset the controls in the game state by 150ms to simulate human reaction time.

Building the AI Script from the Trees

Once your trees are finished, you need to convert them into a form that's usable by your game. Although you could go with some tree interpreter, which is usually fast and efficient, this example translates them into script form, so they can be read and edited by hand. All you really have to do is convert your tree into the scripting language of your choice using conditional statements. For example, the turning tree in Figure 3.1.2 written as a Lua script would look like the code in Listing 3.1.2. (Please note that we used strings in some places for demonstration purposes, whereas a real script would use numbers.)

Listing 3.1.2 Turning Tree as a Lua Script

```
function turn
 --Root node
 if GameState.Distance == "0 to 1" then --Left branch
   if GameState.DirectionFrom == 1 then
     Ship.turn ("LEFT")
   elseif GameState.DirectionFrom == 2 then
     Ship.turn ("NONE")
   elseif GameState.DirectionFrom == 3 then
     Ship.turn ("RIGHT")
   else
     Ship.turn ("NONE")
   end
 elseif GameState.Distance == "1 to 2" then --Center branch
   Ship.turn ("NONE")
 elseif GameState.Distance == "2 to inf" then --Right branch
   if GameState.DirectionFrom == 1 then
     Ship.turn ("RIGHT")
   elseif GameState.DirectionFrom == 2 then
     Ship.turn ("LEFT")
   elseif GameState.DirectionFrom == 3 then
     Ship.turn ("RIGHT")
   else
     Ship.turn ("NONE")
   end
   else
   Ship.turn ("NONE")
 end
end
```

That's all there is to it. When the agent is running, you execute this script function after setting the current game state, and the decision tree does its work. The agent will respond to the state in a way that approximates the human who trained it.

Conclusion

This gem illustrates a very concise and convenient way to make agents that learn behaviors from humans in a simple game. One of the best places to use this technique is for creating those supporting-role characters, like guards, that normally have a very limited behavior, but could benefit from the introduction of some variety, especially in how they respond to the players.

Some of the details we didn't get into here involve expanding the feature space to account for more opponents or obstacles. As you can imagine, adding the distance and direction for each one of those can start to really grow. It gets even worse if you consider needing to add the distance and direction from an ally to an opponent. It is a fully connected graph. The trick in this case is to group the objects and treat them as a large mass with a single distance and direction.

These agents have limited understanding of the passage of time as well. Instead of knowing time directly, they know damage to the ship, which lowers as time goes on. However, if the ship was repaired back up to a certain level they would have no memory of having been damaged in the first place. You could consider adding time as a feature itself, but adding the absolute time poses the same problems as adding absolute position or orientation. However, as you'll see if you play around with the demo on the CD-ROM, it isn't necessary to have that memory to get pretty good behaviors.

ON THE CD

As with anything, "there ain't such a thing as a free lunch." You cannot make the end game super villain with this algorithm, but you can add some variety of behaviors to his (or her) minions. We have set up a forum at http://www.tosos.com to talk about some of the issues and solutions to creating more complex behaviors and dealing with more complex games. There are links there that go into more depth as to why this works and the theoretical background. We would love to have you join us and share your experiences!

References

[Sammut92] Sammut, C., Hurst, S., Kedizer, D., and Michie, D. "Learning to Fly," *Proceedings of the Ninth International Conference on Machine Learning* (ICML–1992), Aberdeen: Morgan Kaufmann, pp. 385–393.

[Witten99] Witten, Ian H., and Frank, Eibe. *Data Mining: Practical Machine Learning Tools and Techniques with Java Implementations,* Morgan Kaufmann, 1999.

3.2

Designing a Realistic and Unified Agent-Sensing Model

Steve Rabin, Nintendo of America Inc.

steve.rabin@gmail.com

Michael Delp, WXP Inc.

michaeljdelp@gmail.com

With increased visual realism, players expect agents to sense the game world with greater fidelity and subtlety. However, agent vision models in games have traditionally been very simplistic, using a combination of view distance, view cone, and line-of-sight checks [Rabin05]. Hearing models, when implemented, have also been fairly simple, usually testing against some cutoff distance to verify whether a sound is heard [Tozour02]. Although these basic agent-sensing models are efficient and simple to program, they are transparent and appear shallow to game players. For example, when agents use a discrete distance check for vision, it results in an absolute blind zone beyond a certain distance. Players intimately know this and routinely use this knowledge to manipulate the enemy AI. This is commonly seen when players lure individual enemies away from enemy groups by repeatedly inching toward them and running away.

Once the developer realizes that current agent-sensing models are rather primitive, dozens of clever ways to enhance these basic models begin to appear. This gem covers many such additions, eventually combining them into a unified sensing model, because all senses should collaboratively inform an agent's awareness of the world. The final model may then be used in any game genre as a core part of the AI.

The Basic Vision Model

Before the gem begins looking at specific enhancements to vision, this section recaps the core vision model used in the majority of games today. The three core vision calculations are view distance, view cone, and line-of-sight. Note that these three checks are usually computed in this order for efficiency reasons, because a radius test is very cheap and a line-of-sight test is very expensive. Figure 3.2.1 illustrates all three tests.

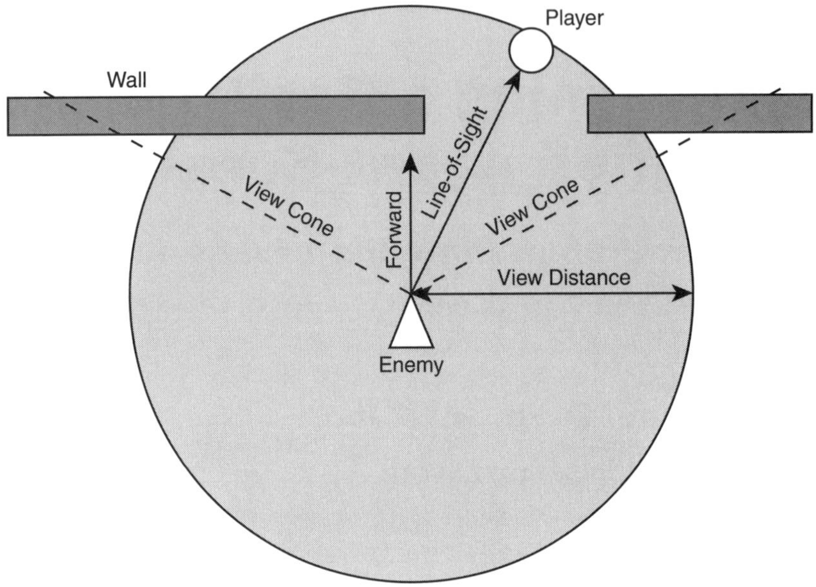

Figure 3.2.1 Example of view distance check, view cone check, and line-of-sight check. In this case, the enemy sees the player because the player passes all three tests.

The computation for the view distance check is a simple distance test. However, it is more efficient to test against the distance squared instead of the actual distance, because it avoids taking a square root. For example, if the agent can see up to 10 meters away, is at coordinate (0,0,0), and the player is at coordinate (5,8,0), you can compare the dot product of the vector between the two entities against the square of the view distance. The dot product of the vector between them is $5^2 + 8^2 + 0^2 = 89$. Compare this against the view distance squared ($10^2 = 100$) and you find that the agent can see the player, because 89 is less than 100. The distance squared optimization can be used because you're only interested in the relative distance, not the actual distance.

The second common step is to do a view cone check. This is done by taking the dot product of the agent's normalized forward vector with the normalized vector that points from the agent to the player (refer to the two vectors in Figure 3.2.1). If the result is greater than zero, the player is within the agent's 180° view cone. If the result is greater than 0.5, the player is within the agent's 120° view cone (cos 60° = 0.5). As an optimization, if only the 180° view cone test is required, there is no need to normalize the vectors (which potentially eliminates two square root calculations).

The final check, the line-of-sight test, is the most costly to perform. This test shoots a ray from the agent's eye level to the location of the player. If it intersects any geometry before it hits the player, the agent can't see the player. This test can be optimized by testing against bounding boxes that surround the level geometry, instead of testing against individual polygons. For testing against objects in the world, the object's lowest LOD can be useful, as well as bounding boxes.

These three tests lay the groundwork for a vision model, but as you'll see later, there are many improvements that can be made.

The Basic Hearing Model

Games that simulate agent hearing, such as games that emphasize stealth, typically implement this feature by having objects emit single-shot sound events that travel a particular distance. For example, each footstep of a player might send out a sound event that gets delivered only to agents within a particular distance from the player. The distance the sound event travels depends on the loudness of each footstep, which in this case usually corresponds to the speed of the player. A tiptoeing player spawns very weak sound events that travel only a meter or so, whereas a running player generates sound events that travel a great distance.

For many games, this is a sufficient hearing model, but it suffers from a similar problem as the vision model, namely that there is an absolute and arbitrary distance cutoff. It seems odd and unnatural that a distance of one centimeter might make the difference between completely hearing and recognizing a sound and not hearing it at all. As you might suspect, there are many improvements that can be made to this basic sensing model.

Augmenting the Vision Model Toolbox with Ellipses

The simple vision tests discussed previously don't model human vision well. In particular, view cones have several drawbacks.

- The agent potentially won't be able to see entities right next to itself.
- Visual acuity is highest in the center of vision and degrades with distance. View cones overestimate the area of vision far away and underestimate the area of vision close by.
- To avoid overly large fields of vision far away, designers tend to make view distances unrealistically short.

One way that designers have dealt with these issues is by testing against multiple cones to model human vision [Leonard03]. However, multiple cones can leave holes in the agent's vision. The left portion of Figure 3.2.2 shows a vision model that uses two cones and a circle to model vision. The narrow cone models the center of focus, which extends to far distances. The wider cone provides a broader field of view at short distances. The circle catches any entities adjacent to the agent or even behind him (as humans tend to have a sense when someone is right behind them). Note the large gaps in the vision model outside the intersection of the two cones.

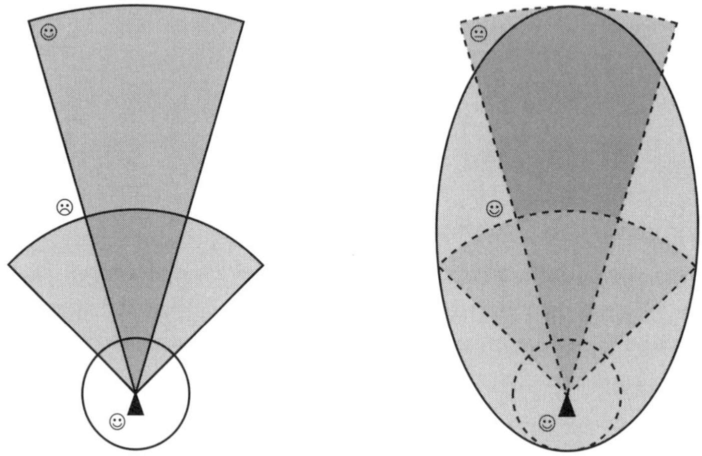

Figure 3.2.2 The left figure illustrates a vision model using two view angles and a circle. Note the holes in the vision system. The right figure illustrates an ellipse overlaying the old model. The ellipse gracefully encompasses the various view angles to give a more accurate model of vision.

A simple solution that solves all of these problems is to use an ellipse for the field of view. As you see in the right side of Figure 3.2.3, an ellipse gracefully deals with the degradation of visual acuity with distance without leaving holes in the vision. The ellipse "starts" a few feet behind the agent to model the sixth sense humans have about people right behind them and encompasses entities adjacent to the agent.

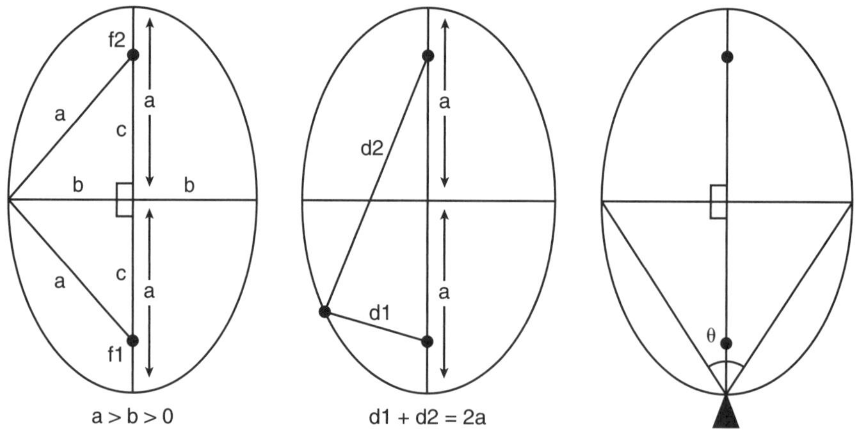

Figure 3.2.3 The left figure shows the important components of an ellipse. The middle figure shows how an example point on the ellipse is calculated. The right figure shows an example view from an agent where [θ] is half the view angle and **a** is half the maximum view distance.

Ellipse Implementation

In order to model vision with an ellipse, it is important to understand its components. Take a look at the left side of Figure 3.2.3. The length of the major axis is *2a*, and the length of the minor axis is *2b*. The two focal points (f1 and f2) are at ± *c* from the center of the ellipse, where $c^2 = a^2 - b^2$. The middle figure illustrates an important fact about ellipses: the distance from the two foci to any point on the outside of the ellipse equals *2a*. To determine whether something is within the ellipse, you must find the positions of the focal points.

To model human vision, you place one end of the ellipse at the agent's eyes. The designer can then specify a view angle much as he or she would with view cones. The view angle will make a triangle with the agent's eyes and the endpoints of the center axis of the ellipse as in the right side of Figure 3.2.3. The designer can also specify a maximum viewing distance; half of which will be the distance from the agent to the center of the ellipse. So given that [θ] is half the view angle, and *a* is half the view distance, you must first find the equation for *c* given θ and *a*:

$$\tan\theta = \frac{b}{a} \tag{3.2.1}$$

$$a\tan\theta = b \tag{3.2.2}$$

$$c^2 = a^2 - b^2 \tag{3.2.3}$$

Substitute Equation 3.2.2 into Equation 3.2.3 to get the following:

$$c^2 = a^2 - (a\tan\theta)^2 \tag{3.2.4}$$

$$c^2 = a^2\left(1 - \tan^2\theta\right) \tag{3.2.5}$$

$$c = a\sqrt{1 - \tan^2\theta} \tag{3.2.6}$$

Equation 3.2.6 can be precalculated at initialization. Now to find the equations for the focal points, you can use the following equations given the agents' eyes are situated at *vPos*, and they are looking in the direction *vDir*.

$$F1, F2 = vPos + vDir\left(a \pm c\right) \tag{3.2.7}$$

You want the ellipse to start `fBehindDist` behind the character (so the character can sense characters right next to him). The final equations are as follows.

$$F1, F2 = vPos + vDir\left(a - fBehindDist \pm c\right) \tag{3.2.8}$$

Of course `fBehindDist` could be subtracted from *a* at initialization in order to save the extra subtractions.

To determine whether an entity is within the agent's field of view, you simply take the entity's distance from each of the focal points, add the distances, and check that they are less than the maximum view distance (*2a*). So two distance checks for each entity is all that is needed per agent. Note that you cannot use squared distances in this equation because you have to add them together. These equations work for 3D or 2D ellipses. Use 3D if height is important to your world.

Using an ellipse to model vision is easy to calculate and is not much more expensive than a cone solution. It is the first building block in providing a more accurate human-sensing model.

Modeling Human Vision with Certainty

As observed previously, the fact that objects are either seen completely or not seen at all is an unfortunate side effect of discrete vision tests. The flaw of the discrete vision test is most obvious when you consider the subtlety of real human vision, such as peripheral vision in which objects are sometimes only partially recognized. In order to understand this more precisely, let's quickly review the mechanics of real human vision.

Human vision has been studied in-depth, from the retina to the neurons in the brain, but for the purposes here, let's extract useful measurements and properties that can be modeled in this artificial vision system. Humans have two eyes, of course, and together they can see a collective range of 200° with 120° of overlap (binocular vision) [Wandell95]. The eye focuses light onto the back of the eye, which uses rod and cone cells to detect light and color. Visual acuity is greatest at the center of fixation and decreases rapidly with distance from the center. Cones detect color and are densely packed toward the center of the retina, whereas rods are 100 times more sensitive to light and are primarily responsible for night vision and peripheral vision. As a result, peripheral vision has very little color response but is extremely sensitive to movement.

With a little more science behind this model now, you can start to make several observations. The first is that visual acuity and color detection is highest in the center of vision and falls off rapidly in the periphery. The second is that, while peripheral vision is poor, it is adept at detecting movement.

Using the discrete tests in the toolbox, a vision model can be created that scores objects by which area they occupy in the range of vision. In Figure 3.2.4, the percentages represent the certainty that a particular object is identified. Objects in the center of vision are fully identified, whereas objects in the near-peripheral, mid-peripheral, far-peripheral, and the behind-the-head (sixth sense) areas have lower certainties.

An important feature of this model is that moving objects get a score increase of 50%, which accounts for the special perception of movement. Depending on the game, walking and running might trigger the 50% increase, whereas sneaking or crawling does not.

If camouflage or hiding (possibly in shadows) plays a significant role, identification can be decreased depending on a combination of contrast and size of exposed profile. For example, when players are crouched in a dark corner, their profiles are smaller and they are difficult to see, which should consequently discount their identification by as much as 100%. Even if the agent is looking directly at the player, the agent might stare for a few seconds and move on, because it can't identify the object 100%. If this level of subtlety is employed, it might be advisable to add a smaller ellipse in which identification is unconditionally 100%, regardless of profile or contrast.

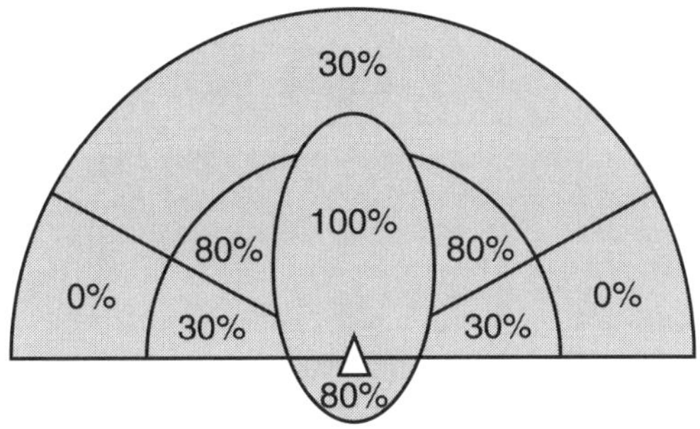

Rule 1: +50% if object is significantly moving.
Rule 2: Decrease certainty appropriately if exposed profile is diminished and/or contrast is poor.

Figure 3.2.4 Certainty in vision as a collection of discrete tests. In this model, objects are fully identified at 100%, highly suspect at or above 80%, and slightly suspect at or above 50%. Moving objects get an extra 50% score increase in order to model peripheral sensitivity to movement. Camouflaged, hiding, or crouching (reduced profile) objects decrease certainty by as much as 50%.

The percentages of certainty can be interpreted in whatever way makes sense within the game design. One approach would be to put thresholds at which the agent would perform particular actions. For example, at 100% certainty the object in question is fully identified and the agent might shoot at the object. At 80% or higher, the agent might turn their head and start approaching the object in question. At 50% or higher, the agent might only turn their head. Anything below 50% might not be enough stimulus to take any action.

One downside of the model in Figure 3.2.4 is that it still contains arbitrary discrete zones. The model can be further refined to support gradual falloff with angle and distance. Figure 3.2.5 shows a vision model in which the inner circle falls off with the angle and the outer circle combines a distance falloff with the angle falloff. The ellipse remains a discrete test with 100% certainty in the forward direction and 80% behind.

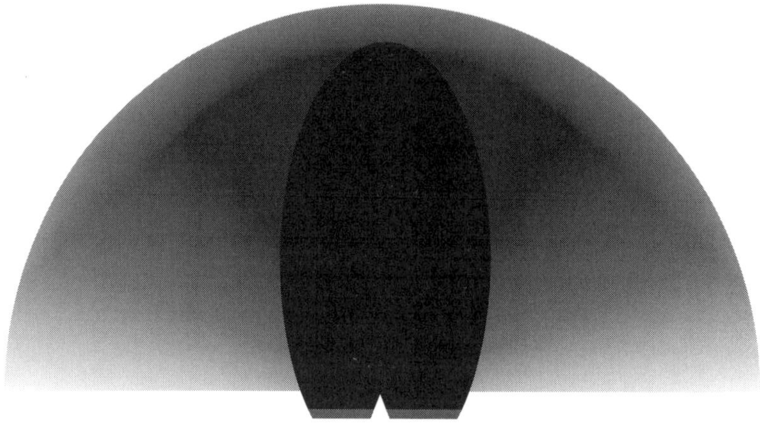

Figure 3.2.5 Vision model with gradient zones of certainty. The inner circle falls off with angle, whereas the outer zone falls off with angle and distance. The ellipse test remains discrete. Note that black equals 100% certainty and white equals 0% certainty.

The arbitrary models depicted in Figures 3.2.4 and 3.2.5 are only examples and should be modified as needed for the game design. They are very coarse approximations of real human vision based on the particular features identified here. Clearly, these models take great liberties and approximate the science. For example, these models favor 180° vision over 200° for simplicity reasons. However, these models are a big improvement in terms of subtlety and sensitivity compared with typical game vision models.

Another important feature of this vision model is to take into account the mental alertness of the agent. When the agent is highly alert, the percentages should be increased and the zones enlarged. If the agent is distracted or sleepy, the percentages should be decreased and the zones reduced.

Modeling Human Hearing with Certainty

As demonstrated with the vision model, calculating sensory identification as a percentage can be an effective way to introduce subtlety into a sensing model. Similarly it's worth constructing a hearing model that produces percentages of certainty. However, before you dive in and create a hearing model, let's look at some issues related to sound and hearing.

The most important property of sound is that intensity falls off exponentially with distance. Although sound propagates easily through air, only lower tones travel well through walls. This makes conversations and many high pitched tones hard to hear from adjacent rooms. Lastly, sound reflects off walls and reverberates within rooms, making sounds capable of getting around most obstacles.

When constructing a hearing model, a simple radius check for whether an agent hears a particular sound could be augmented in several ways. First, the volume of the sound should affect how far it travels, with clear recognition falling off to uncertain recognition. Second, walls might cause some degree of uncertain recognition depending on thickness and such. Third, because sound bounces off surfaces, if the line-of-sight between the source and listener is blocked, a path could be computed to see whether a clear route can be found. If a path is found, the distance of the path can be used to determine the falloff. Alternatively, as a less processor intensive solution, zones could be used in which all sounds made within a particular zone or an adjacent zone can be heard regardless of walls between the source and listener. In some cases, the coarse search space used for hierarchical pathfinding can also be used for determining sound zones.

Figure 3.2.6 demonstrates sound falloff coupled with the zone approach. Based on the sound intensity, the sound will have a radius at which it is recognized at 100%. Beyond that radius the certainty drops off to zero after some distance. However, the sound is heard only if the listener is in the same or adjacent zone from the sound source.

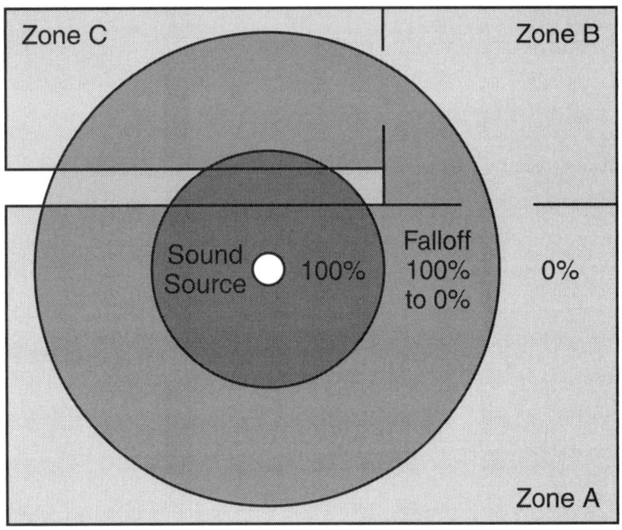

Figure 3.2.6 Hearing model demonstrating sound intensity falloff coupled with zones. An agent can hear a sound only if the sound was made in the same or an adjacent zone. In this example, the sound does not propagate to Zone C even though the radius check would allow it.

If a zone approach requires too much preprocessing of the game world or isn't suitable for randomized maps, the pathfinding engine can be exploited to determine whether a sound can propagate from the source to a listener in the case that the line-of-sight is blocked. Although this is more processor intensive, it can accurately tell if the sound can travel unimpeded to the listener and an approximate distance that the sound traveled.

In the way that walls can block vision, other sounds can drown out a particular sound and make it hard to hear. In order to model this effect, you need to consider all sounds, including ambient sounds, and determine whether a louder sound might be overpowering and masking all other sounds. For example, if a train is rushing by when the player is running, their footsteps might not be heard. However, if the player shoots their gun, the gunshot sound might be reduced by the noise level of the train, making it much more difficult to hear. This kind of modeling opens up new gameplay opportunities because players are then encouraged to time noisy actions with other noisy events.

Similar to how a sixth sense was added to the vision model, the hearing model can also include other senses such as smell. For example, if a rotting corpse creates a smell, that smell travels some distance and then falls off, just like sound. Additionally, stronger smells might overpower weaker smells, so consider modeling this feature as well. Smell might not be interesting in every game, but it can be extra information that can add to the identification of an object when vision isn't sufficient, thus opening up more gameplay opportunities.

Unified Sensing Model

Having created sensing models for vision, hearing, smell, and a sixth sense, the final task is to combine them into a single unified sensing model. The motivation is that all senses should together inform the agents of their surroundings, combining their clues into a complete picture of the current situation as best the agents can sense.

Because this example has been working with percentages representing certainty, the natural extension is to combine them in some way. There are three options. The first is to take the maximum certainty between the vision, hearing, and smell senses, as shown in the left diagram in Figure 3.2.7. For example, if a vision zone has 30% certainty and hearing is 50% certainty, that zone would have max(30%, 50%) = 50% certainty. The second option is to add the certainty of all senses, as shown in the middle diagram of Figure 3.2.7. For example, if a vision zone has 30% certainty and hearing is 50%, that zone would have 30% + 50% = 80% certainty. The third option is to take the vision model certainties and add half of the remaining headroom for hearing/smell, as shown in the right diagram of Figure 3.2.7. For example, if a particular vision zone had 30% certainty, hearing a sound in that zone would add (100 – 30) / 2 = 35% resulting in a total 75% certainty. This last option avoids having any zone with greater than 100% certainty.

To understand the repercussions of this unified sensing model, consider the white circle in Figure 3.2.7 to be the player. If the player was both quiet and motionless, he would go completely undetected by the agent with a certainty of only 30%. If the player makes a loud noise, he is identified at 50%, 80%, or 75%, respectively, using

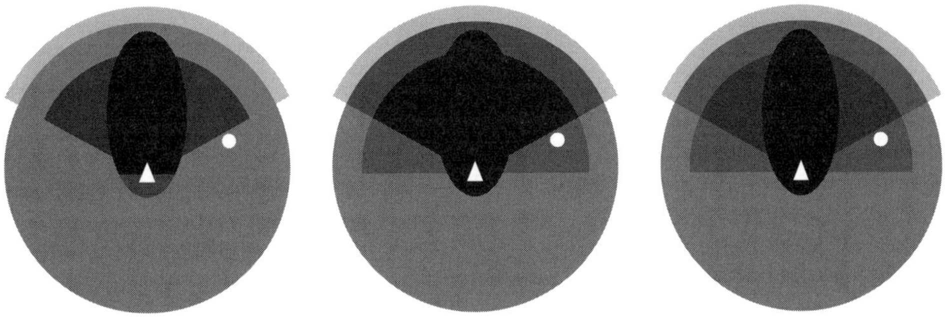

Figure 3.2.7 Three examples of the unified sensing model combining vision with hearing/smell. Hearing has a max certainty of 50% with no falloff shown. The left diagram takes the max sense (vision, hearing) from each zone. The middle diagram adds vision with hearing. The right diagram takes vision and adds half of the remaining overhead due to hearing (to avoid certainties above 100%). In this example, the white circle is the player making a loud sound, which results in 50%, 80%, and 75% certainty respectively in each

each method. This might result in the agents turning their heads in response. If the object was running and fired a loud shot, it would be identified at 80%, 100%, and 90%, respectively, using each method. In this case, the agents might turn their heads and bodies quickly and shoot once they are facing the player.

Adding Memory to the Unified Sensing Model

To achieve a greater degree of realism, agents must have short term memory to augment their sensing model. This is necessary in order for agents to not forget about objects that they have recently identified. For example, if the player moves quickly through the mid-peripheral vision of the agent, the player will be identified at 100%. If the player out-runs the agent, moving into the far-peripheral vision area and stops, the memory of the player at 100% identification needs to be retained for some period of time (even though the player should now technically be identified at only 30%). This makes sense, because the agent identified the player and still has visual contact, making it reasonable to assume that it is the same object that is still fully identified.

In order to implement this type of memory, each object that enters the sensing model needs to be tracked. The object should have some unique identification number that can be associated with varying levels of identification. A timestamp and the location of the object's last known position should also be recorded. This information will be stored in the agent. The general rule is to allow only the certainty level to increase, as clues only add to the knowledge of the object. Once the object is not sensed for several seconds, the structure can be purged from memory.

Conclusion

The unified sensing model brings together vision, hearing, smell, and even a sixth sense to give game agents a coherent and detailed view of the game world. Many very compelling features have been folded into the model, such as movement detection, hiding, and alertness, which allow for very rich and interesting gameplay to emerge. As players better understand the underlying sensing model, they can devise innovative ways to manipulate and deceive the agents, which adds greatly to the quality of the experience.

As presented, the unified sensing model is intended to bring subtlety and added realism to game agents. However, it is a very flexible model. The zones and percentages given are simply suggestions and they will inevitably need to be tweaked for any particular game. Consider each of the tools at your disposal and create your own sensing model that matches and enhances your particular game design.

References

[Leonard03] Leonard, Tom. "GDC 2003: Building an AI Sensory System: Examining the Design of Thief: The Dark Project," available online at http://www.gamasutra.com//gdc2003/features/20030307/leonard_01.htm#, 2003.

[Orkin05] Orkin, Jeff. "Agent Architecture Consideration for Real-Time Planning in Games," AIIDE Proceedings, Artificial Intelligence for Interactive Digital Entertainment Conference, 2005.

[Rabin05] Rabin, Steve. *Introduction to Game Development,* Charles River Media, 2005.

[Tozour02] Tozour, Paul. "First-Person Shooter AI Architecture," *AI Game Programming Wisdom,* edited by Steve Rabin, Charles River Media, 2002, pp. 387–396.

[Wandell95] Wandell, Brian. *Foundations of Vision,* Sinauer Associates, 1995.

3.3

Managing AI Algorithmic Complexity: Generic Programming Approach

Iskander Umarov

Anatoli Beliaev

During the past seven years, TruSoft International Inc. has been focusing on the research and development of behavior-capture AI technologies. These technologies allow a new type of AI game agent to be created that can learn and adapt in the way real humans do. They do this by learning the playing styles of human players and adapting these strategies to achieve set goals.

The system allows game designers to train behavior-capture AI agents directly, by sitting down with a console or a PC and playing the role of the agent to be trained. Agents can then learn tactics and strategies straight from the human controller, without the need for coding. End users can also train game characters using the same system, bringing traditional bot development to a whole new level. By simply playing the game, a behavior-capture enabled system allows the users to create AI-controlled agents that play with very distinct styles.

Introduction

During the work on our behavior-capture AI technology—Artificial Contender—we encountered an interesting challenge common to many AI systems. Sometimes the complexity of AI decision-making related algorithms grows out of control. They start as a simple piece of code and end up as chaos in the form of handcrafted loops and branches. We needed a method of managing this complexity without introducing significant abstraction penalties.

This Artificial Contender technology is an instance-based learning system. It collects instances of learned behaviors and utilizes them during the decision-making process. The data collected while learning may not be applicable directly to the current situation. The learned instances are reevaluated. Possible actions can be filtered out or modified, generalized or specialized, and the priorities can be adjusted. An action should be chosen from a group of actions, and, if the action is not good enough, another group of actions should be analyzed. You might need to apply different algorithms for the next group, or different filtering criteria. However, if the next group does not contain better actions, you might need to reconsider actions from the previous group, compare the consistency of data from each group, and so on. Algorithms of this level of complexity are quite typical.

How might you go about solving this problem? Let's consider the most straightforward implementation first. No over-design, no premature optimization. When you have to deal with a group of actions, you just create a container of objects describing actions. When you have to iterate through actions, you implement a loop. When you have to iterate through a subset of actions, you implement a nested loop. When you have to filter actions, you check the necessary conditions inside the loop. Trying to implement it this way, we ran into problems:

- Each part of the algorithm increases the complexity of the implementation. The code becomes difficult to follow. The approach that appeared simplest and the most straightforward leads to very complex code.
- Maintaining the code in this form becomes very expensive. It is difficult to understand and change. Debugging it is very challenging.
- It also becomes increasingly difficult to optimize the performance of this algorithm. It is difficult to find performance bottlenecks. It is difficult to change the code and make sure it is still correct. It is difficult to create customized versions of the code, optimized for different environments and conditions.
- The pieces of code are tightly coupled, which makes it impossible to reuse them.
- The risk of introducing bugs while making changes is high and unit testing does not eliminate the risk, because often it becomes difficult to determine the expected results for the entire algorithm.

How do you manage this complexity? The most obvious answer is to use decomposition. There are different ways to decompose. We wanted to make the implementation easy to understand, modify, and reuse. We wanted to be able to build these algorithms quickly, and make fast and safe changes. On the other hand, we could not sacrifice the technology's performance characteristics. When you decompose a system into components, you have to deal with inter-component communication issues—sending data back and forward, converting data, and so on. Artificial Contender processes a lot of data, and introducing even a little overhead to processing every single data item can lead to unacceptable processing time and resource consumption increases.

Action Choosing Workflow

"Pipes and Filters" Design Pattern

We have found that *workflow* is the most appropriate metaphor for representing this class of algorithms. The idea is based on the well-known "Pipes and Filters" design pattern [Buschmann96]. Consider the reasons that make this design pattern a good fit, as follows. (Note that we use the term "block" instead of the term "filter" from the original "Pipes and Filters" pattern, in order to avoid ambiguity—*filter* in our workflow metaphor is a block of a special type.)

- We want to construct workflows out of separate blocks.
- Each block should be responsible for exactly one aspect of the algorithm.
- Each block should have well-defined inputs and outputs.
- The structure of the workflow should be homogeneous, so that we can connect blocks in different ways, unless the nature of the implemented aspects does not allow the blocks to be connected.
- We want to be able to create non-linear workflow configurations, containing branches, merges, and loops.
- We want to be able to change workflow configurations with minimum effort.

The advantages of the "Pipes and Filters" pattern are well known [Buschmann96]: flexibility of the processing line configuration, reusability of the components, potential parallel processing, and so on. Let's see how this pattern can help in this case, setting aside the implementation issues for now, but remembering the priorities here—manage complexity and do not sacrifice performance.

The following benefits help to manage complexity:

- *Separation of concerns*. The processing algorithm is broken into a sequence of individual transformations. Every transformation is a distinct and independent task.
- *Modularity*. Every processing task is encapsulated by a separate block, which can be coded independently.
- *Reduced coupling*. Blocks communicate only through well-defined channels. Normally, blocks do not share state and are unaware of surrounding blocks' implementations, as long as the surrounding blocks adhere to the common requirements.
- *Testability*. Every block can be tested independently. It is much easier to specify the required results for a separate simple task than for the entire algorithm. If it is easy to change inputs and check outputs, each block can be treated as a black box. It is also possible to test the result of cooperation of any combination of the blocks.
- *Configuration flexibility*. It is possible to build different configurations out of the same set of blocks. It is also possible to compose simpler blocks into aggregates that can be, in turn, treated as more complex blocks.
- *Specialization flexibility*. Blocks can have alternative replaceable implementations, specialized for different environments.
- *Reusability*. Low coupling allows you to treat blocks as standalone modules that can be easily reused. Avoiding extra dependencies makes blocks more adaptable.

The following benefits help to improve performance:

- *Parallelism*. Blocks performing incremental processing do not have to wait until the surrounding blocks complete their calculations; they can continue working concurrently. This makes the workflow significantly faster, because it takes advantage of multiprocessor architectures.

- *Specialization flexibility.* You can create alternative implementations of blocks specifically for the purposes of performance improvement.
- *Performance profiling.* Breaking the processing down into separate components makes it easier to profile the code and find performance bottlenecks.
- *Partial results.* This aspect is very important for the Artificial Contender decision-making algorithms, and is discussed it in more detail in later sections.

Partial Results

Artificial Contender decision-making algorithms operate on sequences of data describing potential actions. The lowest blocks (sources) generate action data sequences, usually extracting data stored in the knowledge database, or based on statistics, or suggested by heuristic rules. Querying some sources is expensive in terms of processing time. If the current game situation is well known, only the data from the "cheapest" sources is necessary. Only if there is no exact match for the current game situation, is it necessary to query more sophisticated and expensive sources.

In most cases the complete action data sequences are not really needed. Partially calculated sequences may be enough to make the final decision, and expensive calculation can be avoided. If an action is good enough, it can be accepted and calculations can be stopped. If you calculate everything in advance, it is very probable that you'll have to throw away most of the calculated results anyway, and you cannot afford that. It is possible to implement the workflow in a way that the higher blocks control the execution flow. It is up to higher blocks to decide how, when, and for how long they want to continue getting the results from lower blocks. They can interrupt querying lower blocks at any moment, or even not start querying some of the lower blocks. If possible, the lower blocks should not pre-calculate the results until they are asked.

There is one more consideration. Working in real-time environments, sometimes it is better to make a decision that is not perfect, but acceptable, than to spend more time calculating. It is possible to arrange the blocks of the workflow in such a way that they calculate and defer the "acceptable but not perfect" actions first, and then continue calculations while it is not too late to act, and to accept one of the deferred actions if nothing better has been found.

"Pipes and Filters" Liabilities

However, the "Pipes and Filters" pattern is not free from liabilities. Let's take a look at them and what can be done to minimize them.

- *Sharing state information.* If the blocks need to share state information, it can be inefficient or inflexible. It does not seem to be a serious issue for this application, because most of the blocks do not need to share any state information directly. In some exceptional cases, you can relax the "Pipes and Filters" restriction and allow blocks to communicate in special efficient ways, bypassing the "official" block inputs and outputs. Those exceptions should be very rare, though.

- *Communication and data transformation overhead.* Blocks have to exchange data, and this can incur some overhead. Data manipulations that do not contribute directly to the implemented algorithm may be required. If the blocks are interchangeable, they have to agree upon a common communication protocol, sometimes as low as a character stream. Serializing and parsing can be expensive enough to make the pattern not applicable. We are going to address this issue and minimize or completely eliminate this overhead.
- *Parallel processing disappointments.* For different reasons, the performance of parallel processing can be disappointing [Buschmann96]:
  - It can happen because of the communication overhead, but we have already promised to minimize it.
  - It can also happen because of architecture-dependent reasons, such as context-switching and synchronizing overhead, and we are not going to consider these issues for now, because they seem to be common for all parallel-processing solutions.
  - It can happen because of the nature of the processing, or because of bad coding, like when a block consumes all input data before emitting any output data. This block can become a performance bottleneck of the entire workflow. In order to avoid this problem, you should make processing incremental whenever possible.
- *Complex flow control logic.* The workflow processing nature is mostly sequential, so it becomes difficult to implement branches, loops, and other complex constructs. However, in this application, we were almost always able to rethink and redefine algorithms in terms of sequential processing. These new definitions are very beneficial themselves. When a complex task that seems to require complex control of the execution flow is transformed to a sequence of simpler steps, it definitely improves the internal quality of the implementation. In rare cases when you are unable to do it, special constructs outside of the traditional "Pipes and Filters" patterns can be used.
- *Error handling.* In general, error handling can be quite complicated in the "Pipes and Filters" pattern. However, the nature of Artificial Contender decision-making algorithms does not involve any recovery after errors. So, the whole error-handling issue is not important for this application.
- *Complexity, increased maintainability efforts.* The pattern introduces its own complexity and maintainability efforts, because decomposing a monolithic implementation into multiple components increases the number of components and dependencies. This problem is not specific to this pattern, it is rather a consequence of any decomposition. Our solution is as simple and lightweight as possible.

Let's take a closer look at the Artificial Contender decision-making workflows and their specific requirements.

Workflow Diagram

Any workflow can have a visual representation, for instance a block diagram. We developed a special graphical language that allows you to express different workflow configurations in a very compact and vivid form. Using different shapes and connecting lines, you can illustrate sequences of processing steps, data flows, and interdependencies.

Figure 3.3.1 shows an example of a workflow of average complexity. The description of this workflow in English would be cumbersome and perplexing. However, for developers familiar with these diagrams, it is quite easy to understand what is going on.

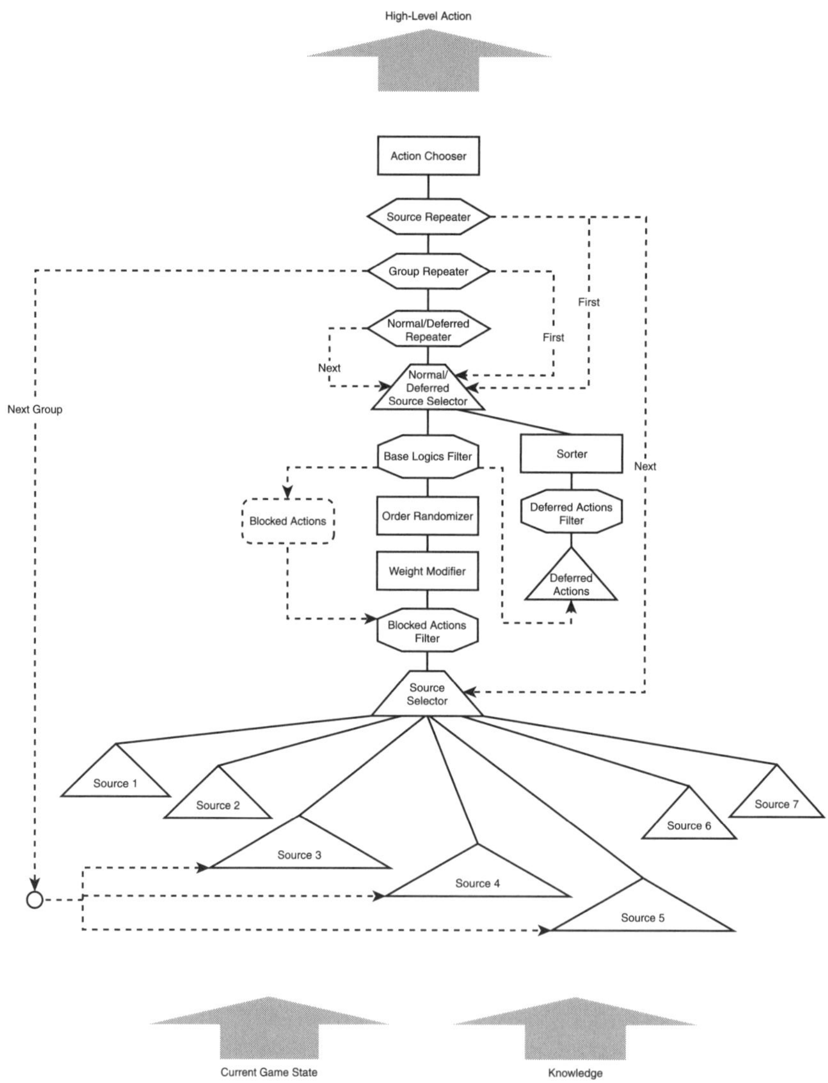

Figure 3.3.1 Artificial Contender decision-making workflow example.

These diagrams are compact and readable. They also make it very easy to modify workflows. You can swap the blocks around, rearrange and reconnect, add and remove. For example, you may want to modify actions before or after filtering. Take a look at the diagram, and you will know what the current workflow does. If you want to change the order, just reconnect the blocks. Compare this to the first straightforward implementation of the algorithm. How long would it take to change the order of action filtering and modification? How can you make sure that the change is correct? The workflow diagrams make the answers obvious.

Execution Flow

A workflow diagram shows just a static picture of the workflow. It represents the workflow configuration in a declarative manner, but it does not illustrate the actual execution sequence. It is enough when the reader of the diagram knows the basic rules. Omitting the details of data and execution flows is what makes the diagrams compact and expressive. But what is going on here?

Blocks work with sequences of separate objects representing some knowledge about a single action or a set of actions. These objects are called *ActionInfo*. Blocks consume, process, and emit sequences of ActionInfo objects. ActionInfo objects travel from lower blocks to higher blocks. On their way, they can be transformed to other ActionInfo objects, they can be filtered out, they can be split into sets of separate ActionInfo objects, they can be merged with other objects, and so on.

How and in what order do blocks process ActionInfo objects? To answer this question, consider a very simple workflow shown in Figure 3.3.2.

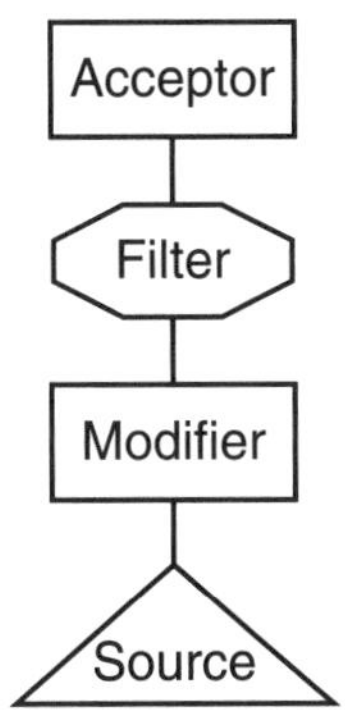

Figure 3.3.2 Very simple workflow.

This is how this workflow is supposed to work:

- *Source* generates ActionInfo objects (based on, for example, the Artificial Contender knowledge base).
- *Modifier* changes ActionInfo objects, adjusting them to the current game situation.

- *Filter* checks whether ActionInfo objects are good enough and lets them through or filters them out.
- *Acceptor* accepts the first ActionInfo that is emitted by Filter.

You could make it work in exactly that sequence, implementing the "push" model—start processing from Source, pass the data generated by Source to Modifier, and so on. This is how many implementations of the "Pipes and Filters" pattern work. However, this is not what you need for the Artificial Contender system. Querying some of the knowledge sources can be expensive in terms of performance.

First of all, it might not be necessary to query all of them. Second, you might not need the whole sequence of ActionInfo from each of them. The workflow in this example may accept the first ActionInfo generated by Source if it makes it through Filter; in that case there is no need to generate more than one ActionInfo. But Source is not supposed to be aware of that fact, so you cannot let Source decide when to generate the whole ActionInfo sequence. Higher blocks must be able to decide which lower blocks to query and when to stop. Although it is theoretically possible to implement this using the "push" model, the "pull" model looks more natural:

- Acceptor asks for one ActionInfo from Filter.
- Filter asks for ActionInfo from Modifier and checks them one by one, looking for ActionInfo that should be returned to Acceptor.
- Modifier queries Source retrieving ActionInfo one by one, modifies them, and returns to Filter in the same manner: one by one.
- Source answers Modifier's requests, emitting ActionInfo objects one by one.
- As soon as the top block (Acceptor) stops asking for more ActionInfo, the workflow stops.

Figure 3.3.3 shows the sequence diagram of a "pull" workflow.

Typical Blocks

There are a few categories of blocks that you usually need for AC decision-making algorithms:

- *Sources* generate ActionInfo objects based on data external relative to the decision-making workflow: from AC knowledge database, from heuristic algorithms, from statistics tables, and so on.
- *Filters* determine whether consumed ActionInfo satisfy specific conditions, and output or ignore these ActionInfo. Usually filters make sure that the potential actions are applicable to the current game situation.
- *Modifiers* change consumed ActionInfo objects and output the changed objects. For example, they can adjust the actions retrieved from the knowledge according to the current game situation, or they can adjust priorities of the actions.

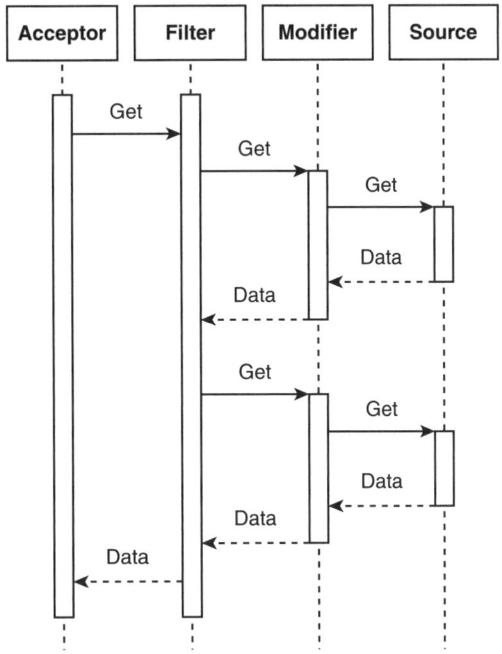

Figure 3.3.3 Pull workflow.

- *Sorters* consume sequences of ActionInfo objects and output the same objects in a new order. For example, they can sort actions by priorities, by estimated effect, by categories, and so on. Sorting criteria can be very flexible and do not have to specify a deterministic order. They can perform weighted random reordering, thus introducing more variety into AC agent's behavior.
- *Splitters* divide the incoming flow of ActionInfo objects into multiple flows and redirect these flows to multiple outputs. Splitters are used to separate some ActionInfo objects for special processing.
- *Mergers* have multiple inputs and redirect the flows of ActionInfo objects from all inputs to a single output. They are often used to query a set of ActionInfo sources sequentially and join the results into one set.
- *Selectors* have multiple inputs and redirect the flow of ActionInfo objects from one of the inputs to a single output. Usually, selectors have a special control channel that makes it possible to switch the active input. They are also often used to query a set of ActionInfo sources sequentially. But, as distinct from mergers, they allow treating the ActionInfo objects from each source as a separate group.
- *Repeaters* consume and output all available ActionInfo objects, and then perform a specified action, and then consume and output all available ActionInfo objects again, and so on. Cooperating with selectors, repeaters make it possible to implement loops that are querying and processing actions from different sources.

Generic implementations of the frequently used blocks are included in the Artificial Contender SDK. However, this is not an exhaustive list of block types. It is possible to develop more customized and specialized blocks. Combining these blocks into different configurations, you can build very versatile and flexible workflows.

Constraints

Blocks can be connected in many different ways. However, system freedom is not unlimited. Some combinations do not make sense, because the nature of the blocks can be very different. For example, if you want a block to perform a weighted random choice of an action, you have to make sure that the inputted ActionInfo objects have weights associated with them. You want to be able to express these constraints and associate them with blocks. Then you can visualize the restrictions and check them automatically, ensuring the correctness of the workflow.

Implementation

Generic Programming and C++

We chose C++ as the main implementation language for Artificial Contender. This language provides tools to deal with abstractions, and still allows control over low-level implementation details in order to achieve high performance. Using C++, we take advantage of the "Pipes and Filters" pattern benefits, and overcome the potential performance hits at the same time.

Generic programming helps us achieve both goals simultaneously. Implementing code in a very general and abstract form without sacrificing efficiency is one of the key ideas of generic programming [JLMS98].

In order to make the workflow flexible enough, we apply generic programming principles while designing workflow blocks. Block implementation should make minimal assumptions about the surrounding environment. The less it relies on implementation details, such as concrete data types, the more adaptable the implementation is. Blocks that have well-defined orthogonal responsibilities should be aware only of the details directly related to those responsibilities, and in the most generic way. The main rule while designing a block is *no over-specification*. If the essential functionality of the block does not depend on a particular data type, do not even mention this data type in the implementation. If it depends on a data type, but still is able work with different types, make this data type a parameter. This lack of concrete details can make the implementation look a little bit vague, but in fact it is exactly the opposite—it becomes succinct and precise.

Polymorphic Workflow Blocks

The most common requirements to workflow blocks is that they should process and output data. If necessary, blocks can also consume data generated by other blocks. At the same time, it must be possible to connect blocks in different ways.

The Dependency Inversion Principle [Martin02] states that blocks should not depend directly on each other. Instead, they should depend on abstract requirements to input and output. In this case, changing one block does not require changing other blocks, as long as all the blocks satisfy the requirements. How abstract are the requirements? More abstraction gives more flexibility, but makes it more difficult to ensure that the developers of the blocks have enough information to really satisfy the requirements in the concrete implementation. You have to balance these issues, considering the requirements and the tools' limitations.

Although the nature of blocks can be absolutely different, they still have a common property: the ability to input and output data items. If you implement this property similarly in all blocks, it will give you an opportunity to build different configurations from the same blocks. You can then connect and reconnect blocks without taking care of different input/output interfaces.

Because we're implementing the "pull" model, blocks should only provide a common way of getting data. If the blocks know how other blocks output data, they automatically have a way to input data. We'll use some form of polymorphism in order to make this process look unified.

How do you make the blocks polymorphic? Developers with object-oriented background might already have an answer—unified interfaces based on virtual functions or another form of dynamic binding.

A block that requires input can hold a reference to an object implementing the Base interface. The block does not need to know the concrete type of other blocks; it can just rely on the interface. See the following code:

```
class BaseBlock {
public:
    virtual OutputData getData() = 0;
};

class Modifier : public BaseBlock {
public:
    Modifier(BaseBlock& input) : input_(input) { }
    virtual OutputData getData() { return modify(input_.getData()); }
private:
    BaseBlock& input_;
};
```

It looks flexible enough, right? But it will not do for this implementation. Why not? The performance of this system is not high enough.

Polymorphism based on virtual functions can introduce significant performance hits. If you follow the Single Responsibility Principle [Martin02] and make the blocks fine-grained, you will end up having a lot of functions with simple or even trivial implementation.

Sometimes you can ignore the overhead of indirect function calls, but you definitely cannot ignore the fact that these indirect calls create optimization bottlenecks for compilers. Usually, compilers can optimize a sequence of static function calls. If the function definition is visible, it is possible to inline it, eliminate the overhead of passing parameters and returning results, and generate very compact and efficient executable code. However, if the compiler does not know which function implementation is going to be called, inlining is not an option anymore, and all this overhead is necessary.

In the previous code example, how would you define the `OutputData` type? You have a similar challenge here. The output data objects should be either fixed or polymorphic, because the blocks should process data objects that are acquired from other blocks. However, the problem looks even more severe in this case. Every block can expect different properties from input data objects. There are almost no common requirements. Most of the requirements are block specific, and do not make any sense in the context of other blocks. If you fix the data type, the type will have to implement all imaginable function and data member placeholders. Only some of them will be really used, and (even more scary) some of them must not be used until initialized properly. Instead, you could try to extract the interface, covering everything possible, and then build the inheritance hierarchy and override virtual functions, providing stub implementations of methods that are not "legal" for particular subtypes. However, it provides perfect opportunities to violate the Liskov Substitution Principle and suffer from the Refused Bequest code smell. And, even if you manage to implement it this way, you'll run into the performance issues described previously.

Why not use other forms of polymorphism? You could use the unbounded dynamic polymorphism, similar to the one available in dynamically typed languages, such as Smalltalk and Ruby. These approaches require additional work for C++ developers, but are definitely possible. You could even introduce reflection and runtime meta-programming capabilities, analyze block requirements dynamically, and build appropriate objects in runtime.

The main obstacle is the same: performance. Although they are incredibly flexible, all kinds of dynamic polymorphism, both bounded and unbounded [Czarnecki00], do not seem to be applicable to this problem, mostly because of performance overhead. The more fine-grained the blocks are, the more visible the performance hit becomes.

Also, it would make the workflows *too* flexible. You would not be able to rely on static type checking anymore, and you would have to execute the workflow just to detect obvious constraint violations. This would make designing workflows overcomplicated, which defeats the purpose of the solution. Reflection and runtime metaprogramming would make the performance problems even worse.

All types of dynamic polymorphism provide you with the ability to substitute objects of different types at runtime, but they make you pay for this ability with performance. You do not want to pay for flexibility that you are not going to use and normally you do not need to change the configuration of the workflow at runtime. You need as much flexibility as possible while the workflow is designed, but you do not need to change it after the code is compiled.

Static polymorphism can help you move as much work as possible from runtime to compile-time. This is why we choose the generic programming approach based on C++ templates. In this scenario, you still can construct workflows out of fine-grained blocks, but you do not have to pay for that with processing time or memory. Also, compile-time type safety is intact. Let's use this idea to implement the Modifier block again, as follows:

```
template <typename Input>
class Modifier {
public:
    Modifier(Input& input) : input_(input) { }
    OutputData getData() { return modify(input_.getData()); }
private:
    Input& input_;
};
```

No inheritance, no virtual functions, but still polymorphic. The "implement `BaseBlock` interface" requirement is replaced with a fuzzy, but much more flexible one: "implement `getData` function returning an object that *behaves like* `OutputData`."

Implementing static polymorphism, you are not losing the opportunity to return to dynamic polymorphism when it is more appropriate (for example, if it is necessary to change the workflow configuration at runtime). You do not have to change the block implementation, you just need a simple adapter that converts the statically polymorphic interface to a similar dynamically polymorphic interface, based on virtual functions or message dispatching. See the next example:

```
template <typename AdaptedBlock>
class Adapter : public BaseBlock {
public:
    Adapter(AdaptedBlock& adapted) : adapted_(adapted) { }
    virtual OutputData getData() { return adapted_.getData(); }
private:
    AdaptedBlock& adapted_;
};

Modifier modifier;
Adapter<Modifier> adaptedModifier(modifier);
```

Similar adapters can be implemented for unbound dynamic polymorphism, too. Obviously, the performance issues come back when these adapters are used. But now you have a choice; you can use it only when necessary.

ActionInfo Flow

What does the output data look like? You need some degree of polymorphic behavior from ActionInfo objects. However, the performance considerations should steer you toward avoiding the involved overhead. The ActionInfo implementation details are discussed later. For now, assume that you have already defined the ActionInfo type that is generic enough to satisfy the requirements of every block in the workflow.

Most of the time you'll work with sequences of ActionInfo objects. How should you store the sequences? How do you pass them between blocks? Should you preallocate memory before querying a block? Should the called block allocate memory itself? Acquiring the whole sequence might be expensive; should you do that if you might end up choosing the first action anyway?

Fortunately, most of the time you don't really need the whole sequence. At least, not at the same time. In most cases, you can process ActionInfo objects one by one, and make appropriate decisions regarding these objects separately. Instead of deciding how to store and pass the data that you might not even need, you can pass functions instead of requesting data. We applied the "tell, don't ask" approach. Instead of asking for all data, you tell the block what to do with the data and when to stop.

Replace the block-interface requirements with the following:

- The block should implement a function with a fixed name (called `forEach`).
- The `forEach` function should accept a function as a parameter.
- The `forEach` function should apply the received function to every ActionInfo instance that should be emitted by the block.

This implies that the function passed to `forEach` should be able to accept ActionInfo objects as a parameter. Note that we don't specify any types in the requirements, so the blocks are free to implement the `forEach` function and the callback function in different ways.

Block Implementation Examples

This next listing shows what *source blocks* (blocks that do not require input) look like:

```
class Source {
public:
    template <typename F>
    void forEach(F f) const {
        ...
        f( generateNext() );
        ...
    }
};
```

You want the `forEach` function to be able to accept any invokable entity, including functions and function objects (*functors*); this is why `F` is a template parameter.

Note that the caller of the `forEach` function does not have to worry about allocating storage for new ActionInfo objects. The Source block manages this storage and can reuse it for every next ActionInfo. Normally, blocks do not have to store previous ActionInfo objects, unless it is required by the nature of the block (for example, sorting blocks usually must collect all input ActionInfo before emitting the first output ActionInfo). This helps minimize the data transfer overhead.

If all the blocks satisfy these requirements, the blocks that require input can expect that the other blocks implement a similar `forEach` function. The following code listing shows a typical modifier's `forEach` function implementation:

```
template <typename F>
void forEach(F f) const {
    input_.forEach(ApplyToModified<F>(f));
}
```

The `input_.forEach` call ensures that ActionInfo objects are retrieved from the input block. The `ApplyToModified` functor's purpose is to modify each ActionInfo object received from `input_` and apply the original `F` function to the modified ActionInfo, as follows:

```
template <typename F>
class ApplyToModified {
public:
  ApplyToModified(F f) : f_(f) { }
  void operator()(const ActionInfo& ai) const { f_(modify(ai)); }
private:
  F f_;
};
```

The following code listing shows a typical filter implementation:

```
template <typename F>
  bool forEach(F f) const {
     return _input.each(ApplyIfAcceptable<F>(f));
  }

  template <typename F>
  class ApplyIfAcceptable {
  public:
     explicit ApplyIfAcceptable (F f) : f_(f) { }

     void operator()(const ActionInfo& ai) const {
         if (isAcceptable(ai)) f_(ai);
     }

  private:
     F f_;
  };
```

Note that there is no physical copying of data here. The ActionInfo objects created by the input block are checked in place, and the original function may be applied. Of course, you do not know anything about the original function, and it might copy or convert data for its own purposes. But there is no copying or conversions for the Filter block purposes, which means that the performance overhead is completely eliminated.

Partial Results

One of the most important requirements is the ability to interrupt the workflow when an acceptable ActionInfo is found, or when there is not enough time to complete the entire decision-making process. It is easy to implement: just make the function passed to `forEach` return a Boolean value, indicating whether the block is allowed to continue emitting ActionInfo objects or not. Each time the function is called, the `forEach` implementation should check the result and exit as soon as possible when necessary. It will effectively stop the whole workflow.

The sequence diagram shown in Figure 3.3.4 illustrates the execution flow.

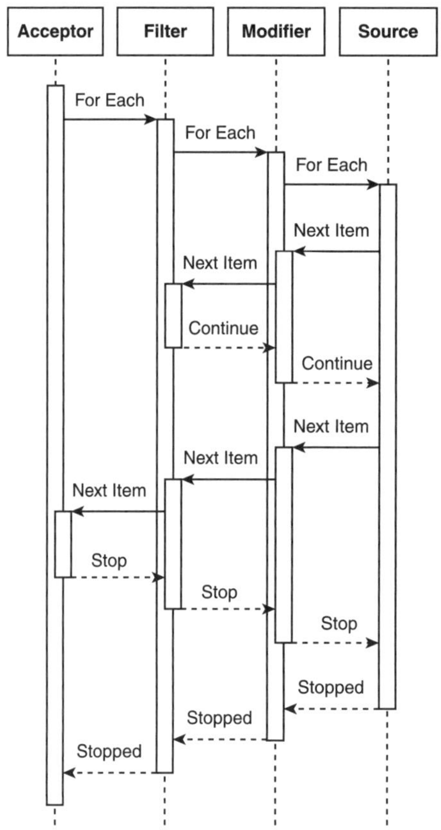

Figure 3.3.4 Pull workflow with callback functions.

Function Pointers versus Functors

You could pass function pointers to `forEach` functions. However, unlike calls through function pointers, calls to functors (function objects) can be inlined, efficiently eliminating most or all of the function call overhead [Meyers01]. Furthermore, empty or trivial implementations may be optimized away altogether. This is a very important way to get an abstraction bonus instead of an abstraction penalty. Imagine the implementation of the previous workflow where all the called code is implemented "in place," even for blocks that are located very far from each other in the workflow, so that there is no more need to really call functions and pass parameters. When inlined properly, the whole algorithm in the resulting executable can be merged into one highly optimized chunk of code that implements the necessary data processing only, without moving and converting data. In the meantime, the developers still deal with a very high-level, abstract, and decomposed representation of this algorithm.

This approach has a caveat, though. Depending on your compiler, the results of inlining may vary.

- First of all, the compiler might not use inlining opportunities fully and might still make real function calls. You may need to experiment, measure, and tweak your code and compiler settings in order to achieve the expected results.
- Secondly, uncontrolled inlining may lead to code bloat when large functions are duplicated. In that case, you can always return to function pointers.

ActionInfo Type

We keep mentioning the ActionInfo type, but we still have not shown you its definition. There is a reason: the generic ActionInfo type simply does not exist. Each block has its own requirements to the incoming ActionInfo flow, and each block can emit ActionInfo objects having specific properties. Combining all properties in one ActionInfo type is inefficient and unsafe. You need to be able to define minimalistic ActionInfo types in the lowest blocks (sources), and add or remove properties moving up the workflow, in compile-time. How can you achieve this? Here is what we did:

- Only sources define concrete ActionInfo types. These types do not have to be the same. Each Source includes only members relevant to this source.
- All other blocks make ActionInfo a template parameter. Then, they derive their output ActionInfo type from input ActionInfo types, using inheritance or aggregation to modify ActionInfo properties. As a result, each block's output ActionInfo type depends on the workflow configuration.
- All blocks use ActionInfo properties that are directly related to a block's responsibility and do not use any other properties. This makes the blocks very adaptable: they accept different input ActionInfo types, but any unknown properties are just propagated to the output and can be used by higher blocks.

Alternative Block Implementations

Another key idea of the generic programming idea is that you can provide alternative implementations of the same generic algorithm, specialized for some particular conditions, in order to make it more efficient when possible. This approach is extremely helpful for our application. For example, it allows us to have different versions of the same block, optimized for different platforms. These versions can be chosen either manually or automatically in compile-time. Also, policy-based design [Alexandrescu01] helps to customize generic block implementations partially, without re-implementing entire blocks and duplicating code.

Constructing Workflows

How do you connect the developed blocks to each other and make the workflow run? In C++, creating and connecting blocks looks as simple as the following listing:

```
template <typename Input>
Filter<Input> makeFilter(const Input& input) {
    return Filter<Input>(input);
}

...

makeFilter( makeModifier( makeSource() ) ).forEach(AcceptFirst());
```

However, you do not have to always do it manually. Because all blocks follow the same rules, the code has a very regular structure, which makes it possible and relatively easy to generate it automatically from scripts or even from the visual representation.

Constraints

Thanks to static polymorphism, you still can take advantage of C++ compile-time type checking. If, for example, the Filter tries to use members of ActionInfo objects received from the Modifier, and these members do not exist or have different types, this code cannot be compiled. In that case, the Filter cannot consume data directly from Modifier's output.

Sometimes it isn't enough, though. Compiler error messages can be unreadable or misleading, especially for code that makes heavy use of templates. This makes it difficult to understand which requirement has been broken. In order to simplify the diagnostics, we use C++ concept checking [Stroustrup03]. Also, we could have used the "Red Code, Green Code" approach suggested by [Meyers07].

The constraints can also be visualized on the workflow diagram:

- A set of labels is attached to block inputs. Every label represents a requirement to the incoming ActionInfo flow.
- Another set of labels is attached to block outputs. Every label represents a property that is added by the block, or a property that is removed by the block.
- When blocks are about to be connected, first of all the label should be analyzed. The requirements of the higher block should be satisfied by the output of the lower block. If they do not contradict, the connection is established. After that, the labels of the lower block's output can be propagated to the higher block's output.

This visual representation makes the process of building workflows quite intuitive and straightforward.

Conclusion

Although generic programming is definitely not a new idea, it still takes some non-trivial efforts to grasp and apply it properly. In addition, prepare for a struggle with C++ compilers and other development tools. Even when they conform to the contemporary C++ standard, efficiency of C++ templates support leaves a lot to be desired. Fortunately, compilers and tools are being improved, and the upcoming new C++ standard is going to facilitate generic programming and template meta-programming.

And the result is worth it, especially if you need to write abstract and reusable code, but have very strict performance requirements. The approach described in this gem makes Artificial Contender very flexible, compact, and fast, all at the same time.

References

[Alexandrescu01] Alexandrescu, A. *Modern C++ Design: Generic Programming and Design Patterns Applied,* Addison-Wesley Professional, 2001.

[Buschmann96] Buschmann, F., Meunier, R., Rohnert, H., Sommerlad, P., and Stal, M. *Pattern-Oriented Software Architecture Volume 1: A System of Patterns,* Wiley and Sons Ltd., 1996.

[Czarnecki00] Czarnecki, K., and Eisenecker, U.W. *Generative Programming: Methods, Tools, and Applications,* Addison-Wesley Professional, 2000.

[JLMS98] Jazayeri, M., Loos, R., Musser, D., and Stepanov, A. Report of the Dagstuhl Seminar 98171 "Generic Programming," Schloss Dagstuhl, April 27–30, 1998.

[Meyers01] Meyers, S. *Effective STL: 50 Specific Ways to Improve Your Use of the Standard Template Library,* Addison-Wesley Professional, 2001.

[Martin02] Martin, R.C. *Agile Software Development. Principles, Patterns, and Practices,* Prentice Hall, 2002.

[Meyers07] Meyers, S. "Red Code, Green Code: Generalizing Const," available online at http://nwcpp.org/Meetings/2007/04.html, 2007.

[Stroustrup03] Stroustrup, B. "Concept Checking—A More Abstract Complement to Type Checking," Technical Report N1510, ISO/IEC SC22/JTC1/WG21, September 2003.

3.4

All About Attitude: Building Blocks for Opinion, Reputation, and NPC Personalities

Michael F. Lynch, Ph. D.,
Rensselaer Polytechnic Institute, Troy, NY.
lynchm2@rpi.edu

The concept of attitude, a positive or negative evaluation about some attitude object, has a long history in psychology. Several games have used this concept in opinion and reputation systems, but the concept of attitude is more general than that. Attitude systems can be used to enrich NPC behavior in other ways besides opinion and reputation systems, for example, as inputs into decision tree or behavior trees, as part of modeling social networks, and to enrich NPC "personalities."

Attitude systems are more appropriate for games where NPCs need to exhibit believable social behaviors toward the player and/or toward one another. These can include game genres like god games, RPGs, dating games, games about political factions or palace intrigue, espionage, and perhaps some types of RTSs. They may also be appealing for use in certain forms of serious games, for example, games that need to simulate political processes, media or propaganda effects, or marketing campaigns.

This gem presents enough basic attitude theory to get started and suggests some lightweight implementations that can be used in conjunction with other parts of the AI.

Introduction

As game consoles and personal computers become more powerful, the prospect of developing games with NPCs that behave something like real human (or maybe alien) beings becomes more and more attractive—and more and more demanded by players. Emotions and attitudes are a large part of what makes us human, and if we are to develop human-like behaviors in our game characters, developers need to tackle these messier aspects of human behavior.

This gem presents the psychological construct called *attitude* that can become part of your toolkit for building more interesting and human-like NPCs. In presenting these ideas, please note that I am going to be doing considerable violence to how these concepts are actually treated in these social sciences, by drastically oversimplifying a number of their more subtle aspects to the point where they will (I hope) become useful in game development. After all, for these concepts to be practical, they ultimately have to be implemented in code.

Fortunately, game characters are caricatures of real humans: simpler, more extreme, and more over-the-top than real people. This should simplify the challenge.

So what you will be doing here is *not* proper science. Call it cognitive engineering or even psychological hacking. One good term for it is "critical technical practice," first proposed by Agre in 1997 and quoted by Michael Mateas [Mateas02].

My own way of describing critical technical practice is that it is a style of engineering practice that's informed by scientific theory but that nevertheless develops along its own trajectory and builds on its own successes. It is nevertheless prepared to reexamine its own premises and techniques in the light of new findings. Game AI certainly fills the bill.

Attitude

What is this thing called *attitude*? Attitude, as defined by social psychologists, has a meaning much like popular usage, as in "having a positive attitude about something," but not in the sense of 'having a bad attitude" or "copping an attitude." The study of attitude in the social sciences has a long history, and there is a vast body of literature about it spanning several disciplines within the social sciences.

Academic researchers strive to be precise in their definitions, and this is no different for attitude. Many different definitions have been offered over the years, but one good one is by Alice Eagly and Shelly Chaiken [Eagly93], who state that attitude "is a psychological tendency that is expressed by evaluating a particular entity with some degree of favor or disfavor." For excellent and in-depth coverage of this subject, the interested reader is directed to their magisterial text [Eagly93].

Central to the attitude construct is the evaluative dimension. Reducing it to the barest essentials, it simply means that the person holding the attitude has made a judgment about the degree to which the holder *likes* or *dislikes* the attitude object; that is, the person has judged how appealing or unappealing the target of the attitude is.

Attitudes can be held for just about anything that can be evaluated; the "target" of an attitude is usually termed the *attitude object*. Attitude objects can be *concrete*, like persons, physical objects, and places; or *abstract*, like notions of freedom, equality, nationalism, or justice. Attitudes about abstract entities that imply a moral dimension (like freedom or equality) are usually termed *values*.

The attitude object can be a singular item or an entire category or class of related items. Humans use the tendency to have attitudes about classes of objects, rightly or wrongly, to reduce cognitive load and streamline decision-making. The dark side of this is that it can lead to unfair prejudice and stereotyping. The bright side is that it can simplify life. If one's attitudes toward Tide detergent are that it smells nice, removes stains, and cleans well, one can, by collapsing down a long chain of reasoning and detergents, lead to the simple behavior outcome "just buy Tide." Humans are "cognitive misers;" we try to keep hard thinking down to the minimum amount needed to get the job done.

Importantly, attitudes can also be about events, attitudes about other attitudes, even attitudes about one's reactions to having an attitude, and so on. When dealing with human attitudes, it can get complicated very quickly.

Attitudes are also the basis for other forms of human cognitions. One way to view a *belief*, for example, is that it is an attitude about a *proposition*, that is, a logical statement. One can believe that the "Earth Is Flat" (a proposition that can be true or false), or that "Bobby Cheated on Danielle" (which might also be true or false).

Attitudes demonstrate what is sometimes called *dispositional liking*. Dispositional liking (the basis of attitude) is not the same thing as *momentary liking*, which is an immediate emotional response to some entity. Attitudes are evaluative beliefs about attitude objects; they are formed though a process sometimes called ABC, for affect, behavior, and cognition. *Affect* (accent on first syllable: *AF-fect*) is (briefly) the technical term for an emotion response. Some attitudes are formed because of an emotionally involving experience with an attitude object. *Behavior* is of course action; a series of pleasant dining experiences in fine restaurants can lead to a positive attitude toward fine dining. *Cognitions* are, of course, thoughts. Thinking about entities or issues can lead to the formation of attitudes; by thinking about what effect freedom has in human affairs may lead to positive attitudes about freedoms, and in turn, about the policies and philosophies that can lead to greater freedom.

Attitudes accumulate through a lifetime of interacting with the world. Attitudes form about attitude objects as you experience them, use them, or think about them. Immediate reactions of liking or disliking become attached to prior experiences and, by doing so, attitudes form and harden.

The distinction between dispositional and momentary liking may seem like a petty or unimportant point; however, you'll see later that attitudes are more or less enduring, and although they can be modified by momentary experiences, they persist beyond those experiences.

Strictly speaking, this discussion is not quite correct. People do not walk around sporting attitude meters that we can read off directly; instead we *infer* that people hold these attitudes based on what we can observe. How exposure to an attitude object (observable) leads to the activation of an internally held attitude (not observable), which can then (although not inevitably) lead to some outward expression of the felt attitude (observable). The expression of an attitude can be through many channels—facial expressions, posture, and other non-verbal communications, spoken language, and actual behaviors.

Complex attitude objects, like people, historical events, and organizations, can be evaluated along as many *attributes* about the attitude object that are of interest. You can love her dimples, hate her cooking, be mildly put off by her political views, enjoy her taste in movies, and detest her horselaugh, all at the same time. This idea will come up later when we look at the matter of love/hate.

Also, because an attitude represents an evaluation held by an individual about something, it is entirely subjective, and because it is, an attitude is not actually a statement of truth or falseness, even if very strongly felt.

Attitudes often (although not always) carry an emotional "charge." Some attitudes are purely intellectual, but others are learned as a result of an emotionally intense experience, and these can become among the most enduring of attitudes. In such cases, the affective (emotional) reaction (along the axis of appealing/unappealing) is noncognitive—we do not think about our reactions but instead experience them immediately and spontaneously. This is because such reactions involve more ancient regions of the brain where much of the emotional apparatus of the brain resides. Emotion is also bound with memory; highly emotional events are nearly always well remembered. It is what happens in extreme cases of Post Traumatic Stress Disorder (PTSD), and it is also why we usually can easily remember what we were doing during 9/11, the Challenger disaster, or the Kennedy assassination.

What's in an Attitude?

Fortunately, by taking some careful liberties with the rigorous social science here, one can produce a reasonably lightweight model of attitude that can be used by AI game programmers. In fact, something very much like attitude has been used in a number of games under various guises, perhaps most notably in the Xbox game *Fable* [Russell06]. Greg Alt and Kristen King mention an earlier approach used in the *Ultima Online* series [Alt02].

Calculations to update values in the attitude system need not be performed every frame; in fact, one nice thing about an attitude system is that attitudes need to be refreshed only when an event in the game that can affect attitudes occurs. Russell [Russell06] called these *opinion events.* More generally, they occur at points in the game story called the *dramatic beat.* How often do these happen? For *Façade,* Michael Mateas [Mateas02] estimated that these occur about every minute or so. An attitude system is therefore not going to stress the CPU budget very much, unless you are dealing with an exceptionally large number of NPCs carrying around a large number of attitudes. If so, the updates can be spread out over multiple frames without causing too many problems or getting them too far out of synch. Memory usage, on the other hand, is likely to be much more of a concern. [Alt02] discusses this point at length.

Let's begin by assuming that each agent capable of holding an attitude will in fact hold a collection of attitudes for as many attitude objects as the game requires. Most likely, the chief attitude object will be the human player or player character (PC), which then forms the basis for an opinion system—how the NPCs in the game world regard the player along some number of dimensions that the designers feel is important.

The agents here are presumably all the significant NPCs in the game, but may also be collections of agents, such as an entire village or even the entire game world. Agents that represent other forms of organizations can also hold attitudes. This was the approach taken in *Fable*, where attitudinal information about the PC was stored globally (called the *hero stats*), then at the village level for each of the 10 villages in the Albion game world, then for each of the many significant individual NPCs [Russell06]. This approach brought many important implementation benefits that are well covered in that article.

Valence

What data should an individual attitude contain? Obviously, the first item has to be that evaluative dimension of liking/disliking, a value commonly called the *valence*. So to start, each attitude needs to carry at least a single integer or floating point value to represent this dimension. Most likely it will be a bipolar value, to express the full range "of like/dislike, love/hate, satisfied/dissatisfied, agree/disagree," and all the rest of the ways an evaluation might be expressed. In some cases, a unipolar value may be more appropriate, as you will see later.

The valence can be stored as a single precision floating point value, especially if the game requires the ability to model small shifts in attitude taking place over time (persuasion). For many uses, however, an integer may be perfectly okay. If there is an anticipated need for storing a large number of attitudes for a large number of NPCs, the valence could be stored in as little as four bits, yielding a –7 to +7 range. (The 16th unused value of –8 (1000b) could be reserved as a sentinel value.)

How valence should be scaled, however, is somewhat less clear-cut. The simplest approach is to use –1.0 to +1.0 (and normalizing integer values in calculations as if they spanned this range), and further assume that liking/disliking is linear within that range. Indeed many systems implicitly assume this. But is it true? First, it is not clear from research how many orders of magnitude a liking/disliking reaction can span. If "mild dislike" is –0.1, does that mean "blind seething hatred" is a –1.0, or is it more like –10.0, or –100.0? Two possible alternatives are as follows.

- One is to still place the evaluation value on a scale from –1.0 to +1.0, but have the response curve be a sigmoid. Chris Crawford suggested this approach for storytelling systems [Crawford04].
- Another possibility is to allow the evaluation value to range over a small span, perhaps {1.0 … 5.0} to represent (for example) five orders of magnitude in logarithmic fashion, in a manner akin to the decibel scale or the Richter scale. Then "mild dislike" is a –1.0, strong dislike –2.0, moderate hatred a –3.0, strong hatred a –4.0, and blind seething hatred a –5.0. The descriptive phrases used here are simply to give an approximate idea of what each level represents. They are not

intended to express linearity of English descriptions (this is another can of worms entirely).

There are some occasions when a unipolar representation may be more appropriate, but these are unlikely to arise in most game design situations. For example, in Rational Emotive psychotherapy, the opposite of love is not hate, but rather indifference [Ellis75]. In that view, hate cannot be the opposite of love because it too requires an intense entanglement with the attitude object, and simply is a different emotion manifested relative to that attitude object, and not one that is 180° apart. The opposite of hate is also indifference.

Use caution here. If the nature of the game you are developing requires modeling this sort of emotional subtlety, expect to spend quite a bit of time developing a model that is up to the task.

Potency

A second value that can be stored in the Attitude class is *potency*. This is a measure of how strongly held the attitude is. Potency is *not* the same as the valence. It is possible, for example, to be very strongly politically moderate, having a valence close to 0.0, while feeling very strongly that way. This occurs because an attitude represents the accumulation of a lifetime of exposures to the attitude object, yet it is expressed as a single snapshot value. As exposures to the attitude object accumulate, the attitude tends to become more and more resistant to change, provided that each exposure does not depart too much from where the attitude is now. A person's first exposure to Brussels sprouts might result in a momentary liking of +0.2. Eventually, as occasions for eating Brussels sprouts pile up, the dispositional liking (the attitude) may settle down to +0.16. It will tend to stay there unless the person experiences some particularly transcendent or horrid (or even traumatic) experience with Brussels sprouts that forces a dramatic reevaluation.

It is possible to omit this potency dimension, but if you do, you will need some other technique to dampen down the large (and not believable) swings in attitude on the part of NPCs that would otherwise result.

This leads to another observation. In real life, a person who has occasion to radically rethink his position about something highly personal generally goes though considerable emotional upheaval along the way. Say, for example, a character learns that her brother has been discovered to be the perpetrator of a number of particularly heinous murders. All at once, her lifetime of accumulated feelings and attitudes about the brother will begin to collapse. She may move through the well-known sequence of denial/anger/guilt/resignation/reconciliation, sequencing (and possibly skipping) through these at a rate that is impossible to know beforehand.

If your game has moments of serious betrayal or treachery, any practical attitude system will probably break down under these conditions. Here, the best advice may simply be to bail out. For this, the Attitude class needs to implement a method that can forcibly reset the valence and potency to any desired values. Then when the dramatically heavy moment arrives, the game scripting system needs only do two things—use that method to forcibly reset all the affected attitudes held by anyone who needs to be "adjusted" to new, more appropriate values, and play the carefully-crafted animations of any NPCs that need to be shown going through their emotional upheavals. Periods of extreme emotional distress in humans are so complex that attempting to model them in game AI is probably hopeless at present.

Duration

Over time, people forget things, and extreme attitudes and bad memories usually soften over time. In many situations, we may want to allow attitudes to weaken or fade away. This is more a matter of getting realistic behavior out of an NPC than of remaining faithful to formal theory. As with most of these issues, the situation for real humans is a lot more complex than we would like it to be for these models.

Duration can be expressed in several ways, and since the fade-out generally follows a more or less logarithmic shape, a *half-life* measure is one way to represent it. If the game spans only a short time frame, attitudes and memories will remain fresh, and duration can be omitted altogether. But if game time frame is to span many years, some sort of decay function will probably be needed. If the game is supposed to span eight game years (to pick a convenient duration) and if memories fade by 50% every two game years, by game's end, attitudes first picked up near the start of the game will decay to only 1/16th of their original strength. Other approaches for decaying attitude strengths or valences are also possible, of course.

Another thing to consider is personality factors of the NPC. You may want some of them to hold grudges, and for them the half-life should be set very long so that very little (or even no) decay in their negative attitudes occurs. [Russell06] describes how this problem was tackled in *Fable*.

The Model

From these factors, the Attitude construct can be implemented with a lightweight class more or less like this:

```
class CAttitude
{
  private:
    Entity* target;     // attitude object;
                        //   points to a game entity
    Valence valence;    // typedef Valence as needed
    Potency potency;    // typedef Potency as needed
  int months;           // game months as half-life
```

```
public:
  CAttitude (Entity*);
  Decay;              // compute another month's decay
  Float Product;      // valence * potency

// etc.
}
```

Complex Attitude Objects

One useful metric often required from the Attitude class is an overall or aggregate evaluation when dealing with complex attitude objects (like the PC) that get evaluated on the multiple attributes that they possess.

At first, it might seem that, for linear representations, a normalized SRSS (square root of sum of squares) would work perfectly well. The game engine's math SDK may even already supply a method for computing this value from a vector of attribute-based evaluation values.

However, this is not what theory calls for. Instead a better value is computed as the normalized sum of the products of each attitude's valence times that attitude's strength, as in:

$$A_{tot} = \frac{\sum_i A_i valence * A_i strength}{\sum_i A_i strength} \quad (3.4.1)$$

If you're using some other representation, like sigmoid or logarithmic curves, generating this aggregate value will naturally require more computational overhead.

A Simple Example

Consider a game in which the player is battling a small but ferocious tribe over a period of time. The enemy NPCs are great warriors and smart enough to know when to retreat or melt away in order to fight another day. In other words, the individual NPCs last a lot longer than the typical 11 or so seconds a typical orc in a typical orc hoard survives in games of this type.

Figure 3.4.1 shows a very simple FSM (Finite State Machine) [Schwab04]. Of course, if the warriors were as good as just described, this FSM would be totally inadequate. A more modern and convenient algorithm would be the behavior tree (actually a DAG) [Isla05]. But to make the point, I'll use this FSM.

If there is no opinion or attitude system in use, you could set up an FSM much like this one, choosing and tuning various values of A (approach distance), R (retreat distance), and H (health) to generate slightly different behaviors among the warriors. You can still use this but now add the attitude system.

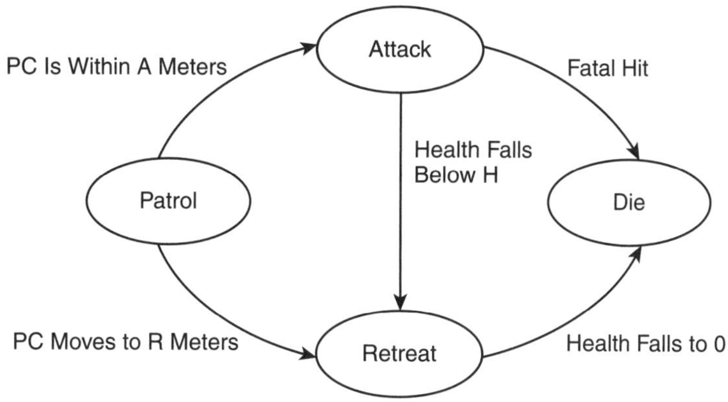

Figure 3.4.1 A simple FSM for a warrior. A is approach distance, R is retreat distance, and H is health.

In that case, each warrior hates the player (to some extent) and fears the player (to some extent) because the attitude system has in some fashion supplied each warrior with hate and fear values about the player to hold as attitudes. But then the player kills off a warrior who is the brother of one of the other warriors. The surviving warrior will now strengthen his hate attitude toward the player, and possibly also change the fear value (depending, perhaps, on how valiantly or cowardly the player fought while killing the brother). From there on, the surviving warrior can communicate his heightened hatred and fear, first of all to his buddies (affinity group), and then, like ripples in a pond, to more remote members of the tribe with ever lessening intensity. How this might be done is discussed briefly in a bit.

You now have a basis for dynamically changing the behavior of the FSM by modifying A, R, and H with attitude values that modify the initial settings upward or downward. Fearful warriors can now retreat at higher values of H. Hate-filled warriors might now require longer R distances before breaking off an attack, and also require longer A distances, on the theory that these hate-filled warriors are much more likely to monitor the environment awaiting the player's return.

Even this simple use of an opinion system can enrich an otherwise simple model. But you need not stop here. Figure 3.4.2 shows an extended FSM with extra nodes added to model the warrior who becomes an implacable foe. Now, if the level of hate (D) rises high enough and the level of fear (F) drops low enough, a tipping point is reached, and the FSM for this warrior now transitions to a new mode, whereby the warrior will pursue, fight, and only briefly retreat from combat with the player, until one or the other is killed. By doing this, you can further add to the believability of the NPC, because it is certainly believable for a warrior to reach a point where the battle with the player becomes personal. Note that you now begin to encroach on the design of the game itself. Once a warrior transitions into "implacable," the nature of the

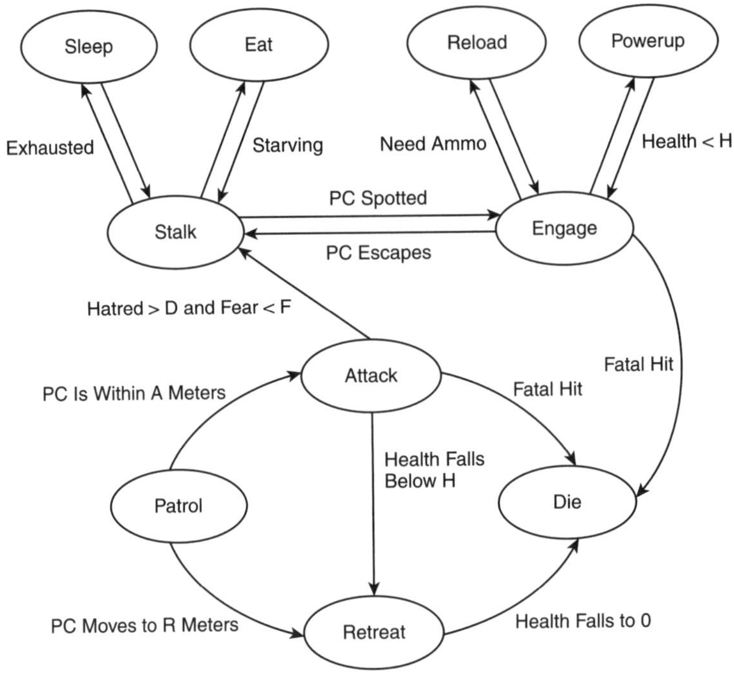

Figure 3.4.2 An extended FSM where attitude influences transitions between the nodes. D is the level of hate and F is the level of fear.

gameplay itself changes, and this sort of decision is probably better handled at the script level and not coded into an NPC's FSM.

So, you might be thinking, "You are creating a nightmare not only for the Q/A testers but for the script and level designers who have to handle all this added complexity!" Sorry, this is true, but cannot be helped as more human-like NPCs are sought. Clearly, better strategies for designing, testing, and tuning these NPCs are part of the challenge.

Attitude and Behavior

This is another area having an extensive body of theories (and their attendant controversies). A human, of course, holds literally millions of attitudes about just about everything she has ever encountered, and only in some cases is a particular attitude—held at a given time and place—followed by an observable behavior. But storing attitudes that don't lead to behaviors that the player can observe in a game environment are wasted.

You want to use attitude data structures only where they are useful, and this means once again cutting through a lot of theory to get at a minimal configuration that gets the job done.

So first, let's introduce two new wrinkles into the model. The first is the notion of an *attitude toward a behavior*. Yes, that is possible. Any action that an NPC is able to take can have associated with it an attitude, which represents the direction and degree the NPC feels that behavior is desirable. In a social game, murder may be possible, but a particular character may view it sufficiently negatively to entirely rule it out, or to commit murder only when the provocation reaches some extreme threshold.

The next notion is *behavioral intention* (abbreviated to BI). BIs sit between attitudes and behaviors, and in this model a behavior has to have a BI connected to it before the behavior can occur. This can turn out to be a welcome simplification, however, and one that lends itself for use in behavior trees or other models of NPC behavior. Let's see how this might work in practice.

Let's say an NPC has developed a positive enough attitude toward the player that he or she wants to help. This NPC has an elaborately scripted behavior tree that contains a number of possible "helping" behaviors—for example, Give Gold, Share Secret, or Arrange Lodging. However, these can only fire when conditions are right. Give Gold and Share Secret can only occur when the player is in proximity with the NPC, whereas Arrange Lodging can be done beforehand and at a distance. (The player can show up at the tavern, expecting to have to beg for a place to stay, only to be told that a room and meal have already been provided for.) Give Gold or Arrange Lodging can happen only if the NPC has sufficient gold to make either of these gifts. Share Secret can happen only if the NPC has a valuable secret to share.

BIs can be used here to "prime" those helping behaviors, which are then further subject to the previous test conditions. So, if the NPC has developed a positive enough attitude toward the PC, the NPC can form a BI to help the PC. The BI can then test the IF portions of the stack of rules in the behavior tree, to determine whether the other conditions are also met. If so, the behavior can actually occur.

Persuasion and Influence

This is yet another complex and messy body of theory, which you need to pare down as well. How much paring is required depends on the kind of game you are building. Serious games that need to model political struggles, or advertising or propaganda campaigns, may need more of the model than games that don't.

In theory, how effectively a person or group *A* can persuade *B* to adopt or shift some position (that is, adopt or shift some attitude) depends on a large number of factors arranged in a causal chain. The persuader, A, is usually called the *sender,* and the target of the persuasive message the *receiver.* At a minimum, the sender needs to be *credible* (to the receiver), *likeable* (by the receiver), and *similar* (to the receiver), in combination to some degree. The receiver, for his part, has to *attend* to the message, be able to *process* the message, and be sufficiently *involved* with what the message is about. The message itself might appeal to reason, emotion, or both. If the appeal is to reason, it has to be logically sound, as the receiver interprets it. Also, the message can easily fail to persuade if it advocates a position too extreme relative to the receiver's current attitude and falls outside of positions the receiver is willing to accept.

In a game, you can do away with a lot of this. First, let's assume that all persuasive communications in a game are important, that receivers will always find them important, attend to them, and are able to understand them. This immediately removes four variables. Categorizing senders into a much smaller number of groups can collapse down credibility, liking, and similarity. It will then be necessary to maintain a matrix of how much Group A trusts messages from Group B.

Note that this matrix is itself a representation of N-by-N attitudes, and could thus also see its values shift over time as groups interacted with each other over the course of the game. If this is too complex for the game, and such attitudes are not going to shift, you should compose the matrix with static values and leave it alone during the game.

This matrix can also be augmented by adding entries for particular individuals (who are also members of groups) to the matrix. This permits members of Group A to mostly distrust messages from Group B, while allowing members of Group A to grudgingly accept messages from Person P (who otherwise happens to be a member of Group B). [Alt02] provides details of a nice implementation of this idea.

Finally, let's assume that you aren't going to worry about how the message is composed; simply that it carries content and persuasive strength. To continue with the example, the surviving warrior who now passionately hates the PC can be shown in an in-game cutscene haranguing his fellow warriors as to why it's now important to make slaughtering the PC top priority. Internally, the message is simply conveyed, and the attitudes of the warrior's buddies are suitably adjusted.

Social Exchanges of Attitudes

As mentioned, the warrior personally affected by the outcome of a battle can communicate his heightened hate and fear about the player to his affinity group. Moreover, if he was close to his brother, and is close to his affinity group, the other members of that group presumably also have liking toward the deceased brother, and will be responsive to the surviving warrior's messages. This gets into *balance theory* [Wikipedia07]. Balance theories are a powerful part of modeling social networks, which is another aspect of human behavior that is outside the scope of this gem. Using the matrix approach in the previous section, possibly with enhancements, can handle much of this.

In many games, all that is important is for the various NPCs to hold attitudes toward the player only, and not hold attitudes about each other. If there is no reason in the design of the game to keep information about inter-NPC attitudes, leaving them out greatly simplifies the design. In fact, [Russell06] was quite explicit about the fact that *Fable* stored opinion data only about the PC and no one else to get complexity under control. The opinion system used in *Fable* is essentially based on the attitude construct, just not by that name.

However, some game designs benefit by having such a system if the gameplay revolves around alliances, treachery, and betrayal. Doing so uncovers a hornet's nest of added complexity.

One such complexity is sheer algorithmic cost. Of course for N characters that can hold attitudes, there are N * (N – 1) pairings, yielding an $O(N^2)$ complexity. You do not even get to divide this by two, because it is unsafe to assume that *A*'s attitude toward *B* will be symmetrical with *B*'s attitude toward *A*. One strategy is to reduce the size of N by assigning less critical NPCs to a much smaller number of groups and tracking those instead.

Another Example

Consider how this can be used in a hypothetical open-world action-adventure game about warring crime syndicates and the sleazy yet colorful NPCs who inhabit this game world. The object of the game is to compete against the NPCs by doing dirty deeds, enforcing the rules laid down by the mob, expanding turf, making money, switching allegiances, and, on occasion, even betraying or killing an NPC when it will do you the most good.

As the PC, you engage in acts that earn the respect or disgust of the NPCs, who form opinions about you as you claw your way to the top. In a manner following the approach used in *Fable* (which used five dimensions of Morality, Renown, Scariness, Agreeableness, and Attractiveness), let's use several dimensions of opinion scale for this example—Competent, Honorable, Ruthless, Charismatic, and Loyal.

Ideally, the selected attributes should be as orthogonal as possible, that is, each attribute is as close to statistically independent of the others as possible. These five seem to meet this requirement. It may seem strange to include Honorable, but consider it as the code of conduct that dictates that innocent "civilians" are not to be harmed (especially one's mother), but that shopkeepers, gamblers, druggies, and johns are fair game, as is anyone who crosses you.

Assume the game features several different competing crime organizations, each with its own style of achieving dominance. One is led by a capo who favors brazen, overt violence (he will probably go down in flames early on); another prefers corrupting police and judges, a third likes to insinuate his organization into legitimate enterprises. Each capo is likely to value a different pattern of attributes of the player or any NPC as best suited for his style of organization.

As the player continues to work up the ranks, different bosses will tend to value different combinations of these perceived attributes. A capo who prefers to keep violence hidden away, used only as a last resort, might well bypass a player who is too hot-headed for that capo's style. A player who botches too many jobs will find that his perceived Competence has deteriorated and so be left off the important missions that could best advance his career. This could lead to the player having to do many more low-level missions in order to get back into the good graces of his superiors in the gang hierarchy.

Just a handful of attribute/attitude dimensions are needed to make this sort of gameplay possible. In *Fable*, the opinion system and hero stats operated using only the five dimensions listed previously. Even if you only consider high/low on each (on the premise that extreme characters are more fun), that leads to 32 possible combinations of how the player is perceived and the player's reputation is built.

Other combinations of these dimensions can be part of the personalities the designers build into the rest of the NPCs. After all, even a dim-witted but ruthless and highly loyal NPC can be useful to a crime syndicate.

Cautions and Conclusion

At this point you may be thinking, "Why not just make games that need NPCs like this be multiplayer games and let real human players handle all this complexity?" To some extent a multiplayer approach will work and already does in many games, but the problem with this approach is analogous to the problem with player-created content—most of it (perhaps 95%) is too poor in quality to be of much use, let alone fun. Not that many people are excellent storytellers, role players, or improvisational actors, and, moreover, it is a lot of work. It seems like it will be the fate of game designers and other talented folk to create the rich game worlds and believable characters that players demand.

This gem introduced a few fundamental concepts about the psychology of attitude. Attitude is only one aspect of the psychology of those most complex of organisms, human beings, but is a useful start and one within reach. Fortunately, the representation of a single attitude can be quite lightweight, although in a game with any complexity they can become quite numerous.

As more and more CPU and RAM budgets are allocated to game AI, game developers will increasingly need to mine the very large body of knowledge about human behavior from psychology, social psychology, and cognitive science. The good news is that game developers need to build caricatures and not real humans, and the challenge is one of adopting what we know of real humans and re-engineering that knowledge into practical implementations.

References

[Agre97] Agre, Phil. *Computation and Human Experience*, Cambridge University Press, 1997.

[Alt02] Alt, Greg and King, Kristen. "A Dynamic Reputation System Based on Event Knowledge." *AI Game Programming Wisdom*, Charles River Media, 2002: pp. 425–435.

[Crawford04] Crawford, Chris. *Chris Crawford on Interactive Storytelling*, New Riders Books, 2004.

[Eagly93] Eagly, Alice and Chaiken, Shelly. *The Psychology of Attitudes*, Harcourt Brace Jovanovich, 1993: pp. 1.

[Ellis75] Ellis, Albert and Harper, Robert A. *A Guide to Rational Living*, Wilshire Book Company, 1975.

[Isla05] Isla, Damien. "Handling Complexity in the Halo 2 AI," GDC 2005 Proceedings, available online at http://www.gamasutra.com/gdc2005/features/20050311/isla_01.shtml.

[Mateas02] Mateas, Michael. *Interactive Drama, Art and Artificial Intelligence*, (Ph. D. Dissertation), Carnegie Mellon University, School of Computer Science, 2002, report CMU-CS-02-206.

[Russell06] Russell, Adam. "Opinion Systems," *AI Game Programming Wisdom 3*, Charles River Media, 2006: pp. 531–554.

[Schwab04] Schwab, Brian. *AI Game Engine Programming*, Charles River Media, 2004.

[Wikipedia07] "Balance Theory," available online at http://en.wikipedia.org/wiki/Balance_theory.

3.5

Understanding Intelligence in Games Using Player Traces and Interactive Player Graphs

G. Michael Youngblood, UNC Charlotte

youngbld@uncc.edu

Priyesh N. Dixit, UNC Charlotte

pndixit@uncc.edu

As the field of game AI has grown, the ability to create characters and game reactions that impart reasonable, challenging, and even insightful actions in their control has improved. However, the basic ability to describe what makes something truly seem generally intelligent has lagged behind. This gem provides some insight into a specific visualization and graph-based AI analyses mindset with some tools and techniques that forward a goal of better understanding both artificial and human intelligence in games. This gem shows how logging player-centric game data can be used to better understand both natural and artificial player behavior through the use of visual data-mining, graph-based interaction representations, and clustering tools.

Introduction

The game AI developer is focused on the creation of an entity, multiple entities, or possibly just a system which the engaged human player must perceive as a challenge in some form or fashion. Satisfying the cognitive needs of human players is what makes the game interesting, fun, and challenging, and it is what ultimately makes the game sell. The interesting problem is that not every human player perceives the same, or even plays the same. What is *intelligent* to one player is *dumb* to another. This makes game AI development very difficult, and it leads to discussions about the tradeoffs between focusing on games that pit human versus human or human versus machine (AI). Fortunately, there is a strong desire for a better single player experience and hence a strong need for better AI—or as the need is often stated, there is a need for human-level AI. There have been numerous discussions about the pursuit of human-level AI [Heinze02, Laird01, Laird02], but there still remain many open questions about how to determine whether you have achieved it.

Is a game AI *turing test* [Russell03] a valid way to determine whether an entity is human or machine controlled? Although it may prove to be an interesting endeavor, it would undoubtedly be mired in much debate and conjecture as with all rather subjective methods. What is needed is a method for objective evaluation of game AI to a human baseline of performance on the same or similar task or scenario. This act requires data.

The current trend in modern computer games is to leave out detailed logging in order to free up system resources for other material; however, this data could be used to enhance the interactive game experience by providing insight into the behaviors of both human and machine players.

The Value of Information

Logging in games is often tied to the game's save features because these subsystems commonly track the progress of the player. However, most games do not log player information; this trend is getting worse, as you can note by the various number of games that now use a checkpoint system for saving rather than being able to save the game at any point. This means that the game will only save when a player reaches a certain location in the level. This way, the developers do not need to track where the player is going at all times—just when they reach certain milestones. As argued by Eilers [Eilers05], this is fine for the first few times that a player plays the level; however, it becomes a hindrance later on once they have already memorized the level. It creates work for the player by them having to drudge through mastered areas to reach the challenge. It also hinders the ability for real logging because there is now no in-game progress monitoring which is a nice place to invoke logging.

Logging is very useful during the play-testing phase because it can make the process more efficient. The development team could capture the tester's session in video form but it is often too time consuming to watch all the videos, analyses may end up very subjective, videos consume a lot of disk space, and objective, automated video processing is a difficult process. Watching the session firsthand can introduce bias from the observer's opinion. Another problem with video or screen capture playback is that it is often difficult to get a complete picture of play just from the player's perspective. Seeing the entire path or desired sections of the player's interaction at once or in a specific focused view in an interactive analysis tool would be very useful in understanding the behavior of that player—whether it was a human or machine.

A good set of logged data and some analysis tools (including visualization tools) also helps to find emergent behaviors, or behaviors that are not expected by the developers. These are not necessarily errors but interesting "accidents" that differentiate games from non-interactive forms of entertainment [Consalvo06].

The most common reason for excluding or oversimplifying logging is that it can slow down the game. For instance, during the development for *Age of Empires II: Age of Kings,* the developers used faster machines for play testing than those targeted for deployment due to the slow down induced by logging play test data [Marselas00]. This does not always have to be the case because one of the most machine expensive steps in logging is file IO, which can be done more opportunistically at periods of lessened hardware need, at cutscenes or designed lulls, or by using multiple threads instead of constantly writing to a file during gameplay. There is also an issue of the needed fidelity for logging. Plenty of information can be gained from 1Hz or slower logging, so 10Hz or better is not always necessary.

Over the past few years, we have been performing AI research with a number of game testbeds of our own creation, some built from the ground up and others modifications of commercial games. We often use the Urban Combat Testbed (UCT), which have been made freely available at www.urban-combat.net. UCT is a total conversion mod of the popular *Quake 3* game by Id Software. The installed base of *Quake* fans has made it easy to find study participants (especially at Quakecon, which is always a great time), and we have captured hundreds of players interacting in our game scenarios. (If the reader is interested in being a study participant for our game studies, please visit our play testing Website at playground.uncc.edu/PlayTesting.)

We often capture logs at 10Hz, but as you can see in Figure 3.5.1, the information from a 1Hz capture can often be just as informative and useful. However, in Human Computer Interface (HCI) analysis work, 10Hz sampling is typically conducted because it is the fastest normal response time for a human using an interface device.

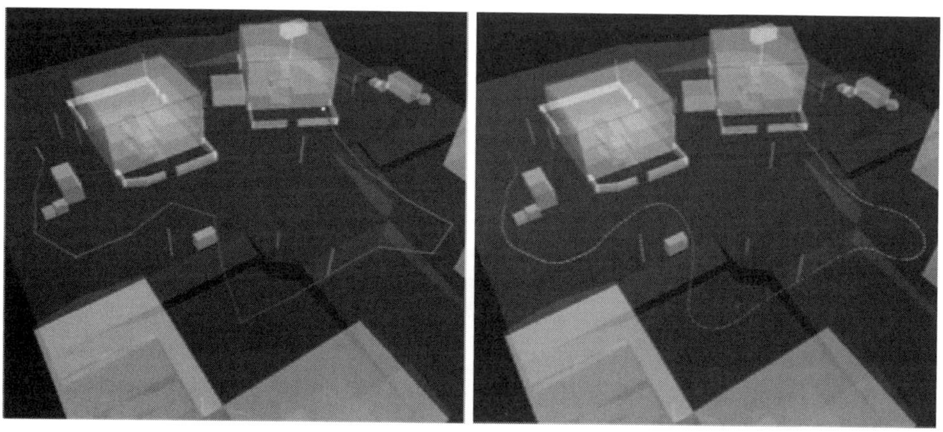

(a) **(b)**

Figure 3.5.1 Player trace from UCT (Urban Combat Testbed) player data showing player movements from logging at (a) 1Hz and (b) 10Hz. The thin line represents the spatial movement of the focused entity over time in the environment.

Our analysis tool whose interactive output is shown in Figure 3.5.1, PlayerViz, requires data files that contain the following information at each timestep:

- Position (x, y, and z)
- Orientation (yaw, pitch, and roll)
- Speed
- Elapsed time
- Time-score
- Health
- Shots fired
- Whether a flag is captured

ON THE CD

The PlayerViz tool is included on the book's CD-ROM and is freely available online at playground.uncc.edu/GameIntelligenceGroup/Projects/CGUL.

The frequency of the timesteps is not fixed and can be adjusted depending on the detail required. Ideally, a logging system could dynamically adjust logging frequency to minimize impact on the game by scaling to the available hardware capabilities. However, even if you log once per second it is enough to do some analysis on player behavior. The implementation of the logging and recorded aspects will vary based on the game, but consideration should be given as to what information is easily available and useful for knowledge discovery and understanding the intelligent actions of entities in the game.

Capturing interaction is the key to understanding the intelligent actions taken in a game by all rational agents participating. So, you log player interactions with the interactive feature points of the environment [Youngblood02]. *Interactive feature points* are elements in a game upon which an entity can perform an action (for example, open, close, push, jump over, stand in, shoot, and lasso). These elements might occupy positive space and represent a real world or fantasy object (for example, window, door, tree, stage coach, crate, and magical potion), they might be negative space areas that can contain other game elements or even the player (for example, a courtyard, inside a room, or in a vehicle), or they might be other agents within the game (for example, an opposing force, a horse you can ride, or a dragon you may fly). Anything with which a player can interact in any fashion can be considered an interactive feature point.

In the real world, the number of interactive feature points is infinite, but in a game world they are finite and determined by the designers and the capabilities of the game engine. All of the interactive feature points in a game or game scenario can be described in a interaction possibilities graph, as shown for a simple example FPS environment in Figure 3.5.2a. The vertices represent interactive feature points and the edges indicate that an interaction may occur next from the current interaction—an extension would be to enumerate the types of interactions possible with each interactive feature point. This graph can be used to look for invalid interactions or design issues when analyzing player traces from logged data.

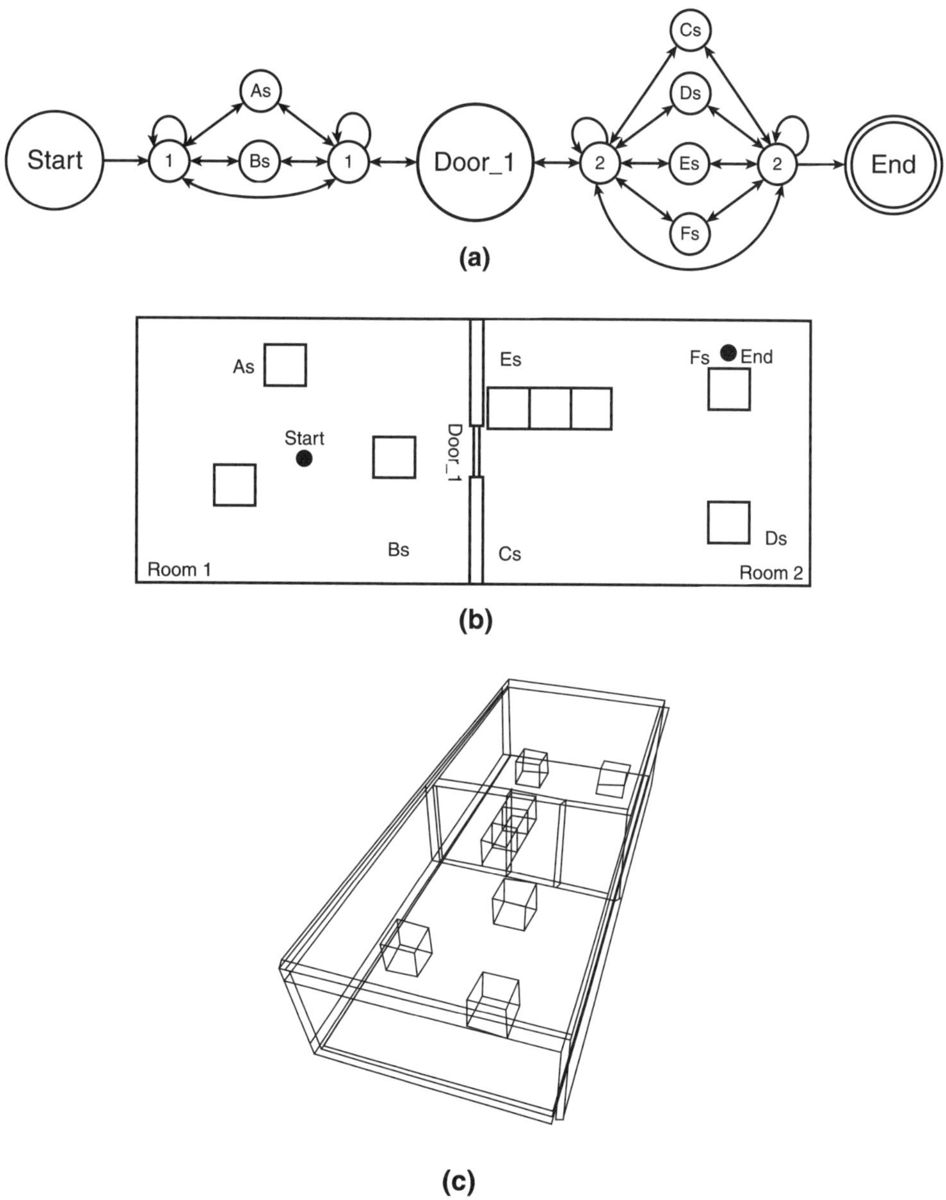

Figure 3.5.2 The interaction feature points of a game can be used to generate an interaction possibilities graph, shown in (a). This illustrates the interaction possibilities in the FPS game scenario shown in (b) from the top and from a 3D perspective in (c).

Generating information for validation from design, capturing information from play testing and agent interaction testing, and creating insightful knowledge as new information from analyses emphasizes how valuable this information is to the design of games and the desired interaction in games, which largely consists of the human and AI driven behaviors. A very important factor in understanding behaviors in games is being able to visualize these behaviors. See Figure 3.5.3.

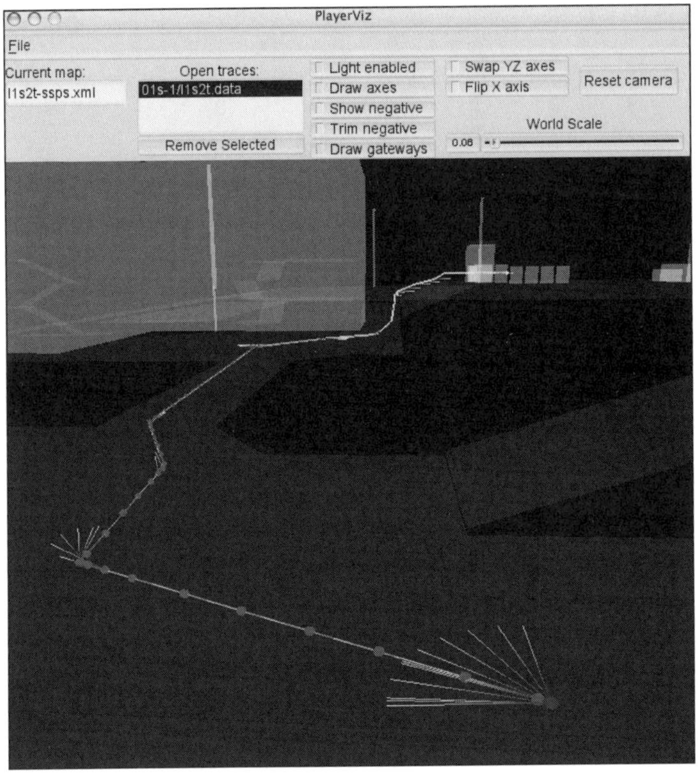

Figure 3.5.3 A screen capture of the PlayerViz tool used for visualizing single or multiple player traces. It shows the path of a player over time, where the spheres represent position and the line segments protruding from the spheres represent orientation.

A Picture Is Worth a Thousand Words

The information gathered from in-game logging of player actions can easily become overwhelming. There are several variables that are all tracked simultaneously, including time, position, orientation, and interaction. This data is easier to comprehend if it is represented visually with a player trace. A *player trace* shows the actions of the player from start to finish in a visual manner. The PlayerViz tool is designed to allow interactive visualization of player trace data from one or more players. As seen in Figure 3.5.3, a player trace is represented as a series of spheres with connecting lines. The color of the spheres cycles through a rainbow color-map, blue to green to red over time, in a way that the colors appear to change faster when moving slower and vice versa. The position of the spheres represents the position of the player, and the player's orientation at that time is portrayed as an oriented line segment coming out of the sphere. A wireframe white sphere represents that the player found the goal and it is usually located at the end of a trace. A red wireframe sphere around the player indicates lost health, and a red solid sphere at the end of the line segment means the player fired a shot. A player trace provides a great overview of physical interactions, but it may not always apply to all games—some games do not have a clear spatial component to them, such as puzzle games.

PlayerViz can also be used to examine multiple player traces at once, which can provide some interesting results. For example, if the players were playing together, their group dynamics can be studied. You could also take the average of their player traces to get an overview of their composite performance. If the players are adversaries, you can examine the strategies taken by each and how they responded to each other's actions. For example, if two players are simultaneously pursuing the same goal, it would be interesting to see the paths taken by each player and where the paths intersect. Player traces can also be utilized to show AI agent behavior and compare it to human behavior. The composite trace of all humans and all agents could be compared to give a general overview of how human-like the AI is for the game.

Simplification of World Data

In order to provide context for the player traces, the world geometry must also be visualized. However, the geometry does not need to be shown in great detail and can be greatly simplified. For PlayerViz, the world is broken down into positive and negative space regions. The 3D modeler manually specifies positive space. It represents an approximation of the external world geometry for an object (for example, a box around a building). These regions are not exact, but you need only a rough estimate of geometry to provide spatial coherence between the player trace and the world. The negative space regions can be manually specified or automatically calculated using methods such as cell decomposition.

In order to simplify the negative space geometry, you must break the world down into a series of convex regions. There are several techniques for decomposing the geometry of a world into regions. The technique we used is called *key vertex cell decomposition* [Youngblood06]. This method involves creating polyhedrons by connecting key vertices on the positive space objects (such as the corners), avoiding crossing segments, and combining adjacent regions to increase size as long as the polyhedrons remain convex.

These regions have a lot of extraneous polygons because negative space generally contains mostly empty regions. However, if you render only the polygons that are roughly parallel to the ground, you generally get useful geometry. You can also identify gateways between spatial regions of the geometry. These gateways are identified by coplanar boundaries between regions. However, the boundaries must be completely coplanar for a gateway to be easily detected. These regions and their connecting gateways can also be used to assist path planning and other spatial tasks for AI agents. The agent can learn about the world around it by keeping track of the regions it has visited. Looking at the player trace for such an agent can be useful in machine learning studies.

A Pixel for Your Thoughts

Even with the help of player trace visualization, it can still be a difficult task to examine all of the player traces if there are several hundred players. One way to make it easier is to use visual data mining [Keim02]. PlayerViz can be used to generate a set of Web pages showing a table of thumbnails of each player trace from different angles. This allows the user to quickly scan through the dataset and find interesting traces, which can then be loaded into PlayerViz to examine further. Once the desired or anomalous artifacts are identified visually, the user can then implement ways to automatically find occurrences of these artifacts, often through the creation of specific feature-finding algorithms. The visual data mining is mainly a bootstrap method to guide the creation of more specific tools for a particular game, but it can be powerful in helping to define what you should be looking for, which is often difficult to determine *a priori.*

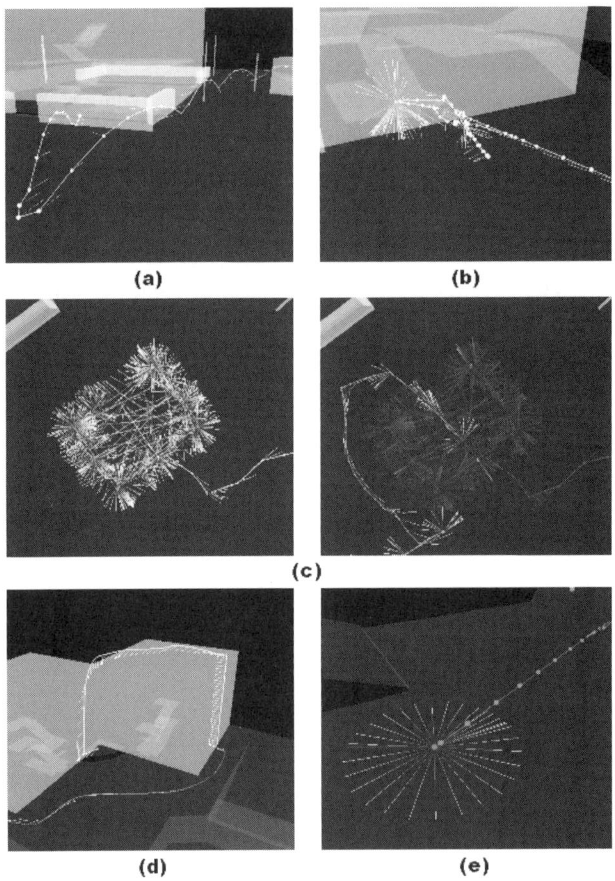

Figure 3.5.4 A table of interesting artifacts found through visual data mining of player traces, as follows—(a) jumper, (b) fluster, (c) positive learning, (d) emergent behavior, and (e) crazy Ivan.

In our own work using these player trace images, as shown in Figure 3.5.4, we can find several interesting artifacts that would be near impossible to find by looking at the numbers alone. For example, Figure 3.5.4a shows a *jumper*. This is a person who likes to jump continuously even when he or she is walking on a flat surface. Another example, shown in Figure 3.5.4b, is called a *fluster*. A fluster is an artifact in the player trace where the player seemingly loses control of his or her cursor. It can be caused by lack of experience with mouse aiming or also by a faulty mouse. These occurrences would be very hard to track without visual data mining.

Figure 3.5.4c shows two player traces of the same player. The left image is the source, or first attempt, and the right image is the target, the second attempt. It can be clearly seen that the player learned from his previous attempt how to get out of that closed-off area. The opposite can also be true when a player finds the goal the first time but forgets it in the second attempt. Thus, you can use this technique to observe both positive and negative learning.

You can also find emergent behaviors using this technique, such as the player trace shown in Figure 3.5.4d. The intent was for the player to climb the wall and find the goal, but instead this player climbed the side of a house and jumped down from the roof. Such behavior is also difficult to track without visual reference. The last example is a crazy Ivan, or an instance where a player turns a full 360° to survey his or her surroundings, as seen in Figure 3.5.4e.

Using this visual data, you can also analyze the areas that are the most visited (or least visited) by the players. This allows the game designers to determine whether their design for the level matches the player experience. For example, if the designer places a clue in an area of the map that very few players ever go to, the designer will know that most players are not likely to find it.

There are several future additions to the PlayerViz tool planned, such as calculating the average player trace using a set of several player traces. This average trace can be used to quickly and easily see the general path taken by most of the players. Another feature might be to generate a congestion map using a set of several player traces to highlight areas that were the most visited. This feature would give game designers a good idea of where future players are more likely to explore, so that they can place interactive feature points accordingly.

Interactive Player Graphs

Understanding the spatial trajectory and observing simple spatiotemporal interactions provides a great deal of understanding about the intelligence of the observed rational agent, but interactive visualization tools still require a lot of manual work for the analyst. A representation of interaction that could be used for comparison with other players would be useful in this case. The trajectory of interaction in the context of a game is a representative of the strategy taken by the individuals playing. The ability to capture and compare strategies could be very useful. The establishment of a finite set of interactive feature points and the introduction and enforcement of a designed interaction possibilities graph along with proper in-game logging come together to allow for the generation of an interactive player graph for each player in a game.

An interactive player graph (IPG) is built either during play or in post-play processing of the running or completed player log file. The game environment needs to capture the desired interactions to make the graph. The vertices of the graph represent an interaction event (for example, pushing a button, picking up a health item, stunning an opposing force, picking up a key, going through a door, or standing in a new region of the map). IPGs can be very detailed, but it is less important and more computationally feasible to reduce the data stream and ignore the minor noise generated from movement, orientation, and other esoteric changes in state. What you need is a somewhat higher abstraction of player activity that gives you the proper resolution for understanding while reducing the extraneous information that can bog down analysis and obscure intention.

Typically, you track spatial movement within the *qualitative convex regions* determined from cell decomposition methods as described in the previous section and report position by those numbered regions when entered—in many game types, especially FPS/3PS, spatial interactions by normal movement can dominate an IPG if tracked at too high a resolution. Other interactions are typically recorded as they occur. So, you build an IPG from a combination of interactions, which come from rough spatial movements through environmental regions and player interactions with specific objects in those regions. However, IPGs do not have to incorporate spatial interaction and are therefore also very useful for analyzing games that do not have a clear spatial component to them.

One problem with the graph representation is that there is a definite issue of timing in many games, and often the real difference between performances in a scenario, especially ones with few paths of choice through the environment, is the time it takes different players to accomplish the same task. Gonzalez [Gonzalez99] and Knauf et al. [Knauf01] also note the importance of time in validation of human models. IPGs capture time by weighting the edges between interaction feature points with the time it had taken the player between interactions. IPGs abstract a player's performance in a game or game scenario, removing the detailed state change noise through the environment while capturing their approach of interaction, moving from one interaction feature point to another and also capturing the time aspect of their performance. Figure 3.5.5 shows a player trace converted to an IPG using the associated spatial decomposition map associated with the scenario—note that the only interaction represented is map traversal; other interactions would merely extend the graph with additional interaction vertices.

To be noted is that there are a number of extensions or variations to the base IPG format described here. For example, it may be useful to associate the type of interaction with an interaction feature point representing each as a separate vertex. Agents may tag internal state to the transitions or interactions as well.

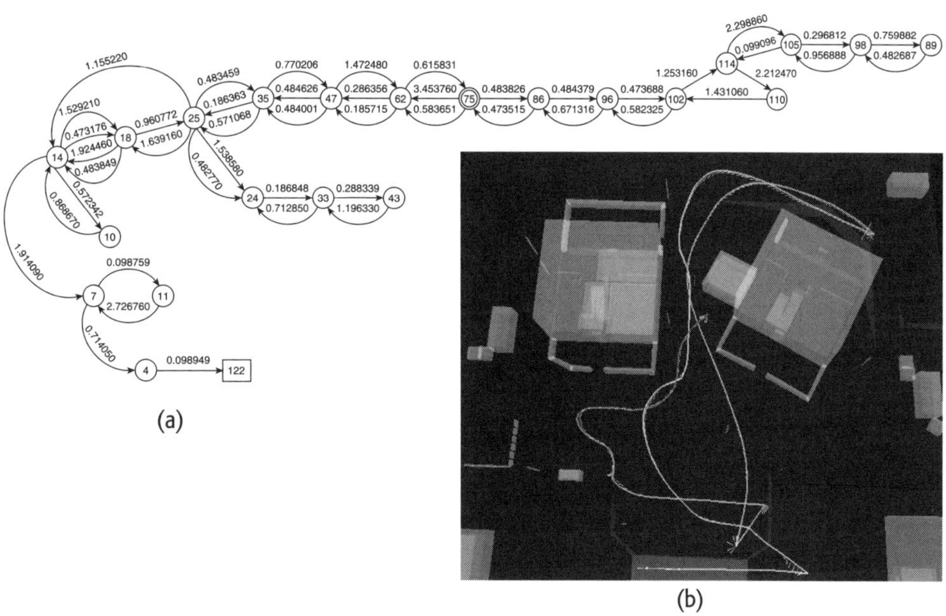

Figure 3.5.5 The interactive player graph in (a) was created from logged data from the player whose same player trace is shown in (b) using PlayerViz. The vertices represent interactive feature points (entry into new spatial map regions in this case), and the edges are weighted by the time between interactions.

Clustering the IPGs

The usefulness of a graph format is that it can be used to compare to other graphs. In order to compare graphs, a measurement of graph similarity is needed. We suggest using *graph edit distance,* which is defined as the minimum number of changes required to change one graph into another. A change is defined as the insertion of an edge, the deletion of an edge, the insertion of a vertex, the deletion of a vertex, an increase in time on an edge by 0.1 seconds, or the decrease in time on an edge of 0.1 seconds. Each change carries an equal weight of one—this can be changed to reduce bias. This scheme gives preference to time since it is the major factor of difference, but in many of the games you'll evaluate, time performance is the major differentiator between players. You can also evaluate graphs without time weights using the same metric, but without the increase/decrease in time weighting.

One goal of comparison is to be able to group or *cluster* players by their IPGs, which essentially represents their strategic choices and performance in the game or game scenario. Figure 3.5.6 illustrates the many different interaction trajectories players may take even in the same game scenarios. If you cluster player performance, you should see clusters of players grouped by their relative skill level [Youngblood02]. If players cluster into their skill levels, this technique can be used for player classification. More interestingly from an AI perspective is that if you evaluate machine-driven

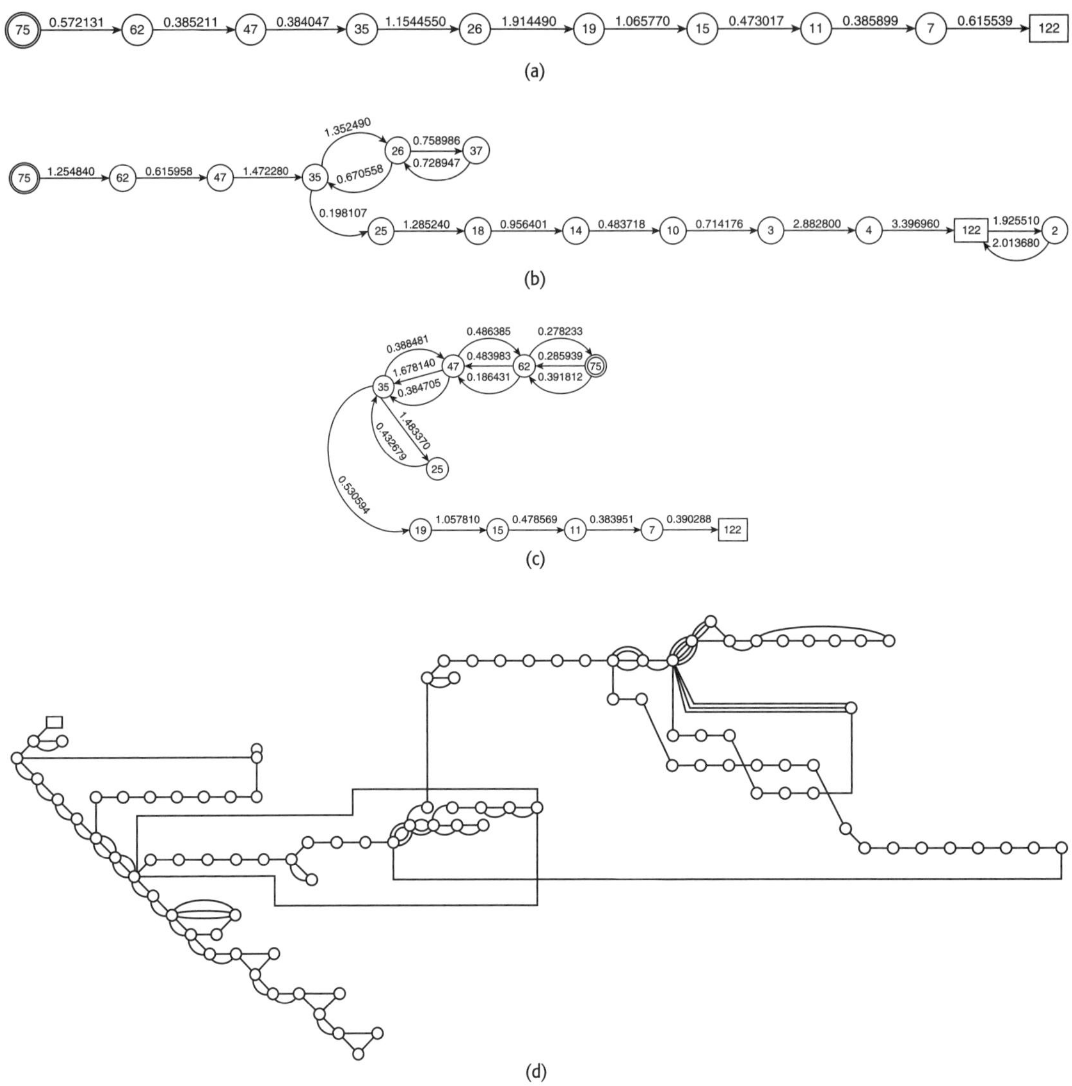

Figure 3.5.6 Interactive player graphs should use different approaches (strategies), as seen in these four examples from the same game scenario and constraints as the previous example in Figure 3.5.5.

agent data with human data and the agents cluster into groups with human players, you can assert that the agent played consistent with that group of humans, or that the agent behaved in a human-consistent manner.

We typically use K-medoids clustering [Friedman99]. K-medoids is an iterative algorithm where based on a given set of data points and *k* clusters with centers approximated by initial representative objects (we seed ours initially with random members of our data set), all members are initially assigned to their nearest *k* cluster representative (or *medoid*).

Then, for each step the cluster medoids are recalculated based on whether one of the non-medoids improves the total distance of the cluster and then members are re-clustered based on their distances to the new centers. This process continues until there is no difference (no improvement) between two consecutive iterations. A clustering criterion function is applied to evaluate clustering quality for that *k* clustering. Due to the high dimensionality of IPGs and seeding with existing members, we iterate our clusters over all possible initial seed values. Due to the abstracted dimensionality of the data, we also suggest exercising *k* from 2 to (*n*–2), where *n* is the number of IPGs being compared, to ensure the discovery of the best clustering in accordance with the clustering quality criterion function.

In clustering IPGs, the clustering criterion functions utilize the distance measure $d(x_{ij},x_{pq})$, which is the distance between the jth member of cluster *i* and the qth member of cluster *p*, where the distance *d* represents the graph edit distance between two members. The mean intra-cluster distance of cluster *i* is as follows, where n_i is the number of members in cluster *i:*

$$\bar{d}^{\,i}_{INTRA} = \frac{\sum_{j=1}^{n_i} \sum_{q=j+1}^{n_i} d(x_{ij}, x_{iq})}{\frac{n_i(n_i-1)}{2}}$$

Achieving a desired clustering of data is moreover a result of optimizing the clustering criterion function [Zhao02]. In our experience clustering IPGs, we have found that the following clustering criterion function to work the best [Youngblood02, Youngblood03].

Minimize, as follows:

$$\sum_{i=1}^{k} \frac{\bar{d}^{\,i}_{INTRA}}{n_i}$$

Utilizing K-medoids on IPGs should produce clusters based on similar strategies and performance in the observed game. Clustering human players and agents can be helpful in determining whether the agents are behaving similar to a known group of human players or even sets of other agent players. Clustering can be used to determine player skill level and distance from the next skill level. Evaluated in-game dynamically, clustering of the current human player could be used to determine the actions of the game AI (based on perceived player skill or strategy). Although K-medoids may be unsuitable for real-time processing in-game, building player type profiles from play testers and utilizing simple and fast methods such as the K-Nearest Neighbors (kNN) to match and respond appropriately can be effective.

Digging in the Graphs

In addition to clustering techniques, there are other methods for discovering knowledge in graph-based data such as that presented by IPGs. The area of graph-based data mining offers tools such as SUBDUE (www.subdue.org) by Larry Holder. SUBDUE has been used to discover common patterns in IPGs for UCT data [Cook07]. Utilizing compression techniques and the *minimum description length* principle, SUBDUE can find common substructures in IPGs. These represent common strategies taken by players regardless of their actual cluster similarity. Game AI using appropriate responses for the anticipated actions could exploit these common sub-strategies.

A Deeper Understanding of Behavior

Data logging and player traces can also be used for other purposes. Players' look directions can be just as useful as their positions. By using the view directions of a player over time, you can derive the surfaces that received maximum or minimal exposure. We have developed a tool called HIIVVE (Highly Interactive Information Value Visualization and Evaluation), designed for this purpose [Dixit07]. The tool, as shown in Figure 3.5.7, uses player trace data to calculate intersections and find the information value for each surface in the world geometry. The information value of a surface represents the likelihood that a player will see information placed on that surface. This data can be used to make design decisions about the placement of art assets or interactive feature points.

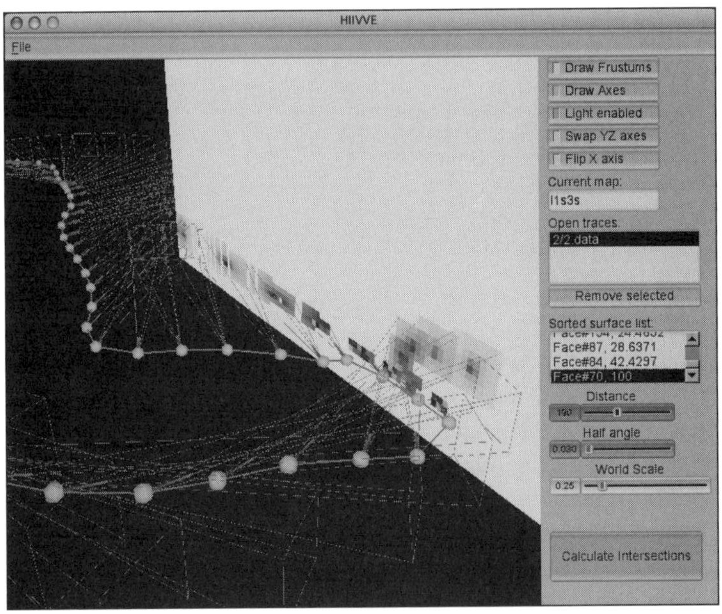

Figure 3.5.7 The Highly Interactive Information Value Visualization and Evaluation (HIIVVE) tool helps determine the information value of game surfaces. Another example of useful in-game logging and knowledge gained from analysis of play testing data.

PlayerViz could also be used to track nearly any type of captured information. For example, something useful for better understanding AI agents and potentially debugging issues within their intelligence mechanisms would be to reflect agent internal state changes (for FSM and FuSM agents) or subsumption level firings. Agent action decisions could also be explicitly represented.

Our group at UNC Charlotte continues research in better understanding both human and agent intelligence in games. We offer a full set of analysis tools and methods for improving game AI through the CGUL (pronounced "seagull") Toolkit—the Common Games Understanding and Learning Toolkit. CGUL is available online for free at playground.uncc.edu/GameIntelligenceGroup/Projects/CGUL.

Conclusion

There are some strong and compelling reasons to include good logging capabilities in games. Data collected from logging human players and AI interacting in a game environment can be used to perform visual data mining with tools such as the provided PlayerViz, which can be used as a bootstrapping process to guide the development of a repertoire of tools for game specific analysis and better understanding of intelligent actions in the game. Player traces tell only half of the story, though. By tracking and constructing interactive player graphs generated from the observed trajectory of player/agent interactions that are analyzed with clustering and knowledge discovery techniques, developers can garner new insights into player performance and classification. This information can then be exploited to develop better game AI.

References

[Consalvo06] Consalvo, Mia and Dutton, Nathan. "Game Analysis: Developing a Methodological Toolkit for the Qualitative Study Of Games," *The Interactive Journal of Computer Game Research,* Vol. 6, No. 1, December 2006.

[Cook07] Cook, Diane J., Holder, Lawrence B., and Youngblood, G. Michael. "Graph-Based Analysis of Human Transfer Learning Using a Game Testbed," *IEEE Transactions on Knowledge and Data Engineering,* 2007.

[Dixit07] Dixit, Priyesh and Youngblood, G. Michael. "Optimal Information Placement in 3D Interactive Environments," *Sandbox Symposium,* 2007.

[Eilers05] Eilers, Michael M. "Soapbox: Difficulty and the Interstitial Gamer," available online at http://www.gamasutra.com/features/20050809/eilers 01.shtml, August, 2005.

[Friedman99] Friedman, Menahem and Kandel, Abraham. *Introduction to Pattern Recognition: Statistical, Structural, Neural, and Fuzzy Logic Approaches,* Imperial College Press, London, 1999.

[Gonzalez99] Gonzalez, Avelino. "Validation of Human Behavioral Models," Twelfth International Florida AI Research Society Conference, Menlo Park, AAAI Press, 1999, pp. 489–493.

[Heinze02] Heinze, Clinton, Goss, Simon, Josefsson, Torgny, Bennett, Kerry, Waugh, Sam, Lloyd, Ian, Murray, Graeme, and Oldfield, John. "Interchanging Agents and Humans in Military Simulation," *AI Magazine,* Vol. 23, No. 2, 2002, pp. 37–47.

[Keim02] Keim, Daniel. "Information Visualization and Visual Data Mining," *IEEE Transactions on Visualization and Computer Graphics,* Vol. 8, No. 1, (March 2002).

[Knauf 01] Knauf, Rainer, Philippow, Ilka, Gonzalez, Avelino, and Jantke, Klaus. "The Character of Human Behavioral Representation and Its Impact on the Validation Issue," Fourteenth International Florida AI Research Society Conference, Menlo Park, AAAI Press, 2001, pp. 635–639.

[Laird01] Laird, John E. and van Lent, Michael. "Human-Level AI's Killer Application: Interactive Computer Games," *AI Magazine,* Vol. 22, No. 2 (2001), pp. 15–25.

[Laird02] Laird, John. "Research in Human-Level AI Using Computer Games," Communications of the ACM, Vol. 45, No. 1, 2002, pp. 32–35.

[Marselas00] Marselas, Herb. "Profiling, Data Analysis, Scalability, and Magic Numbers, Part 1: Meeting the Minimum Requirements for Age of Empires II: The Age of Kings," available online at http://www.gamasutra.com/features/20000809/marselas 01.htm, August 2000.

[Russell03] Russell, Stuart and Norvig, Peter. *Artificial Intelligence: A Modern Approach,* Prentice Hall, 2003.

[Youngblood02] Youngblood, G. Michael. "Agent-Based Simulated Cognitive Intelligence in a Real-Time First-Person Entertainment-Based Artificial Environment," Master's thesis, The University of Texas at Arlington, 2002.

[Youngblood03] Youngblood, G. Michael and Holder, Lawrence B. "Evaluating Human-Consistent Behavior in a Real-Time First-Person Entertainment-Based Artificial Environment," Proceedings of the Sixteenth International FLAIRS Conference, 2003, pp. 32–36.

[Youngblood06] Youngblood, G. Michael, Nolen, Billy, Ross, Michael, and Holder, Lawrence. "Building Test Beds for AI with the Q3 Mod Base," *Artificial Intelligence in Interactive Digital Entertainment* (AIIDE), June 2006.

[Zhao02] Zhao, Ying and Karypis, George. "Evaluation of Hierarchical Clustering Algorithms for Document Datasets," Proceedings of the 11th Conference of Information and Knowledge Management (CIKM), 2002, pp. 515–524.

3.6

Goal-Oriented Plan Merging

Michael Dawe

Using goal-oriented action planning systems to create and manage behavior in automated agents is a powerful technique that has quickly found acceptance among game developers. In game development, planning systems are a relatively new technology, whereas academia has been using planning to solve problems for well over 50 years. Thus, it isn't surprising to find a large base of research that game developers can use to improve their planning systems.

One way planners can be improved is through the use of *plan merging*, a technique used in several ways under academic settings but not yet applied to games. Using plan merging can allow a broader range of behaviors for automated agents and even let them attempt to pursue multiple goals at once. This gem examines one way of implementing a plan-merging system in the context of a real-time game and discusses the implications of using such a system.

Review of Goal-Oriented Planning Systems

Goal-oriented action planning systems are decision-making algorithms designed to take the burden of choosing particular agent behaviors off the programmer and put them into the agent's own sense-think-act cycle. The primary benefit of using these systems is the reduced complexity of designing individual actions for artificial agents while retaining a high level of realism in the agent's total behaviors.

Goal-oriented planning lets particular agents decide their own actions through the pursuit of particular *goals*. An agent's goals might include destroying a target or obtaining an item. Goals are represented as desired world states in whatever system the agent uses to keep track of the state of the world. In traditional planning systems, the agent is restricted to picking one goal as being most important at any given point in time. Once this goal is picked, an agent can create a *plan* by stringing together a sequence of atomic *actions*, sometimes also known as *operators*.

For example, if your agent has decided on the DestroyTarget goal, an action it could pick to accomplish that goal might be the Attack action. Actions have preconditions, which describe conditions on the world that must be true before the action executes, and effects, which describe necessary conditions on the world after the action has completed. In the case of the Attack action, a precondition might be that the agent's weapon is loaded. An effect would be the destruction of the target.

Using the effects and preconditions as guides, any heuristic search can create a plan by listing a sequence of actions an agent can use to achieve the desired goal. Jeff Orkin describes how to use the A* algorithm for planning purposes in [Orkin04]. The completed plan is then just that sequence of actions the agent executes to accomplish its goal.

Some final terminology is needed before discussing plan merging. *Totally-ordered plans* are plans in which the order of each action is completely specified, such that one particular action is first, another occurs second, and so on. *Partially-ordered plans* may specify individual orderings of actions but leave the precise ordering of all actions as unspecified as possible. In other words, a partially-ordered plan doesn't specify the order of actions unless an action satisfies the precondition of another. Totally-ordered plans can be made from partially-ordered plans by giving a specific order to the actions in the plan.

Figure 3.6.1 shows an example of some partially- and totally-ordered plans for making a sandwich. In the partially-ordered version, notice that independent actions (obtaining the meat, cheese, and bread) are unordered relative to each other. Actions can have a relative ordering, though; all the ingredients must be obtained before making the sandwich. In general, the only orderings given to actions are those required by the actions' preconditions. Totally-ordered plans, on the other hand, enforce a specific ordering of all actions, regardless of whether the individual actions satisfy preconditions for other actions. Although you could obtain the meat, cheese, and bread for your sandwich in any order, a totally-ordered plan specifies an order in which to perform these actions. It stands to reason that any partially-ordered plan can be expressed as a totally-ordered one.

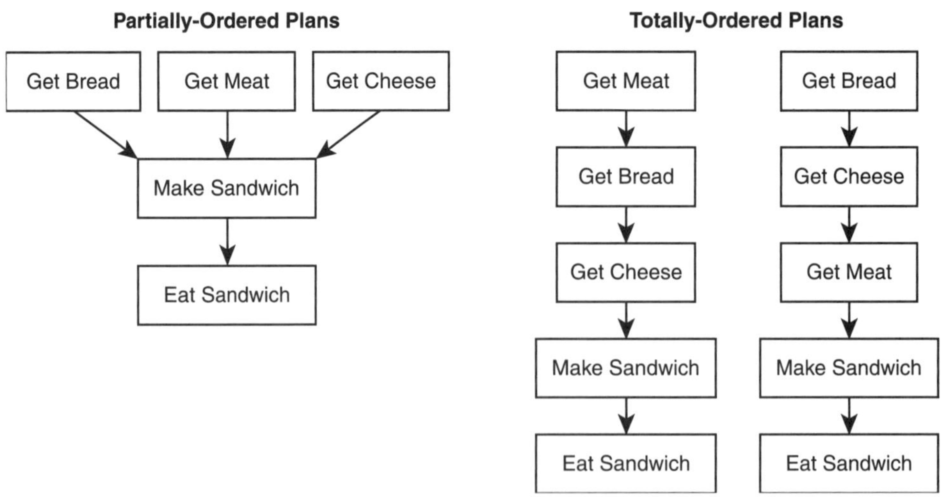

Figure 3.6.1 Partially- and totally-ordered plans. Not all totally-ordered instantiations of the partially-ordered plan are given.

Although the vast majority of academic-based planning algorithms produce partially-ordered plans, these types of planners have not yet found widespread use in games. There are a few reasons why totally-ordered plans are of more immediate use to an NPC:

- First, given a partially-ordered plan, an agent will at some point have to define, either explicitly or implicitly, a totally-ordered plan in order to execute the actions of the plan. In other words, the agent still needs to choose one action to perform first among any number of unordered actions. Given this, there are some reasons why executing one action before another might be advantageous, but the reasons for which the agent might put one action first could easily be abstracted into the planner itself.
- The second major reason that games have traditionally dealt with totally-ordered plans is the ease with which A* is adapted to creating plans. Because A* is such a well known and versatile algorithm, it is an easy choice for use in a goal-oriented planning system, and A* produces totally-ordered plans by its nature.

[Orkin04a], [Orkin04b], and [Orkin06] cover the many practical details of implementing an A* planning system for games.

Plan Merging for Goal-Oriented Plans

Plan merging refers to the process of taking several independently generated plans and creating a single plan out of them, usually with the intention of reducing the overall cost of the plan. Often, a reduced-cost plan has the benefit of also producing more rational-looking behavior. To demonstrate the power of plan merging, let's look at an example before getting into the details of the algorithm.

Suppose an agent has the task of collecting items from around the world and returning those items to a home base. If the agent can carry only one item at a time, it is apparent that it has no better choice than to go to an item, collect it, and return to base. However, if the agent can carry multiple items, it is also evident that many situations exist where the agent could reduce its total distance traveled by collecting several items at once.

There are several ways you could accomplish this behavior utilizing a planning system. Suppose that your goal of collecting items and returning them to base was the ReturnItems goal. You could write a GatherItems action that accomplishes that goal. An agent executing the GatherItems action would look for the nearest items, gather as many as it could, and return them to base. Although this would be a solution, it is clear that the GatherItems action would be quite complicated. It would need to include code to pathfind and travel between items, pick up items, pathfind and travel to base, and drop off the items once arrived. The increased functionality contained within one action works to defeat the purpose of having a flexible planning system.

It is much easier to write smaller, reusable, atomic actions, such as GoTo for pathfinding, GetItem to gather the item from the world, and ReturnItem to drop off the item at base. These multiple actions allow the planner to do the complicated work of stringing together the actions into the right order, and further allow you to reuse the actions among many types of NPCs. Yet none of these actions can communicate to the agent that it should try to gather multiple items at a time. Instead, you can accomplish the desired behavior through plan merging.

The general idea is to take two plans with some overlapping actions and combine the plans to produce a single plan with a lower cost than independently executing each of the original plans. In the current example, the agent could plan to gather each item independently, producing two plans that were unrelated but very similar, as shown on the left in Figure 3.6.2. A possible result from a merge of those two plans would combine as many actions as possible together, producing the single plan shown on the right in Figure 3.6.2. When the agent executes this plan, it collects both items before making the return trip to base.

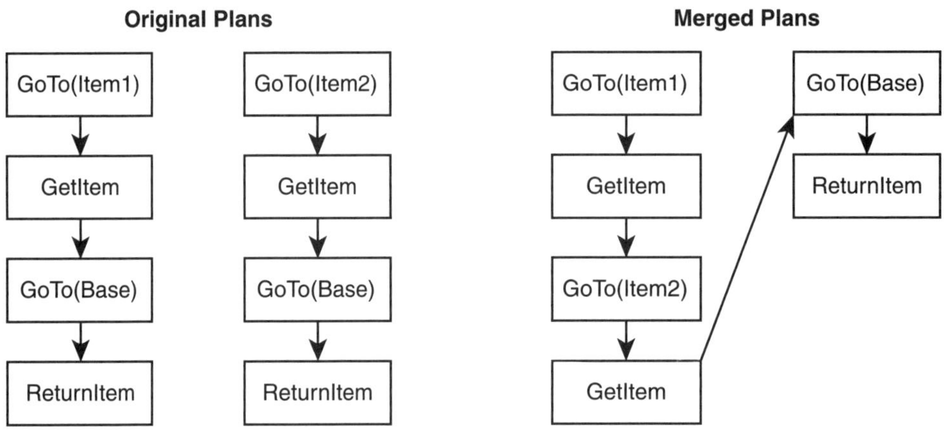

Figure 3.6.2 Two totally-ordered plans and the result of a possible merge between them.

Implementing a Plan-Merging Algorithm

Academically, the interest in plan merging centers mostly on plan optimization. [Foulser92] points out two major components to optimizing a plan: finding actions that can be merged and then computing the optimal way to merge the actions if there exists more than one way to put the operators together. It is easiest to deal with these problems separately, so that is the approach taken in this article.

The first challenge in finding mergeable actions is discovering precisely what kinds of actions can be merged. Put simply, any number of actions can be merged if there is another action that can replace the merged actions with these results:

- If the action has the same useful effects.
- If the replaced action costs less than the sum of the merged actions it is replacing.

Effects are "useful" if they directly establish a precondition of another action in the plan, or a precondition of the goal itself. For example, suppose an agent has a plan to destroy a target using the FireWeapon and ReloadWeapon actions. The ReloadWeapon action has a couple of effects. First, it makes the weapon be loaded, and second, it reduces the agent's ammunition store. The first effect would be a useful effect, because it accomplishes a precondition of another action in the plan. The second effect isn't useful, because it has no bearing on the execution of the plan.

Searching plans for mergeable actions would be incredibly expensive without knowledge of the actions themselves, so it is best to specifically look for actions that are known to be mergeable. In an implemented system, this means either looking for a specific action that can be merged with itself, or looking for a known combination of actions that could be merged. In the earlier resource-gathering example, you know that the agent is likely to have multiple plans, each with an instance of the ReturnItems action. This is an excellent candidate action to look for, because you know it's possible to merge two ReturnItems actions. In this specific case, you might even start the search at the end of the plan, because it is likely to be the last action in each of the plans that are being merged. GoTo(Base) can also be merged with itself, because it obviously accomplishes the same effect.

The second challenge is creating an optimal plan once a possible merge has been discovered. [Foulser92] deals with the difficulties of creating an optimal plan, noting that creating an optimal plan quickly becomes computationally expensive, and probably overkill for games. For the resource-gathering NPC, you've already improved behavior by allowing the agent to collect multiple resources at once. Rather than spend much time worrying about the optimality of the plan, you could just place the rest of the two plans together, as was shown in Figure 3.6.2.

However, to make the agent appear even more intelligent, you could employ critics, special-purpose checks used to help order the remaining actions. For example, you know you have two pairs of GoTo(Item) and Get Item actions to be placed before the merged actions, so you could write a critic to make sure the agent goes to the closest item first. Critics are then general rules written to enforce a desired behavior in plan merges.

At its simplest, then, the plan-merging algorithm accepts two plans generated through the general-purpose A* planning system. The agent could send its two most important goals to the planner, for example, and then send those two independent plans to the plan merger. For every action in the first plan, the algorithm checks to see whether it can be merged with an action in the second. If a merge can be performed, those two actions are put together into a single plan, being careful to put preceding actions from both plans before the merged action, and likewise putting any actions occurring after the merged action afterward. If more precise control over the order of the non-merged actions is needed, critics can be employed to determine the best ordering and rearrange the actions as necessary. For a wider range of possible merges, a complete plan-merging algorithm should examine the net effects of every possible group of actions in each plan, looking for situations where a sequence of actions could be replaced by a single cheaper action. Such an algorithm produces the most impressive improvements to mergeable plans, but is also expensive to run.

Beyond Single-Agent Merges

Although merging two plans for a single agent certainly offers opportunities for improved behavior, plan merging also offers remarkable benefits in the areas of squad-based planning. For instance, an agent utilizing plan merging could merge an individual goal (picking up a weapon or health power-up) with a squad-issued goal (providing cover fire). Utilizing plan merging in these situations allows an agent to maintain its own goals and personality in the face of squad-issued orders and even allows for situations where the agent can accomplish many goals at once.

Strategies for Improving Action Searching

Searching two or more plans for actions with similar effects is expensive, especially if you consider replacing groups of actions with different net effects. If the game is fast-paced, typical of many FPSs, the agent's primary and secondary goals could change more quickly than it could even devise a plan for its secondary goal. Clearly, plan merging is of no use unless you can quickly perform the merge.

One possible strategy to reduce the time needed to search through actions is to look for mergeable actions only when specific actions are present in the plan, something that can be determined in the middle of the plan-making process. For extremely long plans, hooks direct to possibly-mergeable actions could be included in the plan structure itself, directing the algorithm not only into the correct places immediately, but also informing it if a merge is worth looking for at all. In specific kinds of agents, it might even be worth only looking for a specific action to merge in each plan.

Similarly, you might attempt a merge only when the goals being planned for are compatible. Conversely, it makes sense to not even bother to attempt a merge if the two intended goals are incompatible. Indeed, even making a plan for a secondary goal is wasted time if the goals are incompatible. This determination is probably best made by the programmer. It might be obvious to you that an Attack and a Retreat goal will never produce mergeable plans, but a generically written algorithm would search through every action of each plan before reporting that no mergeable actions exist.

Conclusion

Plan merging offers a way to improve the perceived intelligence of an agent acting independently or within a squad. Although potentially a very expensive process, with some careful consideration, it can be accomplished with little extra time spent examining the plans generated.

It should be noted that this is only one way of performing plan merging. [Thangarajah02] and [Thangarajah03] present different systems and ways of performing plan merging that may be more appropriate for agents acting over a longer term than the agent described here. For example, the plan-merging algorithm described in [Thangarajah03] would be especially well suited to a strategy game AI opponent, able to accomplish goals in a variety of different ways and potentially delay actions to take advantage of positive merge opportunities.

Planning is a versatile AI system, with many opportunities for expansion and improvement. Even if plan merging is not useful in a given situation, the ideas it suggests are applicable to other AI systems, or even other planning systems such as hierarchical task networks (HTNs). Thinking about the behavioral improvements afforded by such techniques lends the agents greater intelligence and the players a better experience.

References

[Foulser92] Fousler, David, Li, Ming, and Yang, Qiang. "Theory and Algorithms for Plan Merging." *Artificial Intelligence*, 57(2–3): pp. 143–181, 1992.

[Orkin04a] Orkin, Jeff. "Applying Goal-Oriented Action Planning to Games," *AI Game Programming Wisdom 2*, Charles River Media, 2004.

[Orkin04b] Orkin, Jeff. "Symbolic Representation of Game World State: Toward Real-Time Planning in Games." *AAAI Challenges in Game AI Workshop Technical Report*, 2004.

[Orkin06] Orkin, Jeff. "Three States and a Plan: The A.I. of F.E.A.R.," Proceedings from Game Developers Conference, 2006.

[Thangarajah02] Thangarajah, John, Winikoff, Michael, Padgham, Lin, and Fischer, Klaus. "Avoiding Resource Conflicts in Intelligent Agents," Proceedings of the 15th European Conference on Artificial Intelligence 2002 (ECAI 2002).

[Thangarajah03] Thangarajah, John, Padgham, Lin, and Winikoff, Michael. "Detecting & Exploiting Positive Goal Interaction in Intelligent Agents," *AAMAS* '03, July 14–18, 2003.

COLOR PLATE 1

Screenshot of the "path" command from Gem 1.6, where the user's sketch is highlighted in green and the force vectors are illustrated on the battlefield.

COLOR PLATE 2

Screenshot of the "target" command from Gem 1.6, where the command glyph (spiral) is highlighted in red and the force vectors are illustrated on the battlefield.

COLOR PLATE 3

Screenshot of the "erase" command from Gem 1.6, where the user sketch is highlighted in blue and the force vectors are illustrated on the battlefield.

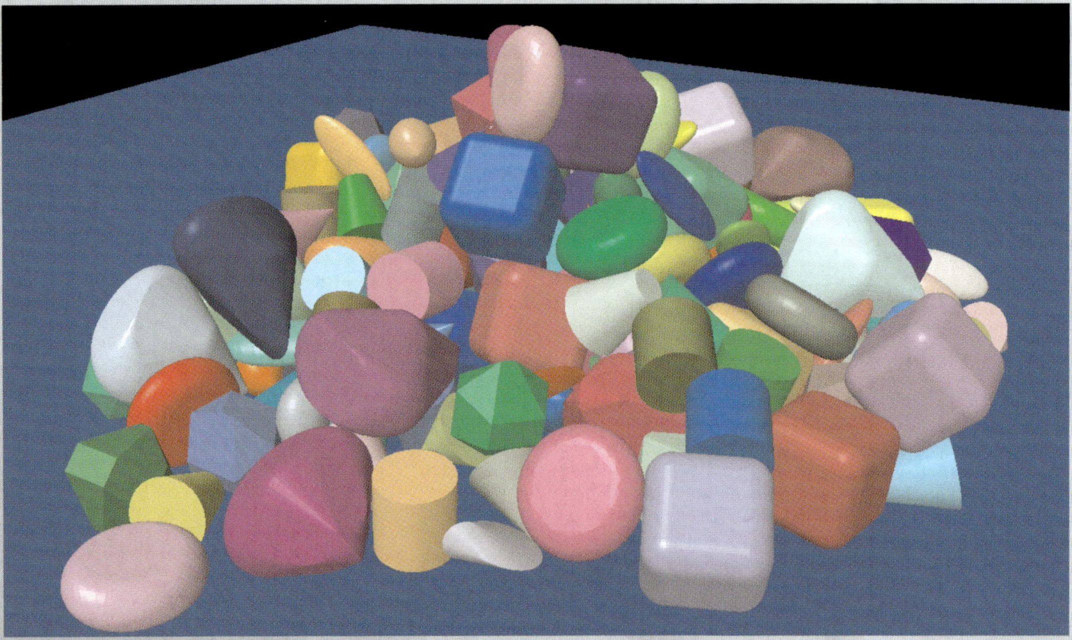

COLOR PLATE 4

A pile of shapes with collisions resolved by the methods in Gem 2.5.

COLOR PLATE 5
A volcano created using advanced particle deposition, as described in Gem 5.1.

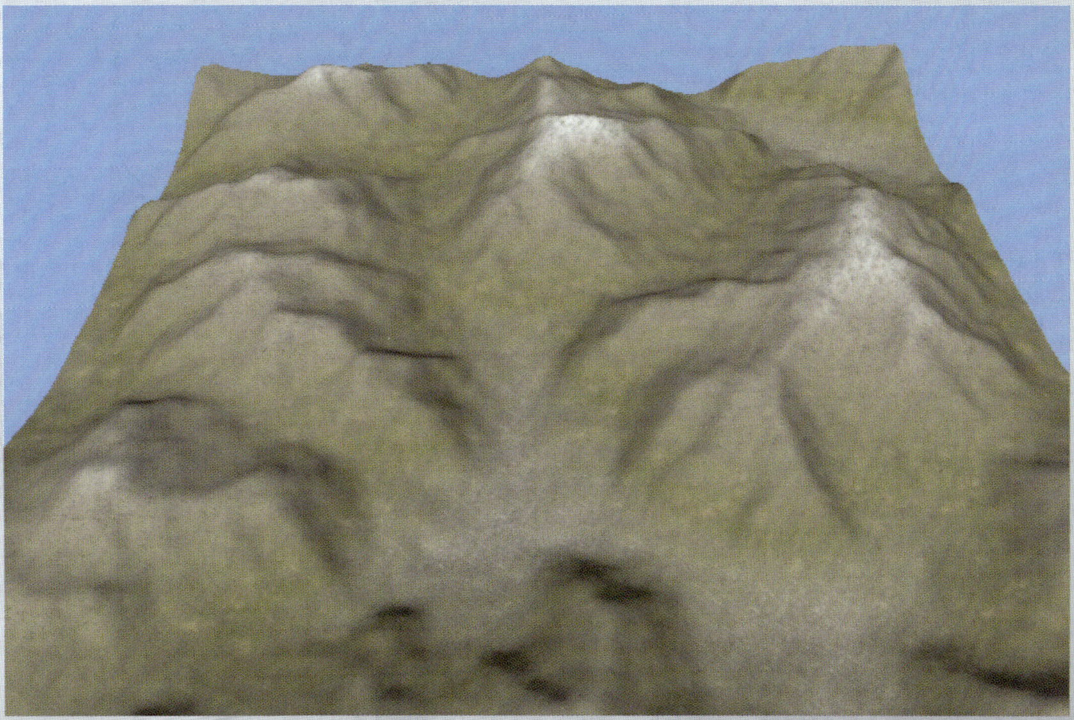

COLOR PLATE 6
Mountains created using advanced particle deposition, as described in Gem 5.1.

COLOR PLATE 7

Dunes created using advanced particle deposition as described in Gem 5.1.

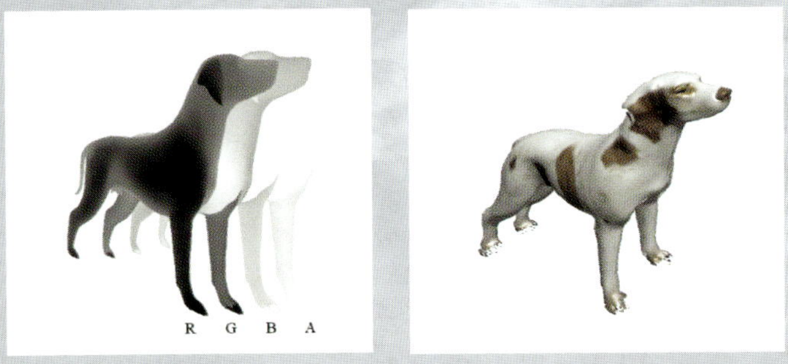

COLOR PLATE 8

A dog impostor from Gem 5.5 modeled as a quad-layer relief texture. The depth values of the progressing layers are stored in the R, G, B and A channels, respectively (left). A view of the rendered dog impostor is shown on the right.

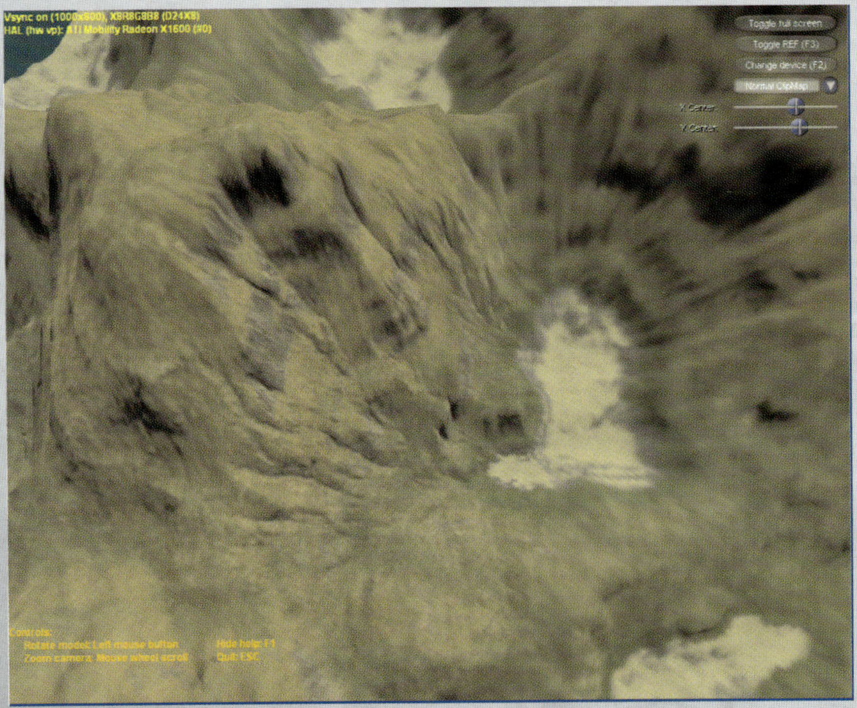

COLOR PLATE 9

Image of a clipped mipmap stack from Gem 5.6.

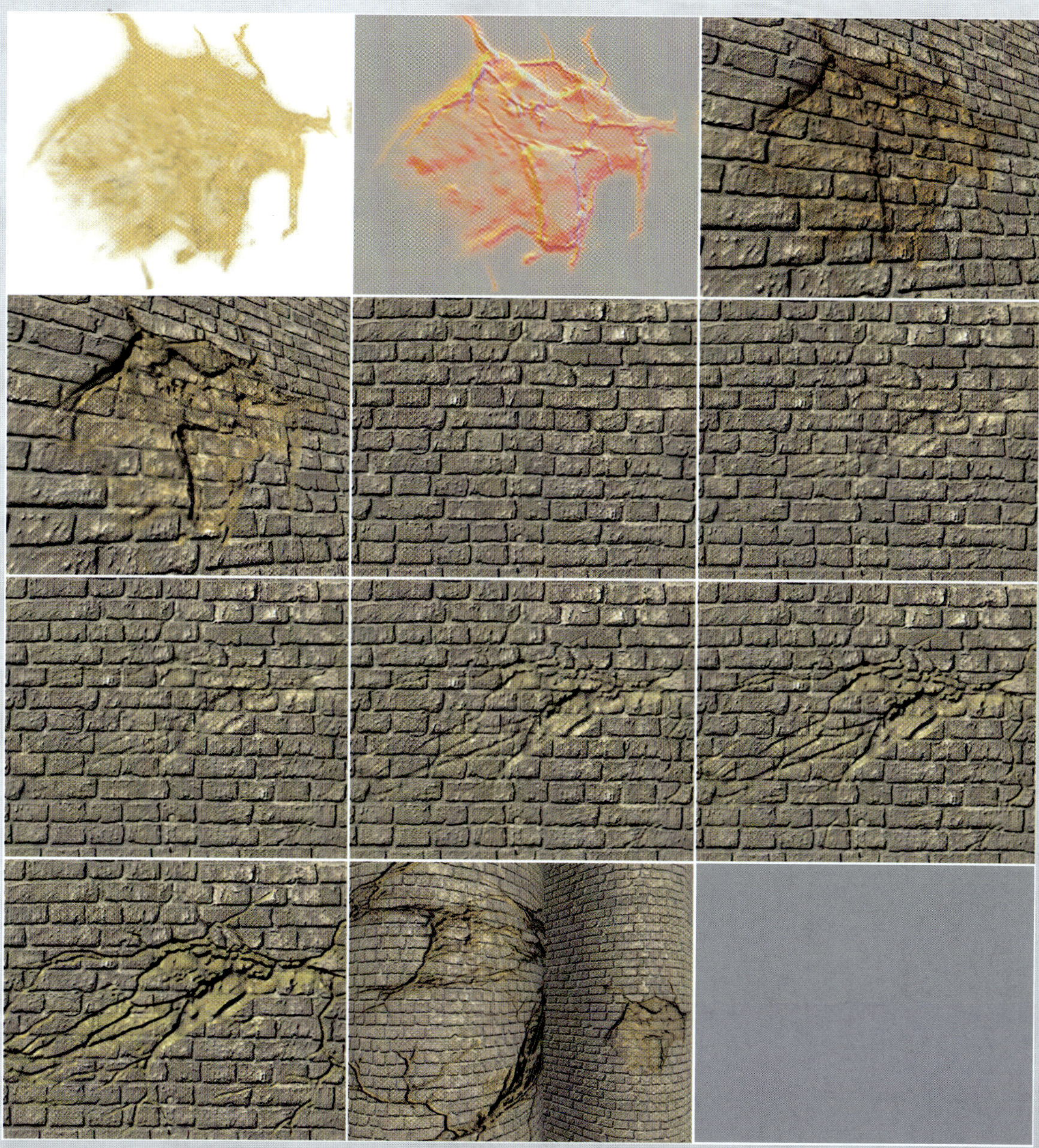

COLOR PLATE 10

Left to right, top to bottom, from Gem 5.7: the example diffuse and bump render targets, traditional decals, decals using the technique in Gem 5.7, erosion over time with opacities of 0, 20, 40, 60, 80, and 100 percent, and decals applied on non-planar geometry.

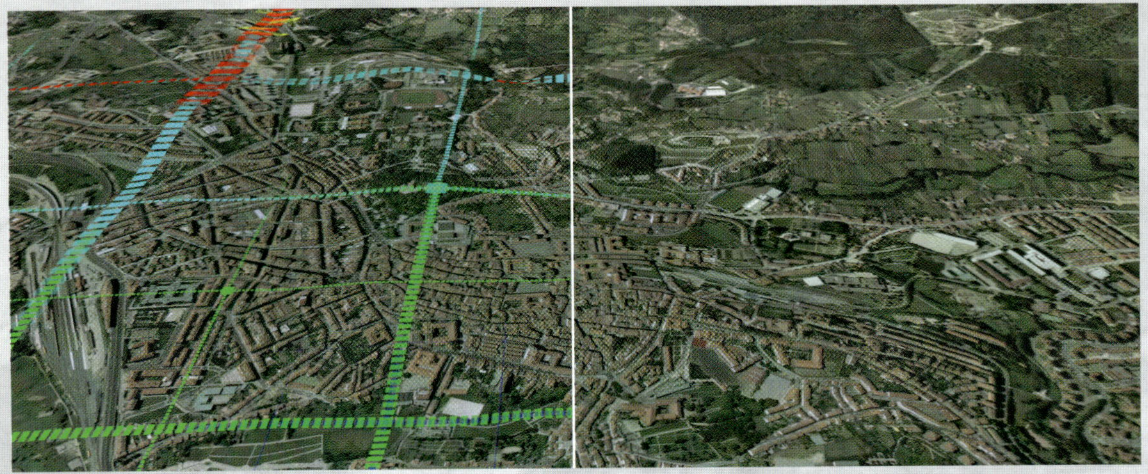

COLOR PLATE 11

Rings of detail and an example of a virtual texture applied to terrain as in Gem 5.8, showing levels of detail using color codes.

COLOR PLATE 12

An example of rendering with graftal imposters from Gem 5.9.

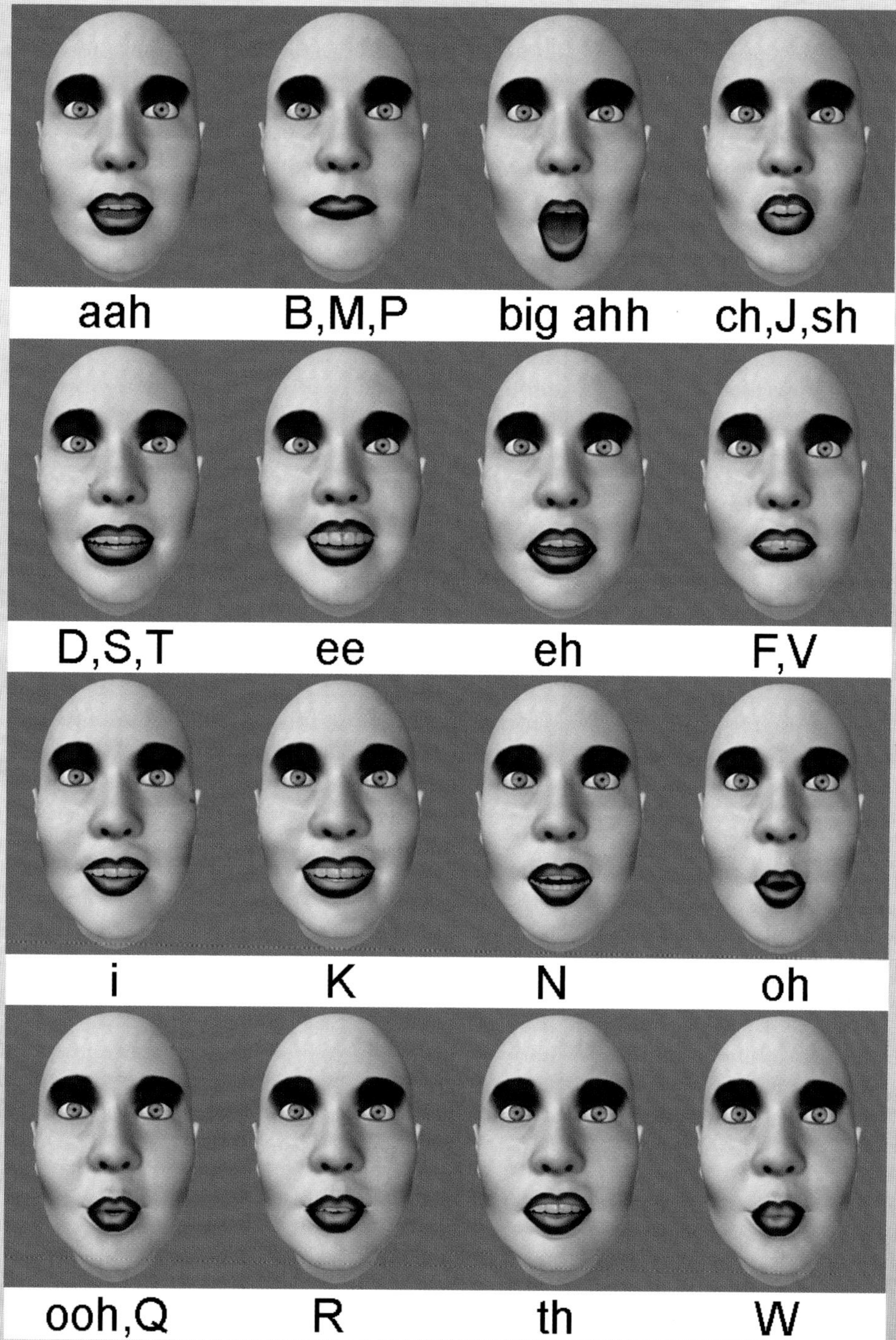

COLOR PLATE 13

Sixteen visemes, each shown at its extreme (1.0) morph, as described in Gem 5.10.

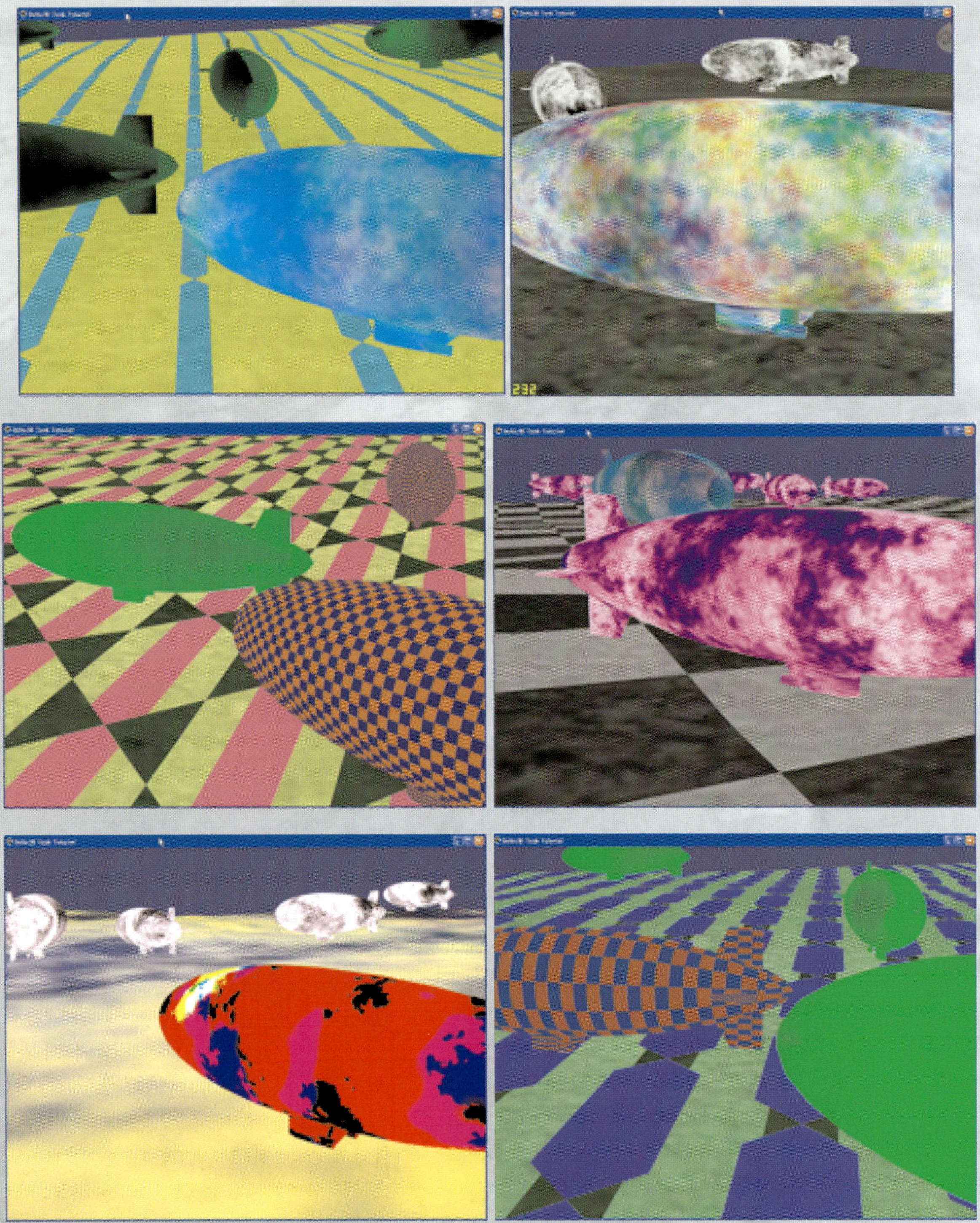

COLOR PLATE 14

Several examples of shaders created with the data-driven shader manager, as described in Gem 7.4.

3.7

Beyond A*: IDA* and Fringe Search

Robert Kirk DeLisle

Graph search techniques are ubiquitous in game programming. Regardless of the game genre, methods of graph search inevitably form a basis for game AI. The currently leading genre of 3D FPS games is heavily dependent on pathfinding approaches that enable non-player characters to move within the environment for the purpose of self-defense or aggressive action. This can also be extended to 2D (or 2.5D) games in which maze or terrain traversal is an integral part of gameplay. Furthermore, games such as checkers, chess, Othello, and even tic-tac-toe involve some level of evaluation of game trees or state graphs in order to develop convincing and competitive artificial intelligence.

Within the realm of path-planning, problems typically take on the form of trees, with the start being considered the root of the tree (see Figure 3.7.1).

The root node can then be expanded into a number of child nodes that represent all the next possible steps in the search. The typical 2D pathfinding process is most obvious with the children representing each of the directions of allowed movement. For example, if the four cardinal directions are allowed, the root node expands into four child nodes, one for each direction, north, south, east, and west. Diagonal movements increase this to eight child nodes with the additional four representing northwest, northeast, southwest, and southeast. Child nodes can be further expanded as you extend the path in search of the goal. This type of problem formulation can also be applied to problems such as searching for the shortest possible solutions for a scrambled Rubik's Cube. The initial, scrambled state of the cube is the root, and each possible turn of a cube face corresponds to a child of that root node. By formulating problems in this way, as graph traversal problems with starting states and goal states within the graph, you open the door to a number of algorithms.

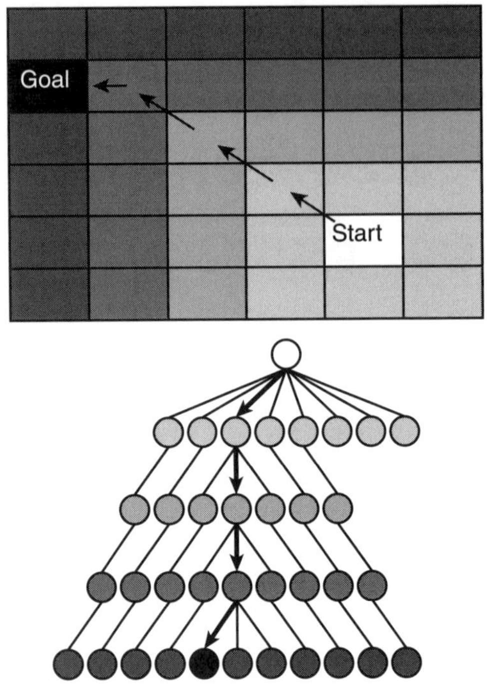

Figure 3.7.1 A search grid and its associated search tree are shown with corresponding grid and tree nodes similarly colored. A path is shown in both with arrows. Paths that result in redundantly visiting the same node have been removed.

A* and Dijkstra

A* has emerged as the most common search algorithm for pathfinding within game AI. The history of A* begins with breadth first search, in which all the children of the root node are expanded and evaluated before moving on to the next level of tree depth. When the goal is not identified at the current depth, the next layer of children are expanded and evaluated. Dijkstra modified this algorithm by adding an "open list" and "closed list" to provide two fundamental capabilities:

- Each node keeps track of the cost of the path to that point, and the open list can be sorted based upon this cost allowing a "best first" search strategy. This is particularly useful when transitions from one node to another do not have the same cost, such as choices in moving through swamp versus dry ground. Allowing expansion of the best path thus far can bias the search away from costly paths.
- Together, the open and closed lists act as a catalog of previously evaluated nodes, thus preventing the re-expansion of already visited nodes. These additions

improve upon Breadth First Search considerably; however, further improvements were to be found by incorporating an "Informed Search" strategy through the use of heuristics.

Up to this stage, the cost of any particular node is considered to be the cost from the goal to this point, and is commonly referred to as *g()*. An uninformed search of this sort is significantly improved upon if you include an estimate of the cost from this point to the goal. This heuristic calculation, typically referred to as *h()*, gives you another method to estimate the total path cost and once again significantly biases the search toward the goal. The resulting overall cost of any particular node becomes *f()* = *g()* + *h()*, and it deserves mentioning that *h()* should always be admissible, or an underestimate of the cost from the node to the goal. If *h()* ever overestimates the cost to the goal, searching potentially fruitful paths may be delayed or missed completely. A* follows the same general algorithm as Dijkstra's, but the cost associated with any particular search node now includes the heuristic cost, that is, the estimated cost to the goal. Algorithm 3.7.1 shows a comparison of Dijkstra's algorithm and A*.

Algorithm 3.7.1 Dijkstra's Algorithm and A*

```
open – priority queue of search nodes
closed – searchable container of search nodes (such as an associative
      array)

root = start node
push root onto open

while goal not found and open not empty
    sort open by f() of each search node
    remove top of open and set to current node
    if current node = goal
        stop
    else
        push current node onto closed

    for each child of current node
        if child present in closed
            continue
        else
            set child's f() = g() + h()(for Dijkstra's, h() = 0)
            push child onto open
```

It comes as no surprise that A*'s most fundamental weakness is the management of the open and closed lists. The open list must be maintained in sorted order with the top of the list being the node with the lowest cost. Perhaps more significantly, the open and closed lists are continuously polled to determine whether a node has already been evaluated, and this can lead to a high computational burden. Although various optimizations of A* have been developed, the overall costs associated with the open and closed lists can lead to loss of performance or even to the complete lack of function if the search space is extremely large. Although simple 2D pathfinding problems may not suffer significantly enough from these drawbacks to warrant different approaches, pathfinding within a complex 3D environment can easily present situations that hinder A*'s capabilities.

Other problems, such as searching for the shortest solution for a scrambled Rubik's Cube, present search spaces so large that A* quickly exceeds the memory capacity of the computer within a few minutes. The $3 \times 3 \times 3$ Rubik's Cube, for example, has as many as 18 child nodes for any particular search node. Even if you restrict the next move to not include certain manipulations (for example, you should not allow the same side to be turned twice), you can only reduce the number of children in the next layer to approximately 13. This leads to over 1 billion possible states after only eight turns! Clearly in such complex search trees, other methods must be used in order to simply enable the identification of a solution.

The Iterative Deepening A* (IDA*)

An extension of A* is Iterative Deepening A* (IDA*), as described in Algorithm 3.7.2. In its most basic form, this algorithm eliminates the open and closed lists. It is true that this imposes the risk of repeated evaluation of states, but this may be accommodated by properly structuring the way in which nodes are expanded (specific ordering, prevention of backtracking, and so on).

Algorithm 3.7.2 Iterative Deepening A* (IDA*)

```
root = start node
threshold  = root's g()

perform a depth-first search starting at root

if goal not found,
    set threshold = minimum g() found that is higher than current
    threshold
    repeat depth-first search starting at root


depth-first search(node):
    if node = goal
        return goal found

    if node's f() > threshold
        return goal not found
    else
        for each child of node, while goal not found, depth-first
        search(child)
```

It may also be self-accommodating due to the fact that a node expanded early will have a lowered value for *g()* than if it is expanded later, and should always have the same value for *h()* regardless of when it was evaluated. In IDA*, a cost threshold is established for *f()* defining the maximum allowable cost above which a node will not be evaluated. All nodes are expanded below this threshold and if the goal node is not found, the threshold is increased. As you have no history maintained, you must reinitiate the search from the original start node and expand all nodes allowed given the new threshold. It may seem counterintuitive to repeat the evaluation of all previous, non-goal nodes, but the cost of expanding and evaluating a node is typically much lower than the cost of maintaining the open and closed lists. In addition, the frontier nodes, those at the edge of the search that were not explored before, will always be greater in number than the number of expanded nodes below the threshold. This fact effectively reduces the cost of re-investigation of previous nodes to a fraction of the cost to expand the new frontier. The ultimate result is minimal overhead in terms of memory at the expense of time required for the search.

The Fringe Search Algorithm

Between A* and IDA* is an algorithm called Fringe Search (see Algorithm 3.7.3), in which nodes are expanded given a cost threshold as in IDA*, but in this case the frontier nodes are not lost. Rather, the frontier nodes are maintained in *now* and *later* lists.

Algorithm 3.7.3 Fringe Search

```
now – linked list of search nodes, list order determines order of
      evaluation
later – linked list of search nodes
root = start node
threshold = root's g()
push root into now

while now not empty
    for each node in now
        if node = goal
            stop

        if node's f() > threshold
            push node onto end of later
        else
            insert children of node into now behind node

        remove node from now and discard

    push later onto now, clear later
    set threshold = minimum g() found that is higher than current
                    threshold
```

The node at the top of the *now* list is evaluated and if its *f ()* value is greater than the threshold, it is moved to the *later* list. If the *f()* value is lower than the threshold, the node's children are expanded and the current node is discarded. The newly expanded child nodes are added to the top of the *now* list and are thus next in line for evaluation.

This procedure maintains the list in a weakly sorted order and effectively expands the nodes in a depth-first fashion much like IDA*. If the goal is not found after the completion of one pass through the *now* list (one iteration), the threshold is increased as it was in IDA*, the later list is transferred to the *now* list, and search is resumed from the top of the *now* list. Although the fringe-search process does require maintenance of the *now* and *later* lists, there is no sorting cost. Furthermore, this extra memory cost is lower than that of A*, because there is no need to store all previously evaluated nodes. Fringe search also does not suffer from speed losses seen with IDA* due to repeated search from iteration to iteration.

In a study by Bjornsson, Enaenberger, Holte, and Schaeffer [Bjornsson05], these algorithms were compared using game maps extracted from *Baldur's Gate II.* It was found that search times for fringe search were reduced as much as 25–40% compared to A* and 10 times compared to IDA*. These improvements in search times over IDA* were maintained even though IDA* was optimized to accommodate repeated visits to nodes in the search tree. Overall, the gains in speed were attributed to the lack of needing to maintain an *open* list in sorted order. The cost for fringe search's performance is obviously increased memory usage due to the requirement to maintain some degree of the search's history in the *now/later* lists. In this way, fringe search seems to represent a useful intermediate between A* and IDA*.

Conclusion

There is no paucity of algorithms for graph search and pathfinding. Although A* represents the most widely used algorithm, the degree of specialization and optimization of the A* algorithm for individual cases expands the set tremendously. The driving force behind algorithm selection has always been and will always be defined by memory and time constraints, and in nearly every case one must be traded for the other. IDA* and fringe search represent useful modifications of the A* family of algorithms and may ultimately provide advantages over traditional approaches to pathfinding.

References

[Bjornsson05] Bjornsson, Yngvi, Enzenberger, Markus, Holte, Robert, and Schaeffer, Jonathan. "Fringe Search: Beating A* at Pathfinding on Game Maps," IEEE Symposium on Computational Intelligence and Games (2005), pp. 125–132.

SECTION

4

AUDIO

Introduction

Alexander Brandon

Game audio programming is becoming more complex than ever. As game audio is getting closer and closer to film post production, a great deal of factors come into play. Where will point-sourced specialized sounds be in relation to the camera? Will they be looped? Will there be a delay on them, or will they be in sequence? How are they triggered? How are they categorized and mixed? The authors in this section have provided some very impressive fresh ways to tackle new issues like these so that your titles can remain competitive with high audio quality.

Jason Page from Sony Computer Entertainment Europe provides some insights into the revolutionary cell processing power of the Playstation 3 and the MultiStream tool Jason and his team has developed. Robert Sparks provides a vital yet elegant solution for multiple layers of mixing groups. Especially with the different hardware playback settings on multiple platforms, this particular gem is a godsend. You might have read recently that the pro studio standard for effects, *Waves*, are in use in *Halo 3*. Check out Mark France's article for more information on how to get this kind of real-time effect functionality. Ken Noland also provides even deeper tips for optimizing these effects. Finally, Stephan Schütze bangs his head against the wall of repetition, which is still all too present in games today.

All of these authors are respected pros in the field with ideas that could make your next game the next award-winning title for audio. Enjoy the gems!

4.1

Audio Signal Processing Using Programmable Graphics Hardware

Mark France

mark@raccoongames.com

Real-time modern audio processing can sometimes be very compute-intensive, as many algorithms often need to be performed simultaneously. Programmable digital signal processors are usually available only to developers and are much too expensive for consumers. Also, modern sound cards are still only fixed function implementations that evolve at a slower pace and can be limiting for audio programmers. This gem suggests techniques that enable you to offload audio routines from the CPU and benefit from the GPU's relatively huge SIMD (Single Instruction Multiple Data) parallel stream processing power (see Figure 4.1.1). This increased flexibility allows creation of customizable, high-quality reverb models that can be calculated in real-time from scene geometry, rather than relying on the use of simple presets found in previous generation hardware.

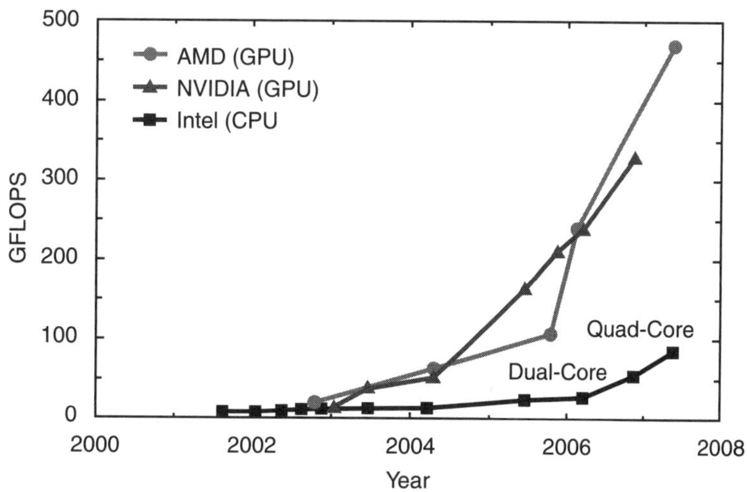

FIGURE 4.1.1 Comparison of computational power for GPUs and CPUs [Owens07].

GPGPU Programming Overview

The GPU's shift to a programmable pipeline and its increasing programmability has allowed it to be used as a powerful general purpose coprocessor. The pipeline shown in Figure 4.1.2 can be programmed for use in applications other than the specific graphical ones it was designed for. This is known as GPGPU (General Purpose computation on a Graphics Processing Unit) programming and has been successfully used for applications from artificial neural networks [Rolfes04] to cloth physics simulations [Zeller05].

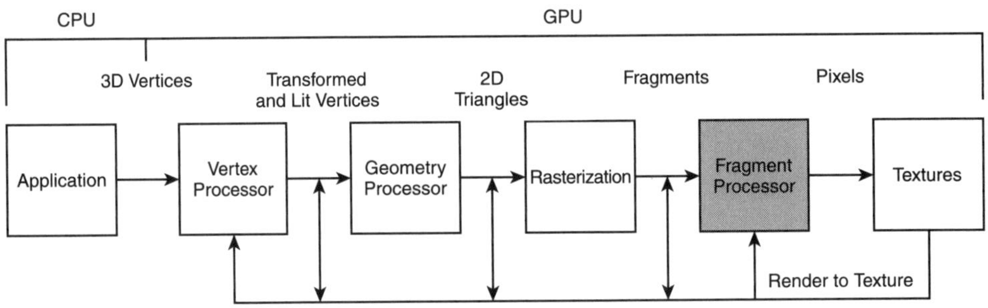

FIGURE 4.1.2 The recent graphics pipeline.

For GPGPU, fragment shaders are more useful because there are more fragment pipelines than vertex pipelines and, because the fragment processor is at the end of the pipeline, it allows for direct output. Shader programs can be written in assembly language or high-level shader languages such as Cg, HLSL, and GLSL. My preferred language for this purpose is Brook for GPUs, which is specifically designed for stream processing and runs directly on GPUs by generating Cg code with a C++ runtime. More information on GPGPU programming can be found at [GPGPU07].

GPU Audio Optimization

GPU features such as multiple execution units or multiply-accumulate instructions are similar to those of professional audio DSP hardware [Gallo04], therefore it can be suggested that the ubiquitous GPU can be used as an efficient DSP substitute.

GPUs operate on vectors containing four floats, often representing the RGBA components. Therefore, audio sample data is often stored in one of these components and 1D arrays of samples are mapped to 2D square textures before being processed on the GPU.

Does using the GPU for audio calculations significantly optimize performance? Whalen [Whalen05] asked this question by using shading languages to process an array of DSP effects on both graphics hardware and CPU. The point was to discover which was fastest. It was discovered that algorithms such as chorus and compression had a significant decrease in execution times when processed on the GPU; others such as Filter and Delay effects were slightly slower. The GPU excels at certain tasks that are suited to its model of stream processing—that is, many processors executing the same code in parallel—therefore, not all audio programming techniques may be optimized by running them on the GPU.

Audio Effects

This section concentrates on describing algorithms for chorus and compression audio processing effects. A chorus effect introduces a short delay and slight pitch change to an audio signal in order to add an audible "thickness" to the sound. The chorus effect can be used in games to help create a surreal "dreamy" effect. The processing of this effect requires two texture lookups; interpolation between them is shown here:

```
lookahead(coord, index)
{
   coord.x = coord.x + index * step;

   if(coord.x > 1.0)
   {
      rowsUp = floor(coord.x / rowSize);
      coord.x = coord.x - rowsUp * (1 + step);
      coord.y = coord.y + rowsUp * step;
   }

   return coord;
}

chorus(coord, texture)
{
s1 = lookUp(texture, coord);
   s2 = lookUp(texture, lookahead(coord, 20 * sin(coord.x)));
   return interpolate(s1, s2, 0.5);
}
```

Audio compression effects that are unrelated to data compression reduce the dynamic range of audio signals and are useful for balancing the game's overall audio mix. This effect needs one texture lookup and the logarithmic compression calculation to be performed:

```
compress(coord, texture)
{
   s1 = lookUp(texture, coord);
   return pow(abs(s1), 1 - level / 10);
}
```

Many other audio effects, such as delay and normalization, can be optimized using similar techniques.

Room Acoustics

Another type of audio-processing technique that could be made more efficient using GPU is calculating real-time room acoustics, as demonstrated by [Jedrzejewski06].

Calculating echoes, occlusions, and obstructions in real-time from environment geometry requires a lot of computation; a ray tracing method can be used to implement this, which is well suited to GPU processing. Ray tracing for acoustics is different from graphical ray tracing because the scenes that are computed don't need to be visually accurate and smaller render targets are often used. Rays are traced from the sound source until they reach the listener's position.

Precomputation

The scene geometry consists of polygons that represent walls; other game objects that are considered large enough to affect the audio environment can be approximated as boxes. During the precomputation stage of this algorithm, the geometry is partitioned to a BSP tree with solid convex regions for leaves. After the BSP tree is computed, it is used to create a portal graph that shows the paths between each leaf. If a portal and polygon lay on the same plane in a certain leaf, additional leaf splits need to be made; new portal and paths computation might be needed if there is need for additional leaf splitting. Information on portals and planes is stored in separate 1D textures that contain data such as whether it is a portal or plane, and its absorption values. The leaf data contains indexes into the plane texture and how many planes it contains. This stage can be performed every time the scene geometry is changed.

Real-Time Rendering

Fragment shaders are executed that first compute intersections in the current leaf for each ray, and then the propagation to new leaf, and then the reflected ray and intersection with listener. The listener's position can be approximated as a bounding sphere; often the bounding volume for the player's avatar is used if the listener object is intended to represent the player. Pseudocode for the shader programs is shown here:

```
LeafPlaneIntersect(Ray)
{
   Get plane index for current Ray
for (i=1; i<=6; i++)
{
      Intersect with plane for current leaf
      Store data for closest intersected rays
}
}

PropagateRay(Ray)
{
   Check if currentLeaf contains more planes
```

```
            if(currentLeaf == listener.leaf)
            Intersect Ray with boundingsphere

            if(intersection with plane)
               Reflect ray and its absorption

            If(intersection with portal)
               Set new leaf for ray
     }
```

The environmental reverberation model is then constructed. It involves retrieval of the render target texture and final ray data. Three render target textures are used, one for state information, one for the ray origin, and one for the ray direction.

Conclusion

Not all audio algorithms can take advantage of the GPU's parallel computation; however, certain tasks such as some audio effect algorithms and acoustical ray tracing excel when executed on graphics hardware. Other than the audio techniques described in this gem, GPUs have also been shown to greatly outperform CPUs for techniques such as FFT (Fast Fourier Transforms), which are ubiquitous in audio processing. With PCI-Express cards becoming common, transfering large amounts of data from video memory to system is no longer a significant bottleneck. These techniques show that the GPU can be utilized as a practical optimization for many audio algorithms and even a feasible replacement for specialized audio DSP hardware.

References

[Buck04] Buck, Ian, et al. "GPGPU: General Purpose Computation on Graphics Hardware," SIGGRAPH, 2004.

[Gallo04] Gallo, Emmanuel, and Tsingos, Nicolas. "Efficient 3D Audio Processing with the GPU," Proceedings of the ACM Workshop on General Purpose Computing on Graphics Processors, ACM, 2004.

[GPGPU07] "General Purpose Computing Using Graphics Hardware," available online at www.gpgpu.org.

[Jedrzejewski06] Jedrzejewski, Marcin, and Krzysztof, Marasek. "Computation of Room Acoustics Using Programmable Video Hardware," *Computer Vision and Graphics*, Springer Netherlands, 2006.

[Owens07] Owens, John D., Luebke, David, Govindaraju, Naga, Harris, Mark, Krüger, Jens, Lefohn, Aaron E., and Purcell, Tim. "A Survey of General-Purpose Computation on Graphics Hardware," Computer Graphics Forum, 26(1), pp. 80–113, March 2007.

[Rolfes04] Rolfes, Thomas. "Artificial Neural Networks on Programmable Graphics Hardware," *Game Programming Gems 4*, Charles River Media, 2004.

[Whalen05] Whalen, Sean. "Audio and the Graphics Processing Unit," available at http://www.node99.org/projects/gpuaudio/, 2005.

[Zeller05] Zeller, Cyril. "Cloth Simulation on the GPU," SIGGRAPH, NVIDIA Corporation, 2005.

4.2

MultiStream—The Art of Writing a Next-Gen Audio Engine

Jason Page, Sony Computer Entertainment, Europe

Jason_Page@scee.net

For the past three years, the SCEE R&D's audio team has been writing a "next-gen" audio engine for the Playstation 3 that was to be part of the official SDK. My aim for this gem is, having been a part of the SCEE engine project, to give you an idea of the work involved in designing and creating your own audio engine. In turn, this information may be useful in allowing you to create your own audio engine, or by knowing the magnitude of the job depending on your goals, you might decide to use something from an SDK or middleware provider instead.

I'm not going to cover the MultiStream function calls in detail—any licensed PS3 developer can look at the docs at any time, but I would like to bring your attention to the issues that my team had to overcome. At the end of this gem, I will look at new problems that might also need resolving due to the expectations of next-gen audio.

At the very beginning of the project, we had no idea what hardware would be available for us; no idea of how much RAM we would require or the expected performance.

We decided to take the approach of creating everything in software and to expect there to be no help from hardware DSPs. Later, we found that this was indeed the correct choice, as there was to be no audio hardware in the PS3. I also find that planning audio engines around known hardware or game requirements can mean that the final result is rather mediocre. If you know that a game requires a low-pass filter for occlusion and obstruction but don't allow the capability for such a filter to handle high-pass, band-pass, notch—or indeed the many other filter types—how many creative possibilities have you lost? Thinking big means you can trim down areas that might not be feasible in the long term, and also means you've got something different from everyone else.

A "stream" in MultiStream consists of audio data to play (up to eight channels), playback frequency, volume parameter/surround sound position, amplitude envelope, DSP effects, and output routing locations.

How It All Began

Apart from the technical aspects of creating an audio engine, we also had to decide on other features to include to make MultiStream "next-gen." The following sections explain a little more about the questions we had to answer. Again, the idea of creating your own audio engine might be appealing, but such a project could end up taking years to complete, and there are many things that you need to have planned for in detail first. Having a team working on an audio engine for three years does not come cheap. The following sections describe the design process we used before writing any code.

Understanding "Next-Gen" Audio

Although it should seem simple, creating an audio engine that makes games sound better than ever before isn't as straightforward as it may seem. The ability to play CD quality audio tracks has been available to game developers for over a decade. The ability to add high-quality reverb (although perhaps not to the standard of professional audio plug-ins by companies such as Yamaha or Lexicon) to hundreds of audio channels has been with us since the late 90s. Would just upping these values create a "next-gen" feel? After all, it is not we who decide this—it's Jimmy and Jenny who just spent $60 on a game and need to be impressed.

If you are thinking of writing your own audio engine, first ask yourself what it needs to do. For MultiStream, one purpose was to allow game audio to sound better than, and in a certain sense, different than current generations. More channels but with the same audio capabilities as previous audio engines—this might make a game sound better by creating a richer environment, but it's unlikely that it will really stand out of the crown as being "next-gen." Sure, you can do what you want with offline processing, but the real power of next-gen is to do it all in real-time. There's a whole load of great sounding effects like vocoders or convolution reverb that have never been done before in real-time, but these all need frequency domain processing. This has previously been seen as impractical to run in real-time along with a full game, but we wanted it. It soon became obvious that next-gen audio means gaining expertise in a number of areas we'd never had to worry about before.

Wish Lists

From my experience with audio on the PS3, it seems that a good approach for anyone to take is to make a wish list of what kind of audio processing they require. At the time of writing, it seems like just about any type of audio process is not only possible, but is also possible in real-time. To give you an example, MultiStream can process over 50 mono convolution reverb effects in real-time. However, this also means that there is no processing left for any audio channels! But, it does mean that even if you require one convolution reverb, which was previously thought of as not being possible for games, it is now a reality. Programming audio on the PS3 does literally allow for new approaches to audio, where techniques that had previously only been seen in professional music packages can now be used.

How Many Audio Channels?

It is presumed that for any audio engine, it must be able to process enough audio channels of data to meet expectations. Yes, more channels do help produce "better audio," but as Mozart once said, "The silences between the notes are as important as the notes themselves." Even so, today's (and tomorrow's) game requirements mean more audio channels are required for creating the same game sounds as before. It would be reasonable to think that a car engine sound might be created with at least 25–30 audio channels:

- Car engine rev loops * eight (each for, say a 1000 RPM rev range)
- Car exhaust loops * eight (recorded at the same time as the car engine)
- Skid sounds (four looping skid sounds, one for each wheel)
- Road rumble sounds (four sounds, one for each wheel)
- Gear changing noises

Due to the number of channels required for a single car in the standard race game, it was previously only the player's car that used such a detailed model. All other AI cars might be using a far lower channel count, due to hardware constraints, CPU and/or RAM constraints.

Today, this is not such a problem. MultiStream has limited its maximum channel count to 512. In a racing game, this would make it possible to handle 20 race cars, all with the same audio capabilities as the player's own car. Of course you could go beyond 512 voices (depending on platform you're developing for), but you have to draw the line somewhere. In our case, sticking with this limit still means there's plenty of processing time to spare for DSP effects, buss routing, re-sampling, and amplitude envelopes.

Finally, in the case of car engines, it must also be noted that by the time you read this, the method of cross-fading loops for engines may well be a thing of the past. Methods that use granular synthesis techniques, whereby playback of small sections—or "grains"—of a car engine sample, create a far more realistic engine sound than loops alone. Again, this was not really possible until now. The RAM footprint required for such samples without the ability to use file formats such as MP3 or ATRAC3 meant that these techniques, although tried and tested in theory, used too much RAM.

Sample Formats

Playback of an audio file must also take into consideration the format of the sample data and the number of channels. Note that stereo files do not necessarily take twice as much processing or RAM as mono files; this depends on the file format. MP3 joint stereo mode for example records some of the audio in mono, where if the left and right channels contain the same frequencies, there's no need to store them twice. Actually, there are indeed many books and Websites explaining why you *should* store them twice, but again, explaining this would take too many pages!

For game audio, one of the main issues is accessibility. Sample accurate playback is something you really need to aim for. For the MP3 format, it is relatively simple to play back audio approximately +/–1000 samples from where is required. Therefore, extra work (and RAM and CPU) is required to make MP3 fully sample accurate, or as I like to call it, "game-compatible."

The file formats your audio engine accepts also have to be considered, as shown in Table 4.2.1.

Table 4.2.1 Audio Engine File Formats

Format	Pros and Cons	Notes
Float32 PCM	*Pros:* No decoding required Best quality audio Easy to loop to sample boundaries *Cons:* Large memory footprint	Faster processing means more CPU spare for other tasks.
16-bit PCM	*Pros:* Good "CD-quality" audio Easy to loop to sample boundaries Smaller memory footprint than Float32 *Cons:* Still quite a large memory footprint. Unlikely that a game will have enough RAM to store all samples in this format.	More usable in games than float32 format, but in many cases, the listeners aren't going to notice the difference.
ADPCM	*Pros:* Passable quality Smaller memory footprint than PCM Quite fast to decode *Cons:* Possible that decoders only handle mono input files Higher CPU overhead required for decoding Looping to sample boundaries may not be possible	In many cases, this is still used as a standard game audio format. It offers compression and a fast decode. Sample accurate seeking or looping might not be possible; it does not require too much tweaking of the input data to align loop markers to boundaries.
MP3	*Pros:* Good quality Excellent compression Many decoders can handle multiple channel data *Cons:* High CPU overhead Not easy to seek to sample accurate positions	Best for getting as many sounds in RAM at one time, but you must consider the processing required to decode such formats.

It also has to be noted that codecs such as MP3 require data buffers per audio channel too, where decoded data and other information needs to be stored. Considering that MultiStream can play 512 MP3s at once, even if each audio channel only required a 2KB buffer, the codec still requires 1MB. Although this may seem obvious, it is areas such as this that are best explained to game producers and designers early on in the development cycle when they request such codecs.

Also, as shown in Table 4.2.1, although float32 input would offer the best quality, another issue can be DMA bandwidth (a method for transferring data around a system). In which case, using 16-bit data could half the bandwidth, while still producing audio of CD quality.

Loop markers need to be considered too. The loop markers may be stored in the file header (such as .WAV), within the sample data (such as the SCE's .VAG ADPCM format), or not at all (such as .MP3s converted from .WAVs, where the loop information is lost). Handling looping of audio is not as simple as it may seem. If the sample is memory resident, you just play the sample and know where in RAM the address of the loop position is. If you are streaming audio content, care needs to be taken so the loop point is in memory when it comes time to loop.

To Stream or Not to Stream

Most audio systems need to be aware that data may be streamed. Here, your audio engine has to cater for some kind of buffer mechanism, where data is copied into an area of RAM for playback (this data is normally loaded from disk, but there could also be PCM data obtained from a decoded .MP3 via a codec outside of your audio engine).

From experience I would not recommend handling data-loading functions within your audio engine. If the audio engine requires more data for a streaming buffer, it should request this. (In MultiStream, this is handled via a callback function.) If you start handling data loading in your audio engine, expect a world of pain later on. Here's why:

- You need to sync other game data-loading with your audio engine loading.
- You need to handle all cases of corrupt data loads (disk removed during loading or a damage disk).

Essentially, your audio engine becomes far trickier to optimize and maintain. It must also be noted though, that any audio streaming needs to take priority over any other data loading. Why? Simply due to the fact that if audio is not streamed in time, you will have to either repeat playback of the last buffer of data (which sounds like a broken CD player) or play silence. Either of these may well cause your title to fail during any QA process.

Even if your audio system is not going to handle streaming of data from disk directly, the programmer(s) in charge of the IO systems must be aware of the following priorities in order of importance:

- Currently playing streams must be updated first
- Newly requested streams can be updated next
- Data load for the game happens last

Using this method, if a player keeps requesting more audio to be streamed, say, each game frame, any currently playing music will still play correctly without skipping or jumping. In many cases, streaming is used for areas such as sports commentary. This is also usually in context with the current action on-screen, which is why the playing of such audio is, as far as I am concerned, more important than game data loading. There is nothing worse than a commentator saying the wrong thing at the wrong time.

The size of stream buffers is not an exact science. This will depend on the sample rate and format of the data you are streaming, along with how often you expect to be loading data. Streaming data from hard disk is by no means as tricky as loading from DVD, where the time taken for the DVD head mechanism to physically move to the correct place and the time taken for data to load is also a factor. In many cases, having multiple copies of the same file on a disk is a common technique for speeding up DVD loading. The current head position is kept track of in software, and then the streaming engine (note that the streaming engine and the audio engine are separate engines) will choose which file on the disk is closest to this position.

This method can also help with prioritizing audio data streaming. If multiple audio channels need more data, you need to choose which should be the first to be loaded. Again, this is not an exact science. If multiple streams require more data, then you need to make sure that they all get that data as soon as possible. If you can't load the data in time, a simple solution is to either increase the stream buffer sizes or reduce the sample rate of the audio. Halving the sample rate has the same effect as doubling the stream buffer size. For example, playing 48000 samples at 24kHz will take twice as long as playing 48000 samples at 48kHz.

The method of reducing the playback frequency of a stream is also very useful for determining whether pops or clicks in audio playback are caused by the system running out of data to process. This modification is normally very simple to make to any audio calls, compared to increasing streaming buffer sizes, which can be limited in size due to the restrictions set by other non-audio game requirements.

For streaming audio with loop markers, depending on the sample data format, the only time you might know that you need to loop the data is when you've reached the loop marker, which is too late. For MultiStream, we decided to ignore all loop markers within the audio engine. It is therefore up to the user to either decode .WAV headers, or stream correctly to the required data. Not only does this allow the user to feel in control, but it also takes care of any of the issues mentioned previously.

So if we are required to loop to a certain offset within a file, we can first check to see if that portion of the file is indeed in RAM. If it isn't, we need to load this portion first so that playback will continue as desired.

Volume Parameters

Setting volume levels of an audio channel, along with setting its frequency, are the two most basic audio DSP effects.

For MultiStream, you still had a number of issues to decide upon: As the PS3 can output audio up to 7.1, you needed to allow any audio channel to be routed to any number of speakers. For example, a mono audio signal may want to be heard on both the front-left and the rear-right speakers. This means that any single audio channel requires eight volume parameters. Furthermore, as MultiStream can play data containing up to eight audio channels, there are a total of 64 volume parameters available per stream. Finally, MultiStream can process up to 512 channels and these volume parameters can be Float32s. This means that $512 \times 64 \times 4$ bytes are required just for volume parameters alone.

You could reduce the memory footprint if you used 16-bit volume parameters, or maybe even less. Imagine that MIDI volume parameters range from 0–127, giving you 128 possible settings. Why do you need to use floats that give you millions of possible settings? First, you must ask when you set a volume parameter in MIDI, is the hardware (or software plug-in) using this value directly? It could be that this value is then scaled to work in a floating point system where volumes are ramped toward the required volume level. Secondly, for ease of use, having a system that uses floats can make the rest of the audio engine quicker in general. There will be less need for conversion of volume levels between various formats, for a start.

Playback Frequency

As stated in the "Volume Parameters" section, volume and frequency are the two most basic audio DSP effects.

With a purely software-based system, even setting the playback frequency of a sample needs consideration. Any resampling is going to take CPU time and it would be foolish to waste this time on such basic functionality. Not only does the resampling algorithm need to be considered, but also the fact that playing back audio at high frequencies can in turn take longer to process. Therefore, a system that can process 4000 audio channels may only be able to do so at a maximum playback sample rate of, say, 48kHz.

To explain a little more, if you need to create one second worth of audio data for playback at 48kHz, you need to process 48000 samples to do so. If you need to play back at 96kHz, you need to process 96000 samples. "Processing" in this sense could mean decoding of MP3 files. So again, playing back a 48kHz MP3 at 96kHz means you need to decode twice as much of the MP3 file.

Perhaps this processing time could have been spent more wisely? If you require a sample to be played at an octave higher than its original pitch, it may make sense to resample it down to 24kHz, which in turn means that going one octave higher would put it at 48kHz. Simply put, by halving your audio files sample rate, you can cut the processing required to resample in half.

Frequency Domain Processing

For any frequency domain processing, you are looking at requiring a FFT/iFFT routine. Understanding the fine detail of the FFT is not as important as it may seem. Yes, there's a lot of math involved here, but once written, it's not something that you really have to worry about again. Using it is a different issue.

The main problem with frequency domain processing is choosing the correct window size. If the effect you're working on needs high-frequency resolution (for example, say you're implementing some kind of parametric EQ), you need a large window. Large windows give very poor time resolution, so it's not possible to change parameters quickly. Large windows also result in greater latency, require more memory, and use more CPU. Although shorter windows do not suffer from these problems, they lead to poor frequency domain resolution, which defeats the objective of trying to implement a frequency domain effect.

The answer really lies in finding the right window size for your application, tuning it to make the best use of the available resources, and listening to hear if it sounds right. Even then, different effects may require different window sizes. Are you prepared to switch window sizes in the signal path, or is a "one-size-fits-all" solution good enough?

Basics of FFT

There are a number of issues to consider when using FFT. First, the number of input samples needs to be double the number of output samples. So, for example, you need to feed the FFT 1024 samples for it to output 512. They have implications for other routines too. For things like amplitude envelopes, you may need to actually process all 1024 samples but then rewind the envelope parameters by 512 samples so that the next time the amplitude envelope is processed, you are using the correct values.

FIGURE 4.2.1 Simple amplitude envelope (fade in/fade out) over 2048 samples.

The very big plus point of FFT (and windowing) is that you'll find it can remove a lot of possible pops and clicks normally heard with large volume changes or looping to boundaries where samples do not match up.

As you can see in Figure 4.2.2, on each step, the envelope needs to be re-calculated for the first half of the data packet, even though it has already just calculated it for the second half of the previous packet.

Note that some systems would also include a step before this, where, being the inverse of the last step, the fade-in part of the amplitude envelope would only process the first 512 samples. This is illustrated in Figure 4.2.3.

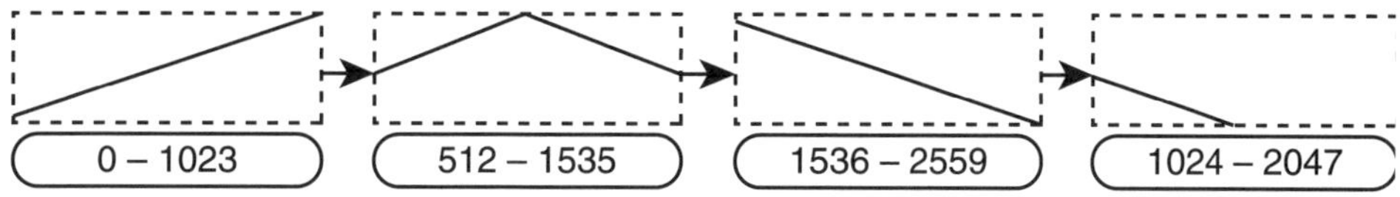

FIGURE 4.2.2 At least four passes of the data are required when processing in 1024 sample packets if you're using windowing techniques.

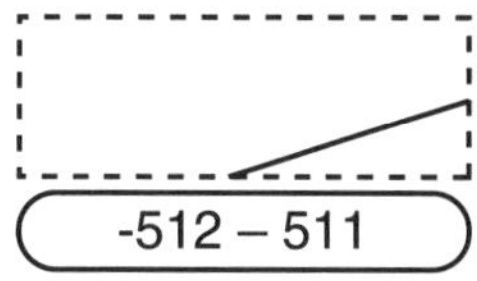

FIGURE 4.2.3 Some systems use a fading that processes only the first 512 samples.

This step adds a lot of latency to the final output, which we found to be far too noticeable in real-time applications.

Latency

Real-time applications obviously require a low latency. For MultiStream, we decided that it should generate 512 samples per channel each time the update routine is processed (this technique is known as granularity). When using FFT, outputting 512 samples requires 1024 input samples due to windowing functions (see the section called "Basics of FFT").

With 512 sample granularity, this gives the FFT function enough data to meet two goals:

- Latency is low enough for most game requirements.
- 512 bands (where MultiStream requires 1024 samples as input data) gives enough scope for many FFT-based DSP effects but keeps the quality high. If you drop to 256 bands (512 samples as input data), you would find the audio quality to be too poor to be of any use for just about any application.

Processing of 512 samples means that the update routine will need to be called 93.75 times per second (every 10.66 milliseconds):

```
48000 samples = 1 second of playback
48000 / 512 = 93.75 Hz (Number of audio updates required per second)
1000/93.75 = Audio engine will be called every 10.66 milliseconds
```

This is generally fast enough to keep the audio in sync with any graphic updates running at a maximum of 60 updates per second. Even though outputting 512 samples may seem like an easy task (remember that there are 48000 samples required for one second of playback), processes such as MIDI sequencers run at a faster rate than this. In many cases, they run up to 240Hz or even 384Hz (between 2–4 milliseconds!) Therefore, the problem may be that if a MIDI sequence requires an instrument to start playing, it will not actually start until the next audio update. Now, many people will not notice this, but those who have very good hearing (such as the audio engineers who are going to be listening to their work played through your audio engine) will notice. If a lower latency than 512 samples is required, FFT processing may not be the one for you.

For MultiStream, we have both frequency and time domain processing modes. So if you do not require frequency domain effects, it is possible to process totally in time domain. This means window size is no longer an issue and we can offer optional granularity settings of 128 or 256.

Packet Smoothing

As discussed in the "Latency" section, granularity is the number of samples generated on each audio update. On the simplest level, each update would use the settings the user has required for each audio channel, such as what frequency and volume with which to play back. One issue to consider here is that if each packet just uses the required volume, it is possible to get aliasing artifacts due to the sudden jump of volume. Another artifact is clicking or popping, which is noticeable on audio such as car engines where multiple audio channels would be cross-faded depending on the motor rev required.

For time-domain processing, a filter process is required so that volume changes are smoothed, whereas for frequency domain processing, you will find that the windowing which is required for FFT (such as a *hamming* or *hanning window*) does all of the hard work for you.

As first discussed in the "Frequency Domain Processing" section, windowing techniques are used when processing frequency data. The reason for windowing when converting to frequency domain is that when you process the data, you only focus on a single portion of the data. Analysis therefore knows nothing about what audio signals proceeded or follow this data and if you don't take this into consideration, there will be discontinuity between each data packet (known as pops and clicks to you and me). Window types such as hanning or hamming are essentially just algorithms used to modify each packet of data. Each packet of data is then processed and mixed with the previous packet, producing an output which resembles the desired data. This is a *really* simplified paragraph on what would normally require chapters in other books, but hopefully there's enough information here to give you something to Google with!

Windowing may also mask a multitude of sins that normally cause pops and clicks to be output, such as looping samples whose start and end samples do not match. Note that care must be taken here still. Although looping to any sample might sound fine when using window techniques, if for any reason you need to move your audio engine to a pure "time domain" mode, where no such windowing or filtering colors the audio output, you will hear these pops again. Source data that loops perfectly by default is always preferred.

Surround Sound

Consideration must be taken on how to handle surround sound. There are two main approaches to take:

- User supplies X, Y, and Z coordinates of both the source and listener positions
- User supplies an angle and distance for the source compared to the listener position

MultiStream uses the X, Y, Z approach, using OpenAL 1.1 algorithms, although it would also be sensible for such a routine to accept either approach considering that the X, Y, Z system creates a surround sound panning position (angle) and an overall volume (distance) from this position anyway.

Processing multi-channel audio in surround sound must also be considered.

Again, MultiStream will fold multi-channel audio down to a single point source if it requires positioning in surround sound. Another way to handle multi-channel audio is to play each channel as mono (for example, channel 0 = front-left and channel 1 = front-right for a stereo channel), and set the surround sound X, Y, Z position for each speaker. Figure 4.2.4 shows six channels of audio.

6 channel .WAV
Ch 0 = Front Left
Ch 1 = Front Right
Ch 2 = Front Center
Ch 3 = Rear Left
Ch 4 = Rear Right
Ch 5 = LFE

FIGURE 4.2.4 Six channels of audio. Splitting the .WAV into separate channels, you can position each speaker's position in the game world to replicate the desired effect.

This approach can be also used for car race games, where moving the camera position from behind to inside a player's car means all the audio playback works correctly, such as the exhaust being heard from behind the player (see Figure 4.2.5).

For certain types of games, a common approach for game audio is to keep non-player audio as mono (point source) and player-specific audio can be multi-channel if desired. As the player is always in front of a camera, it is safe to presume that no surround

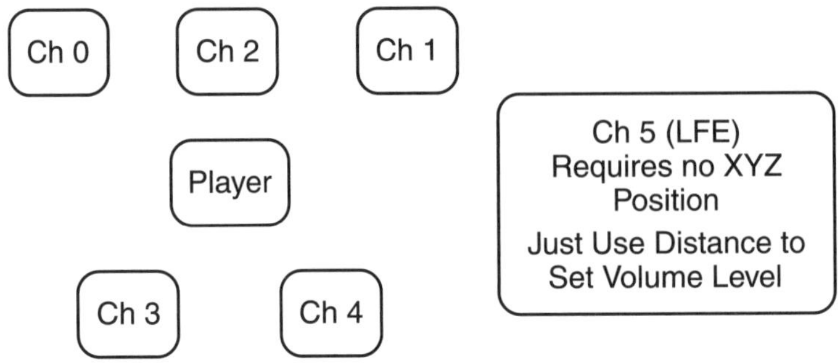

FIGURE 4.2.5 Channel location relative to the player.

sound processing of their audio is required and just playing their audio as stereo will be fine. Not only does this allow for higher quality samples, but it also reduces processing overheads because there are fewer surround sound objects in the game world.

Syncing Channels

One problem that often occurs in audio programming is being able to sync multiple channels. This allows the starting, stopping, and pitch changing of multiple channels to happen at the same time. You might hear phasing or chorus effects if this is not taken into consideration.

The reason for this can be seen in Figure 4.2.6.

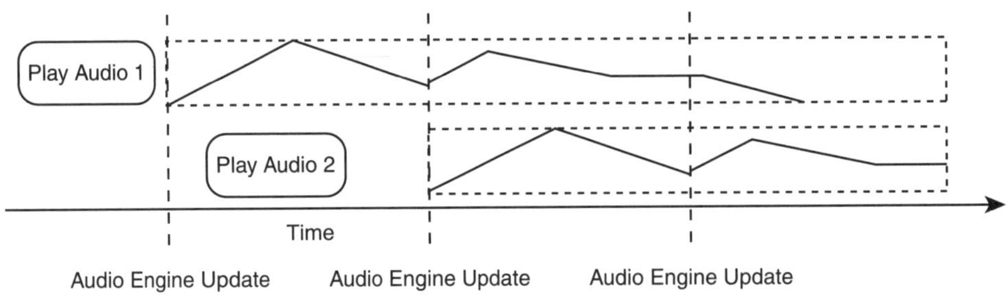

FIGURE 4.2.6 Channels can become out of sync if the audio engine updates between play audio commands.

In Figure 4.2.6, you can see that two audio channels have been requested to play, but due to the audio engine's update routine firing in between the initialization of these two audio channels, the output of "Audio 1" is now one data packet ahead of "Audio 2." In real life MultiStream terms, this means that "Audio 1" is 512 samples ahead of "Audio 2." This can also occur if you pause and resume channels, or set the pitch of multiple channels, except that in both of these cases it is possible for the audio to drift farther and farther out of sync!

For a solution to this problem, you need to make sure that any phase-causing functions (the Play or Pitch Change functions) are not split by the audio update routine. The simplest method for this is to have two functions:

```
Void Sync_On(void)
Void Sync_Off(void)
```

Here, any Play or Pitch functions called between these calls are "remembered" and are processed in the next audio update function after `Sync_Off`, as illustrated in Figure 4.2.7.

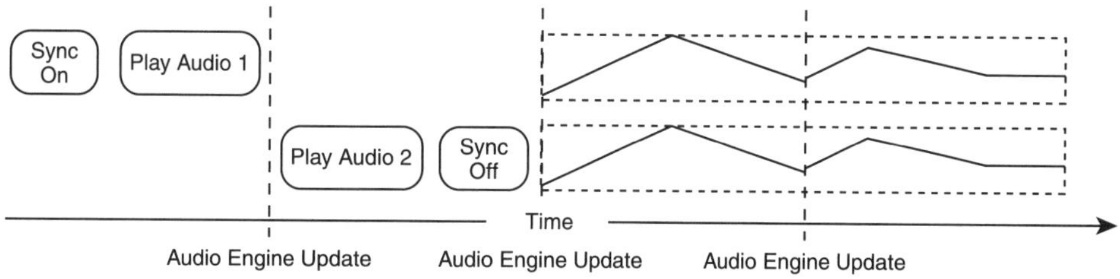

FIGURE 4.2.7 The Play Audio commands are queued up to be synchronously started during the same audio engine update.

As you can see in Figure 4.2.7, "Audio 1" has now waited until the "Sync Off" function has processed, which means both channels are now playing in sync as desired.

DSP Effects

DSP effects separate the "next-gen" from current or last-gen titles. The processing power available, again from my experience on the PS3, means that it is possible to process audio in real-time, and using a minimal amount CPU at the quality normally only experienced in professional effect units.

The purpose of this gem is not to discuss each DSP effect. There are many books already available covering filter design, FFT and so on. Therefore, I will leave it to you to research this area.

Rest assured, having only a low-pass filter to use as occlusion/obstruction is not going to make your title sound next-gen. You will need to go a little further to impress people! Just think about the amount of DSP effects available for general music or sound effect creation and then think of how any of these effects could be used within your game title. Think about every room in every level having its own reverb type, for example. As "anything is possible," a good start is having programmers communicate to audio engineers about what effects they would like to see in real-time and why.

Of course, processing DSP effects in real-time also means that there is less pre-processing required for audio samples. Considering that a game title may contain tens of thousands of samples, it can make sense to process these in-game, allowing the developer to tweak and change parameters at will, rather than needing to go back to the audio engineer and ask for changes or just put up with an effect that's close enough to what you want. Imagine a sample of a human voice that you decide would sound better if it were talking through a radio headset. Having the ability to test these effects without the need to waste time pre-processing data not only speeds up development, but also allows for far more creativity when creating your audio.

Routing

The number of busses an audio channel can be mixed to cannot be underestimated. For MultiStream, we currently have 31 sub-busses and one master buss. It is already becoming apparent that these values should be increased in the future. The grouping of sound sources has previously been used for volume scaling. For example, all SFX would route to one bus, all music to another, and all commentary to another. The volume parameters can then be modified in, say, game "option" menus and will then just set the volumes for these busses, scaling all audio playing through them.

Today, with the number of audio channels required for creating things like car engines, busses can be used for far more than just volume scaling. By adding DSP effects to busses, it is easier and less CPU intensive to set such effects for all of these components in one go (see Figure 4.2.8). Imagine a car game where you see a car go behind an object. Instead of processing low-pass filters for 30 or more audio channels, you could just do it once.

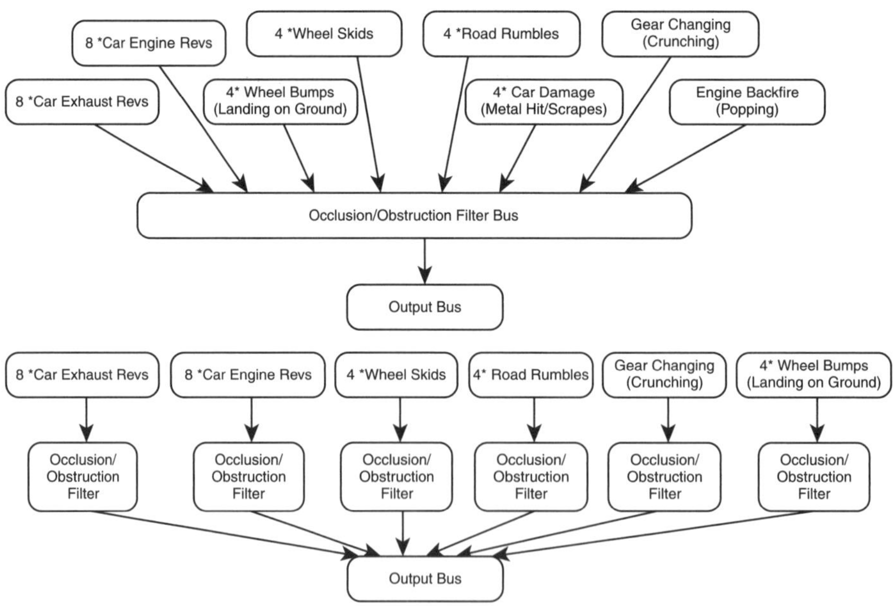

FIGURE 4.2.8 Putting DSP effects into the buss can reduce the amount of processing done per channel.

Conclusion

Creating a good master mix is still seen as something of a black art. Indeed, it can be seen as something that you will never get right. It should go without saying that games, unlike film, are unpredictable. You can never be sure where the camera is pointing or which situation the player is in. Trying to work out what audio should be heard is not simple.

Ducking techniques have been used previously to provide a little clarity. Most sports titles will automatically reduce the volume of all other audio whenever commentary is played. This has previously been handled by a simple "if I am playing commentary, reduce all other volume by x percent" approach. In the real world, a ducker (or side chain compressor) would be used. This analyzes the audio input signal (in this case, the voice of the commentator) and then reduces another input signal (all other audio) accordingly.

This technique can now easily be introduced into a next-gen title and gives a far more realistic result. The previous method does not check for what commentary is playing, it just knows it is. If there is a long silence in the commentary audio sample, all other audio volume will still be reduced. Using a ducker DSP effect will not cause this problem.

Priority systems can also be used to make sure that you hear audio that's more important to a scene. The choice of what is important in a scene is still really up to the game engine. For example, imagine a game where 10 enemies who are all the same distance from the player are shooting; you may need to choose which ones are more important. Perhaps you need to order this by the direction the enemies are shooting or by what kind of weapons they are shooting (laser rifles being more powerful than pistols perhaps).

The number of priority levels is also a factor (where, say, a higher level will give one sound priority over another). I have previously written systems that give the user 256 priority levels for any SFX. Although this feels like a good idea, in practice it is not common for there to be any noticeable difference between using a priority level of 122 compared to 121. A smaller range of something like 0–7 is far more usable.

Mixing the two techniques of both the ducker and a priority system can allow you to automate a master mix. Here, a number of busses are used—one buss for each priority level. On each buss apart from one (which has the highest priority), a ducker is placed and each buss also feeds into the adjacent buss. Buss 0 will duck busses 1–6. Buss 1 will duck busses 2–6. Buss 2 will duck busses 3–6, and so on. Simply by making sure your audio routes to the selected buss, it should be possible that volume levels are controlled correctly. This requires minimum input from the users; they just select the buss for audio to route to in the same way as you select the sound's priority.

Under MultiStream, this would be a feasible routing and DSP setup, although I admit that there are still other considerations. Other busses may contain reverb effects and you will need to know how to route from the six priority busses to these other busses. Even so, I believe this is an area that may well make games feel far more "film-like" with regard to post-production values, and it is only possible to do this now, under the next-gen banner.

4.3

Listen Carefully, You Probably Won't Hear This Again

Removing Repetition from Audio Environments in Games and Discussing a New Approach to Sound Design

Stephan Schütze

Being REALLY Different

Drop a coin on a table and listen to the sound it makes. Drop the same coin a second, third, or hundredth time and the chance of the sound it makes being the same is incredibly unlikely. The creation of sound is influenced by a staggering number of factors and apart from scientifically measurable sounds, such as a sine wave, is extremely variable. Sounds used in most games, however, are generally static or limited in their variation. In some cases this may be desirable. For the most part, though, having the same sound effect repeat with little or no change not only reduces the realism of a game environment but, more importantly, it is often a source of frustration or annoyance for the players.

The technology to create real-time variable in-game sound effects has been available for some time. These techniques not only remove the issue of repetitive sounds, but they also allow for far more complex audio assets to exist in a game than would have generally been possible with the limited resources of some game consoles. With the advance into the newest generation of game consoles, these methods can allow an audio designer to create rich audio environments featuring complex reactive and truly interactive sound and music. At last developers can achieve a level of sound design comparable to the incredible levels of graphics that have been achieved in interactive entertainment in the past few years.

This gem discusses the methodology behind creating these more complex and variable sound environments, as well as illustrates a need to shift our thinking as creators of audio assets. I will also look at some of the tools available to asset creators. The goal of this gem is to inform about the techniques available but also to generate thought amongst sound designers about how we practice our craft. I also hope to inform producers of the potential that exists for incredible audio environments.

How It Works; Thinking Differently

The first step is to move away from the traditional static linear audio used in film and television. Games do not function in a linear fashion, but for want of a better role model the industry has often strived to achieve movie industry standards of quality and production. Initially as game technology was developing, this was a useful benchmark, but the closer games come to meeting the standards of big budget film and television productions, the more we should look at exceeding them. It is apparent now that in the very near future games will surpass film and television in the potential to deliver entertainment. As a result, the benchmarks for production quality may also move beyond those of linear media. Audio can and should be one of the leading areas in which interactive entertainment production methods surpass film standards. A selection of static pre-made sounds to be triggered as required in-game, although adequate, completely fails to utilize the creative possibilities available to designers and developers.

The basic principle of this technique is to construct complex sounds from their individual raw component sounds. Although this may be inefficient on a sound-by-sound basis, when implemented for the entire audio environment it often actually takes less memory and fewer resources to create sounds that are infinitely variable and often far more interesting than pre-made sound effects. It also provides the sound designer with a much bigger selection of possibilities for sounds in-game. So you can actually have more sounds in-game with no repetition and for less memory. Initially this process has a steeper learning curve for designers, and may take longer to set up. However, the resources gathered will provide ongoing material for future projects without the risk of sounding like you are simply reusing the same sound library.

Going Bang!

To begin with, it is useful to think of the sounds we record and add to the engine as being the core building blocks from which we will create all in-game sounds. This is no different than going out and recording raw source material, preparing the source sounds and mixing them together to produce a finished sound effect. The difference here being that creating the actual sound happens in-game each time a sound is needed. This approach does preclude your ability to simply drop in pre-made library sound effects, but the benefits are worth the effort.

Explosions are common sounds required in a great many games. I will refer to them as "pops." I use the term "pop" because it encompasses a lot more than simply saying explosion. Pops appear in most shooter-style games as sounds for grenades, missiles, or rockets detonating or for objects in the world exploding. Pops however also exist in many platform games to represent an adversary being defeated, an item being collected, or a special effect such as teleporting, turning invisible, or gaining invulnerability. An actual explosion effect is very similar in structure to a literal "pop" sound or many of the other sounds I have mentioned, as they contain many or all of the same elements.

It is important to understand that a real explosion is a release of energy, usually through some kind of chemical reaction. The actual release of energy will create a basic BANG, which will then echo or reverberate with a fading effect. The extraordinary explosions heard in Hollywood films are a result of the initial energy affecting other things in the world. So smashing glass, splintering wood, bending metal, and so on are not actually apart of the initial explosion of energy; they are consequences of this energy rushing out and meeting wooden, metal or glass objects and having an effect on them, in some destructive way. Those items then react in a similar manner; you get an initial sharp attack sound followed by a drop-off. When the item affected is a plate-glass window, the result is of thousands of small attacks and drop-offs combined to spectacular effect.

Often, when creating sounds, the recorded material alone can sound dull or lifeless. The recorded sound of a real gun being fired can be quite unsatisfying in its raw state. Sound designers will often combine several raw sounds together to create a single new sound. Sometimes the raw material used is to accentuate certain frequency ranges to add depth to the final assets. A low frequency impact can add considerable weight to a sound, whereas high frequencies can make a sound seem much louder and brighter. EQing can add further depth to the final sound and is often helpful if you want a particular sound to stand out from the rest of the audio environment. Balancing the final audio environment should consider the mix of frequencies used as well as the amplitude levels of the sounds. Too much of any particular frequency range can quickly tire the listener and become annoying.

To better understand how to construct a sound, it helps to first deconstruct it:

- **An initial sharp attack sound/surge of energy**. A very short, hard attack, zero drop-off sound. Think of a handclap or gunshot.
- **A drop-off and fade sound**. Think of the echo of a handclap in a church or a gunshot. This is actually part of the initial sound, but it is useful to think of it as a separate element when deconstructing sounds.
- **Affected elements**. These are the sounds of everything that are affected by the initial surge of energy.
- **The drop-off of every affected element.**
- **Major subsidiary effects**. Elements returning to a state of rest. Think large falling debris.
- **Minor subsidiary effect**. As the previous entry, but smaller debris, such as dust, and so on.

This example deconstructs a traditional explosion into its basic sound elements. Sometimes the inclusion of extra sound material can significantly improve the final result. The same thing can be done for any game pop. For example, a musical pickup sound in a children's platform game.

- **An initial sharp attack sound/surge of energy**. A very short, hard attack zero drop-off sound, such as striking a chime or bell tree.

- **A drop-off and fade sound.** The actual ring of the bell and its fade over time.
- **Affected elements often occur in a cascade of sounds.** The bell chime moves and hits the surrounding chimes, but with less energy and in a random pattern.
- **The drop-off of every affected element.** The other bells all ring.
- **Major subsidiary effects.** The overtones or harmonics of the initial bell and further minor contact between chimes.
- **Minor subsidiary effect.** The fading rings of all chimes as they return to a state of rest.

After deconstructing explosions, bubble pops, or chimes ringing, you can then reconstruct those sounds from their individual components. When you understand exactly how these components sound in their raw state, you can construct a convincing pop using a very limited number of raw components and cleverly combining them.

So, let's actually make a sound effect. Previously, I deconstructed a sound so that you can understand the elements you need to construct the same type of sound effect. Let's use the following elements:

- Big_Bang01–03: A short sharp metallic impact sound
- Stone_Fall01–02: Stone objects affected by the energy
- Debris01–02: Small objects returning to a state of rest

ON THE CD

These base sounds are included on the CD-ROM in standard PCM .wav file format. Also included are seven in-game sounds (Ingame_Sound01a–Ingame_Sound03) created using only the seven base sounds.

Seven wav files totalling 629KB were combined to create seven new in-game sounds totalling 1.38MB. All the new sounds were created and recorded directly out of the Microsoft XACT (Cross-Platform Audio Creation Tool) authoring tool using the initial seven base sounds. The three variations of Ingame_sound01 and Ingame-Sound02 are examples to show the variation, which is essentially limitless. Ingame_Sound03 was constructed simply to illustrate an entirely different result from the base material.

I allowed myself only one hour for gathering the base sounds, setting up the XACT project and creation, audition and recording of the new sounds. This was an intentional limitation to demonstrate the speed at which the tool can be used. I'm not saying these new sounds are going to win any awards, but they show how a few simple definitions allow you to create infinite realistic variations quickly in real-time. I purposely did not descriptively name the sounds, as I did not want to influence the listener's thoughts when they were first played.

The Old and the New

Figure 4.3.1 illustrates various files laid out as they might be in a traditional linear sound-editing program to create an explosion sound effect. The tracks allow for sounds to be triggered with varying degrees of overlap and the horizontal axis is used to position the sounds relative to each other in time. The sounds themselves can be any combination that produces the desired final sound effect.

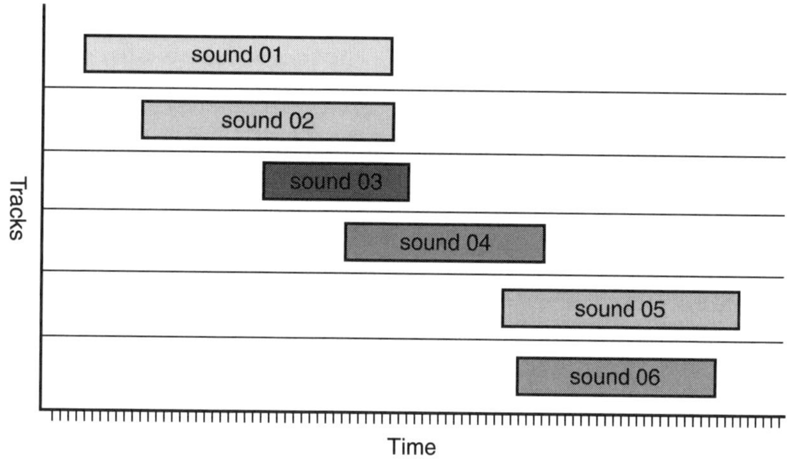

FIGURE 4.3.1 Standard editing software shows linear progression.

This is a traditional linear editing method as used for audio and video; once the designer is happy with the result the sounds are combined by rendering them together to produce a new file in the desired file format.

Figure 4.3.2 illustrates the same layout of sounds events with the same temporal positioning and overlap as Figure 4.3.1. In Figure 4.3.2 however, the layout is just a representation of how you would like the sounds to be combined in real-time by the game engine; there is no rendering process. The sound events are also not limited to an individual sound file. The number in brackets in each sound event represents a pool of sound files that are drawn from randomly to create the desired final output sound. The number of sounds available for each sound event is limited only by the physical memory available on the end platform.

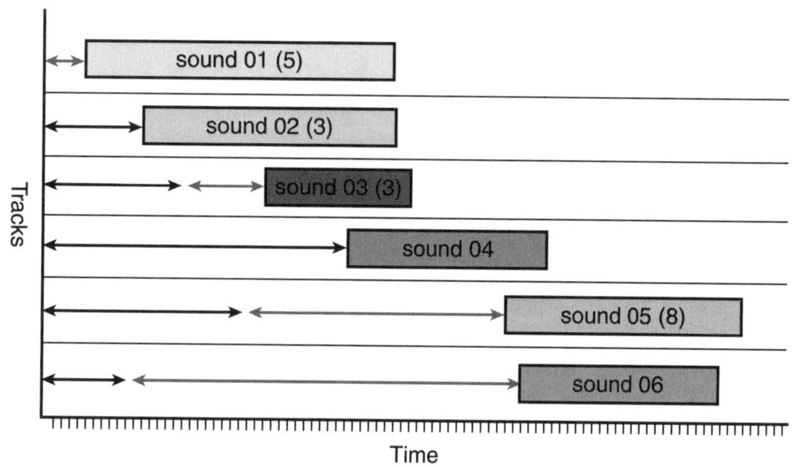

FIGURE 4.3.2 Sound tool layout.

Another difference with this method is the ability to alter the sound's position randomly in time. The black arrows represent a time-offset value. Each time a sound is played, each of the tracks will count its time offset before the sound is triggered. The gray arrows represent a variable time offset. In this case, the time before the sound is triggered is randomized up to the maximum value set. For example, sound 01 will randomly wait a short period of time each time it is played. By comparison, sound 02 will wait a set time approximately twice that of sound 01 each time it is played. Sound 03 combines a set wait time with a further randomized wait time. This means it can sometimes play almost directly after sound 02 triggers, and sometimes as late as halfway through sound 02 triggering.

The main tools used to create sound effects are amplitude, pitch, and time manipulation. Combinations of these three factors can change an original source sound into a new sound completely unrecognizable from the original. Sound designers in all media use these tools to create the sounds they want to use and render out a new altered sound in the required format. This method replaces the tools that manipulate the sounds. The manipulation occurs in real-time in the game. No permanent rendering occurs; a sound is created as it is needed according to the parameters provided using a source sound and then it is discarded. Each time the required sound is called, the process is repeated, the variable parameters are applied, and a unique sound is created.

New Tools for a New Approach

Figure 4.3.3 shows the FMOD sound designer interface. In many ways it appears similar to the two previous diagrams. There are sound events arranged horizontally on two track layers. FMOD's use of sound events rather than actual wave files in the design tool allows for a sound event to include multiple sound files as described in Figure 4.3.2. In Figure 4.3.3, the sound events overlap to allow for a cross-fade between them.

A significant feature in FMOD is that the horizontal axis is not limited to representing time alone. This is another way in which moving away from traditional methods can be extremely effective. In Figure 4.3.3, movement along the horizontal axis represents the RPM of an engine, but it could just as easily represent altitude, speed, or number of hit-points. As any of these parameters are affected, the sounds change as defined. The strength of these systems is that they allow the content creator to set the desired parameters and how they will affect the audio environment. This frees up coder time considerably, because the coder can be provided with a few simple tags to link up. In the case of the car example, once the sound is added, all that is needed in code is for the RPM data from the game to be linked to the RPM tag from FMOD.

Microsoft's XACT audio tool in Figure 4.3.4 has a considerably different interface than FMOD's Sound Designer, but many of the same features and strengths. XACT uses wavebanks and soundbanks that are defined by the designer. The soundbanks are representative of the end sound that is desired, and each sound event can consist of multiple sound files in the same way as FMOD. Parameters for randomizing pitch and volume are accessible at multiple levels when creating a sound. As such, it is possible to

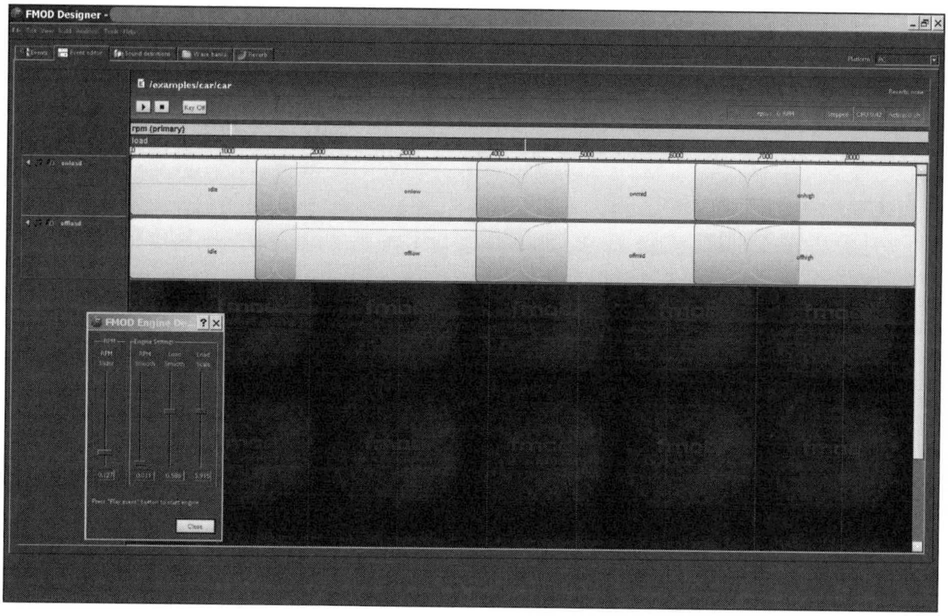

FIGURE 4.3.3 FMOD Designer.

randomize each smaller component making up a sound event, and then pitch or alter the final event as needed. XACT works in the same way as the example in Figure 4.3.2, it just does not use a traditional linear type of editing window.

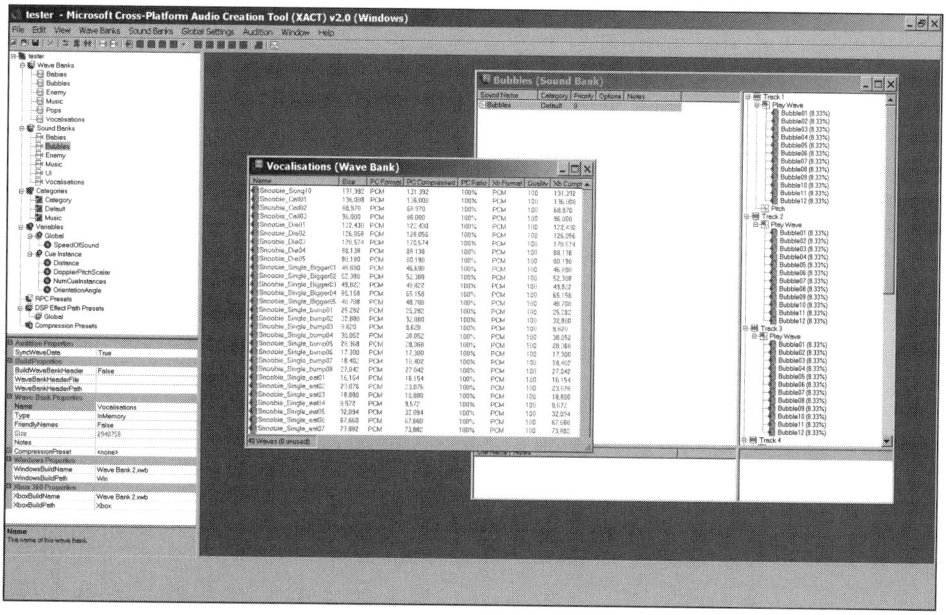

FIGURE 4.3.4 Microsoft XNA XACT audio tool.

In some ways this is a good thing, because it forces the user to approach asset creation in a different way. Although FMOD supports nearly all currently available platforms, XACT is limited to the Microsoft platforms and PC. Hardly surprisingly though, it does interface extremely well with the supported platforms and is easy to use.

Micromanagement

All but the simplest sounds (such as a sine wave) are made up of many smaller sounds. By dividing sounds into their smaller components, you increase their usefulness to the overall sound environment. For example, the click/clunk sound of a car door being closed is reasonably characteristic, and will provide only so much usefulness as a sound for another purpose, even with some pitch shifting of the sound. If, however, the sound is divided into the separate elements that create the final sound (click and clunk), not only do you have two new source sounds that can be combined into other complex sounds, but you can also add some slight variation to the original car door sound by subtle pitch shifting or varying slightly the time between the click and the clunk.

This is a relatively basic example, and a non-repetitive car door sound will probably not win you any awards, but it is certainly relevant when thinking about how to approach sound design for greater realism. Go and open and close a car door a few dozen times and see how different the sounds are each time. It is also worth noting that dividing the two sounds will not add significantly to memory. The combined wav data is the same length.

This method will however drastically increase the number of files you will be dealing with and as a result there will be increases in resources. If nothing else, your header files or wherever you have your assets listed will be bigger. These changes are quite small and with third-generation consoles they should be completely ignorable. The benefits of a more dynamic audio environment far outweigh the issues of having to wrangle more files. That is our job, after all.

Why Are We Doing This Again?

The ultimate goal with this system is to have every sound rendered in-game and to avoid repetition and create a dynamic and effective audio environment. Implementation time can take longer, especially initially as the designer learns to get the most out of the system, depending on the level of complexity of the audio environment. Obviously spending a lot of time on very minor sounds may not be cost effective, but the freedom exists in the system for the designers to choose how detailed they want to be in creating sounds.

The time it would take to randomize simple footsteps by separating the foot impact and gravel crunch underneath, and then replacing the gravel sound as required when different surfaces are walked on is trivial when compared to the benefits of not having annoyingly repetitive footsteps. Add in pitch and volume randomization and it might even sound real. The player will probably never notice; that's often a sign of good sound design.

The designer creates the sounds by choosing the raw material and setting the variables that will control how the sound is created in real-time. Because of the random nature of the sounds, it is important that the designer audition a considerable selection of each sound to ensure it doesn't output undesirable results. Often regular tweaking might be necessary as more sounds are added to the audio environment and they need to balance with each other. One of the best aspects of this method is that once a sound is in the game it can be tweaked using the parameters in the tools.

This means often drastic changes can be made to the sound environment with nothing more than the changing of a single data file. This should not require a full rebuild of the game engine. As a result, the sound department should be able to work with considerably less support from the code team, balancing and changing the audio environment regularly and easily. This method is also incredibly useful for online content, as new sounds could be included in game updates without the need to download large amounts of data. The designer uses the available assets that each player will already have installed and creates new sound assets by making new definitions only. An MMORPG could have hundreds of new sounds added to it by simply downloading a new definitions file and a new EXE file of only a few hundred kilobytes.

Going Further

This gem has focused on the most basic tools for sound production and manipulation: time, pitch, and amplitude, and their most basic uses. The available software tools do, however, offer far more advanced tools such as filtering, effects, and implementation tools. More importantly, though, these tools can allow you to create incredibly complex audio environments. A series of musical motifs or even individual note events could be combined in real-time to predefined parameters and played in-game to react and interact with a player's actions. If you want an ascending and descending musical pattern as Doofy Duck runs up and down the stairs, you can do it. If the player wants to test you by stopping halfway and jumping up and down, that's okay too; the music can respond appropriately.

Although this method certainly isn't limitless, it allows a freedom of creativity that benefits greatly from thinking outside the box. An entire game could center on a musical score that grows organically from the actions of the player, or where every possible interaction in the game world was supported by a unique audio representation. Insert your idea here and go and make it happen!

Even though I refer to this method as rendering or creating the sounds in real-time, these ideas will not reduce or replace the work of a sound designer. In fact, it makes the role even more critical and requires the sound designer to work far beyond simply using library sounds. This method will very quickly expose a designer with weak skills or poor imagination. Conversely, a great designer could use this system to create an audio experience worthy of the best titles in the industry. This method will have an impact on the time required to create and implement audio at least for the first project on which it's utilized. However, once developers overcome the initial learning curve, this method can be extremely flexible. The method allows for last minute changes and alterations to the sound assets far more easily than traditional methods of game sound design.

Conclusion

Game production standards have increased dramatically in the last five years, and as studios better understand the importance of good tools and production processes, the increase in quality should continue. In the past, game audio was often overlooked or given minimal attention. The development of new middleware software and production tools such as XACT allows audio content producers to approach content design and creation in a whole new way. Once designers unlearn some of the traditional approaches to sound construction, these new methods can allow for incredible flexibility and variety. The ability to create audio environments never before possible is not only a great opportunity for talented audio teams, but will hopefully provide entertainment for players that exceed the experiences available through any other media.

4.4

Real-Time Audio Effects Applied

Ken Noland

The purpose of this gem is to outline some of the more basic fundamentals of audio processing from a high-level perspective, taking into account all the tips and tricks I've learned over the years in designing an audio engine for video games. Some of these tips are straightforward and others require a little more thought to work around.

A quick search on the Web will show you how to efficiently create a graphics rendering pipeline or perhaps an AI framework. However, when it comes to creating your own sound system, a large portion of articles are, in my opinion, too API specific or too general and don't cover the niche cases that always tend to show up with audio programming. Lately this has been changing, and a much larger focus has been put on audio programming from the perspective of a digital signal analysis perspective.

This gem is less API specific, although I do mention a couple APIs available and some of the more interesting features, but instead this gem is focused on the general principles of building an audio system. As a note of caution though—as the gem progresses, I will go into more and more advanced topics that will likely require further reading.

Before I begin, I want to introduce a very basic concept. *Sound* is perceived as a difference in samples. Be very mindful of this. If you've seen a waveform, you know that it consists of mostly oscillating values that are constantly changing. Those changes denote the frequency over time. If the signal is flat, there is no frequency. If a signal changes very rapidly, there is a very high frequency.

This is a very important concept to know. Keeping in mind that the values are constantly oscillating, if you drop from one high value to another, because say you want to clear the buffer and fill it with all zeros during the middle of a peak oscillating value, you introduce a frequency change that can be perceived as a tick or a pop. A much more accurate way to deal with clearing a sound buffer is covered in the following sections.

A quick note about the two primary APIs available—you have DirectSound (for Win32 and Vista) and OpenAL (available on most platforms, including Win32, Vista, Linux, and most consoles). Both APIs do what they do well and support a wide variety of formats and effects. I have no preference when it comes to choosing one API over another and it depends on what environment you are developing for.

With that being said, both sound APIs have their benefits and drawbacks. Because of the distinct difference in drivers for DirectSound and OpenAL, I recommend writing a sound system that is abstract enough that the end user can readily switch between the two different sound APIs depending on the card and drivers they have installed. I also recommend including an option for software processing for both APIs; that way any driver-related problems are addressed.

OpenAL and DirectSound have two very distinct design methodologies and are much like their graphical counterparts. If you have worked with OpenGL, OpenAL will come very naturally to you. If you've worked primarily with DirectX, DirectSound is going to be very straightforward.

Overview of a Sound System

There are four concepts to understand when dealing with a high-level overview of a sound system—the primary buffer, the listener, the sound, and any effects applied to the sound or the listener.

The Primary Buffer

The primary buffer is the final resting place for the PCM samples you send to it. Under most sound systems you won't be filling the primary buffer directly, but you will be dealing with it from the perspective of the listener. The only thing that you are concerned about with the primary buffer is how much it advances from frame to frame.

The Listener

The listener is a special object that exists in 3D space. It listens to the incoming sounds and applies any special transformations and effects such as panning and falloff, and advanced filters like Doppler Shifting and Head Relative Transfer Delay.

You should always assume that under any given API you are going to have only one listener. Normally this is not a problem, but for those of us who write games that have multiple viewports or monitors, it represents a slight challenge. The solution to this problem is actually very easy. Simply transform all sounds to the listener and record things such as velocity in the sound properties so that effects, such as Doppler shifting, can still be correctly calculated. Things get a little more complex when listeners have effects applied to them and those effects are different from listener to listener, but I'll explore effects in a little while.

The Sound Sources

The sound sources themselves are typically mono channel signals coming from within the world. Sound sources typically have properties such as position, falloff, and velocity. Those properties are then used by the listener and the effects to process the sound.

Under any sound system, you should differentiate between sound sources and the actual sound data. Sound sources contain a reference to the sound data as well as the position and orientation of the particular sound and the current play position within the actual sound data. The actual sound data is merely the container for the PCM data as well as any other audio designer related properties, such as falloff reference, maximum number of instances, and any general effects to be applied to all instances of the sound itself.

The Sound Effects

Sound sources also contain effects. Some of those effects are inherited from the sound data and other effects are applied from its position within the world. Either way, it is a good idea to stack up the effects so that you can easily collapse them upon request.

Putting these concepts together, you'll see that the primary buffer requests data from the listener, the listener then goes out and determines what sounds to play and requests the samples from the sound sources. Upon getting that request, the sound sources collapse the effect stack and fill the listener with the correct data. The listener then runs a digital signal peak limiter on the sound effects and collapses its own effects stack; then it presents the contents to the final buffer.

One thing to note in this entire example of a sound system is that it uses a model-view-controller architecture. The data is encapsulated in the sound data (the model) and is requested by the sound source (the controller), which then applies the individual sound effects (more controllers), which in turn is requested by the listener and then finally outputted to the primary buffer (the view).

Sound Buffers

On almost all machines you are limited to the amount of sounds the hardware can play. Even when processed in software mode, you should still clamp the number of available sound buffers to something within the range of your performance targets. As of writing this gem, the maximum available hardware accelerated sounds on the average top-of-the-line consumer sound card is 128 sounds. Keep this in mind for later.

This does not take into account that Vista will force you to use software processing under DirectSound at the time of writing this gem. The only alternative is OpenAL if you want to utilize the hardware processing under Windows Vista.

In most cases, you will want to allocate enough sound samples in your sound buffers so that continuous playback is possible, even in the most dramatic frame rate drops. I typically create my buffers with enough room for one second's worth of sound data at 44100kHz.

One thing I've picked up is that it can actually take more time and more resources to stop and start sound buffers than to let them play beyond the duration of their sound (making sure to clear the sound buffer so that they are not heard!). But do this within reason. For instance, using the previous example, where you have 128 sound buffers, you should start playing eight of them. As soon as all eight sounds are occupied by sound data, you start playing eight more. Once it drops below a certain threshold and the sound buffers haven't been accessed in a while, you go ahead and stop them. This kind of balancing is not necessary, but I found it to help in situations when I had a lot of short sounds playing one right after the other.

Once you get a request to play a sound, populate as much of the sound buffer as you can at the current write position, remembering that you're likely to have already started playing this buffer. You can get the playback advancement by recording where your previous playback cursor was to where it is now from frame to frame. One thing to note here is that drivers will sometimes give you the wrong playback position. The position is sometimes off by only a couple of samples, but other times it can be significantly off. In order to compensate for that, take half the size of the buffer and fill that on the first request. Thus, the one second buffer actually only contains half a second of data.

So let's say you've got a 44100 sample size buffer and the write position is at 44000 and your playback has advanced 150 samples in the last frame. Using this knowledge, you can request 22050 samples (1/2 buffer size) from the sound source on the first pass. Now that you've got those samples from the sound source, you need to write 100 samples to fill the current write position to the end of the buffer and then the remaining 21950 samples go to the start of the buffer at offset 0. This is simply known as a *circular buffer*.

On the next update, all you have to do is continue to fill the buffer at the last written position with the amount of samples that playback has progressed. In the last example, you'd then be writing 150 samples to buffer position 21950.

As a safety precaution, you also want to clear out the previously played samples. When you do this, you'll want to stay three to four frames behind the playback cursor's current position, remembering that the playback cursor could be off as well. Another safety precaution is to set a callback at the last written position, clearing any previous callbacks. When the play cursor gets to that position, it triggers the callback, which then should fade the entire buffer into silence. Because sound is generally processed on a separate thread, this should work in all cases. This way, you'll never get those repeating sounds looping in the event that the main update thread locks up.

Rank Buffers

Using the example of the sound card from before, I'm going to say that you will have 128 sounds in total that you can play at any given time. The problem is that within your 3D world you have hundreds, perhaps even thousands, of sounds coming from all different directions. This is where you want to implement a special kind of buffer known as a *rank buffer*.

A rank buffer is a very simple concept. You algorithmically generate a rank and then you request a buffer. If all buffers are full and the rank exceeds another already playing sound buffer then the lowest ranking sound is booted out and the new sound is played.

The rank can be calculated any number of ways. The most general way to calculate the rank is to determine the attenuation (distance, falloff, and volume), and then multiply that by a value given to you by the audio designer. This works in most cases, but not all. It's best to take into account all properties of the sound such as distance, falloff, effects, and other items associated with the sound so you can get a clear idea of the sound rank. It's not acceptable to have a high priority sound just repeating its subtle echo effect, as another lower priority, but potentially more noticeable, sound is getting skipped.

Also worth noting is that audio designers like to specify how many instances of a particular sound or sound category can be played. For instance, if you're in a room with tons of machine gun fire going off, it only makes sense to play 10 or so of these types of sounds. Be sure to take this into consideration when building your rank buffer algorithm. One thing I did was to allow the sound data to figure out its rank given its particular context by abstracting a simple function that took in the parameters passed to the sound, like its position relative to the listener and the general world data.

There are some catches to the rank buffer solution that you must address specific to audio processing. The primary catch is that you can't just stop a sound and then follow that up with another sound. Remember earlier when I stated that sound is perceived as the difference in samples. If you stop playing one sound abruptly, you'll hear a tick or a pop. Instead, you have to transition one sound to the next, fading out the previous sound.

Things get even more complex when the previous sound has effects applied to it. Because of the way audio drivers handle the effects applied to the sound buffer, you should not just linearly transition the effect, but instead you have to wait until the previous sound has finished fading and then you can switch the effects properties over. Thus, once your gain (volume) has reached zero for the previous sound source, you can apply the new effects and start copying over the new sound. One thing to note is that you do not want to commit the switch in effects until the playback cursor, not the write cursor, reaches the desired switch point.

Remember previously when you copied half a second of sound samples into the buffer to accommodate for drops in frame rate? You want to be able to transition immediately. Keep in mind that once you send the data to the sound buffer, it's up to the driver's implementation if it wants to keep that data around, so I wouldn't count on it still being there. To get around this, you should keep copies of all the samples you copy over to the sound buffer so that you can go back in time and fade out at the playback buffer's current write position.

The fade sample amount varies, but I generally keep it at around five milliseconds, or roughly 220 samples at 44100kHz playback. You can set this up to be a property of the sound data so the audio designer can adjust this value.

Effects and Filters

Effect objects should be created through an abstract factory method generated by your individual sound system API, so that hardware processing is possible, and then attached to the sound source or listener so that they can be collapsed when requested.

Effects are different from filters. An effect can contain multiple filters or simply generate sound data or perhaps contain a wrapper for a hardware accelerated feature. In any case, think of the effect as the middleman between the sound source and, if the effect calls for it, the filter. When designing filters, keep in mind that filters should be as generic as possible and that any implementation details should be gathered and stored in the effect object itself, thus allowing you to abstract new effects quickly. To put it simply, effects are implementation specific and filters are not.

There are two types of filters to be concerned with, as follows:

- Infinite impulse response (IIR) filters, which recursively work on the sound samples.
- Finite impulse response (FIR) filters, which just deal with transforming the sound samples in some manner without regard to prior output.

You'll have to differentiate the two filters when designing the effect.

Within the filters, there is a concept known as wet/dry mix. Wet samples are samples that have been previously transformed and dry samples are the raw incoming samples without any transformation. You should have a distinguishing factor of wet/dry mix and allow for your effects to change that ratio.

To complicate matters even more, there are multiple ways of transforming the samples. One of the most common methods is through the use of Fast Fourier Transform (FFT). This type of calculation, although extremely useful and applicable, is very time- and processor-consuming and much research has been done to improve the speed of this operation. Be sure to run this type of operation only when absolutely needed, caching any data that you can from it. This means that you should be able to transform the sound in the effect object to the frequency domain, run all of the filters in the transformed frequency domain (ensuring that the filters can use the frequency domain data), and then transform back to sample space in the effect itself when all filters have been processed, if the effect calls for it.

FIR filters are the easiest to deal with because all you have to do is feed it the data (dry mix) and it spits out the result. IIR filters are a little more complex because they rely on the previously generated result (wet mix). The easiest way to deal with this is to have a separate buffer set up within the effect that records the output from the filter (the wet mix buffer). The size of that buffer is specified when the effect is created, thus setting the delay line. In some effects, this delay line can be set up using the inputs for the effect, such as feedback delay, which can then be translated to buffer size. Otherwise, you can optionally explicitly set the buffer size, thus clamping your window.

IIR and FIR filters can also be arranged in a directed graph, allowing the filter to reference other filters in a cyclical manner, running until it has reached the extents as specified by delay line. This is the style of filter design outlined in *Game Programming Gems 5* in the article entitled "Fast Environmental Reverb Based on Feedback Delay Networks" [Schüler05]. Using these types of filters is very handy, because you can design new effects quickly as well as extend those effects to simulate audible characteristics of the world around you.

I have yet to talk about signal timing—all those cases where you have looping sounds combined with effects that elongate a sound beyond the original sound length, such as with an echo. I've outlined a system where you request samples and those samples are filled via collapsing a stack of effects resulting in the final data, thus a sound is finished when no samples are returned via the listener. However, there is a caveat to this. Simply waiting for the request to return no samples on a looping sound source with an IIR filter will result in a sound that never loops. Therefore, you do have to push a separate flag that informs the sound source that it is looping and that when an effect reaches the end of reading the sound data, it should loop back to the beginning.

Compression and Streaming

There are many audio compression formats available, each one focusing on a particular need. Some formats, such as ADPCM, are focused on performance and quick decoding, whereas others, such as MP3 and OGG, are focused heavily on compression ratio, giving you small file size while maintaining quality. Here's a quick comparison between those three formats.

- ADPCM is the simplest of the three formats. It uses a simple predictive algorithm to generate deltas on blocks of audio. Those deltas are stored in four-bit values, thus making the decompression algorithm as simple as two table lookups and decoding a four-bit delta, coupled with two multiplies and an add makes this the least CPU intensive algorithm with the highest payoff in compression. However, the compression ratio is a measly 4:1 compared to the other formats and the signal restoration at low sampling is not nearly as good as the other formats.
- MP3 is a common format, widely known and used across multiple platforms. MP3 uses frames, similar to chunks used in ADPCM. These frames contain information on the acoustical makeup of the sound signal in transformed frequency domain, which then is broken down into a quantized lookup table [MP307a] [MP307b]. MP3 allows for many encoding options such as variable bit rate and ID3 tags.
- OGG Vorbis uses the modified discrete cosine transform to convert from signal space to frequency domain, similar to MP3, and then clamps the floor value.

Afterward it quantizes the entropy coding and then stores the delta into a lookup table [OGG07]. This kind of encoding allows for lossy compression at variable bit rates and is specially tuned for fast decompression, but still not as efficient as ADPCM.

You might be wondering why I'm going into detail about these three compression techniques. There are many libraries out there that will handle the conversions for you ([MP307a], [MP307b], [OGG07]), and aside from the performance related data, there's really no need to go into detail about each format. But then again, there's something there that you may have picked up. OGG and MP3 store their information in the frequency domain, which means that the really expensive FFT that I mentioned earlier is already present.

What this means is that using the libraries from each respective format, you can extract the frequency data and use that information to run your frequency domain effects, and then translate into the signal space for final presentation!

Another reason for going into detail about each respective format is that you'll notice each compression scheme has "frames" or "blocks" that they work with. Using this information, you can create a separate rank buffer mechanism for caching decoded PCM samples or decoded frequency data. When you're streaming from disk, it means that you can cache certain frames or blocks in an already decoded fashion as opposed to having to store the entire decoded file. For music, this is extremely important. You want to read ahead as much as you can and cache the decoded data, but you don't want to dedicate 300MB or more of memory just to your sound track. By decoding on a frame-by-frame basis, you can limit your memory usage to any arbitrary number and by utilizing the rank buffer (without the need for fading samples), you have a mechanism for streaming files from disk efficiently.

Conclusion

Building an entire audio system from scratch seems like a daunting task at first look, but by utilizing the methods you know as a programmer and using the concepts outlined here, you should be able to get up and running fairly quick. There are many other topics to learn about and a ton of resources to get you started—a few of which I've noted in the references section. I would also go so far as to suggest reading up on the many dedicated forums and newsgroups. They contain some of the best information available.

Audio programming is both rewarding and challenging. After you develop your own sound system, tailored to your game's needs and performance requirements, expanding upon that knowledge and implementation to facilitate design decisions and extended effects makes a difference in the overall playability of the final video game. That difference is then perceived by the players, and they leave the game with a better sense of immersion, so in my opinion, it is one of the most important areas of video game programming.

References

[dsnd07] Microsoft "DirectSound," available online at http://msdn2.microsoft.com/en-us/library/bb219818.aspx, August 1, 2007.

[MP307a] Underbit Technologies. "MAD: MPEG Audio Decoder," available online at http://www.underbit.com/products/mad/, August, 2007.

[MP307b] Mike Cheng. "The LAME Project," available online at http://lame.sourceforge.net/index.php, August, 2007.

[OGG07] Xiph.Org "Vorbis audio compression," available online at http://xiph.org/vorbis/, August, 2007.

[openal07] Creative. "OpenAL: A Free (LGPL-ed) and Open Source, Cross-Platform Audio Library Used for 3D and 2D Sound," available online at http://www.openal.org, August 1st, 2007.

[Schüler05] Schüler, Christian. "Fast Environmental Reverb Based on Feedback Delay Networks," *Game Programming Gems 5,* Charles River Media, 2005.

4.5

Context-Driven, Layered Mixing

Robert Sparks

sparks.robert@gmail.com

The technical quality of sound in our industry is beginning to approach that of the film industry. Next-generation consoles are here. Games support Dolby Digital and DTS; they use high sampling rates; they have virtually unlimited numbers of voices; and they use perceptually lossless compression algorithms. That said, the film industry still has great advantages over us when it comes to overall control of the final product.

Consider the process of sound mixing. A film can be mixed with total control of every sound effect. Each scene can be mixed with purpose and deliver a specific emotional experience. A game is mixed with much less control. For the most part, we can't change much from scene to scene. We rely on positional and environmental simulation to do the rest.

This gem presents a mixing system that brings the overall sound of a game under greater human control. A similar system was used with great success in developing *Scarface: The World Is Yours* and supported a three-week final mixing session of the game at Skywalker Sound.

Overview

This mixing system takes for granted the idea that game parameters can be tuned in real-time. It concerns itself with organizing that tuning experience into an effective workflow—a workflow based on the mixing of films.

The system presents sound parameters (for example, volume, pitch, and filter settings) as if they were the rows of faders and knobs on a mixing board. Each of the rows controls whole groups of related sounds (for example, music, dialogue, or footsteps).

The system also divides the action of the game into logical scenes. Unlike the scenes of a film, which can be defined chronologically, the scenes of a game must be defined by actions of the player.

Associating a set of mixing parameters with each logical scene allows precise control of the overall sound (see Figure 4.5.1). It also allows each scene to be mixed independently in real-time in a series of mixing sessions.

The scene-by-scene approach of this system makes it context-driven. Later, you'll see that scenes can overlap and modify each other, making it also a layered mixing system.

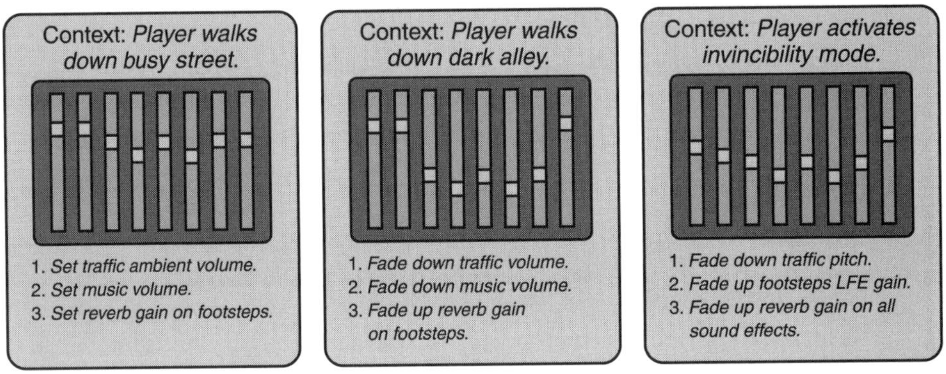

FIGURE 4.5.1 An example of context-driven mixing in which the player enters a dark alley and activates "invincibility mode."

Implementation

ON THE CD

What follows is a high-level description of the mixing system logic and its main classes. A more detailed C++ implementation is available on the CD-ROM.

Mixing System

The *mixing system* provides a central mixing interface to other systems in the game. It manages component lifetimes and performs calculations.

Mixing Categories

The mixing system groups related sounds into *mixing categories*. The system works only in terms of these categories rather than in terms of individual sounds.

Possible mixing categories include music, ambience, explosion, glass, footsteps, or birds. When a sound plays in the game, it is assigned a mixing category.

The Central Mix

The mixing system centralizes the mixing (or tuning) parameters for all sounds into a single logical object, the *central mix*. Parameters may include volume, pitch, LFE gain, auxiliary effect gain, or parameters related to positional simulation. The central mix provides a set of parameters for each mixing category.

Conceptually, the central mix is like a mixing board through which all sounds in the game are routed. As sounds play in the game, they do so according to the parameters assigned to their mixing category in the central mix (see Figure 4.5.2).

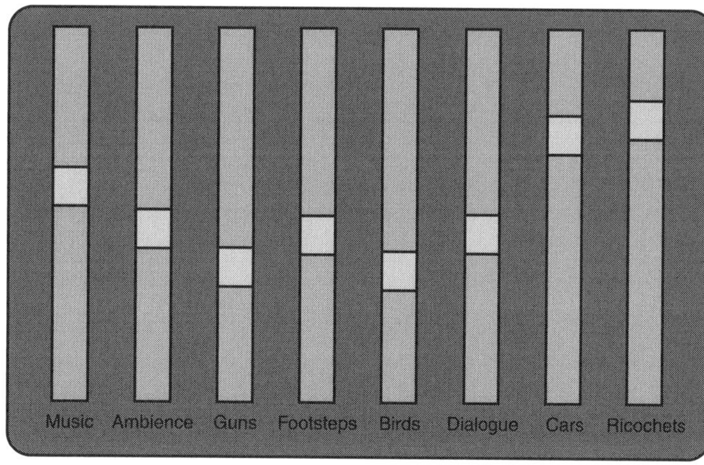

FIGURE 4.5.2 The central mix acts as a mixing board for the game, controlling the playback of groups of sounds.

Mixing Snapshots

The sound designer works with the central mix in terms of sets of parameter values known as *mixing snapshots*. The state of the central mix is calculated using these snapshots (see Figure 4.5.3). Mixing snapshots are like mixing board presets or fader automation controls for the central mix.

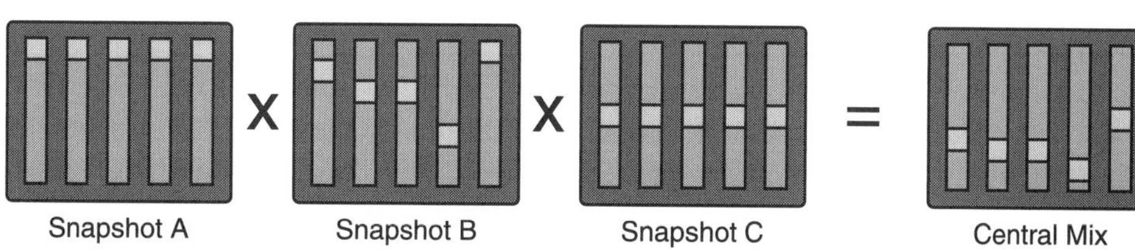

FIGURE 4.5.3 The mixing system calculates the central mix using mixing snapshots provided by the sound designer.

The sound designer defines a mixing snapshot for each logical scene of the game. When the scene begins, a *mixing event* triggers, adding the associated snapshot to the central mix calculations. When the scene ends, another mixing event triggers, removing the snapshot. The snapshots provide fade-in durations and fade-out durations that smooth transitions as the snapshots are added and removed from the calculations.

Mixing snapshots give the designer complete control over each scene. The granularity of this control depends on the number of scenes and the number of mixing categories.

Scenes can be very general and appear throughout the game or they can be very specific. Scenes may overlap and be defined as modifications of other scenes. Table 4.5.1 defines some example mixing snapshots and scenes.

Table 4.5.1 Example Mixing Snapshots

Snapshot Name	Scene Description	Sound Highlights
`on_foot_night`	Active when the player is on foot at night.	Footsteps and foley. Nighttime ambient sounds. Nighttime reverb settings and roll-off settings.
`on_foot_day`	Active when the player is on foot in the daytime.	Daytime ambient sounds Footsteps and foley. Daytime reverb settings and roll-off settings.
`in_car`	Active when the player is driving a vehicle.	Player's vehicle sounds. Reduced ambient sounds. In car reverb settings. Traffic levels increased.
`interior`	Active when the player enters a building. This snapshot may install at the same time as `on_foot_day` or `on_foot_night`.	Reduced outdoor sounds.
`dialogue_duck`	Active when the player speaks. This may install at the same time as almost any other snapshot.	Emphasis on dialogue clarity. Reduction of music and other interfering sounds.
`invincible`	Active when the player enters a special invincibility mode. This may install with almost any other snapshot.	Pitch lowering of specific sound effects. Increased volume of the sub-woofer.
`nis_2`	Active during the cinematic, non-interactive sequence (NIS) named `nis_2`.	All in-game sound effects removed from the mix except those required by the NIS.
`pre_mix`	Active at all times.	Allows for global adjustments in all sounds.

Mixing Layers

Mixing layers organize the mixing snapshots that are active. The mixing snapshots are assigned to layers by the sound designer. Three mixing layers exist, each exhibiting a specific behavior:

- The *pre-mix layer* contains one snapshot that is always present and never changes. This layer allows sound properties to be changed globally in all contexts.
- The *base layer* always contains one snapshot and never more than one. As new base layer snapshots become active, they replace previous base layer snapshots.
- The *modifying layer* contains any number of snapshots at a time, allowing scenes to overlap. These snapshots act as modifiers to other snapshots, typically reducing specific volumes and applying special filters or pitch effects. For example, a modifying snapshot will duck music during dialogue or apply special filters during key game play moments.

Figure 4.5.4 illustrates the three mixing layers.

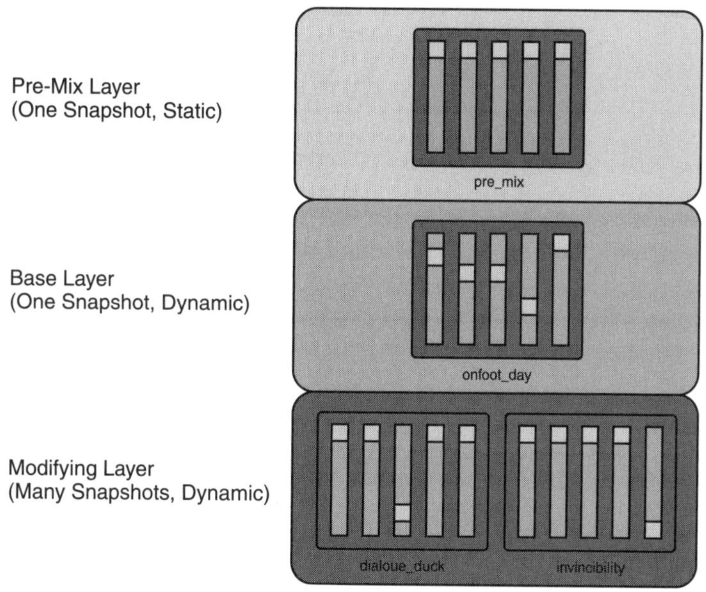

FIGURE 4.5.4 Three mixing layers organize the active mixing snapshots.

Extending the Concept with Live Tuning

A remote tuning application is essential for achieving a truly efficient mixing workflow. Only live tuning enables the sound designer to fix problems as they are heard and to precisely adjust volume levels and other settings.

The tuning application can present parameters with simple arrays of numbers or with a graphical representation of a mixing board. It is useful for the application to display both the active mixing snapshots and the state of the central mix. This allows mixing snapshots for each scene to be selected and tuned individually.

The resulting workflow is very sophisticated. Typically, the process involves teleporting to the location or mission that requires mixing, selecting the appropriate mixing snapshot in the remote tuning application, and then mixing the scene while playing through it.

For *Scarface: The World Is Yours,* our team implemented a MIDI interface between our tuning application and a physical mixing board. This interface made it easy for people from outside the video game industry to work on our project (see Figure 4.5.5).

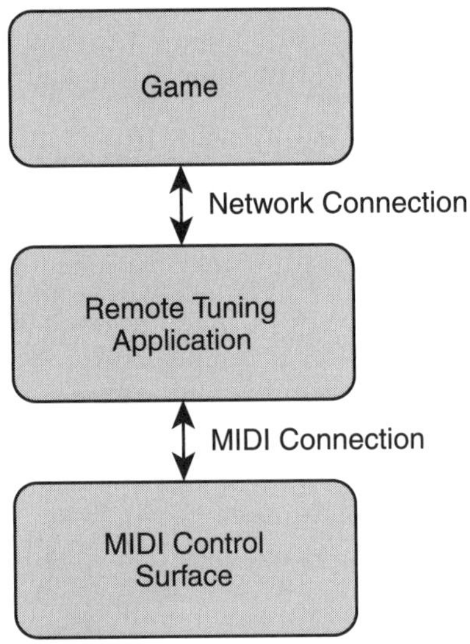

FIGURE 4.5.5 Live mixing through a MIDI control surface.

Performance

CPU requirements of the mixing system are low. Calculating the central mix consumes most of its energy, which involves combining the parameters of the active mixing snapshots. Typically there may be four active mixing snapshots and 20 sound categories with four parameters each. The parameters are often combined using addition or multiplication.

Memory requirements grow with the number of mixing snapshots and the number of sound categories. Large games may require several hundred mixing snapshots and a few dozen sound categories. An un-optimized mixing snapshot may require 512 bytes. As a result, 200 snapshots will consume 100KB of memory. Optimization reduces the memory footprint of the system considerably.

The most effective optimization reduces the number of mixing snapshots held in memory at a time by loading snapshots only when needed (for example, bundling snapshots with art for a mission, a location, a cinematic sequence, or a character). This requires pipeline work and coordination with other content loading systems.

Another optimization stores mixing snapshot parameters as shorts instead of floats, which halves the size of a mixing snapshot.

Combining these optimizations, a 512 byte mixing snapshot becomes 256 bytes; 200 snapshots in memory become 10 in memory. Therefore, a 100KB footprint reduces to 2.5KB.

Sample Program

ON THE CD

The CD-ROM includes a sample program for this article. The program presents a very simple game and an equally simple mixing environment. Click the buttons to trigger sound effects and mixing events. Use the mixing board and related controls to select and tune mixing snapshots and experience context-driven, layered mixing.

Conclusion

This gem discussed a powerful approach to sound mixing that has proven itself practical and effective in the field.

Workflow is paramount when it comes to delivering quality sound. Well-defined, intuitive processes enable creative and polished work. Established, effective processes are available to be borrowed from the film industry. Technical decisions should focus on establishing these processes in the gaming industry.

SECTION

5

GRAPHICS

Introduction

Timothy E. Roden, Angelo State University

troden@angelo.edu

In the early days of 3D computer games, developers were generally concerned with keeping polygon counts low and reducing scene complexity. Graphics engines had fixed function pipelines that allowed very narrow creative freedom in terms of rendering and animation. It is amazing how things have changed. The graphics section of this edition of *Game Programming Gems* presents a wide range of articles covering topics as diverse as content creation, animation, and rendering.

Jeremy Hayes of Intel expands on the work Jason Shankel did to show advanced methods of procedural terrain generation using a method called particle deposition. New techniques are described for volcano placement, mountain ranges, dunes, and overhanging terrain. These new methods add more control, which enable a level designer to better define the placement of important terrain features. Because crafting interesting and useful terrain is not only a function of geometry, another gem explores the mapping of textures onto terrain. Antonio Seoane, Javier Taibo, Luis Hernández, and Alberto Jaspe present a method for mapping very large textures onto outdoor terrain and Ben Garney provides an implementation of that idea with pointers for enabling the technique on SM 1.0-level graphics cards.

The graphics section features several excellent gems that cover rendering. Joris Mans and Dmitry Andreev of 10Tacle Studios describe an advanced decal system that properly blends bump and diffuse maps under a decal, thereby removing the "on top of" look that decals can sometimes exhibit. A system for real-time rendering of diffuse lighting for rough materials is presented in the gem by Tony Barrera, Anders Hast, and Ewert Bengtsson. Chris Lomont presents a comprehensive overview of high-performance subdivision surfaces. Joshua Doss demonstrates the use of graftal imposters in rendering cartoon-style plants and fur effects.

Animation receives a good treatment in this edition of the Gems series. Bill Budge of Sony Entertainment of America explains techniques for dealing with cumulative errors in skeletal animation sequences. A technique for animating relief impostors is described by Vitor Fernando Pamplona, Manuel M. Oliveria, and Luciana Porcher Nedel. Finally, I have contributed a gem on procedural generation of lipsync data for human models using a freely available phonetic dictionary.

5.1

Advanced Particle Deposition

Jeremy Hayes, Intel Corporation

armyofzin@gmail.com

Particle deposition is a procedural terrain generation technique that has so far been limited to creating topography for volcanic mountain ranges. However, the beauty of particle deposition lies within its versatility. This gem demonstrates several advancements to particle deposition that allow the creation of new types of terrain topography as well as improved volcanic mountain ranges. These advances to particle deposition also improve artistic control by allowing a level designer to preview and refine the position and size of terrain features.

Why Particles?

The surface layer of the earth is called the continental crust. The continental crust floats on another layer of the earth, called the mantle, because it is less dense than the mantle. Over very long periods of time, the continental crust behaves like a ductile solid (like hot wax) [Grotzinger07]. The earth's topography is created by forces above and below the surface. The continental crust is fractured, rippled, and twisted by plate tectonics, which are powered by geothermal forces inside the earth. Above the surface, the earth's climate also molds the topography. Erosion by wind, water, and ice can cause dramatic changes over time.

Particles can be used to naturally simulate the deformation of terrain by plate tectonics and erosion. Particles can be used to simulate the flow of material and they can be joined to form solids. In other words, particles provide a simple and versatile mechanism to generate the topography of virtual terrain.

Particle Deposition

Shankel proposed the original particle deposition algorithm as a way to generate terrain that looks similar to volcanic mountain ranges [Shankel00]. Particle deposition traverses a height field with a random walker. The random walker drops at least one particle at each location it visits. The particle must check the height of the adjacent positions after it lands on the height field. If a lower adjacent position is found, the particle moves to that position. The particle repeats this process until it can no longer move to an adjacent position of lower elevation. Figure 5.1.1 demonstrates a single particle descending a one-dimensional height field. The algorithm can be stopped when a predetermined number of particles have been dropped or when the user is content with the results. Figure 5.1.2 shows an example of terrain created with particle deposition.

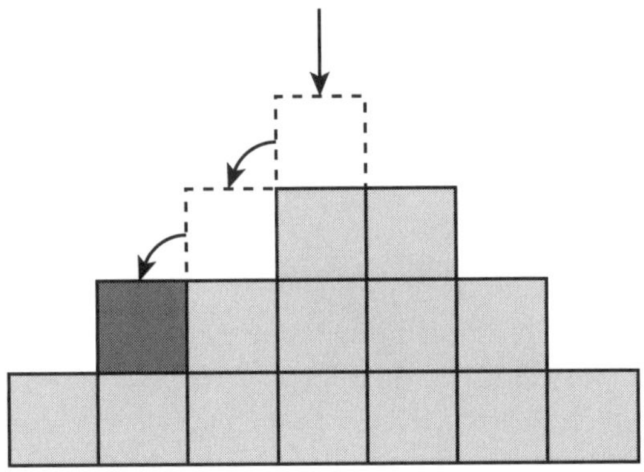

FIGURE 5.1.1 Depositing a single particle.

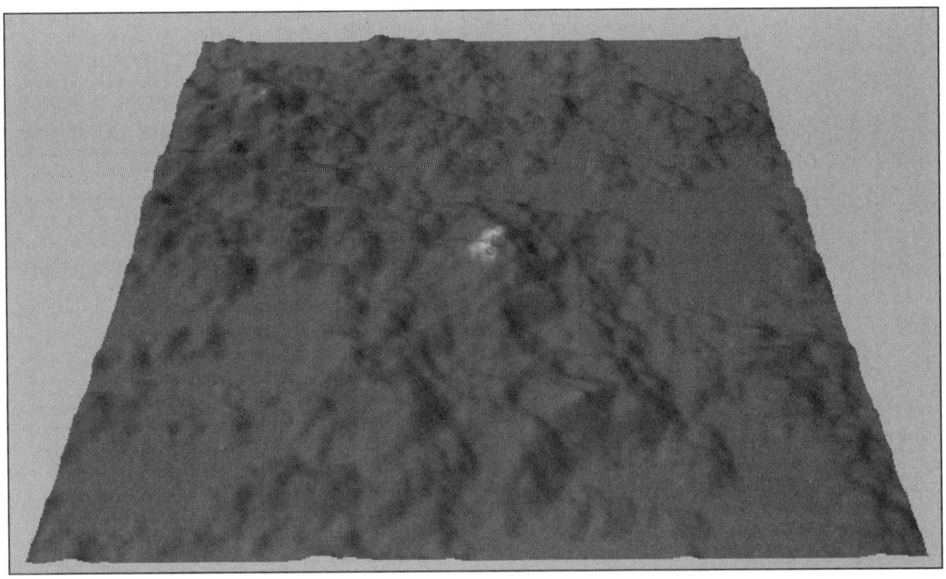

FIGURE 5.1.2 A screenshot of terrain generated with the original particle deposition algorithm.

Improving Particle Deposition

Although particle deposition does create interesting topography for volcanic mountain ranges, it is easy to see it has some limitations. Notice that the slope of the terrain formed by the particles is almost always 45°, which is a consequence of the heuristic used to settle the particles on the terrain. Particles are not allowed to stack if there is a lower adjacent position, so the slope will never be greater than 45°. Sometimes particles will briefly form slopes less than 45°. This usually occurs when particles are accumulating in a valley or near an existing peak. Unfortunately, these gentler slopes will never span more than a few positions. Developers would like to be able to create more interesting terrain slopes composed of various angles that span small and large distances, as shown in Figure 5.1.3.

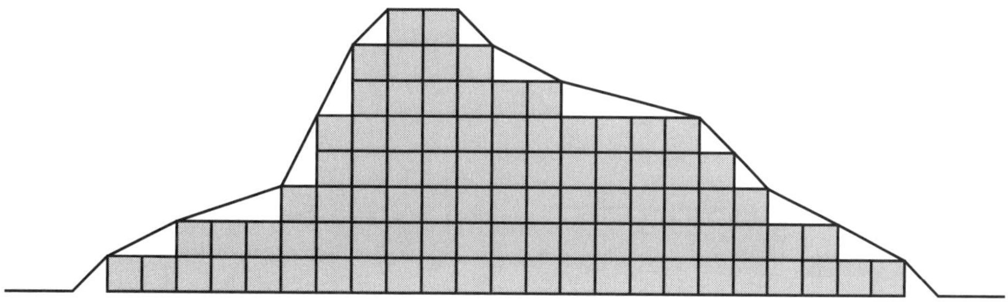

FIGURE 5.1.3 An example of ideal terrain composed of various angles.

Another limitation of particle deposition is there is no control over the placement of major terrain features such as the volcano's peak. It is also hard to control how many peaks to create. The outcome of the terrain is almost entirely random. This is a big disadvantage if a level designer wants to create a certain number of volcanoes at specific locations. It would be nice to give a level designer more control over the major terrain features (for example, size, general shape, and placement). Perhaps the biggest limitation to particle deposition is that it only creates topography that is suitable for a volcanic mountain range. What if you want to create other types of terrain? Fortunately, all of these limitations can be overcome with simple modifications to particle deposition.

Notice that particle deposition can be broken into two main steps. The first step defines where to initially drop the particles. The second step defines where the particles settle after they have been dropped. Let's refer to the first step as particle placement, and the second step as particle dynamics. In order to overcome the limitations of particle deposition, you need to improve both particle placement and particle dynamics. Let's start by examining particle dynamics.

Improving Particle Dynamics

Particle dynamics are required to simulate the effects of erosion. After a particle is dropped on the height field, it begins randomly searching the adjacent positions to determine if the particle can move to a lower elevation. The slope of the terrain is implicitly defined by how far away the particle is allowed to search. The monotony of the terrain's slope can be broken up by varying the search radius and elevation threshold of the particles placed on the slope. If the search radius is large, the slope will be shallow, as shown in Figure 5.1.4.a. Conversely, if the search radius is small, the slope will be steep. Figure 5.1.4.b shows how particles can accumulate to form a very steep slope. To make this possible, the particle dynamics need to be changed so that particles will not move to an adjacent position until the difference in elevation reaches a certain threshold.

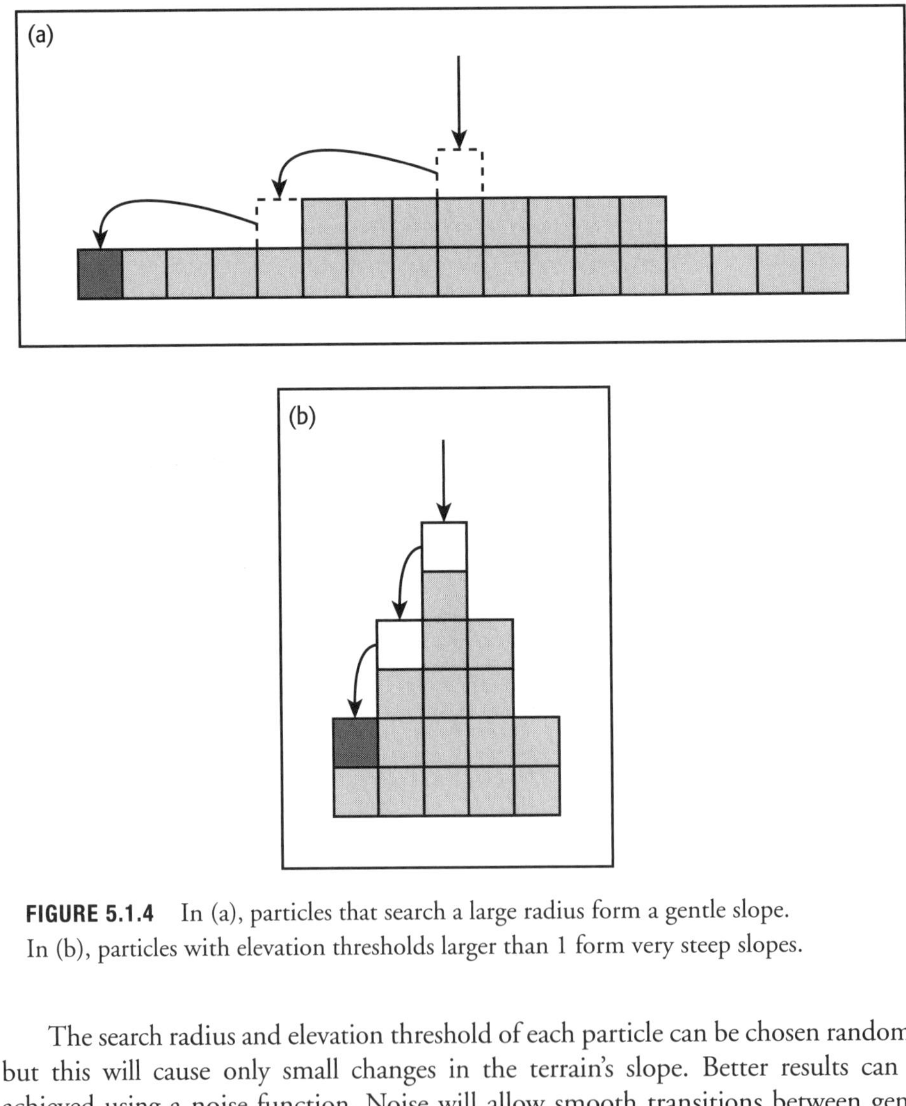

FIGURE 5.1.4 In (a), particles that search a large radius form a gentle slope. In (b), particles with elevation thresholds larger than 1 form very steep slopes.

The search radius and elevation threshold of each particle can be chosen randomly, but this will cause only small changes in the terrain's slope. Better results can be achieved using a noise function. Noise will allow smooth transitions between gentle and steep slopes. There are several widely known noise functions but for simplicity the results in this gem were obtained using value noise. Refer to [Ebert03] for a thorough discussion of noise functions. Figure 5.1.5 demonstrates the difference between using a constant search radius and a search radius defined by a noise function. In Figure 5.1.5, all of the particles were dropped at the same location to emphasize the change in slope characteristics. In a similar manner, the elevation threshold can be varied to create terrain with even more extreme slopes. The following pseudocode represents the particle dynamics used in this article:

```
for each dropped particle:
  determine the search radius using a 2D (or 3D) noise function
  while there is a lower position (within the search radius):
     move to the closest position that is lower
     increment the height field at the final position
```

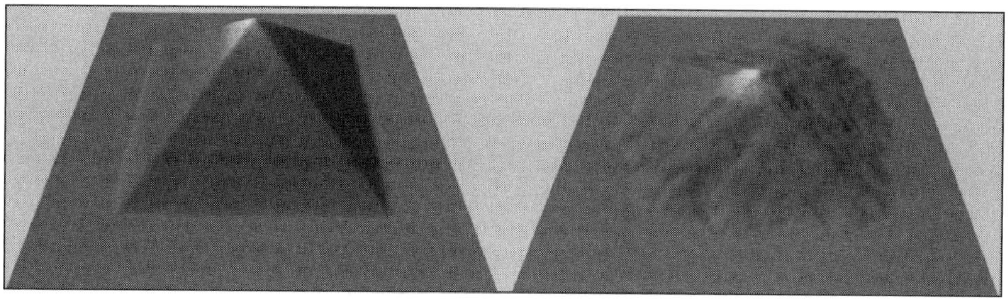

FIGURE 5.1.5 The terrain on the left was created using a constant search radius equal to 1, and terrain on the right was created using value noise to vary the search radius between 1 and 4.

Improving Particle Placement

The particle placement heuristic defines where particles are initially dropped on the height field. This is a very important step in particle deposition. If particle placement is random, the terrain features are going appear random. Different particle placement heuristics will generate different types of terrain. The next three sections investigate different particle placement heuristics—each one designed to create a specific type of terrain.

Volcanoes

Before you consider a suitable particle placement heuristic for volcanoes, it helps to know how real volcanoes are formed. A volcano is formed by layers of ash and lava that are ejected from its central vent. The layers of ash and lava accumulate, over many years, to create a cone-like shape. The exact shape of the cone is determined by the type of magma ejected from the volcano. Different magma types result in different types of eruptions and landforms. Some volcanoes also have side vents and radiating fissures, which create more asymmetric shapes. Volcanoes can have gentle slopes or steep slopes, and they can have symmetric shapes or asymmetric shapes. Like all landforms, the shape of a volcano is also defined by erosion of the surface.

One possible particle placement heuristic for volcanoes would be to dump a lot of particles at a single location until the stopping criteria are met. Although this might be adequate, the resulting shape would be fairly symmetric and somewhat boring. A more interesting particle placement heuristic, as demonstrated in Figure 5.1.6, is to loosely simulate the lava streams that wander radially from the central vent of the volcano. The pseudocode for this particle placement heuristic follows:

```
choose a position for the central vent
choose the number of streams
choose a random length and direction for each stream
while the stopping criteria has not been met:
  for each stream:
     start at the central vent
     while the end of the stream has not been reached:
       drop a particle and compute particle dynamics
       move in the direction of the stream (+/- small random angle)
```

Using this heuristic, the shape of the volcano is defined by the number of streams, the length of each stream (which doesn't have to be the same for every stream), and the total amount of particles dropped. The stopping criteria can be when a certain number of particles have been dropped or when the peak of the volcano has reached a certain elevation. If you implement particle deposition in a way that allows users to watch the terrain being generated in real-time, the users can stop the algorithm when they are content with the results.

If a caldera at the peak of the volcano is desired, you can use the same inversion algorithm used in [Shankel00] to invert the peak of the volcano. Begin by arbitrarily choosing the elevation of the caldera plane, and invert the elevation at the central vent's position across the caldera plane. Then check the neighboring positions, invert them if they lie above the caldera plane, and check their neighbors. Repeat this process until there are no more neighbors to invert.

Notice the shape of the volcano can now be more easily defined by a level designer. A level designer can choose the location of the volcano by deciding where to place the central vent. In addition, the paths of the lava streams can be precomputed, as shown in Figure 5.1.7, and overlaid on the height field. This would allow a level designer to preview the size and general shape without dropping a single particle.

Mountains

Particle deposition can also create realistic mountains by using a clever particle placement heuristic. The ridges between mountain peaks form a very distinct tree-like structure. For obvious reasons, this will be referred to as the mountain's ridge structure. This is the result of many years of erosion, and the tree-like structure of the surrounding river network is correlated to the mountain's ridge structure. The ridge structure is important because it provides ideal locations where particles should be dropped, hence the particle placement heuristic to generate mountains.

FIGURE 5.1.6 A volcano created using advanced particle deposition. See the color insert section for color versions of the photos from this gem.

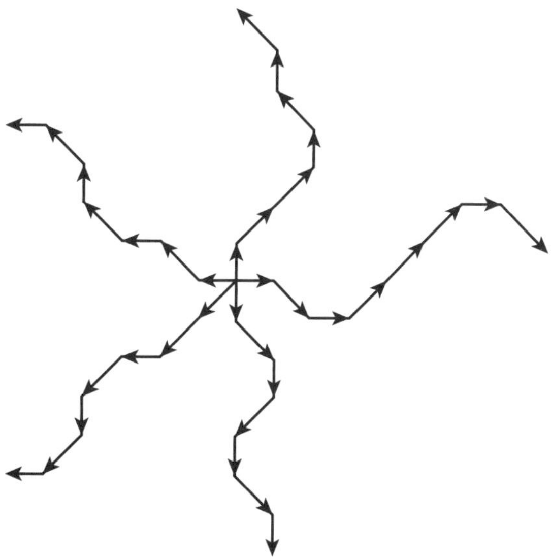

FIGURE 5.1.7 An example of the paths taken by simulated lava streams.

Now you need a way to procedurally create a realistic ridge structure. Fortunately, a suitable algorithm already exists. Diffusion limited aggregation (DLA) is a physical process that forms dendrite-like structures known as Brownian trees. Figure 5.1.8 shows a Brownian tree that was created using DLA on a two-dimensional lattice.

Qualitatively this looks similar to the ridge structure of mountains. The pseudocode to create a Brownian tree on a two-dimensional lattice follows:

```
choose one or more seed positions
while stopping criteria has not been met:
  place a random walker at a random position
  move the random walker until it is adjacent to a seed
  (i.e. touching)
  place a new seed at the random walker's position
```

The most obvious stopping criteria for a Brownian tree are when a desired number of particles have been dropped or when the Brownian tree covers a desired area or volume. After the Brownian tree has been generated, it is straightforward to define the particle placement heuristic to generate mountains. First, overlay the Brownian tree on the height field. Then traverse the entire height field and drop a particle at every location covered by the Brownian tree. You'll need to traverse the height field several times until the terrain features reach a desired size. Figure 5.1.9 shows the results using this particle placement heuristic with the particle dynamics discussed earlier.

FIGURE 5.1.8 An example of a Brownian tree created with DLA.

Notice the Brownian tree provides a nice way to preview the shape of a mountain range, like the lava streams of volcanoes, without needing to drop a single particle. A level designer can use the Brownian tree to easily decide the position and size of the mountains. The general shape of the Brownian tree can also be controlled by starting the random walkers at positions that lie in the direction of desired growth.

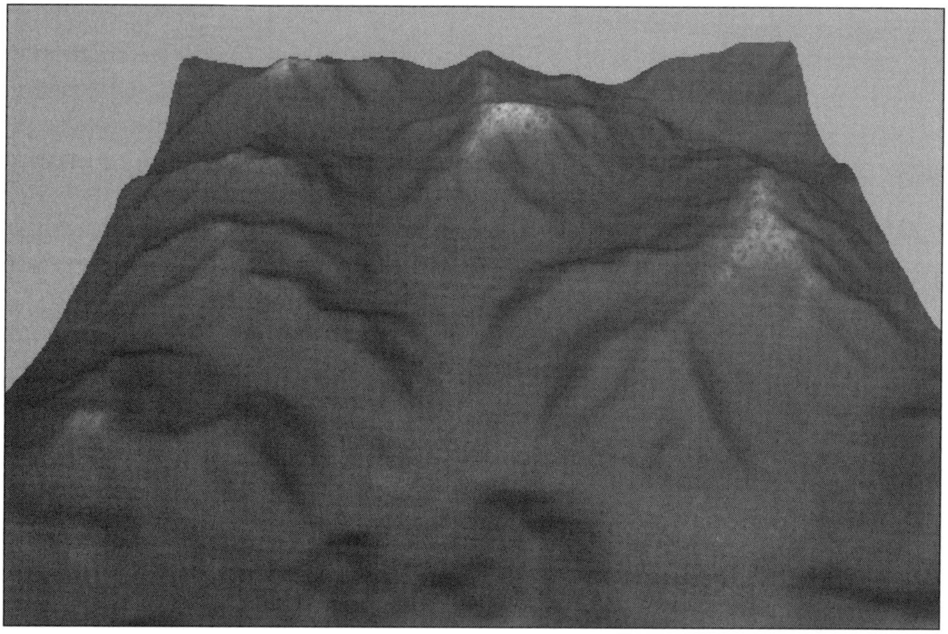

FIGURE 5.1.9 Mountains created using advanced particle deposition. (Also shown in color in the color insert section.)

If you are familiar with L-systems (see [Prusinkiewicz96]), you may wonder if L-systems can be used to generate a tree-like structure suitable for the particle placement heuristic. The answer is yes. However, L-systems require a grammar to define the tree's structure. The simplicity of Brownian trees was preferred for this article, but the potential of L-systems should not go unmentioned.

Dunes

Dunes are very interesting landforms that are usually associated with deserts, but can also form underwater. Dunes found in the desert are formed by the wind so they are constantly moving and changing shape. In fact, dunes have been recorded moving as much as 20 meters per year. There are several types of dunes, but this gem focuses on a common type of dune called a traverse dune. Traverse dunes form a ridge that is perpendicular to the direction of the prevailing wind. As shown in Figure 5.1.10, a dune is formed as the wind rolls and tosses particles up the windward slope, and deposits the particles on the leeward slope. This motion can be easily simulated using particle deposition.

One obvious solution is to randomly pick particles off the height field and displace them by a small random distance in the direction of the wind. However, this does not quite work. The missing key is that particles are more likely to be deposited on the leeward slope than they are on windward slope because of wind's "shadow" on the leeward slope. To simulate this, you can assign a cost to the distance each particle traverses. The cost of traveling up the windward slope should be less than the cost of

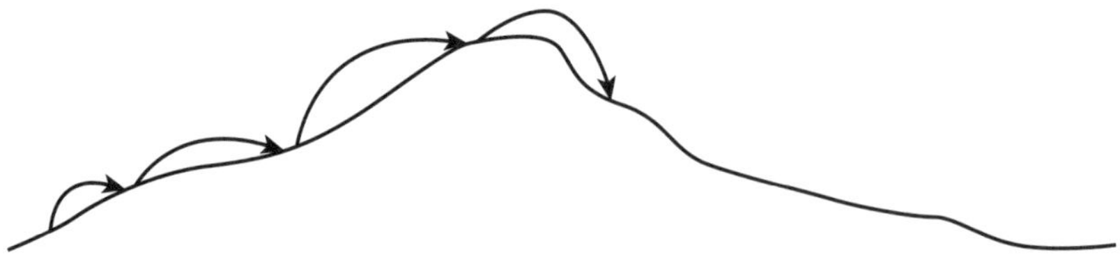

FIGURE 5.1.10 Dunes are formed as particles are carried up the windward slope and deposited on the leeward slope.

traveling down the leeward slop. The following pseudocode implements a suitable cost function, and Figure 5.1.11 demonstrates the results:

```
while stopping criteria has not been met:
  choose a random position and remove a particle
  displacement = small random number
  while displacement >= 0:
     move the particle one position in the direction of the wind
     if the particle moves up
        displacement -= 1
     else
        displacement -= 2
  drop the particle and compute particle dynamics
```

FIGURE 5.1.11 Dunes created using advanced particle deposition.

In this example the cost of traveling up the windward slope is only the horizontal distance traveled (i.e. no vertical cost), and the cost of traveling down the leeward slope is the horizontal and vertical distance traveled. This is a very simple, yet effective, cost function. Different cost functions will yield different dune shapes and dynamics so experimentation is encouraged.

Overhanging Terrain

As shown in Figure 5.1.12, overhanging terrain is terrain that protrudes over other terrain. Particle deposition can create this type of terrain with some minor modifications to the particle dynamics. Assign a stickiness attribute to each particle that is dropped on the terrain, and look at the path a particle takes as it falls toward the terrain. If a particle touches another particle at an adjacent position before landing on the terrain, the stickiness of the falling particle will determine if the particle stops or continues to fall. As shown in Figure 5.1.13, when very sticky particles brush the face of a steep slope they will accumulate to form an overhang. The stickiness of a region can be user-defined or it can be defined by a noise function. The following pseudocode provides more details:

```
choose an arbitrary threshold, S
for each dropped particle:
  determine the particle's stickiness, Sp (3D noise)
  check the particle's path as it falls toward the height field
  if the particle touches an adjacent particle
     determine the adjacent particle's stickiness, Sa (3D noise)
     if (Sp >= S) and (Sa >= S)
        leave the particle at this position
  else
     use the heuristic discussed in the particle dynamics section
```

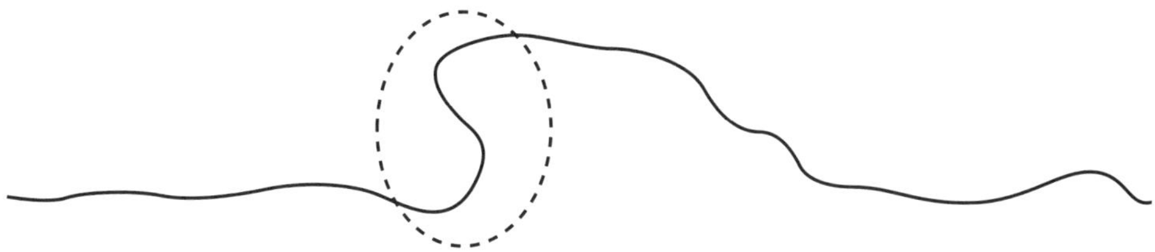

FIGURE 5.1.12 An example of overhanging terrain.

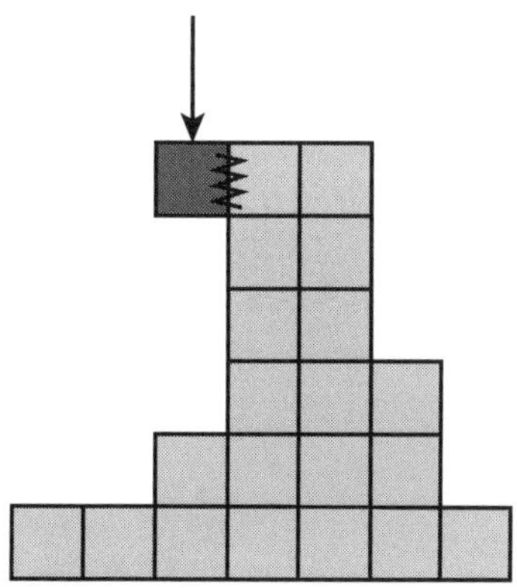

FIGURE 5.1.13 Sticky particles attach to steep slopes as they fall to the surface.

Notice that traditional height fields cannot be used to define overhanging terrain because a height field is a two-dimensional lattice with elevation assigned to each position (that is, a two-dimensional scalar field). Voxels can represent volumes in a three-dimensional lattice (that is, a three-dimensional scalar field), and they are ideal for modeling overhanging terrain because they can be polygonalized using a marching cubes/tetrahedrons algorithm. Voxel representations will increase the space and time complexity of particle deposition. Hybrid representations, which only use voxels where they are needed, can ameliorate some of this cost.

Conclusion

Particle deposition is a powerful tool for creating various types of realistic terrain. The terrain types shown here do not represent an exhaustive list of what is possible with particle deposition. Canyons, craters, caves, plateaus, terraces, and various outcroppings are just a few other examples of what might be possible using particle deposition.

References

[Ebert03] Ebert, David S., Musgrave, F. Kenton, Peachey, Darwyn, Perlin, Ken, and Worley, Steven. *Texturing & Modeling: A Procedural Approach,* Morgan Kaufmann Publishers, 2003.

[Grotzinger07] Grotzinger, John, et al. *Understanding Earth,* W. H. Freeman and Company, 2007.

[Prusinkiewicz96] Prusinkiewicz, Przemyslaw, and Lindenmayer, Aristid. *The Algorithmic Beauty of Plants,* Springer Verlag, 1996.

[Shankel00] Shankel, Jason. "Fractal Terrain Generation—Particle Deposition," *Game Programming Gems,* pp. 508–511. Charles River Media, 2000.

5.2

Reducing Cumulative Errors in Skeletal Animations

Bill Budge, Sony Entertainment of America

bill_budge@playstation.sony.com

This gem describes a simple trick to reduce the amount of cumulative error during playback of skeletal animations. It is applied during the offline processing of animation data, as part of the normal animation tool chain, and doesn't affect the size of the animation data. No changes are required in the runtime animation playback engine.

A Quick Tour of Game Animation Systems

In the pioneering 3D game *Quake*, characters were animated by storing a separate mesh for each pose and rendering a different one each frame [Eldawy06]. This kind of animation is simple and in theory capable of the highest quality, but it is difficult to modify and blend animations, and a lot of memory is needed to store the meshes. For these reasons, skeletal animation is now the standard in 3D games.

Skeletal animation works by attaching the vertices of a single character mesh to a collection of coordinate transforms—the bones of a "skeleton"—and animating the bones to deform the mesh. The vertices of the character mesh are positioned in a single coordinate space, together with the transforms that align the bones with the mesh. These transforms make up what is called the "default" or "rest" pose of the skeleton. To deform the mesh into a new pose, you first use the inverses of the rest transforms to take the vertices from their original space to "bone" space and then use the new bone transforms to move the vertices to their final positions. The equation for each vertex is as follows:

$$\mathbf{V}' = \mathbf{M}_{pose}\left(\mathbf{M}_{rest}^{-1}\mathbf{V}\right) \tag{5.2.1}$$

Skeletal animation works well because most game characters and objects are not shapeless blobs, but can be closely approximated by collections of rigid bodies. This leads to a great reduction in data because there are far fewer bones than mesh vertices to animate, and a great increase in flexibility, because it is much easier to modify and blend bone transforms than meshes.

A further observation leads to a trick that reduces the animation data by almost half again. Game characters and objects are not just random collections of rigid bodies; they are jointed (at least until you blow them to pieces!). Each bone is connected to others at these joints, so you can organize the transforms into a hierarchy and make all but the root transform relative to its parent transform. Because jointed bones don't move relative to each other, all of the child translations reduce to constant vectors, which can be removed from the animation and stored with the skeleton. In fact, they're already there in the rest pose. Thus animations need only have a single translation track for the root and rotation tracks for every bone.

Playback of the parent-relative transforms is straightforward. First, you construct the root transform from the root translation and rotation tracks. Next, for each child of the root, you construct the child transform by concatenating the child rotation with the parent transform. This process is repeated for the children's children, and so on, until you have reconstructed the transform for every bone in the hierarchy.

For a more in-depth description of skeletal animation and an introduction to skinning techniques to improve mesh deformation around joints, see [Lander98].

Cumulative Error

Unfortunately, there is a price to pay for the data reduction that you achieved by making the transforms parent-relative. It's not so much the extra work—by doing the reconstruction in breadth-first order as described, you only require one additional matrix concatenation per bone. The real problem is that Equation 5.2.1 has effectively become:

$$\mathbf{V}' = \mathbf{M}_{\text{root}} \ldots \mathbf{M}_{\text{parent}} \mathbf{M}_{\text{child}} \left(\mathbf{M}_{\text{rest}}^{-1} \mathbf{V} \right) \tag{5.2.2}$$

The reconstruction of the transforms using Equation 5.2.2 is less robust than Equation 5.2.1. There are two reasons for this. First, any error at a transform higher in the hierarchy will affect every transform below it. An error at the root transform, for example, will affect every other transform. Second, the error at each step will naturally tend to accumulate, creating a larger error. For the purposes of this gem, we assume that the error at each transform behaves like a random variable (otherwise, you would be able to compensate for it). Therefore, the second effect due to concatenating rotations is like adding random variables

These two effects mean that the greatest error will be at bones that are furthest from the root. These are usually the character's hands and feet. Such artifacts can be seen in many games. The classic example is a standing idle animation where the feet appear to slide over the ground. An even worse situation is when a character is gripping a bat or sword with two hands. The gripped object is a leaf bone, parented to one of the hands. The other hand, being at the end of a different transform chain, will appear to be swimming around and through the object.

For parent-relative animations, you should be mostly concerned with rotation error. Where does this error come from? A small amount is due to the use of floating point arithmetic, which introduces round-off and precision error. However, by far the most important sources of error are lossy compression schemes that most games use to further reduce the size of animation data.

There are many ways to compress rotation data. Some are lossless. For example, joints like the knees and elbows have only a single degree of freedom. Storing a full rotation such as a quaternion for each pose is wasteful. Instead, the axis of rotation can be stored, and the animation data reduced to a series of angles.

Lossy compression algorithms can lead to even greater reductions in storage cost. One of the simplest techniques is key frame reduction, which looks at the rotation values and tries to remove those values that can be interpolated from neighboring values without exceeding some error threshold. The problem with key frame reduction is that it is difficult to know which values to keep and which to reject. A better technique is to use a curve fitting algorithm to convert the rotation values into a multidimensional spline curve that approximates the data to some tolerance [Muratori03]. Spline curves are a good fit to real-world rotational data, are very compact, and are easy to evaluate at runtime. Wavelet compression is another popular technique [Beaudoin07].

Even if an efficient representation is found, storing lots of floating point data can be inefficient if the numbers are in a known small range. If you are using quaternions, all numbers are in the range [–1...1], so the eight bits of exponent for each is wasteful. You can compress the numbers to 12- or 16-bit fixed point form. For an entire gem on quaternion compression, see [Zarb-Adami02].

It is common to push the compression algorithms to the point where artifacts due to cumulative errors just become visible. In this case, you will always have significant errors at each rotation.

Figure 5.2.1 shows a simple 2D hierarchy of two bones in the original pose and some possible reconstructed poses, given the same random error at each transform. The parent transform is shown with its error range as a gray region. Three child transforms are shown with their error ranges, one aligned with the actual child transform, and the other two where the parent has the greatest error. Note how the error at the ends of the bones increases from parent to child.

Eliminating Cumulative Rotation Errors

The conventional algorithm for processing the animation begins by extracting all of the transform data from the authored representation into a common coordinate space. Next, all child transforms are made parent-relative by concatenating with the parent's inverse transform. Finally, the relative transforms are compressed and formatted for the runtime playback engine. Let's call this the naive algorithm, because it assumes that there is no error introduced by compression and reconstruction by the runtime.

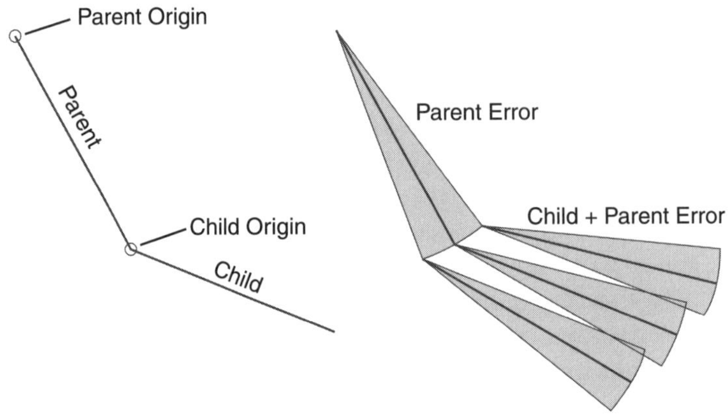

FIGURE 5.2.1 Cumulative error increases from parent to child.

The idea of this gem is to take reconstruction errors into account and use the reconstruction algorithm to get the parent transform with error, and make the child transforms parent-relative to that transform rather than the original.

This leads to the following procedure, which we call Algorithm 1:

1. Compress and format the root transform data.
2. Run the decompression algorithm on the result of Step 1 and replace the original transform with the results.
3. For each child of the root, make its transform data relative to the decompressed root transform data. Compress and format the parent-relative rotation data.
4. Run the decompression algorithm on each child from Step 3 to get its final transform data and replace the original child data with the result.
5. Continue down the hierarchy until all bones have been processed.

This completely eliminates the accumulation of rotational error because for each child transform, Step 3 subtracts the rotational error of the parent transform. However, the parent's rotation error does more than just rotate the child. It also translates the child (unless the child's origin is at the parent's origin). That means that the parent-relative transform resulting from Step 3 will generally have a translation that is different from the constant one you store with the skeleton. This translation error can't be eliminated by any child rotation. Although you could correct it by adding a new translation, that would defeat the whole purpose of making the transforms parent relative, which was to eliminate these translations in the first place! So translation error is still accumulating, although total error is less than with the naive algorithm because the rotation error is less.

Figure 5.2.2 shows the results of the naive algorithm and Algorithm 1. Note how the child bones all have the same orientation as in the true pose (although still with local error), and how they are offset by the translation error as a result of the rotational error of the parent bone.

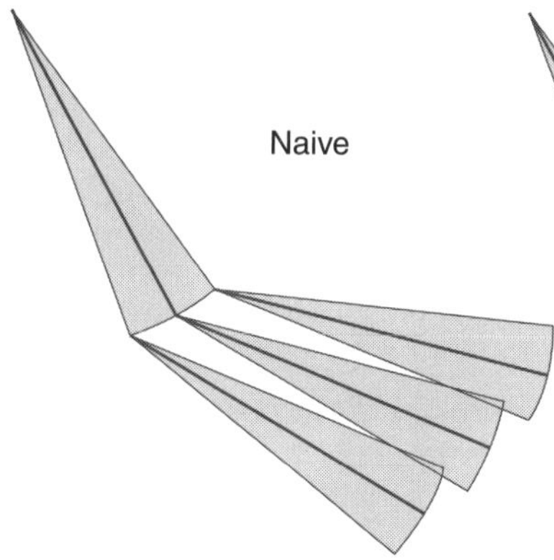

FIGURE 5.2.2 Removing cumulative rotational error.

It is possible to reduce this translation error, but to do this you have to rotate the child bone away from its true orientation. To calculate this rotation, you first select a fixed point on the bone where you would like to minimize the translation error. Let's call it a significant point. A significant point could be the origin of a child bone, or some arbitrary point that identifies the "end" of the bone. You rotate the reconstructed bone from Algorithm 1 so as to move the significant point closest to its true position. Figure 5.2.3 shows the geometry.

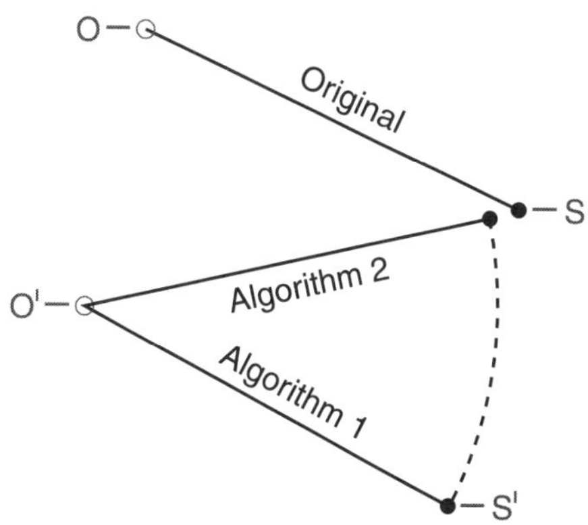

FIGURE 5.2.3 Reducing translation error at the significant point.

The rotation is computed by the following equations:

$$\mathbf{Axis} = \mathbf{O'S'} \times \mathbf{O'S} \tag{5.2.3}$$

$$\text{angle} = \cos^{-1}\left(\mathbf{O'S'} \cdot \mathbf{O'S}\right) \tag{5.2.4}$$

Modify Step 3 of Algorithm 1 to get Algorithm 2:

1. Compress and format the root transform data.
2. Run the decompression algorithm on the result of Step 1 and replace the original transform with the results.
3. For each child of the root:
   a. Make its transform data relative to the decompressed root transform data.
   b. Concatenate this with the decompressed parent transform to get the reconstructed transform, without error.
   c. Compute the rotation that takes the significant point in this reconstructed transform closest to its actual position, and add it to the transform.
   d. Compress and format the parent-relative rotation data.
4. Run the decompression algorithm on each child from Step 3 to get its final transform data and replace the original child data with the result.
5. Continue down the hierarchy until all bones have been processed.

Figure 5.2.4 shows the results of the naive algorithm and Algorithm 2. Note how the child bones now have slight rotation errors (although they don't accumulate, as each step still corrects for the parent's error) and how the translation error has been reduced.

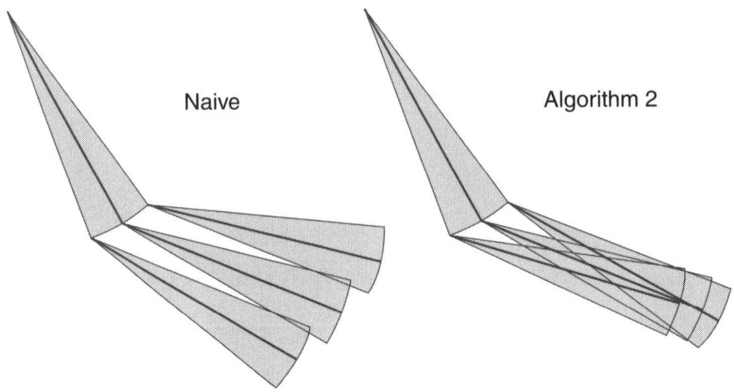

FIGURE 5.2.4 Reducing cumulative translational error.

Algorithm 2 does not completely eliminate translational error. One way to address this is to add translation tracks at leaf bones to combat any objectionable artifacts. Another way is to employ an inverse kinematics system to make sure that bones are where they should be. Even if a game uses an IK system, these error reduction techniques are useful because they improve the quality of the pose reconstruction so that it is closer to the artist's original version.

Conclusion

You have seen how skeletal animation systems suffer from cumulative error, and how conventional processing of animation data can lead to noticeable artifacts on playback. With a simple modification to the processing algorithm, however, you can eliminate cumulative rotational error and reduce the translation errors.

Only the preprocessing of animation is changed, so it has no performance or memory impact on the game runtime. Finally, translation tracks can be added at important bones to eliminate any remaining artifacts.

References

[Beaudoin07] Beaudoin, Philippe. "Adapting Wavelet Compression to Human Motion Capture Clips," available online at http://www.cs.ubc.ca/~van/papers/2007-gi-compression.pdf.

[Eldawy06] Eldawy, Mohamed. "Trends of Character Animation in Games," available online at http://adlcommunity.net/file.php/23/GrooveFiles/Games%20Madison/charAnimation.pdf.

[Lander98] Lander, Jeff. "Skin Them Bones: Game Programming for the Web Generation," *Game Developer Magazine*, May 1998, pp. 11–16, www.gamasutra.com/features/gdcarchive/2000/lander.doc.

[Muratori03] Muratori, Casey. "Discontinuous Curve Report," available online at http://funkytroll.com/curves/emails.txt.

[Zarb-Adami02] Zarb-Adami, Mark. "Quaternion Compression," *Game Programming Gems 3,* Charles River Media Press, 2002.

5.3

An Alternative Model for Shading of Diffuse Light for Rough Materials

Tony Barrera, Barrera Kristiansen AB

tony.barrera@spray.se

Anders Hast, Creative Media Lab, University of Gävle

aht@hig.se

Ewert Bengtsson, Centre For Image Analysis, Uppsala University

ewert@cb.uu.se

This gem shows how it is possible to improve the shading of rough materials with a rather simple shading model. This gem discusses both the flattening effect, which is visible for rough materials, as well as the possible methods for creating the backscattering effect.

Introduction

Usually Lambert's model (cosine law) [Foley97] is used to compute the diffuse light, especially if speed is crucial. This model is used for both Gouraud [Gouraud71] and Phong [Phong75] shading. However, this model is known to produce plastic looking materials. The reason for this is that the model assumes that the object itself is perfect in the sense that the surface scatters light equally in all directions. However, in real life there are no such perfect materials.

A number of models have been introduced in literature that can be used for metals [Blinn77, Cook82]. These models assume that the surface consists of small v-shaped cavities. Oren and Nayar proposed a model for diffuse light suitable for rough surfaces [Oren94, Oren95a, Oren95b]. This model can be used for rough surfaces, like clay and sand. However, this model is quite computationally expensive, even in its simplified form. Nonetheless, the benefit of using their model is that it produces more accurate diffuse light for rough surfaces. They showed that a cylindrical clay vase will appear almost equally bright over the entire lit surface except for the edges where the intensity drops quite suddenly.

The Lambert model will produce shadings which drop off gradually and this is seldom the case in real life. This effect is shown in Figures 5.3.1 and 5.3.2. Note that the intensity is not scaled down for the Lambert shaded teapot in Figure 5.3.1 and therefore it appears brighter than the teapot rendered with the Oren-Nayar model in Figure 5.3.2. Nonetheless, it is apparent that the intensity is almost equally bright over the surface for the Oren-Nayar model.

FIGURE 5.3.1 A Lambert shaded teapot.

We proposed earlier in a poster a model that simulates the same behavior, but is much simpler and faster to compute [Barrera05]. This gem develops the idea further.

FIGURE 5.3.2 An Oren-Nayar shaded teapot.

The Flattening Effect

One of the main differences between Lambert's model and the Oren-Nayar model is that the Oren-Nayar model produces diffuse light that is almost equally bright over the surface. This flattening effect can be modeled by forcing the diffuse light to be closer to the maximum intensity, except on the edge where it should drop down rather quickly to zero. Thus, the shading curve will be horizontally flat over a large portion of the interval. The following function could be used for this purpose:

$$I_d = k\left(1 - \frac{1}{1+\rho\cos\theta}\right) \tag{5.3.1}$$

where $cos\theta = \mathbf{n}\cdot\mathbf{l}$ is the Lambert's law, ρ is the surface roughness property that tells how flat (or close to one) the function should be, and k is a constant.

$$k = \frac{1+\rho}{\rho} \tag{5.3.2}$$

The constant k makes sure that $I_d=1$ for $cos\theta=1$. Note that k can be precomputed and can also contain surface color.

The roughness property ρ is not derived in a way that it describes the physical behavior in the way that Oren and Nayar does for the distribution of cavities. Instead it can be used to adjust the slope of the curve, thus simulating different degrees of roughness. Figure 5.3.3 shows Lambert (*cos* θ), the steepest curve, compared to the new model with ρ = {0.75, 1.5, 3.0, and 6.0}. The larger the value for ρ that is used, the closer to 1 the curve will be over the interval.

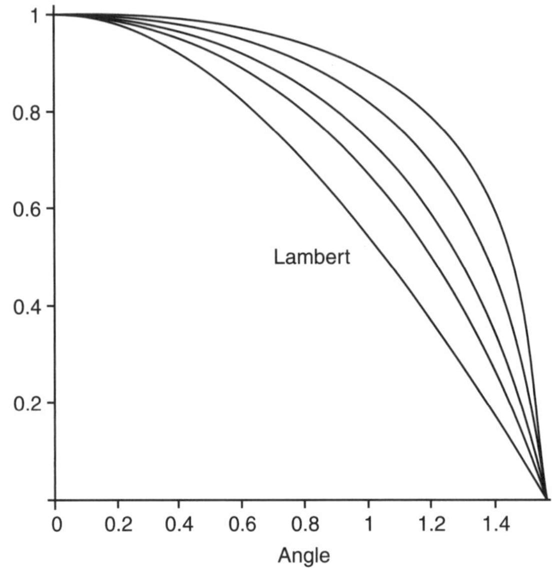

FIGURE 5.3.3 Intensity for different angles between the normal and the light source vector for ρ = {0.75, 1.5, 3.0, and 6.0}.

In Figures 5.3.4 through 5.3.7, the effect of using the method is shown for a shaded teapot. Notice how the surface appears flatter when ρ increases.

The shader code in GLSL looks like this:

```
uniform float shininess;
varying vec3 normal, color, pos;

void main()
{
   vec3 l = normalize(gl_LightSource[0].position.xyz - pos);
   vec3 n = normalize(normal);

   float nl=max(0.0, (dot(n,l)));

   // Flattening
   float rho=6.0;
   float k=(1.0+rho)/rho;
   float diff = k*(1.0-1.0/(1.0+rho*nl));

   gl_FragColor = vec4(color * diff, 1);
}
```

FIGURE 5.3.4 ρ is the surface roughness property that tells how flat (or close to one) the function should be; here ρ is 0.75.

FIGURE 5.3.5 Here the surface roughness property, ρ, is 1.5.

FIGURE 5.3.6 Here, ρ is 3.0. Notice how the surface appears flatter when ρ increases.

FIGURE 5.3.7 Here, ρ is 6.0. The flattest surface of all.

Backscattering

The backscattering effect is visible in many materials and it is a contributing reason to why you can see things quite well in the dark using a flashlight. However, it is a rather subtle effect and it is quite hard to notice it in real life and it should therefore be used with care. Because it is visible only when the light source is in the same direction as the viewer, it could be modeled using $\mathbf{l} \cdot \mathbf{v}$. The following equation was used as an attenuation factor that is multiplied with the diffuse light:

$$F_{bs} = \frac{f(\mathbf{l} \bullet \mathbf{v}) + b}{1 + b} \tag{5.3.3}$$

We used the power function for f but the Schlick model [Schlick94] can also be used. This function determines how the effect will be distributed over the surface in a similar manner as for the specular light.

The constant b will determine how much impact the backscattering effect should have on the diffuse light. A large b will yield a small effect and vice versa. In Figure 5.3.8, a small b is used only to demonstrate the effect.

In Figure 5.3.9, it is clear that the backscattering effect vanishes as the viewer is looking at the object from a different direction than the light source direction.

FIGURE 5.3.8 Note how the center of the teapot appears brighter because the light source is in the same direction as the viewer.

FIGURE 5.3.9 The light source is no longer in the direction of the viewer and the backscattering is not visible.

The extra code needed for computing the backscattering is as follows:

```
vec3 v = normalize(-pos);

float lv=max(0.0, (dot(l,v)));

// Backscattering
float b=1.00000;
float bs=(pow(lv,80.0)+b)/(1.0+b);

gl_FragColor = vec4(color*diff*bs, 1);
```

Another possibility is to add the effect as a term of its own to the Phong-Blinn model. The following equation was used for Figure 5.3.10.

$$I_{bs} = K_{bs} f(\mathbf{l} \bullet \mathbf{v}) \tag{5.3.4}$$

The constant K_{ks} determines how much the effect will be visible and once again the function f determines how the effect will be distributed over the surface. It should be mentioned that the backscattering intensity was multiplied with the color of the surface in the picture.

FIGURE 5.3.10 Once again the teapot appears brighter in the center because the light source is in the same direction as the viewer.

Change the code as follows:

```
float kks=0.3;
float bs=kks*pow(lv,80.0);

gl_FragColor = vec4(color *(diff+bs), 1);
```

Conclusion

The Oren-Nayar model is rather complex while the proposed model is quite simple and easy to use. Still it produces a result that mimics behavior typical for rough materials. You saw two possible ways of computing the backscattering effect and it is hard to tell which one is the better method. You can used large values for the power function to make the difference visible in the images, but when an object is rotated interactively it is clear that a much lower value gives a more pleasing result.

References

[Barrera05] Barrera, T., Hast, A., and Bengtsson, E. "An Alternative Model for Real-Time Rendering of Diffuse Light for Rough Materials," SCCG'05 Proceedings II, pp. 27–28, 2005.

[Blinn77] Blinn. J.F. "Models of Light Reflection for Computer Synthesized Pictures," Proceedings of the 4th Annual Conference on Computer Graphics and Interactive Techniques, 1977, pp. 192–198.

[Cook82] Cook, R.L., and Torrance, K.E. "A Reflectance Model for Computer Graphics," *ACM Transactions on Graphics (TOG),* 1, 1, 1982, pp. 7–24.

[Foley97] Foley, J.D. van Dam, A., Feiner, S.K., and Hughes, J.F. *Computer Graphics: Principles and Practice, Second Edition in C,* 1997, pp. 723–724.

[Gouraud71] Gouraud H. "Continuous Shading of Curved Surfaces," *IEEE Transactions on Computers,* Vol. c–20, No. 6, June, 1971.

[Oren94] Oren, M., and Nayar, S.K. "Generalization of Lambert's Reflectance Model," Proceedings of the 21st Annual Conference on Computer Graphics and Interactive Techniques, 1994, pp. 239–246.

[Oren95a] Oren, M., and Nayar, S.K. "Generalization of the Lambertian Model and Implications for Machine Vision," *International Journal of Computer Vision,* 1995, pp. 227–251.

[Oren95b] Oren, M., and Nayar, S.K. "Visual Appearance of Matte Surfaces," *Science,* 267, 5201, 1995, pp. 1153–1156.

[Phong75] Phong, B.T. "Illumination for Computer Generated Pictures," Communications of the ACM, Vol. 18, No. 6, June, 1975.

[Schlick94] Schlick, C. "A Fast Alternative to Phong's Specular Model," *Graphics Gems 4,* 1994, pp. 385–387.

5.4

High-Performance Subdivision Surfaces

Chris Lomont

chris@lomont.org

Subdivision surfaces are a method of representing smooth surfaces using a coarser polygon mesh, often used for storing and generating high-detail geometry (usually dynamically) from low-detail meshes coupled with various scalar maps. They have become popular in modeling and animation tools due to their ease of use, support for multi-resolution editing, ability to model arbitrary topology, and numerical robustness. This gem presents extensions to Loop subdivision, blending results from numerous places and adding useful implementation details. The result is a complete set of subdivision rules for geometry, texture, and other attributes. The surfaces are suitable for terrain, characters, and any geometry used in a game.

This gem also presents a general overview of methods for fast subdivision and rendering. After learning the material presented, you'll be able to implement subdivision surfaces in a production environment in either tools or in the game engine itself.

Introduction to Subdivision Schemes

There are many types of subdivision schemes, with varying properties. Some of the properties are as follows:

- Mesh type—Usually the mesh is made of triangles or quads.
- Smoothness—This is the continuity of the limit surface, and is usually denoted C^1, C^2..., and so on, or G^1, G^2...., and so on.
- Interpolating [Zorin96] or approximating—Interpolating schemes go through the original data points, whereas approximating schemes may not.
- Support size—This is the amount of neighboring geometry affecting the final position of a given surface point.
- Split—Some schemes work by replacing faces with more faces, others work by replacing vertices with new sets of vertices. A few more work by replacing the entire previous mesh, making a "new" mesh.

Table 5.4.1 lists common schemes and some data about them.

Table 5.4.1 Subdivision Schemes

Method	Mesh	Smoothness*	Split	Scheme
Catmull-Clark	Quads	C^2	Face	Approximating
Doo-Sabin	Any	C^1	Vertex	Approximating
Loop	Triangles	C^2	Face	Approximating
Butterfly	Triangles	C^1	Face	Interpolating
Kobbelt	Quads	C^1	Face	Interpolating
Reif-Peters	Any	C^1	New	Approximating
Sqrt(3) (Kobbelt)	Triangles	C^2	Face	Approximating
Midedge	Quads	C^1	Vertex	Approximating
Biquartic	Quads	C^2	Vertex	Approximating

*Smoothness generally has one degree less of continuity at exceptional points.

Although this gem focuses mainly on generating geometry and rendering issues, subdivision surfaces have many other uses, including:

- Progressive meshes
- Mesh compression
- Multi-resolution mesh editing ([Zorin97])
- Surface and curve fitting ([Lee98] and [Levin99])
- Point set to mesh generation

Most 3D animation and rendering packages support subdivision surfaces as a primitive, although there is no standard type used throughout the industry. (See http://www.et.byu.edu/~csharp2/#A_SubD [as of 2007] for a partial list of toolsets supporting subdivision.) Catmull-Clark and Loop subdivision are the most commonly used, because they are arguably the simplest, are well documented, and are well suited to real-time rendering.

A related topic is PN triangles [Vlachos00], which provide a way to replace triangles at the rendering level with a smoother primitive. The basic idea is to quadratically interpolate surface normals, similar to Phong shading, and to use this cubically to interpolate new geometry. A good overview of subdivision is [Zorin00].

Subdivision Schemes Usage

For a production tool chain for interactive games, one method for using subdivision surfaces is to create art using high-resolution geometry and textures (and the geometry might be modeled in whatever subdivision flavors the tools support). The art is then exported as high-density polygon models and associated data. Tools then reduce the assets to a low poly count mesh with associated displaced subdivision maps, textures, and animation data. A subdivision kernel in the GPU dynamically converts assets back to needed poly counts at runtime based on speed, distance from camera, hardware support, and so on. This allows different subdivision surfaces to be used in the asset creation and asset rendering stages, which has advantages.

A tool along these lines is ZBrush, which allows you to edit meshes using subdivision surfaces in order to add geometry at multiple resolution levels, and then converts the resulting high-detail geometry to low-detail meshes and displacement maps.

Choice of Subdivision Type

This gem covers implementing Loop subdivision [Loop87]. Some reasons are that it is triangle based, making it (perhaps) easier to implement on GPUs, most artists and tools already work with triangle meshes, it is well studied, and it produces nice-looking surfaces. Another common choice is Catmull-Clark subdivision [Catmull78], but being quad-based, it seems less suitable for gaming. Pixar uses Catmull-Clark subdivision for animating characters. Many ideas presented in this article are applicable to quad-based subdivision as well as other schemes.

Loop Subdivision Features and Options

A single iteration of the original Loop Subdivision algorithm applied to a closed triangle mesh returns another closed triangle mesh with more faces. Repeated applications result in a smooth limit surface. Extensions to the original method are needed to model more features; a full-featured subdivision toolset includes the following:

- Boundaries—Allow non-closed meshes.
- Creases—Allow sharp edges and surface ridges. Adding boundaries gives creases. (Creases technically should have the techniques in [Biermann06] to prevent minor corner errors, but [Zorin00] claims these errors are visually minor. The corrections require more computation than what is presented and intended: a technique suited for real-time rendering.)
- Corners—Useful for making pointed items.
- Semi-sharpness—Modifies the basic rules for boundaries, creases, and corners to get varying degrees of sharpness.
- Colors and textures—Easy extensions of the subdivision process needed for rendering and gaming.
- Exact positions—After a few subdivisions, vertices can be pushed to what would be their final position if the subdivision were carried out to the limit. This computation is not very expensive.
- Exact normals—Computing exact normals for shading is not very expensive, and is less costly than face normal averaging.
- Displacement mapping—Adds geometry to the subdivided surface, and is a very nice feature to have, but not implemented in this gem. Instead, see [Lee00] and [Bunnell05].

- Evaluation at arbitrary points—Allows for computing the limit surface at an arbitrary position on the surface [Stam99]. This is useful for ray tracing or very detailed collision detection, but for game rendering is not likely to be needed.
- Prescribed normals—Allows for requesting specific normals on the limit surface at given vertices [Biermann06], and is useful for modeling. However, it is more expensive to implement than what is presented in this gem, and for this and space reasons details, it is omitted.
- Multi-resolution editing support—By storing all the levels of the subdivided mesh, users can work on any level of the subdivision, making many editing features easier [Zorin97].
- Collision detection—Needed for game dynamics; one method is in [DeRose98].
- Adaptive subdivision—Subdivides parts of the mesh into different amounts based on some metric, patching any holes formed in the process. Adaptive subdivision is useful for keeping polygon counts low while still giving nice curves, silhouettes, and level of detail. The decision on where to subdivide the mesh is usually based on curvature.

Features are added to the mesh by tagging vertices, faces, and edges with parameters to direct the subdivision algorithm. Tag combination restrictions can be enforced in software to prevent degenerate cases if needed.

Geometry Creation

To implement boundaries, creases, corners, and semi-smooth features, each vertex and edge is tagged with a floating-point weight $0 \leq w < \infty$. A weight of 0 denotes standard Loop subdivision, and ∞ denotes an infinitely sharp crease or boundary. Infinity need not be encoded in the data structures, because the weight is really a counter for the levels of subdivision affected. Any number larger than the highest level of subdivision performed will suffice. For example, 32767 should suffice, because it is unlikely that any mesh will be subdivided this many times.

Loop subdivision takes a mesh and creates a new mesh by splitting each old triangular face into four new faces, as shown in Figure 5.4.5. This is done in two steps. The first step inserts a new vertex on each existing edge, and the second step modifies old vertices (not those inserted on the edges).

Most of these geometry rules are from [Hoppe94a] and [Hoppe94b], with some ideas merged from [DeRose98] and [Schweitzer96].

Edges

The first step inserts a new vertex on each edge using a weighted sum of nearby vertices. The edge weights and the types of vertices at each endpoint of the edge serve to categorize the edges. Vertex categories are listed in the next section.

Each (non-boundary) edge has two adjacent triangles; the new vertex has the position $\frac{3}{8}(v_0 + v_1)$, where v_0 and v_1 are the vertices on the edge to split, and the other two vertices are the remaining vertices on the two adjacent triangles. This is illustrated in Figure 5.4.1, where the circle denotes the new vertex on the edge between the triangles. The weights can be written $\left(\frac{3}{8},\frac{3}{8},\frac{1}{8},\frac{1}{8}\right)$, where position j corresponds to vertex j (0-indexed).

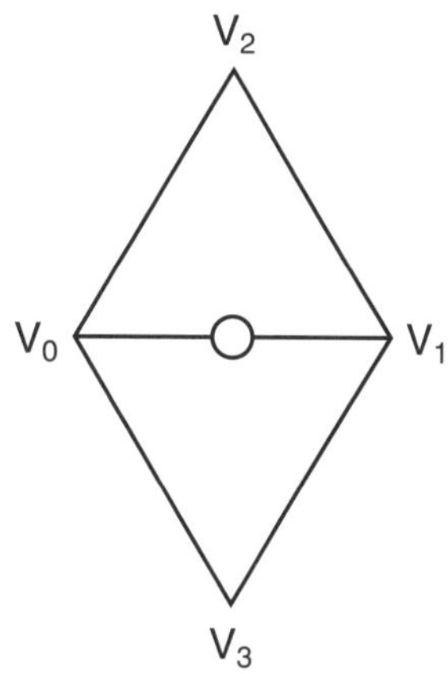

FIGURE 5.4.1 Edge mask.

The weights used to create a new edge depend on the edge weight and the vertex types of the two vertices that define the edge: v_0 and v_1. Given the two vertices on an edge, Table 5.4.2 shows which type of weights to use to create the new edge vertex. Weights are as follows:

- Type 1 weights : $\left(\frac{3}{8},\frac{3}{8},\frac{1}{8},\frac{1}{8}\right)$.
- Type 2 weights : $\left(\frac{1}{2},\frac{1}{2},0,0\right)$.
- Type 3 weights : $\left(\frac{3}{8},\frac{5}{8},0,0\right)$, where the $\frac{3}{8}$ weight goes with the corner edge.

An edge is *smooth* if it has weight $w = 0$. An edge is *sharp* if its weight is $w \geq 0$. If an edge has weight $0 < w < 1$, the new vertex is linearly interpolated between the two cases $w = 0$ and $w = 1$, keeping the end vertex types fixed.

Table 5.4.2 Edge Mask Selection

	Dart	Regular Crease	Non-Regular Crease	Corner
Dart	1	1	1	1
Regular crease	1	2	3	3
Non-regular crease	1	3	2	2
Corner	1	3	2	2

When an edge is split, each new edge gets weight $\bar{w} = \max\{w-1,0\}$. This gives finer control over sharpness because the crease rules are applied to a few levels, and then the smooth rules are applied, with possible interpolation on one step. An option for more control is to tag each end of an edge with a weight, giving two weights per edge, to interpolate the new edges, and then to make the corresponding changes throughout.

Note in all cases the total weight sums to 1 (also true for vertex masks).

Vertices

The *type* of a vertex depends on the vertex weight and the types of incident edges. A *smooth* vertex is one with zero incident sharp edges and weight 0. A *dart* vertex has one sharp incident edge and weight 0. A *crease* vertex has two sharp incident edges and weight 0. A *corner* vertex has > 2 sharp incident edges or has weight $w \geq 1$. An interior crease vertex is *regular* if it has six neighbors and exactly two non-sharp edges on each side of the crease; a boundary crease vertex is *regular* if it has four neighbors. Otherwise, crease and boundary vertices are *non-regular*. If an edge has weight $0 < w < 1$, it suffices to call it smooth for vertex classification.

The second step of Loop subdivision modifies all the original vertices (not the vertices inserted on each edge in step one) using a weighted sum of the original vertex and all neighboring vertices.

The weighting is dependent on the number n of neighboring vertices. For smooth and dart vertices, this is illustrated in Figure 5.4.2. The value of b is usually $b(n) = \frac{1}{64}\left(40 - \left\{3 + 2\cos\frac{2\pi}{n}\right\}^2\right)$, although other values are in the literature. (For example, [Warren95] proposes $b(n) = 3/(8n)$ for $n > 1$ and $b(3) = 3/16$, but this has unbounded curvature for a few valences.) The old vertex is given weight $1 - b(n)$ and each old neighbor (not the vertices created in step one!) is given weight $b(n)/n$ to determine the new vertex position, which is then the weighted sum of all these vertices: $v_{new} = (1 - b(n)) \cdot v_{old} + \frac{b(n)}{n}\sum_{j=1}^{n} v_j$.

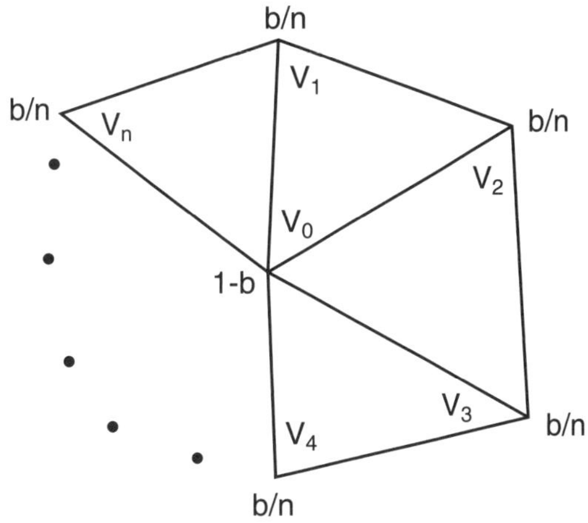

FIGURE 5.4.2 Vertex mask.

For corner vertices, the vertex position does not move, so $v_{new} = v_{old}$.

For crease vertices, the new vertex is the sum of $\frac{3}{4}$ of the original vertex and $\frac{1}{8}$ of each of the two neighbors on the crease.

If a vertex has weight $0 < w < 1$, the new vertex is linearly interpolated between the two cases $w = 0$ and $w = 1$. A new vertex also has a new weight $\tilde{w} = \max\{w-1,0\}$.

The final case is when a vertex has weight $0 < w_v < 1$ and some neighboring edge has weight $0 < w_e < 1$, leading to many possible combinations of interpolation. In this case evaluate each with weights 0 and weights 1, and interpolate on w_v, instead bilinearly interpolating the four cases of the weights (0,0), (0,1), (1,0), and (1,1).

Another option is to require integer weights, avoiding interpolation cases entirely at the loss of control on semi-sharp creases.

Displacement-mapped surfaces are implemented by moving the vertices as needed according to a displacement map. Vertices are also modified using [Biermann06] to implement prescribed normals, and this also splits crease rules into convex and concave cases, avoiding certain degenerate cases.

Limit Positions

Vertices can be projected to the position they would take if the surface were subdivided infinitely many times. This is often done after a few subdivision levels have been applied. This is optional and often doesn't modify the surface much.

Limit positions v^∞ are computed from a weighted sum of the current vertex v_0 and n neighbors v_j. Corner vertices stay fixed, that is $v^\infty = v_0$. Smooth vertices are projected using $v^\infty = \frac{3}{8b(n)(n+1)} v_0 + \frac{1}{n+1}\sum_{j=1}^{n} v_j$. A regular crease uses weights $\left(\frac{1}{6}, \frac{2}{3}, \frac{1}{6}\right)$ with v_0, getting $\frac{2}{3}$. The two crease neighbors get weight $\frac{1}{6}$, and the rest of the neighbors get weight 0. Similarly, non-regular creases use weights $\left(\frac{1}{5},\frac{3}{5},\frac{1}{5}\right)$.

Vertex and Crease Normals

True normals can be computed for each vertex, which should be done after computing limit positions for each final vertex. Surprisingly this is faster than computing approximate normals by averaging each adjacent face normal (partitioned to each side of a crease).

Computing two true tangents and taking a cross product computes true normals at each vertex.

For a smooth or dart vertex, the two tangents are $t_1 = \sum_{j=1}^{n} v_j \cos\left(\frac{2\pi * j}{n}\right)$ and $t_2 = \sum_{j=1}^{n} v_j \cos\left(\frac{2\pi * (j+1)}{n}\right)$.

Crease and boundary vertices require more work. Normals are not defined per vertex for corners, and must be done for each face. Tangents need to be computed for each side of the crease. Along a crease (or boundary), one tangent is –1 times one crease neighbor plus 1 times the other crease neighbor. The second tangent is more complicated to compute and is done as follows. Weights w_j are computed for each vertex, with $j = 0$ being the vertex where a normal is desired. Then the other indices are numbered $j = 0,2...,n$ from one crease to another. The weights depend on the number of vertices and for each case are as follows:

$$(w_0, w_1, w_2) = (-2,1,1)$$

$$(w_0, w_1, w_2, w_3) = (-1,0,10)$$

$$(w_0, w_1, w_2, w_3, w_4) = (-2,-1,2,2,-1)$$

$$w_0 = 0,\ w_1 = w_n = \sin(z),\ w_i = (2\cos(z) - 2)(\sin(i-1)z),\quad z = \frac{\pi}{n-1} \text{ for } n \geq 5.$$

This creates over four subdivision levels from a tagged cube, with one face missing and marked as boundary, as in Figure 5.4.3. Notice that some corners have varying semi-sharpness.

Feature Implementation

Besides geometry, a full solution needs colors, textures, and other per-vertex or per-face information.

Face parameters like color and texture coordinates can be interpolated using the same subdivision methods when new vertices are added. A simple method is to interpolate by distance after the old vertices are modified, giving new values for the new faces. Many features can be subdivided per vertex except at exceptional places, like along an edge where texture coordinates form a seam. Some details for Catmull-Clark

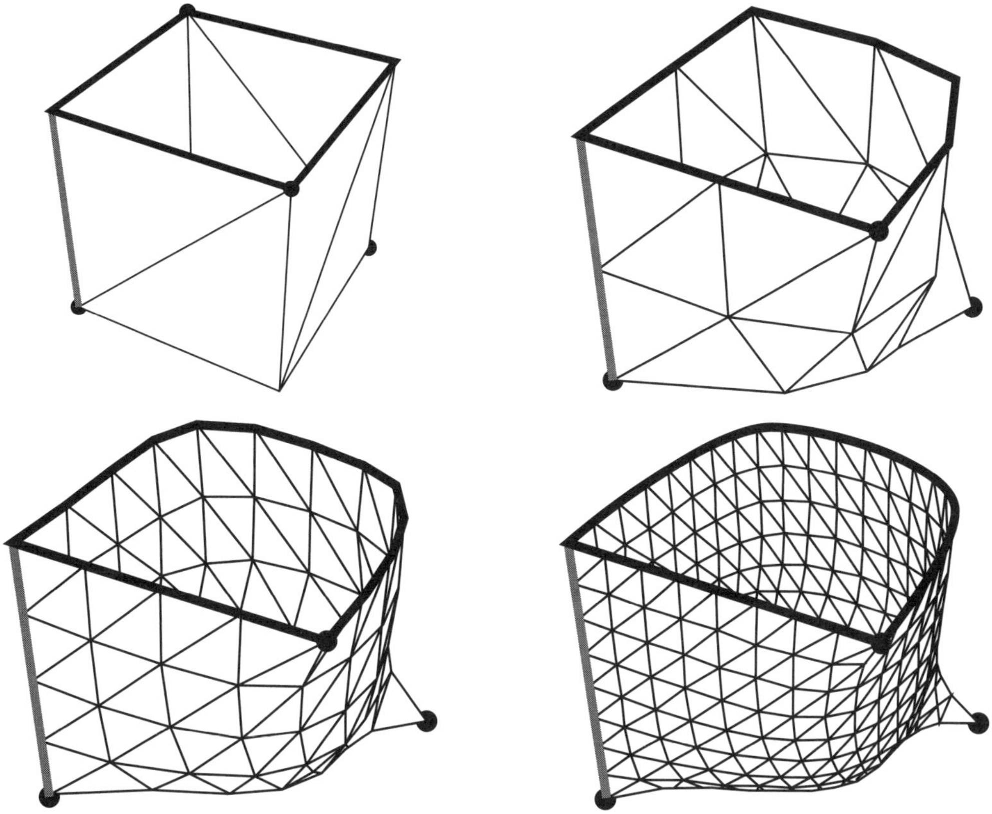

FIGURE 5.4.3 Example geometry.

surfaces (but applicable to Loop surfaces) are in [DeRose98]. Basically, per-vertex parameters are interpolated like vertex coordinates, so adding (u,v) texture coordinates is as simple as treating vertex points as (x,y,z,u,v) coordinates. Per-vertex textures don't allow easy handling of seams, in which case per-face texture coordinates are useful. However, all internal points on a subdivided face become per-vertex parameters.

Possible features to add but not covered in this article for lack of space are adaptive tessellation (where only part of the mesh is subdivided as needed for curvature, such as with silhouettes, clipping, and so on, and making sure cracks aren't introduced), and displaced subdivision surfaces (which add geometry by using a "texture" map to offset generated vertices as they are computed). Adaptive tessellation is covered in [Bunnell05] and displaced subdivision surfaces are covered in [Bunnell05] and [Lee00].

Collision Detection

If prescribed normals are not implemented, the surface has the convex hull property; that is, sits inside the convex hull of the bounding mesh. This can be used for coarse collision detection. More accurate (and more expensive) collision between subdivision surfaces is covered in [Wu04] using a novel "interval triangle" that tightly bounds the limit surface. [Severn06] efficiently computes the intersection of two subdivision surfaces at arbitrary resolutions. Collision detection will not be covered here further.

In the next section, a data structure is presented that accommodates Loop subdivision on a triangle mesh. An algorithm follows that performs one level of subdivision, returning a new mesh. This structure supports most of the features described in this gem, and is extensible to many of the other features.

Subdivision Data Structure

There are many approaches in the literature for data structures used to store and manipulate subdivision surfaces including half-edge, winged-edge, hybrid, and grids [Müller00]. For Loop subdivision, the data structure should allow finding neighbor vertices and incident edges easily, and preserve this ability on each level of subdivision.

There are many factors when designing the data structure. Converting a mesh to a Loop-subdivided mesh is the main goal, leading to certain structures, but other times the end purpose is GPU rendering, in which case optimizing data structures for this use makes sense. The approach presented here is somewhat of a hybrid, resulting in a data structure that ports easily to a GPU. A later section covers performance issues when moving to a GPU.

The following data structure is easy to read/write from files or elsewhere, fast to use internally, and does not use pointers. Avoiding pointers makes it easier to move to GPUs or languages not as pointer friendly as C/C++, and makes the memory footprint smaller than the previously mentioned schemes (useful for large mesh tools), because instead of storing connectivity information explicitly, it is deduced from index positions. This structure also makes sending meshes to a GPU easier because items are arranged into vertex arrays, normal arrays, and so on, using indices to render polygons.

Data Structure

See Figures 5.4.4 and 5.4.5 for insight. Extensions allow storing all the levels of subdivision for multi-resolution editing.

The mesh and supported features are stored in various arrays. Each array is 0-based. There is one array for each of the following:

- Vertices array VA—Each vertex is a three-tuple x, y, z of floats, and a float sharpness weight $0 \le w < \infty$, with 0 being smooth, and a half-edge index v_h of a half-edge ending on this vertex (for fast lookup later). If the vertex is a boundary, v_h is the boundary half-edge index ending on the vertex. Optional per-vertex color, texture, or index to a normal can also be stored.
- Faces array FA—Each face represents a triangle, stored as three indices v_0,v_1,v_2 into the vertex array. Also stored are three indices n_0,n_1,n_2 into the normal array

NA, corresponding to the three vertex indices. Each face can optionally store color, texture, and other rendering information, per face or per vertex as desired. Faces are oriented clockwise or counter-clockwise as desired, but all must be oriented the same way.

- Half-edge array HA—Each face has three (half) edges in the half-edge array, stored in the same order. Thus, a face with index f and (ordered) vertex indices $\{v_0,v_1,v_2\}$ has ordered half-edges with indices 3f, 3f+1, and 3f+2, denoting half-edges from vertex v_0 to v_1, v_1 to v_2, and v_2 to v_0, respectively. Note that half-edges are directed edges, with the two half-edges of a pair having opposite directions. A half-edge entry is two values: an integer marking the pair half-edge index or a –1 if it's a boundary, and a floating-point sharpness weight $0 \leq w < \infty$ denoting the crease value, 0 being smooth, and larger values denoting sharpness. Each matching half-edge pair must have the same crease values to avoid ambiguity. Note that a half-edge index determines the corresponding face index, which in turn determines a start and end vertex for the directed half-edge.
- Normals Array NA—Normals can be included in the scheme in numerous ways with varying tradeoffs. In order to handle creases, boundaries, and semi-sharp features cleanly, you need one normal per vertex per face, but for many vertices (for example, smooth and regular) only a single normal is needed. An array of normals accommodate this; each has a unit vector and a weight $0 \leq w < \infty$ telling how fast a vertex normal converges to a prescribed normal, with 0 meaning no prescribed normal. Normals are referenced by index, thus avoiding redundant stores.

Besides storing the size of each array, the number of edges E (where a matching pair of half-edges or a boundary edge constitutes a single edge) is stored. This is not too costly to compute if the mesh has no boundary (E=# half-edges/2 = #faces*3/2), and can be computed otherwise by scanning the half-edge array and setting E=(size of HA+# of boundary edges in HA)/2.

Information about vertex types (smooth, crease, and so on) may also be stored on a vertex tag for speed. Other items may also be tagged, but the algorithm described here needs to be modified to maintain the invariants across subdivisions.

Unneeded features can be dropped, such as three normals per face, prescribed normals, or semi-sharp creases, but this loses finer grained control.

A well-formed mesh requires a few rules. If a half-edge is not paired (it is on a boundary), it has pair index –1, and must have infinite crease weight. Otherwise, the edge will shrink. Each half-edge of the same edge must have the same weight; otherwise the edges will subdivide differently, creating cracks.

File Format

Based on the data structure described here, a file format is defined as an extension to the popular text based Wavefront *.OBJ format. An entry is a line of text, starting with a token denoting the line type followed by space-separated fields. Various pieces of data are stored to speed up loading so all items such as paired edges do not need to be recomputed each load. The format in order of file reading/writing is in Table 5.4.3.

Table 5.4.3 File Format Entries

Entry	Description
`#SubdivisionSurfL 0.1`	Denotes a non-standard OBJ file, versioned.
`si v f e n`	Optional subdivision info giving number of vertices, faces, edges, and normals. Allows pre-allocation of arrays.
`v x y z`	One entry per vertex with floating point position.
`f v1 v2 v3`	One entry per face with one-based vertex indices, oriented.
`hd j wt`	Half-edge data, one entry for each half-edge, in the order described by the faces, in half-edge order $v_0 \rightarrow v_1$, $v_1 \rightarrow v_2$, $v_2 \rightarrow v_0$. Each entry is a one-based integer edge pair index j (or –1 for a boundary) and a floating-point weight `wt`.
`fc r1 g1 b1 a1 r2 g2 b2 a2 r3 g3 b3 a3`	Optional face colors, one per vertex, RGBA, [0,1] floats. Not allowed with per-vertex colors `vc`.
`vc r g b a`	Optional per-vertex color data, RGBA, [0,1] floats. Not allowed with per-face colors `fc`.
`ft u1 v1 u2 v2 u3 v3 texname`	Optional face textures with (`u,v`) floats in [0,1]. `texname` is application dependent.
`fn nx ny nz w`	Optional normal data, with weights for prescribed normals. 0 is default weight.
`fni n1 n2 n3`	Optional face normal indices into the normal table, one normal per vertex. Requires `fn` entries.
`vs wt`	Optional vertex sharpness,$[0,\infty)$, with 0 being smooth and default; one per vertex.

Subdivision Algorithm Details

This is an overview of the Loop subdivision algorithm. Let V = # old vertices, F = # old faces, H = 3F = # of half-edges, and #E = number of edges = (H + # boundary edges)/2.

One level of subdivision consists of six steps:

1. Compute new edge vertices.
2. Update the original vertices.
3. Split the faces.
4. Create new half-edge information.
5. Update the other features.
6. Replace the arrays in the data structure with the new ones, and discard, store, or free the old ones as desired.

These steps are described in detail in the following sections.

Computing New Edge Vertices

Follow these steps to compute the new edge vertices:

1. Because each existing vertex will soon be modified (and originals need to be kept around until all are done), and because new vertices are going to be added per edge, you allocate an array NV for all new vertices of size (# old vertices + # edges). When creating new edge vertices, the first V positions in the array are skipped so the original vertices can be placed back in the same positions as they are modified.
2. Allocate an array EM (edge map) of integers of size (# half-edges) to store indices mapping half-edges to new vertex indices. Initialize all to –1 to indicate half-edges not yet mapped.
3. For each half-edge h, if EM[h] = –1, insert a vertex on the edge using the edge split rules. Store the new vertex in an unused slot in NV past the original V, and store the resulting NV index in EM[h]. If h_2=E[h] is not –1, h has a paired half-edge h_2, so store the NV index in EM[h_2] also.

Updating the Original Vertices

Now you must move each original vertex to a new position, placing the new vertex in the new vertex array NV, in the same order and position as before to make splitting faces easy. This is done using the vertex modification rules from before. During updating, reduce vertex weights by 1, clamping at 0. New vertices have weight 0. Each vertex stores a half-edge index v_h ending on the vertex, which is used to quickly walk neighboring vertices and determine edge types, as shown in Figure 5.4.4. Given a half-edge index h ending at the vertex, the joined neighbor vertex is VA[FA[Floor[h/3]].vertexIndex[h mod 3]]. Given e_A, the next half-edge of interest is found by $e_B = EA[e_A]$ and $e_C = 3Floor\left[\frac{e_B}{3}\right] + ((e_B + 2) \bmod 3)$. With this information, the edges and neighboring vertices can be queried rapidly.

The reason for requiring a boundary vertex to be tagged with an incoming crease is so traversal only needs to go in one direction, thus making the code simpler.

After all updates, change all vertices (new and old) to have a half-edge index of –1, which denotes no incoming matching half-edge. These will be filled in during the face splitting.

Splitting the Faces

Each old face will become four new faces, split as shown in Figure 5.4.5. Figure 5.4.5 shows the original triangle with edge and face orientations, and how this maps to new edge and face orientations, along with the order (0, 1, 2, 3) in which the new faces are stored.

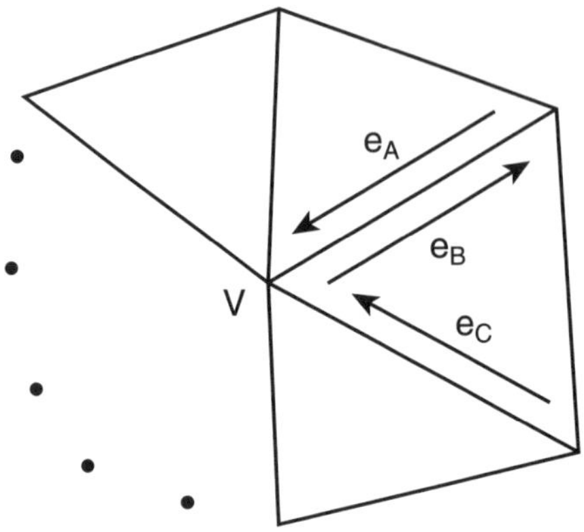

FIGURE 5.4.4 Vertex neighbors.

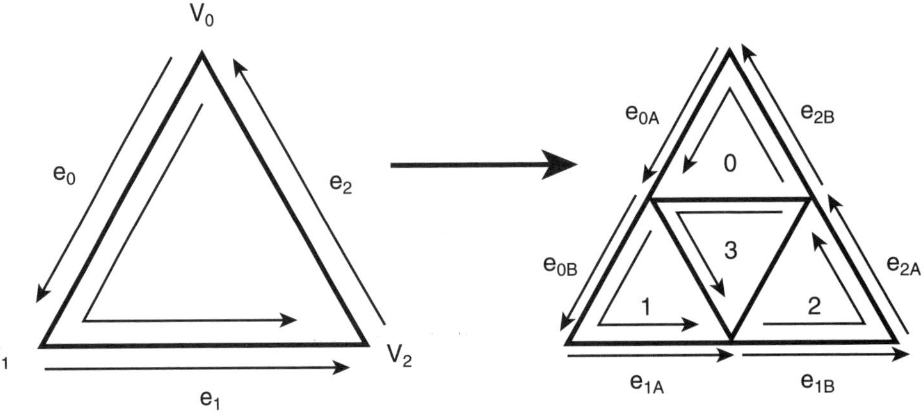

FIGURE 5.4.5 Face splitting.

1. Allocate an array NF for new faces of size 4F.
2. For each face f, with vertex indices v_0,v_1,v_2, look up the three edge vertex indices as j_0=NV[3f+V], j_1=NV[3f+1+V], and j_2=NV[3f+2+V].
3. Split the faces in the order shown in Figure 5.4.5. To NFm add faces $\{j_2,v_0,j_0\}$, $\{j_0,v_1,j_1\}$, $\{j_1,v_2,j_2\}$, $\{j_2,j_0,j_1\}$ at positions 4f, 4f+1, 4f+2, and 4f+3. This order is important! Each parent half-edge e_k is conceptually split into two descendent half-edges e_{kA}, followed by e_{kB}.
4. During the face split, tag each vertex (which still has a –1 tag from the previous steps) with an incident half-edge index ending on the vertex, giving preference to an incoming boundary.

Creating the New Half-Edge Information

This step could be merged with the split-face step, but is separated for clarity. A new list of half-edges is needed, correctly paired and weighted. Create a new half-edge array NE of size 12*F (three per new face, each old face becomes four new faces, producing 12).

Define a function `nIndex(j,type)` to compute new half-edge pair indices, where `j` is the old half-edge index, and type is 0=A or 1=B, denoting which part of the new half-edge is being matched. This function is as follows:

```
function nIndex( j, type)
  /* data table for index offsets - matches new half-edges */
  offsets[] = {3,1,6,4,0,7}
  /* original half-edge pair index */
  op = EV[ei]
  if (op == -1)
     return –1    /* boundary edge */
  /* new position of the split-edges for the face with pair op */
  bp = 12*Floor[op/3]
  /* return the matching new index */
  return bp + offsets[2*(op mod 3) + type]
```

The {3,1,6,4,0,7} array comes from matching half-edges to neighboring half-edges and is dependent on inserting items in arrays as indicated. For each original face index f, do the following:

1. Let b=12*f be the base half-edge index for a set of new half-edges, which will be stored in NE at the 12 indices b through b+11.
2. Store the 12 new half-edge pair indices at b,b+1,…,b+11 in the following order: $\{e_2B, e_0A, b+9, e_0B, e_1A, b+10, e_1B, e_2A, b+11, b+2, b+5, b+8\}$, where e_iT is `nIndex(ei,type)` with `ei` being the edge index. `type` = 0 for $T = A$ and `type` = 1 for $T = B$. These are grouped three per face in the order of faces created in Figure 5.4.5.
3. In the previous 12 entries, update the half-edge weights, with descendent half-edges getting the parent half-edge weights –1, clamped at 0. New half-edges with no parent get weight 0.

Updating Other Features

Per-vertex colors and per-vertex texture coordinates can be updated during the edge vertex creation and during the vertex re-positioning steps by simple interpolation. Per face per vertex colors and textures coordinates can be interpolated in the previous steps also, or can be done as a final step.

Displaced subdivision surface modifications can also be applied here by modifying the current vertex positions using a displacement map.

If the surface is about to be rendered, temporary normals can be computed using standard averaging techniques or by using the exact normals. Exact normals are more appropriate on a surface with vertices at limit points. Normals don't usually need to be computed until render time.

Final Step

The final step is to replace the arrays in the data structure with the new ones, and discard, store, or free the old ones as desired.

Finally, if the mesh is not going to be subdivided further, vertices can be pushed to limit positions, and true normals can be computed. In a rendering engine where the object is about to be drawn, this is an appropriate step.

Performance Issues

This section contains an overview of hardware rendering techniques for this algorithm.

Performance Enhancements

There are many places to improve the performance of the algorithm itself, especially if all the features are not needed. If all you need is a simple, smooth, closed mesh, you can remove all the special cases, making subdivision very fast.

Consider these implementation tips:

- Use tables for the $b(n)$ based weights, the tangent weights, normal weights, limit position weights, as well as any other items. A given mesh has a maximum valence vertex and all new vertices have valence at most, which makes using tables feasible.
- Make the half-edge array spaced out by four entries per face instead of three, allowing many divide by three and mod three operations to be replaced with shifts. This is the traditional space-for-speed tradeoff.
- Most interior vertices will have valence 6 and be smooth, so make that code fast, with special cases for the other situations. Most boundary vertices will be regular with valence 4. Most edges will be weight 0 and connect valence 6 smooth vertices.
- Tag edges and vertices for whether they are smooth or need special case code, allowing faster decisions, instead of determining vertex and edge types by walking neighbors. Once a vertex or edge type is determined it is easy to tag descendents.
- Pre-compute one level of subdivision to isolate the special case vertices, and then at runtime use a simpler version of the algorithm since there are fewer cases. This is a minor speed improvement, and is used for some hardware implementations.
- A pointer-based data structure like a half-edge structure can speed up subdivision at the cost of using more (and likely less contiguous) memory and making reading/writing harder. It is not clear which is really faster until you do some tests.

- Move per-vertex per-face parameters to per-vertex when possible. For example, creases require per-vertex per-face normals because neighboring faces require different normals along the crease, but once a face has been subdivided, the interior smooth new vertices can (and should) use per-vertex normals.
- Do multiple subdivision steps at once if desired, storing only the resulting triangles, and not updating all the connectivity info. This is detailed in the GPU section.
- Implement adaptive subdivision. Having fewer triangles to split after a few steps will speed things up a lot (but will break the simple algorithm operating on the data structure presented).

GPU Subdivision and Rendering

I dropped my original plan to present a state-of-the art GPU subdivision renderer once I reviewed the literature and learned how fast such articles become obsolete. Instead the focus here is putting in one place unified rules for a subdivision scheme. This will assist future hardware and software implementations, making this gem useful for a longer period.

For GPU rendering, the following is a chronological review of several papers, most of which can be found on the Internet. The papers are roughly evenly divided between Catmull-Clark methods, Loop methods, and universal methods:

- [Pulli96] presents an efficient Loop rendering method. It works by grouping triangles into pairs during a precomputation phase, effectively passing squares and a 1-neighborhood to a rendering function, which then renders the two triangles to an arbitrary subdivision depth.
- [Bischoff00] presents a very memory efficient and fast Loop rendering solution. The main concept is using multivariate forward differencing to generate triangles several subdivision levels deep without having to generate the intermediate levels. Rendering is done patch by patch.
- [Müller00] presents an extension to [Pulli96], and details a triangle paring algorithm and a sliding window method. Details are also presented for adaptive subdivision and crack prevention.
- [Leeson02] covers a few subdivision methods, and gives an overview of some rendering tips such as hierarchical backface culling.
- [Bolz02] implements Catmull-Clark subdivision, using a static array to hold the results. The methods are good for SIMD implementation.
- [Bolz03] implements Catmull-Clark subdivision on a GPU, with special attention given to avoiding cracks and pixel dropout caused through floating point errors.
- [Boubekeur05] presents a general method useful for rendering many types of subdivision surfaces. The main idea is to implement a "refinement pattern" on the GPU. Each triangle or other primitive passed to the GPU is then refined using the pattern.
- [Bunnell05] and [Shiue05] both implement Catmull-Clark subdivision on a GPU, with ample details.

Fast Subdivision Surface Rendering

A fast subdivision routine suited for a GPU is based on the following observation. For each triangle, upon subdividing, the new items (vertices, edges, faces, colors, and so on) are a *linear* combination of a 1-neighborhood of the triangle. Second subdivision items are then linear combinations of first subdivided items, hence a linear combination of the original neighborhood. This is exploited in various ways in the preceding references, and will be explained in a simple case.

A *patch* is single triangle T and the surrounding triangles (those that influence descendent triangles from the triangle T). See Figure 5.4.6 for a patch illustration—on the left, T is shaded and a 1-neighborhood is included. The right side shows T subdivided once, with a new 1-neighborhood (without all edge lines drawn).

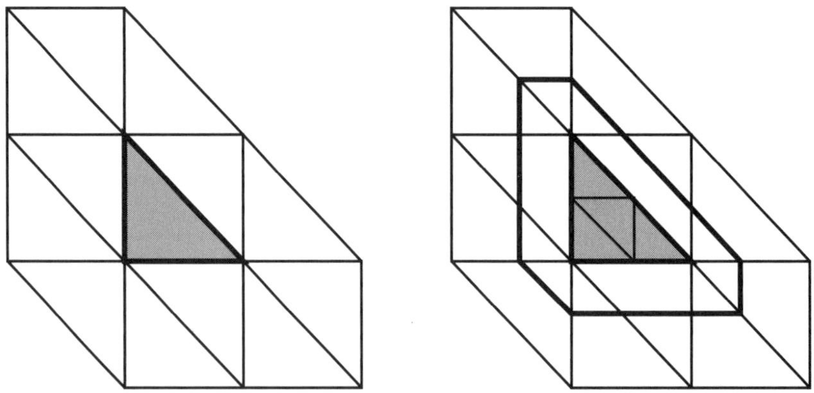

FIGURE 5.4.6 Subdividing a patch.

Assume for the moment there are no creases or boundaries (which can be added back in later). All the subdivision levels beneath T can be generated from linear combinations of existing vertices, so for each level of desired subdivision a mask can be computed in terms of neighboring vertices that outputs all the triangles descended from T, *without needing to compute intermediate levels.* Connectivity information does not need to be computed or stored either—all that is desired are the vertices of the faces, which naturally fall into a grid arrangement and are suitable for GPU rendering.

Mesh precomputation gathers needed data for each patch, stored per triangle. At render time, a subdivision level is selected, and each patch is passed to a GPU kernel. The GPU kernel then takes the low-resolution triangle, creates subdivided triangles in one pass, and renders the resulting triangles. In order to incorporate all the features from the gem, different kernels should be implemented. Alternatively preprocessing could simplify the numbers of cases, resulting in fewer GPU kernel variations.

A final point is this method might result in pixel dropout or cracks, because neighboring triangles may be evaluated using floating point operations in different orders. This is addressed in [Bolz03] for Catmull-Clark surfaces.

Conclusion

This article showed details of how to implement Loop subdivision surfaces with additional features and provides a starting point for the literature on subdivision surfaces. Geometry features such as creases, boundaries, semi-sharp items, and normals were covered, as well as surface tags like colors and textures. Future directions would be to add displaced subdivision surfaces and adaptive subdivision to the algorithm.

References

[Biermann06] Biermann, Henning, Levin, Adi, and Zorin, Denis. "Piecewise Smooth Subdivision Surfaces with Normal Control," Proceedings of the 27th Annual Conference on Computer Graphics and Interactive Techniques, pp. 113–120, 2006.

[Bischoff00] Bischoff, Stephan, Kobbelt, Leif, and Seidel, Hans-Peter. "Towards Hardware Implementation of Loop Subdivision," Eurographics SIGGRAPH Graphics Hardware Workshop, 2000 Proceedings.

[Bolz02] Bolz, Jeffery, and Schröder, Peter. "Rapid Evaluation of Catmull-Clark Subdivision Surfaces," Web3d 2002 Symposium, available online at http://www.multires.caltech.edu/pubs/fastsubd.pdf.

[Bolz03] Bolz, Jeffery, and Schröder, Peter. "Evaluation of Subdivision Surfaces on Programmable Graphics hardware," available online at http://www.multires.caltech.edu/pubs/GPUSubD.pdf.

[Boubekeur05] Boubekeur, Tamy, and Schlick, Christophe. "Generic Mesh Refinement on GPU," ACM SIGGRAPH/Eurographics Graphics Hardware, 2005.

[Bunnell05] Bunnell, Michael. "Adaptive Tesselation of Subdivision Surfaces with Displacement Mapping," *GPU Gems 2,* 2005, pp. 109–122.

[Catmull78] Catmull, E., and Clark, J. "Recursively Generated B-Spline Surfaces on Arbitrary Topological Meshes," *Computer Aided Design 10,* 6(1978), pp. 350–355.

[DeRose98] DeRose, Tony, Kass, Michael, and Truong, Tien. "Subdivision Surfaces in Character Animation," International Conference on Computer Graphics and Interactive Techniques, SIGGRAPH 1998, pp. 85–94.

[Hoppe94a] Hoppe, Huges. "Surface Reconstruction from Unorganized Points," PhD Thesis, University of Washington, 1994, http://research.microsoft.com/~hoppe/.

[Hoppe94b] Hoppe, Huges, DeRose, Tony, DuChamp, Tom, et. al. "Piecewise Smooth Surface Reconstruction," Computer Graphics, SIGGRAPH 94 Proceedings, 1994, pp. 295–302.

[Lee98] Lee, Aaron, Sweldens, Win, et. al. "MAPS: Multiresolution Adaptive Parameterization of Surfaces," Proceedings of SIGGRAPH 1998.

[Lee00] Lee, Aaron, Moreton, Henry, and Hoppe, Huges. "Displaced Subdivision Surfaces," SIGGRAPH 2000, pp. 95–94.

[Leeson02] Leeson, William. "Subdivision Surfaces for Character Animation," *Game Programming Gems 3,* 2003, pp. 372–383.

[Levin99] Levin, Adi. "Interpolating Nets of Curves by Smooth Subdivision Surfaces," Proceedings of SIGGRAPH 99, Computer Graphics Proceedings, Annual Conference Series, 1999.

[Loop87] Loop, Charles. "Smooth Subdivision Surfaces Based on Triangles," Master's Thesis, University of Utah, Dept. of Mathematics, 1987, available online at http://research.microsoft.com/~cloop/thesis.pdf.

[Müller00] Müeller, Kerstin, and Havemann, Sven. "Subdivision Surface Tesselation on the Fly Using a Versatile Mesh Data Structure," *Comput. Graph. Forum,* Vol. 19, No. 3, 2000, available online at http://citeseer.ist.psu.edu/.

[Pulli96] Pulli, Kari, and Segal, Mark. "Fast Rendering of Subdivision Surfaces," Proceedings of 7th Eurographics Workshop on Rendering, pp. 61–70, 282, Porto, Portugal, June 1996.

[Schweitzer96] Schweitzer, J.E. "Analysis and Application of Subdivision Surfaces," PhD Thesis, University of Washington, Seattle, 1996, available online at http://citeseer.ist.psu.edu/.

[Severn06] Severn, Aaron, and Samavati, Faramarz. "Fast Intersections for Subdivision Surfaces," In International Conference on Computational Science and its Applications, 2006.

[Shiue05] Shiue, L.J., Jones, Ian, and Peters, Jörg. "A Realtime GPU Subdivision Kernel," ACM SIGGRAPH Computer Graphics Proceedings, 2005.

[Stam99] Stam, Jos. "Evaluation of Loop Subdivision Surfaces," SIGGRAPH 99 Course Notes, 1999, http://www.dgp.toronto.edu/people/stam/.

[Vlachos00] Vlachos, Alex, Peters, Jörg, Boyd, Chas, and Mitchell, Jason. "Curved PN Triangles," ID3G 2001, http://www.cise.ufl.edu/research/SurfLab/papers/.

[Warren95] Warren, J. "Subdivision Methods for Geometric Design," Unpublished manuscript, November 1995.

[Wu04] Wu, Xiaobin, and Jörg Peters, "Interference Detection for Subdivision Surfaces," *EUROGRAPHICS,* 2004. Vol. 23, 3.

[Zorin96] Zorin, Denis, Schröder, Peter, and Sweldens, Wim. "Interpolating Subdivision for Meshes with Arbitrary Topology," Proceedings of SIGGRAPH 1996, ACM SIGGRAPH, 1996, pp. 189–192.

[Zorin97] Zorin, Denis, Peter Schröder, and Wim Sweldens. "Interactive Multi-Resolution Mesh Editing," CS-TR-97-06, Department of Computer Science, Caltech, January 1997, available online at http://graphics.stanford.edu/~dzorin/multires/meshed/.

[Zorin00] Zorin, Denis and Schröder, Peter. "Subdivision for Modeling and Animation," Technical Report, ACM SIGGRAPH Course Notes 2000, available online at http://mrl.nyu.edu/~dzorin/sig00course/.

5.5

Animating Relief Impostors Using Radial Basis Functions Textures

Vitor Fernando Pamplona,
Instituto de Informática: UFRGS
vfpamplona@inf.ufrgs.br

Manuel M. Oliveira,
Instituto de Informática: UFRGS
oliveira@inf.ufrgs.br

Luciana Porcher Nedel,
Instituto de Informática: UFRGS
nedel@inf.ufrgs.br

Games often use simplified representations of scene elements in order to achieve real-time performance. For instance, simple polygonal models extended with normal maps and carefully crafted textures are used to produce impressive scenarios [IdSoftware], while billboards and impostors replace distant objects. More recently, *relief textures* [Oliveira00] (textures containing depth and normal data on a per-texel basis) have been used to create impostors of detailed 3D objects using single quadrilaterals and preserving self-occlusions, self-shadowing, view-motion parallax, and object silhouettes [Policarpo06].

Relief rendering simulates the appearance of geometric surface detail by using the depth and surface normal information to shade individual fragments. This is obtained by performing ray-height-field intersection in 2D texture space, entirely on the GPU [Policarpo05]. The mapping of relief details to a polygonal model is done in the conventional way, by assigning a pair of texture coordinates to each vertex of the model.

Relief impostors are obtained by mapping relief textures containing multiple layers of depth, normals, and color data per texel onto quadrilaterals [Policarpo06].

Introduction

Textures in general can be used to represent both static and animated objects, and texture-based animation traditionally uses techniques such as image warping or a set of static textures cyclically mapped onto some polygons. Although conventional image warping techniques are limited to some planar deformations, the second approach requires as many textures as frames in the animation sequence, which, in turn, tends to need a significant amount of artwork.

This gem describes a new technique for animating relief impostors based on a single multilayer relief texture using radial basis functions (RBF). The technique preserves the relief-impostor properties, allowing the viewer to observe changes in occlusion and parallax during the animation. This is illustrated in Figure 5.5.1, which shows three frames of a dog walking animation sequence created from a dog relief impostor. Note the changes in the positions of the dog's legs.

FIGURE 5.5.1 Three frames of a dog walking animation created by warping a relief impostor. Note the changes in the positions of the legs.

In order to produce these animations, during a pre-processing step, the user specifies a set of control points over the texture of the relief impostor. Moving the control points in 2D warps the texture, thus bringing the represented objects into new poses. Such poses are the key poses to be interpolated during the animation. Note that these poses are only implicitly represented by the control points and by a single texture. This situation is illustrated in Figure 5.5.2.

As part of the pre-processing, the algorithm also interpolates the positions of these control points for the desired number of frames in the animation and, for each of them, solves a linear system to obtain a set of RBF coefficients. The control points and their corresponding RBF coefficients define a series of warping functions that produce the actual animation. For efficiency reasons, these control points and coefficients are stored in a texture (usually 16×16 or 32×32 texels). At runtime, this data is used to recreate the animation on the GPU.

The proposed technique can be used to animate essentially any kind of texture-based representations, such as relief textures [Oliveira00], billboards with normal mapping, and displacement maps [Cook84]. Note that it is also possible to replace the RBFs with any other method that describes the desired transformation and that can be evaluated on a GPU. The proposed technique produces real-time realistic animations of live and moving objects undergoing repetitive motions.

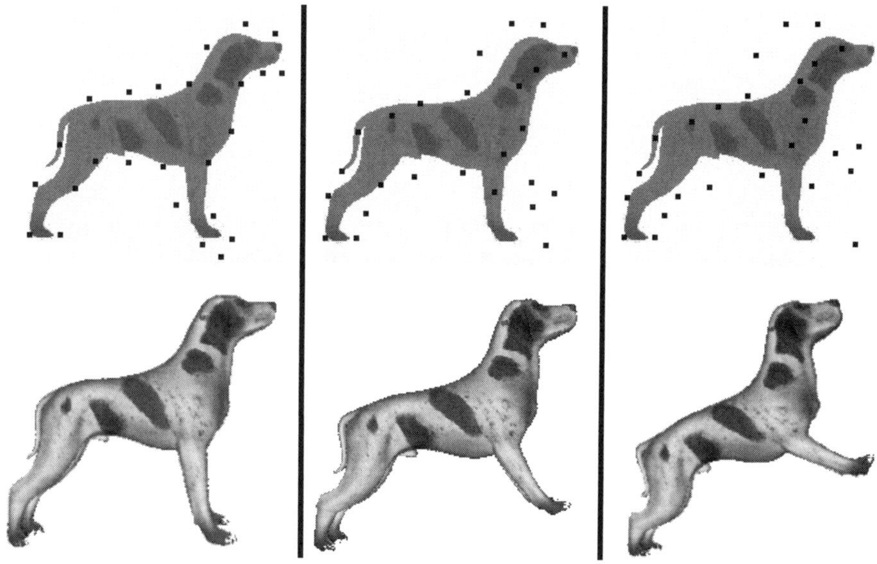

FIGURE 5.5.2 Control points (dark dots) placed over the texture of the relief impostor (top row) warp the texture, changing the pose of the rendered dog (bottom row). All poses are implicitly represented by a single texture and the sets of control points.

Image Warping

Warping-based texture animation evaluates a function over the source image in order to compute each frame of the sequence. Given a source image, a warping function produces an output image by computing new coordinates for each source pixel. Image warping then comprises two steps:

- A mapping stage that associates source and target pixels' coordinates.
- A re-sampling stage.

The mapping is usually computed using a global analytic function built from a set of correspondences involving control points in the source and the target images. Many techniques, such as triangulation based, inverse-distance weighted interpolation, radial basis functions, and locally bounded radial basis functions, are available to generate the mapping function from a set of corresponding points [Ruprecht95].

Radial Basis Functions

Radial basis function (RBFs) methods are a mathematical way to produce multivariate approximation and one of the most popular choices when interpolating scattered data [Buhmann03]. In computer graphics, RBFs have been used for surface reconstruction from point clouds [Carr01], for image warping [Ruprecht95], and for animation [Noh00]. An RBF is defined in Equation 5.5.1:

$$f(x) = \sum_{i=1}^{N} \lambda_i \phi(\|x - c_i\|) \tag{5.5.1}$$

Here, N is the number of centers, ϕ is a basis function, λ_i is the i-th coefficient for the RBF representation, c_i is the i-th center, and x is a point for which the function will be evaluated. In the case of image warping, c_i represents the pixel coordinates of the control points, and x represents the pixel coordinates of any pixel in the image. In this case, a good choice of ϕ is the multiquadrics, originally proposed by Hardy [Hardy71]:

$$\phi(d_i) = \sqrt{r^2 + d_i^2} \tag{5.5.2}$$

where $d_i = \|x - c_i\|$ and r is a positive arbitrary characteristic radius that can be a constant or a different value per control point. In Equation 5.5.2, r represents the smoothness of the interpolation and is critical for good image warping results. In our experiments, we used $r = 0.5$, as suggested in [Ruprecht95].

The warping problem can be modeled using the linear system shown in Equation 5.5.3, where ϕ_{ij} is the distance between control points c_i and c_j expressed in pixel coordinates, f_{kx} and f_{ky} are, respectively, the x and y image coordinates of control point c_k. λ_{kx} and λ_{ky} are the RBF coefficients that you want to solve for. Once such coefficients have been obtained, you can use RBFs as warping functions.

$$\begin{bmatrix} \phi_{11} & \phi_{12} & \phi_{13} & \cdots & \phi_{1m} \\ \phi_{21} & \phi_{22} & \phi_{23} & \cdots & \phi_{2m} \\ \phi_{31} & \phi_{32} & \phi_{33} & \cdots & \phi_{3m} \\ \cdots & \cdots & \cdots & \cdots & \cdots \\ \phi_{n1} & \phi_{n2} & \phi_{n3} & \cdots & \phi_{nm} \end{bmatrix} \begin{bmatrix} \lambda_{1x} & \lambda_{1y} \\ \lambda_{2x} & \lambda_{2y} \\ \lambda_{3x} & \lambda_{3y} \\ \cdots & \cdots \\ \lambda_{nx} & \lambda_{ny} \end{bmatrix} = \begin{bmatrix} f_{1x} & f_{1y} \\ f_{2x} & f_{2y} \\ f_{3x} & f_{3y} \\ \cdots & \cdots \\ f_{nx} & f_{ny} \end{bmatrix} \tag{5.5.3}$$

Interpolating the Warping Functions

Given two sets of control points S_t and S_{t+k} specified by the user for two key poses at times t and $(t+k)$, respectively, the RBF coefficients for the intermediate poses are obtained by interpolating the coordinates of the corresponding pairs of control points in S_t and S_{t+k}, and solving Equation 5.5.3 for the interpolated λs. To achieve some smooth interpolation, we used a cubic Hermite spline, where the end points of the tangents are given by the vector $0.5(S_t + S_{t+k})$. This is illustrated in Figure 5.5.3. When using normal maps, the same warping approach has to be applied to the normal map as well. Thus, both textures must be evaluated using the same RBF for each frame.

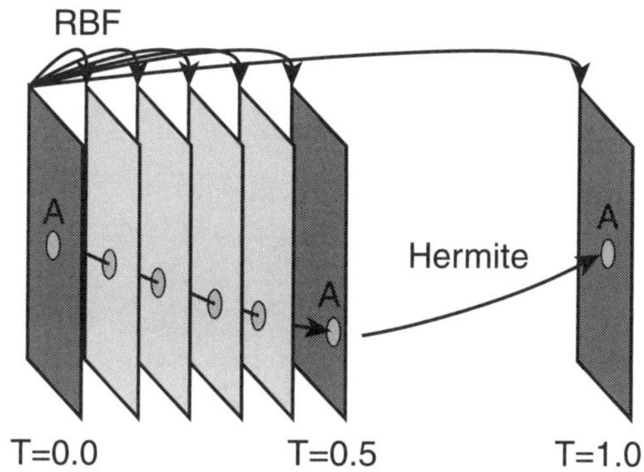

FIGURE 5.5.3 The light gray frames between time 0.0 and 0.5 used a cubic Hermite spline to interpolate the control point.

Evaluating the Warping Function Using Shaders

Modern GPUs can execute programs called *shaders*. As the warping function needs to be executed for each texel, it is clear that the RBF should be evaluated on a fragment shader. But for this, it is necessary to invert the warping functions because, given a fragment f, you must be able to obtain the texture coordinates that were mapped to f under the warping transformation. Fortunately, inverting the warping function using Equation 5.5.3 only requires two steps:

- Compute ϕ_{ij} using the coordinates of the control points of the current (desired) pose.
- Use the x and y coordinates of the unmodified (before moving) control points as f_{kx} and f_{ky}.

For the example shown in Figure 5.5.2, the RBF coefficients used for rendering the image in the bottom center were computed as follows: ϕ_{ij} are the distances between the control points c_i and c_j shown in the top center, whereas f_{kx} and f_{ky} are the coordinates of the k-th control point shown in the top left. Note that the re-sampling needed as the second step of an image warping operation is provided for free by the texture filtering hardware.

As previously mentioned, you store the RBF data (coordinates of the control points and lambda values) into a texture for access by the shader during runtime. The j-th row of this a texture represents the j-th frame of the animation. The RGBA channels of the i-th texel store the (x,y) coordinates as well as the λ_{ix} and λ_{iy} coefficients of c_i, respectively (see Figure 5.5.4). We used a float32 non-normalized texture, because the values of λ may not be in [0,1] range.

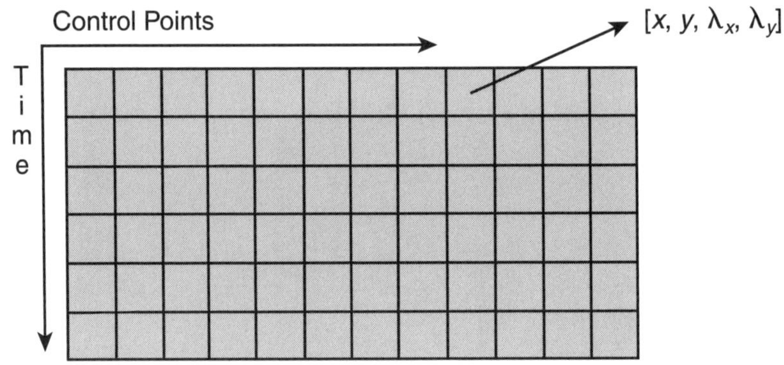

FIGURE 5.5.4 The animation data is stored in single texture. Each row of the texture represents a frame of the animation. Along a row, the i-th texel stores the (x,y) coordinates of the control point c_i as well as its λ_{ix} and λ_{iy} coefficients.

The shader for evaluating the RBF-based warping function is shown next. It maps texture coordinates of the current fragment (obtained after rendering a texture-mapped quadrilateral) into texture coordinates on the original texture.

Listing 5.5.1 Evaluating the RBF-Based Warping Function

```
// Computes the Phi function.
float multiquadric(float r, float h) {
    return sqrt(r*r+h*h);
}

// Evaluates the RBF for texCoord with a pre-defined number
// of control points, the actual time and smoothness.
float2 evaluateRBF(float2 i_texCoord, float points, float keyTime,
              float smoothness, samplerRECT rbfTexture) {
    float2 newTexCoord;
    newTexCoord.xy = float2(0.0, 0.0);
    for (int i=0; i<points; i++) {
        float2 access = float2(i, keyTime);
        float4 rbf = texRECT(rbfTexture, access);
```

```
            float distance = sqrt((pow(rbf.x - i_texCoord.x,2))
                             + (pow(rbf.y - i_texCoord.y,2)));
            float temp = multiquadric(distance, smoothness);

            newTexCoord.xy += temp * rbf.zw;
        }

        return newTexCoord;
    }
```

Animating Relief Maps

You can produce RBF-based animations of relief maps by adding a couple of extra lines to a relief mapping pixel shader [Policarpo05]. Just before the call to the linear search, you should clamp the original texture coordinates to the [0,1] range. This is required if the entire relief map covers only part of the polygon. In this case, the texture coordinates for some fragments will be out of the [0,1] range needed for the RBF evaluation. This clamping does not hurt the animation because there is no depth or normal information outside the region not covered by the texture. You then need to add the code in Listing 5.5.2 to a relief mapping shader, immediately before calling the linear search.

Listing 5.5.2 Actions Required for Relief Warping That Need to Be Executed Before Calling the Linear Search

```
// s is the texture coordinate used in the relief mapping shader
float2 sZeroOne = clamp (s.xy, 0.0, 1.0);

  // Evaluating RBFs
  float2 sRBFEval = evaluateRBF(sZeroOne.xy, points, keyTime,
                                smoothness, rbfTexture);
  // Compensating the clamp.
  s.xy += sRBFEval - sZeroOne;

  ... // Call linear search.
```

Animating Relief Impostors

Relief impostors [Policarpo06] are rendered using multilayer relief representations. Figure 5.5.5 (right) shows a dog impostor modeled as a quad-layer relief texture, whose depth values are shown on the left. For the case of relief impostors, the warping strategy described earlier will cause all layers to be subject to the same warping function and, consequently, undergo the same motion. Thus, although a single warping function can be used to animate a running dog, it would not produce a convincing dog motion. In this case, for instance, the two front legs would always move together instead of moving in opposite directions.

Thus, for multilayer relief representations, you might want to animate each individual layer independently. A walking dog motion is illustrated in Figure 5.5.1. In this example, however, the animation was created using a single warping function by exploiting the symmetry of the walking motion of bipeds and quadrupeds—for each frame *f* at time *t*, the first two layers were rendered using time *t*, while the last two layers were rendered using time (1–*t*). Thus, while the right front (back) leg is moving forward, the left front (back) leg is moving backward. *t* is used in the evaluation of the function `evaluateRBF` as the parameter `keyTime` in the code fragment shown in Listing 5.5.2.

In this case, the linear and binary search calls in Listing 5.5.3 receive two new parameters: `sFront` and `sBack`. These parameters represent the warped texture coordinates for the front and back layers, respectively. These coordinates are used to sample both the depth and normal maps from different layers. This is illustrated in Listing 5.5.4 for the case of the x-component of the normal map, where the retrieved values are combined in a single RGBA variable (`normal_x`). (The x and y components of the normal map are stored in separate textures, `normal_map_x` and `normal_map_y`, respectively. The z component is computed on the fly from the other two components [Policarpo06].)

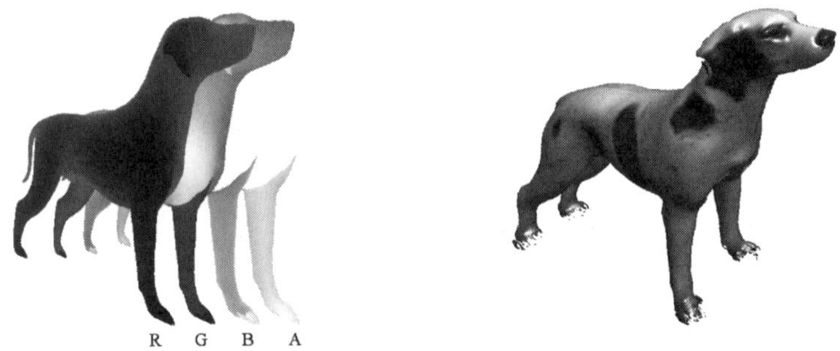

FIGURE 5.5.5 A dog impostor modeled as a quad-layer relief texture. The depth values of the progressing layers are stored in the R, G, B, and A channels, respectively (left). A view of the rendered dog impostor is shown on the right. See Color Plate 8 for a color version of this image.

Listing 5.5.3 Using a Single Warping Function to Produce the Walking Motion Shown in Figure 5.5.1

```
float2 sZeroOne = clamp (s.xy, 0.0, 1.0);

  sFront = evaluateRBF(sZeroOne, points, keyTime,
                       smoothness, rbfTexture);
  sFront = s.xy + (sFront - sZeroOne);

  int keyTimeBack = (int)(keyTime+maxKeyTime/2) % (int)maxKeyTime;
```

```
sBack   = evaluateRBF(sZeroOne.xy, points, keyTimeBack,
                      smoothness, rbfTexture);
sBack   = s.xy + (sBack - sZeroOne);

... // Call the linear search with sBack and sFront.
```

Listing 5.5.4 Sampling the Multilayer x-Component of the Normal at Two Positions, Using Texture Coordinates *sFront* and *sBack*

```
float4 normal_x;
normal_x.xy=tex2D(normal_map_x,sFront.xy).xy;
normal_x.zw=tex2D(normal_map_x,sBack.xy).zw;
```

A similar operation is performed for the y-component of the normal.

The following code fragment uses `sFront` and `sBack` to sample the color texture.

Listing 5.5.5 Sampling the Color Texture Using Texture Coordinates *sFront* and *sBack* and Checking the Relative Position of the Viewing Ray with Respect to Several Layers

```
// get color at intersection
float4 c;
float4 cFront = tex2D(texture,sFront.xy);
float4 cBack  = tex2D(texture,sBack.xy);

float4 z=abs(s.z-q); // q is the quad-depth value joined.
float zt=z.x;
c = cFront;           // hits the first layer.
if (z.y<zt) c=cFront; // hits the second layer.
if (z.z<zt) c=cBack;  // hits the third layer.
if (z.w<zt) c=cBack;  // hits the fourth layer.
```

Results

We have implemented the described algorithms using C++ and Cg and used them to animate several textures and relief impostors. In all our experiments, the textures had 400 × 400 texels. On a 2.21GHz PC with 2.0GB of memory and an NVIDIA GeForce 8800 GTX with 768MB, our implementation achieves 3,000fps, 710fps, and 500fps, when rendering animations of textures with normal maps, relief maps, and relief impostors, respectively.

Figure 5.5.6 depicts the control points (small dark dots) used to define the walking dog animation shown in Figure 5.5.1. The user defined a set of control points positioned on top of the dog image (left). Some of these points were then interactively moved defining the configurations shown in Figure 5.5.6 (center) and (right). As the user moves a control point, the underlying texture is automatically warped, providing immediate visual feedback that allows the user to plan and define the animation (see Figure 5.5.2).

FIGURE 5.5.6 Control points (dark dots) used to define the RBF-based warping functions used to create the dog walking animation illustrated in Figure 5.5.1. Besides these 12 control points, four extra control points were positioned at the corners of the texture to anchor it.

Figure 5.5.7 shows a few frames of a horse animation. On the left is the original relief impostor. The images to its right show different poses, seen from the same viewpoint, obtained with RBF-based warping functions. The accompanying video on the CD-ROM shows these animations.

ON THE CD

FIGURE 5.5.7 Horse animation. The image on the left shows a view of the original relief impostor. The three images to its right show frames from an animation seen from the same viewpoint. Note the changes on the horse's body and tail. A total of 27 control points were used to produce this animation, including 4 anchors at the corners of the texture.

Conclusion

This gem presented a technique for animating relief impostors in real-time using RBF-based warping functions. This approach produces realistic animations of live and moving objects undergoing repetitive motions. Given its generality, it can be used to animate essentially any kind of texture representation. During a pre-processing stage, the user specifies a set of control points, which are the centers for an RBF representation. By moving such control points around in 2D, the user obtains immediate feedback on the resulting animation. Once the key deformations have been specified, the system interpolates the control points for intermediate frames and solves the linear system defined by Equation 5.5.3 to find a set of RBF coefficients (λs), which are saved into a texture with the 2D coordinates of the control points. The stored information is then read during runtime by a shader that performs the actual animation via texture resampling.

Our technique can be used to define separate warping functions to individual layers of a relief texture. As a result, it supports the definition of complex animations using a simple interface, thus reducing the amount of time and artwork usually associated with texture animation. As any other technique, this approach has some limitations: large deformations tend to distort the texture too much, leading to poor results. Also, the use of the clamping function shown in Listings 5.5.2 and 5.5.3 may introduce some artifacts when the polygon used to render the impostor is seen at a grazing angle. Under such viewing configurations, these artifacts can be avoided by calling the function `evaluateRBF` at each step of both the linear and binary searches, at the cost of some performance penalty.

ON THE CD

The accompanying CD-ROM contains a video and a demo (including source code and shaders) for animating normal maps and multi-layer relief maps.

Acknowledgements

We would like to thank NVIDIA for donating the GeForce 8800 GTX video card used in this work.

References

[Buhmann03] Buhmann, Martin. *Radial Basis Functions,* Cambridge University Press, 2003.

[Carr01] Carr, Jonathan et al. "Reconstruction and Representation of 3D Objects with Radial Basis Functions," Proceedings of SIGGRAPH 2001, ACM Press, New York, NY, pp. 67–76.

[Cook84] Cook, Robert L. "Shade Trees," In *Computer Graphics* (SIGGRAPH 84) 18(3), pp. 223–231, 1984.

[Donnelly05] Donnelly, William. "Per-Pixel Displacement Mapping with Distance Functions," *GPU Gems 2,* 2005.

[Hardy71] Hardy, Roland L. "Multiquadric Equations of Topography and Other Irregular Surfaces," *J. Geophys. Res.,* 1971, Vol. 73, pp. 1905–1915.

[IdSoftware] Id Software. DOOM 3, available online at http://www.idsoftware.com/games/doom/doom3/.

[Litwinowicz94] Litwinowicz, Peter, and Williams, Lance. "Animating Images with Drawings," Proceedings of the 21st Annual Conference on Computer Graphics and Interactive Techniques SIGGRAPH, 1994, ACM Press, New York, NY, pp. 409–412.

[Noh00] Noh, Jun-yong, et al. "Animated Deformations with Radial Basis Functions," Proceedings of the ACM Symposium on Virtual Reality Software and Technology, Seoul, Korea, October 22–25, 2000, VRST '00. ACM Press, New York, NY, pp. 166–174.

[Oliveira00] Oliveira, Manuel M., Bishop, Gary, and McAllister, David. "Relief Texture Mapping," Proceedings of SIGGRAPH 2000, New Orleans, LA, July 23–28, 2000, pp. 359–368.

[Policarpo05] Policarpo, Fabio, Oliveira, Manuel M., and Comba, João. "Real-Time Relief Mapping on Arbitrary Polygonal Surfaces," ACM SIGGRAPH, 2005, Symposium on Interactive 3D Graphics and Games, Washington, DC, April 3–6, 2005, pp. 155–162.

[Policarpo06] Policarpo, Fabio, and Oliveira, Manuel M. "Relief Mapping of Non-Height-Field Surface Details," ACM SIGGRAPH 2006 Symposium on Interactive 3D Graphics and Games, Redwood City, CA, March 14–17, 2006, pp. 55–62.

[Policarpo06b] Policarpo, Fabio, and Oliveira, Manuel M. "Rendering Surface Details in Games with Relief Mapping Using a Minimally Invasive Approach," In Wolfgang Engel (Ed.), *SHADER X4: Lighting & Rendering.* Charles River Media, Inc., Hingham, Massachusetts, 2006, pp. 109–119.

[Ruprecht95] Ruprecht, Detlef, and Müller, Heinrich. "Image Warping with Scattered Data Interpolation," IEEE Computer Graphics and Applications, Vol. 15, No. 2, 1995, pp. 37–43.

5.6

Clipmapping on SM1.1 and Higher

Ben Garney

GarageGames

Clipmaps are a fast and robust technique for texturing terrains. This gem provides a brief introduction to the theory behind clipmaps, and discusses their implementation on Shader Model 2.0 hardware. Finally, it explores some advanced topics, such as support on fixed function, SM1.x, and SM3.0+ hardware, as well as different sources for image data.

Basic Concepts of Clipmaps

When rendering to a 1024 × 768, 32bpp display, only 786,432 pieces of color information are necessary at any given moment to give a fully detailed, unique view. This is exactly 3MB of data. If you want to run at 60Hz, you need to transfer only 180MB/sec to the display, which is well within the capabilities of most game platforms.

Suppose you draw a model on-screen. Regardless of how much detail its texture might contain, you cannot display more texels than the screen has pixels. For the case of a small object, like a character or power-up, you can discard more detailed mip levels of the texture (see [Forsyth07]). However, for environments where the camera spends most of its time looking only at a small portion of the mesh, dropping mip levels is impractical. If any part of the model requires high detail, you need all or most of the mips, and with a terrain or other environment, you'll almost always need high detail on some part.

What can be done to deal with terrain textures efficiently? Only load partial mipmaps! Ideally, you would only load texels onto the GPU that are needed for the current frame—meaning that you could have an arbitrarily detailed terrain that fits in only 3MB of VRAM. Unfortunately, GPU manufacturers haven't built their hardware to support this kind of operation.

Clipmaps are a generalization of mipmapping that allow you to only load subsections of each mip level. If a texel that is sampled isn't loaded, lower-resolution data that's already loaded is used instead. This means you can upload a relatively small dataset, get efficient rendering, and degrade gracefully if the viewpoint manages to outrun your texture paging. Although clipmaps aren't directly supported by current graphics hardware, you can emulate them efficiently using shaders.

Implementation of Clipmaps

Building on the concept of mipmapping, SGI developed clipmapping for the purpose of virtualizing a single large texture [Tanner96].

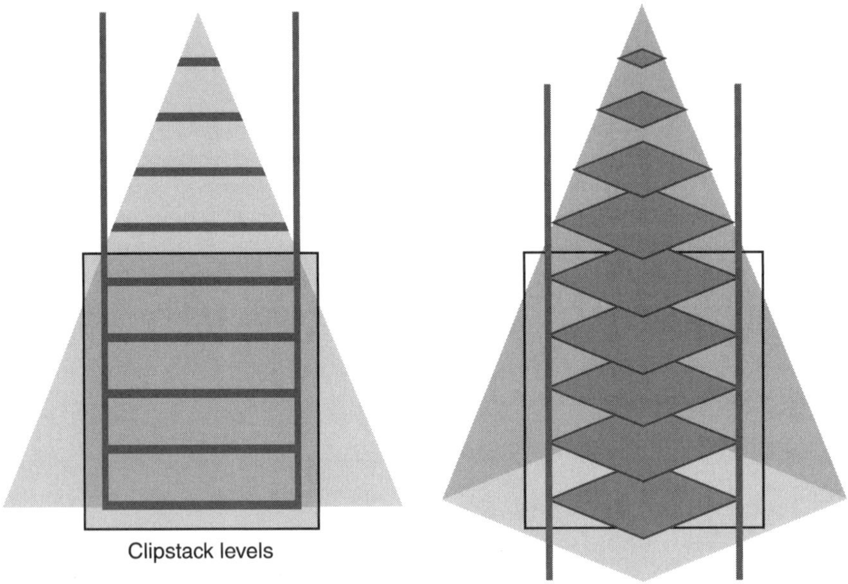

FIGURE 5.6.1 Image of a clipped mipmap stack.

Recall that a mipmap is used to reduce aliasing and localize memory accesses. Conceptually, when a given pixel of a triangle is rendered, the pixel's bounds are projected into texture space, and based on its size, a mipmap is selected and from it a point is sampled. The result of this is that as a triangle becomes more distant it selects from less detailed mip levels and the memory accesses are less scattered than they would otherwise be.

Clipmaps take the same basic idea, but the more detailed levels of the mip pyramid are clipped to limit memory usage. This means that a 32KB px texture, which would normally have 15 mip levels and consume half a gig of memory, if put into a clipmap with a maximum level size of 512px, would only use six 512px textures' worth of memory, plus a "cap" 512px texture with a full mip chain. The memory footprint for this is only 7.3MB.

In SGI's InfiniteReality2 hardware platform, the hardware, when accessing mip levels, checked to see if the cached clipmap region in memory covered the area of the mip level it wanted to read from. If so, it would sample as normal. If not, it would bump up to the next less detailed mip level and try again, with the result that if detailed data was not available for an area, less detailed data would be used instead.

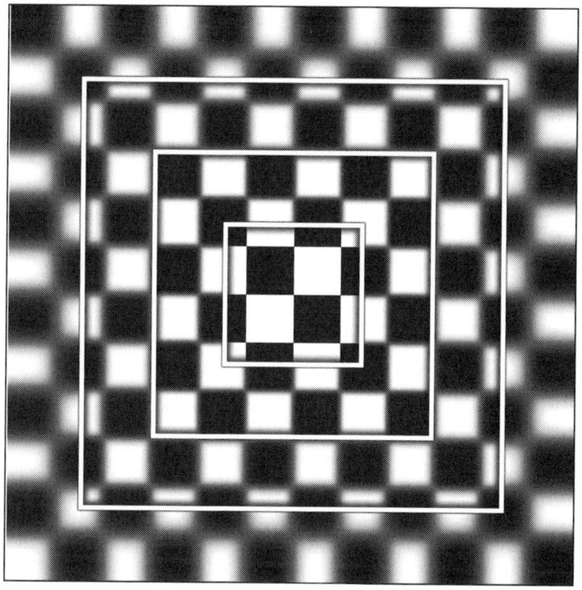

FIGURE 5.6.2 Updating clipmaps affect which areas are contained in each detail level.

On the CPU, SGI's Performer scenegraph was responsible for adjusting the data in each layer of the clipmap by purging old data and uploading new data from a database on disk.

Advantages of Clipmaps

Clipmaps bring several major benefits compared to the other strategies discussed, as follows:

- They always have smooth transitions between LOD levels, and no specific LOD level is required to render geometry—worst case, things will just be a bit blurry.
- They have a fixed memory cost; no dynamic allocation of GPU resources is needed either during rendering or updating. This is important as most GPU drivers don't deal well with frequent allocations and deallocations.
- They are view independent provided you place the focal point for detail at the camera position; data is available with a smooth fall-off in all directions, meaning that spinning in place has no effect on performance.
- Clipmaps are straightforward to implement on any hardware with programmable shaders. Even on fixed-function hardware, it's possible to emulate them. Implementing update region determination is a bit tricky, but the system as a whole is straightforward to work with, with no complex caching logic.

- They have well-defined relationships between image quality and resources allocated to the clipmap, so it's easy to tune the visual experience based on user preference.
- They can receive data from many sources. Unique data from files, CPU synthesis of data, or GPU synthesis are all supported.
- Finally, they have excellent update characteristics, because the quantum of update is variable. The minimal amount of update required is usually quite small and bounded—just the new texels that need to be uploaded for a single clipmap level, which is often only a few thousand. The worst case is a full upload of the whole clipmap, which is only a dozen megabytes or so.

Drawbacks of Clipmaps

The major drawback of clipmapping is that it cannot deal with varying detail levels. Detail simply falls off linearly in texture space from the focal point. This makes them unsuitable for dealing with a complex interior environment, where multiple regions in texture space may need to be high detail (for instance, the floor and walls may have different UV regions that they use). If you can require mid-range SM2 or higher, there are some good options to check out, like [Lefebvre04].

The full un-optimized shader for clipmapping is also expensive and requires at least SM2. However, with some geometry conditioning, this can be optimized significantly, as you'll read later on. It might also be possible to use the gradient operators in SM3 and higher to write a more efficient clipmapping shader.

Details of Clipmaps

The following sections explain and describe the details related to clipmaps, including clipstack size, the focus point, and methods for updating clipmaps.

Clipstack Size

The size of the textures in the clipmap stack is the main variable when working with clipmaps, and it can be controlled quite simply—it should be the power of 2 nearest to the display resolution. For higher-quality results, bias up, and for lower quality, bias down. The reason for this goes back to the original discussion of the amount of texel data needed for an optimal renderer; the most demanding situation possible, texture-wise, is for the view to be looking straight on at a clipmapped surface, zoomed in as much as possible without magnification of the original texture. In this case, a texture equal in size to the screen would be needed to give the illusion of full detail.

The Focus Point

Selecting the *focus point,* which is the location in UV space of the clipmap where detail should be highest, is another open question when working with clipmaps. There are many possible heuristics, but the one that gives the most consistent results is to simply project down from the camera position onto the plane of the clipmapped geometry and use those coordinates as the new focal point.

Methods for Updating

There are three broad paths for getting data into the style of clipmap discussed here. They all do roughly the same thing: updated regions are identified by the clipmap code and data is supplied to fill them.

First, you can blast data into them from files on the disk. In this case, once the data is in system memory, you only need to directly upload it to the GPU. Second, you can synthesize data on the CPU and upload it. I found this to be inferior to the next method, but if you have an existing fast synthesis routine, it might be useful. Finally, you can perform synthesis on GPU by doing render to texture operations. This requires allocating the clipstack textures as render targets to begin with, but otherwise operation is identical to the other modes.

Implementing Clipmaps

The following sections cover the details related to implementing your clipmaps.

The SM2.0 Path

For simplicity's sake, this gem discusses only the SM2.0 clipmap path in-depth. Once you have the 2.0 path done, the majority of work is done, so getting the SM1.x and SM3.0+ paths going is straightforward.

ON THE CD

This is the core pixel shader code that drives the clipmap effect in the demo app on the CD-ROM:

```
PS_OUTPUT Output;

// The base level can always be sampled as there's nothing behind
// it... so save some math.
float3 colAccum = tex2D(clipSamplers[0], In.TextureUV[0]);

// Grab the rest, fading based on distance from each layer's center.
for(int i=1; i<CLIP_LAYER_COUNT; i++)
{
   float fade = smoothstep(0.4, 0.5, distance(In.TextureUV[i],
            g_clipLayerAndCenter[i].xy));
   float4 curColor = tex2D(clipSamplers[i], In.TextureUV[i]);
   colAccum = lerp(curColor, colAccum, fade);
}

// Store accumulated result and return.
Output.RGBColor = float4(colAccum,1);
```

In the SM2.0 path, you do all the clipmap level selection calculations per-pixel. At each pixel, you must determine the UV coordinate and, using information passed via uniform shader constants, produce a texture coordinate for each clipstack entry by scaling and offsetting the original UVs. You also generate a "fade" value for each clipstack entry based on distance in texture space from its focal point. Then, using the fade values as coefficients, you *lerp* the colors from each clipstack entry in order from least to most detailed.

Toroidal Updates and the Rectangle Clipper

A major optimization in the clipmap scheme is to treat the clipstack textures as toroidal buffers. This means that shifting the stack is done as efficiently as possible—you only do work to upload new data. However, determining the regions that need to be updated is a little tricky.

Consider a level of the clipstack. At any given moment, there's a rectangle of data that's contained in the clipstack's texture. Let's call this rectangle *currentRect*. It's the currently loaded subset of the full set of data available at some miplevel of the virtualized texture. As you move the focus point, this rectangle shifts around to center on it.

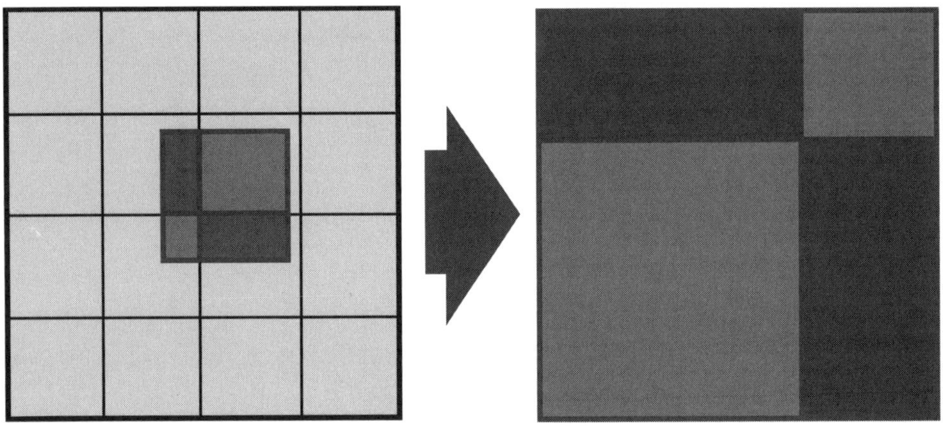

FIGURE 5.6.3 The size of the clipstack texture is only 1/16th the size of the full source level.

Suppose you're on the third level of the clipmap from the top. This means that the size of the clipstack texture is only 1/16th the size of the full source level. The situation is illustrated in Figure 5.6.3. The grid shows how the texture is mapped to the geometry. You scale unit UV coordinates by four, so the texture is repeated four times in each direction. However, the *currentRect* isn't aligned to this grid; it's somewhere in the middle. By uploading the texture data in the pattern shown to the right, you end up with every piece of data where you want it on the geometry.

You then clip the *currentRect* against this grid, which is spaced equal to the size of the clipstack textures. You'll always end up with different pieces (in the common case, four, but if you're aligned to the grid in various ways, it can be less). This gives you the basic idea of what's going on and how uploaded data has to map into the texture to be displayed properly. ClipMap::fillWithTextureData implements this to refill the clipstack entirely.

What about updating? When you move the rectangle, you tend to get something that looks like Figure 5.6.4.

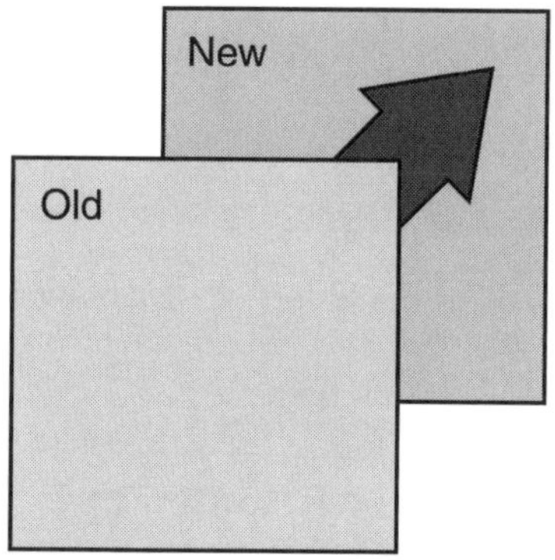

FIGURE 5.6.4 The inverted L-shaped region is what needs to be uploaded during an update.

The inverted L-shaped region is what you need to upload. So when you're updating what *currentRect* contains, you determine what this update region is, and then clip and wrap it just as you did above with the *currentRect* itself, ending up with rectangular regions in the texture where data is to be uploaded. This allows very efficient clipmap updates—moving the focus point one pixel means a rectangle only one pixel wide would be uploaded. See ClipMap::recent for the implementation of this.

Basic CPU Synthesis

A helpful aid in debugging is a simple checkerboard synthesizer. A 1px checkerboard makes it easy to spot any sampling issues or other problems. Applying a gradient makes it simple to spot any incorrect updates—the colors won't match.

Look in ClipMap::uploadToTexture for an example of this. The #if block can be toggled to 1 to enable a simple CPU synthesis that chooses a random color for each clipmap upload. This is useful for seeing how updates happen and what regions they cover.

Basic CPU Upload

By default, the example app loads data into the clipmap from a large image stored in system memory. (This allows you to avoid the complexity of a paged loader.) This is a straightforward bitblt operation.

Advanced Clipmapping

The following sections cover some advanced issues related to clipmaps, including adding background paging, budgeting updates for better performance, optimizing fill-rate, and more.

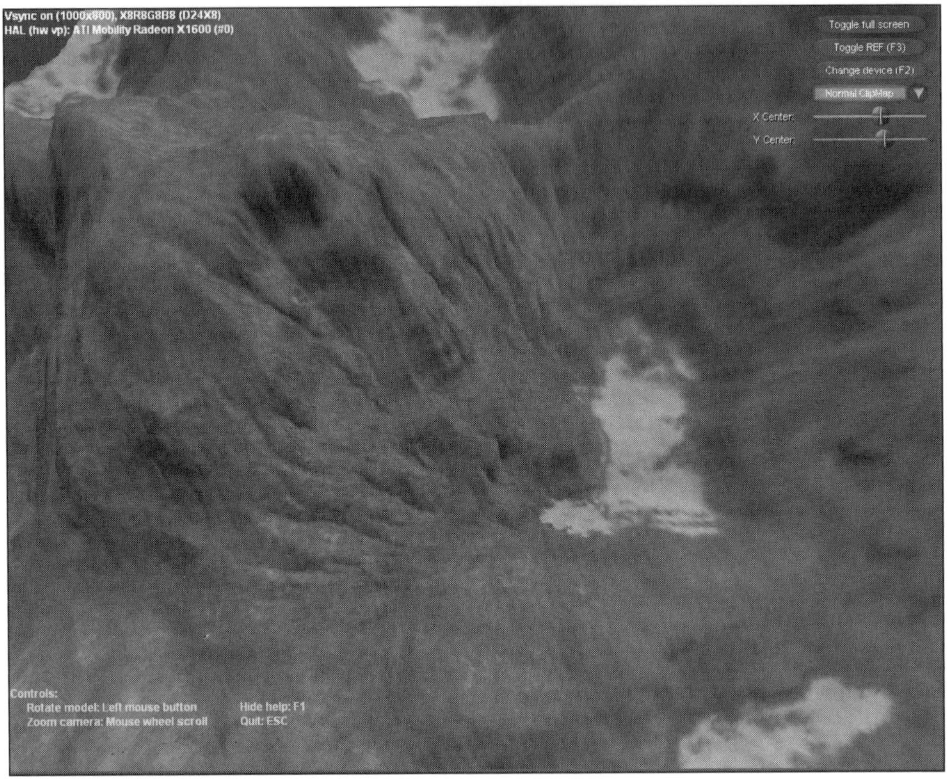

FIGURE 5.6.5 An image from the clipmapping app provided on the CD-ROM. See Color Plate 9 for a color version of this image.

Background Paging

Conceptually this is simple (although implementing a performant pager takes work!). Break your source image and its mip levels into tiles. Maintain a cache in system RAM of all the tiles that the clipstack levels overlap, plus a border of data so that adjustments to the focal point can be fulfilled rapidly.

Make sure you have a fast copy from your tiles into the clipstack textures. If data isn't available to update a clipstack level, make sure the data has been requested, and defer the update until a later time. I find that working from the bottom up gives good results—high detail follows the user around, whereas mid-level data sometimes takes a while to appear.

Budgeting Updates

This is one of the major victories of clipmaps as opposed to other techniques. Most surface caching approaches require a fixed quantum of work to be done—say, synthesizing a 128 × 128px tile. As texel density increases the quantum does, too, until you're looking at a minimum of doing a 512px or 1024px tile! No good.

Instead, clipmaps generally require frequent small updates as the focal point moves. The typical update is just a few slices along the horizontal or vertical edges of a clipstack layer—for a 512px clipmap, this might be only a thousand pixels to upload.

Thus, you can set a texel upload budget and, after each level is updated, check to see if you've overrun it. If so, just stop updating, and let the next frame's update take care of it. This is also helpful in cases when the camera is moving—you don't waste much time on detail that will only be visible for a frame. It's also possible to budget based on available time until the next present, using the same methodology.

As long as you always update at least one level each time through before aborting, all the required data will eventually make it into the clipmap, and you may avoid lots of work that would be seen for only a frame or two.

Optimizing Fillrate/Low-End Support

By conditioning your geometry into chunks with known texture coordinate bounds, it's possible to determine efficiently at runtime what clipstack levels are needed to texture that chunk, thus allowing you to reduce the number of textures that have to be bound to the clipmap shader.

This also begins to enable SM1.0 support, because you can get down to four or fewer active textures, under the four texture sampler limit of SM1.0. By then, moving the level fade calculations into the vertex shader (and ensuring a certain minimal vertex density!), you can fit the clipmap logic into an SM1.x pixel shader.

Using an SM1.x-compatible path is a good idea even on higher end cards because it's much faster than the naive SM2.0 shader. Especially on cards that report high capabilities but can't do them quickly, like the X300, this can be a huge win.

By extending this idea, it's also possible to target FF cards. You can either bind the smallest clipstack level that contains the chunk's texcoords, or you can hack up transitions between two or three levels using register combiners and approximating the shaders.

Taking Advantage of the High End

In shader models where the pixel gradient operators are available, you can do the mipmap calculations yourself, and look up the exact levels of the clipmap that are needed for the pixel in question. This cuts the fillrate significantly, although the shader may then be costly to evaluate.

In higher-end contexts, it's also feasible to consider maintaining several clipmaps for different attributes. For instance, one for normal maps, another for diffuse, a third for specularity. For "localized" attributes, which tend to average to nothing in the distance, like normal maps, it might also be profitable to maintain just the two or three most detailed levels of the clipmap.

If You Want To Save Some Time...

If you want to just grab an existing implementation off the shelf, Torque Game Engine Advanced, which my employer, GarageGames, sells, contains the Atlas terrain system. TGEA comes with full source and liberal licensing terms, and Atlas has a fully paged and optimized clipmapping implementation with support for SM1 and higher. TorqueX's 3D terrain system also includes a comparable implementation in C# on XNA. Check them out; they might save you a lot of time and money.

ON THE CD

L3DT, 3d Studio Max, and the Panda DirectX exporter were used to create the assets for the demo included on the CD-ROM.

References

[Forsyth07] Forsyth, Tom. "TomF's Tech Blog—Knowing Which Mipmap Levels Are Needed," available online at http://home.comcast.net/~tom_forsyth/blog.wiki.html, 2007.

[Lefebvre04] Lefebvre, Sylvain, Darbon, Jerome, and Neyret, Fabrice. "Unified Texture Management for Arbitrary Meshes," 2004.

[Tanner96] Tanner, Migdal, Jones. "The Clipmap: A Virtual Mipmap," available online at www.cs.virginia.edu/~gfx/Courses/2002/BigData/papers/Texturing/Clipmap.pdf, 1996.

5.7

An Advanced Decal System

Joris Mans

joris.mans@10tacle.be

Dmitry Andreev

dmitry.andreev@10tacle.be

Most games these days use decals in one way or another; for instance, to show bullet marks on the environment, or to add variation on repetitive geometry. Usually this is done by rendering a transparent polygon on top of the existing geometry. This technique, however, has some drawbacks, especially if you want to apply bump mapping in your decals. When rendering a bump mapped decal on top of existing bump mapped geometry, the lighting is not correct, because the pixels underneath the decal should also have been lit using a combination of the decal bump map and the geometry bump map. This gem explains how to render decals that actually replace the bump and the diffuse map of the geometry (this can be extended to any kind of texture map you use), thereby giving correct lighting results and a higher image quality.

Requirements

An implementation of this gem can be done on any platform supporting render targets and shader logic capable of sampling and interpolating between values obtained from at least two different maps (if you only want to use it for diffuse textures), or four (if you want to add bump map support). The best image quality is obtained by using render targets that are the same resolution as the screen, but smaller ones will also work, with a decrease in image quality. The demo provided runs on any PC with a DirectX 9 compatible graphics card supporting pixel shader version 2.0.

Normal Decals Method

In a traditional engine using a decal system, you first render all the geometry in the frame buffer, and on top of that you render polygons containing the decals, usually using some kind of blending.

Advanced Decals Method

In this example, you'll do things slightly differently. First, you need to create the necessary tools in the runtime to accomplish the decal renderer. In this case, we will create two full-screen render targets. The first one is in 32-bit RGBA format; it's called the DiffuseRenderTarget. The second one will also be in 32-bit RGBA format; it's called BumpRenderTarget. For this second one, you could use a 16-bit per component buffer or any other format of render target if your bump maps are stored in higher precision. In our demo, we use DXT5 compressed bump maps so 32-bit RGBA will suffice.

Rendering the scene can be split up into two parts. First, you generate the decal buffers, and next you render the scene with the decals applied. To generate the decal buffers, execute the following steps:

- Render all depth values of the geometry in the main z buffer (excluding the decals). The depth compare function used is the same as the one you use to do the normal scene rendering.
- Select the DiffuseRenderTarget as the current render target, while still using the main z buffer. The render target is cleared, using black as the clear color.
- Render all decal geometry into that render target, using the same depth compare function used previously for the depth pass, but don't render the complete shader as you would in the normal decal case. The rendering uses a special shader that just outputs the color of the diffuse texture, pre-multiplied with the opacity texture (or diffuse alpha depending on your art pipeline). In the alpha component of the render target, output the opacity value used to scale the diffuse value.
- In the BumpRenderTarget, you do something similar. Render the decal geometry, this time using the bump map texture value in world space as output. This step can be combined with the previous one if your target hardware supports multiple render target rendering. Sample results are shown in Figures 5.7.1 and 5.7.2.

Finally, you render the scene. The thing you have to do in the shaders used for the geometry is change the code that makes the diffuse texture lookup and the bump texture lookup. You must actually combine the diffuse value from the texture applied to the geometry and the values found in the DiffuseRenderTarget/BumpRenderTarget textures. This works as follows:

- Take the screen space position of the pixel you are currently rendering. This will be used as texture coordinates to read out the values of the render targets.
- Use the texture coordinates to read the diffuse RGB value from the decal diffuse map; call this value *drt*.

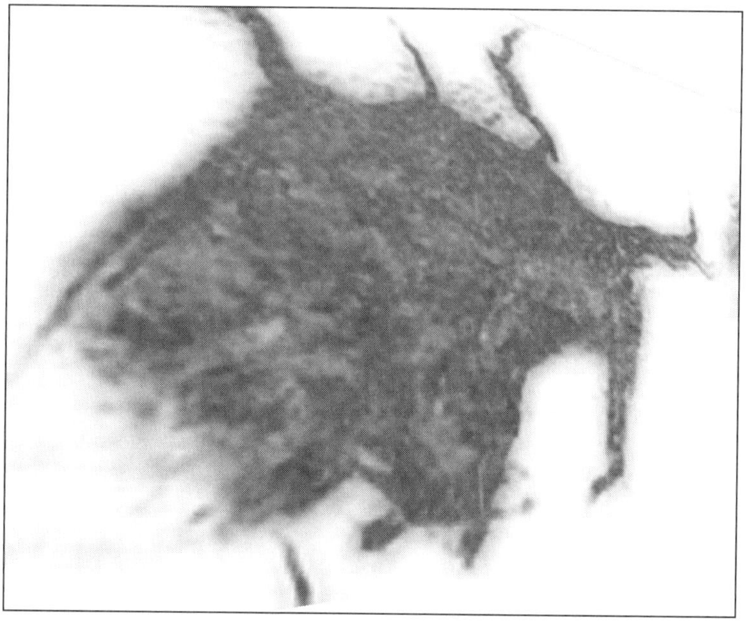

FIGURE 5.7.1 The DiffuseRenderTarget used by the decal system.

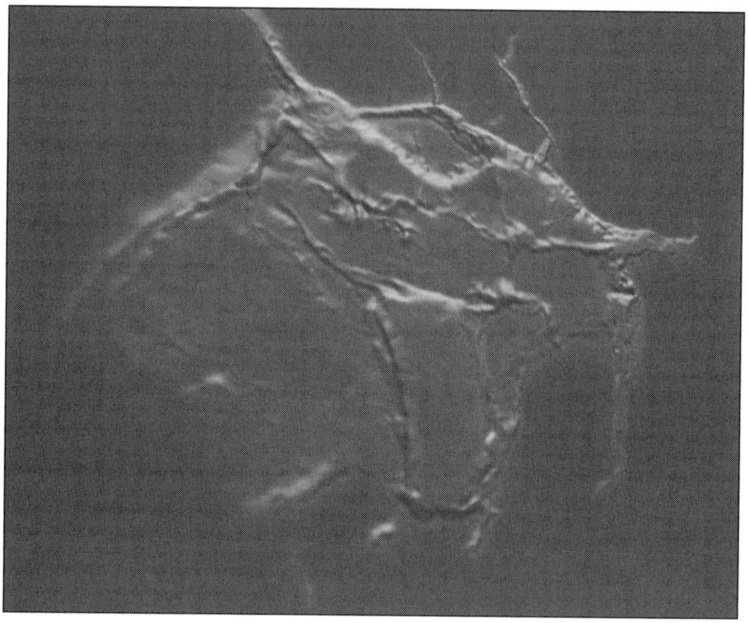

FIGURE 5.7.2 The BumpRenderTarget used by the decal system.

- Combine it with the RGB value read from the diffuse texture used on the geometry, using the alpha value read from the render target. This gives you the following formula, where *dt* is the diffuse texture of the object, *drt* is the render target texture containing the decal diffuse value, and *d* is the resulting diffuse value:

$$d_{rgb} = dt_{rgb} * (1 - drt_a) + drt_{rgb} \tag{5.7.1}$$

- Read the value stored in the decal bump map; store it in the variable *brt*.
- Combine it with the bump map of the object according to the following formula. Here *bt* is the bump texture of the object, *wsb* is the bump vector in world space, *drt* is the render target texture containing the decal diffuse value, *brt* is the render target texture containing the decal bump value in world space, and *b* is the resulting bump value:

$$\begin{aligned} wsb &= TransformToWorldSpace\left(DecodeBump\left(bt_{rgba}\right)\right) \\ b_{xyz} &= wsb * \left(1 - drt_a\right) + DecodeBump\left(brt_{rgba}\right) * drt_a \\ b &= normalize\left(b\right) \end{aligned} \tag{5.7.2}$$

`DecodeBump` is the function that converts your RGBA texel into a bump vector, depending on the way you store your bump maps. Of course, interpolating bump vectors like this isn't really mathematically correct, but the visual results in this case are fine, so you need not look for a more advanced solution.

Figures 5.7.3 and 5.7.4 show a comparison of the traditional method and the technique explained in this gem.

FIGURE 5.7.3 Decals using the traditional technique.

FIGURE 5.7.4 Decals using this technique.

DecodeBump

As mentioned in the previous paragraph, this example uses a function called `DecodeBump` to decode the bump maps. There are several ways of storing bump maps. The choice of which one to use depends on hardware support, quality, and speed. Explaining in detail the different approaches is beyond the scope of this gem, but it does include some examples of how this can be done. The easiest solution is to use an RGB render target with 8bits per component and store the bump maps as color values, scaled and biased to fit in the 0..255 range of the pixel color.

Encoding a bump vector into this format would look like this:

$$color.rgb = (bumpvector.xyz + 1)*127.5 \quad (5.7.3)$$

The corresponding `DecodeBump` function would be something similar to this:

$$bumpvector.xyz = color.rgb * 2 - 1 \quad (5.7.4)$$

Recall, although you wrote byte values in the range of 0..255 when encoding, in the pixel shader, all values are normalized floats, where 0 maps to 0 and 255 maps to 1.0. The disadvantage of this way of storing is that the bump maps are uncompressed, and that compression using DXT1 gives rather bad visual results.

Another approach sometimes used is to store the bump values in a DXT5 compressed surface, using the green component to store the x value of the bump vector, and the alpha component to store the y value. When reading the bump map, you can reconstruct the z value using x and y.

Encoding the bump vector would look like this:

$$\begin{aligned} color.r &= 0 \\ color.g &= (bumpvector.x + 1) * 127.5 \\ color.b &= 0 \\ color.a &= (bumpvector.y + 1) * 127.5 \end{aligned} \tag{5.7.5}$$

The `DecodeBump` function reconstructs the third component:

$$\begin{aligned} bumpvector.x &= color.b * 2 + 1 \\ bumpvector.y &= color.a * 2 + 1 \\ bumpvector.z &= \sqrt{(bumpvector.x)^2 + (bumpvector.y)^2} \end{aligned} \tag{5.7.6}$$

This allows you to store bump maps in a compressed format, while still maintaining a good level of quality by exploiting the fact that the green component in a DXT5 compressed texture contains six bits of precision, and that the alpha component is compressed separately. The tradeoff is, of course, that there are more calculations needed to recreate the bump vector—calculations that are not available on all platforms or that might be too expensive. There is a tradeoff between storage requirements and pixel shading speed, but on some platforms the fact that the data is compressed gives you fewer cache misses and actually is faster, even with the calculation of the z component, than reading decompressed values directly.

Advantages of This Advanced Decal System

The main advantage of this system is the increased quality of the image, compared to normal bump maps. It also allows decals to be used in different ways. For instance, imagine using decals that only contain bump maps to influence the look of a repetitive wall by adding cracks, noise, or other variations. Instead of only using decals in the runtime to add bullet and explosion marks, you can also use them in the level editor when building the scene.

Creating the same diversity in an engine supporting standard decals would require an entirely different approach. Because you cannot replace bump maps with normal decals, you would have to actually create bump maps for each part of the scene where you want variations, replacing the original bump map used with the variant one. Not only does this mean that you will have a lot more bump maps in memory, but it also requires more work from artists to create and place those bump maps on the geometry.

As shown in Figure 5.7.5, playing with the opacity of the decals can simulate wear and tear on geometry over time. Because you have coherent lighting here, you can perfectly blend in an erosion bump map by playing with the opacity value of the decal.

It can also be used to create variations in a scene that uses a lot of instancing. You can instance the same geometry all over, using hardware instancing support if that is

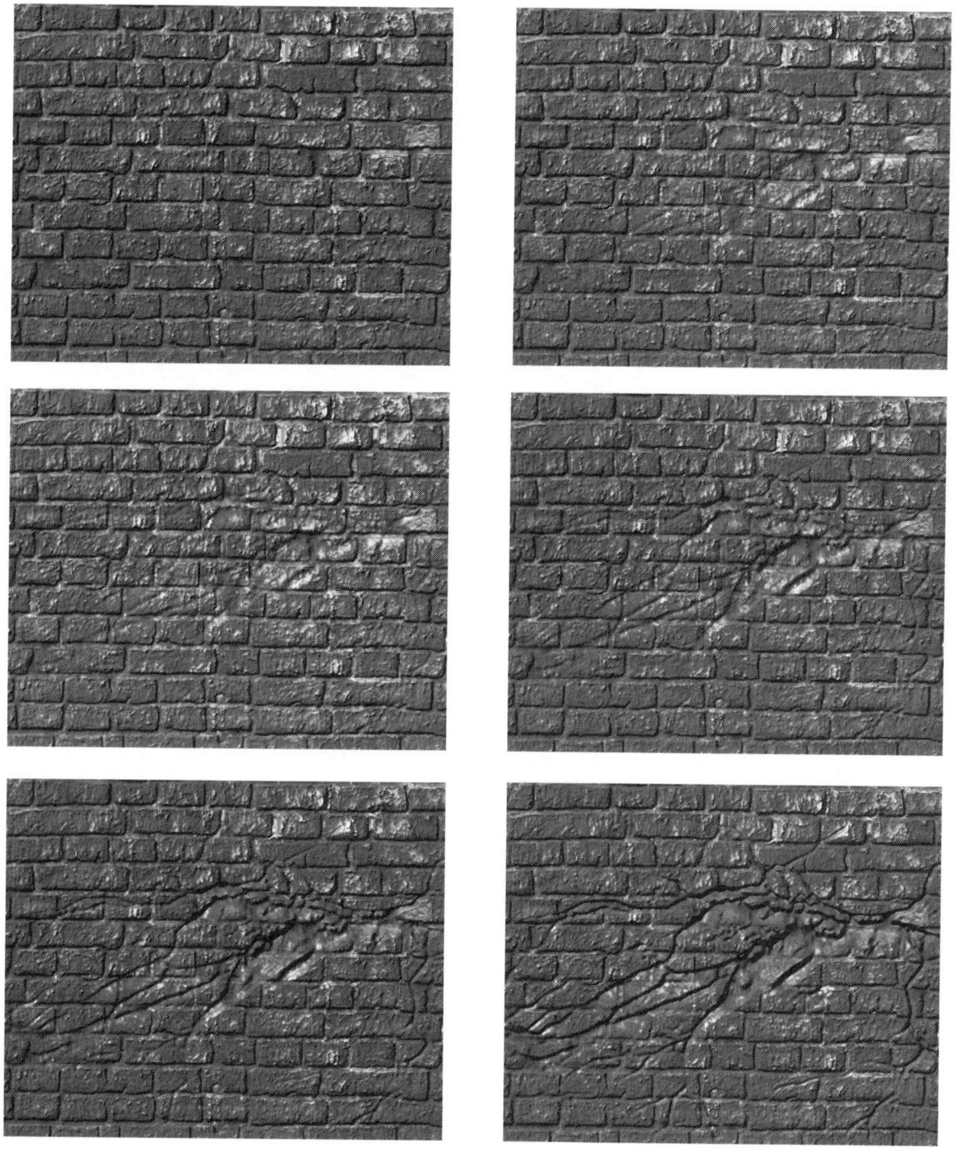

FIGURE 5.7.5 Uses of decals for erosion over time. From left to right and top to bottom, the opacity values are 0, 20, 40, 60, 80, and 100 percent, respectively.

available, but thanks to the decal system, you can add variations on the surface of each instance, without requiring the memory footprint of having each instance separately in memory. Because you use the depth buffer in the decal system, it supports non-planar decals. The only constraint is that the decals have to follow the geometry underneath them as closely as possible. Apart from that, the topology of the decal has no restrictions whatsoever. An example of decals on non-planar geometry is shown in Figure 5.7.6.

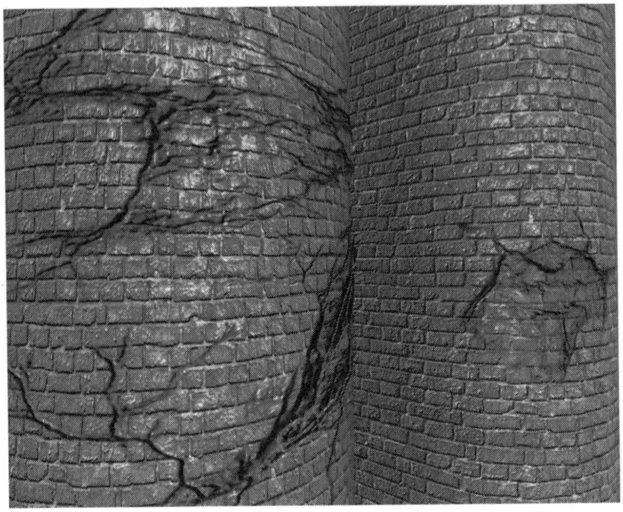

FIGURE 5.7.6 Decals on non-planar geometry.

It is also quite easy to implement, and integrating it in existing technology does usually not require major changes in the rendering pipeline. If the z pre-pass is already available, you can add the render to the two decal render targets right after that pre-pass, and you just need to change the shader code that samples the diffuse and bump map textures when rendering the scene in order to read from the decal buffers. (See the color insert for color versions of many of the images shown in this gem.)

Performance and Experimental Results

ON THE CD

This section shows the results of our implementation of the technique described here, along with some performance tests and potential issues. The demo on the CD-ROM is just another simplified implementation of advanced decals we are using in our gaming engine. It shows the main parts of the technique and yields clear performance tendencies. All tests were performed on a 3.0GHz P4 with NVIDIA's GeForce 6800 GT and GeForce 7800 GT.

We used four rendering presets of the demo to show different aspects of performance:

- Original—A standard lighting model that already exists in almost all modern engines, without using decals. In this case, it is based on two per-pixel computed light sources using tangent-space normal maps, diffuse maps, and specular maps.
- Normal decals—Regular decals rendered on top of the geometry rendered using the original shaders. A decal consists of a diffuse texture and a bump texture.
- Advanced (Original)—Renders the decals into the decal buffers, but uses the shader of the original to render the objects on the scene, so no decals are shown. This allows you to see the cost of filling the two decal buffers.
- Advanced—Renders the decals into the decal buffers and applies them to the objects in the scene.

The primary question is what is the performance difference between normal and advanced decals. Figures 5.7.7 and 5.7.8 show performance in frames per second. There are two 512 × 512 × 32 (diffuse and specular) and one 1024 × 1024 × 32 (normal map) textures assigned to each object. There are also the same amount of textures of the same sizes assigned to decals.

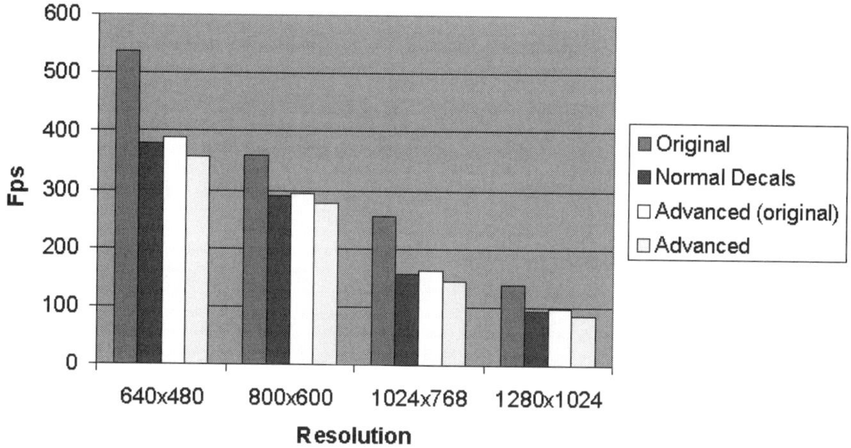

FIGURE 5.7.7 Full scene test.

For these two tests, we used non-compressed textures with 8x anisotropic filtering of normal maps. In the "full scene test" in Figure 5.7.7, the camera was pointed such that almost all decals were visible covering both close and distant scene objects. Whereas the close up test shown in Figure 5.7.8 was completed with the camera pointed only at one single object covering the full screen, so that all others would be Z culled.

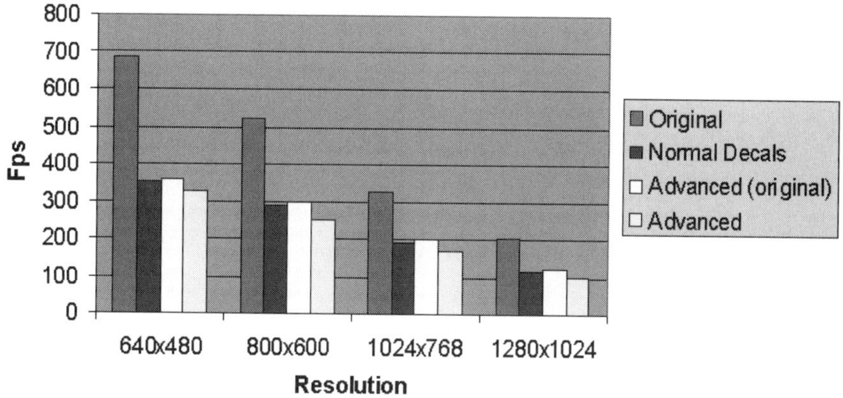

FIGURE 5.7.8 Close up test.

No matter what resolution we render in, or whether rendering an entire scene or close up, the "Advanced" technique is about 11% slower than the "Advanced (Original)" technique. The same tests have been done but with compressed textures and they gave us a 23% difference between "Advanced" and "Advanced (Original)," and higher frame rates. So those few additional texture fetches and blending instructions in the main shader cost us about 11–23% speed.

But how does that difference depend on the complexity of decals? To answer that question we've made two tests showing that dependency. We rendered one full-screen decal multiple times on our scene to see how this would influence performance. As the cost of the lookup in the decal buffers is independent of the number of decals used, the test we did previously already showed the performance implications of those lookups. The second test shows the cost of actually rendering the decals themselves.

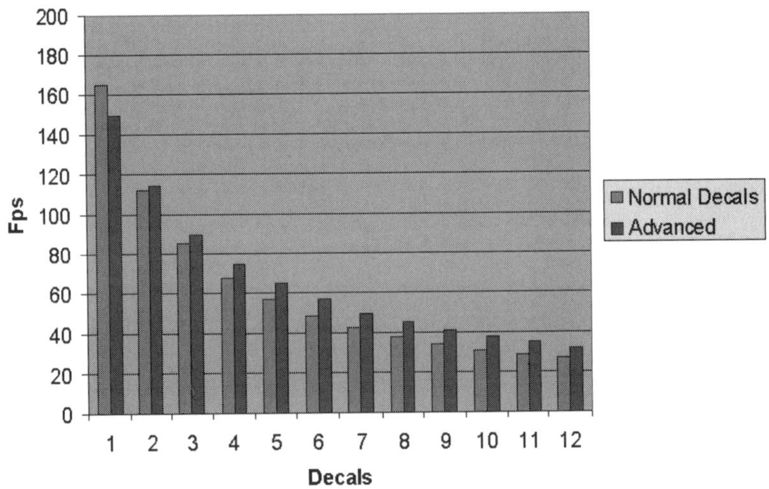

FIGURE 5.7.9 Non-compressed textures.

As you can see in Figures 5.7.9 and 5.7.10, when only using one decal the standard decal technique is faster, but when drawing multiple decals on top of each other, the advanced technique actually renders faster. This is due to the fact that when rendering multiple standard decals on top of each other, the complex shader, which does the lighting and bump mapping, is executed once for each decal being rendered, while in the advanced decal's case, the complex shader is only executed once, even when multiple decals overlap.

If your rendering pipeline is memory or API-call bound, all decal buffers (textures) could be filled at once using multiple render targets. In this demo it only shows that it doesn't cause any additional performance issues. But using it will just minimize texture state changes and API calls, simply because in that case you need to render decals only one time.

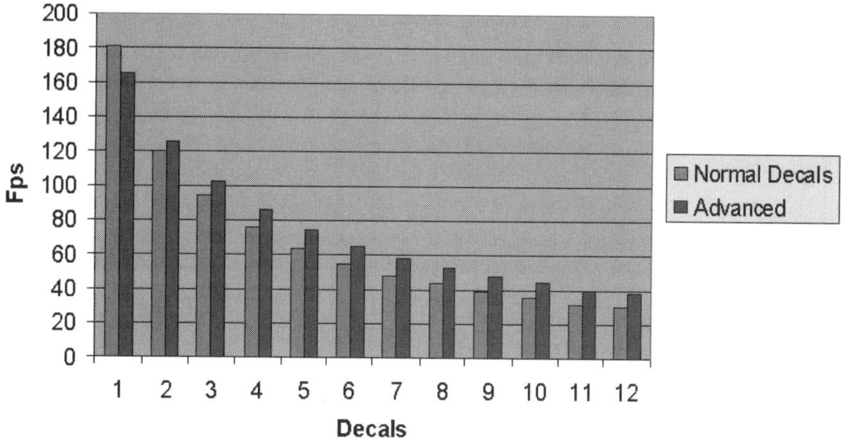

FIGURE 5.7.10 DXT 1/5 compressed textures.

Although we can conclude there is a performance cost of about 12% in our test scene, we should not forget that these are test cases and that a rendering engine does much more rendering than just rendering objects with decals. When taking into account the cost of the other things going on during the rendering (for example, full-screen effects, particle systems, shadowmapping, and so on), the total performance hit percentage will be smaller. Something else to consider is that by using these decals, you can build scenes with a smaller amount of different textures, resulting in available memory gains, fewer state changes, and bigger batches, which might actually increase rendering performance. So the cost of using those decals ends up being less than 12%, while gaining available memory. You can even see performance benefits when there are lots of overlapping decals.

Demo

ON THE CD

On the CD-ROM, you can find a demo of this decal system. There are several parameters exposed so you can see and test the differences between this system and traditional decals, and tweak certain rendering settings. You can also see how the diffuse and bump maps are combined with the decal maps, to get a better understanding of the algorithm. There are some more screenshots found in the "screenshots" subfolder. The demo requires a DirectX 9 compatible video card supporting shader model 2.0.

Conclusion

This gem covered a way of rendering decals that has several advantages over the traditional approach. It results in better image quality, consistent lighting of the parts covered with decals, and it allows uses of decals that were previously not possible. For instance, decals can be applied that only contain a bump map and no diffuse texture. The method presented here can easily be integrated in existing technology, without requiring massive changes to the production or rendering pipeline, and the performance cost is relatively small. Moreover, when pushing this further, you can use decals to replace any texture used on the scene geometry. Another possibility is to add decals on the scene when building the geometry in the editor, thereby allowing for many variations on top of generic, tiled textures without having to resort to using detail textures.

References

[Jing06] Jing, YingHui, et. al. "A Post-Processing Decal Texture Mapping Algorithm on Graphics Hardware," Proceedings of the 2006 ACM International Conference on Virtual Reality Continuum and Its Applications, pp. 99–104.

[Lengyel01] Lengyel, Eric. "Applying Decals to Arbitrary Surfaces," *Game Programming Gems 2,* 2001, Charles River Media, pp. 411–415.

5.8

Mapping Large Textures for Outdoor Terrain Rendering

Antonio Seoane, Javier Taibo, Luis Hernández, and Alberto Jaspe
VideaLAB, University of La Coruña
(antonio.seoane@videalab.udc.es), (jtaibo@udc.es), (lhernandez@udc.es), and (jaspe@videalab.udc.es)

Texturing highly detailed large terrain areas is a requirement in many games, especially flight simulators. Fortunately, hardware supports large textures, up to 8192 texels square. Classical techniques are based on the tiling of large textures or blending detail textures. The problem with these techniques is that, in one case, geometry must be divided into segments with borders exactly matching the texture tile boundaries and, in the other case, the appearance is repetitive, unnatural, and unrealistic. This gem explains a method that allows the use of huge textures, based on clipmaps. The technique can be used with any geometry algorithm without the need to divide textures into tiles adapted to the geometry boundaries. Moreover, it allows dynamic geometry deformation.

Introduction

In the case of online games huge textures can be stored on game servers, so they can be downloaded in real time. This allows textures that would exceed the storage capacity of the user's computer and also enables easy updates on the game server to add more detail, new features, and so on. Moreover, allowing huge textures is more natural and easy for game artists, who can use a large canvas to paint with as much detail as possible and also eliminate artifacts due to repeating tiled textures.

In order to successfully deal with textures that are larger than system and video memory, some specific techniques are needed. On the Virtual Terrain Project Website, there is a large compilation of papers about the problem of mapping large textures over terrain [VTerrain07]. One drawback in the vast majority of existing solutions is the strong coupling between texture and geometry databases. This requires subdivision of the texture in order to adapt it to the geometry or vice versa.

Clipmapping is one of the best approaches to manage large textures that cannot fit into system memory [Tanner98]. This technique decouples the handling of texture and geometry, allowing independence between both databases. The first implementation of this technique was made in Silicon Graphics systems and required expensive, specific hardware [Montrym97].

The main idea of clipmapping is to handle a large size mipmap pyramid (where large means larger than the texture size limit and/or the available video memory), keeping only a subset of the pyramid in video memory. The portion of each level that is kept resident is limited by a user-specified parameter called the *clipsize*. The levels with size lower than or equal to the clipsize are always in video memory, and the larger levels are clipped to this limit. The area of incomplete levels that is resident is centered around a point called the center of detail or the *clipcenter*. As the camera moves, the clipcenter is dynamically updated and the region cached for each level in video memory is consequently updated. This way, there is always the best possible quality available to map the geometry into the region being visualized. They can be large areas with low resolution or small areas with very fine detail.

The main advantage of clipmapping is that a huge texture can be handled using a limited portion of memory. For instance, a 65536 × 65536 texel cliptexture (21.3GB using 32 bits depth in a storage device) using a 1024 clipsize requires only 29.34MB of video memory. The system can be adjusted to use any clipsize depending on the amount of video memory that is allocated to it.

Next, this gem describes a technique that allows the handling of a large amount of texture using current PC and console hardware. The technique stores the image in tiles that are not used directly as textures. These tiles are combined in a texture stack that caches the region of interest, following the clipmap idea. Although inspired by clipmapping, there are important differences in its structure, video memory management, and the way the texture is applied. This allows implementation on any graphics card without special hardware requirements—only OpenGL or Direct3D fixed function pipeline is required to implement this technique.

The technique described in this gem has been successfully used in several projects using texture details of 0.25 m/texel in geographical areas of about 60,000km^2 [Santi07]. It has also been successfully used with different geometry algorithms, based on grids as well as TINs.

The main advantages of this technique are as follows:

- It can be implemented using a fixed-function pipeline API such as OpenGL or Direct3D.
- It maintains independence between geometry and texture databases.
- Texture coordinates can be automatically computed in the GPU, avoiding their transference to the graphics system. This allows modification of the geometry in real-time, while keeping the right texture mapping.
- Texture aliasing is avoided using trilinear and anisotropic filtering hardware capabilities.

- It allows the visualization of high-resolution textures with the possibility of including higher-resolution regions.
- It allows the use of several independent large textures that can be combined to show different information types simultaneously on the terrain.

Structure

The technique proposed manages a virtually unlimited texture that we call the *virtual texture*. It is stored using a pyramidal mipmap scheme [Williams83]. The highest detail level of this pyramid is formed by $2^{l-1} \times 2^{l-1}$ texels at most (such as in case of a square texture), with l being the number of levels in the pyramid. Levels are numbered from 0 to 2^i, the largest side size for level i, as illustrated in Figure 5.8.1.

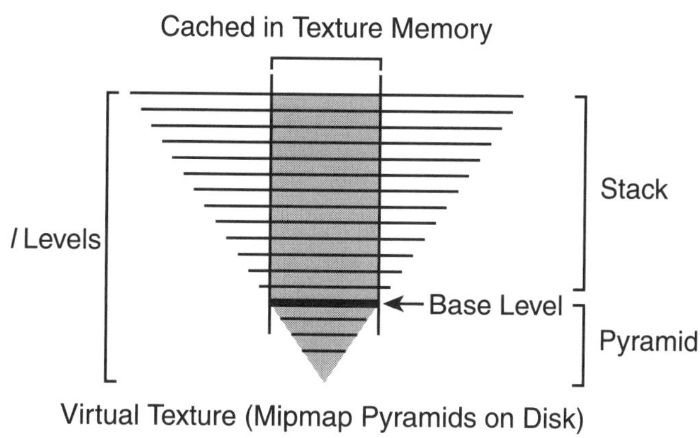

FIGURE 5.8.1 Virtual texture.

The virtual texture is stored complete on persistent storage, either on a local disk or remotely requested from a server. This virtual texture is structured in the persistent storage level in square tiles with a side size in texels power of two. An exception to this is those levels of the pyramid in which the texture size is smaller than the tile size. Tiles are addressed with a vector (column, row, and level).

The pre-filtered mipmap levels of the virtual texture increase by a third the storage space required, but this is needed to map the texture in an efficient way that avoids aliasing artifacts.

Texture Cache

Following the clipmap concept, a subset of the full pyramid is cached in texture memory to apply the adequate detail level to the area being visualized. This virtual texture is managed through a two-level cache system. The second-level cache is located in main memory and uses a pool of buffers to store the least recently used tiles.

Tiles are asynchronously loaded on demand. Requests are prioritized by level with coarser levels given higher priority. This way, larger areas are covered as quickly as possible and the detail around the center of interest is progressively refined as higher level tiles become available. The tile size is a critical parameter, as it can impact the transfer rate from persistent storage to main memory.

The first-level cache is a subset of the virtual texture levels that is resident in texture memory. The virtual pyramid is fully stored in texture memory from the apex to the base level. This set of levels is called the pyramid and it will be managed as a regular mipmapped texture. The size of the base level is called the clipsize. The base level (l_b) is calculated from the clipsize (c) as $l_b=log_2(c)$.

From the base level up, only a subregion of the whole level is stored. The set of incomplete levels is called the stack. The levels of the stack are all the same size in texels and, progressively from the coarser to the finer detail level, half the terrain region. The levels that make up the stack are incomplete subsets (with size $c \times c$ texels) of the corresponding virtual texture levels. These levels are centered on a point of interest, called the center of detail. These concepts are shown in Figure 5.8.1.

You'll use $l-l_b+1$ independent textures in texture memory, as shown in Figure 5.8.2. The first one (t_0) corresponding to the pyramid's finest level. Subsequent textures t_i cache the virtual level l_b+i.

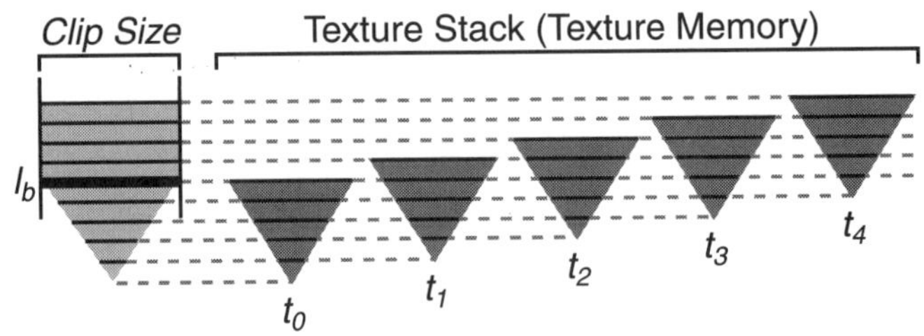

FIGURE 5.8.2 Texture stack.

Trilinear Filtering

In order to allow the graphics system to perform a trilinear filtering to avoid aliasing, mipmap levels for every texture are needed. Let t_{ij} be the mipmap level j of the texture i; it caches level l_b+i-j of the virtual texture.

As shown in Figure 5.8.3, it is not necessary to have all mipmap levels in the textures corresponding to the stack. This can save valuable bandwidth during cache updating. Our experience proves that about four or five mipmap levels in the textures of the stack are enough to achieve good quality without noticeable artifacts with a clipsize of 1024×1024 texels.

Figure 5.8.4 illustrates the terrain area covered by different levels of the stack. There, you can see the application of those levels to a real terrain, represented by a color-coded grid (see Color Plate 11 in the color insert of this book for the full-color version of this image).

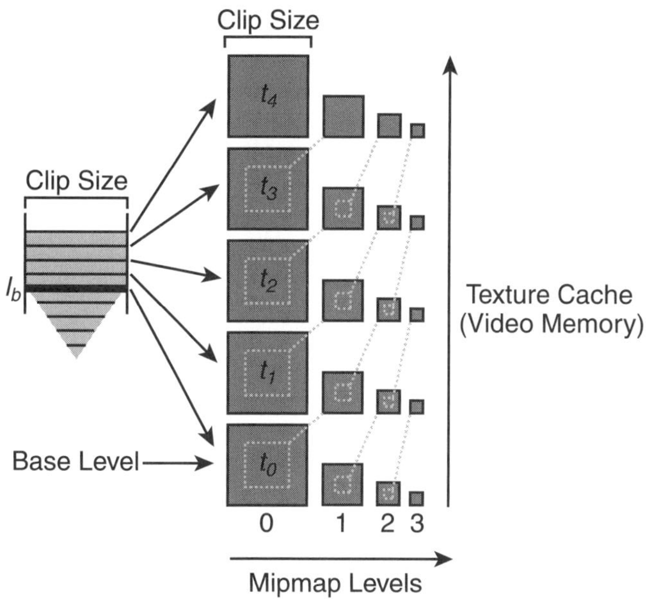

FIGURE 5.8.3 Texture stack with mipmap levels correspondence.

FIGURE 5.8.4 Rings of detail and an example of a virtual texture applied to the terrain, showing levels of detail using color codes.

Texture Memory Usage

For an l level virtual texture with a clipsize c, m mipmap levels for the stack textures and a texel depth of b bytes, the usage of texture memory for the cache can be computed as follows:

$$texture\_memory = \left((l - l_b - 1) \cdot \sum_{i=0}^{m-1} \left(\frac{c}{2^i} \right)^2 + \sum_{i=0}^{l_b} 2^{2i} \right) \cdot b \tag{5.8.1}$$

Higher levels in the pyramid can be incomplete, allowing the inclusion of additional detail for special interest areas over a constant overall image detail. It is quite usual in games such as flight simulators to have a medium detail satellite texture over all the terrain and increase detail in some areas in which the plane is likely to fly low or approximate, such as an airport.

Updating the Contents of the Cache

Data stored on the texture cache corresponds to a zone of the terrain covered by the virtual texture around the center of detail. As this center of detail is moved, contents of the cache need to be updated.

Detail Center Computation

Every frame, the application must place the center of detail in the location where the maximum quality is desired. Several strategies can be used. Typically, you'll use camera position and orientation. The trivial approach is placing the center of detail in the vertical projection of the camera location over the ground. Better results can be achieved by placing it on a point of the visible terrain close to the camera, and then computing the intersection with the terrain of the eye view direction.

Texture Stack Update

Whatever strategy is used, once the center of detail is placed, stack texture levels must be updated. Each level is updated sequentially from coarser to finer.

Textures corresponding to these levels are considered divided in square blocks with side size power of two. These blocks are called subtiles to differentiate them from the tiles stored in the second level cache. The subtile is the texture updating atomic unit. Subtile size (s) must be a divisor of the clipsize (c) and the tile size (t), where

$$s = 2^i\ ,\ t = 2^j\ ,\ c = 2^k\ ,\ \text{with } i <= j\ ,\ i < k \qquad (5.8.2)$$

As the center of detail is moved, some subtiles will become invalid and will have to be updated, whereas others will retain useful data. For each texture, there is a subtile state matrix indicating the validity of each subtile in the texture. Immediately after placing the center of detail, these matrices will need updating for the new position.

After the state matrices are updated, each texture is processed, from coarser to finer detail. For each invalid subtile, you compute the address of the tile containing the subtile data. This tile is requested from the second level cache. If it is resident the subtile data is uploaded to the texture memory; otherwise, the asynchronous load of the tile will be requested by the RAM tile cache and will be available in the next few frames. In case of incomplete levels, invalid subtiles absent from persistent storage will never be updated.

The virtual texture window cached in each stack level is accessed toroidally in the corresponding real texture. This allows partial updates of each level, which drastically improves the efficiency. As seen in Figure 5.8.6, when the center of detail is updated, the window position is changed. Using the wraparound addressing only the new subtiles not present in the previous window position have to be loaded, while the overlapping area remains in place.

A subtile update of a texture implies updating the related area in each mipmap level of this texture. In the mipmap level updating process, consider that subtile size for mipmap level m is $s/2^m$. Update of levels t_{ij}, where $j > 0$ can be made from coarser textures, because mipmap levels data is replicated, as shown in Figure 5.8.3.

Load Control

Texture upload time is critical for a real-time graphics application like a game to sustain the frame rate. The render time plus the texture update time must not exceed the frame time. For this reason, updating subtiles is limited in duration for each frame. That means that for quick movements of the center of detail, it will not be possible to reach the finest detail in one single frame. This usually is not a problem because fast movements do not usually allow the viewer to appreciate details in the image and a blurry aspect is normally acceptable.

When deciding the subtile size, it is important to find a tradeoff between an adequate load control and a high transfer rate. The smaller the subtile size, the higher the accuracy to measure the update time. Even though the subtile update time is strongly dependent on the hardware used, the smaller sizes typically have a very poor efficiency. Our experience has shown that subtile sizes of 128×128 give the best performance.

Concentric Rings Update

Because of the previously mentioned update time limit, textures in the stack are not always completely updated. It is necessary to decide when a texture is updated with enough data to be applied. The simple approach is to exclude a texture from use in the stack until it is completely updated. The problem here is that every time the center of detail is moved the distance of a subtile, it will be invalidated until being completely updated again. This problem is reduced by applying the texture even though only a partial area of the full texture is loaded.

You update the subtiles of each texture in concentric rings, innermost to outermost, so the coverage grows as the subtile rings are updated (see Figure 5.8.5). This way, the texture is useful from the moment it begins to have some valid subtiles. Beginning from the center, the highest interest zone is available sooner. Also, the center subtiles are the ones with higher life expectancy.

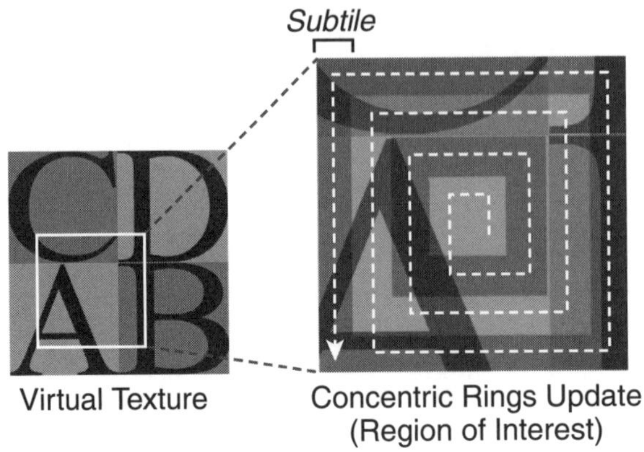

FIGURE 5.8.5 Circular update.

Pseudocode

The virtual texture update is summarized in the following pseudocode:

```
Compute the center of detail position
For each texture level of the stack
   update the subtile validity matrix

For each texture level of the stack from coarser to finer detail
   For each subtile of the level (innermost to outermost)
   and while update time limit is not surpassed
       If the subtile state is invalid
          Compute the address of the disk tile
          Request the tile to the RAM tile cache
          If the tile is cached
          Update the subtile in all mipmap levels
          Set subtile state to valid
```

Rendering Issues

Geometry management algorithms can be adapted and used with the described technique. There are two possible ways to map a virtual texture to a geometry model. The first way, considering the geometry model is divided into patches, is to apply the finest available texture that covers each geometry patch. In this case, you would follow these steps:

```
For each geometry patch
  Apply the finest texture level that covers the patch
  Compute the texture coordinates for the selected texture
  Draw the patch
```

The second way is to select each texture level, asking for its coverage and drawing the geometry covered by the selected level but not for the finer ones. In this case, you would follow these steps:

```
For each texture level
  Select and apply the texture
  Compute the texture coordinates for the selected texture
  Compute geometry covered by the level but not finer ones
  Draw the geometry set computed
```

No matter which way is used, texture coordinates must be computed for every vertex of the geometry. These coordinates are computed for the finest level of the virtual texture. Because each texture level from the stack covers half the virtual space of the coarser one, you need to scale the texture coordinates computed to translate it to the virtual texture level applied. The scale factor for level i is 2^{l-i-1}. The toroidal updating of the textures in the stack assures that the mapping will be correct if the texture repeats (see Figure 5.8.6).

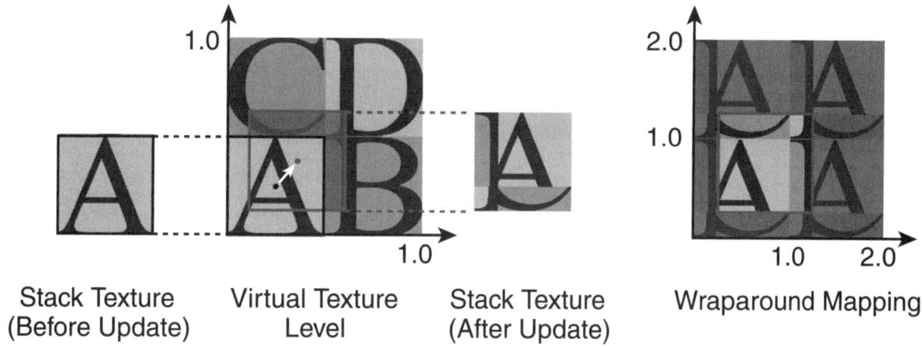

FIGURE 5.8.6 Toroidal update and mapping example.

The texture coordinate computation just described can be done in several ways. For static geometry, texture coordinates can be precomputed and stored statically in texture coordinate arrays. This way, all the computation can be done with the texture matrix scaling and texture repeat mode, so no shaders are needed at all. Only the standard fixed function graphics pipeline available in both OpenGL and DirectX is needed.

In the case of dynamic geometry, texture coordinates must be computed every time the vertices are modified. In both cases, but especially with dynamic geometry, it is very helpful to automatically compute the texture coordinates in a vertex shader. This way, you avoid their computation in CPU, the transfer from main memory to video memory, and the storage for texture coordinate arrays in video memory. The following pseudocode shows how to calculate texture coordinates:

```
L: left texture limit, R: right texture limit,
T: top texture limit, B: bottom texture limit,
(x,y,z): vertex position, i: virtual texture level selected
scale = 2^(l-i-1)
u = scale * (x-L)/(R-L)
v = scale * (y-B)/(T-B)
```

Texture coordinate computation can include additional transformations in case there are different coordinate systems for the texture database and the geometry database. By using only one GPU texture stage for the mapping of the virtual texture, this allows you to easily combine the virtual texture with other virtual or regular textures, each one bound to a texture stage.

Results

The presented technique has been tested using a proprietary terrain navigation system with a data set containing a virtual texture of aerial terrain photographs covering an area of about 250 × 200Km [Santi07]. The resolution of this image is 0.5m per texel, which is a stack of 19 levels.

Figure 5.8.7 shows the results of a stress test executed on a low-end computer using a programmed flight at 3000Km/h over the terrain, using a large clipsize (2048 square texels), and an update time limit of only 1ms.

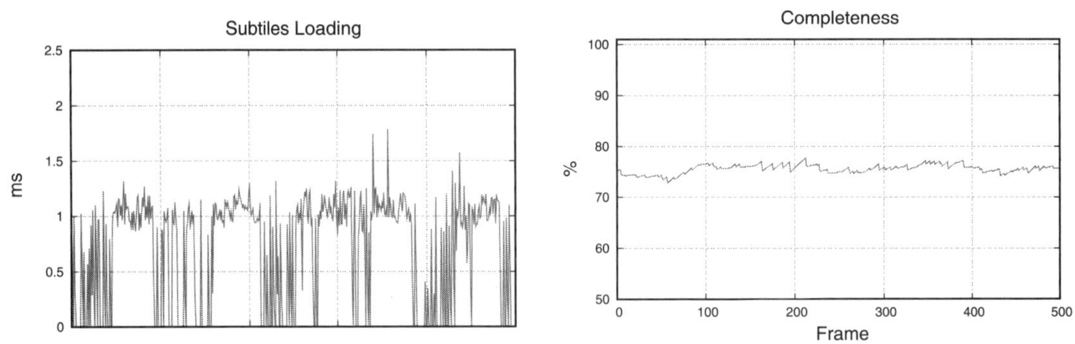

FIGURE 5.8.7 Test results.

Table 5.8.1 System Configuration for Testing

Graphics hardware	AGP 8x NVIDIA GeForce 7800 GS
Clipsize	2048 texels
Tile size	512 texels
Subtile size	128 texels
Updating-time limit	1ms
Virtual texture size	~ 1M × 1M
Virtual texture color depth	24 bits (RGB888)
Filtering	Trilinear
Anisotropic filtering	4x
Flight speed	3000Km/h

Figure 5.8.7 shows the graphs for a six-second interval, using the configuration shown in Table 5.8.1. The first graph shows the time used by the system to upload texture subtiles to VRAM. The system attempts to limit update times to 1ms in order to leave time to process the rest of the application.

The second graph shows the completeness of the texture stack which can be used as a measure of the quality of the texture shown by the system. In spite of the stress conditions of the test, it holds a completeness level of about 75%, that means a texture detail of 1m per texel.

Table 5.8.2 Statistics

	Min.	Max.	Avg.	Std. Dev.
Subtiles per frame	0	4	2.15	1.55
Subtiles load (ms)	0.19	1.09	0.33	0.09
Completeness (%)	72.83	77.69	75.53	0.86

Table 5.8.2 shows some interesting statistics, such as an average of two subtiles uploaded to video memory per frame or an average of 0.33ms used per frame for updating. Tests with more favorable conditions, such as reducing the clipsize to 1024 texels, maintain averages over 95% quality (0.5m per texel) during all the executions, even using only 1ms as the update time limit, which proves the efficiency of the technique.

Conclusion

The technique described in this gem makes it possible to efficiently manage large textures beyond hardware limits. They can be used in a variety of real-time applications due to configurable load control. The technique stores the image in tiles that are not used directly as textures. These tiles are combined in a texture stack that caches the region of interest, following the clipmap idea. You do not need to subdivide the geometry to make the patches match the texture tile boundaries, as occurs in many terrain visualization techniques. Whatever the geometry algorithm, there will always be a texture to map each patch.

The limitation of this technique is more about patch size than geometry structure, subdivision, or tessellation. The implementation of this texturing technique has been successfully used with different geometry algorithms, based on grids as well as TINs, with some slight level dropping when using large geometry patches for close views, which can be usually avoided.

References

[Montrym97] Montrym, J.S., Baum, D.R., Dignam, D.L. and Migdal, C.J. "InfiniteReality: A Real-Time Graphics System," SIGGRAPH 97, Proceedings of the 24th Annual Conference on Computer Graphics and Interactive Techniques, pp. 293–302. ACM Press/Addison-Wesley Publishing Co, 1997.

[Santi07] The SANTI Project Web Page, available at http://videalab.udc.es/santi.

[Tanner98] Tanner, C.C., Migdal, C.J., and Jones, M.T. "The Clipmap: A Virtual Mipmap," In Proceedings of the 25th Annual Conference on Computer Graphics and Interactive Techniques, pp. 151–158. ACM Press, 1998.

[VTerrain07] The Virtual Terrain Project Website, http://vterrain.org.

[Williams83] Williams, L. "Pyramidal Parametrics," SIGGRAPH 83, Proceedings of the 10th Annual Conference on Computer Graphics and Interactive Techniques, pp. 1–11. ACM Press, 1983.

5.9

Art-Based Rendering with Graftal Imposters

Joshua A. Doss, Advanced Visual Computing, Intel Corporation

joshua.a.doss@intel.com

Graftals are used to express the shape and formation of plants in a formal grammar for use in computer graphics. A close relative of fractals, *graftals* allow for a compact representation of foliage [Smith84]. Graftals have also been used in a non-photorealistic cartoon rendering implementation at interactive frame rates [Kowalski98]. Graftal imposters are used as a real-time method of drawing cartoon-style plants and fur using the geometry shader in modern GPUs. The particular style we aim to produce is inspired by Dr. Seuss's children's book illustrations [Seuss71].

An artist will provide sketches of graftal imposters along with a set of textures that place the foliage in a scene with a high amount of control over the final look and feel. The imposters are placed along the silhouette edges of the object. See Color Plate 12 for a full-color example.

Assets

Creating graftal imposters requires a set of assets in addition to the geometry—a texture atlas, control texture, and a vector field texture. The texture atlas contains three types of graftal imposters along with several variations of each type. A control texture provides information about what type of graftal imposter should be placed at a certain location on the mesh. The vector field gives a direction and the color texture provides information on the coloring of the landscape mesh as well as the graftal imposters.

Texture Atlas

The texture atlas contains the graftal imposter itself. It is created by specifying a few different types of graftal imposter types, in different rows. The exterior of each graftal imposter should have an RGB and alpha value of zero for all components. As you near the soft edge of the graftal imposter, the alpha value should go smoothly from zero to one in the middle of the stroke, giving you a smooth transition and reducing any aliasing effects. The red, green, and blue channels should remain zero until the alpha channel is saturated, as shown in Figure 5.9.1.

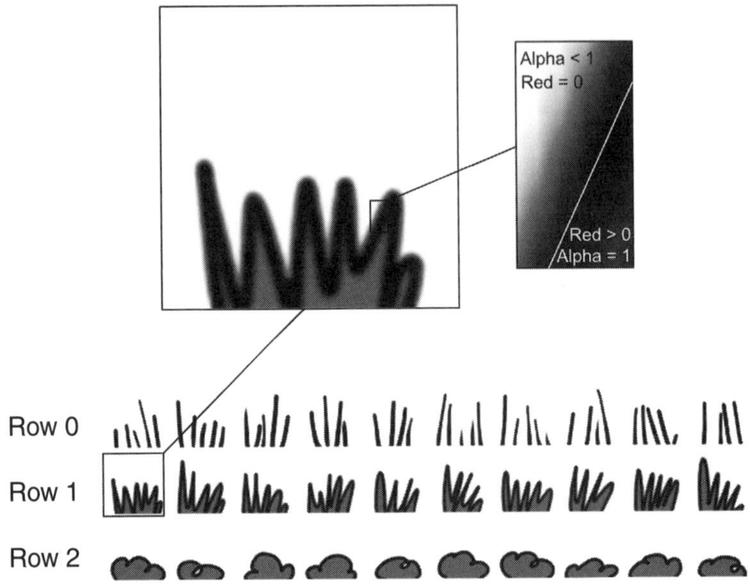

FIGURE 5.9.1 The texture atlas uses red as a color key inside of the graftal imposter and the alpha channel to smoothly blend the graftal imposter with the rest of the scene.

Once you reach the middle of the outline, it blends smoothly into solid red, leaving the alpha channel saturated. The inside of graftal imposters will be blended with the color of the underlying geometry while the outside will be blended with the rest of the scene.

Control Texture

The control texture enables the designer to specify where a graftal imposter may be placed and the type of graftal imposter to be drawn. The alpha channel is used to indicate areas where no graftal imposters can be drawn. Red should be used where the designer wants graftal imposters from the first row of the texture atlas, green for the second row, and blue for the third and final row. Using three color channels isn't the optimal encoding; however, it simplifies the asset-creation process.

Vector Field

It is often desirable to indicate a direction, or flow of the graftal imposters. One example of this comes when using this technique to create fur (or hair) on a character. You could use the normal as an extrusion direction; however, this limits the amount of control the end user has over the final look of the scene. Hair, plants, trees, and so on, don't always grow at a right angle to the surface from which they protrude. To solve this, you can create the vector field, which gives you the direction. See Figure 5.9.3.

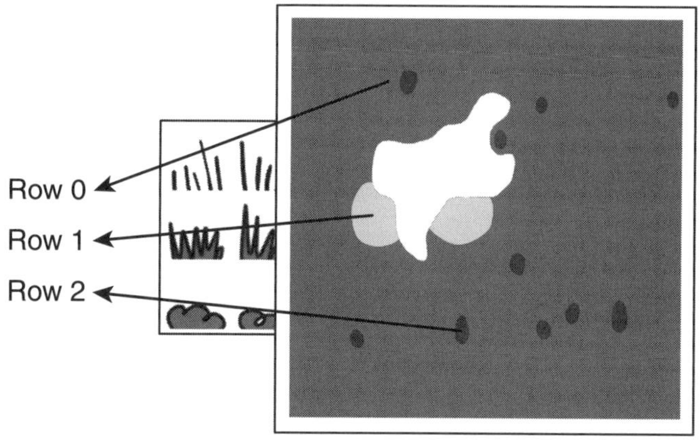

FIGURE 5.9.2 The control texture indicates coverage and row selection.

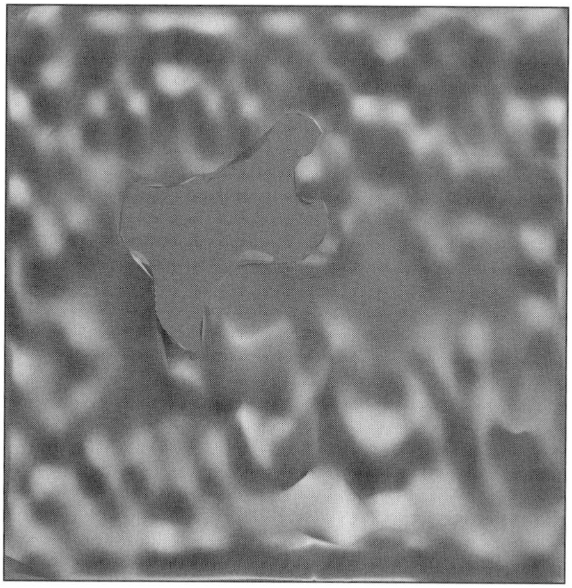

FIGURE 5.9.3 The vector field texture indicates the direction of the graftal imposters.

To create the vector field, you leverage existing digital content-creation applications and plug-ins. After creating a mesh of the desired resolution, the designer saves it and substantially reduces the tessellation of the mesh. You want to be sure to preserve the original normals, as they are used in another step and passed with the mesh. Next, the designer manipulates the normals to indicate which direction the graftal imposters should go; this can be done on a per-face basis or by selecting several normals at the same time. Once the manipulation is complete, these new values can be saved using a normal map plug-in creating the vector field. The result will look like Figure 5.9.3.

Color Texture and Mesh

The color texture is used to indicate the color of the mesh as well as the internal coloring of the graftal imposters. Figure 5.9.4 is the color texture for the scene. This technique creates the graftal imposters along the edges. Large differences in edge length result in visible irregularities in the width of the graftal imposters; therefore, the mesh should contain triangles of roughly uniform size. In areas with a high level of detail where extremely small triangles are required, it might be best to use the control texture to omit the creation of graftal imposters.

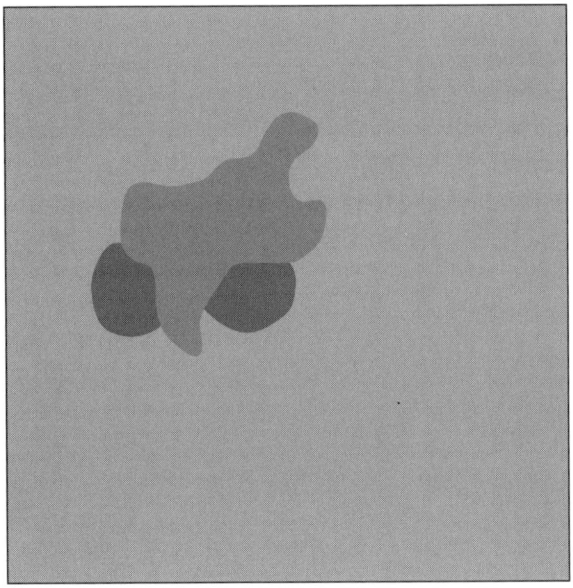

FIGURE 5.9.4 The color texture is used to color the base mesh and the graftal imposters.

Runtime

You can now use the assets created in the previous step during the runtime component of the algorithm. This implementation of graftal imposters requires the use of a programmable graphics language with a geometry shader. First, you draw the original mesh and apply the color texture. Next, you use the geometry shader to determine where to place the graftal imposters as well as which type of graftal imposter to place. Finally, you use the pixel shader to give the final color to the graftal imposters and blend them with the rest of the scene.

The control texture was created earlier to dictate where you can create graftal imposters as well as what type of graftal imposter to draw in a given area. You need to test the triangle to determine whether the primitive is eligible for a graftal imposter and assign a type if it is.

```
texCoordCentroid = ( vertex1uv + vertex2uv + vertex3uv ) / 3;
controlSample = controlTexture.sample( sampler, texCoordCentroid );
if( controlSample.a == 1 )
   if( controlSample.r == 1)
      glyphType = 0;
   elseif( controlSample.g == 1)
      glyphType = 1;
   else
      glyphType = 2;
```

Sampling a texture from within the geometry shader is allowed using the unified instruction set provided with Direct3D 10. You need to choose a point at which to sample the texture, since you have access to multiple vertices. The previous pseudocode shows how you can sample the control texture using the centroid of the triangle currently being processed.

Now that you know the triangle is eligible for graftal imposter(s), you need to test each edge to see whether it is a silhouette edge. A silhouette edge is an edge that's shared by both a front and a back facing triangle. In order to test an edge to see whether it is a silhouette edge, calculate the dot product of the face normal $\mathbf{N_1}$,$\mathbf{N_2}$ with the view direction $\mathbf{V}$ for both faces and test to see if the signs differ [Lake00].

$$(\mathbf{N}_1 \bullet \mathbf{V}) * (\mathbf{N}_2 \bullet \mathbf{V}) \leq 0 \tag{5.9.1}$$

To create the new geometry at the silhouette edge, you extrude vertices $\mathbf{V}_0$ and $\mathbf{V}_1$ in a direction $\mathbf{D}$ obtained from the vector field sampled using the texture coordinates at the midpoint M of the edge. See Figure 5.9.5.

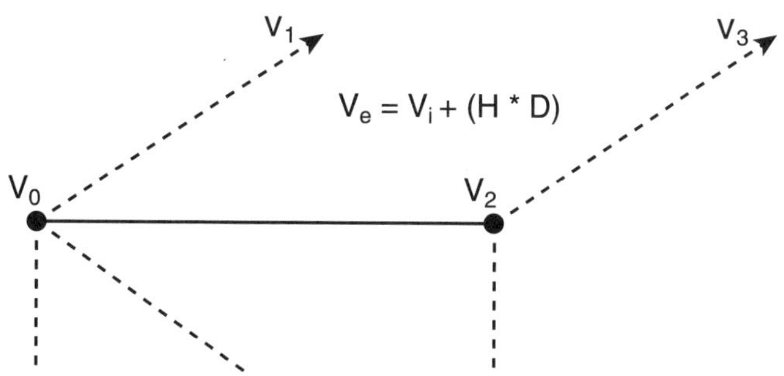

FIGURE 5.9.5 New vertices are created by extruding each vertex along the edge where graftal imposters are desired.

```
//Recreate the original vertex V0
Position = Input.Position;
Output.Position = mul(Position, ObjectToProjection);
Output.GraftalImposterColor = V0Color = ColorTexture.sample
                                (sampler, Input.V0.Texcoord);
. . .
AppendVertex();

//Create a new vertex in the appropriate direction
Position = Input.Position * Direction + GraftalHeight;
Output.Position = mul(Position, ObjectToProjection);
Output.GraftalImposterColor = V0Color;
. . .
AppendVertex();

//Recreate the original vertex V1
Position = Input.Position;
Output.Position = mul(Position, ObjectToProjection);
Output.GraftalImposterColor = V1Color = ColorTexture.sample
                                (sampler, Input.V1.Texcoord);
. . .
AppendVertex();

//Create final new vertex, finishing the quad
Position = Input.Position * Direction + GraftalHeight;
Output.Position = mul(Position, ObjectToProjection);
Output.GraftalImposterColor = V1Color;
. . .
AppendVertex();
```

This pseudocode shows how to create the graftal imposter surface as well as sampling the color texture in order to shade the graftal imposter. Selecting the color once per incoming vertex allows you to have a graftal imposter that crosses a color boundary, because the value is interpolated as it is passed to the pixel shader.

Next, you assign texture coordinates to the newly created geometry to place the graftal imposter on the newly created surface by indexing into the texture atlas. You use the graftal imposter type G to index into the correct row of the texture and a pseudorandom value such as a sample into a noise texture to determine the column C. N_C is the number of variations, or columns, the texture atlas contains (see Equations 5.9.2–5.9.5).

$$uv_{V_0} = \frac{C}{N_c}, \frac{G}{3} + \frac{1}{3} \tag{5.9.2}$$

$$uv_{V_{0New}} = \frac{C}{N_c}, \frac{G}{3} \tag{5.9.3}$$

$$uv_{V_1} = \frac{C}{N_c} + \frac{1}{N_c}, \frac{G}{3} + \frac{1}{3} \quad (5.9.4)$$

$$uv_{V_{1New}} = \frac{C}{N_c} + \frac{1}{N_c}, \frac{G}{3} \quad (5.9.5)$$

The final step is to sample the texture atlas using the texture coordinates calculated in the geometry shader. You want to have a smooth transition from the graftal imposter's black outline to the internal color passed in by the vertex shader. To accomplish this, the red channel of the result is masked off and the sample is linearly interpolated with the color value passed in via the geometry shader. The red channel is used as the blending factor in the interpolation.

```
//coloring the graftal imposter
AtlasColor = AtlasTexture.Sample(Sampler,
             GraftalImposterTextureCoords);
RedZero = float3(0,AtlasColor.gb);
GraftalImposterColor = lerp(RedZero.rgb, IncomingColor.rgb,
                       AtlasColor.rrr);
GraftalImposterColor.a = AtlasColor.a;
```

The incoming color is interpolated across the two vertices that you sampled within the geometry shader. You blend the graftal imposter's soft edge by doing a linear interpolation with the red channel masked out. Preserving the alpha value enables you to blend the outside of the smooth edge with the underlying landscape color. See Color Plate 12 for a full-color example of rendering with graftal imposters.

Acknowledgements

The author would like to thank Jeffery A. Williams, Rahul Sathe, David Bookout, Nico Galoppo, Adam Lake, and the Advanced Visual Computing team at Intel for their assistance, support, and contributions.

Conclusion and Future Work

This gem has shown how to create a scene in a style similar to that found in Dr. Seuss's children's books. The technique utilizes the new technology capabilities of geometry shaders in this GPU-centric technique, leaving more CPU cycles for game logic and other tasks. Currently, we are applying graftal imposters only to the silhouette edges. In our future work, we would like to automatically generate the vector field used for extrusion directions without an artist having to encode it for the entire geometry.

When implementing this technique for production, a couple of additional features may be desired. Adapting the introduction and removal of graftal imposters to provide for inter-frame coherence by scaling or "fading" in the graftal imposters is one possible solution. Another important consideration is handling of z-fighting.

References

[Doss07] Doss, Joshua A. "Inking the Cube: Edge Detection with Direct3D 10," *Game Developer Magazine,* June/July 2007, pp. 13–18.

[Kowalski98] Kowalski, Michael A., et. al. "Art-Based Rendering of Fur, Grass, and Trees," Proceedings of the 26th Annual Conference on Computer Graphics and Interactive Techniques, SIGGRAPH 1998, pp. 433–438.

[Lake00] Lake, Adam, et. al. "Stylized Rendering Techniques for Real-Time 3D Animation and Rendering," Proceedings of the 1st International Symposium on Non-photorealistic Animation and Rendering, NPAR, 2000, pp. 13–20.

[Rost06] Rost, Randi J. *OpenGL Shading Language,* Addison Wesley, 2006.

[Seuss71] Seuss, Dr. *The Lorax,* Random House, Inc., 1971.

[Smith84] Smith, Alvy Ray. "Plants, Fractals, and Formal Languages," *Computer Graphics,* Vol. 18, No. 3, SIGGRAPH 1984, pp. 1–10.

5.10

Cheap Talk: Dynamic Real-Time Lipsync

Timothy E. Roden, Angelo State University
troden@angelo.edu

Game developers are increasingly using lipsyncing for in-game 3D characters. One problem is that getting lipsyncing up and running can be both time-consuming and expensive. A custom solution may involve valuable programmer time while a more expedient method, involving purchased middleware, can have other drawbacks. Particularly for developers wanting to experiment with lipsyncing, perhaps as part of a proof-of-concept demo, a quicker, less expensive solution is desirable. Fortunately, you can incorporate lipsyncing into a game on the cheap and in a minimum amount of time. The result is at least adequate for a proof-of-concept and might be sufficient for a packaged game. This gem explains a method for quick and easy lipsyncing.

Requirements

In order to use this method, several general requirements need to be met. First, you need a 3D character. Because the example animates the lips, you need at least a pair of lips and preferably an entire head. This gem's examples use a head generated with Singular Inversion's FaceGen® software. The head model we are using is shown in Figure 5.10.1. The model consists of 7,341 vertices and 12,960 triangles, not including the hair.

The head model needs to have some parametric controls for mouth positions that can be manipulated dynamically. A set of morph targets works great. If you are not versed in how morph targets work, Lever provides a good explanation [Lever02]. A nice thing about the FaceGen® models is that they come with a large set of morph targets for both facial expressions and lip positions, which correspond to various basic units of speech. As shown in Figure 5.10.2, the head used here has 16 morph targets for *visemes,* which are visual representations of speech such as "aah" and "ee." Watt and Policarpo describe visemes as the basic units of visual speech that are described by extreme lip shapes, which correspond to basic auditory speech units [Watt03]. A set of visemes constitutes a minimally distinct set representing the sounds in a language.

You can probably imagine more lip positions than the 16 shown in Figure 5.10.2. However, this minimal set is actually quite good for the purposes here and will allow you to generate very convincing lipsync animation.

FIGURE 5.10.1 A head model generated using Singular Inversion's FaceGen® software.

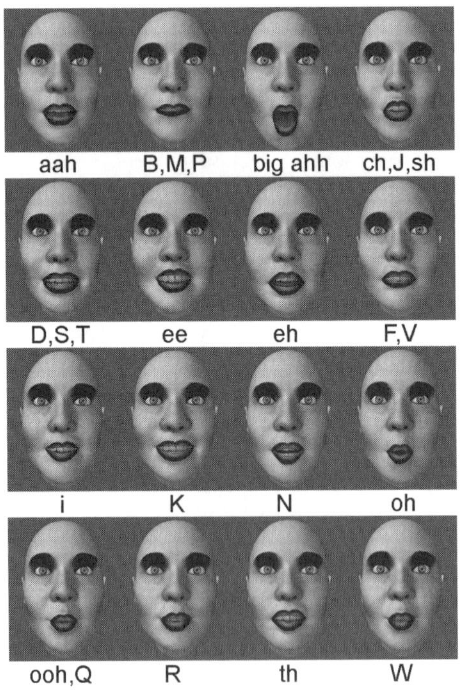

FIGURE 5.10.2 The 16 visemes used here, each shown at its extreme (1.0) morph. See Color Plate 13.

You'll need the ability in your program to independently adjust each of the 16 visemes using a float value that ranges from 0.0 to 1.0. Values of 0.0 effectively turn off the viseme, whereas values of 1.0 mean the viseme is at full strength. Figure 5.10.3 illustrates how a value of 0.0 adds nothing to the mouth position, whereas higher values cause the mouth to morph into the desired shape. This example allows any set of combinations. So, for example, you could have the mouth change shape by applying the "aah" viseme at a value of 1.0 combined with 0.5 of the "ee" viseme. In fact, this ability is crucial to enabling you to generate realistic dynamic lipsync.

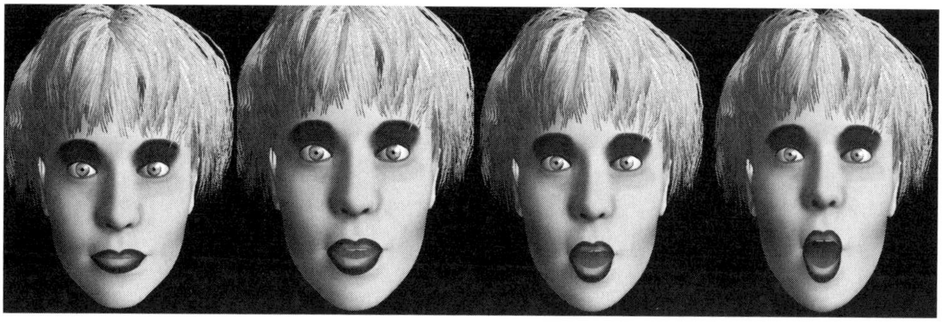

FIGURE 5.10.3 The "aah" viseme at varying values (from left: 0, 0.33, 0.66, and 1.0).

For audio, you can use pre-recorded speech or audio generated speech at runtime, such as the output of text-to-speech engine. You will also need the text of what is being spoken. Using a text-to-speech engine works nicely because the audio is generated at runtime based on a text string, so you get the text and audio at the same time.

General Procedure

For each lipsynced audio sample, the general runtime procedure is as follows:

1. Translate each word of the text into its corresponding set of phonemes.
2. Translate each phoneme into its corresponding viseme.
3. Generate animation data based on the set of visemes.
4. Start playing the audio.
5. Use the animation data to drive the 3D model during audio playback.

ON THE CD

The companion CD-ROM contains source code written in C++ for a static library that implements Steps 1 through 3 of this procedure.

Word to Phoneme Mapping

Phonemes are different from visemes. *Phonemes* are the basic distinctive units of how speech is heard in a language. Individual words can be broken down into phonemes based on the individual sounds that make up a word. Visemes, on the other hand, are the basic visual units of speech. There is a close correspondence between phonemes and visemes. There are typically more phonemes in a language than visemes. That is because several different sounds may be represented by the same lip position. For example, "s" and "z" are audibly different sounds, but the position of the lips can be similar.

Translating words into phonemes couldn't be easier than using the Carnegie Mellon Pronouncing Dictionary [CMU07]. The CMU dictionary is available online and can be used for any research or commercial purpose without restriction. It is a text file containing over 118,000 English words and their corresponding phonetic translations. For example, the word "hello" translates to the four phonemes HH, AH, L, and OW. There are a total of 39 distinct phonemes in the CMU dictionary. Table 5.10.1 lists each phoneme and an example word found in the dictionary that uses the phoneme. Because the dictionary is already in alphabetical order in the text file, it is a fairly simple programming task to read the dictionary into an array and perform a binary search to look up words and retrieve their corresponding phonemes.

Table 5.10.1 The 39 CMU Phonemes

Phoneme	Example	Translation (of the Example)
AA	Odd	AA D
AE	At	AE T
AH	Hut	HH AH T
AO	Ought	AO T
AW	Cow	K AW
AY	Hide	HH AY D
B	Be	B IY
CH	Cheese	CH IY Z
D	Dee	D IY
DH	Thee	DH IY
EH	Ed	EH D
ER	Hurt	HH ER T
EY	Ate	EY T
F	Fee	F IY
G	Green	G R IY N
HH	He	HH IY
IH	It	IH T
IY	Eat	IY T
JH	Gee	JH IY
K	Key	K IY
L	Lee	L IY
M	Me	M IY
N	Knee	N IY
NG	Ping	P IH NG
OW	Oat	OW T

→

Phoneme	Example	Translation (of the Example)
OY	Toy	T OY
P	Pee	P IY
R	Read	R IY D
S	Sea	S IY
SH	She	SH IY
T	Tea	T IY
TH	Theta	TH EY T AH
UH	Hood	HH UH D
UW	Two	T UW
V	Vee	V IY
W	We	W IY
Y	Yield	Y IY L D
Z	Zee	Z IY
ZH	Seizure	S IY ZH ER

Phoneme to Viseme Mapping

Translating phonemes to visemes is a direct lookup based on a table you need to create beforehand. The dictionary contains 39 separate phonemes and the 3D model used here has 16 visemes. A little creativity is required here to determine the correct viseme for each of the phonemes. Probably the easiest way to do this is in front of a mirror. Using Table 5.10.1, pronounce each example word and notice the position of your lips as you sound out the particular phoneme in the word. Match your lip position with the closest viseme in Figure 5.10.2. For the purposes of this gem, we will use the mapping shown in Table 5.10.2.

Table 5.10.2 Phoneme to Viseme Mapping

Phoneme	Viseme	Phoneme	Viseme	Phoneme	Viseme
AA	Big aah	F	F,V	P	B,M,P
AE	Aah	G	Ch,J,sh	R	R
AH	Aah	HH	Eh	S	D,S,T
AO	Big aah	IH	I	SH	Ch,J,sh
AW	Big aah	IY	Ee	T	D,S,T
AY	Aah	JH	Ch,J,sh	TH	Th
B	B,M,P	K	Ch,J,sh	UH	Oh
CH	Ch,J,sh	L	Th	UV	Ooh,Q
D	D,S,T	M	B,M,P	V	F,V
DH	Th	N	N	W	W
EH	Eh	NG	D,S,T	Y	Ee
ER	R	OW	Oh	Z	W
EY	Eh	OY	Ooh,Q	ZH	Ch,J,sh

Real-Time Lipsyncing

ON THE CD

At runtime, for each audio sample you want lipsynced, you have to convert the string containing the text into phonemes and then into visemes. Using the code supplied on the companion CD-ROM, this consists of making two functions calls. A third function is then called to translate the visemes into lipsync animation data that can be used to animate the 3D model during playback of the audio. Let's first examine how the lipsync data is generated.

Several methods could be used that vary in complexity with more complex methods providing possibly more accurate data. However, for the purposes of this gem, let's use an easy approach that gives quite remarkable results given its simplicity. The idea is to divide the duration of the spoken audio by the number of visemes and assign each viseme a time slot to become active during audio playback.

For example, Figure 5.10.4 illustrates the word "hello." The word consists of four visemes. At time 0, you begin to morph the viseme "eh" from 0 to 1 and then back to 0. Before "eh" becomes inactive, you must begin to morph the "ahh" viseme, and so on. The idea is to overlap the visemes slightly from one to the next. This results in more natural looking lipsync.

By varying the amount of overlap, you can achieve some interesting effects. For example, a long overlap period tends to make the speaker appear to slur words together, at least visually. A short overlap period produces very distinct visemes as might be expected when someone is angry. Too short or too long of an overlap produces unnatural looking results.

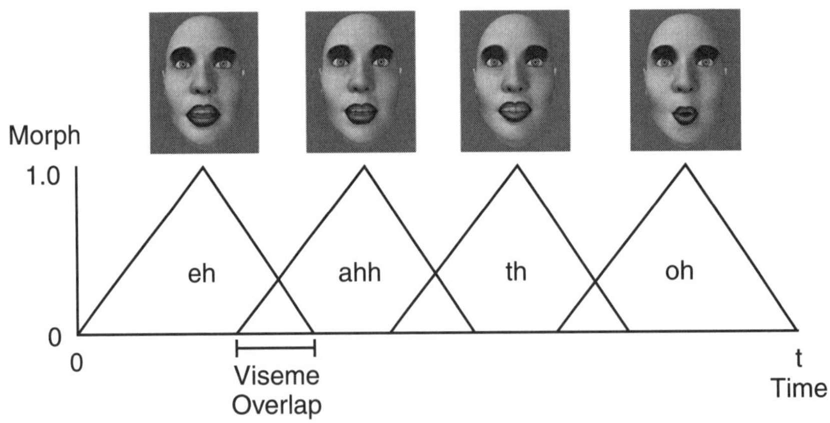

FIGURE 5.10.4 The word "hello" and its corresponding visemes animated over time.

A few details of word timing need to be addressed in any solution. For multi-sentence audio, the text should contain periods to indicate the end of sentences. Each period can then be assigned a timeslot so the last viseme at the end of a sentence does not bleed over into the first viseme at the start of the next sentence. The amount of

ON THE CD

time for this end-of-sentence delay will likely need to be discovered by trial and error. The code on the companion CD-ROM uses 500 milliseconds. If using a text-to-speech engine, one trick is to save a few text-to-speech audio files that contain multiple sentences and then review them in a WAV file editor. Looking at the WAV data, it is easy to see the duration of the end-of-sentence delay.

There are obvious drawbacks to the proposed solution. Perhaps the biggest problem is with actual human voice files. Unlike text-to-speech engines, which typically speak at a constant rate, humans often speak at varying rates even within the same sentence. This can be problematic with the simple lipsync algorithm described here, because it relies on a constant rate of speech. Still, the advantage of this method is the lipsync data is generated on the fly, which can be very useful in a rapid prototyping environment where you want to get lipsync up and running quickly.

Conclusion

Creating a dynamic real-time system for lipsync animation using the method presented is likely a few days work, at most, for an experienced programmer. For better results, the method could be enhanced. One idea is to take into account the coarticulation effect, which refers to changes in audio for a particular sound as a function of what sounds have come before and what sounds will follow. Implementation ideas are given in [Watt03].

References

[CMU07] The Carnegie Mellon Pronouncing Dictionary, available online at http://www.speech.cs.cmu.edu/cgi-bin/cmudict, July 2007.

[Lever02] Lever, Nik. *Real-Time 3D Character Animation with Visual C++,* Focal Press, 2002.

[Watt03] Watt, Alan, and Policarpo, Fabio. *3D Games: Animation and Advanced Real-Time Rendering,* Vol. 2, Addison-Wesley, 2003.

SECTION

6

NETWORKING AND MULTIPLAYER

Introduction

Diana Stelmack

The number of game genres that are using multiplayer gameplay is growing by leaps and bounds. The accessibility of the Internet is reaching more platforms than ever before. The consoles are getting in the act. Console makers are providing Internet services to entice their customers to play online with their friends. All this networking means there is a growing need for network programming, and all these genres and services mean there are more game programmers who need to interface with networking. What does this mean? This means that the complex systems that come together to form games need to have more clearly defined interfaces for non-networking programmers to use, tools to help find those bugs during crunch time, methodologies in place to deal with security issues as they arise, and so much more. This section contains some gems that just might help you address one or more of these issues.

The first gem, by Hyun-jik Baeb, describes a technique called High Level Abstraction, or HLA. This technique describes a tool that could be developed to make it easier for the non-networking programmer to interact with the networking engine. Whether you are a network programmer trying to make it easier, or a non-networking programmer who wants it easy, take a look at this gem.

As we all know, if there is a program running on a machine, there is someone that will try to hack it. Keeping up with network security is a never-ending job. This means that network programmers need to consider a strategy for keeping the player's information safe. It is busy on that "Information Superhighway" and consumers don't know how many stops there really are between their PCs and the hosts they are connecting to. The second gem, by Jon Watte, explores the myriad of security approaches and presents a well-rounded solution to address most security needs of today.

Take a game with a lot of simulation. Slow down the frame rate to do lots of cool graphics. Now, for fun, add network latency to data that impacts the simulation, and hence the rendering of the scene. By the way, now the multiple human players who exist in the networked session are shooting at each other and someone wants credit for that kill. All of this involves a lot of network traffic, all of which needs to get from Point A to Point B in a reasonable amount of time with reasonable accuracy. Put in a breakpoint, and that can be the end of that testing session, unless you happen to have a smart packet sniffer. The third gem, by David Koenig, explores the mechanism to create a game-specific packet sniffer to make finding those network issues easier. Understanding the data is half the battle when you are debugging a gameplay issue on the network.

6.1

High-Level Abstraction of Game World Synchronization

Hyun-jik Baeb

One of the important roles of networked gaming hosts is communicating with other hosts to maintain game world synchronization, which involves keeping the game worlds in the same states on all hosts around the world. Synchronization of the game world across multiple hosts requires that game programmers write code that:

- Collects changes occurring on the local host
- Packs the changes into one or more messages
- Transmits the messages to remote hosts
- Applies the messages to the game world states of the remote hosts

Writing code for these tasks can be simplified by techniques such as the Remote Procedure Call (RPC) system [HyunJik04]. RPC sends or receives messages for the cost of writing only one line of code for each message type. However, you still have to manually write routines that manage the game world state, gather information to synchronize, and send and process it. This work grows quickly if your game designer has developed hundreds of diverse battle units that cannot be easily generalized within your program architecture.

The power of meta-programming [Wikipedia07] increases productivity over writing code manually. RPC is, of course, a kind of meta-programming technique. This gem introduces another meta-programming technique that synchronizes the game worlds using High Level Abstraction (HLA). RPC abstracts source code lines that exchange messages among hosts in a few lines in the lower code layer; however, HLA abstracts them in a higher layer, where the messages are exchanged for synchronizing the game world state, which is why it's called *high-level abstraction*.

Raw memory synchronization techniques also allow game world synchronization. However, they are lacking in some aspects:

- Actual working multiplayer gaming requires latency hiding techniques such as dead reckoning [Aronson97]. Synchronizing raw memory has no way of doing this.
- Raw memory synchronization requires game world data to be stored in a block. It is difficult in a situation where automatic memory managers or garbage collectors are used.

- Not every last byte of data has to be synchronized precisely in actual multiplayer gaming worlds. For example, a unit located far from the viewport might not require full precision synchronization.

In an HLA world, game world synchronization can be done by declaring object types and synchronization behavior for each of them, instead of writing code that sends or receives messages. The actual code is automatically generated by the source code generator provided in this gem.

This gem discusses an HLA usage case and explains the overall system of the game world synchronization, and then constructs an HLA system.

HLA Usage

The goal of HLA is to offer a feasible method for abstracting game world synchronization. It is composed of object type definitions, their synchronization behaviors, and a facility that determines the visibility of each object.

The definitions for synchronized objects are stored in a source file in a grammar you define. You can name it the SWD (Synchronized World Definition) file. It will be compiled to several source files and then built within your project files.

The facility that determines synchronization range will actually be a function. You will be able to extend it differently, as you wish.

Anatomy of Game World Synchronization

Because this example involves writing your own HLA infrastructure, there's no limitation when you adopt the HLA technique to your game project. This gem assumes client/server topology, which can be explained like this:

- The game hosts are composed of one server and the other clients. The server owns all game world objects and takes control of them.
- One or more messages are sent from the clients to the server when a change of game world occurs in a client. Then they are applied to server's game world and broadcast to other clients for updating.
- Messages are sent from a server to the clients when a change of game world occurs in a server. The clients receive them and update based on the changes.

Figure 6.1.1 illustrates this collaboration.

You can categorize the changes in the game world state. These are the conditions for sending messages:

- Value modification of an object
- Creation of an object
- Destruction of an object
- Appearance or disappearance of an object, discussed later
- Every time interval

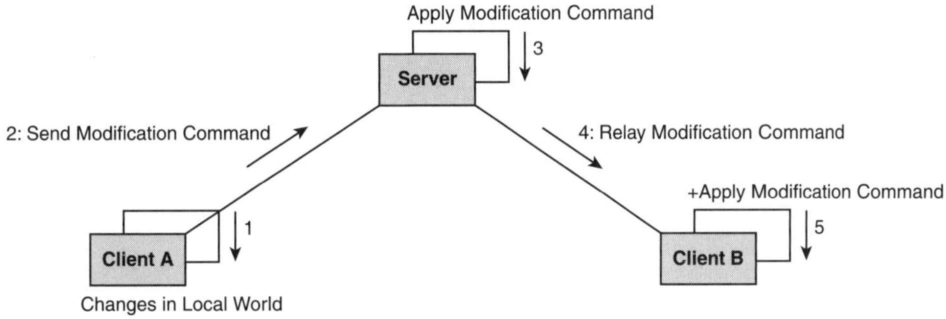

FIGURE 6.1.1 HLA collaboration diagram.

The condition *every time interval* is needed when data changes are frequent, but every change is not necessarily propagated. A good example of this is a character's position. These kinds of changes can be announced by way of an unreliable messaging protocol such as User Datagram Protocol (UDP).

In many actual game products, not every object is synchronized for every remote host due to suffocation of network traffic bandwidth. This is critical to a massive multiplayer game, where every client holds only a very small area of the game world state, while their server holds all of it. (The server-side game world is even incomplete on any single server if the server system consists of distributed processes.) The synchronization range every host occupies is determined by rules that are unique to every game project.

Figure 6.1.2 shows an example that culls the synchronization by a circle defined by a radius from the center of each observer. One circle reflects a viewport of a host and each star represents an object to synchronize. After an object outside two viewports goes into a viewport or a viewport approaches it and envelopes it, the host of the viewport gets the message "a new object has appeared" and the host creates an object in its game world state. In contrast, when the object leaves a viewport by moving the viewport or the object, the "disappear" message arrives to the appropriate host.

Changes that cause corruption of the game world must be prohibited. For example, no one wants his or her loving avatar to be unwillingly moved by opposing forces. You can classify kinds of permissions, as shown in Table 6.1.1.

Table 6.1.1 Permissions of World State Modification

	Change by Server Is Permitted	Change by Local Host Is Permitted	Change by Remote Host Is Permitted
Server-only	Yes	No	No
Server-and-local-only	Yes	Yes	No
Everyone	Yes	Yes	No

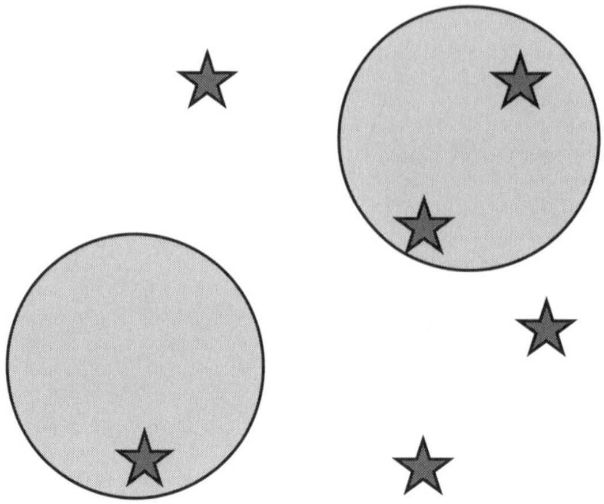

FIGURE 6.1.2 Viewports and objects.

When the change arrives at the receiver, the game world is not updated with the exact data in the change, but rather updated in an interpolated manner. One of the favorite techniques for doing this is dead reckoning [Aronson97].

Now that you've put this world synchronization logic in order, you can implement the HLA infrastructure that follows it. This is an example of synchronizing world state, so you might want to design your own HLA infrastructure by determining what synchronization system your game project requires.

HLA Components

The HLA system consists of an SWD compiler and an HLA runtime, as well as the SWD files. The grammar of the SWD file depends on which factors are defined as important for the synchronized objects. The SWD file discussed in this gem has these factors:

- Object types, AKA classes
- The classes have, of course, member variables
- The variables have synchronization behaviors

Now you can define the major portion of SWD grammar in a simplified BNF form, as in Listing 6.1.1. (Note that the symbols and keywords are omitted.)

Listing 6.1.1 Pseudo-Grammar of an SWD File

```
compilation_unit  :=  (first_id,class*)
class := (name,member*)
member := (behavior,type,name)
behavior := (behavior_selection,additional_attribute)
```

The grammar definition `compilation_unit` is the entry point of parsing.

Listing 6.1.2 is an example of the SWD file that follows the grammar in Listing 6.1.1. The keywords `conditional`, `periodic`, and so on are explained later.

Listing 6.1.2 An Example of an SWD File

```
world MedivalWorld
{
    synch_class Knight
    {
        conditional float Life;
        periodic(interval=0.2,duration=1) int MotionState;
        periodic(interval=0.2,duration=1) float rotationY;
        dead_reckon Vector3 Position,Velocity;
        conditional int Type;
        static ItemList Inventory;
    }

    synch_class Mountain
    {
        conditional int Type;
        // No mountain moves, of course.
        conditional Vector3 Position;
    }
}
```

The code generated by the SWD compiler does the following:

- Manages the synchronized objects and collects any changes to them (creation and destruction of objects or member variable changes)
- Converts the changes to messages and sends them to the networking layer
- Receives messages from the networking layer and processes them

The code generated by the SWD compiler should do everything for world synchronization in an ideal situation. However, this is inefficient in the practical programming world, when a small change to the HLA source code is needed. So, let's drive much of HLA infrastructure into a common library.

Now you might be able to imagine how the HLA system fits into program's architecture. This is shown in Figure 6.1.3.

The recommended way of compiling an SWD file is putting it into the custom build configuration, which was introduced in [HyunJik04].

The Synchronized Object

Let's call the synchronized object *SynchEntity* for avoiding ambiguity with the term *object*. A SynchEntity is one of the classes defined in an SWD file.

A SynchEntity is an ordinary class in practice; however, it has more attributes and behaviors, which are explained next.

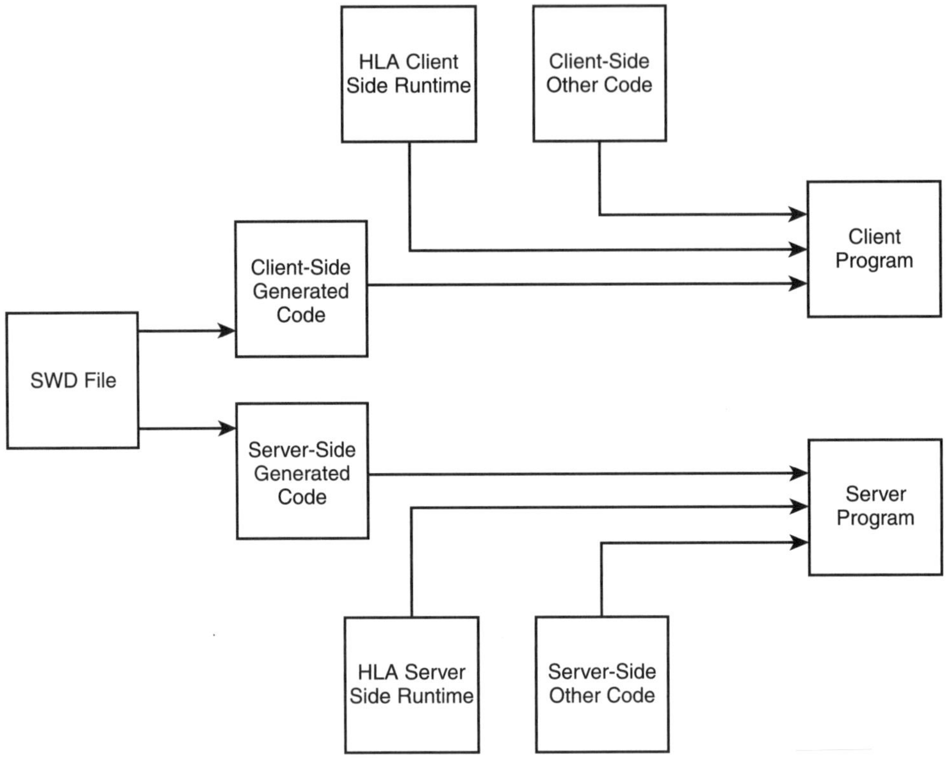

FIGURE 6.1.3 HLA activities within a program's architecture.

A SynchEntity exists as the original or the replica, depending on which host has the ownership (and full permission to modify any values) of it. The host that has ownership is the subject of the SynchEntity. So SynchEntity has an attribute *subject.*

Each object identified across multiple network hosts must be unique. So every SynchEntity instance will have a unique identifier value, which is issued by the server.

Every member variable in a SynchEntity is actually a *property* member. The property member consists of a `set/get` function pair and an alias declaration that binds the two functions into a virtual member variable. Many contemporary compilers support property features such as the `__declspec(property)` keyword in Visual C++. You can also work around this feature's absence by using a casting operator and an assign operator even if your compiler doesn't support the *property* feature. Listings 6.1.3 and 6.1.4 show these two cases.

Listing 6.1.3 Using the *__property* Keyword

```
class MyClass
{
public:
```

```
        __declspec(property(get=getX,put=setX)) int X;
        void setX(int);
        int getX();
    };
```

Listing 6.1.4 Using a Casting Operator and an Assign Operator

```
class XType
{
public:
    XType();
    XType(int value); // takes a value into self
    XType& operator=(int value); // takes a value into self
    operator int(); // outputs the internal value
};

class MyClass
{
public:
    XType X;
};
```

The synchronization behavior for each member variable can be defined in an SWD file. The SWD compiler then generates appropriate source code depending on which behavior is defined for each member variable. Some of the code may monitor to see if any changes are made to the variable. You can get better performance by substituting it with code similar to Listing 6.1.5, which can help to quickly skip comparisons when there are no changes.

Listing 6.1.5 Flagging a Variable as Changed While Assigning a Value

```
void SetXXX(int newVal)
{
    m_maybeChanged=true;
    m_value=newVal;
}
```

The synchronization behavior to be bound to a SynchEntity member variable is typically one of static, conditional, periodic, or dead reckoning.

Static behavior means it is never synchronized. If there were no the static behavior, you should define a class derived from the SynchEntity just for adding member variables that don't have to be synchronized.

Conditional behavior means that the value is synchronized when its value changes. This is the most commonly used behavior; however, it can flood network traffic if the value changes are too frequent.

Periodic behavior resolves the potential problems with conditional behavior by sending the value at specified intervals. This behavior needs send interval value and send duration. If the value of a periodic behavior member variable changes, it will be sent to remote hosts in the interval of send interval value until the send duration time elapses. Assuming, for example, that you set the send interval to 0.2 second and the duration to 1 second for a periodic behavioral variable, the value will be sent to remote hosts five times every 0.2 seconds. Periodic behavior is typically used together with unreliable messaging protocols such as UDP.

Listing 6.1.6 is an example of a conditional behavioral member variable that is used in the SWD file, whereas Listing 6.1.7 shows its compiled code.

Listing 6.1.6 An Example Conditional Behavioral Member Variable Used in an SWD File

```
synch_class Knight
{
    conditional int life;
    <...and more...>
}
```

Listing 6.1.7 Generated Code for the Conditional Behavioral Member Variable

```
class Knight
{
private:
    int m_private_life;
    bool m_private_life_changed;
    inline void set_life(int value)
    {
        if(value!=m_private_life)
        {
            // A variable whose *_changed
            // is true will be broadcasted soon.
            m_private_life_changed=true;
            m_private_life=value;
        }
    }
    inline int get_life(int value)
    {
        return m_private_life;
    }
public:
    __declspec(property(get=get_life,put=set_life)) int life;

    <...and more...>
};
```

Dead reckoning behavior allows you to hide the jittering values that occur due to network latency. A simple dead reckoning model involves three variables to reference: the actual value of the sender, the predicted value of the receiver side, and the interpolated value. So the SWD compiler should generate these three variables for each dead reckoning behavioral variable.

The flag that indicates whether the value is changed (`m_private_life_changed` in Listing 6.1.7) is then used for collecting change information from the game world. One simple model is to iterate over each SynchEntity and gather the changed ones by reading the flag. Because the HLA runtime itself cannot know what the flag values are, the iteration routine should be generated by the SWD compiler. Listing 6.1.8 shows an example for the variable in Listing 6.1.6.

Listing 6.1.8 Generated Code That Identifies the Change and Collects It to the Output Message Object

```
class MedivalWorld_Runtime
{
public:
    void GatherTheChangeToMessage(SynchEntity* entity,
        CMessage &outputMessage)
    {
        // the identifier SynchEntity_Knight is
        // generated enumeration value from the SWD compiler.
        if(entity->GetType()==SynchEntity_Knight)
        {
            Knight* typedEntity=(Knight*)entity;
            if(typedEntity->m_private_life_changed)
            {
                outputMessage.Write(typedEntity->m_private_life);
                typedEntity->m_private_life_changed=false;
            }
            <...and more...>
        }
    }
};
```

One more part to investigate is the routine that receives messages from other HLA runtimes and applies them to the local game world. This task, which is called *deserialization*, is mentioned in [HyunJik04].

Communication Between HLA Runtimes

The major cases during world synchronization that were classified here are SynchEntity creation, destruction, appearance, disappearance, and value change. Each of these cases corresponds to a messaging sequence.

Almost all SynchEntities are created only after the server decides that a creation is necessary (that is, creating the object in the server side at first) and its event is broadcast to the clients. Then the received client creates the replica of the new SynchEntity after receiving the message. The required parameters for creating the SynchEntity are its ID and its initial member variable values. These values are serialized to a message and then sent to the clients that need to know about the newly created SynchEntity.

SynchEntities that are trivial in presence but sensitive in performance (machine gun projectiles, for example) can be created by the client side even if the server does not permit it yet. In this case, the client first creates it and notifies the server, and then the rest is the same as before. The identifier value of a SynchEntity that's created client side always exists in a value range that has been issued by the server when the client joined the game world. [Yongha06] shows more details about doing this.

The destruction of a SynchEntity is similar to the creation case, except for the fact that the message type has only the ID of the destructed SynchEntity. A SynchEntity is destroyed at the server, the server sends the event to the clients that view the object, and the clients also destroy the replica. The additional sequence needed for a trivial SynchEntity is a client-side decision to destroy the entity, at which point the server is notified.

All changes in the SynchEntity variables are collected and sent to the clients that possess replicas. Messages containing these changes have the SynchEntity ID and a list of changed values with their variable ID numbers. Then, each of the clients receives these messages and applies the changes to its replicas.

Consider one more case: the client first decides to change and announces it to the server, but only if it is trivial enough that a client has permissions to call for the modifications or the subject of the SynchEntity is the client.

The visibility of every SynchEntity can be changed as time goes on because its position or the position of each viewer changes. If one SynchEntity enters a viewport, the client that owns the viewport creates the replica of the SynchEntity after the server sends the appearance message with the SynchEntity ID and its serialized values. In contrast, the disappearance message with the SynchEntity ID is received at the client and then it removes the corresponding replica.

Viewports in HLA Runtime

The viewport in HLA runtime maintains the current state (position and such) as well as a network host identifier for sending or receiving messages for synchronization. Typically a viewport has a camera position (or more, depending on what radar the player has) and a host identifier value. SynchEntity and the base class of viewport SynchViewport are both abstracted classes.

A simple implementation of the entity-viewport visibility check is calling a function that takes two parameters: a SynchEntity and a SynchViewport. This function is normally called $N \times M$ times, where N is the number of all SynchEntity instances and M is the number of all SynchViewport instances. You may want to implement the function to meet your own needs. For example, your method could be based upon geographical range, parent-child relationship of each scene graph node, or portal partition of BSP/PVS. The prototype of this function is shown in Listing 6.1.9.

Listing 6.1.9 A Function for Entity-Viewport Visibility Determination

```
bool IsOneEntityVisibleToOneViewport(SynchViewport *viewport,
                                     SynchEntity* SynchEntity);
```

The client/server topology discussed here allows this functionality to be on the server. So this function exists only on the server side.

HLA Event Handlers

You may need to handle something at the exact time when the world state changes. Examples of this are the *appear* and *disappear* events of a SynchEntity. These cases are useful for loading just-in-time (JIT) resource files for a character type, for example.

You can add these event handler interfaces without any limitation because you are using your own HLA system. You just inject these event handler prototypes and the invoker code into the HLA compiler or HLA runtime source lines.

Construction of HLA Runtime

The HLA runtime fits in with the structure of what you've investigated so far. Keeping that in mind, the HLA runtime's design is shown in Figure 6.1.4.

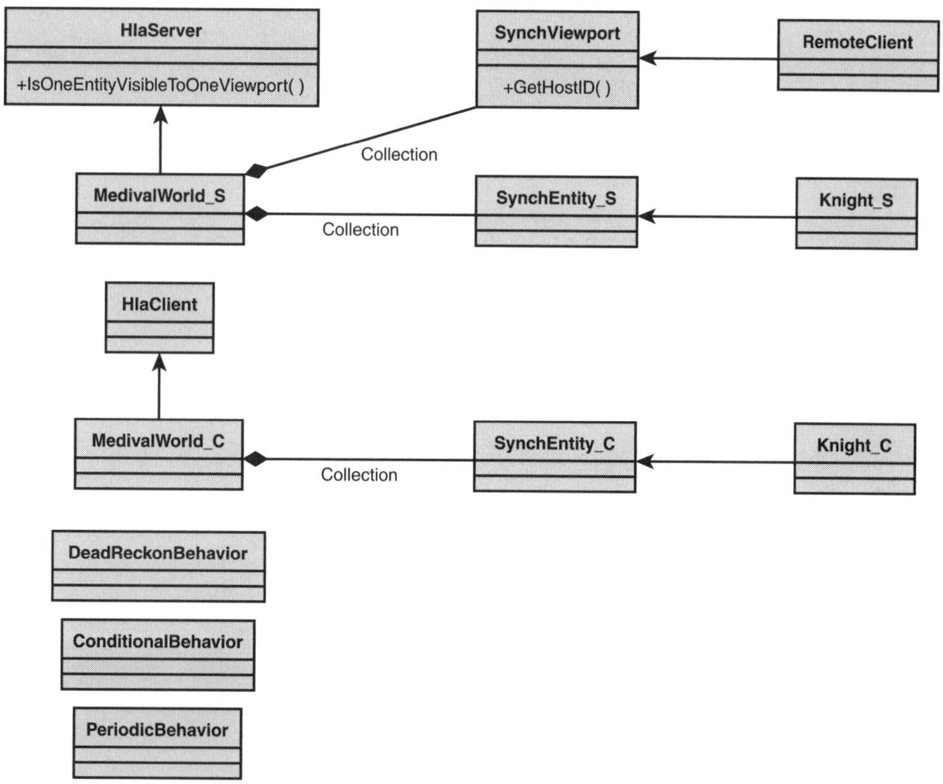

FIGURE 6.1.4 UML class diagram of major classes of HLA system.

`HlaServer` has these features:

- `HlaServer` has every instance of SynchEntity_S-derived objects and SynchViewport-derived objects as well as an entity-viewport visibility decision maker. (Note that `_C` and `_S` postfixes stand for server and client.)
- `HlaServer` monitors the state of every SynchEntity_S and SynchViewport instance. If a change is detected, `HlaServer` serializes the changes into several messages and sends them to the remote hosts.
- `HlaServer` interfaces with a networking engine to send or receive messages related to world synchronization.

`HlaClient` keeps instances of SynchEntity_C replicated from the server. Like `HlaServer`, it also interfaces with the networking engine and has routines for keeping the state of every SynchEntity_C synchronized with the server.

`Knight_S` and `Knight_C` are generated classes from an example class `Knight` in the SWD file.

Class `Knight_C` and class `Knight_S` have members, each of whose type is one of the classes `DeadReckonBehavior`, `ConditionalBehavior`, and `PeriodicBehavior`. These classes help `HlaClient` and `HlaServer` determine whether these member variables should be broadcasted. The code in Listing 6.1.7 can become more concise if it uses `ConditionalBehavior` class.

Further Issues

The implementation of the HLA system in this article is just a simple networking model focused on ease of reading and discussion. These features are worth extending based on the HLA system in this gem:

- Besides the conditional, periodic, static, and dead reckoning behaviors, there are more models for synchronization. For example, synchronization based on timestamp value.
- The SynchEntity types discussed so far have no member functions. They could be added to the HLA system by sending event messages to the remote host. There are two invocation behaviors—running the member functions only on a host that has the original (this can be in an object-oriented remote procedure call manner), or on every host that has the original or replica. This may be specified where the invocation begins or pre-specified in the SWD file.
- Duplicated definitions in similar classes could be refactored into common objects. This also applies to the SWD files.
- Optimization of comparison bottlenecks may be helpful for better performance. The HLA in this gem checks visibility for every SynchEntity and every SynchViewport, which then results in $O(n^2)$ time complexity. You could cull some of them by adding a Boolean variable called "this object is changed" to the SynchEntity and SynchViewport classes and use it before the actual comparison.

Conclusion

If you find yourself writing a lot of similar code to keep your game world synchronized, implementing your own High Level Abstraction (HLA) system based on this design can greatly ease your subsequent efforts at game world synchronization. The HLA system introduced in this gem can be a guide for the first step as you write your own HLA system.

References

[Aronson97] Aronson. "Dead Reckoning: Latency Hiding for Networked Games," available online at http://www.gamasutra.com/features/19970919/aronson_01.htm.

[HyunJik04] Bae, Hyun-jik. "Fast and Efficient Implementation of a Remote Procedure Call System," *Game Programming Gems 5,* edited by Kim Pallister, Charles River Media, 2005, pp. 627-642.

[Wikipedia07] "Meta-Programming," available online at http://en.wikipedia.org/wiki/Meta_programming.

[Yongha06] Kim, Yongha. "Generating Globally Unique Identifiers for Game Objects," *Game Programming Gems 6,* edited by Michael Dickheiser, Charles River Media, 2006, pp. 623-628.

6.2

Authentication for Online Games

Jon Watte

gpg-7@mindcontrol.org

Authentication for games, where un-trusted clients connect to one or more trusted servers, is an interesting special case of general authentication. This article presents some alternatives that you should consider when designing authentication for an online game system, and proposes one particular set of internally cohesive design choices.

Introduction

Authentication is the process of making sure that someone is who they say they are, and by extension, that a given communication comes from a given party. For computer games, this comes in two flavors:

- *Game login*—Given credentials (a user name and password) match the information against a database of allowed players.
- *Game session*—A network packet was sent by the logged in player it says it came from.

Note that authentication, consisting of the ability to determine who sent a specific message, does not have much to do with encryption, which is the ability to hide a message from unintended recipients. The one exception is that one kind of cryptosystem (public/private key systems) has the ability to provide both functions at once. Unfortunately, these cryptosystems are usually computationally expensive, and thus are not a great match for real-time, online services like computer games.

Securing Game Logins

To secure game logins, you need to worry about a few kinds of problems:

- *Insecure passwords*—Players may have a password that is a common word (like "secret"), the player's name, or even a blank. Your password setting mechanism should detect weak passwords and require better ones.

- *Insecure password storage*—Are your servers secure? Someone might break into them. If they can read the password in clear text at that point, that's a problem. Also, are the operators of your system trustworthy? What if you have to lay them off or fire one?
- *Sniffed passwords*—If you don't use Secure Sockets Layer or some similar heavy-weight encrypted protocol, it's possible that someone can use a packet sniffer to read a password sent in clear text, and then impersonate the user in question. Although this kind of attack is rare, it has actually happened, typically as part of a partial data center compromise.
- *Keyboard sniffers*—Some kinds of malware or Trojan programs will install themselves on users' computers, and then log all the keystrokes that the users make. Someone familiar with the game in question can quickly deduce the login name and password used from reading such a log.
- *Uneducated users*—In many online games, there are users who will try to get the account name and password directly from communication with other players. Once these "keys" are obtained, the account is typically plundered of any valuable virtual goods, and the password is changed to something random, so the original user can no longer play.
- *Multiple logins*—The system should not allow the same user to log in more than once at the same time. Otherwise, a single player will pay for the game and share the login with all his or her friends. Although this is a small bit of lost revenue, the bigger problem comes when you have to ban the account because some of those "friends" didn't play by the rules. That kind of situation is a customer service nightmare.

The main point of this gem is to examine authentication in your client/server design a little closer.

One tradeoff you have to make is whether you want the passwords to be recoverable from the database or not. Depending on this choice, you have the following options:

- *Recoverable passwords*—If the password is recoverable, you can use the Challenge Hash Authentication scheme, as described later. However, the passwords are more vulnerable when they are recoverable in the database, because an untrustworthy operator, or system intruder, might get hold of the list of passwords.

  Don't store the passwords in clear text in the database. At least scramble them using some key that you build into the code, to make it harder for the casual inspector to "accidentally" see the password. There's still a danger that the passwords can be compromised, so be vigilant against human factors that can compromise your data.
- *One-way hash passwords*—When setting a password, you calculate a one-way hash of the password (such as an SHA256 checksum), and store the checksum. When users log in the next time, they give you a password, and you calculate an SHA256

checksum of that, and compare to the stored checksum. If they match, you assume the password provided is correct.

The main benefit here is security on the system side; reading an SHA256 checksum will not let anyone know what the actual password is. Finding another password that generates the same checksum is computationally very hard. However, when doing this, you must use Secret Exchange Authentication (described later), which is more vulnerable than Challenge Hash Authentication.

- *Public key infrastructure*—If you have a private/public key cryptosystem, such as RSA or SSL, you can publish the public key of the game servers, and even hardcode it into the game client executable. The user's password is then transmitted over this link, safe from eavesdropping. The added benefit is that nobody but the authentic server can decrypt the message, so the client has a reasonable assurance that it is talking to the real server, not an impostor. The drawback is significant complexity in implementation (the best choice here is probably to go with an open cryptosystem library such as OpenSLL).

Challenge Hash Authentication

In Challenge Hash Authentication, the server issues some random number, called a *challenge* or *nonce*, to the client. The client computes a hash of this random number and the client-side entered password, and sends the hash value back to the server. The server then computes a hash of the remembered challenge value and the stored (plaintext) password, and compares it to what the client submitted. If the hashes match, the right password was supplied.

There are three main properties of this system:

- *Passwords are not transmitted*—Thus someone sniffing the regular login traffic cannot determine what the password is.
- *The challenge is specific to each login attempt*—Thus, if you sniff the connection, you cannot remember what the hash is and then just re-supply the same hash value later to log in, because the random challenge generated by the server for a specific login attempt is different each time.
- *The server has the clear-text password*—This is a security problem if the server side becomes compromised, but the clear-text password, which is a secret shared by both sides of the communication, can be used to encrypt any data coming to/from that particular client. Care has to be taken to use an encryption algorithm from which the key cannot be too easily recovered—XOR or ROT-13 would not be appropriate!

A common-sense precaution is to use a hash of the clear-text password as a key for the communication, but not the same hash as used for authentication, or the benefit of an "unsniffable" shared secret is lost.

Secret Exchange Authentication

In Secret Exchange Authentication, the server stores a hash of the password. The client submits a plain-text password, and the server hashes this plain-text password, and compares the hash to the stored hash. If they match, the right password was supplied.

There is one strength and two weaknesses in this system:

- *The server doesn't store the plain-text password*—If someone breaks in and steals the password file, it doesn't matter, because you can't guess what a password is just by knowing its (cryptographic strength) hash. On old UNIX machines, the strength of the cryptography is not that high, so you should still keep your /etc/shadow file secure, but with a 256-bit SHA hash, you should be pretty safe. If you can't trust your backup operators, or if you get hacked, this is a major benefit!
- *The password is transmitted on each login attempt*—If someone can sniff the connection, they could recover the password. Thus, you have to secure the login attempt using some kind of encryption—but it's not clear what you should use as a key to achieve good security. The most secure way involves a Diffie-Hellman key exchange, which is fairly tricky code to implement correctly, but will provide for a secure, encrypted channel between two endpoints, without prior exchange of keys. If you wanted to protect against a sophisticated attacker inserting himself in the middle of the network, you would additionally have to introduce a public key–based cryptographic authentication system, which is a significant additional burden.
- *The server has the clear-text password*—Because the client sends the clear-text password, the server has at least temporary access to the clear-text password, and can use this as a key for future communication encryption, after the initial login. Unfortunately, this means that if someone can impersonate your server, or read the memory of your server process, they can still recover plain-text passwords, even if the password storage file itself is secure.

Public Key Infrastructure

If you have a private/public key cryptosystem, such as RSA or SSL, you can publish the public key of the game servers, or even hard-code it into the game client executable. The user's credentials are then transmitted over this link, safe from eavesdropping on the wire. An additional option is to generate a private key for the user when setting up the account, storing the matching public key on the server side, and encrypting the private key locally with the user's password (known as a pass phrase).

Such a system has the following properties:

- *The server never sees the pass phrase*—Thus, disgruntled employees or server system intruders cannot easily steal the credentials through packet sniffing or log skimming. A determined attacker who disassembles the server binary can still get the credentials, but at that point, your entire game is compromised, and you probably have bigger problems to worry about.

- *The user has a good assurance against server impersonation*—As long as the server private key is not compromised, nobody else can pretend to be your server and extract user credentials.
- *The user credentials are not portable*—If the user accesses your game from more than one location, he or she needs to make a copy of the private key used for his or her game account, so that the client can authenticate itself on logon. This is not something users generally expect, and will likely lead to a customer support headache.

Securing Game Sessions

Once the player has logged in, your troubles are not over. You often need to transfer a player from one machine to another, or to allow the player to disconnect from the server (perhaps through crashing) and then re-connect, resuming where the player left off. You clearly can't just let the client claim any identity, and have the server blindly trust that, because it would be trivial for one player to suddenly impersonate another player. Instead, you have to use one of three techniques: identity by IP address, identity by authentication token, or identity by cryptography.

Identity by IP Address

In this method, the server looks at the source IP address and port number of the arriving packet, and internally has a table that tells which player is connected on which address/port pair. This is secure, as long as you know that the player will keep sending from the same port, and as long as you trust that the Internet will not accept spoofed addresses in packets—or, if a packet is spoofed, that some round-trip confirmation with the real client can take place.

Such round-trip confirmation can come in the form of explicit acknowledgement of particularly suspect commands ("surrender game," for example), or implicitly by using a rotating sequence number starting from a random initial starting point.

Sadly, if you use TCP for your connections, or if you need to hand connections off between servers, the port part of the client's address will not necessarily stay the same. TCP allocates a new port for each connection for each machine it connects to, and even UDP can suffer port renumbering when you switch destination machines, if it's behind a non-friendly NAT gateway (although most home NAT routers don't impose this limitation).

Identity by Authentication Token

When the player logs in, the server determines the duration for which the connection is good—for example, one hour. The server then calculates a hash of a few pieces of data: the client ID, the expiration time of the login session, and a secret number that only the game server knows. The server then sends a token to the client, which contains the client ID, the expiration time, and the hash of the three pieces of data.

When the client sends data, it precedes the data with this token. The server picks apart the identity, time, and hash parts, and recomputes the hash with its internal secret number. If the hash matches the hash in the supplied token, the server knows that the packet comes from the player who initially authenticated with the server, or at least that the claimed identity and session duration is one that the server has signed off on.

If the client crashes and then reconnects, it could read the cookie from disk and re-supply it, and as long as the session is still valid, no new authentication would be necessary. If game sessions last more than an hour, the server that the player is currently talking to would extend the cookie by half an hour each time the cookie is at least half an hour old by re-generating a new token based on client ID, new expiration time, and a hash of those entities and the server secret number. That way, a client can crash and then keep playing as long as it reconnects within half an hour, without having to log in again.

Identity by Cryptography

If you use a shared secret between the server and the client, such as a plain-text password, you can use that secret as a key, or perhaps better, a hash of that password and some known salt or nonce different from that used to authenticate the connection initially. Each packet sent by the client contains the client ID in plain text, followed by the packet data, encrypted by the shared secret, followed by a checksum of the (unencrypted) data.

When the server receives a packet, it looks up the client password in an internal table, decrypts the message, and verifies the checksum. If the checksum doesn't match, the data was not encrypted with the right password, and thus the packet did not come from the right client.

Best practice says that part of the encrypted data should be a sequence number, so that successive identical packets will still encrypt differently, and so that capturing and replaying a packet will have a low likelihood of being accepted for real.

Other Considerations with Game Sessions

The other problems mentioned in part two of this gem also bear mentioning, although the solutions aren't spelled out in as much detail as with the main topic of the article:

- *Insecure passwords*—When the player generates or changes a password, you should verify that the password contains at least six characters (and allow up to 24). Additionally, verify that the password contains at least one character from each of the three groups—letters, digits, and non-alpha-numeric characters.
- *Insecure password storage*—To protect server secrets against malicious internal operators, follow best IT practices. Don't let anyone in the company have access to all the servers. Store any plain-text password data in a scrambled format, using some key that's hard-coded into the executable. Store extra sensitive data, such as credit card

information or user home addresses, in a server separate from the main game servers, with an additional firewall between game and billing information.

- *Keyboard sniffers*—If you worry about keyboard sniffers, make the users enter their passwords using an on-screen keyboard (point-and-click) instead of using the keyboard. Also beware that a malicious piece of software could read out all data in standard text edit controls, so you might want to use a custom GUI control for reading passwords.
- *Uneducated users*—Create a comprehensive set of rules for user conduct and safety, and require acceptance when users sign up. However, make sure you boil down the most important bits into quick sound bites like "never give out your password, even if someone says they are from our company." Add one of those sound bites to each loading screen, perhaps on a rotating basis, to reinforce the message.
- *Multiple logins*—When one session ticket or cookie is generated, invalidate all previous such tickets/cookies. This means that a second login on the same account will kick out the first logged-in user. However, if a user disconnects and logs in again, that user will not be affected, because the old session ticket is no longer used.

Conclusion

If you are reading this, it's a good sign—you care about security and want to do it right! A good encryption algorithm to use when both sides know the key (such as when using secret exchange authentication and identity by cryptography identification) is the Tiny Encryption Algorithm, which is easy to implement, yet cryptographically strong. True sticklers for security recommend only using standardized protocols, such as AES, because they undergo more study and publication, and any weaknesses will thus be known sooner and wider, giving you early warning when it is time to change cryptosystems.

SHA256 is a commonly used and standardized hashing (digest) function, and has not yet shown the weaknesses of the older MD5 hashing algorithm. Other alternatives are available, such as Tiger (see http://www.cs.technion.ac.il/~biham/Reports/Tiger/tiger/tiger.html).

A sufficient implementation of authentication and identity for a cluster of collaborating trusted servers (such as for an MMORPG or Virtual World) would look something like this:

- At setup, all servers in the cluster share a large random number, known as the cluster secret.
- Client connects to login server using unencrypted TCP or UDP.
- The server issues a challenge to the client, consisting of a 256-bit random number (nonce).
- Client calculates a hash of this number concatenated with the password the user enters, and supplies the hash to the server.

- Server verifies that the hash of the challenge and stored password matches what the client supplied, and issues an authentication ticket consisting of a user ID, ticket expiration time, and hash of a cluster secret combined with these two items, and supplies the ticket to the client.
- Login server also generates a random key for use by this client during this session, and supplies it to the client. It also records the key for the user, and the expiry time of the ticket. The key is encrypted by a key generated by hashing the user password and a known salt (say, the string "abcd") before sending it to the client.
- Client connects to any server that is part of the game server cluster.
- Client starts the connection to a new server within the cluster by sending the authentication ticket previously issued.
- The new server verifies that the ticket has not expired, and that the hash is correct. Using the user ID in the ticket, the new server retrieves the encryption key for the client from the login server.
- The new server and the client also negotiate sequence numbers for future communications at this point.
- Once authenticated, the new server and client exchange data encrypted with the session key, where the encrypted data includes a hash of the data proper (as checksum) and a sequence number. Each of these packets needs to have only the client ID and ticket identifier (a small integer) as a header, not the full authentication ticket.
- Periodically, the server that the client is currently connected to checks whether the session authentication ticket is about to expire; if this is the case, it contacts the login server to get a new ticket and forwards it to the client.

This scheme will protect against the dangers of someone sniffing your passwords on the open Internet, and against the dangers of someone trying to use sniffed packets in a playback attack. For a man-in-the-middle attack, the session being compromised would be insecure, but the man in the middle would not gain the authentication credentials to re-authenticate at a later time. To make sure there is no tampering in the middle, you would have to add public/private key encryption and authentication.

It is also worth noting that no technique protects against a user looking at all the data sent to his or her client machine—the user controls the machine running the client, so he or she could always inspect the data in memory. This means your game design has to be cheat-proof, or you must provide incentives for users not to cheat, to get around that problem. Authentication and encryption save you only from third parties getting hold of secret information, not the two first parties (the client and server).

References

AES, the Advanced Encryption Standard algorithm. The successor to the Data Encryption Standard, and the current U.S. Federal Information Processing Standard encryption algorithm, available online at http://csrc.nist.gov/CryptoToolkit/aes/aesfact.html.

OpenSSL. A high-quality Secure Sockets Layer library, using an Apache-style Open Source license, available online at http://www.openssl.org/.

[Schneier95] Schneier, Bruce. *Applied Cryptography: Protocols, Algorithms, and Source Code in C,* 2nd edition, Wiley, 1995.

SHA, Secure Hash Algorithm. The successor to MD5, and the current U.S. Federal Information Processing Standard hash/digest function, available online at http://csrc.nist.gov/publications/fips/fips180-2/fips180-2withchangenotice.pdf.

Tiger. A fast hashing (digest) function, with no known patent encumbrance, available online at http://www.cs.technion.ac.il/~biham/Reports/Tiger/tiger/tiger.html and http://en.wikipedia.org/wiki/Tiger_(hash).

X-Tea and Corrected Block TEA. A fast, high-strength, simple-to-implement symmetric encryption algorithm, with no known patent encumbrance, available online at http://en.wikipedia.org/wiki/XXTEA.

6.3

Game Network Debugging with Smart Packet Sniffers

David L. Koenig, The Whole Experience, Inc.

yarnhammer@hotmail.com

In general, most network traffic in games is very sensitive to long delays in between game packets. This can be problematic when attempting to debug network code in real-time. The standard practice is to use a packet sniffer application that collects network traffic on the network during gameplay so that it can be later analyzed. Packet sniffers give easy access to information about packet source and destination, and other network protocol stack information. What these do not provide are the specifics of your game protocol when that data goes out over the network.

The Smart Packet Sniffer Concept

The concept of a smart packet sniffer or, perhaps better-named, game message sniffer, is the idea that you are not just looking at the raw binary data sent across the wire, or TCP/IP protocol data. You are looking at more detailed information in a human readable form. In its most basic description, this is a packet sniffer that has specific knowledge of the internals of your game protocol.

This smart packet sniffer application was developed while working on *Greg Hastings' Tournament Paintball Max'd* for PlayStation 2 (GHTP), which was released in late 2006. An engineer who was no longer with the company wrote the baseline game message system and network code. With no documentation provided for the network code and message system, it was certainly overwhelming to start working with it. The first place to start is to look over the code. Doing so will give you a good idea of the architecture of the underlying system. Exactly what game messages are sent across the wire and when can be very difficult to grasp initially. This is where a smart packet sniffer can come in handy.

An Example

On the GHTP project, the sniffer showed us that our server was sending a large number of 100- and sub-100-byte player position packets to the clients. With 42 bytes of that consisting of Ethernet frame, IP, and UDP header information, our packet header overhead was around 40 percent. We were able to improve efficiency by coalescing our packet data and greatly reducing our overall overhead. By using a standard packet sniffer, we probably could have examined the binary data of a number of packets and come to the same conclusion. It only took a quick glance, with our sniffer, to see exactly what network messages were being sent, and how much bandwidth they were consuming. Needless to say, this saved us a great deal of time.

Gotchas with Traditional Debugging Techniques

You don't want to completely abandon your standard debugging functions when working with network code. However, you should be aware of the artifacts they can introduce. What you want to avoid is causing bugs that don't really exist for end users. This is usually the result of changing the code path or changing the code timing. The following are examples that can result in either of these two issues.

Breakpoints

These are generally the developer's first line of defense when testing a piece of code for validity. They allow you to see if an operation is following the expected path. They allow you to see the values of important variables and register values. This information is invaluable to a developer. The problem that is introduced when it comes to network code is that you are only stopping one side of the simulation. The other side, which is the other host connected to the game, keeps running. At some point this secondary host will assume that the connection has dropped and will timeout. Now you may not care about this depending on what type of issues you are trying to debug. If you are just trying to find out if a given piece of code is ever executed, this is a quick way to obtain that information. However, if you're trying to figure out how many heartbeat packets are being sent to the server, or which messages are coming out of order most frequently, breakpoints quickly lose their potency.

Tracepoints

The concept of tracepoints was introduced into Visual Studio with version 8.0, also known as Visual Studio .NET 2005. These allow you to place points in the code that, when hit, do not necessarily cause the game to halt. You can do all sorts of things. You can choose to halt progress. You can also run scripts, print to the debug window, or print a callstack. Although these are great advances in debugging options, they can change the timing of your code.

Debug Output

This is usually in the form of a call to `printf`, `OutputDebugString`, or an equivalent function. These can be useful for obtaining information such as bandwidth usage per second, or percentage of packets dropped. The problem is that anytime you add additional code to a given operation, the timing is going to change. With additional code comes additional processor instructions. This can cause issues seen in the non-instrumented code to go away, or may introduce other artifacts. Be sure to use caution when using the debug output pipeline to debug time sensitive code.

Implementation

The base implementation for a smart packet sniffer is simple. The following sections outline the basic steps we took when creating our sniffer.

Expose Network Structures

The basics of a smart packet sniffer require that you expose internal game protocol information. This can usually be done by simply including the same header files for both the game and the sniffer. One suggestion is to set up a shared directory for any code that is common between the game and sniffer. This will help you keep the protocol version synchronized between the two applications.

Packet Acquisition

You are going to need a way to pull data off of the network. There are several options available. You can write the code for capturing packets yourself. An alternative, and recommended solution, is to use a third-party library like pcap [Pcap]. This is the route we took with our sniffer. The benefit of using pcap is that the code has been around and tested for many years, as well as being Open Source and easy to use.

Packet Decoding

ON THE CD

Once you have obtained a group of packets, you are going to want to translate them into game messages. That is where the parsing code comes in. This is basically your protocol codec and what differentiates the smart sniffer from a standard packet sniffing application. In the sample, included on the CD-ROM, we took a plug-in approach. The decoding for our simple example protocol is handled by a DLL, loaded at runtime. This allows you to support as many protocols as you want. It also allows you to keep the specifics of your protocol out of the packet sniffer core code.

Display

There are a number of ways you can represent the data. Utilities such as tcpdump [Tcpd] use a command-line interface. On the GHTP sniffer, we went with an MFC user interface [Mfc]. The List Control is pretty basic, but lends itself very well to the data we wanted to display. It allows you to set up a simple multi-row, multi-column view. There are a number of options out there for building interactive user interfaces. Do your homework and find what works best for your project. See Figure 6.3.1.

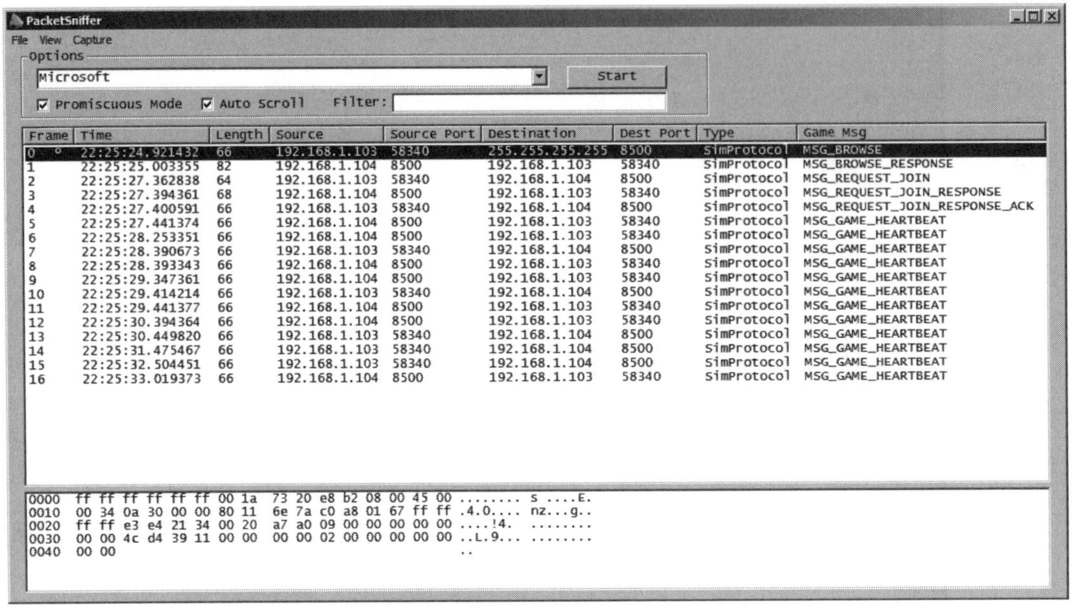

FIGURE 6.3.1 A view of the user interface of our smart packet sniffer.

Using the WinPcap Library

The pcap library is used in the Wireshark Open Source packet sniffer among many other network tools [Wireshark]. WinPcap is the Windows version of this library. It allows developers to easily capture packets being sent across the network. Developers only need to use a small subset of the full library in order to get started. Make sure to look at the sample code on the CD-ROM for a working example of the functions covered in this section. To save space, and your sanity, I only list function prototypes here. Read over the pcap documentation for more in-depth information on these functions.

ON THE CD

Enumerating Devices

In order to start capturing packets, you need to define which local network device you want to listen to. First, you need to know what devices are available on your system. Pcap provides the following two functions for obtaining device information and for flushing the memory used for the query.

```
int     pcap_findalldevs(pcap_if_t **, char *);
void    pcap_freealldevs(pcap_if_t *);
```

Initializing Pcap

Before you can start capturing packets, you have to initialize pcap. This sets up which network device you would like to use for capturing packets. You can set filters for capture as well. You might, for example, want to filter out everything except UDP packets. Our packet sniffer sample assumes this to be true.

```
//Obtain a handle to the pcap device.
pcap_t *pcap_open_live(const char *, int, int, int, char *);

//Determine the medium for this device. (such as Ethernet)
int    pcap_datalink(pcap_t *);

//Compile the packet capture filter from text.
// (pcap documentation covers the specifics of the filter grammar.)
int    pcap_compile(pcap_t *,
          struct bpf_program *,
          char *,
          int,          bpf_u_int32);

//Set the packet filter.
int    pcap_setfilter(pcap_t *, struct bpf_program *);

//Release the pcap device
void  pcap_close(pcap_t *);
```

Acquiring Packets

ON THE CD

The next step is to set up the pipeline for handling the packets. To do that, we use the `pcap_dispatch` function. In the sample code included on the CD-ROM, after initializing pcap, we set a timer via the SetTimer Windows API function. In the timer handler, we call the `pcap_dispatch` function to access the captured packet data.

```
//Callback prototype
typedef void (*pcap_handler)(u_char *,
             const struct pcap_pkthdr *,
             const u_char *);

int  pcap_dispatch(pcap_t *, int, pcap_handler, u_char *);
```

The packet handler callback is where your code gains access to the packet data. This is where your protocol codec will handle the raw network data and turn it into something useful.

Security Risk Reduction

A tool that can decode and display all of the internals of your network code is a great aid for the engineers working on debugging your protocol. At the same time, it's also a great tool for those who might want to exploit your protocol. This makes it a potentially dangerous tool. You should therefore put some thought into how you can limit the potential misuse.

Limit Deployment

Make sure that only those who need direct access to the tool can get it. As a network engineer, the last thing you want to see is your protocol hacked, on the first day of release, by a tool you created to make development life easier.

Encryption

If your protocol includes some level of encryption, you may have an inherent untapped line of defense. It is a good idea to provide the ability to disable encryption for ease of debugging. You can do this a number of ways. You can link against an unencrypted version for your networking library. Another option is to have a separate build target that includes a preprocessor define to disable encryption.

Perhaps your packet sniffer is only able to evaluate packets that are sent out across the wire with encryption disabled. This should help mitigate the risks with developing a tool like this. Even if it were to make its way to the public channels, users would not be able to use it directly to analyze your network traffic. This solution is not perfect. Someone could analyze the sniffer assembly code to reverse-engineer your internal network code structures. This will certainly make it easier for a hacker to find the corresponding structures in your game binary.

An Alternative

There are options available if you would rather not write an application from the ground up. The Wireshark packet sniffer has a plug-in architecture that allows you to define your protocol specifics. You could, for example, write a packet dissector for your protocol. What this does is expose the internals of your protocol to Wireshark. This adds a great deal of extensibility to an already powerful tool. There are a number of third-party packet dissectors that are packaged with Wireshark. For example, there is a dissector for the *Quake 3* protocol included with the main distribution. As a network programmer, you should make sure to have a full-featured packet sniffer available.

Sample Code

ON THE CD

The example on the CD-ROM includes a simple command-line client and server simulation application set, as well as a simple smart packet sniffer application. Full source code is included to all applications. The project files included require Visual Studio 2005 and the WinPcap development library.

Conclusion

Sometimes small efforts end up with huge wins when you take your time. The core sniffer took us about a half a day to write. The end result was a big help in reducing developer time when debugging our protocol. Try to make the time early on in your project to think about the information you need to collect from your game in order to best debug it. Put the hooks in as early as possible. It will pay off later in the project.

References

[Mfc] Microsoft Foundation Classes documentation. Available online at http://msdn2.microsoft.com/en-us/library/d06h2x6e(VS.80).aspx.

[Pcap] WinPcap Website. Available online at http://www.winpcap.org.

[Tcpd] tcpdump Website. Avaliable online at http://www.tcpdump.org.

[Wireshark] Wireshark Website. Available online at http://www.wireshark.org.

SECTION

7

SCRIPTING AND DATA-DRIVEN SYSTEMS

Introduction

Scott Jacobs

Tom Forsyth

Maximizing performance is a perpetual endeavor when developing games. Traditionally, the performance focus has been on the game software's runtime characteristics. Therefore, compiled languages have been and currently remain the bedrock of game programming. But often developers find they need to increase performance in other areas: implementing speed and rate of iterative development come immediately to mind. This is where scripting and data-driven solutions are most frequently put to effective use. This section introduces five scripting and data-driven gems, each one with accompanying code on the CD-ROM.

ON THE CD

First, Julien Hamaide provides a method for automatically binding C++ classes to the popular game scripting language Lua. His implementation is particularly focused on performance, efficient memory usage, and thread safety. Next to interface with C++ classes is Joris Mans, who wrote a gem about serializing class instances to and from relational databases such as PostgreSQL. Storing class instance data in this way opens up whole new avenues for data manipulation, sharing, calculating metrics, and balancing.

Martin Linklater shares a design he calls *dataports*, which provide a common communication API for code to manipulate data in other pieces of code. This generic interface can reduce coupling between modules and allow for more flexible interfaces.

A data-driven approach for managing shaders is presented by Curtiss Murphy. The architecture he introduces is configured by XML files and can conceivably allow for shader iteration and development with little to no graphics programmer involvement after the initial implementation investment.

Finally, Zou Guangxian explores the idea of directly manipulating Python's AST to create string tables. This gem makes use of powerful functionality inherent in Python to hook into Python's parsing and compiling stages in order to either extract useful information about the code's structure or to dynamically affect and customize the compilation results, which you will hopefully find interesting and inspiring.

7.1

Automatic Lua Binding System

Julien Hamaide

julien.hamaide@gmail.com

With game content growing faster than ever, programmers cannot hand-code all the behavior anymore. They need the help of game and content creators. Scripting languages have already been used in games for decades, but today's console can take advantage of them to increase the player's experience further. This gem focuses on an implementation of a Lua binding. This technique allows programmers to expose their C++ classes to Lua without any knowledge about the system. The tools presented here can apply to other languages as well. The design has been driven by usability, performance, memory footprint, and multithreading.

Introduction

The binding explained in this gem allows creation, access, and use of C++ objects inside a Lua script. As an example, if a list of `ENTITY` instances is stored inside a singleton class `WORLD`, the following script can be used to set the health of the player:

```
local entity = WORLD:GetEntity( "player" )
entity:SetHealth( 50 )
```

The binding used in this example is defined by the following declarations:

```
// in .h and class definition
SCRIPTABLE_DefineClass( WORLD )

// in .cpp
SCRIPTABLE_Class( WORLD )
{
   SCRIPTABLE_ResultMethod1( GetEntity, ENTITY, std::string )
}
SCRIPTABLE_End()
```

Binding a class is as simple as that. No other step is required, allowing the programmers to expose a C++ class and its methods to the Lua binding very simply.

Features

The system has been designed with several objectives in mind:

- Low memory footprint
- High-performance binding
- Support of C++ inheritance
- Ease of use
- Thread safety between scripts

Binding of C Functions

To bind a function, Lua requires a specific interface. The function must have the type defined in the following code. Lua binding is stack-based, the `lua_State` contains all arguments passed to the function. Those arguments must be retrieved with `lua_to*` methods using stack indexes. In this example, the function accepts a string as the first argument, a number as the second argument, and returns another number. More information on binding of C functions can be found in the Lua manual [Ierusalimschy06]. The C function binding is the only way you can bind Lua to C/C++, and will be the base of the system.

```
int binding_method( lua_State * state )
{
  const char * some_string;
  double some_number, another_number;
  some_string = lua_tostring( state, 1 );
  some_number = lua_tonumber( state, 2 );
  // Do some stuff here, including setting the return value
  // another_number
  lua_pushnumber( state, another_number );
  return 1; //Just say we returned one argument.
}
```

Object-Oriented in Lua

Lua is a versatile language that can be used to implement a lot of programming paradigms. This gem explains how Lua can become object-oriented. To help, the Lua authors have defined a set of tools providing "syntactic sugar." The one we use in this system is shown in the following code. In it, `the_object` is an initialized variable, and this code simulates a `this_call` on the method returned.

```
the_object:Test( 5 ) == the_object["Test"]( the_object, 5 )
```

Object-oriented methods can be implemented using this syntactic sugar. The object is accessed as an array with the name of the method and returns the function to be called. Lua has a mechanism that allows any type of variable to react to an array access, using a metatable. (This is a feature of Lua 5.1. Lua 5.0 restricted metatables to table and userdata objects.) Metatables are Lua tables that are assigned to an object that contains special fields: `__index`, `__newindex`, and so on [Ierusalimschy06b]. The functions set in those special fields are called depending on the situation. When an object is accessed as an array, `__index` is called. The following code shows how to set up a metatable on an object:

```
metatable = {}
metatable.__index = function( table, key ) return key end
setmetatable( object, metatable )
test_return = object[ "Test" ] -- call the __index function in
                                  metatable
```

Lua native types are number (double or float), string, table, nil, function (Lua or C), thread, and (light) user data. We use the latter to store the object in Lua. Light user data and user data are slightly different. The first is used as a raw pointer, has no metatable, and is not garbage collected. The second is a complete Lua object that can have a metatable.

Binding C++ Objects in Lua

The binding requires several mechanisms: the representation of the C++ object in Lua, the storage of bound functions, and finally the registering of each C++ object in the binding data. In this gem, the overall technique is given, and special cases are explained later.

The Binding Data Structure

In existing implementations [Celes05], the binding is directly stored in Lua. Binding data is then stored in each script. But if the number of scripts the system must support is high, binding data is duplicated unnecessarily. To avoid this, we decided to store the binding data in C++ in a class called `SCRIPTABLE_BINDING_DATA`. Each class to be bound is assigned an index. `SCRIPTABLE_BINDING_DATA` contains a map between the class name and its index, and this map is stored in `ClassIndexTable`. Each class then has a map between a function name and the corresponding binding function. `MethodTable` is an array of these maps indexed by the value in `ClassIndexTable`. Because the `delete` operator has no name, its binding is put in a separate array called `DeleteTable`. Finally, the `ParentTable` contains the index of the parent of each class. When a class has no parent, the `ParentTable` entry is set to –1.

ON THE CD

A series of helper functions to access these maps can be found on the CD-ROM in scriptable_binding_data.h.

```
class SCRIPTABLE_BINDING_DATA
{
   typedef int (* BINDING_FUNCTION) (lua_State *);
```

```
    std::map<std:string, int>
        ClassIndexTable;
    std::vector<std::map<std::string, BINDING_FUNCTION>*>
        MethodTable;
    std::vector<BINDING_FUNCTION>
        DeleteTable;
    std::vector<int>
        ParentTable;
};
```

A pointer to this binding data and the index of the class is stored inside `lua_State`. The space for this data is allocated by setting the `LUAI_EXTRASPACE` constant in `luaconf.h`, and the extra memory is allocated before `lua_State`.

C++ Objects as Lua Objects

A bound C++ object needs to store its class index—the result of looking up its class name in `ClassIndexTable`. This class index is used to search for bound functions in the binding data. As previously said, we represent C++ objects as user data in Lua. This user data contains the pointer to the bound object and its class index. The `SCRIPTABLE_BINDING_HELPER` structure helps the readability of the code.

Inside each bound class, an inner class called `CLASS_SCRIPT_TYPE` is declared. This is used in several parts of the binding process, explained individually. The interest right now is that it stores the index of the class, making the storage of C++ objects in a Lua object simpler. `_VALUE_::CLASS_SCRIPT_TYPE::GetClassIndex()` recovers the class index.

The following functions are used by C++ code when reading the arguments of a call made from Lua, and returning the results to Lua.

```
template< typename _VALUE_>
void SCRIPTABLE_PushValue(
    lua_State * state, _VALUE_ & object, _VALUE_ * dummy )
{
    SCRIPTABLE_BINDING_HELPER
        *helper;
    helper
       = lua_createuserdata( state, sizeof(SCRIPTABLE_BINDING_
                                            HELPER ) );
    helper->Object = & object;
    helper->ClassIndex = _VALUE_::CLASS_SCRIPT_TYPE::GetClassIndex();
}

template<typename _VALUE_>
_VALUE_& SCRIPTABLE_GetValue( lua_State * state, int index, _VALUE_
                              *dummy )
{
```

```
        SCRIPTABLE_BINDING_HELPER
            *helper;
        helper = lua_touserdata( state, index );
        return *(helper->Object);
    }
```

By default, `SCRIPTABLE_GetValue` returns a reference to the object. But these functions can be specialized to support specific types, such as string, by value. A version is defined for each C++ type that can convert to a Lua primitive: string, integer, and float.

```
std::string SCRIPTABLE_GetValue(
   lua_State * state, int index, std::string * dummy )
{
   return lua_tostring( state, index );
}
```

The function signature contains a trick. A dummy pointer is passed in as the third argument. This argument selects the correct overloaded function. If template specialization was used, the return value would always be a reference to the object. By using the dummy pointer trick, the return value can be changed depending on the type—objects can be returned by reference, whereas primitives such as strings and floats can be returned by value.

The code is still not complete. A metatable must be assigned to the user data. This metatable defines a method for `__index` (array access) and `__gc` (garbage collection). As all binding data is stored in `SCRIPTABLE_BINDING_DATA`, only one instance per script of this metatable is needed and it can be assigned to all C++ objects.

Binding Function Creation

The binding function recovers the arguments from the Lua stack and performs the actual call. With the help of `SCRIPTABLE_GetValue` and `SCRIPTABLE_SetValue`, the binding function creation is simple. The `this` pointer is always passed as argument one. The function arguments are indexed from two.

```
int ENTITY_AddHealth( lua_state * state )
{
   ENTITY &entity = SCRIPTABLE_GetValue( state, 1, ( ENTITY*) 0 );
   float health_add = SCRIPTABLE_GetValue( state, 2, (float*) 0 );
   float new_health = entity.AddHealth ( health_add );
   SCRIPTABLE_PushValue( state, new_health, (float*) 0 );

   return 1; // One return value
}
```

Although binding code like this is easy to create, the task is repetitive and error-prone. A macro-based system is used to generate this function instead. An example of such a macro is as follows:

```
#define SCRIPTABLE_ResultMethod1( _RETURN_, _METHOD_, _
                                  PARAMETER_0_ ) \
int _RETURN_##_METHOD_##_PARAMETER_0_( lua_State * state ) \
{ \
    CLASS \
        &self = SCRIPTABLE_GetValue( state, 1, (CLASS *) 0 ); \
    SCRIPTABLE_PushValue( \
        state, \
        self._METHOD_( SCRIPTABLE_GetValue( state,
                       2,(_PARAMETER_0_*)0 )), \
        (_RETURN_*) 0 \
        ); \
    return 1; \
}
```

This macro only creates the binding function. It also needs to be registered into the system. With a little C++ trick, you can do both at the same time. By using a function inner class with a static method, you can create and register the method at the same time, as shown in the following code:

```
void register_ENTITY( BINDING_DATA & binding_data )
{
    class float_AddHealth
    {
    public:

        static int Call( lua_State * state )
        {
            // ... ENTITY_AddHealth() code as above...
            return 1;
        }
    }
    binding_data.Register(
        "ENTITY", "AddHealth", &float_AddHealth::Call );
}
```

This pattern can be made into a set of general macros, as follows:

```
#define SCRIPTABLE_Class( _CLASS_ ) \
void register_##_CLASS_ ( BINDING_DATA & binding_data )\
{

#define SCRIPTABLE_End( _CLASS_ ) \
}

#define SCRIPTABLE_ResultMethod1( _RETURN_, _METHOD_,
                                  _PARAMETER_0_ ) \
class _RETURN_##_METHOD_##_PARAMETER_0_ \
{ \
    public: \
    static int Call( lua_State * state ) \
```

```
        { \
            ... SCRIPTABLE_ResultMethod1 () code as above...
            return 1; \
        } \
    } \
    binding_data.Register( class_name, #_METHOD_, \
      &#_RETURN__#_METHOD__#_PARAMETER_0_::Call );
```

These macros are used in the following way:

```
SCIPTABLE_Class(ENTITY)
{
    SCRIPTABLE_ResultMethod1(float,AddHealth,float)
}
SCRIPTABLE_End(ENTITY)

//...and then at start of day, register the class...
register_ENTITY(binding_data);
```

Attributes (such as data members of a class) are also handled by the system. Typical binding allows the access of attributes by doing `object.attribute`. To handle such an access, the `__index` and `__newindex` metamethods must be adapted. To avoid this, when an attribute is bound with `SCRIPTABLE_Attribute`, `Set` and `Get` functions are created in Lua. The demo on the CD-ROM contains a definition of this macro and an example use of it in the `vector_3` class.

ON THE CD

As shown, the creation of the binding and registration function for each class is now handled by some macros. But you still need a simple way to call these functions.

Automatic Type Registering

To try to keep the system as transparent to the user as possible, we decided to encapsulate the registration function into a class. Each object that is bound declares an inner class derived from `SCRIPTABLE_TYPE`. This class has a static member whose constructor adds it to a global table. This table is then walked at program invocation, calling each registration function.

```
class SCRIPTABLE_TYPE
{
   public:
       SCRIPTABLE_TYPE()
       {
           SCRIPTABLE_TYPE_TABLE::Add( this );
       }

       virtual void Register( BINDING_DATA & binding ) = 0;
}
```

Then, in the bound class, the following code is inserted:

```
class CLASS_SCRIPT_TYPE;
friend class CLASS_SCRIPT_TYPE;
class CLASS_SCRIPT_TYPE :
    public SCRIPTABLE_TYPE
{
    public :

    typedef GAME_ENTITY CLASS;
    CLASS_SCRIPT_TYPE( void );
    static const char * GetClassName() { return "GAME_ENTITY"; }
    static int & GetClassIndex()
    {
        static int index = -1;
        return index;
    }
    static int Delete( lua_State * lua_state );
    virtual const char * GetName() const { return GetClassName(); }
    virtual int & GetIndex(){ return GetClassIndex(); }
    virtual void Register( SCRIPTABLE_BINDING_DATA & binding );
};
```

ON THE CD

The inner class contains the `Register` function, the `Delete` function, the bound class name, and its index. Its definition is hidden inside the `SCRIPTABLE_DefineClass` macro. The details on this macro can be found in the demo on the CD-ROM.

```
class GAME_ENTITY
{
public:
SCRIPTABLE_DefineClass( GAME_ENTITY )

};
```

With the whole system in place, you can call all registration functions by walking the table, as shown in the following code:

```
void SCRIPTABLE_TYPE_TABLE::Register( BINDING_DATA & binding_data )
{
    int type_index;

    for( type_index = 0, type_index < TypeTable.size(); ++type_index )
    {
        TypeTable[ type_index ]->Register( binding_data );
    }
}
```

Extending the Binding System

The following sections explain some ways to extend this binding system.

Reference Counting and Raw Objects

The Lua instance of an object contains its pointer. If an object is destroyed while Lua still has a variable containing the object, bugs can occur. To prevent such situations, we handle the object in two ways:

- If the object is reference counted, Lua increases the reference count. Even if the C++ object is not referenced on the C++ side of the program, the object will not be deleted as long as Lua does not release its reference. The `Delete` function associated on the `__gc` metamethod will be called when a Lua variable is being collected, and this function will decrease the reference count.
- If the object is an uncounted object such as a vector, create a copy of it. In this case, the `Delete` function just deletes the object.

The choice between the two methods is done for each class. Two defines are available—`SCRIPTABLE_Class` for counted objects and `SCRIPTABLE_UncountedClass` for uncounted objects. These macros must be placed in the class definition. The demo shows both techniques at work.

Inheritance

Inheritance is implemented by storing the class index of the parent in the `ParentTable`. If a method cannot be found in the current class binding, it searches in its parent binding. The function `BINDING_DATA::GetFunction` does this search, and can be found on the CD-ROM. The registration function created by the macros contains a call that sets the parent for the current class. `SCRIPTABLE_Class` is used for baseless classes, otherwise `SCRIPTABLE_InheritedClass` can be used.

Supporting inheritance also means that inherited classes can be pushed as arguments to a method. The `SCRIPTABLE_PushValue` macro has the class index hard-coded. To bypass this issue, the binding function is put in a virtual function of the class. The template version of `SCRIPTABLE_PushValue` is shown next, calling the derived version of `LuaPushValue`. This function is hidden inside `SCRIPTABLE_DefineClass` (virtual) and `SCRIPTABLE_DefineRawClass` (non-virtual).

```
template< typename _VALUE_>
void SCRIPTABLE_PushValue(
    lua_State * state, _VALUE_ & object, _VALUE_ * dummy )
{
    object.LuaPushValue( state );
}
```

Singletons, Static Functions, and Attributes

Singletons, static functions, and attributes share a property: no object is associated with function calls. To follow the C++ syntax as closely as possible, the call to such functions is done by prefixing the class name with the method name, as if the class was the object. For example, WORLD:GetEntity(). This call triggers a lookup for the variable WORLD in the global table (in Lua, all global variables are stored by name in a table called _G). An easy way to allow this is to create a Lua variable for every C++ class. But this solution breaks the memory consumption target. Even if your script is not using a class function, or if a class does not have any static functions, a variable would have been created and inserted into the global table.

The chosen solution is to use the __index mechanism on the global table. When a script accesses a global variable that does not exist in the global table, the SCRIPTABLE_LUA_REGISTERER::GlobalIndexEventHandler is called. If the access variable name matches a class name, a new object with a null pointer is created and inserted into the global table with the class name. If it does not match, the handler returns nil as Lua does if no table entry is found. This way, only class variables that are used are created, and once the event handler has been called, the variable is available in the global scope. This mechanism is transparent to all other variable access.

Template Classes

The binding is also able to handle template classes. The template does not need to be a bound class, but in this case, it should define its name in Lua by using SCRIPTABLE_DeclareScriptableTypeName. All the native types are already declared. The name of the class in Lua is the name of the template class suffixed by the name of the parameter. The codebase requires all template class to be of the form CLASS_TO_ or CLASS_OF_, therefore RANGE_OF_<VECTOR_3> becomes RANGE_OF_VECTOR_3 in Lua, which is quite consistent. If this convention does not suit your needs, the system is easy to change.

The macros used are the same as the non-template ones with the word "Template" added. For exampe, SCRIPTABLE_Class becomes SCRIPTABLE_TemplateClass. The binding requires a cpp file to contain all definitions. The binding must also be explicitly instantiated with the help of the macro SCRIPTABLE_InstantiateTemplateClass. The demo shows a dummy template class to show how the binding works.

The binding has only been implemented for a single-parameter template class, but it can be easily extended to any number of parameters if needed.

Support of Enums

Enums are supported in our system. SCRIPTABLE_PushValue and GetValue are redefined to treat them as integers by using SCRIPTABLE_CastValue(ENUM_TYPE, int). To allow the user to use the name of the enum in the code, a preprocessor pass is done on the code, replacing all matching enum entries by their values. A macro system is also used to create and register the text as a #define in the preprocessor, but the details of this are beyond the scope of this gem.

Binding Overloaded Functions

C++ allows the overloading of a function. In a variant, SetValue can exist for bool, int, real, and so on. Lua does not support overloading. Two solutions exist. The first is that BINDING_DATA::GetFunction can implement an argument type matcher, but this is expensive. The other solution is to rename the function in Lua. The SCRIPTABLE_Renamed* macros allow methods to be renamed in Lua so that SetValue can be renamed to SetBoolValue, SetRealValue, and so on.

Debug Helper

Because the binding functions are being created by macro instances, adding debugging functions and asserts to all bound functions is simple. The debugging system is enabled by the preprocessor define _LUA_DEBUG_. The debug helper checks the argument count and the class type. If errors are detected, a Lua error is triggered. This debugging is designed to be usable in a C++ release build, allowing the scripts to be debugged at full speed. The advantage of using Lua errors is that the game does not crash; it just exits the call. The behavior is also compatible with any Lua debugger you use. The binding error can be treated the same way as a Lua error. The debug helpers can be completely deactivated for a retail build, increasing the binding overall speed.

Summary

To bind a class, this macro SCRIPTABLE_DefineClass(MY_CLASS) must be put in the class definition. Four options are available:

```
SCRIPTABLE_DefineClass : LuaPushValue is virtual
SCRIPTABLE_DefineRawClass : LuaPushValue not virtual
SCRIPTABLE_DefineTemplateClass : template class, LuaPushValue is
                                 virtual
SCRIPTABLE_DefineRawTemplateClass : template class, LuaPushValue
                                    not virtual
```

The template parameter is passed as the second argument of the macro. In the cpp file, the class binding implementation must be set up as follows:

```
SCRIPTABLE_Class( MY_CLASS )
{
   SCRIPTABLE_VoidMethod( SetValue, float )
}
SCRIPTABLE_End()
```

The options are SCRIPTABLE_(Uncounted)(Inherited)(Template)Class. If the object is not reference counted, the Uncounted version of the macro should be used. If the class inherits from another, use the Inherited version. The demo code covers the definition of almost all types of object.

Future Work

The following sections address some possible extensions to this system.

Overloading of C++ Methods in Lua

C++ objects exist in Lua and can be used as Lua objects. Overloading the C++ object may be an interesting extension. For example, this would allow hooking of function calls. To intercept each call to `GetHealth` and print the current health, the `GetHealth` method can be overloaded, as shown in the following code:

```
Object.GetHealth =
   function( self )
       local health = ENTITY.GetHealth( self ) -- Do the call to C/C++
       print( "Health of object " .. self .. " is " .. health )
       return health;
   end
```

When a value is set by array access, the metatable's `__newindex` entry is called. It stores the Lua function into a table as a replacement of the C function. The `__index` function is also changed to reflect a new behavior: on array access, it searches the Lua function table first, and then searches the C++ binding data. Although this solution should work, it causes another problem—the object must be kept by Lua in some way. If it is garbage collected, its overloading will be lost. The implementation in the demo does not support overloading, but does support the persistence of objects. Every time a call to `SCRIPTABLE_PushValue` is made, the Lua version of the object is sought in a table called `_object`. If it exists, it is reused; otherwise, the Lua version of the object is created. This code can be found in the demo.

Sand-Boxing and Type Filtering

The presented system allows the binding of objects to Lua. But you may want to sand-box some scripts, limiting their access. Low-level scripts can be used as configuration files, accessing features such as file I/O or graphics configuration, whereas user-level scripts can only access a selected set of classes. The definition of the access level can be set up in the macros and stored in `SCRIPT_TYPE`. The Register method can be called with the access level wanted. In the following code, the class `WORLD` is declared as being at user level. The `SCRIPT_MANAGER` contains the `BINDING_DATA`. Several managers can be created with different access levels. When a manager is initialized, it calls `SCRIPT_TYPE_TABLE::Register` with its binding data and its access level. The binding data contains only classes that are available for its access level. Scripts are created by and associated with a manager, and use its binding data.

```
SCRIPTABLE_Class( WORLD, ACCESS_LEVEL_User )

void SCRIPT_TYPE_TABLE::Register(
   BINDING_DATA & binding_data, const ACCESS_LEVEL access_level )
{
   int type_index;

   for( type_index = 0, type_index < TypeTable.size(); ++type_index )
   {
       if( TypeTable[ type_index ]->GetAccessLevel() >= access_level )
           TypeTable[ type_index ]->Register( binding_data );
    }
}
```

Optimization of Generated Code Size

The technique presented here creates a binding function for all bound methods. It generates lots of code that does the same duty again and again. A solution is to create function descriptions instead of binding functions. The binding data can be a class that stores this `FUNCTION_DESCRIPTION`:

```
struct FUNCTION_DESCRIPTION
{
   const char * FunctionName;
   const void * FunctionPointer
   int ArgumentCount;
   ARGUMENT_DESCRIPTION * ArgumentDescription;
   RETURN_DESCRIPTION * ReturnValueDescription;
}
```

The macro system fills an array of these descriptions:

```
#define SCRIPTABLE_VoidMethod1( _METHOD_, _PARAMETER_0_ ) \
{ #_METHOD_, &CLASS::_METHOD_, 1,
   { GetArgumentDescription<_PARAMETER_0_>() }, 0 },
```

Now only a single binding function is necessary. Its pseudocode is as follows:

```
for each argument_index  < description.ArgumentCount
   description.ArgumentDescription[
     argument_index ].PushArgumentOnCStack();

call( decription.FunctionPointer );

if( description.ReturnValueDescription )
    description.ReturnValueDescription->StoreResultValueInLua();
```

This code must be partially written in assembly, because it accesses the C stack. This system, although a little slower, saves some memory, which is useful if your system is memory-bound.

Demo

ON THE CD

The code on the CD-ROM provides the binding in full functionality, and it should be simple to plug it into a codebase without any problem. The demo tries to cover all the features explained here. If you launch the demo, you won't see much except some text. Single-stepping the code is the best way to understand how the system works. Once the broad details are clear, expand the macros manually and step into the expanded code to see the detailed workings.

Conclusion

This gem presents an automatic binding system. The user only has to set up some declarations about a bound class, recompile, and the class is accessible from scripts. No knowledge of either the system or the Lua binding is needed. The system has been designed to be CPU and memory friendly. The system provides debug helpers such as argument checking that can be disabled for retail builds. This gem also presents several C++ tricks, such as automatic type registering and dummy pointer function selection. With these tools in hand, anybody should be able to write or adapt this binding to their engine and script language.

References

[Celes05] Celes, W., de Figueiredo, L.H., and Ierusalimschy, R. "Binding C/C++ Objects to Lua," *Game Programming Gems 6,* edited by Michael Dickheiser, Charles River Media, 2005, pp. 341-356.

[Ierusalimschy06] Ierusalimschy, R., de Figueiredo, L.H., and Celes, W. "Lua 5.1 Reference Manual," available online at Lua.org, 2006.

[Ierusalimschy06b] Ierusalimschy, R. "Programming in Lua (second edition)," available online at Lua.org, 2006.

7.2

Serializing C++ Objects into a Database Using Introspection

Joris Mans

joris.mans@10tacle.be

With the ever-increasing amount of assets that need to be managed by content-creation tools, managing those assets becomes more difficult, especially when confronted with quantities that cannot simply all be loaded in memory at the same time. Users of these tools want to be able to navigate through all those assets in order to quickly find the one they need. Keyword searches, categories, and hierarchical views are ways of exposing this to the end user. Another issue is that there are many people working on content creation who want to use the same shared assets, and the asset creators want to have them exposed to all the users as soon as possible.

One of the possible ways to implement this is by using a database backend. This gem presents a system that allows storage of C++ objects into an SQL database, and their retrieval using filters. The implementation and examples were created using PostgreSQL 8.2 and Microsoft Visual Studio 2005.

Metadata

Before you can start serializing in the database, you need some introspection tools in the codebase. The implementation of a robust and complete metadata system (hereafter referred to as *meta-system*) is beyond the scope of this gem, so I will restrict it to a basic implementation that has support for everything necessary for database serialization.

The metadata of a class is saved in an instance of a class called `MetaType`. For the system to work, you need to be able to retrieve the following information from this class:

- Classname
- Parent classname
- AttributeTable containing an instance of `MetaAttribute` for each serializable attribute
- Size of an instance of the object in bytes

This class allows you to manipulate objects of arbitrary types without having to resort to RTTI or use polymorphism.

Attributes

For every attribute in the class you want to serialize, you add its information to the metadata. For this, you create a class called `MetaAttribute` containing the following information.

- AttributeName
- Attribute metatype
- Memory offset in bytes from the start of the object
- Whether the attribute is a pointer
- Whether the attribute is an array

Each `MetaAttribute` instance will be added to the AttributeTable list of the corresponding MetaType instance. Code for these classes can be found on the demo on the CD-ROM.

ON THE CD

Arrays

This gem uses a special array class. This is a template class inheriting from a class called `ArrayBase`. This base class contains an interface that allows you to retrieve the number of items in an array, to set the number of items, and to retrieve the metatype of the item class used in the array. It also allows you to get the pointer to the data in the array. This way you can manipulate arrays without having to know what type of object is stored inside them, an ability that you'll need when manipulating objects in the database system.

Serializing in Text

There is one more thing you need before you can start implementing the database system. You need to be able to serialize simple attributes into text format. This demo uses some overloaded C functions to do this.

```
void WriteObjectToText(
   const void * object,
   const MetaType & meta_type,
   std::string & output_text
   );

void ReadObjectFromText(
   void * object,
   const MetaType & meta_type,
   const std::string & input_text
   );
```

These functions have support for reading and writing objects of scalar types and strings. For example:

```
int a = 5;
std::string output_text;
WriteObjectToText( &a, META_TYPE_GetStaticMetaType( a ),
                   output_text);
```

This will result in `output_text` containing the string `"5"`.

The Database System

Before you start serializing into a database, consider that you'll want to serialize C++ objects. What do those objects contain?

A C++ class consists of a combination of the following:

- Scalar members (for example, `int`, `float`, `char`, and so on)
- One or more parent classes, if present
- Pointers
- Instances of other C++ classes

In this case I will slightly change this list. For the purposes here, a C++ class will consist of the following:

- Scalar members
- Strings
- One parent class, if present
- Pointers
- Instances of other C++ classes
- Arrays of pointers, instances of other C++ classes or scalars, using our own array type

The system described in this gem can be extended to support more features of C++ classes (multiple inheritance, other collection types, and so on), but it would extend the scope too far so I restrict the explanation to classes fitting the previous description.

The Tables

Because you'll store the objects in a relational SQL database, you need to define the tables used to store those objects.

Each table corresponds to one class. The primary key for a table is a field called `_Identifier` and contains an auto-incrementing integer. (You can give this key any other name you want as long as it does not conflict with the name of an attribute of an object you want to serialize.)

Using the list of attribute types previously defined, you'll see how to store each type in a field in the database. For each attribute, the field name corresponds to its name.

Scalar Members

Each scalar member is stored as a scalar field of type `integer` or `real` in the database.

Strings

Each string is stored in a `varchar` field.

The Parent Class

You can use any table in a database as the type of a field of another table. This example creates a field called `_Parent` that will be of the type of the table created to store the parent class. (You could also name this field any other name you want as long as it doesn't conflict with the name of an attribute in your class.) An example will clarify this class:

```
class Base
{
   int a;
};

class Subclass : public Base
{
   int b;
};
```

Now create a table called `Base`:

```
CREATE TABLE "Base"
(
   "_Identifier" serial,
   "a" integer
) ;
```

and a table called `Subclass`:

```
CREATE TABLE "Subclass"
(
   "_Identifier" serial,
   "_Parent" "Base",
   "b" integer
);
```

Pointers

There are several ways to store a pointer to an object in the database. At first you might think that a pointer could be considered a foreign key, corresponding to the primary key of the table containing the object pointed to. For example:

```
class Base
{
   int a;
};

class StoreInDatabase
{
   Base * basePointer;
};
```

You could create a table called `Base` like this:

```
CREATE TABLE "Base"
(
    "_Identifier" serial,
    "a" integer
);
```

and a table called `StoreInDatabase` like this:

```
CREATE TABLE "StoreInDatabase"
(
    "_Identifier" serial,
    "basePointer" integer,
);
```

Now imagine creating some instances:

```
Base * base_object = new Base;
StoreInDatabase * store_object = new StoreInDatabase;

base_object->a = 10;
store_object->basePointer = base_object;
```

You could store them in the database like so:

Table `Base`:

_Identifier	a
1	10

Table `StoreInDatabase`:

_Identifier	basePointer
1	1

Retrieving the object from the database seems straightforward. You read out the contents of table `StoreInDatabase`, use the value found in the field `basePointer`, and get the corresponding row from `Base` to instantiate the object pointed to. A simple solution...or maybe not?

Check the following example:

```
class Base
{
   int a;
};

class Subclass : public Base
{
   int b;
};

class StoreInDatabase
{
   Base * basePointer;
};
Subclass * subclass_object = new Subclass;
StoreInDatabase * store_object = new StoreInDatabase;

subclass_object->a = 10;
subclass_object->b = 20;
store_object->basePointer = subclass_object;
```

If you were to apply the same system to these objects, you get into trouble. Saving the objects would result in this:

Table `Subclass`:

_Identifier	b	_Parent
1	20	{10}

Table `StoreInDatabase`:

_Identifier	basePointer
1	1

When you're trying to get the object from the database, you have an issue. When you're retrieving the value stored in `basePointer`, there is no way of knowing that you are not storing a pointer to an object of type `Base` but an object of type `Subclass`. You do not know which table corresponds to the key stored in `basePointer`.

There are several solutions to this problem. This gem sticks to one solution, but feel free to experiment with others. Instead of storing an integer that refers to the primary key of the object pointed to, let's try storing a string with the following layout:

```
"( primaryKeyValue, tableName )"
```

Applying this to the previous example gives this result:

```
CREATE TABLE "Base"
(
    "_Identifier" serial,
    "a" integer
);

CREATE TABLE "Subclass"
(
    "_Identifier" serial,
    "_Parent" "Base",
    "a" integer
);

CREATE TABLE "StoreInDatabase"
(
    "_Identifier" serial,
    "basePointer" varchar,
);
```

Storing the same objects will result in these table values:

Table `Subclass`:

```
_Identifier     b          _Parent
1               20           {10}
```

Table `StoreInDatabase`

```
_Identifier        basePointer
1                  "(1,Subclass)"
```

When reading the field values, you can use string manipulation to get the primary key part and the tablename part of the field value stored in `basePointer`, and use the corresponding table to receive the contents of the pointed to object.

Another solution is to store a table containing all names of the classes stored in the database, and instead of using a pair containing `( primaryKeyValue, tableName )` to store a pointer, the field will contain `( primaryKeyValue, classNamePrimaryKeyValue )`, where `classNamePrimaryKeyValue` contains the primary key value of the corresponding classname stored in the table. Especially with big databases, this would be a more efficient solution, because the amount of data to retrieve from the database is smaller, as would be the size of the database, because classnames aren't replicated in different tables.

Instances of Other C++ Classes

You could store instances of classes in the same way that you store the parent class, by adding a field with an attribute type corresponding to the table of the associated class. For example:

```
class Base
{
    int a;
};

class StoreInDatabase
{
    Base baseInstance;
};

CREATE TABLE "Base"
(
    "_Identifier" serial,
    "a" integer
);

CREATE TABLE "StoreInDatabase"
(
    "_Identifier" serial,
    "baseInstance" "Base"
);
```

This will work, unless you have objects containing pointers to members of other objects. For example:

```
class Base
{
    int a;
};

class StoreInDatabase
{
   Base baseInstance;
};

class AnotherToStoreInDatabase
{
    Base * basePointer;
    int b;
};

StoreInDatabase * store_1 = new StoreInDatabase;
AnotherToStoreInDatabase * store_2 = new AnotherToStoreInDatabase;

store_1->baseInstance.a = 10;
store_2->basePointer = &store_1->baseInstance;
store_2->b = 20;
```

There is no way you can store the pointer value in `store_2->basePointer`, because it references part of another object and not an entire row in a database table.

A solution to this issue is to store instances of C++ objects the same way you store pointers. You store the instance in the table corresponding to its class, make a `varchar` field in the table corresponding to the object containing the instance, and write the string containing the primary key and the tablename in the field. Here's an example using the same objects presented previously:

```
CREATE TABLE "Base"
(
    "_Identifier" serial,
    "a" integer
);

CREATE TABLE "StoreInDatabase"
(
   "_Identifier" serial,
   "baseInstance" varchar
);

CREATE TABLE "AnotherToStoreInDatabase"
(
   "_Identifier" serial,
   "basePointer" varchar,
   "b" integer
);
```

And the result of storing the objects will look like this:

Table `Base`:

_Identifier	a
1	10

Table `StoreInDatabase`:

_Identifier	baseInstance
1	"(1,Base)"

Table `AnotherToStoreInDatabase`:

_Identifier	basePointer	b
1	"(1,Base)"	20

Arrays

Because an array is a data type supported by the database, you can apply the same rules used for the previous types, but store them in an array in the field. For a scalar it will simply be an array of scalars; for a pointer, it's an array of `varchar`, and so on.

Creating the Tables

By using the `MetaType` instance of each class, you can generate the tables in the database. You generate a string containing the SQL statement to create the table using the following pseudocode:

```
procedure AddTypeToDatabase( meta_type )
begin
  if meta_type.HasParent()
      if NOT(TypeExistsInDatabase( meta_type.parentClassName )
          AddTypeToDatabase( GetMetaType( meta_type.parentClassName ) )
      endif
   endif

  sql_statement =  "CREATE TABLE" + meta_type.className
  sql_statement +=  "_Identifier serial,"

  foreach attribute in meta_type.attributeTable
      sql_statement += GenerateCreateAttributeStatement( attribute )
  endfor

  if meta_type.HasParent()
      sql_statement += "_Parent " + meta_type.parentClassName
  endif

  ExecuteSqlStatement( sql_statement )
end
```

In this pseudocode, `GenerateCreateAttributeStatement` generates the part of the SQL statement needed to create the field corresponding to the kind of attribute. For a string attribute called `myText`, it will generate something along the lines of `"myText varchar"`. The actual code will need to take some more things into account, such as generating the commas between the field declarations and generating the right quotes in the SQL statement so there are no case issues.

One thing to take into consideration when executing the generated SQL statement is that you need to make sure to create the tables for the base classes before those of the subclasses. Otherwise the database will give an error stating that the `_Parent` field has been declared with an unknown type, hence the `TypeExistsInDatabase` test in the beginning of the procedure.

ON THE CD

The corresponding code on the CD-ROM demo can be found in the method called:

```
bool DatabaseManager::CreateTable( const MetaType & meta_type )
```

Storing an Object

Storing an object happens in several phases. First, you get a new primary key value for the corresponding table. Next, you insert the object in the table, which is completely empty except for its primary key value. Finally, you update the object in the table, filling in its attributes. Why all this fuss? Why not just insert the object in the table, have the database autogenerate the primary key value, and be done with it? The reason will become clear when you go to retrieve objects.

Remember that each instance of an object in a database table is uniquely identified by its primary key value. On the C++ side, each instance of an object of a certain type is uniquely identified by its memory address. Imagine running your application and having one object in a table in your database. You ask the database system to give you that object. The program will execute a query, will receive the contents of the fields, construct a new instance in memory of the C++ object, and return you its pointer. So far, so good.

Now somewhere down the line, you execute exactly the same query. If this scenario repeats itself, you are in trouble, because the system will actually create a second instance in memory of an object that exists only once in the database. Instead, the database manager should return the pointer to the same instance created before.

A way to solve this issue is by having an instance table inside the database manager. This cache stores the relationship between a primary key value, a tablename, and an instance of an object. What will happen the first time you retrieve the object from the database? The system will instantiate the C++ object, fill in its values, and store the pointer to the object, its tablename, and its primary key value in the cache. The next time you ask for a certain object, the database system will take the primary keys it receives from the database and match those with the tablename in the cache. If the object already exists in the cache, it will return the stored pointer instead of creating a new instance.

But what has this got to do with storing the object? Well, imagine this scenario. The program inserts an object in the database, and somewhere later on tries to retrieve it. The original object that was inserted still exists in memory. Here, the database system should return the pointer to the original object, and not create a new instance, so at insertion time the object should be added to the cache too. Because you need the primary key value to store the object, you need to retrieve this up front. If you were to insert the object there is no way of retrieving its primary key value by any robust method. Even a SQL `SELECT` with a `WHERE` clause of all the attribute values of the object will not be robust, because there could be multiple identical objects in the database.

This is why you must retrieve the primary key value explicitly. But why insert an empty object first, and update it afterward? This is purely for code simplicity. Because the SQL syntax for insert and update commands is different, it requires less code if you can use the same codepath for insertion of new objects and updates of existing objects.

To store an object in the database, you execute the following pseudocode:

```
procedure StoreObjectInDatabase(object, meta_type )
begin
   BeginTransaction();
   InsertObjectAndAttributePrimaryKeys( object, meta_type );
   UpdateObject( object, meta_type );
   EndTransaction();
end
```

Something important to note are the calls to `BeginTransaction` and `EndTransaction`. Because you execute multiple consecutive SQL statements, it is very important to keep the database in a consistent state at all times. Using transactions allows you to roll back the database if between a `BeginTransaction` and `EndTransaction` something was to happen that crashed the application. Imagine having your application crash right after inserting the empty object only containing a primary key value. Next time you use the application there will be corrupt data in the database. Guarding these blocks of statements with a transaction block will make sure none of the statements executed will be permanently stored in the database until `EndTransaction` is called.

Let's take a closer look at the important parts of the two functions used to store the object. The first function is `InsertObjectAndAttributePrimaryKeys`. Inside this function, you execute the following steps:

- If the object already exists in the instance table, or if it is a native database type (for example, integer, string, and so on), then return.
- Iterate over all attributes of the object and its ancestors and call `InsertObjectAndAttributePrimaryKeys` on each of them.
- Check if the table corresponding to the class of the object actually exists in the database. If not, create it.
- Finally, at this point in the function, all the attributes of the object and its ancestors have been processed (recursively), so now you generate a primary key value for the object itself and insert the object in the database with this value.

The second function is `UpdateObject`. Here, you have the following steps:

- If the object is a native database type, return.
- Iterate over all attributes of the object and its ancestors and call `UpdateObject` on each of them.
- Create and execute the SQL statement to update the object's contents.

Updating the Object's Contents

Generating an SQL `UPDATE` statement consists of four parts. First is the name of the table you want to update, next is the list of the field names you want to update, after that are the field values you want to store, and finally the condition that decides what rows are getting updated.

Selecting the name of the table you are going to update is quite easy; the table has the same name as the classname stored in the metatype of the object. The condition part of the statement is also straightforward. You use the primary key value corresponding to the object pointer. This value can be retrieved from the instance table.

The interesting part is generating the field names and values. Let's start by looking at how to generate those field names.

The data in a C++ class consists of a group of attributes found in the class and its ancestors. When creating the list of field names, start with the attributes in the class itself. This is quite simple as the field name is the same as the attribute name. For the parent class, you store the complete contents in a field called `_Parent`. Attributes in that field can be referenced just like accessing a member of a class in C++, by writing it in the form `_Parent.attributeName`. If the parent class has a parent class containing attributes, you can access those fields in a similar way, by doing `_Parent._Parent.attributeName`. So, if you want to generate the list of field names for the SQL statement for the ancestors, you iterate over each ancestor's attributes, write out the names, and prefix each name with one or more `_Parent.` strings. For each level you go up in the hierarchy, you add one extra `_Parent.` string in front of the attribute name.

For example:

```
class Base
{
   int a;
};

class Subclass : public Base
{
   int b;
};

Class SubSubclass : public Subclass
{
   int c;
};
```

Generating the names of the attributes of class `SubSubclass` results in the following:

```
c
_Parent.b
_Parent._Parent.a
```

Generating the values for each field should of course happen in the same order as generating the names; otherwise the data will get mangled up. You iterate over each attribute and depending on what type of attribute it is, generate the field value in a different way. There are three cases, described in the next three sections.

Native Database Type

This is a scalar or a string. Use the `WriteObjectToText` function to convert the attribute to a string, which you can use in the SQL statement.

Object or Pointer to an Object

In this case, you take the memory address of the object (or of the object pointed to in the case of a pointer), get its metatype, and get the primary key value from the instance table. Remember that the instance table is guaranteed to contain those values because you generated them before generating the `UPDATE` statement. With this primary key, you construct the string containing the primary key-classname pair, as described in the "Pointers" section.

Array

When encountering an array, you construct a string corresponding to an array representation in SQL. The format is `"{ item1, item2, …,itemN}"`. Something you need to know when retrieving the object later on is the number of items in the array. You simply store the item count as the first element of the array, for easy retrieval later. To generate the rest of the string, you take the metatype of the object stored in the array, iterate over each of the items, take a pointer to the item in the array, and execute the generation of the attribute value for that item.

If the array contains pointers to objects, you can iterate over those using the following code:

```
item_address = *( array_data + sizeof( void * ) * item_index )
```

Where `array_data` is the start of the array buffer and `item_index` is the index of the item you want to use in the array.

If the array contains instances of objects, the code looks like this:

```
item_address = array_data + item_meta_type.GetByteCount() * item_index
```

In this case `item_meta_type` is the metatype of the items in the array (in a typical templated array class it will be the metatype of the template argument type).

Using these strings, you can assemble the SQL `UPDATE` statement and change the contents of the objects in the database.

Retrieving an Object

As with insertion, object retrieval happens in two steps. First, you execute a SELECT statement, which returns a list of primary key values. Next, for each primary key value, you check whether the object already exists in the instance table. If it does, you return its pointer. If it does not exist, you build a SELECT statement to fetch the field values. The result of this query is used to fill in the attributes of the object you want to retrieve. In pseudocode, it looks like this:

```
procedure GetObjectsFromDatabase( object_table, meta_type, predicate )
begin
   key_table = GetAllPrimaryKeysCorrespondingToPredicate( predicate )
   foreach key in key_table do
      if HasObjectInInstanceTable( key, meta_type )
         object_table.Add( GetObjectFromInstanceTable( key,
                                 meta_type ) )
      else
         object_table.Add( CreateNewObject( key, meta_type ) )
      endif
   endfor
end
```

predicate contains the filter applied to the query, meta_type is the metatype of the class you want to retrieve instances from, and object_table is the table that will contain the result of the query, a list of pointers to the instances.

In the case of creating a new object, you use its metatype to construct a new instance. The MetaType class has a method called CreateNewInstance to accomplish this.

Next, you generate the SELECT statement. As is the case for the UPDATE statement, you generate a list of the field names of the attributes of the class and its ancestors, which will be used to specify the field values you want to recover and the order in which they will be recovered. When iterating through the result of this query, you need to consider the different types of attributes you'll encounter.

Native Database Type

ReadObjectFromText is used to convert the string version of the value into the scalar or string value of the attribute.

Pointer to an Object

You retrieve a primary key + classname pair in a string. First, check whether an object corresponding to this pair already exists in the instance table. If it does, get its address and store it in the pointer attribute. If it does not, create a new instance, execute the code to retrieve that object's contents from the database, and store the new instance's address in the pointer.

Object

As in the previous case, you retrieve a primary key + classname pair in a string. Because this is an attribute, you do not have its address in the instance table. You add the address in the instance table, together with its primary key value and metatype, execute a `SELECT` statement to retrieve its attribute's values, and fill in its contents.

Array

An array is represented by a string of the format `"{ item_count, item1, item2, …, itemN}"`. Using some string manipulation, you get the `item_count` of the array. You take the pointer to the attribute, cast it into a pointer to an object of type `BaseArray`, and set its `item_count`. Next, you get the pointer to the data and iterate over each of its elements. Using the item's metatype you get from the `BaseArray` class, you can categorize the elements in the array (native database type, pointer to an object, or object). For each of those elements, you get its address and its string representation found in the array text received from the database, and use this to fill in the element value.

The Demo

ON THE CD

The demo is not supposed to represent an industrial-strength full-fledged database serialization implementation, but more of a proof of concept, where all the code that's not directly related to this gem has been kept to a minimum for the sake of clarity. In order to use this demo, you first need to do some things, because it requires a running PostgreSQL server. There is a version of PostgreSQL included with the demo, so if you do not have one on your machine you can use this. Install it with the default options, and when asked to create a database superuser with the name "postgres," use `gem` as your password. Once you do this, the database will be ready for use and you can run the test application.

Just running the application will not show much, but if it runs without errors you know the application is functioning correctly. To understand what is going on in the database system, you are encouraged to trace through the code. Just by following the steps executed in the main function of the application, you can see which kinds of objects are created, inserted in, and retrieved from the database. There are some tests after object retrieval that verify that the object returned is correct.

Using pgAdmin, you can look at the tables created and the way the objects are stored in the database.

Issues and Future Improvements

As with most things in life, the system presented here is far from perfect and there are a number of improvements that can be made to it.

There are things you can do in a C++ object that are not supported by this system. For example, storing a pointer to a string, a pointer to an integer, or any other native database type. These issues can all be solved, but are beyond the scope of this gem.

Currently, the system supports pointers to objects stored as attributes in a class (the demo has an example of this); however, this will not work if the attribute pointed to will be processed by the database after encountering the pointer that points to the attribute. This issue can be solved by implementing a two-pass approach, where first all attribute addresses are stored in a table before beginning the serialization process.

Memory management has not been touched upon. Imagine having a pointer to an object stored in the database instance table, but the application has already deleted this object, creating a dangling pointer. Using smart pointers and reference counting is one of the ways to address this issue.

One of the strengths of using a database is that you can execute queries with predicates. In this demo, the database manager supports only simple filters that work directly on an attribute of the class you are trying to retrieve (for example, `"a = 5"`). There is still a lot of room for improvement. You could add functionality that allows for more complicated filters or supports filters in a more human-readable format, which would then be converted to an SQL statement internally.

When working on a centralized database with many users, one of the challenges is to keep every user's local view synchronized with the database contents. One of the improvements to this system is to implement some kind of notification mechanism that notifies the database manager of user X when user Y modifies some content that's relevant to user X.

Conclusion

This gem presents a way of storing C++ objects in a database using a metadata system. The mechanism is non-intrusive, meaning that there are no changes needed to classes whose objects need to be stored. There are several advantages to this kind of approach. You can store many small objects in a database and quickly retrieve the ones you're interested in, without having to read a lot of files on disk. Because the database is centralized, there can be multiple users accessing the same data, adding new objects, reading them and modifying them, and a database system has all the mechanisms needed to work with concurrent access, something that's much more difficult to accomplish using regular files on a shared network drive, especially when dealing with large amounts of relatively small data. It also allows any C++ programmer to store objects in a database and retrieve them, without needing any knowledge of SQL, because all the implementation details are hidden inside the database manager.

References

[Abrahams06] Abrahams, D., and Gurtovoy, A. *C++ Template Metaprogramming: Concepts, Tools and Techniques from Boost and Beyond,* Addison-Wesley Professional, 2004.

[Postgresql06] The PostgreSQL Global Development Group. "PostgreSQL 8.2.4 Documentation," available online at http://www.postgresql.org/docs/8.2/static/index.html, 2006.

7.3

Dataports

Martin Linklater

mslinklater@mac.com

One of the apparent laws of game programming is that as game projects grow in size they become more complex and more difficult to manage. Because games are obviously getting bigger, game programmers have to deal with increasing amounts of complexity. There are two ways to manage this complexity—you either work harder and longer or you create better systems to manage the complexity. I for one would rather go for the second option. One aspect of this complexity is managing how data is routed through the various systems present in the game code. Code modules communicate by passing data around between themselves and exposing certain parts of their internal data to their modules. This data needs to be stored in a format that each of the modules involved can understand. The need for common knowledge shared between modules creates both runtime and compile-time dependencies and more dependencies means more complex code structure and longer compilation times. Dataports are a way of helping to manage this complexity by reducing compile-time dependencies and making the runtime behavior more flexible and data-driven.

There are two basic ways of controlling communication between code modules—you either code it up, binding pointers to data explicitly in the source code, or you create a data-driven system and define the data linkage by loading and parsing external linkage definition files. Coding behavior explicitly suffers from two main disadvantages—first you have to rebuild your code whenever you change data connections, and second, because the behavior is explicitly encoded in the executable, it can be problematic to extend or alter the behavior at runtime or post release. Dataports are a tool to help you create a more dynamic and data-driven flow in your programs.

Conceptual Overview

Conceptually, dataports are very simple. A *dataport* is a piece of data that has a unique global identity. This data can be a structure, a class, or a simple C++ data type. Once they are created, dataports register their identity with a manager class. Code elsewhere in the program can then get access to the dataport by creating a dataport pointer and asking the manager class to bind it to the desired dataport. There are various nuances to the implementation, but the basic pattern that you need to visualize is that of data structures and pointers.

The Dataport

The dataport itself is just a template wrapper for a programmer-defined piece of data. There are only a couple of basic methods of a dataport, as follows:

```
void Register( std::string ID );
```

Once created, the dataport needs to register its identity. Once registered, the data is public and available for other pieces of code to interrogate.

```
void DeRegister( void );
```

Calling `DeRegister` removes the dataport from public view.

The Dataport Pointer

The dataport pointer is in most respects a traditional pointer. The difference is that the actual binding of pointer to data is done by the Dataport Manager, rather than being statically defined by source code and bound by the linker. The two methods of dataport pointers are as follows:

```
Dataport<T>* Attach( std::string );
```

This call asks the Dataport Manager to attach your dataport pointer to your requested dataport. This call returns the pointer to the dataport object, so the actual line of C++ is as follows:

```
pDataport = pDataportMgr->Attach( "Dataport ID" );
```

To detach a dataport pointer from the data it points to, you need to call the following:

```
Detach();
```

The return value tells you whether this was successful or whether an error occurred.

After you have attached a dataport pointer to a dataport, you access the data contained by using the `data` member.

```
pDataport->data.<member variable>
```

The Dataport Manager

The Dataport Manager is the hidden backbone to the dataport system. At its heart, the Dataport Manager is a storage and retrieval system containing a list of dataports that have been registered. The Dataport Manager deals with pointer binding and manages reference counting. It is worth thinking a little about the implementation of the Dataport Manager because you need to optimize the internal algorithms to suit your application's usage patterns.

If you will be creating and deleting dataports rapidly and binding infrequently, you need a representation that has good create and delete performance, but that does not necessarily have good search performance. On the other hand, if you create and delete dataports infrequently and bind pointers often, you might need a representation that has a fast searching performance compared to create and delete performance.

Because this example uses C++ for this particular implementation, it capitalizes on the STL library and uses an STL `<list>` as the internal storage mechanism. I recommend this as a general and easy solution unless your profiling later shows that you need a customized solution. The STL library was written with runtime performance as a primary aim, and it's a shame not to use tested and robust code that's already been written.

The Dataport Manager is a singleton class, meaning that there is always only one instance in memory at runtime. This is because dataports have a universal unique identity and, although it is possible, there is little benefit to be gained by running multiple Dataport Managers in parallel.

Type Safety

The first time I implemented a dataport system, I didn't have any form of type checking in place. It didn't take long before I refactored the code to include type checking, because it was entirely possible to bind one type of data to a pointer of a different type. This is certain to introduce some difficult-to-track-down bugs in your code. Implementing type safety is definitely a good thing. The code contains a handy C++ template function (`GetID<T>`) which, when given a class, returns a unique 32-bit number identifying that class. It is essentially a pointer to an instance of a static class function. This ID is used by the Dataport Manager to prevent name collisions between different types.

Reference Counting

Whenever you work with data and pointers, there is a danger of a pointer that was once valid becoming invalid for some reason. These *hanging pointers* can be very difficult to track down because the ensuing crash might happen a long time after the data has become invalid. Ideally, you should not be able to make data invalid if there are still pointers pointing to it.

Dataports use reference counting to help debug problems like these. Although not strictly required for functionality, reference counting is a huge help in debugging potential problems.

The dataport template defines an `m_refCount` member that all dataports inherit:

- When the dataport is registered, this reference count is set to zero.
- When dataport pointers attach to a dataport, its reference count is incremented by one.

- When dataport pointers detach from a dataport, its reference count is decremented by one.
- When a dataport is de-registered, its reference count is checked. If it does not equal zero, there has been a mismatch somewhere and an error is returned (`kErrorNonZeroRefCount`).

Dataport reference counting is a great help with debugging, but it does incur a small runtime performance penalty. You should consider removing reference counting from your final release builds to remove this performance penalty. As long as you keep reference counting in your debug builds, you will gain the extra debugging information that reference counting gives.

Practical Examples

I have been using dataports since 2000 and they have proven to be a very useful addition to my programming toolkit. The following sections explain a few examples of how I have used dataports in the past.

Camera Systems

It is very useful to encode a level of abstraction into the camera system in a game. I abstract the camera system into tripods and cameras. Tripods are classed as camera "attach points" and can be placed in the scene at will. The player controller object has multiple tripods, and things like the debug fly cam have a tripod. These tripods are created as dataports. The actual cameras that drive the renderer have a tripod dataport pointer as a member variable. To move a camera to a new location, the camera's tripod dataport pointer was simply detached and reattached to a different tripod.

Once this system is in place it is very easy for people on the team to create new tripod attach points and attach the cameras to them at runtime. Because all of this can be driven by human readable text identifiers, a great deal of flexibility is added to the code. Once the tripod and camera classes are set up, there is little or no maintenance needed to introduce new camera viewpoints.

Ship Handling Debug Values

The handling stats for the ships in both *Quantum Redshift* and *Wipeout Pure* were held in human readable XML file format. The filenames for these files included the team names that were associated with the statistics. On program boot these files were loaded and given dataport names derived from their filenames. Then, when ships were created in-game, they could bind with their corresponding handling statistics very easily. New teams could be added to the code without having to explicitly add extra bindings to their handling statistics. This simple data-driven model simplified the task for both programmer and designer.

Broadcasting Positional Information

One of the most infuriating things when coding game logic is getting hold of data buried inside different classes. Drilling into game class data while maintaining object-orientated encapsulation and data access rights can become a tricky engineering job in itself. Commonly accessed game object data can be wrapped in a dataport and exposed to the rest of the game engine in a very simple manner. Rather than trying to memorize how you navigate through your class hierarchy to get at data, you just need to know its type and its ID, and then let the Dataport Manager find it for you. Things like game object positional information can be wrapped in dataports for easy access by other systems.

In the past, I have also set up HUD dataports so the in-game HUD can be dynamically driven by different game objects very easily. Once you have your dataport structures locked down and you decide on a sensible ID scheme, you can get hold of data very easily.

Problems

Dataports are certainly not the silver bullet that will make your code easy to use and bring about world peace. Sadly, they also have some drawbacks.

If you use any form of hashing in your Dataport Manager, it is entirely possible that you will get hash collisions. You can mitigate this problem a little by including the dataport type into your storage, but you will have to deal with hash clashes in a sensible manner. In the example code, I don't use hashing at all, but for performance reasons you might want to introduce hashing into your release builds.

Dataports are harder to debug. By their very nature, dataports introduce a level of dynamism and freedom into your data binding that you may find makes debugging harder. You can mitigate this difficulty by introducing more debug and logging code into the dataport system, but you are going to have to live with the idea that you are making the code harder to debug.

Heavy use of a dataport system can introduce some fairly substantial performance penalties. Dataports are not meant to be a direct replacement for all your pointer usage, and you need to balance the need for flexibility against the added CPU overhead needed to create, delete, and bind dataports with dataport pointers.

My personal choice is to use dataports for commonly accessed game elements that need to have global scope and need to be dynamically accessed by multiple code modules. As long as you are sensible you shouldn't see dataports hit your frame rate at all. In fact, I have yet to see dataport operations show up during performance measurement with final game code.

Conclusion

The current implementation does not encode any sort of access behavior into the dataport system—all dataports are read/write and have global access. People used to `const` pointers might feel decidedly uneasy about this freedom, and might want to add "`const`-ness" into the dataport API. So far, I have not yet felt the need to add this to my implementation, but I can appreciate the desire for that extra layer of support that `const` pointers can give the API.

7.4

Support Your Local Artist: Adding Shaders to Your Engine

Curtiss Murphy; Alion Science and Technology

cmmurphy@alionscience.com

Recent advances in hardware have made shaders an essential part of visually compelling games. There are now dozens of books, including this one, filled with thousands of shader techniques and best practice examples. Your team is raring to go. So what now? How are you going to integrate shaders into your engine? As a developer, it is tempting to just code the shaders directly into your actors. Unfortunately that approach leads to a dangerous coupling of code, art assets, and shader parameters as well as a hard-coded, inflexible solution that is averse to scaling. So, what are you going to do? This gem is here to help.

Following is a data-driven design to help you incorporate shaders into your engine. This design presents good techniques for isolating most shader parameters from your actor logic. It provides support for simple parameters such as floats and integers as well as more complex parameters such as textures and automatic oscillating values. The resulting implementation allows artists and level designers to define shaders and parameters in XML with little programmer involvement. An example use case shows a blimp that hovers in three dimensions and applies an animated pink highlight; the example is integrated into the engine with zero lines of code. This gem includes a fully working implementation that can be used as the basis of a more complete solution.

Shader Terminology

There are several terms that often confuse newcomers to shader development. The first is the basic definition of *shader* itself. Originally, shaders got their name because of the way pixels were shaded. Now, there are two kinds of shaders—the vertex shader can manipulate vertices and the geometry shader can manipulate an entire model.

A better term is *processor*. After all, shaders can process all sorts of data and are used for much more than just shading. However, the term shader has become the standard and will be used by this gem.

Another source of confusion is use of the terms *fragment shader* and *pixel shader*. They sound like they should be different, but in actuality they are the same. The term fragment means that the shader is only computing a "potential" pixel. That is, a pixel that is computed as part of the graphics pipeline but that might not become part of the final frame buffer. So, for example, "per-pixel-lighting" is really "per-fragment-lighting." In an ideal world all fragments would become real pixels—there would be no overdraw—so you would only need one term. However, in practice, it is more efficient for the GPU to compute extra fragments than it is to perfectly isolate each pixel.

This gem presents general concepts that can be used in both OpenGL and DirectX. Because they are both state-driven, the mechanics and concepts are easily transferable. *State* refers to the entire rendering pipeline, including bound shaders, render states, bound textures, and so on. *Mesh* refers to any object, geometry, node, or primitive that can be drawn with a single state. For simplicity, this gem generally uses OpenGL terms and the OpenGL Shading Language (GLSL). The example application is built using OpenSceneGraph (see http://www.openscenegraph.org) within the Delta3D Open Source Game Engine (see http://www.delta3d.org).

Programs and Parameters and Managers, Oh My!

The primary classes of this solution are the `ShaderProgram`, the `ShaderParameter`, and the `ShaderManager`. This section describes the general purpose of these three classes.

The *ShaderProgram* Class

The `ShaderProgram` class is the heart of this solution. It corresponds directly to the concept of a program (in OpenGL) or effect (in DirectX). The program is what most people mean when they refer to a shader. It is the compiled executable associated with the vertex and fragment shaders. The `ShaderProgram` class holds onto the actual OpenGL program. A program can have a vertex shader, a fragment shader, or both. However, the most important job of the `ShaderProgram` class is to hold a list of the shader parameters.

The *ShaderParameter* Class

The `ShaderParameter` class holds onto a single uniform variable. Each parameter value is bound directly to a mesh via its state and is the primary way that an application communicates with shaders. A parameter can be a base color highlight, a gloss texture, a blur weight, an offset point, particle density, alpha strength, or almost any type of value that you want to pass into the shader. The parameters are uniform because they stay the same for every vertex and pixel drawn by that node during a single frame. Most parameters are simple data types such as `float`, `int`, `vec3`, and texture2D that are used to affect shader output. This architecture also supports complex parameters that have their own behavior, as seen in the time-based oscillating parameter (explained in a later section).

The *ShaderManager* Class

ShaderManager is the class that holds this architecture together. It is responsible for loading shader prototypes from the XML definition file, assigning and unassigning the parameters to a state, tracking the assigned shaders, and managing a cache of compiled programs. The manager is what you use to find a shader program and assign it to the meshes in your game engine. This class is based on the Singleton Design Pattern [Gamma95].

To put it all together, the manager holds onto the programs and the programs hold onto the parameters. Together, the three classes appear as shown in Figure 7.4.1.

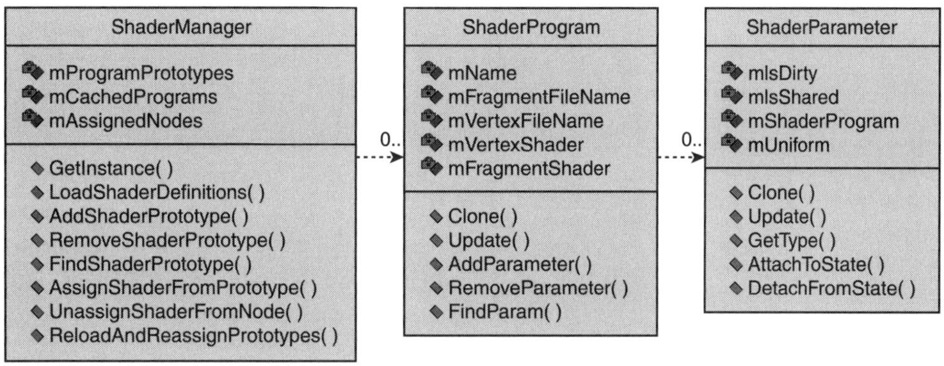

FIGURE 7.4.1 The ShaderManager class diagram.

Flexibility Is Key

Why go through all this trouble? After all, if you are already coding the behavior of your actor, why not just add the shader code directly? The answer is flexibility. Games are now vast, complicated software behemoths [Blow04]. They require huge teams of artists, designers, and programmers working in concert. In fact, it is becoming increasingly common to have more artists than programmers. In such an environment, it is critical to ensure the pipeline is as smooth as possible. Artists need to be able to test models and shader effects without having to involve a programmer. Shader developers need to be able to edit the parameters of a shader, or even add an entirely new shader without having to edit or recompile code. This design provides a flexible system that meets those needs and helps remove the dependency between programmers and artists.

This architecture is especially helpful in allowing artists to visualize their changes live within the real engine. In most studios, the art pipeline involves a suite of tools that is outside of the actual engine. Often, models are created in one tool, textures in another, and shader code in yet a third. This means that what the artist sees while creating an asset is disjoint from what a player will see in the actual engine. Sometimes, there are additional tools to preview the asset combined with the shader to make it as close to real as possible. However, regardless of how good the tool, it's never going to be more than just an approximation unless it is viewed live, in the actual game, with actual actors, lights, weapons, shadows, and cameras. There is simply no replacement for seeing the final, combined result. Getting this level of realism was a primary motivation for the data-driven nature of this architecture. Because the shaders are easy to define and integrate, artists can test their assets in the real engine almost immediately, and they can do it with little programmer involvement.

Test Mode

Another aspect of this solution is the ability to dynamically reload shaders at runtime. Shader development is an art. As such, it can take hundreds of iterations to get one "just right." Maybe the lighting is too bright, the fog decays too quickly, or the gloss highlights are too sharp. Fortunately, the data-driven nature of this architecture makes it easy to reload all the shaders in the system at any time. The `ShaderManager` knows whenever a new shader is created, keeps a list of all active programs, and has access to all parameters. It has everything it needs to reload the shader definition XML and systematically replace existing programs and parameters with the updated values. This behavior is provided by the `ReloadAndReassignShaderDefinitions()` method on `ShaderManager`. With a single key press, the new shader is loaded and the artist can immediately visualize their tweaks in the real engine. Whether using this or some other shader system, engine programmers should do everything in their power to introduce an in-game test system that will allow artists and designers to reload shaders at runtime without restarting.

Prototypes

This architecture is based on the Prototype Design Pattern [Gamma95]. As a refresher, a prototype is a prototypical instance that is copied to create a new object. In this case, the `ShaderProgram` that is loaded from the XML file is really just metadata that is not applied to an actual mesh. When the manager reads the definition file, it creates new instances of `ShaderProgram` and adds them to its list of prototypes. The manager then loads the shader source code and parameter variables for each instance. Once complete, it precompiles the shaders into a program and adds it to a cache.

The prototypes should be loaded and compiled when loading a map or at startup time. That way there is no spike in CPU work when applying a shader to a new object in the middle of the game. This design is further optimized so that any unique shader combination (vertex plus fragment) should be compiled only once. To do this, the manager looks for programs that can be shared across prototypes and stores them in `mCachedPrograms`. Essentially, if two prototypes use the same vertex and fragment source code and only differ by the values of the assigned parameters, they both use the same cached program. For instance, this is used to specify unique prototypes that only differ by a gloss map texture based on the vehicle type.

Notice that most of the methods on `ShaderManager` have the word "prototype" in them. That is because there are only two times when the manager is working with an actual instance instead of a prototype—first, when assigning a prototype shader to a mesh and second, when unassigning (that is, destroying) a shader instance from a mesh. In the first case (for example, `AssignShaderFromPrototype()`), the manager clones the prototype to create a unique shader instance. To support this, both `ShaderProgram` and `ShaderParameter` provide a `Clone()` method. The program is a fairly light class, so when it is cloned, it simply grabs a few references and sets a few strings. Then it makes clones of all the parameters and adds them to its parameter map. For each new parameter, it calls `AttachToState()`. This method binds the parameter to the actual mesh. Finally, the manager adds the new program instance to a list called `mAssignedNodes`.

The second case is much simpler. The `UnassignShaderFromNode()` method ensures that each parameter is unbound from the state by calling `DetachFromState()` and then removes the shader instance from the active list. Because the implementation uses smart pointers, all objects are cleaned up correctly. The whole process of assigning and unassigning results in a unique program instance whose parameters are part of a specific mesh's state. The program is precompiled and shared as a prototype, but applied as an instance.

State Sets and Scene Graphs

This architecture has some added benefits if the engine happens to support scene graphs and state sets. A *scene graph* is just a hierarchical way of storing the meshes in a scene. A *state set* is a mechanism that allows each mesh to have its own unique state values and provides the ability to switch between them at draw time. When these two ideas are combined, you get a hierarchy of meshes that can manage their own state. This type of hierarchy typically allows the values of the state to pass down from parent to child. In other words, each child mesh can set some state values of its own and inherit the rest from its parent. The total collection of individual and inherited values becomes the mesh's active state.

During the draw phase, a shader program is composed from both the compiled shader code and the associated parameters. This distinction is exactly analogous to the code block and data block used by the operating system. Typically, in a state-based scene graph, the shader program and the parameters are tracked as independent state variables. In other words, you can assign the executable shader program to a mesh with or without setting the parameter variables, and vice versa.

Using this gem, you can leverage this type of hierarchy to allow a generic, high-level shader program to cascade down from the top of the scene to any child that doesn't have its own shader. This could be used to define various default settings such as a lighting model. You could also specify "global" shader uniforms without knowing which program will eventually use them.

For example, you could set up global values for an HDR light modifier, custom fog variables, beginning and end values for tunnel vision, or the parameters for fish eye or water blur effect. Because the values cascade down through the scene graph, they become part of each mesh's state. This should make it easier to tweak global values for common render effects and result in less overall management of your shader parameters. Note that it is possible to achieve a similar effect in the current design by using the `mIsShared` flag on `ShaderParameter` (discussed in a later section).

Shader Parameters

After this general overview of the architecture, you should be ready to visit shader parameters in more detail. Before you can do that, you need to take a closer look at the way a shader receives data. Generally speaking, there are three types of variables that are sent to the vertex or fragment shader. In OpenGL, they are referred to as uniform, attribute, and varying parameters:

- *Uniform parameters* are values that remain the same across an entire piece of geometry. These values do not change during a frame and often they may not change at all.
- *Attributes* are like uniforms in that they don't change very often, but different because they are unique to each vertex. That is to say, each vertex can have a different value for each attribute used by a shader. Vertex attributes are typically used to pass data such as a vertex normal, vertex color, and tangent-space vector.
- *Varying parameters* are computed in the vertex shader and sent down to the fragment shader. The GPU interpolates the values across the surface of a triangle using the outputs sent down from each of the three vertices.

Uniforms 'R Us

Which of these types of data should be supported by the `ShaderParameter` class? Because varying parameters are defined entirely in the vertex and fragment shader and are generated by the GPU, they are obviously out. That leaves only two types: uniforms and attributes. Consider attributes first. By definition, an attribute parameter has to be set for every vertex. Because each vertex requires its own value for each attribute, it is likely that the artist is going to use a 3D modeling tool to set values such as a vertex normal or a vertex color. Alternately, some attributes may be computed by the engine, such as the tangent and bi-tangent vectors. In either case, the attribute parameters are essential elements of the art pipeline that need to be agreed upon by the whole team and integrated into both the art tools and game engine. Consequently, there's no reason for `ShaderParameter` to manage them. So, with varying and attributes both out of the picture, you just need to support uniforms.

Fortunately, uniforms are what you want to manage anyway. Uniforms are typically used to pass down lights, fog conditions, clipping regions, and so on. Additionally, uniforms are also perfect for sending general customizations over to the shader. They are the best way to pass down textures such as a gloss map, detail map, or bump map. They are the obvious choice for control values such as depth for tunnel vision or any value that is time-based. So the goal is to design parameters in such a way that the artist can easily define their own uniforms.

Are You My Type?

There are many types of parameters supported by shader languages, including integers, floats, textures, and vectors of all different sizes. This means you will need to be able to support multiple types. Further, you should provide a mechanism to allow for more complex types. After all, the goal is to eliminate the need for programmer involvement, so it would be nice if the design supported parameters with built-in behavior. Clearly, `ShaderParameter` cannot be all of these types at once, so it needs to be a base class. Each specific parameter type then becomes a subclass. The class diagram for this is shown in Figure 7.4.2.

The base class provides base data members such as the actual uniform variable, parent program, and whether the shader is currently dirty. It exposes behaviors required by each parameter type such as the ability to clone itself and the ability to attach and detach itself from a mesh's state. Each subclass then has control over how it binds itself to the state and what type of value it manages.

Figure 7.4.2 shows simple types such as `ShaderParamFloat` and `ShaderParamInt`. It shows data-heavy types such as `ShaderParamTexture2D`, which has to load an image from file or cache and bind it to the texture unit. It also shows `ShaderParamOscillator` as an example of a complex data type. This oscillating parameter cycles its value between a minimum and maximum value over some time. The default behavior cycles the uniform from 0 up to 1 and back down to 0 every two seconds. The artist can customize the min/max range values, time interval, offset value, and how the value oscillates. You can easily expand this system by adding your own custom types.

Clone

In order to support the prototype design pattern, each parameter type needs to be able to clone itself. Simple types such as `int` and `float` merely create a new instance and assign the value.

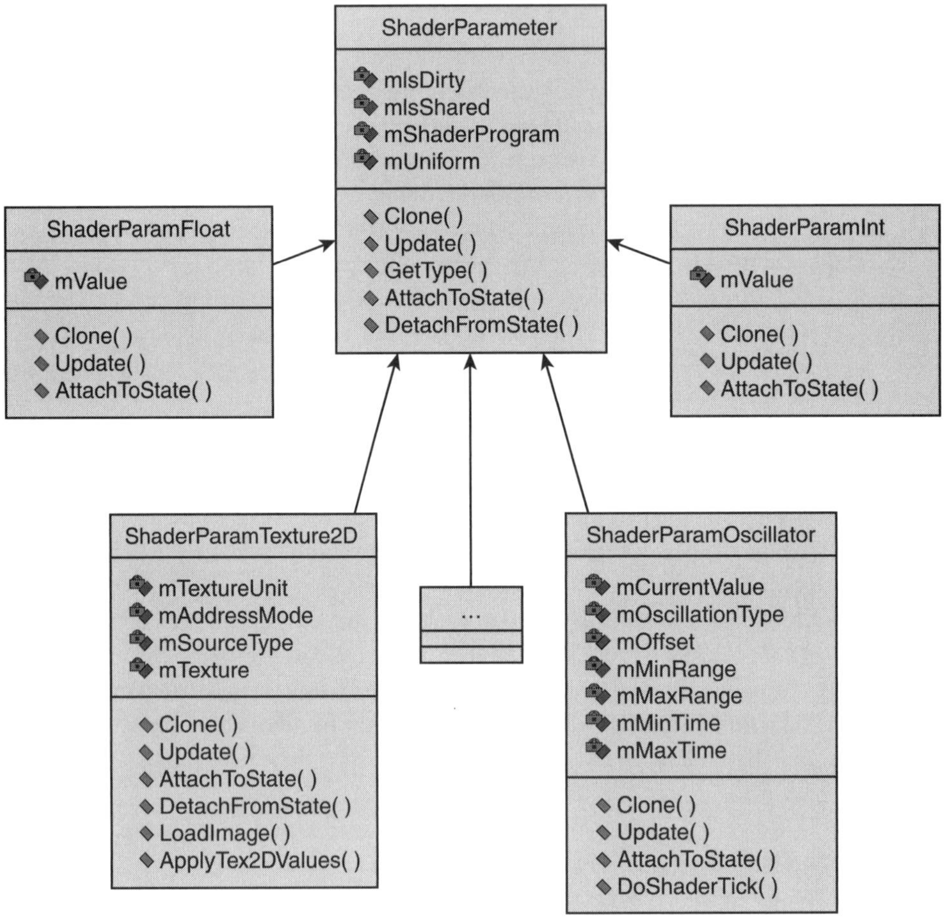

FIGURE 7.4.2 The `ShaderParameter` class diagram.

Data-heavy types should take extreme care to correctly manage a shared reference or other cache mechanism. An early version of the `ShaderParamTexture2D` failed to correctly manage instance referencing and brought the system to its knees when it allocated over 500MB of duplicate texture data.

The cloning process enables a very interesting bit of behavior for sharing parameters. Right before the new parameter instance is created, `Clone()` checks `mIsShared` to see if the parameter should be shared between cloned instances. A shared parameter essentially acts like a global value for all instances of a shader prototype. So, if `mIsShared` is false, the method performs as expected by creating a new parameter instance and copying the values over appropriately. However, if `mIsShared` is true, the prototype's parameter instance is returned instead. The return value is then added to the shader program. The result is that two programs will have exactly the same parameter. Although this can possibly result in weird values, it also sets up the ability to have multiple objects respond to a single parameter. For example, this would allow multiple objects to oscillate in exactly the same way and would allow all instances of a vehicle to use the same detail texture map.

Use Case—The Blimp Target

To see how the architecture works, let's examine a simple use case involving a blimp. In this case, the artist wants the blimp to appear to hover in the air with a slight bounce in all three dimensions. The artist also wants to apply an animated swirl effect to make it look highlighted. To achieve this effect, the artist creates the blimp model and defines the following shaders.

Blimp Vertex Shader

The vertex shader is extremely simple. To create the hover, it needs three instances of the `ShaderParamOscillator`. It processes the X, Y, and Z dilation values and moves each vertex in a sinusoidal pattern, as follows:

```
uniform float MoveXDilation;
uniform float MoveYDilation;
uniform float MoveZDilation;

// Vertex - Simple blimp shader for 'Hover' and 'Highlight'
// Lighting was removed for simplicity
void main()
{
  gl_TexCoord[0] = gl_TextureMatrix[0] * gl_MultiTexCoord0;

  gl_Vertex.x += 1.5 * sin(3.14159 * MoveXDilation);
  gl_Vertex.y += 1.5 * sin(3.14159 * MoveYDilation);
  gl_Vertex.z += 2.0 * sin(3.14159 * MoveZDilation);

  gl_Position = ftransform();
}
```

Now, let's take a look at the fragment shader.

Blimp Fragment Shader

The fragment shader is a bit more complex. Take a look at the code first:

```
uniform sampler2D DiffuseTexture;
uniform sampler2D HighlightTexture;
uniform float TimeDilation;
```

```
// FRAGMENT - Provides highlight by blending from a detail texture
void main()
{
  float whackyOffset = sqrt(abs(TimeDilation - 0.5) + 1.0);
  float x = gl_TexCoord[0].x;
  float y = gl_TexCoord[0].y;

  // look up the three oscillating colors
  vec2 lookup1 = vec2(x + TimeDilation, y + TimeDilation+.25);
  vec2 lookup2 = vec2(x - whackyOffset, y + whackyOffset);
  vec2 lookup3 = vec2(x - (TimeDilation*2.0), y + TimeDilation);
  vec4 color1 = texture2D(HighlightTexture, lookup1);
  vec4 color2 = texture2D(HighlightTexture, lookup2);
  vec4 color3 = texture2D(HighlightTexture, lookup3);

  // Now blend the three colors together to make the highlight
  vec4 highlightColor;
  highlightColor.a = 1.0;
  highlightColor.r = color1.r*0.6 + color2.r*0.3 + color3.r*0.3;
  highlightColor.g = color1.g*0.2 + color2.g*0.7 + color3.g*0.2;
  highlightColor.b = color1.b*0.2 + color2.b*0.2 + color3.b*0.8;

  // Finally, blend the original color and highlight color
  vec4 diffuseColor = texture2D(diffuseTexture, gl_TexCoord[0].st);
  gl_FragColor = (0.2 * diffuseColor) + (0.8 * highlightColor);
}
```

This processor takes in one float uniform and two texture uniforms (`ShaderParamOscillator` and `ShaderParamTexture2D`, respectively). To create the swirling highlight, it does three separate look ups into the detail texture. Each lookup is a permutation of the `TimeDilation` uniform variable. Then, it uses the lookup to compute a final highlight color and blends that color in with the original diffuse texture.

To integrate the new shaders into the engine, the artist adds the following snippet to the shader definition XML file:

```
<shader name="Green">
  <source type="Vertex">Shaders/green_vert.glsl</source>
  <source type="Fragment">Shaders/green_frag.glsl</source>
  <parameter name="diffuseTexture">
    <texture2D textureUnit="0">
       <source type="Auto"/>
    </texture2D>
  </parameter>
  <parameter name="TimeDilation">
    <oscillator cycletimemin="2.0" cycletimemax="4.0"/>
  </parameter>
  <parameter name="MoveXDilation">
    <oscillator cycletimemin="5.0" cycletimemax="8.0"/>
  </parameter>
```

```
    <parameter name="MoveYDilation">
      <oscillator cycletimemin="5.0" cycletimemax="8.0"/>
    </parameter>
    <parameter name="MoveZDilation">
      <oscillator cycletimemin="5.0" cycletimemax="8.0"/>
    </parameter>
    <parameter name="HighlightTexture">
      <texture2D textureUnit="1">
         <source type="Image">Textures/green_detail.png</source>
         <wrap axis="S" mode="Repeat"/>
         <wrap axis="T" mode="Repeat"/>
      </texture2D>
    </parameter>
  </shader>
```

This entry defines a shader program called `Green`. For that, it specifies the vertex and fragment shader files. It also specifies two texture parameters and four oscillating float values that cycle between 0 and 1. Note that the oscillator uses reasonable defaults, so the artist only had to set the oscillation time.

ON THE CD

The entire effect is realized with zero lines of code. The artist created the vertex and fragment shaders and then added an entry to the definition XML file. The artist was able to see the effect in game and was able to repeatedly tweak the magic numbers at runtime without having to repeatedly restart. The significant code snippets are provided on the CD-ROM and the complete working example with source can be found as part of Delta3D (see the section called "Conclusion"). Color Plate 14 in the color insert shows a few examples of dramatically different results that were generated without a restart.

Advanced Techniques

The previous sections define a basic architecture that can be added directly to an engine. In addition, there are several advanced techniques that are used in the complete implementation of this system that might be useful in your environment.

Shader Groups

Shader groups allows several related shaders to be lumped together into one group. This allows the definition of separate shaders for each type of actor, such as damaged mode, destroyed mode, and normal mode. Alternatively, you could define a shader group with a targeted and non-targeted shader, or daytime and nighttime shaders for all the actor categories in the system.

To implement this, add a new class called `ShaderGroup` that sits between `ShaderManager` and `ShaderProgram`. This changes the original design in two ways. First, the manager now holds onto group prototypes instead of program prototypes. Second, you have to look up the group by name before you can find the shader within the group. Note that each group tags one of its shaders as the default; there is always one to use. In the full example, the blimp has a group with two shaders—one for the green highlight and one for the normal, untargeted look. The following snippet shows an example of an XML definition with groups:

```
<shaderlist>

  <shadergroup name="Target Shaders">
    <shader name="Normal" default="yes">
      ...
    </shader>

    <shader name="Green" default="no">
      ...
    </shader>
  </shadergroup>

  <shadergroup name="Tank Shader">
    <shader name="Normal" default="yes">
      ...
    </shader>
  </shadergroup>

</shaderlist>
```

Combining Shaders with Actors and Properties

Another advanced feature leverages actors and actor properties. This feature allows an artist or level designer to specify which shader to use for an object by setting the shader group actor property. Just as the XML definition allows the artists to easily define their shaders, the actor property system allows the artists to easily define which shader should be assigned to an actor. The result is an API that is friendly to both the programmer and the artist. For fun, the artist used this feature to add a new shader to the terrain. For a complete explanation of actors and actor properties, see [Campbell06].

The following snippet shows all the code necessary to change the shader applied to an actor. This method is automatically called whenever the `string` property for the shader gets set. The shader property is just a string that can easily be defined in a map or received across a network in an actor update message. To apply the shader to the mesh, the programmer calls the three important methods on the manager: `FindShaderGroupPrototype()`, `GetDefaultShader()`, and `AssignShaderFromPrototype()`. Note that all error checking is omitted for brevity and that this method reduces down to only two calls if shader groups are not supported.

```
// Set the Actor Property for Shader Group
void GameActor::SetShaderGroup(const std::string &groupName)
{
  ShaderManager &sm = ShaderManager::GetInstance();
```

```
    // Make sure any old shaders are cleaned up. Better safe than sorry.
    sm.UnassignShaderFromNode(*GetOSGNode());

    // Get the shader group & the default shader
    const ShaderGroup *group = sm.FindShaderGroupPrototype(groupName);
    const Shader *defaultShader = shaderGroup->GetDefaultShader();

    // Make a new cloned instance of the shader from the prototype
    // and assign it to the state set for the mesh
    sm.AssignShaderFromPrototype(*defaultShader, *GetOSGNode());
}
```

Future Work

Although this version of the design is completely functional, there are many possible enhancements. The following list is presented as features to consider for your own engine and that may eventually be added to the host game engine, Delta3D (see the "Conclusion" section).

- *Geometry shaders*—This gem does not support geometry shaders. However, based on the 4.0 specification, it should be a relatively straightforward addition.
- *XML editor tool*—Add a tool that helps the artist create the XML shader definition file. This is similar to the level editor described in *Game Programming Gems 6* [Campbell06].
- *Generated shader source*—Some engines support the ability to generate shader source code at runtime. This design could be augmented to support such a technique by inserting the generated shader code into the program prototype instead of loading it from disk. The design would benefit from the optimized runtime code while still allowing the artist to test new uniforms.
- *Actor property parameter*—Add a new data type to automatically update a mesh's state whenever an actor property (such as health or velocity) changes.
- *Enhanced cache*—Maintain separate caches for vertex and fragment shaders.

Conclusion

This gem presents a ready-to-use shader architecture that can be integrated directly with your engine. It makes a case for building a data-driven shader system that can be manipulated outside of engine code, which gives artists the ability to visualize their assets inside the real game. It discusses the three primary classes of `ShaderManager`, `ShaderProgram`, and `ShaderParameter`. It describes how to use the prototype design pattern to provide a flexible system with good performance. It explains why uniform variables are critical and how to support many different data types. Finally, this gem demonstrates a real use case allowing an artist to hover and animate a blimp without involving a developer.

ON THE CD

For more examples of this concept, see the source snippets available on the CD-ROM. In addition, a complete and fully working implementation of this design is available in the Tank Target Example provided by the Open Source Delta3D project (see www.delta3d.org).

References

[Blow04] Blow, Jonathan. "Game Development: Harder Than You Think," available online at http://www.acmqueue.org/modules.php?name=Content&pa=showpage&pid=114, 2004.

[Campbell06] Campbell, Matt and Murphy, Curtiss. "Exposing Actor Properties Using Nonintrusive Proxies," *Game Programming Gems 6*, edited by Michael Dickheiser, Charles River Media, 2006, pp. 383–392.

[Gamma95] Gamma, Erich, Helm, Richard, Johnson, Ralph, and Vlissides, John. *Design Patterns—Elements of Reusable Object Oriented Software*, Addison-Wesley, 1995, pp. 117–126.

7.5

Dance with Python's AST

Zou Guangxian

In any MMORPG, there are plenty of conversations between NPC and player. It takes processor time to encrypt them and costs a lot of bandwidth to transfer them. Python is a dynamic object-oriented programming language, and is widely adopted in MMORPG development. It is also powerful, and with the Python compiler package, a developer can manipulate the Abstract Syntax Tree (AST) and the process of analyzing and generating Python bytecode can be controlled at runtime.

This gem describes how to replace strings with numbers (ID) by manipulating the AST. This way, bandwidth and runtime costs can be saved. A tool based on this idea is also given here.

Introduction

In computer science, AST means Abstract Syntax Tree. It is generated by the parsing phase, and it is used as the source of the bytecode generator. Its internal nodes are labeled with operators such as addition or concatenation, and the leaf nodes represent the operands of the operators. Thus, the grammar rules of the language can be illustrated with an AST. By visiting the nodes in the AST in order, code generation can be performed and the bytecode will be emitted.

Each node in the AST has special meaning and information, including whether it is a variable or a constant, and if it is a constant, what is its value? By making use of this information or changing it, the programmer can control the bytecode generated, that is, to change the meaning of source code.

Background

The standard way to handle text in games is to use a translation table. Each string in the game is assigned an ID, and the ID is looked up in a table of strings each time it is displayed. The advantages of using IDs instead of raw strings are that they save bandwidth and memory, they can refer to any audio speech that goes with them, and the language can be changed easily when translating to different territories without changing the code.

However, tracking all these IDs takes a lot of time and management during the development of the project. It is much easier and quicker to simply use the strings directly when trying out concepts. However, this means they then need to be tracked down later and replaced by string ID lookups, and the code needs to be changed to perform the string lookup. This is a time-consuming task, and it is easy to make mistakes or miss instances.

It is useful to have a way to examine existing code to find all the strings, enter them in a database, and then track them. As a bonus, once you can inspect code for strings, it is just as easy to edit code and change strings. Instead of changing the code to do an indirection through a table each time, it is far simpler to edit the code to point directly at the string. In the rare event that the player changes language or the server updates some text, the edits can be performed again, but otherwise there are no extra indirections in the places where the strings are used, reducing code complexity.

Solution

Python strings are enclosed in single quotes (' and ') or double quotes (" and "). For example:

```
companyName = 'NetEase.Co'
projectName = "Tang Dynasty"
address = """
GuangZhou,
China
"""
```

For general programs, it is not easy to extract these strings. Writing a parser to do it is tricky and not something to be attempted lightly.

Furthermore, there can be cases where replacing the text of the string with the lookup function in the source text will produce problems, such as being in the wrong scope, or when it's part of a compile-time macro.

Fortunately, Python already has a good mechanism to simplify this job. In the compiler package, there are five functions:

```
compile( source, filename, mode, flags=None, dont_inherit=None )
compileFile( source )
parse( buf )
parseFile( path )
walk( ast, visitor[, verbose] )
```

`compile` and `compileFile` both compile the source code; however, `compileFile` generates a .pyc file and `compile` returns a code object.

`parse/parseFile` returns an AST for the Python source code in the buffer or in the file specified by path.

The `walk` function does an ordered walk over the AST and calls the appropriate method on the visitor instance for each node encountered. For example, when a `Const` is encountered, a `visitConst` function will be called. In general, for a node `Type`, if the `visitType` exists, `visitType` will be called; otherwise `ASTVisitor.default` will be called. So, if you can provide a visitor to the `walk` function with appropriate method, the node information in AST can be extracted.

To solve this problem, a visitor that implements `visitCallFunc` should be provided. There are two phases to the solution. First, find all the constant strings in the code, assign an ID to each string `const` found, and save the relationship between the string and the ID to a file called stringres.txt. In the second phase, the walk is performed again, the string is replaced with the ID, and the new .pyc file is generated.

ON THE CD

To help understand the AST, astshow.py is provided on the CD-ROM, and it will produce the formatted output of the AST. Here, I explain what you will get when a function was called in source code.

For example, if a file called sample.py contains this:

```
import game
game.msg2player( "hello" )
```

Use the `walk` function to walk through the AST of the previous source code, and the node passed to `visitCallFunc` will be:

```
CallFunc(Getattr(Name('game'), 'msg2player'),
               [Const('hello')], None, None)
```

Its child node is `"Getattr(Name('game'), 'msg2player')"` and its argments are `"[Const('hello')]"`.

The full name of a function can be extracted with the following function:

```
def getFunctionName( node ):
  if isinstance(node, compiler.ast.Name):
     return node.name
  elif isinstance(node, compiler.ast.Getattr):
     return getFunctionName(node.getChildNodes()[0])
                               + '.' + node.attrname
  else:
     return ''
```

In the first phase, `visitCallFunc` can be implemented as:

```
import os
from compiler import ast, pycodegen
import utils

class Visitor:
  def visitCallFunc(self, node):
     func_name = utils.getFullName( node.node )
     if func_name in utils.helper.functions :
         for arg in node.args :
            if isinstance( arg, ast.Const ) :
                if isinstance( arg.value, basestring ):
                    utils.helper.append( arg.value )
```

```
    # the rest is copied from pycodegen
    # and simply continues to walk the AST.
    pos = 0
    kw = 0
    self.visit(node.node)
    for arg in node.args:
        self.visit(arg)
        if isinstance(arg, ast.Keyword):
            kw = kw + 1
        else:
            pos = pos + 1
    if node.star_args is not None:
        self.visit(node.star_args)
    if node.dstar_args is not None:
        self.visit(node.dstar_args)
```

In this function, the argument will be checked and any `const` string argument will be added to the ID-string map by the `utils.helper.append` function.

In the second phase, the bytecode will be generated by calling `compile/compileFile`. `compile/compileFile` have a strong coupling with CodeGenerator so that you cannot define a class inherited from CodeGenerator to affect the result. Instead, you can assign a custom function as the `visitCallFunc` to the CodeGenerator, taking control of the generation process. The `visitCallFunc` is given here, and when `arg.value` is a `const` string, it is replaced by the ID.

```
import os
from compiler import ast, pycodegen
import utils

def visitCallFunc(self, node):
  func_name = utils.getFullName( node.node )

  if func_name in utils.helper.functions :
     for arg in node.args :
         if isinstance( arg, ast.Const ) :
             if isinstance( arg.value, basestring ):
                arg.value = utils.helper.get( arg.value )

  # the rest is copied from pycodegen
  # and simply continues to walk the AST.
  pos = 0
  kw = 0
  self.set_lineno(node)
  self.visit(node.node)
  for arg in node.args:
     self.visit(arg)
     if isinstance(arg, ast.Keyword):
         kw = kw + 1
     else:
         pos = pos + 1
```

```
if node.star_args is not None:
   self.visit(node.star_args)
if node.dstar_args is not None:
   self.visit(node.dstar_args)
have_star = node.star_args is not None
have_dstar = node.dstar_args is not None
opcode = pycodegen.callfunc_opcode_info[have_star, have_dstar]
self.emit(opcode, kw << 8 | pos)
```

ON THE CD

Please refer to the full source code on the CD-ROM for more details.

Conclusion

In this article, with Python's compiler package, you have the ability to access and modify the AST. Based on this idea, you get an elegant solution to constructing a string table without programmer help. In addition, the script writer can worry less about later translations. This process is transparent and can be integrated seamlessly.

References

[Python] Python language Website, available online at http://www.python.org.

About the CD-ROM

About the *Game Programming Gems 7* CD-ROM

The CD-ROM included with this book contains source code, executable demos, libraries, images, and text. All are meant to demonstrate or supplement the gems in this book. Full appreciation of the book requires perusal of the CD-ROM materials. Every effort has been made to ensure the enclosed source code is bug-free and able to be compiled, the executables run trouble-free, and the images and text are freely viewable. Please refer to the book's Website, http://www.gameprogramminggems.com/, for the most recent details regarding the contents of the CD-ROM.

Contents

For ease of location, the materials on the CD-ROM are organized into folders that correspond to the sections and gems of the book. For your convenience, an auto-run Windows executable is provided that helps you locate each folder, but the executable is not required to browse the CD-ROM's contents. Source code in each folder has been verified to compile with Microsoft Visual Studio C++ 7.0 and Visual Studio 2005 solution and project files are usually provided. In many cases, precompiled binaries are also included. When possible, supplemental libraries have also been included but in a few instances additional libraries must be obtained by the user. Examples of these include the Windows version of OpenAL, available from http://developer.creative.com/ and the DirectX SDK, available from http://msdn.microsoft.com/directx/sdk/.

System Requirements for Windows

Windows 2000, XP, or Vista is required. A document reader capable of displaying Microsoft Word or PDF documents is needed for article supplements. Examples using or demonstrating graphical techniques require a 3D card supporting DirectX 9.

INDEX

Numbers with "GPG" proceeding refer to previous editions of the Game Programming Gems Series. Numbers without this notation refer to the current volume.

Numbers

2D Gaussian distribution, construction of, 202
3 × 3 matrix, example of, 180
10Hz, capturing logs at, 267
16-bit PCM audio engine file format, pros and cons of, 308–309
" (double quotes), using with Python strings, 556
' (single quotes), using with Python strings, 556
Symbols
< and >, use in formulas, 163

A

A&C (age and cost), function in cache replacement, 12–13
A* search algorithm
  use of, 290–292
  weaknesses of, 291–292
AABB (axis-aligned bounding box), use in scenes, 184
AABB-trees, considering in collision tests, 187
absolute values, impact on behavior cloning, 211
Abstract Syntax Tree (Abstract), using to replace strings with numbers, 555–559
AC decision-making algorithms, blocks for, 236–238
acoustics, raytracing for, 302
action searching, improving, 286
ActionInfo flow, use in Artificial Contender, 241–242
ActionInfo objects
  retrieving from input blocks, 243
  use in Artificial Contender, 235, 245
actions, merging, 284–285
actors, combining with shaders, 552–553
Adaptive Replacement Cache (ARC) algorithm, use of, 6
AddRegion() function, use in optical flow, 31
AddressingScheme class, using with hexagonal grids, 54
ADPCM audio engine file format, pros and cons of, 308, 337
affect, relationship to attitudes, 251
affine mappings, extracting semantics from, 181
affine matrices, inverting, 181–182
affine transforms, use of, 180
Age algorithm
  benefits of, 9
  expansion of, 10–11
  using in cache replacement, 8–13
age and cost (A&C), function in cache replacement, 12–13
Age Percentage Cost (APC)
  calculating, 9
  relationship to RC (relative cost), 12–13
agents
  attitudes held by, 252–253
  creating with behavior cloning, 210–216
  training, 211–212
  training for acceleration, 211
  vision-modeling considerations for, 224
agent-sensing model
  hearing model for, 219
  vision model for, 217–219
AI (artificial intelligence). See agents
AI script, building from trees in behavior cloning, 215–216

AIShooter demo, running, 212
algorithms
  A* search algorithm, 290–292
  ARC (Adaptive Replacement Cache), 6
  blocks for AC decision-making algorithms, 236–238
  cache replacement, 6–8
  central limit theorem, 201
  chorus and compression audio processing effects, 301
  collision detection using MPR, 171–176
  components of, 153
  CSG (constructive solid geometry), 159
  Dijkstra's algorithm and A*, 291
  farthest feature map, 150
  Fringe Search, 293–294
  IDA* (Iterative Deepening A*), 292
  K-medoids clustering, 276–277
  Loop subdivision, 383–390
  LRU (Least Recently Used), 6
  Lucas and Kanade, 31–33
  Lucas and Kanade algorithm in optical flow, 29–30
  page-replacement, 6
  particle deposition, 353–354
  plan-merging algorithm, 284–286
  polar-rejection, 200
  polygon cutting, 162–163
  raytracing, 127
  recursive node learning, 213
  ridge structures, 359–360
  RP^2 operations, 161–164
  skeletal animation, 367, 370
  sum-of-uniforms, 201
  victim page determination, 6
  WELL algorithm, 120–121
  whitening algorithms used with RNGs, 116
  workflow for Artificial Contender, 230–232
allocated blocks, resizing, 23
allocation hooks
  implementing, 101–102
  using with memory leaks, 100–101
amplitude envelope, example of, 312
animating
  relief imposters, 407–409
  relief maps, 407
animation data, storing in textures, 406
animation systems, overview of, 365–366
  See also relief imposters
APC (Age Percentage Cost)
  calculating, 9
  relationship to RC (relative cost), 12–13
APC variables, deriving, 10
APIs, using in audio processing, 332
application crashes, exception handling, 97–98
Application Recovery and Restart API, availability in Windows Vista, 103
ApplyToModified functor, code for, 243
ARC (Adaptive Replacement Cache) algorithm, use of, 6
array of pointers, using with heap allocators, 21
array of vectors, optical flow as, 26
arrays, use with subdivision data structures, 390–391
Artificial Contender
  decision-making algorithms for, 232
  development of, 229
  execution flow in, 235–236
  partial results in, 232
  using "Pipes and Filters" design pattern with, 230–232
  workflow algorithms for, 230–232
  workflow diagram for, 234–235
Artificial Contender implementation
  ActionInfo flow, 241–242
  ActionInfo type, 245
  alternative block implementations, 245–246
  constraints, 246–247
  constructing workflows, 246
  function pointers versus functors in, 244–245
  generic programming and C++, 238
  partial results in, 244
  polymorphic workflow blocks, 238–241
artificial intelligence (AI). See agents
ARToolkit
  obtaining marker position with, 74
  retrieving transformation matrix used by, 74
  sample programs in, 72–73
  using with foot-based navigation, 71–72
AST (Abstract Syntax Tree), using to replace strings with numbers, 555–559
asynchronous events, notifications as, 81–83
asynchronous versus synchronous exceptions, 97
Atlas terrain system, availability of, 421–422
attitude components
  duration, 255
  potency, 254–255
  valence, 253–254
attitude objects, example of, 252, 256–258
attitude systems
  example of, 261–262
  features of, 250–252

model for, 255–256
persuasion and influence in, 259–260
setting half-lives in, 255
updating values in, 252
use of, 249
attitudes
accumulation of, 251
emotional charges of, 252
and social exchanges, 260–261
toward behavior, 258–259
use in Fable, 253
attributes, serializing into text format, 518–519
audio
calculating room acoustics, 302–303
keeping in sync with graphic updates, 314
on PS3, 306
streaming with loop markers, 310
surround sound, 315–318
See also mixing system; next-gen audio engine; sounds
audio channels
mixing to busses, 318
processing relative to playback frequency, 311
requirements for, 307
setting volume levels of, 311
splitting, 315
audio compression formats
ADPCM, 337
MP3, 337
OGG Vorbis, 337–338
audio data streaming, prioritizing, 310
audio effects, using, 301
audio engines
considering, 306
file formats for, 308
loop markers used with, 309
audio files, playback of, 307–309
audio optimization, implementing with GPUs, 300–301
audio processing
APIs available for, 332
compression and streaming, 337–338
effects and filters in, 336–337
rank buffers in, 334–336
sound buffers in, 333–334
audio samples, clearing out, 334
audio tools, using, 326–328
authentication
Challenge Hash Authentication, 483
implementation of, 487–488
and password recovery, 482–483
process of, 481
public key infrastructure, 484–485
Secret Exchange Authentication, 484
AVG usage, finding for pages, 10
axis-aligned bounding box (AABB), use in scenes, 184

B

B-A Minkowski difference, considering as convex shape, 170
backscattering effect, applying for diffuse-light shading, 377–379
balance theory, relationship to attitude systems, 260
battlefield, navigating in RTS (real-time strategy) games, 63, 65
behavior, attitudes toward, 258–259
behavior cloning
building AI script from trees for, 215–216
demo game for, 210–216
explanation of, 209
behavior-capture AI technology. See Artificial Contender
behaviors, finding in player traces, 272
Belady's Min (OPT) algorithm, use of, 6–13
best-fitting spheres, relationship to farthest feature map, 143, 148
BI (behavioral intention), relationship to attitudes, 259
bin, selecting based on heap-allocation size, 16–17
binding
C functions, 504
classes, 503, 513
binding function, creating for Lua, 507–509
Biquantic subdivision scheme, features of, 382
bit array, using with heap allocators, 21
blimp, invoking in shader architecture, 549–551
blimp fragment shader code sample, 549–550
blimp vertex shader, creating hover for, 549
blocks
for AC decision-making algorithms, 236–238
ActionInfo objects processed by, 235
alternative implementations of, 245–246
constraints on, 238
function in execution flow, 235
implementation examples, 242–243
polymorphic workflow blocks, 238–241

blocks *(continued)*
properties of, 239
See also workflow blocks
Bloom, Charles, 184–185
Blum Blum Shub RNG method, description of, 121
bones, cumulative error associated with, 366
book, use in debugging heap allocation, 22
Boolean operations, performing on convex polygons, 161, 163
bounding boxes, use in scenes, 184
bounding volume hierarchies, use in narrow phase, 185–188
box, support mapping for, 168
box-box overlap test, use in narrow phase, 186–187
breakpoints, using with network code, 492
broad phase of collision detection, speeding up, 184–185
Brownian trees, use in particle deposition, 359–360
BSP tree, kD-tree as, 129
bucket organization, parameters for WER, 102
bump maps, storing for advanced decals method, 427–428
bump vectors, encoding, 428
busses, mixing audio channels to, 318
Butterfly subdivision scheme, features of, 382

C

C functions, binding, 504
C++, use with Artificial Contender, 238
C++ classes, components of, 519
C++ compile-time checking, use with Artificial Contender, 246
C++ methods, overloading in Lua, 514
C++ objects
and arrays, 530, 532
binding in Lua, 505–510
improving, 533
native database type for, 530–531
objects or pointers to objects, 530–531
retrieving, 531
storing, 527–530
storing instances of, 525
updating contents of, 529–530
See also objects
C++ STL, using with hexagonal grids, 51–52
cache, direct-mapping main memory to, 43
cache, function of, 5–6
cache coherency, use in multithread job and dependency system, 90
cache misses
occurrence of, 5
types of, 43
cache replacement
A&C (age and cost) considerations, 12–13
Age and Cost metrics, 8–13
cost of, 11–12
cache systems, difficulty associated with, 5
cached memory, reading from, 6
cache-replacement algorithms
Belady's Min (OPT), 6–7
LRU (Least Recently Used), 7
MRU (Most Recently Used), 7
NFU (Not Frequently Used), 7–8
use of, 5
capsule, support mapping for, 169
car race games, using surround sound in, 315
Catmull-Clark subdivision scheme
features of, 382, 388–389
for GPU rendering, 397
CD contents
AddressingScheme for hexagonal grid, 52
AIShooter demo, 212
astshow.py file, 557
C++ object serialization, 532
clipmap demo, 422
clipmap effect, 417
debugging framework, 103–104
decal system, 430, 433
deferred function caller, 84
foot-based navigation, 70
heap allocator, 23
hexagonal tile (grid) example, 47
hiroPatt.pdf file for foot-based navigation, 72
horse animations, 410
lipsyncing example, 457, 460
Lua binding, 516
Lua binding data structure, 505
mixing system, 347
multithread job and dependency system, 87
optical flow example, 33
PlayerViz tool, 268
projective space example, 164
raytracing demo, 139–140
relief imposters, 410
shaders integrated into engine, 551
smart packet sniffer, 493, 496
sound effects, 324
tables for database backend, 526

threading system, 36
cellular automata
RNG method, 119
using hexagonal grids with, 56–57
using in RTS (real-time strategy) games, 64
central limit theorem, use with GRNGs, 201–202
centroids, connecting for farthest feature map, 149
Challenge Hash Authentication, properties of, 483
chorus effects, using, 301
circular buffer, role in audio processing, 334
cities, depicting with square tiles, 50
classes, binding, 503, 513
client/server topology, considering in game world synchronization, 468
clipmaps
advantages of, 415–416
background paging, 420
budgeting updates, 420–421
and clipstack size, 416
CPU synthesis and upload, 419
drawbacks of, 416
implementing, 417–419
managing large textures with, 436
methods for updating, 417
optimizing fillrate/low-end support, 421
purpose of, 414
selecting focus points, 416
toroidal updates and rectangle clipper, 418–419
use of, 413
closed lists, eliminating with IDA*, 292–294
CMU phonemes, 458–459
code samples
ApplyToModified function, 243
attitude system, 255–256
audio effects, 301
backscattering, 378–379
binding function for Lua, 507–509
blimp fragment shader, 549–550
blimp vertex shader, 549
Brownian tree, 360
C++ methods overloaded in Lua, 514
C++ object update, 529
C++ objects as Lua objects, 506–507
C++ objects stored, 528
clipmap effect, 417
dataports, 536
dependency group and links, 93
dunes created with particle deposition, 362
farthest feature map, 148, 150
foot-based navigation, 73–75
forEach function implementation for modifier, 243
Gaussian distribution, 201
GLRCachePad macro, 43
graftal imposters, 451–453
half-edge pair indices in Loop subdivision, 395
job class in multithread job and dependency system, 88–89
job selection in multithread job and dependency system, 91
kD-tree EventBoxSide, 135
kD-tree traversal, 136–137
KdTreeNode structure, 130
LFSR113, 119–120
Lua binding, 503
Lua binding and automatic type registering, 509–510
Lua binding data structure, 505–506
Lua binding function, 509
Lua binding metatable for object-oriented method, 505
Lua binding of C function, 504
Lua binding optimization of generated code size, 515
Lua binding sand-boxing and type filtering, 515
Lucas and Kanade algorithm in optical flow, 29
manager class in multithread job and dependency system, 89
Modifier block for Artificial Contender, 241
motion history in OpenCV, 28–29
mWebCam.AddRegion(), 32
non-collinear surface points in XenoCollide, 172
OpenCV, 26
overhanging terrain, 363
packet sniffer, 495
particle dynamics, 357
particle placement for volcanoes, 358
pathfinding with hexagonal grids, 56
pointers for database backend, 521–523
polymorphic workflow blocks, 239
Python's AST, 556–557
raytracing, 127
room acoustics real-time rendering, 302–303
scheduler class in multithread job and dependency system, 90
serializing attributes into text format, 518–519
shader groups, 552
shader in GLSL, 376
shaders combined with actors and properties, 552–553
shaders integrated into engine, 550–551

code samples *(continued)*
source blocks, 242
spatial search with hexagonal grids, 55
static polymorphism, 241
tables for database backend, 526
texture-coordinate calculation, 443
trigonometric functions, 194–195
variables allocated memory for OpenCV, 26–27
webcamInput class cvAbsDiff function, 27
webcamInput class public interface, 31
WELL algorithm, 120–121
worker threads in multithread job and dependency system, 90
XenoCollide pseudocode, 171
See also Listings
codecs, requirements of, 309
CodeGenerator, using with Python's AST, 558–559
cognitions, relationship to attitudes, 251
collinear cases, detecting, 153
collision algorithm. See XenoCollide
collision culling, explanation of, 184
collision detection
broad phase task of, 184–185
and Loop subdivision, 389–390
modeling, 144
between models in scenes, 180
narrow phase of, 185–188
simplifying using Minkowski differences, 170–171
using Minkowsi Portal Refinement (MPR), 171–176
collision detection tasks, using semantics for, 184–188
collision systems, creating, 165
collision tests, considering AABB-trees in, 187
collision-detection steps
choose_new_candidate(), 173–174
choose_new_portal() step of, 175
find_candidate_portal(), 172
find_origin_ray() step of, 171
find_support_in_direction_of_portal(), 174
if () return hit; step of, 174
if (origin outside support plane) return miss, 174
if (support plane close to portal) return miss, 175
while (origin ray does not intersect candidate), 172
command lifetime, use with RTS games, 65–66
compression, considering in audio processing, 337–338
compression algorithms, using with skeletal animation, 367
computer vision games, optical flow in, 26
computer vision, using with foot-based navigation, 71–72
cones
creating, 169
support mapping for, 170
testing of model human vision, 219
constructive solid geometry (CSG) algorithms, use of, 159
contact information, acquiring with MPR, 176–178
continuous collision detection, approach toward, 144
control points
interpolating for relief imposters, 404–405
for walking dog animation, 409–410
convex polygon, describing, 161
convex shapes, manipulating, 170
coplanar cases, detecting, 153
cosine law, use of, 373
crashes, reasons for, 97
CSG (constructive solid geometry) algorithms, use of, 159
CSPRNGs (cryptographically Secure PRNGs)
Blum Blum Shub, 121
/dev/random, 121–122
Fortuna, 122
ISAAC, ISAAC+, 121
Microsoft's CryptGenRandom, 122
Yarrow, 122
cube-map, relationship to farthest feature map, 144–145
custom texture cache, design of, 8–13
cylinder, support mapping for, 169

D

DA (direct-argument) functions, adding deferred calls to, 84
data loading, considering in streaming audio, 309
data structures, designing for subdivision surfaces, 390–392
database backend for C++ objects
array class used in, 518
metadata for, 517–518
database backend tables for C++ objects
arrays, 525
creating, 526
instances of classes, 523–525
parent class, 520
pointers, 520–523

scalar members, 520
strings, 520
dataport examples
broadcasting positional information, 539
camera systems, 538
problems with, 539
ship handling debug values, 538
Dataport Manager
using, 536–537
using hashing in, 539
dataport pointers, use of, 536
dataports
and reference counting, 537–538
and type safety, 537
use of, 535–536
debug output, using with network code, 492–493
debugging framework
exception handling, 104
memory leak detector, 104
debugging support, adding for heap allocation, 22
debugging techniques, maintaining for network code, 492–493
decal system, requirements for, 423
decals method (advanced)
advantages of, 428–430
DecodeBump function used in, 427–428
performance and experimental results, 430–433
using, 424–428
decision tree implementation, using with agents, 211–215
decision-making algorithms, for goal-oriented planning systems, 281–286
decomposition
effects of, 230
of worlds into regions, 271
deferred functions, use of, 82–85
deferred_proch system
header file for, 84
parameters used with, 84
demos. See CD contents
Dependency Inversion Principle, applying to workflow blocks, 239
dependency manager system
dependency graph in, 92
dependency storage in, 93–94
entries in, 91
group entry in, 94
job entry in, 94
design patterns
iterator used with hexagonal grids, 53
Prototype Design Pattern used with shaders, 544
/dev/random RNG method, description of, 121–122
dfpProcessAndClear deferred function caller, use of, 84
DIEHARD randomness-testing suite, features of, 116
diffuse light
computation of, 373
model for, 374
producing, 375
diffuse-light shading
backscattering, 377–379
flattening effect of, 375–377
diffusion limited aggregation (DLA), creating ridge structures with, 359–360
Dijkstra, modification of A* search algorithm by, 290–292
direct-argument (DA) functions, adding deferred calls to, 84
directed lines
computing in R^2 projective space, 159
cutting polygons with, 161
operations on, 157–158
DirectSound API, features of, 332
disc, support mapping for, 168
discrete collision detection, approach toward, 144
dispositional liking, demonstration by attitudes, 251
DLA (diffusion limited aggregation), creating ridge structures with, 359–360
Doo-Sabin subdivision scheme, features of, 382
double quotes ("), using with Python strings, 556
dramatic beat, function in attitude systems, 252
DSP effects, considering in surround sound, 317–318
dump file, controlling information in, 98
dunes, improving particle placement of, 361–362
duration, purpose in attitude systems, 255
DXT5 compressed surfaces, storing bump values in, 427
dynamic geometry, computing texture coordinates in, 443

E

echoes, calculating, 302–303
edge vertices, computing with Loop subdivision, 393
edges, manipulating in Loop subdivision, 384–386
effects versus filters, considering in audio processing, 336–337

ellipses
augmenting vision model toolbox with, 219–222
Equation for, 195
implementing for vision model, 221–222
support mapping for, 168
ellipsoid, support mapping for, 168
entities, roles in game worlds, 55
Enumerator class, using with hexagonal grids, 53
epsilon values
using in foot-based navigation, 75
using with collinear and coplanar cases, 153
Equations
affine transform, 180
attitude objects, 256
backscattering, 377–378
bump-vector encoding, 428
clustering IPGs, 277
cost of split, 133
decals method (advanced), 426
decision tree implementation for agents, 213
ellipse, 195
ellipse implementation for vision model, 221
flattening effect of diffuse-light shading, 375
graftal-imposter texture coordinates, 452–453
Hermite spline, 192–194
inverse of affine matrix, 181–183
MA and MB matrices, 186
matrix multiplication over vertex, 181
Minkowski differences, 171
origin shift, 181
Phong-Blinn model applied to backscattering, 378–379
points and directed lines in RP^2, 155
polygon cutting, 163
ray intersection with axis-aligned plane, 130
RBFs (radial basis functions) and relief imposters, 404
skeletal animation and cumulative error, 366
skeletal animation rotation computation, 369
SLERP (spherical linear interpolation), 194
sphere with support mapping, 167
support mapping for rotated and translated object, 168
texture memory usage for large terrain areas, 439
texture stack update for large terrains, 440
vertex and crease normals in Loop subdivision, 388
vertices in Loop subdivision, 386
vertices in skeletal animation, 365
erosion, simulating effects of, 355–356, 429
errors
application crashes, 97–100
memory leaks, 100–102
WER (Windows Error Reporting), 102–103
EventBox, use with kD-tree, 134–135
exception handling, 97–98, 104
exceptions, types of, 97
explosions
considering as "pops," 322
qualities of, 323
Eye Toy: Play, optical flow experiment with, 30–33
eyes. See vision model

F

FA (faces array), use with subdivision data structures, 390–391
Fable
opinion system in, 260
use of attitude in, 252–253
Façade, opinion events in, 252
fade sample amount, specifying for rank buffers, 336
fading, use with FFT, 312–313
farthest feature map
2D case of, 145–146
3D case of, 147
algorithm for, 150
and best-fitting spheres, 143
and mean curvatures, 143
oversampling, 148
and preprocessing, 144–148
and principle curvatures, 143
and runtime queries, 148–150
storage of vertices for, 148
use of, 143
visualizing, 145
Fast Fourier Transforms (FFT)
relationship to audio engines, 312–313
relationship to effects and filters, 336
feature space output, setting up for behavior cloning, 210–211
FFT (Fast Fourier Transforms)
relationship to audio engines, 312–313
relationship to effects and filters, 336
windowing required for, 314
field of view
determining entities in, 222
using ellipse for, 220

Figures
2D case of farthest feature map, 145–146
3D case of farthest feature map, 147
AABB fitting model, 185
amplitude envelope, 312
Artificial Contender decision-making workflow, 234
audio-channel location relative to player, 316
backscattering, 378–379
best fitting circle in 2D, 149
bin selection based on heap-allocation size, 16
bin with single page for small allocator, 17
Boolean operations on polygons, 163
bounding box start and end events for kD-tree, 134
Brownian tree created with DLA, 360
cellular automata and hexagonal grids, 57
cellular automaton grid in RTS game, 64
circular update for large terrain, 442
clipmap update, 415
clipped mipmap stack, 414
clipstack-texture size, 418
decal techniques, 426–427
decal-methods tests, 431
decals method (advanced), 425
decision tree for agents, 214
dependency graph, 91, 93
dependency graph after propagation, 92
dog imposter, 408
DSP effects in buss, 318
dunes formed as particles, 362
DXT 1/5 compressed textures, 433
edge mask in Loop subdivision, 385
ellipse components for vision model, 220
Enumerator class used with hexagonal grid, 53
erosion using decals, 429
face splitting in Loop subdivision, 394
feature space, 210–211
FFT (Fast Fourier Transforms), 313
flattening effect of diffuse-light shading, 376–377
Flock of Birds motion capture device, 70
FMOD Designer interface, 327
foot-based navigation, 71
FSM (Finite State Machine) for warrior, 257–258
game circuit for foot-based navigation, 76
game start indicator for foot-based navigation, 76
Gaussian distribution, 200, 202
geometry for Loop subdivision, 389
GLR thread library, 37
goal-oriented planning systems, 282
GPGPU graphics pipeline, 300
GPU versus CPU computational power, 299
graftal imposters, 449–450
graftal-imposter vertices, 451
grid partitioned into rectangular cells, 54
head model for lipsyncing, 456–457
hexagonal tiles, 48
hexagonal tiles with axes of symmetry, 50–51
HIVVE (Highly Interactive Information Value Visualization and Evaluation), 278
HLA activities, 472
HLA collaboration diagram, 469
HLA viewports and objects, 470
HLA-runtime entity-viewport visibility, 476
HLA-system UML class diagram, 477
horse animation, 410
interaction feature points, 269
IPGs (interactive player graphs), 275–276
kD-tree split plane position, 132
kD-tree splitting process, 129
kD-tree traversal cases, 138
kD-tree with node reduction, 130
Lambert shaded teapot, 374
large allocator memory use, 18
lava streams, 359
LCG bias, 123
Microsoft XNA XACT audio tool, 327
mixing layers in mixing system, 345
mixing system, 342
mixing system with central mix, 343
mixing through MIDI control surface, 346
mountain created with particle deposition, 361
movements of soldier troops in RTS game, 60
nil node's place in tree, 20
optical-flow game, 30, 32
Oren-Nayar shaded teapot, 375
origin ray, 172
overhanging terrain, 363
particle deposition, 354
particles and slope of terrain, 356
Play Audio commands relative to surround sound, 317
PlayerViz tool, 270
polygon cut with line, 162
polygon intersection, 162
portal for XenoCollide and MPR, 173–174, 176
pull workflow for Artificial Contender, 237
pull workflow with callback functions, 244
ray components, 128
raytracing demo application, 140

Figures *(continued)*
rectangular domain for hexagonal grid, 52
red-black-tree nodes for large allocator, 19
relief imposters with control points, 403
relief-imposter warping, 402
rotational error removed, 369
RP^2 projective space, 154
RP^2 projective space points and lines, 156
RTS (real-time strategy) games, 60
RTS (real-time strategy) sketches, 65
RTS focus-context interface combination, 61
RTS games with integrated interfaces, 66
RTS-game implementation, 63
search grid with search tree, 290
sensing-model unification, 227
ShaderManager class diagram, 543
ShaderParameter class diagram, 548
skeletal animation cumulative error, 368
skeletal animation reduction in cumulative translational error, 370
skeletal animation translation error reduction, 369
smart packet sniffer, 494
sound falloff with zone approach, 225
sound-layout comparison, 325
sphere with support mapping, 167
square grid relative to neighborhoods and marching, 48
stack overflow, 100
sticky particles used with overhanging terrain, 363
subdividing patch, 398
support mapping as moving plane, 166
support mappings combined, 169
support point, 167
support point in direction of portal, 175
surround sound, 315
surround sound with channels synced, 316
terrain composed of angles, 355
terrain created with search radius, 357
terrain generated with particle deposition algorithm, 354
terrain navigation system results, 444
texture atlas for graftal imposters, 448
texture stack for large terrain, 438
texture stack with mipmap levels, 439
textures (non-compressed) for decals method, 432
threaded and multithreaded models, 38
tiles, 50
toroidal update and mapping for virtual texture, 443
totally-ordered plans, 284
transformation semantics, 186
trigonometric curve for circle, 196
trigonometric curve with constraints, 193
UCT player trace, 267
vertex mask in Loop subdivision, 387
vertex neighbors in Loop subdivision, 394
view distance check in agent-sensing model, 218
virtual texture, 437
visemes for "hello," 460
vision certainty, 223
vision model with gradient zones of certainty, 224
vision model with view angles and circle, 220
visual data mining of player traces, 272
volcano created with particle deposition, 359
Walker class used with hexagonal grid, 53
walking-dog control points, 410
workflow for Artificial Contender, 235
filter, use in Artificial Contender, 231
Filters block, use in AC decision-making algorithms, 236
filters versus effects, considering in audio processing, 336–337
Finite State Machine (FSM), use with attitude systems, 256–257
FIR (finite impulse response) filters, using in audio processing, 336–337
first-person shooting (FPS) games, interaction control in, 69
flattening effect, applying for diffuse-light shading, 375–377
Float32 PCM audio engine file format, pros and cons of, 308–309
Flow Regions() function, using in optical flow, 31
fluster, displaying for player trace, 272
FMOD Designer interface
features of, 326–328
goals of, 328–329
See also sounds
folklore algorithm mistakes, occurrence with RNGs, 123–124
foot-based navigation
capabilities of, 69–71
implementation of, 69–70, 72–75
requirements for use with computer vision, 71–72
sample game, 75–77
tests with users, 77–78
footsteps, randomizing, 328–329

formulas. See Equations
Fortuna RNG method, description of, 122
Fourier series, constructing trigonometric spline from, 192
FPS (first-person shooting) games, interaction control in, 69
fragment shaders, use with room acoustics, 302–303
fragment versus pixel shaders, 542
frames, storing information per, 10
free nodes, managing with large allocator, 18
free-list
  accessing with small allocator, 17
  function in heap allocation, 16
frequency data, using windowing techniques used with, 312, 314
Fringe Search algorithm, using, 293–294
frustum, support mapping for, 170
FSM (Finite State Machine), use with attitude systems, 256–257
function calls, categorizing for asynchronous events, 83–84
function pointers versus functors, use in Artificial Contender, 244–245

G

g() cost, purpose in A* search algorithm, 291, 293
gain, finding in behavior cloning example, 214
game animation systems, overview of, 365–366
game architecture, planning for multithreaded programs, 36
game logins, securing, 481–485
game sessions, securing, 485–487
game world state
  categorizing changes in, 468–469
  sending messages in, 468–469
game world synchronization. See synchronizing game worlds
game worlds, entities in, 55
gateways, identifying between spatial regions, 271
Gaussian distributions
  example of, 201
  in nature, 203
  use of, 199
  using in RNGs, 115
Gaussian random number generators (GRNGs)
  application for, 202
  and central limit theorem, 201
  polar-rejection, 200
  use of, 200–203
  ziggurat method, 201
Gaussian randomness, use of, 203
General Purpose computation on a Graphics Processing Unit (GPGPU), overview of, 300
general purpose registers (GPRs), use with asynchronous events, 84
generic programming
  alternative block implementations in, 245–246
  use with Artificial Contender, 238
geometry creation in Loop subdivision
  edges, 384–386
  limit positions, 387–388
  vertex and crease normals, 388
  vertices, 386–387
geometry models, mapping virtual textures to, 442–443
GHTP project, smart packet sniffer used in, 491–492
GJK (Gilbert, Johnson, Keerthy) algorithm
  versus MPR (Minkowski Portal Refinement), 177–178
  use of, 171
GLRCachePad macro, using in threaded systems, 43–44
GLRThread interface
  capabilities of, 39
  size of, 40
GLRThreadFoundation singleton, usage of, 38
GLRThreading library
  components of, 36–38
  creating cache-aligned data structures with, 43–44
  features of, 36
  threading capabilities in, 42
  using, 44–45
GLRThreading system, submitting objects to, 42
GLRThreadProperties mechanism, use in threading systems, 39–40
GNU C library
  hooking functions related to, 102
  replacing memory functions with, 101
goal-oriented planning systems
  overview of, 281–283
  partially-ordered plans in, 282
  plan merging for, 283–286
  totally-ordered plans in, 282
GPGPU (General Purpose computation on a Graphics Processing Unit), overview of, 300
GPRs (general purpose registers), use with asynchronous events, 84

GPU subdivision, considering in Loop subdivision, 397–398
GPUs, relationship to audio optimization, 300–301
graftal imposters
 assigning texture coordinates to, 452–453
 sampling texture atlas for, 453
 using assets during runtime, 450–453
graftal-imposter assets
 color texture and mesh, 450
 control textures, 448, 451
 texture atlas, 447–448
 vector fields, 448–450
graftals, use of, 447
granularity, role in next-gen audio engine, 313–314
graph edit distance, using, 275–277
graph searches, techniques for, 289
graph-based data, discovering knowledge in, 278
grids
 hexagonal versus square types of, 47
 impact on visual appearance of games, 49
 representing playing fields with, 49
 use in games, 47
GRNGs (Gaussian random number generators)
 application for, 202
 and central limit theorem, 201
 polar-rejection, 200
 use of, 200–203
 ziggurat method, 201

H

h() cost, purpose in A* search algorithm, 291, 293
HA (half-edge array), use with subdivision data structures, 391
half-edge array (HA), use with subdivision data structures, 391, 395
half-life, setting in attitude systems, 255
handheld gaming systems, relationship to vertical blanking period, 82
hanging pointers, tracking down, 537
hanning and hamming window types, use of, 314
head model, using for lipsyncing, 455
header file, use with asynchronous events, 84
heap allocation
 adding debugging support for, 22
 combining allocators, 21
 example on CD, 23
 extensions of, 23
 hybrid approach toward, 15–23
 with large allocator, 18–21
 and multithreading, 22
 perception of, 15
 with per-size template pool-style allocator, 16
 with small allocator, 16–18
hearing model
 with certainty, 224–226
 considering in agent-sensing model, 219
 including other senses in, 226
height fields, traversing with random walkers, 353–354
Hermite spline, Equation for, 192–193
hexagonal grids
 access layer of, 53
 address layer in, 51–53
 implementing, 54–55
hexagonal tiles
 advantage of, 48
 axes of symmetry, 50–51
 equidistant neighbors on, 48
 forming organic shapes with, 50
 isotropy and packing density considerations, 49
hexagonal-grid applications
 cellular automata, 56–57
 pathfinding, 55–56
 spatial search, 55
hit-test computations, using with hexagonal grids, 54
HIVVE (Highly Interactive Information Value Visualization and Evaluation) tool, features of, 278
HLA (High Level Abstraction)
 collaboration diagram for, 469
 components of, 470–476
 usage of, 461
HLA event handlers, use of, 477
HLA runtimes
 communication between, 475–476
 construction of, 477–478
 viewports in, 476–478
HLA system, extending, 478
hook function, use with memory leaks, 101–102
horse-animation example, 410
human cognitions, attitudes as basis for, 251
human hearing. See hearing model
human vision. See vision model

I

IA (indirect-argument) functions, adding deferred calls to, 84
IDA* (Iterative Deepening A*), eliminating open and closed lists with, 292–293

identity
by authentication method, 485–486
by cryptography method, 486
by IP address method, 485
IDs, replacing strings with, 555–559
IIR (infinite impulse response) filters, using in audio processing, 336–337
image warping, using with relief imposters, 403
index dispenser, use in dependency storage, 93
indirect argument data blocks, storage of, 83–84
indirect-argument (IA) functions, adding deferred calls to, 84
InfiniteReality2 hardware platform, access of miplevels in, 414
influence and persuasion, considering in attitude systems, 259–260
information theory, applying to behavior cloning, 214
instance-based machine learning
Artificial Contender example of, 229–230
feature space in, 210–211
integer representation, finding length in prospective space, 160
interactions, capturing, 268
Inversive Congruential Generator RNG method, description of, 118
IP address, identity by, 485
IPGs (interactive player graphs)
building, 274–278
clustering, 275–277
clustering players by, 275
ISAAC, ISAAC+ RNG method, description of, 121
iterator design pattern, using with hexagonal grids, 53

J

jittering values, hiding, 474
job selection, use in multithread job and dependency system, 91
jobs versus threads, 87
job-system objects
cache coherency, 90
job, 88–89
job selection, 91
manager class, 89
scheduler, 89–90
worker threads, 90
jumper, displaying for player trace, 272

K

kD-tree
axis-aligning split planes in, 130
construction of, 132–135
cost of splits in, 133
determining split plane position, 132
EventBox used with, 134–135
traversal of, 135–138
use in raytracing, 128
use of, 129
See also raytracing
kD-tree nodes, contents of, 130
KdTreeNode structure, 130
key vertex cell decomposition, applying to worlds, 271
keyboard sniffers, concerns about, 482, 487
K-medoids clustering, using on IPGs, 276–277
Knuth mistake, occurrence with RNGs, 122–123
Kobbelt subdivision scheme, features of, 382

L

Lagged Fibonacci Generator (LFG) RNG method, description of, 118
Lambert's model
effects of, 374
versus Oren-Nayar model, 375
use of, 373
large allocator
combining with small allocator, 21
function in heap allocation, 18–21
latency, relationship to audio engines, 313–314
later and now lists, use in Fringe Search algorithm, 293–294
LCG (Linear Congruential Generator) RNG method, description of, 116–117
leak detector, allocation registry managed by, 101–102
Least Recently Used (LRU) algorithm
efficiency of, 6
use of, 7
least used pages, identifying, 10
LFG (Lagged Fibonacci Generator) RNG method, description of, 118
LFSR (Linear Feedback Shift Register) RNG method, description of, 118
LFSR113, LFSR258, use of, 119–120
liking/disliking, evaluating in attitude systems, 253–254
Linear Congruential Generator (LCG) RNG method, description of, 116–117
Linear Recurrence Generators (LRGs)
LFSR113, LFSR258, 119–120
Mersenne Twister, 119
WELL algorithm, 120–121
line-of-sight test, doing in agent-sensing model, 218–219

lines
  cutting polygons with, 162
  defining relative to projective space, 156
  finding intersection points of, 157–158
  leading through pair of points, 157
links, creating for dependency manager system, 94
lipsyncing
  head model used for, 455
  in real-time, 460–461
  requirements for, 455–457
  use of, 455
  word to phoneme mapping for, 457–459
listener, role in sound systems, 332
Listings
  GLRThreading library executing test objects, 45
  GLRThreading library test game object, 44
  GLRThreading library threadable function for game function, 44
  RBF-based warping function, 406–407
  recursive node learning algorithm, 213
  sFront and sBack for relief imposters, 409
  SWD file, 471
  SWD file for synchronized object, 474
  SWD file pseudo-grammar, 470–471
  synchronized object _property keyword, 472–473
  synchronized object casting and assign operators, 473
  walking motion, 408–409
  See also code samples
LOD levels, smooth transitions between, 415
logging
  excluding and oversimplifying, 267
  implementation of, 268
  usefulness of, 266
logins, securing, 481–485
logs, capturing at 10Hz, 267
loop markers
  streaming audio with, 310
  use with audio engines, 309
Loop subdivision algorithm
  collision detection, 389–390
  computing new edge vertices with, 393
  creating new half-edge information, 395
  data structure for, 390–392
  edge weights in, 385
  extensions to, 381
  feature implementation, 388–389
  features of, 382
  geometry creation, 384–388
  GPU subdivision and rendering, 397–398
  levels of subdivision in, 392
  performance enhancements, 396–397
  relief warping requirements, 407
  splitting faces with, 393–394
  toolset for, 383–384
  updating features, 395–396
  updating original vertices, 393
  See also subdivision surfaces
lossy compression algorithms, using with skeletal animation, 367
lozenge, support mapping for, 169
LRGs (Linear Recurrence Generators)
  LFSR113, LFSR258, 119–120
  Mersenne Twister, 119
  WELL algorithm, 120–121
LRU (Least Recently Used) algorithm
  efficiency of, 6
  use of, 7
L-systems, use with particle deposition, 361
Lua binding
  attributes, 511–512
  and automatic type registering, 509–510
  of C functions, 504
  of C++ objects, 505–510
  creating binding function for, 507–509
  debug helper, 513
  enum support, 512
  inheritance, 511
  making object-oriented, 504–505
  native types for, 505
  optimization of generated code size, 515–516
  overloaded functions, 513
  overloading C++ methods in, 514
  reference counting and raw objects, 511
  sand-boxing and type filtering, 514–515
  singletons, 511–512
  static functions, 511–512
  template classes, 512
  use of, 503–504
Lua script, turning tree as, 215
Lucas and Kanade algorithm
  turning tree as Lua script, 215
  use in optical flow, 29–30
  use with optical flow, 31–33

M

MA and MB matrices, use in narrow phase, 185–186
main memory, direct-mapping to cache, 43
  See also memory

malloc/free replacement, heap allocator for, 22
manager class, use in multithread job and dependency system, 89
marker position, obtaining with ARToolkit, 74
matrices, extracting semantics from, 181–184
matrix m, values for, 75
MAX analysis, using with pages, 10
mean curvatures, relationship to farthest feature map, 143
memory
  adding to unified sensing model, 227
  association with threads, 40
  management by small allocator, 17
  use in large allocator, 18
  See also main memory
memory leak detector, using, 100–102, 104
Mergers block, use in AC decision-making algorithms, 237
merging plans for agents, 284–286
Mersenne Twister Linear Recurrence Generator, use of, 119
mesh, storing for subdivision data structures, 390–391
MetaAttribute class, use with database backend, 518
metals, models for, 374
MetaType class
  class metadata saved in, 517–518
  using with database backend, 526
Microsoft CRT, using allocation hooks in, 101
Microsoft's CryptGenRandom RNG method, description of, 122
Microsoft's XACT audio tool, features of, 326
Middle Square RNG method, description of, 116
Midedge subdivision scheme, features of, 382
MIDI interface, implementation for *Scarface: The World Is Yours,* 346
mini-dump, creating for running process, 98
MiniDumpCallback function, use in debugging, 104
Minkowski differences
  finding points on interiors of, 171
  simplifying collision detection with, 170–171
mipmapping, generalizing with clipmaps, 413–414
mixing system
  features of, 341–342
  implementation of, 342–345
  performance of, 346–347
  tuning application for, 345–346
  See also audio
Modifier block
  implementing, 241
  use in AC decision-making algorithms, 236
momentary versus dispositional liking, 251
Most Recently Used (MRU) algorithm, use of, 7
mountains, improving particle placement of, 358–361
MP3 audio compression format, explanation of, 337
MP3 audio engine file format
  playing back audio in, 307–308
  pros and cons of, 308
  requirements of, 309
MPR (Minkowski Portal Refinement)
  versus GJK (Gilbert, Johnson, Keerthy) algorithm, 177–178
  relationship to XenoCollide algorithm, 166, 171–176
  using for contact information, 176–178
MRU (Most Recently Used) algorithm, use of, 7
MultiStream
  busses for audio channels in, 318
  latency considerations, 313
  processing capabilities of, 306, 309
  role in SCEE audio engine, 305
  surround-sound management by, 315
  and volume parameters, 311
multithread job and dependency system. See job-system objects
multithreaded programs, designing, 36
multithreading
  hiding complexity of, 87
  relationship to heap allocation, 22
  synchronization problems associated with, 87
multivariate normal distribution, example of, 202
mutex per bin, using in heap allocation, 22
mWebCam.AddRegion() function, using in optical flow, 32

N

NA (normals array), use with subdivision data structures, 391
narrow phase of collision detection, implementing, 185–188
navigation. See foot-based navigation
N-by-N attitudes, use in attitude systems, 260
Neighborhood instance, using with hexagonal grids, 54
neighborhoods, role in square tiling, 48
neighbors, coalescing with large allocator, 20
Netscape mistake, occurrence with RNGs, 123
network code, maintaining debugging techniques for, 492–493
Newton-Raphson method, use in optical flow, 29
next-gen, separating from last-gen titles, 317

next-gen audio engine
  channels for, 307
  and FFT (Fast Fourier Transforms), 312–313
  and frequency domain processing, 312
  and latency, 313–314
  packet smoothing, 314–315
  playback frequency of, 311
  routing, 318
  sample formats for, 307–309
  streaming, 309–310
  volume parameters for, 311
  See also audio
NFU (Not Frequently Used) algorithm, use of, 7–8
nil node, use with red-black trees, 20
nodes, managing with large allocators, 19–20
noise functions, using with particles, 356–357
normal distribution, use of, 199
normals array (NA), use with subdivision data structures, 391
Not Frequently Used (NFU) algorithm, use of, 7–8
notifications, considering as asynchronous events, 81–83
now and later lists, use in Fringe Search algorithm, 293–294
NPC behavior. See attitude systems
NPCs, use of totally-ordered plans with, 283
numbers, replacing strings with, 555–559

O

OBB (oriented bounding box), use in scenes, 184
object oriented programming, applying to hexagonal grids, 51–53
object threading, implementing, 42
objects
  instantiating in optical flow, 31–33
  in R^2 projective space, 155
  use in R^2 projective space, 159
  See also C++ objects
OGG Vorbis audio compression format, explanation of, 337–338
O(log(N)) search, guaranteeing with large allocator, 18
open lists, eliminating with IDA*, 292–294
OpenAL API, features of, 332
OpenCV library
  functions of webcamInput class in, 26–27
  use with optical flow, 25–26
OpenCV methods
  cvAbsDiff function, 27
  image differences, 27–28
  Lucas and Kanade algorithm, 29–30
  motion history, 28–29
OpenGL, shader parameters in, 546
opinion events, function in attitude systems, 252
opinion system
  example of, 257
  in Fable, 260
OPT (Belady's Min) algorithm, use of, 6–13
optical flow
  as array of vectors, 26
  in computer vision games, 26
  definition of, 25
  game sample, 30–33
  and image differences, 27–28
  instantiating objects in, 31–33
  Lucas and Kanade algorithm used in, 29–33
  and motion history, 28–29
  and OpenCV library, 25–26
  partitioning queries for, 32
Oren-Nayar model, versus Lambert's model, 375
oriented bounding box (OBB), use in scenes, 184
origin shift, example of, 181
outdoor terrain rendering. See terrain areas
OutputData type, defining for polymorphic workflow blocks, 240
overhanging terrain, creating with particle deposition, 362–364

P

PA_HARD and PA_SOFT labels, using with threads, 40
packets, capturing with WinPcap library, 494–496
page-replacement algorithms, use of, 6
pages
  accessing relative to Age algorithm, 8–13
  APC/RC ratios for, 12
  costs associated with, 11–12
  determining for eviction from cache, 10
  placement with small allocator, 18
  relationship to cache, 5
  requesting from OS in heap allocation, 17
parent side index, use with large allocators, 19–20
partially-ordered plans, use in plan merging, 282–283
particle deposition
  explanation of, 353
  improving, 354–355
  limitations of, 355
particle dynamics, improving, 355–357

particle-placement improvements
dunes, 361–362
mountains, 358–361
overhanging terrain, 362–364
volcanoes, 357–358
particles
behavior of, 355
search radius and elevation threshold of, 356–357
using noise functions with, 356–357
password recovery, considering in authentication, 482–483
passwords
insecurity of, 486–487
protection in Challenge Hash Authentication, 483
transmitting in Secret Exchange Authentication, 484
pathfinding approaches
A* search algorithm, 290–292
use of, 289
using hexagonal grids in, 55–56
pcap, initializing, 495
PCS (potentially colliding set) of triangles, discovering at runtime, 143
per bin marker, using with large allocator, 21
perspective projection, applying to planes, 156
persuasion and influence, considering in attitude systems, 259–260
phase-causing functions, managing for surround sound, 317
phonemes
mapping to visemes, 459
mapping words to, 457–459
versus visemes, 457–458
Phong-Blinn model, applying to backscattering, 378–379
"Pipes and Filters" design pattern
liabilities of, 232–233
using with Artificial Contender, 230–232
pixel movement. See optical flow
pixel versus fragment shaders, 542
plan merging, use with goal-oriented planning systems, 283–286
planes, applying perspective projection to, 156
plan-merging algorithm, implementing, 284–286
plants, expressing shape and formation of, 447
Play or Pitch functions, managing in surround sound, 317
playback frequency
considering in audio engines, 311
reducing for audio streams, 310
player traces
examining, 272
finding emergent behaviors in, 272
providing contexts for, 271
using visual data mining with, 272
visualizing, 270
players, clustering by IPGs, 275
PlayerViz tool
capturing captured information with, 279
design of, 270–271
generating thumbnails of player traces with, 272
information contained in, 268
world data in, 271
playing fields, representing with grids, 49
Playstation 3, next-gen audio engine for, 305
PN triangles, relationship to subdivision surfaces, 382
point, support mapping for, 168
pointers, using with large allocators, 19
point-line test, using in projective space, 157
points
consecutive operations on, 158–159
finding in interior of Minkowski difference, 171
operations on, 157–158
representing in projective space, 155
polar coordinates, use with Gaussian distribution, 202
polar-rejection, function in GRNGs, 200
polygon, support mapping for, 170
polygon meshes, generation of T-intersections in, 163–164
polygons
convex quality of, 161
cutting with lines, 162
polyhedron, support mapping for, 170
polymorphic workflow blocks, use in Artificial Contender, 238–241
"pops"
deconstructing, 323–324
explosions as, 322
potency, purpose in attitude systems, 254–255
potentially colliding set (PCS) of triangles, discovering at runtime, 143
preempting, purpose in threading architecture, 36
primary buffer, role in sound systems, 332
principle curvatures, relationship to farthest feature map, 143
PRNGs (pseudo-random number generators), use of, 114–115
procedural modeling, potential of, 110

programming errors
application crashes, 97–100
memory leaks, 100–102
WER (Windows Error Reporting), 102–103
projectile paths, adding random variation to, 202
projective space
objects in RP^2, 155
use of, 153–154
Prototype Design Pattern, use with shaders, 544, 547–548
PS3, audio on, 306
pseudocode. See code samples
pseudo-random number generators (PRNGs), use of, 114–115
public key infrastructure, using, 484–485
pull model, use in workflow, 236, 239
push model, use in workflow, 236
Python's AST, using to replace strings with numbers, 555–559

Q

Quake, animation of characters in, 365
Quake 3, conversion mod of, 267
QueryFlow() function
calling in optical flow, 31
preventing calling in optical flow, 33
quotes (' and "), using with Python strings, 556

R

R^2 projective space
converting vectors from, 155
number range limits in, 158–161
objects in, 155
operations in, 157–158, 161–164
points and directed lines in, 155–156
using integer coordinates in, 158
radial basis functions (RBFs)
animating relief imposters with, 402
and relief imposters, 404
See also relief imposters
random number generators (RNGs)
distributions of, 115
hardware RNGs, 114
PRNGs (pseudo-random number generators), 114–115
and software whitening, 116
uses of, 113–114
random variation, adding to projectile paths, 202
random walker, use in particle deposition, 353–354
randomness testing, conducting, 116
RANDU mistake, occurrence with RNGs, 123
rank buffers, role in audio processing, 334–336
ray, components of, 128
ray casting, explanation of, 127
ray queries, support for, 128
raytracing
for acoustics, 302
demo application, 139–140
dynamic scenes, 139
use of, 127
and visibility queries, 128
See also kD-tree
raydir array, use of, 137
rays, finding intersections of, 130
RBF coefficients, using with warping function and shaders, 405–406
RBFs (radial basis functions)
animating relief imposters with, 402
and relief imposters, 404
See also relief imposters
RC (relative cost), function in cache replacement, 12–13
real-time strategy (RTS) games
focus-context control level in, 61–63
integrating sketch- and unit-based interfaces in, 66
moving soldiers in, 63–64
moving troops through battlefields in, 65
popularity of, 59
using sketch-based approach with, 66
rectangle, support mapping for, 168
recursion, adding to raytracing, 127
red-black tree
combining with book container, 22
using with large allocators, 18
red-black tree node
searching for appropriate size, 20
storing, 19
use in non-default alignment, 21
Reif-Peters subdivision scheme, features of, 382
relative cost (RC), function in cache replacement, 12–13
relief imposters
animating, 407–409
and image warping, 403
interpolating warping functions for, 404–405
obtaining, 402

producing, 402
and RBFs (radial basis functions), 404
rendering, 407
texels for textures used with, 409
See also animation systems; RBFs (radial basis functions); warping functions
relief maps, animating, 407
relief rendering, explanation of, 401
rendering
considering in Loop subdivision, 397–398
of large terrain areas, 442–444
methods for, 381
relief imposters, 407
subdivision surfaces, 398
Repeaters block, use in AC decision-making algorithms, 237
ridge structures, creating, 359–360
RNG methods (cryptographic)
Blum Blum Shub, 121
/dev/random, 121–122
Fortuna, 122
ISAAC, ISAAC+, 121
Microsoft's CryptGenRandom, 122
Yarrow, 122
RNG methods (non-cryptographic)
cellular automata, 119
Inversive Congruential Generator, 118
LCG (Linear Congruential Generator), 116–117
LFG (Lagged Fibonacci Generator), 118
LFSR (Linear Feedback Shift Register), 118
LRGs (Linear Recurrence Generators), 119–121
Middle Square, 116
TLCG (Truncated Linear Congruential Generator), 117–118
RNGs (random number generators)
distributions of, 115
hardware RNGs, 114
mistakes associated with, 122–124
PRNGs (pseudo-random number generators), 114–115
and software whitening, 116
uses of, 113–114
room acoustics, calculating, 302–303
rotated objects, finding support mappings for, 168
rotation error
eliminating, 367–370
occurrence in skeletal animation, 367
rough surfaces, model for, 374–376
rounded box, support mapping for, 169
RP^2 projective space, use of, 154
RTS (real-time strategy) games
focus-context control level in, 61–62
integrating sketch- and unit-based interfaces in, 66
moving soldiers in, 63–64
moving troops through battlefields in, 65
path sketching in, 62–63
popularity of, 59
using sketch-based approach with, 66
runtime queries, using with farthest feature map, 148–150

S

SAH (surface area heuristic), relationship to kD-tree, 133
SAT (Separating Axis Theorem), use of box-box text with, 187
Scarface: The World Is Yours, MIDI interface implemented for, 346
SCEE audio engine project, goals of, 305
scheduler class, use in multithread job and dependency system, 89–90
SCRIPTABLE_DefineClass(MY_CLASS) macro, binding classes with, 513
search algorithms, A*, 290–292
Secret Exchange Authentication, using, 484
securing
game logins, 481–485
game sessions, 485–487
segment, support mapping for, 168
Selectors block, use in AC decision-making algorithms, 237
sensing model
adding memory to, 227
components of, 226–227
SGI's InfiniteReality2 hardware platform, access of miplevels in, 414
shader architecture, invoking blimp in, 549–551
shader groups, using, 551–552
shader in GLSL code sample, 376
shader languages, parameters supported by, 547
shader parameters, use in OpenGL, 546
shader programs, using with room acoustics, 302–303
ShaderManager class
methods on, 545
using, 543

ShaderParameter class
types of data supported by, 546–547
using, 542–543
ShaderProgram class, using, 542
shaders
cloning of parameter types for, 547–549
combining with actors and properties, 552–553
evaluating warping functions with, 405–407
fragment versus pixel shaders, 542
prototypes for, 544–546
reloading at runtime, 544
state sets and scene graphs, 545–546
terminology for, 541–542
shadings, producing with Lambert model, 374
shapes
finding support points for, 169
representing with support mappings, 166–170
shrink-wrapping, 169
support mappings for, 167–168
SIMD (Single Instruction Multiple Data), role in audio, 299
single quotes ('), using with Python strings, 556
singletons, use of GLRThreadFoundation in threading architectures, 37
skeletal animation
bone and rotation errors in, 366–367
and cumulative error, 366–370
functionality of, 365–366
reconstruction errors in, 368
sketches, creation by users in RTS games, 62
SLERP (spherical linear interpolation), use with trigonometric splines, 194
slope of terrain, defining, 355–356
SM2.0 clipmap path, implementing clipmaps with, 417–418
small allocator
combining with large allocator, 21
function in heap allocation, 16–18
using reserved virtual address range for, 21
smart packet sniffer
alternative for, 496
example of, 491–492, 496
features of, 491
implementation of, 493
reducing security risks for, 495–496
smooth edges and vertices, determining in Loop subdivision, 385–386
smooth surfaces, representing, 381
snapshots, mixing in mixing system, 344
sniffed passwords, concerns about, 482
social exchanges, relationship to attitudes, 260–261
soldiers, moving in RTS (real-time strategy) games, 63–64
Sorters block, use in AC decision-making algorithms, 237
sound buffers, role in audio processing, 333–334
sound designers, interaction with mixing system, 343
sound effects
creating, 324
and rank buffers, 335
tools used in creation of, 326
sound environment, making changes to, 329
sound falloff, demonstration of, 225–226
sound files, comparing layouts of, 324–326
sound instances, specifying playing of, 335
sounds
components of, 328
composition of, 322
conceptualizing, 322
constructing and deconstructing, 323–324
creating with FMOD Designer interface, 329
in-game rendering of, 328
perception of, 331
playing limitations of, 334–335
properties of, 224
See also audio; FMOD Designer interface
sound-system overview
listener, 332
primary buffer, 332
sound effects, 333
sound sources, 333
Sources block, use in AC decision-making algorithms, 236
Space War game, use in behavior-cloning example, 210
spatial movement, tracking, 274
spatial search, using hexagonal grids in, 55
sphere, support mapping for, 167–168
splines, use of, 192–194
Splitters block, use in AC decision-making algorithms, 237
sqrt(d) (Kobbelt) subdivision scheme, features of, 382
square tiling, neighborhoods in, 48
stack overflows, handling, 99–100
static polymorphism, implementing, 241
sticky particles, use with overhanging terrain, 363
streaming audio, 309–310, 337–338

strings, replacing with numbers, 555–559
subdivision, methods for, 381
subdivision data structure, file format for, 391–392
subdivision schemes
  properties of, 381–382
  usage of, 382–383
subdivision surfaces
  explanation of, 381
  fast rendering of, 398
  toolsets for, 382
  uses of, 382
  See also Loop subdivision algorithm
subdivision type, choosing, 383
SUBDUE tool, features of, 278
sum-of-of uniforms algorithm, use with GRNGs, 201–202
support mappings
  combining, 169–170
  translating and rotating, 168
  using with shapes, 167–168
  using with XenoCollide algorithm, 166–170
surface area heuristic (SAH), relationship to kD-tree, 133
surround sound
  approaches toward, 315–316
  DSP effects, 317–318
  syncing channels, 316–317
SWD compiler, code generated by, 471
SWD files
  defining synchronization behavior in, 473
  use in HLA systems, 470–471
SynchEntity class
  creation of, 475–476
  destruction and visibility of, 476
  synchronization bound to, 473–474
  use in HLA (High Level Abstraction), 471–472
synchronization behavior, defining in SWD files, 473
synchronizing game worlds
  overview of, 468–470
  synchronized objects in, 471–475
  techniques for, 467–468
synchronous versus asynchronous exceptions, 97

T

Tables
  audio engine file formats, 308
  CMU phonemes, 458–459
  edge mask selection in Loop subdivision, 386
  feature-space calculations, 211
  game state data for behavior cloning, 212
  LCGs (Linear Congruential Generators) in use, 117
  matrix inversion methods, 183
  mixing system mixing snapshots, 344
  motion detection algorithm times for optical flow, 30
  phoneme to viseme mapping, 459
  phonemes, 458–459
  projective space numerical ranges of results, 160
  shapes with support mappings, 168
  subdivision data structure file-format entries, 392
  subdivision schemes, 382
  support mappings for compound shapes, 169
  terrain navigation system configuration for testing, 444
  terrain navigation system statistics, 445
  world state modification permissions, 469
target victim page, determining via age, 9
tasks
  in multithread job and dependency system, 95
  synchronization with dependency manager, 91–94
terrain
  defining slope of, 355–356
  overhanging terrain, 362–364
terrain areas
  applying textures to, 435–437
  concentric rings update for, 441
  managing virtual textures for, 437–440
  rendering issues associated with, 442–444
  texture cache for, 437–438
  texture memory usage for, 439–440
  texture upload time for, 441
  updating virtual textures for, 442
  using trilinear filtering with, 438–439
terrain deformation, simulating with particles, 353
terrain formed by particles, slope of, 354–355
terrain navigation system, results of, 444–445
terrain texturing. See clipmaps
TestSystem game object, use of GLRThreading library with, 44–45
text, handling with translation tables, 555
texture atlas, using with graftal imposters, 447–448
texture cache
  design of, 8–13
  updating contents of, 440–442
  using with large terrains, 437–438
texture coordinates, computing in dynamic geometry, 443
texture memory usage, considering for large terrain areas, 439–440

texture pages, using in cache replacement examples, 10–11
texture stack, updating for large terrains, 440–441
texture upload time, considering for terrain areas, 441
texture-based representations, animating, 403
textures
  applying to large terrain areas, 435
  managing with clipmaps, 436
  representing objects with, 402
  storage of, 435
  storing animation data in, 406
  texels for relief imposters, 409
  See also virtual textures
texturing terrains. See clipmaps
thrash, occurrence of, 5
thread allocation strategies
  naive allocation, 41
  thread pools, 41–42
thread context switching, speed of, 40
thread handles, storage of, 39–40
thread local storage, using in heap allocation, 22
thread pools, use of, 41–42
thread stack size, altering default for, 39–40
threading architecture, designing, 36
threading engine, development of, 35
threading systems
  engineering, 39
  execution of, 37
  GLRThreading library sample, 44–45
threads
  and cache coherency, 43–44
  designating task priority of, 41
  execution properties of, 40
  versus jobs, 87
  object threading, 42
  preemption and simultaneous execution of, 39
  and processor affinity, 40
  properties of, 39–40
  safety, reentrancy, object synchronicity, and data access, 43
  use of, 38–39
tiling
  creation of, 47
  use with textures for large terrains, 438
T-intersections, generation in polygon meshes, 163–164
TLCG (Truncated Linear Congruential Generator), description of, 117–118
totalistic cellular automaton, use in RTS games, 64
totally-ordered plans, use in plan merging, 282–283
tracepoints, using with network code, 492
transformation matrices
  example of, 182–184
  inverting, 179
  retrieving for ARToolkit, 74
transformation semantics
  coordinate systems used in, 187
  explanation of, 180
  extracting from matrices, 181–184
  flexibility of, 186
  requirements for, 183
  use with box-box test and SAT, 187
  using for collision detection tasks, 184–188
triangles
  finding intersections of, 144
  testing for graftal imposters, 451
  testing for XenoCollide and MPR, 172
trigonometric functions, fast evaluation of, 194–195
trigonometric splines, use of, 192–194
trilinear filtering, using with large terrain areas, 438–439
troops, moving through battlefields in RTS games, 65
Truncated Linear Congruential Generator (TLCG), description of, 117–118
truncation, effect of, 153
tuning application, using with mixing system, 345–346

U

UCT (Urban Combat Testbed), use of, 267
unhandled exceptions, reporting, 98–99
unified sensing model
  adding memory to, 227
  components of, 226–227
uniform distribution, using in RNGs, 115
UNIX platforms, creating core dump on, 99
Update() function, using in optical flow, 33
Urban Combat Testbed (UCT), use of, 267
user input, capturing in RTS (real-time strategy) games, 62–63

V

VA (vertices array), use with subdivision data structures, 390
valence, purpose in attitude systems, 253–254
values
  relationship to attitudes, 250
  updating in attitude systems, 252

variables, allocation in OpenCV, 26–27
vector of C++ STL, use with hexagonal grids, 51–52
vector spaces, mapping between, 180
vectors
 use in projective space, 157–158
 use with GPUs, 300
vertical blanking period
 with limited time, 82–83
 relationship to handheld gaming systems, 82–83
vertices
 in Loop subdivision, 384, 386–387
 updating with Loop subdivision algorithm, 393
vertices array (VA), use with subdivision data structures, 390
victim pages, finding, 10
view cone check, doing in agent-sensing model, 218
view distance, computing in agent-sensing model, 218
virtual textures
 managing for large terrains, 437–440
 mapping to geometry models, 442–443
 updating for large terrain, 442
 See also textures
visemes
 mapping phonemes to, 459
 versus phonemes, 457–458
 use with head model for lipsyncing, 455–457
vision, modeling with certainty, 222–224
vision model
 augmenting with ellipses, 219–222
 considering in agent-sensing model, 217–219
 creating, 222–224
visitCallFunc, using with AST, 557–558
Vista, API for WER, 103
visual appearance of games, impact of grids on, 49
visual data mining, using with player traces, 272
volcanoes, improving particle placement of, 357–358
volume levels, setting for audio channels, 311
voxels, using with overhanging terrain, 364

W

walk function, using with AST, 557–558
Walker class, using with hexagonal grids, 53–54
walking, controlling in FPS games, 71
walking dog animation, control points for, 409–410
walking motions, producing, 408–409
warping functions
 evaluating using shaders, 405–407
 interpolating for relief imposters, 404–405
 See also relief imposters
warrior attitudes, FSM for, 257–258
waveforms, oscillating values in, 331
Webcam resolution, considering in optical flow, 33
webcamInput class
 cvAbsDiff function in, 27–28
 encapsulation of functionality in, 31
 functions in OpenCV, 26–27
Websites
 ARToolkit, 71
 L'Ecuyer's papers on RNG algorithms, 124
 random noise, 114
 subdivision surface toolsets, 382
 SUBDUE tool, 278
 UCT (Urban Combat Testbed), 267
WELL algorithm, use of, 120–121
WER (Windows Error Reporting), 102–103
wheel, support mapping for, 170
whitening algorithms, using with RNGs, 116
Win32 model for threading architecture, standard for, 36
windowing techniques
 using with FFT, 312–314
 using with frequency data, 312, 314
Windows Error Reporting (WER), 102–103
Windows Vista, API for WER, 103
WinPcap library, capturing packets with, 494–496
WinQual online portal, features of, 102
words, mapping to phonemes for lipsyncing, 457–459
workflow algorithms, using with Artificial Contender, 230–232
workflow blocks, requirements for, 238
 See also blocks
workflow diagram
 using with Artificial Contender, 234–235
 visualizing constraints on, 246
workflows
 constructing, 246
 interrupting, 244
 process of, 235–236
world coordinates, transforming model to, 182
world geometry
 finding information values for surfaces in, 278
 visualizing for player traces, 271
worlds, decomposing into regions, 271
WriteCoreDump function, using on UNIX platforms, 99

X

X, Y, Z approach, using with surround sound, 315
XACT audio tool, features of, 326
Xbox 360, implementation in threading systems, 37
XenoCollide algorithm
  and MPR (Minkowski Portal Refinement), 166
  optimizing, 177
  support mappings used with, 166–170
  use of, 171–176

Y

Yarrow RNG method, description of, 122

Z

ziggurat method, use with GRNGs, 201
zone approach, applying to hearing model, 225–226

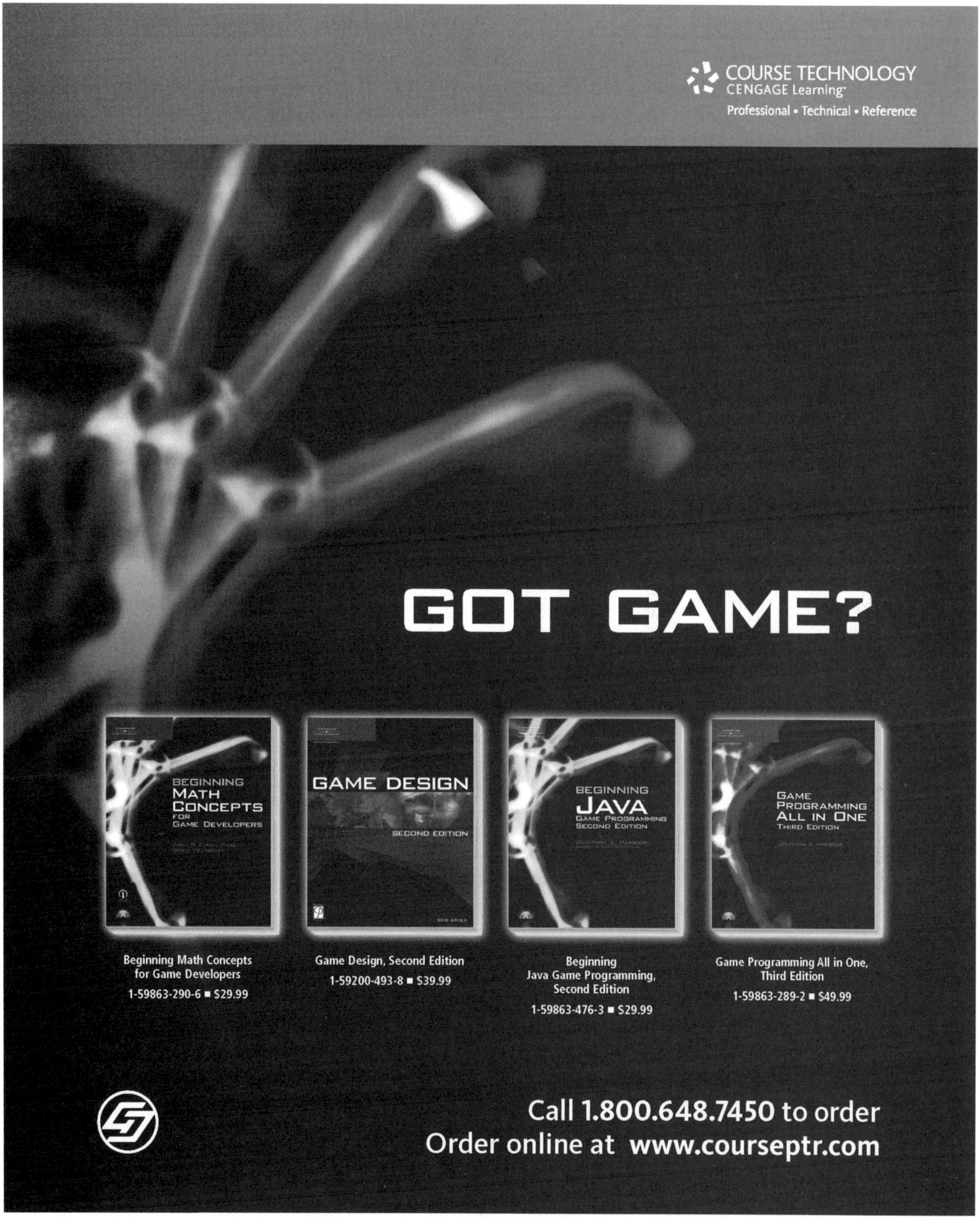
COURSE TECHNOLOGY
CENGAGE Learning
Professional • Technical • Reference
GOT GAME?
BEGINNING MATH CONCEPTS FOR GAME DEVELOPERS
GAME DESIGN
SECOND EDITION
BEGINNING JAVA GAME PROGRAMMING SECOND EDITION
GAME PROGRAMMING ALL IN ONE THIRD EDITION
Beginning Math Concepts for Game Developers
1-59863-290-6 ■ $29.99
Game Design, Second Edition
1-59200-493-8 ■ $39.99
Beginning Java Game Programming, Second Edition
1-59863-476-3 ■ $29.99
Game Programming All in One, Third Edition
1-59863-289-2 ■ $49.99
Call 1.800.648.7450 to order
Order online at www.courseptr.com

License Agreement/Notice of Limited Warranty

By opening the sealed disc container in this book, you agree to the following terms and conditions. If, upon reading the following license agreement and notice of limited warranty, you cannot agree to the terms and conditions set forth, return the unused book with unopened disc to the place where you purchased it for a refund.

License:

The enclosed software is copyrighted by the copyright holder(s) indicated on the software disc. You are licensed to copy the software onto a single computer for use by a single user and to a backup disc. You may not reproduce, make copies, or distribute copies or rent or lease the software in whole or in part, except with written permission of the copyright holder(s). You may transfer the enclosed disc only together with this license, and only if you destroy all other copies of the software and the transferee agrees to the terms of the license. You may not decompile, reverse assemble, or reverse engineer the software.

Notice of Limited Warranty:

The enclosed disc is warranted by Course Technology to be free of physical defects in materials and workmanship for a period of sixty (60) days from end user's purchase of the book/disc combination. During the sixty-day term of the limited warranty, Course Technology will provide a replacement disc upon the return of a defective disc.

Limited Liability:

THE SOLE REMEDY FOR BREACH OF THIS LIMITED WARRANTY SHALL CONSIST ENTIRELY OF REPLACEMENT OF THE DEFECTIVE DISC. IN NO EVENT SHALL COURSE TECHNOLOGY OR THE AUTHOR BE LIABLE FOR ANY OTHER DAMAGES, INCLUDING LOSS OR CORRUPTION OF DATA, CHANGES IN THE FUNCTIONAL CHARACTERISTICS OF THE HARDWARE OR OPERATING SYSTEM, DELETERIOUS INTERACTION WITH OTHER SOFTWARE, OR ANY OTHER SPECIAL, INCIDENTAL, OR CONSEQUENTIAL DAMAGES THAT MAY ARISE, EVEN IF COURSE TECHNOLOGY AND/OR THE AUTHOR HAS PREVIOUSLY BEEN NOTIFIED THAT THE POSSIBILITY OF SUCH DAMAGES EXISTS.

Disclaimer of Warranties:

COURSE TECHNOLOGY AND THE AUTHOR SPECIFICALLY DISCLAIM ANY AND ALL OTHER WARRANTIES, EITHER EXPRESS OR IMPLIED, INCLUDING WARRANTIES OF MERCHANTABILITY, SUITABILITY TO A PARTICULAR TASK OR PURPOSE, OR FREEDOM FROM ERRORS. SOME STATES DO NOT ALLOW FOR EXCLUSION OF IMPLIED WARRANTIES OR LIMITATION OF INCIDENTAL OR CONSEQUENTIAL DAMAGES, SO THESE LIMITATIONS MIGHT NOT APPLY TO YOU.

Other:

This Agreement is governed by the laws of the State of Massachusetts without regard to choice of law principles. The United Convention of Contracts for the International Sale of Goods is specifically disclaimed. This Agreement constitutes the entire agreement between you and Course Technology regarding use of the software.